MR. PUTIN

NEW AND EXPANDED

MR. PUTIN
OPERATIVE IN THE KREMLIN

Fiona Hill
Clifford G. Gaddy

BROOKINGS INSTITUTION PRESS
Washington, D.C.

The Brookings Institution is a private nonprofit organization devoted to research,
education, and publication on important issues of domestic and foreign policy. Its
principal purpose is to bring the highest quality independent research and analysis
to bear on current and emerging policy problems. Interpretations or conclusions in
Brookings publications should be understood to be solely those of the authors.

The Library of Congress has cataloged the hardcover edition as follows:

Hill, Fiona, 1965–
  Mr. Putin : operative in the Kremlin / Fiona Hill and Clifford G. Gaddy.
    pages ; cm. — (Brookings focus book)
  Includes bibliographical references and index.
  ISBN 978-0-8157-2376-9 (hardcover : alk. paper)
  1. Putin, Vladimir Vladimirovich, 1952– 2. Presidents—Russia (Federation)
3. Russia (Federation)—Politics and government—1991– I. Gaddy, Clifford G.
II. Title. III. Series: Brookings focus books.
  DK510.766.P87H55 2012
  947.086'2092—dc23
  [B]   2012041470
ISBN 978-0-8157-2617-3 (pbk. : alk. paper)
ISBN 978-0-8157-2618-0 (e-book)

9 8 7 6 5 4 3 2 1

Printed on acid-free paper

Typeset in Sabon

Composition by Cynthia Stock
Silver Spring, Maryland

CONTENTS

CONTENTS

ACKNOWLEDGMENTS

THIS BOOK IS THE REVISED and considerably expanded version of the first edition of *Mr. Putin: Operative in the Kremlin,* which we finished writing in September 2012 and was published in 2013. The original manuscript was the result of a long-standing collaboration between Fiona Hill and Clifford Gaddy as colleagues at the Brookings Institution, dating to the beginning of Mr. Putin's presidency in 2000. The background for the authors' research work (individually and jointly) was outlined in the acknowledgments to the 2013 edition. These acknowledgments also thanked all the colleagues and contacts who assisted in fleshing out specific ideas and identifying source material.

Fiona Hill researched and wrote the additional material for this second edition, which moves the narrative frame of the original book from its focus on the Russian domestic scene to the international arena. Between the launch of the first edition in early 2013 and September 2014, Fiona Hill collected and analyzed new source material and embarked on a series of international research trips to conduct supplemental interviews with analysts, policymakers, government officials, and private sector representatives on the key themes of the book. Some of these trips were sponsored by external organizations, including the Embassy of the United States in Berlin and the U.S. consulates in Germany (through the U.S. Department of State's Strategic Speaker Program); the Ministry of Foreign Affairs of Japan (through its official visitors and speakers program); and the Department of National Defence of Canada (through the National Defence, Defence Engagement Program). Other trips and interviews were facilitated through meetings and conferences arranged by partner organizations, including the Aspen Institute, Chatham House, the Council on the United States and Italy, the Ditchley Foundation, the European Council on Foreign Relations, the EU Institute for Strategic Studies, the German Marshall Fund, the Heinrich Böll Foundation, the French Institute of International Relations (IFRI), the Körber Stiftung, the London School of Economics, and the Munich Security Conference. Participation in numerous Brookings Institution conferences, seminars, and private meetings in Washington, D.C., and Europe also provided opportunities to engage in one-on-one or small-group discussions with a range of U.S., European, and Russian officials, as well as U.S. and international business figures active in Russia.

Other interviews with officials were conducted in Washington, D.C. (as indicated in the endnotes), with the assistance of the embassies of many foreign countries, including Australia, Canada, the Czech Republic, Estonia, Finland, France, Georgia, Germany, Israel, Italy, Japan, Moldova, Norway, Poland, Romania, Serbia, Slovakia, Sweden, Turkey, Ukraine, the United Kingdom, and the Delegation of the European Union.

Clifford Gaddy contributed new material and conclusions from two separate research projects: on the reform of the Russian military and the evolution of Russia's new military doctrine (conducted with Michael O'Hanlon), and on the state of the Russian economy (conducted with Barry Ickes). Some of this material will also be reflected in Clifford Gaddy and Barry Ickes's forthcoming book: *Russia's Addiction. The Political Economy of Resource Dependence.*

The book was written between June and September 2014 with the help and hard work of Brookings senior research assistant Hannah Thoburn. Hannah was a genuine collaborator on both editions of the book, carrying out painstaking work on Russian source material and playing an essential role in all aspects of the manuscript preparation.

Irina Angelescu played a critical role in the final stages of completing the manuscript, checking sources, editing, and thinking through the organization of concepts and material. Bilyana Lilly, Jan Malaskowski, and Catherine Trainor also assisted with the identification of Russian language source material.

Jill Dougherty, Michael O'Hanlon, Robert Otto, and Angela Stent all reviewed the text and gave invaluable editorial, conceptual, and organizational suggestions for the final manuscript. Also at Brookings, Andrew Moffatt provided moral support, kept everything on track, and made sure that time and the necessary funding were carved out so the work could get done. Other colleagues shared sources and ideas, and offered critiques, including Strobe Talbott, Tim Boersma, Charley Ebinger, Kai Eide, Michael Doran, Erica Downs, Bruce Jones, Kenneth Lieberthal, Tanvi Madan, Suzanne Maloney, Ted Piccone, Natan Sachs, Mireya Solis, Harold Trinkunas, and Thomas Wright.

Colleagues at the Center on the United States and Europe—Riccardo Alcaro, Pavel Baev, Carlo Bastasin, Caitlyn Davis, Jutta Falke-Ischinger, Richard Kauzlarich, Kemal Kirişci, Steven Pifer, and Jeremy Shapiro—all generously took the time to brainstorm on core concepts.

Valentina Kalk, Janet Walker, and other colleagues at Brookings Institution Press embraced the idea of an expanded second edition of the book and assisted the project all along the way. The Brookings Institution Press also covered the new editorial and production costs for the book. Independent editor John Felton gave editorial support and suggestions for improving the final manuscript. Laura Mooney and other colleagues at the Brookings library helped with difficult sourcing. Gail Chalef and Tina Trenkner pitched in with a range of ideas on outreach as the new version of the book moved toward completion.

As the second phase of research moved along, several people who had read the first edition raised important questions about core ideas, flagged articles in the Russian and international press, suggested individuals for interviews (or offered themselves for interview), and very generously sent their own and other publications for reference. These included Hannes Adomeit, Ellen Barry, Samuel Bendett, Lynn Berry, J. D. Bindenagel, Samuel Charap, William Courtney, Igor Danchenko, Jaba Devdariani, William Drozdiak, John Evans, Florence Fee, Katja Gloger, Paul Goble, Tomas Gomart, Charles Grant, Zuhra Halimova, Michael Haltzel, Andrej Heinke, Marc Hujer, Shinji Hyodo, Shoichi Ito, Akihiro Iwashita, Barbara Junge, Alisher Khamidov, Nina Khrushcheva, Hiroshi Kimura, Thomas Kleine-Brockhoff, Martin Klingst, John Kornblum, Ivan Krastev, Johann Legner, Bobo Lo, Jenny Lo, Alexander Lukin, Georg Mascolo, Steven Lee Myers, James Nixey, Rene Nyberg, Craig Oliphant, Tim Oliver, Bruce Parrott, William Partlett, Volker Perthes, Simon Saradzhyan, Yukio Satoh, Zachary Shore, Mary Springer, Holger Stark, Constanze Steltzenmüller, Stephen Szabo, Michael Thumann,

Kazuhiko Togo, Mikhail Troitsky, Charles Undeland, David Du Vivier, Thomas de Waal, Kyle Wilson, Igor Zevelev, and Nikolai Zlobin.

Finally, our dear friend and colleague Clara O'Donnell was a great source of inspiration and ideas at the beginning of the new edition. Clara passed away in January 2014 and did not see the project completed. Her loss is keenly felt, and perhaps this second edition of the book may serve in some small measure as a testament to her accomplishments and memory.

We are grateful for the generous support of Stephen and Barbara Friedman, whose contributions to the Brookings Foreign Policy program made this book possible. This revised edition is part of Foreign Policy's project, Order from Chaos. The book's findings are in keeping with Brookings's mission: to conduct high-quality and independent research and, based on that research, to provide innovative, practical recommendations for policymakers and the public. The conclusions and recommendations of any Brookings research are solely those of its authors and do not reflect the views of the Institution, its management, or its other scholars.

PART ONE

THE OPERATIVE EMERGES

CHAPTER ONE

WHO IS MR. PUTIN?

ON MARCH 18, 2014, still bathed in the afterglow of the Winter Olympics that he had hosted in the Black Sea resort of Sochi, Russian president Vladimir Putin stepped up to a podium in the Kremlin to address the nation. Before an assembly of Russian officials and parliamentarians, Putin signed the documents officially reuniting the Russian Federation and the peninsular republic of Crimea, the home base of Russia's Black Sea Fleet. Crimea had seceded from Ukraine only two days earlier, on March 16. The Russian president gave what was intended to be a historic speech. The events were fresh, but his address was laden with references to several centuries of Russian history.

Putin invoked the origins of Orthodox Christianity in Russia. He referenced military victories on land and sea that had helped forge the Russian Empire. He noted the grievances that had festered in Russia since the 1990s, when the state was unable to protect its interests after the disintegration of the Soviet Union. At the center of his narrative was Crimea. Crimea "has always been an inseparable part of Russia," Putin declared. Moscow's decision to annex Crimea was rooted in the need to right an "outrageous historical injustice." That injustice began with the Bolsheviks, who put lands that Russia had conquered into their new Soviet republic of Ukraine. Then, Soviet leader Nikita Khrushchev made the fateful decision in 1954 to transfer Crimea from the Russian Federation to Ukraine. When the Soviet state fell apart in 1991, Russian-speaking Crimea was left in Ukraine "like a sack of potatoes," Putin said.[1] The Russian nation was divided by borders.

Vladimir Putin's speech and the ceremony reuniting Russia with its "lost province" came after several months of political upheaval in Ukraine. Demonstrations that had begun in late November 2013 as a protest against Ukrainian president Viktor Yanukovych's decision to back out of the planned signing of an association agreement with the European Union soon turned into a large-scale protest movement against his government. By February 2014, protesters were engaged in clashes with Ukrainian police that left over 100 people dead on both sides.[2] On February 21, 2014, talks between Yanukovych and the opposition were brokered by outside parties, including Russia. A provisional agreement, intended to end the violence and pave the way for new presidential elections at the end of 2014, was upended when Yanukovych abruptly fled the country. After several days of confusion, Yanukovych resurfaced in Russia. Meanwhile, the opposition in Ukraine formed an interim government and set presidential elections for May 25, 2014.

At about the same time that Yanukovych left Ukraine, unidentified armed men began to seize control of strategic infrastructure on the Crimean Peninsula. On March 6, the Crimean parliament voted to hold a snap referendum on independence and the prospect of joining Russia. On March 16, the results of the referendum indicated that 97 percent of those voting had opted to unite with Russia. It was this referendum that Putin used to justify Russia's reincorporation, its annexation, of Crimea. He opened his speech with a reference to the referendum and how more than 82 percent of eligible voters had turned out to make this momentous and overwhelming choice in favor of becoming part of Russia. The people of Crimea had exercised their right—the right of all nations—to self-determination. They had chosen to restore the unity of the Russian world and historical Russia. But by annexing the Crimean Peninsula, immediately after the referendum, Putin had dealt the greatest blow to European security since the end of the Cold War. In the eyes of most external observers, Putin's Russia was now a definitively revisionist power. In a short span of time, between February 21 and March 18, 2014, Russia had moved from brokering peace to taking a piece of Ukraine.

As Western leaders deliberated how to punish Putin for seizing Crimea and deter him from similar actions in the rest of Ukraine and elsewhere, questions arose: Why did Putin do this? What does he want? Many commentators turned back to questions that had been asked nearly 15 years earlier, when Vladimir Putin first emerged from near-obscurity to become the leader of Russia: "Who is Mr. Putin?" For some observers, the answer was easy: Putin was who he had always been—a corrupt, avaricious, and power-hungry authoritarian leader. What Putin did in Ukraine was just a logical next step to what he had been doing in Russia since 2000: trying to tighten his grip on power. Annexing Crimea and the nationalist rhetoric Putin used to justify it were merely ploys to bolster his flagging public support and distract the population from problems at home. Other commentators saw Putin's shift toward nationalist rhetoric and his decision to annex Crimea as evidence of new "imperial" thinking, and as dangerously genuine. Putin's goal, they proposed, was to restore the Soviet Union or the old Russian Empire. But if that was true, where were the patterns and key indicators of neo-imperialist revisionism in Putin's past behavior? Many world leaders and analysts wondered what they had missed. Unable to reconcile their old understanding of Putin with his behavior in Ukraine, some concluded that Putin himself had changed. A "new Putin" must have appeared in the Kremlin.

If, in fact, Putin's behavior in the Ukraine crisis was really different from the past, it could provide an opportunity to understand him better. In his 2014 book, *A Sense of the Enemy: The High-Stakes History of Reading Your Rival's Mind,* Zachary Shore argues that it is precisely when people break with previous patterns of behavior that we can begin to gain an understanding of their real character. Patterns of past behavior are a poor predictor of how a person will act in the future. Contexts change and alter people's actions. Pattern breaks are key for analyzing individual behavior. They push us to focus on the invariant aspects of the person's self. They help reveal the hidden drivers, the underlying motivations, and what an actor, a leader, values most.[3]

This is the essence of our approach in this book. The book is an effort to figure out who Mr. Putin is in terms of his motivations—what drives him to act as he does? Rather than present a chronicle of events in which Putin played a role, we concentrate on events that *shaped* him. We look at formative experiences of Putin's past. And where we do examine his actions, we focus on the *circumstances* in which he acted. Our reasoning is that if Putin's actions and words differed during the crisis in Ukraine in 2014 from what we might have expected in the past, it is likely that the circumstances changed. Indeed, as we will lay out and describe in the two parts of this book, Vladimir Putin's behavior is driven by the imperative to adapt and respond to changing—especially, unpredicted—circumstances.

This book is not intended to be a definitive biography or a comprehensive study of everything about Vladimir Putin. Although personal and even intimate life experiences shape the way an individual thinks and views the world, we do not delve into Putin's family life or close friendships. We also do not critique all the different stories about him, and we try to avoid retreading ground that has been covered extensively in other analyses and biographies. Our purpose is to look for new insights in all the material we have on Vladimir Putin.

THE ELUSIVE NATURE OF FACTS

It is remarkable—almost hard to believe—that for 15 years there has not been a single substantive biography published in Russian, by a Russian, of President Putin. It is true that a few very incomplete books—limited in their scope—appeared in his first months as president. There is also, of course, Putin's own autobiography, *Ot pervogo litsa* (First person), which appeared in early 2000.[4] Arguably the only other true biography with wide circulation in Russia is a translation of Alexander Rahr's *Wladimir Putin: Der "Deutsche" im Kreml* (Vladimir Putin: the "German" in the Kremlin).[5] By contrast, there have been a number of serious biographies of Putin in English. The West, particularly the United States, is used to a steady flow of memoirs, and tell-alls, from former associates of our leaders. There has been nothing like that in Russia. Rather than the flow of information about the man who has led the country for a decade and a half growing stronger, it has actually declined over time. Above all, the information that does emerge has been increasingly controlled and manipulated. Instead of independently verifiable new facts from identified sources, there are only "stories" about Putin from unidentified sources, sources who are—we are invariably assured by those who tell the stories—"close to the Kremlin." There is also the phenomenon of old stories being recycled as astonishing new revelations.

Attempting to write about Vladimir Putin is thus a challenge for many reasons. One that we ourselves never imagined until we were well into this venture is that, like it or not, when you delve into his hidden aspects, whether in the past or present, you are playing a game with Putin. It is a game where he is in charge. He controls the facts and the "stories." For that reason, every apparent fact or story needs to be regarded with suspicion. It has to be traced back to original sources. If that turns out to be impossible, or the source seems unreliable, what does one do with the information? As the reader will soon find out, we too use stories about Putin. But we do so with caution. We have tested the sources. When we were unable to do so to the fullest extent, we make that clear. Most important, we have learned to ask the question, "Why has this story been circulated?"

The most obvious reason we cannot take any story or so-called fact at face value when it comes to Vladimir Putin is that we are dealing with someone who is a master at manipulating information, suppressing information, and creating pseudo-information. In the course of studying Putin, and Putin's Russia, we have learned this the hard way. In today's world of social media, the public has the impression that we know, or easily can know, everything about everybody. Nothing, it seems, is private or secret. And still, after 15 years, we remain ignorant of some of the most basic facts about a man who is arguably the most powerful individual in the world, the leader of an important nation. When there is no certifiably real and solid information, any tidbit becomes precious.

THE PUTIN BIOGRAPHY

Where then do we start? The basic biographical data, surely, are beyond dispute. Vladimir Putin was born in the Soviet city of Leningrad in October 1952 and was his parents' only surviving child. His childhood was spent in Leningrad, where his youthful pursuits included training first in sambo (a martial art combining judo and wrestling that was developed by the Soviet Red Army) and then in judo. After school, Putin studied law at Leningrad State University (LGU), graduated in 1975, and immediately joined the Soviet intelligence service, the KGB. He was posted to Dresden in East Germany in 1985, after completing a year of study at the KGB's academy in Moscow. He was recalled from Dresden to Leningrad in 1990, just as the USSR was on the verge of collapse.

During his time in the KGB, Putin worked as a case officer (the "operative" of our title) and attained the rank of lieutenant colonel. In 1990–91, he moved into the intelligence service's "active reserve" and returned to Leningrad State University as a deputy to the vice rector. He became an adviser to one of his former law professors, Anatoly Sobchak, who left the university to become chairman of Leningrad's city soviet, or council. Putin worked with Sobchak during Sobchak's successful electoral campaign to become the first democratically elected mayor of what was now St. Petersburg. In June 1991, Putin became a deputy mayor of St. Petersburg and was put in charge of the city's Committee for External Relations. He officially resigned from the KGB in August 1991.

In 1996, after Mayor Sobchak lost his bid for reelection, Vladimir Putin moved to Moscow to work in the Kremlin in the department that managed presidential property. In March 1997, Putin was elevated to deputy chief of the presidential staff. He assumed a number of other responsibilities within the Kremlin before being appointed head of the Russian Federal Security Service (the FSB, the successor to the KGB) in July 1998. A year later, in August 1999, Vladimir Putin was named, in rapid succession, one of Russia's first deputy prime ministers and then prime minister by President Boris Yeltsin, who also indicated Putin was his preferred successor as president. Finally, on December 31, 1999, Putin became acting president of Russia after Yeltsin resigned. He was officially elected to the position of president in March 2000. Putin served two terms as Russia's president from 2000 to 2004 and from 2004 to 2008, before stepping aside—in line with Russia's constitutional prohibition against three consecutive presidential terms—to assume the position of prime minister. In March 2012, Putin was reelected to serve another term as Russia's president until 2018, thanks to a constitutional amendment pushed through by then President Dmitry Medvedev in December 2008 extending the presidential term from four to six years.

These basic facts have been covered in books and newspaper articles. Yet there is some uncertainty in the sources about specific dates and the sequencing of Vladimir Putin's professional trajectory. This is especially the case for his KGB service, but also for some of the period when he was in the St. Petersburg mayor's office, including how long he was technically part of the KGB's "active reserve." Personal information, including on key childhood events, his 1983 marriage to his wife, Lyudmila (whom he divorced in 2014), the birth of two daughters in 1985 and 1986 (Maria and Yekaterina), and his friendships with politicians and businessmen from Leningrad/St. Petersburg is remarkably scant for such a prominent public figure. His wife, daughters, and other family members, for example, are conspicuously absent from the public domain. Information about him that was available at the beginning of his presidency has also been suppressed, distorted, or lost in a morass of competing and often contradictory versions swirling with rumor and innuendo. Some materials—related to a notorious 1990s food scandal in St. Petersburg, which almost upended Putin's early political career—have been expunged, along with those with access to them. When it comes to Mr. Putin, very little information is definitive, confirmable, or reliable.

As a result, there are many important and enduring mysteries about Vladimir Putin that we will not address in detail in this book. Take something so fundamental as his initial rise to power as Russian president. In less than two-and-a-half years from 1997 to 99, Vladimir Putin was promoted to increasingly lofty positions, from deputy chief of the presidential staff, to head of the FSB, to prime minister, then to acting president. How could this happen? Who facilitated Putin's rise? Putin does not have a story about that in his official biographical interviews. He leaves it to others to spin their versions. The fact that there are multiple competing answers to such a basic question as who chose Putin to be Boris Yeltsin's successor in 1999 is one of the reasons we decided to write this book and to adopt the specific approach we have. All the versions of who made this important decision are based on retrospective accounts, including from Boris Yeltsin himself in his memoir *Midnight Diaries*. Almost nothing comes from real-time statements or reliable accounts of actions taken. Even then—if this kind of information were available— we would not know what really happened behind the scenes. It is clear that many of the after-the-fact statements are self-serving. None of them seem completely credible. They are from people trying to claim credit, or avoid blame, for a set of decisions that proved monumental for Russia.

Rather than spending time parsing the course of events in this period and analyzing the various people who may or may not have influenced the decision to install Vladimir Putin as Boris Yeltsin's successor, we parse and analyze Putin himself. We focus on a series of vignettes from his basic biography that form part of a more coherent, larger story. We also emphasize Putin's own role in getting where he did. We stress the one thing we are certain about: Putin shaped his own fate. We do not deny there was an element of accident or chance in his ultimate rise to power. Nor do we deny there were real people who acted on his behalf—people who thought at a particular time that he was "their man" who would promote their interests. But, for us, it was what Mr. Putin did that is the most critical element in his biography.

As a good KGB operative, Vladimir Putin kept his own ambitions tightly under wraps. Like most ambitious people, he took advantage of the opportunities that presented themselves. Mr. Putin paid close attention to individuals who might further his career. He studied them, strengthened his personal and professional ties to them, did favors for them, and manipulated them. He allowed—even actively encouraged—people to underestimate him even as he maneuvered himself into influential positions and quietly accumulated real power. Instead of providing a "Who's Who" of Vladimir Putin's political circle, we highlight some of the people who played important roles for Putin at different junctures. These include Russian historical figures whose biographies and ideas Putin appropriated and tailored to suit his own personal narrative. They also include a few people from his inner circle whose relationships and roles illuminate the connections Putin developed to put himself in a position to become Russian president and, more important, to become a president with the power to implement his goals. None of Vladimir Putin's personal ties, however, made his rise to power inevitable.

To understand our approach, it might be useful to present a couple of examples of the specious "stories" that have circulated about Putin and have been taken at face value by some authors. One is the story of Putin's alleged personal fortune. The other relates to an apparent KGB assessment of Putin as a dangerously risk-prone individual who likes to gamble.

PUTIN'S PERSONAL WEALTH

In the wake of Putin's actions in Ukraine in the spring of 2014 and the search by politicians in the West for effective levers to "punish Putin," one tempting option was to focus on the Russian president's personal wealth. Over the years, there have been repeated stories about how Mr. Putin had accumulated a vast fortune thanks to massive corruption within the inner circle of what we call Russia, Inc.[6] Early on, it was rumored that Putin's net worth was $20 billion. With each retelling, the number grew—$30 billion, $40 billion, $70 billion, up (at last count) to

$100 billion. These stories date back to Putin's time in the St. Petersburg mayor's office, they implicate his family and close associates, and they have been frequently featured in Russian as well as Western media. There is, however, little hard documentary evidence to back up even the most credible reporting.[7]

Some of the world's top financial institutions have conducted serious research on how the corrupt hide their stolen assets.[8] We did not have the means to undertake the kind of detailed and laborious technical work necessary to pursue Mr. Putin's purported ill-gotten gains, nor did we want to engage in further conjecture on this subject. As we indicate in the book, there is notable circumstantial evidence—including expensive watches and suits—of Mr. Putin's supposedly luxurious lifestyle beyond the official trappings of the Russian presidency. These extravagances on their own do not make the case that he has amassed a fortune in the tens of billions of dollars. There are competing narratives that Putin's day-to-day lifestyle is ascetic rather than luxurious. It is certainly true that individuals with close and long-standing personal ties to Vladimir Putin now occupy positions of great responsibility within the Russian economy and are some of Russia's (and the world's) richest men. In interviews, they are remarkably frank in discussing the links between their political connections, their economic roles, and their money.

There might also be political reasons for Putin to accumulate and flaunt personal wealth. Indeed, some of the stories in the Russian press, and some related to us by Russian colleagues, suggest that Mr. Putin himself might even encourage rumors that he is the richest of the rich to curb political ambitions among Russia's billionaire businessmen, the so-called oligarchs. They cannot even compete in the realm of personal wealth with Vladimir Putin, and it is he who has supreme power in Russia. But this is all speculation about facts that remain, for now, unproven.

The problem arises when this so-called fact of huge personal wealth leads to the conclusion that greed must necessarily be Vladimir Putin's principal motivation, or that somehow the fear of losing his personal fortune, or his associates' fortunes, would restrain his actions in the international arena. Even if Vladimir Putin has enriched himself and those around him, we do not believe a quest for personal wealth is primarily what drives him. We need to understand what else motivates Putin's actions as head of the Russian state.

A "DIMINISHED SENSE OF DANGER"

One idea that gained currency during the crisis in Ukraine is that Putin is a reckless gambler who takes dangerous risks.[9] This argument is based on the alleged fact that Putin's KGB trainers deemed that he suffered from a "diminished sense of danger" (*ponizhennoye chuvstvo opasnosti*). Although presented in a couple of recent books about Putin as if it were a new revelation, this is a story familiar to anyone who has read Putin's 2000 book, *Ot pervogo litsa*.[10] There, Putin describes how, when he was studying at the KGB academy, one characteristic ascribed to him as a "negative trait" was a "diminished" or "lowered sense of danger"—a deficiency that was considered very serious, he noted.[11]

In fact, the Putin book turns out to be the only source for this story, something that ought to have set off alarm bells. *Ot pervogo litsa* was intended to be a campaign biography, or "semi-autobiography." The publication of the book was orchestrated by Putin's staff in the spring of 2000 based on a series of one-on-one interviews with a carefully selected troika of Russian journalists. Putin's team's task was to stage-manage the initial presentation, to all of Russia, of this relatively unknown person who was now standing for election as president of the country. It was crafted as a set of conversations with Putin himself, his wife, and other people close to him in his childhood and early life. Every vignette, every new fact presented in the book was chosen for a specific political purpose. The journalists who interviewed Putin also used some of the material for articles in their own newspapers and other publications.

What, then, could Putin's purpose have been in revealing such a character flaw? The answer becomes evident when one reflects on the curious ending of the book. *Ot pervogo litsa* ends with the interviewers noting that Putin seems, after all the episodes in his life that they have gone through, to be a predictable and rather boring person. Had he never done anything on a whim perhaps? Putin responded by recounting an incident when he risked his own life and that of his passenger, his martial arts coach, while driving on a road outside Leningrad (in fact when he was at university). He tried to grab a piece of hay through his open car window from a passing farm truck and very nearly lost control of the car. At the end of the harrowing ride, his white-faced (and presumably furious) coach turned to Putin and said, "You take risks." Why did Putin do that? "I guess I thought the hay smelled good" (*Navernoye, seno vkusno pakhlo*), said Putin.[12] This is the last line in the book. The reader clearly is meant to identify with Putin's coach and ask: "Wait! What was that all about? Just who is this guy?"

This story offers a classic case of Putin and his team imparting and spinning information in a confusing manner so that it can be interpreted in multiple ways. Putin tells contradictory versions of the story in the same passages of his book. Immediately after stating that the characteristic was ascribed to him during his KGB studies, Putin then suggests that his "lowered sense of danger" was well-known to him and all his friends already in his university days (that is, before he was ever in the KGB).[13] Putin wants people to see him in certain ways, and yet be confused. He promotes the idea of himself both as a risk-taker and as someone who takes calculated risks and always has a fallback option. Which version is the real one? Both have a certain power and useful effect. The end result of Putin's misinformation and contradictory information is to create the image that he is unknowable and unpredictable and therefore even dangerous. It is part of his play in the domestic and international political game—to keep everyone guessing about, and in some cases fearing, how he might react.

Putin is hardly the first world leader to engage in this sort of conscious image manipulation to create doubts about their rationality or even sanity. Richard Nixon's notorious "Madman Theory" during the Vietnam War is a case in point. In 1972, believing he had a chance to bluff the North Vietnamese to the negotiating table to end the war, Nixon instructed his national security advisor, Henry Kissinger, to convey the message to the North Vietnamese, via their Soviet backers, that Nixon was prepared to use a nuclear weapon. As James Rosen and Luke Nichter write in a recent article, "Nixon wanted to impress upon the Soviets that the president of the United States was, in a word, mad: unstable, erratic in his decision-making, and capable of anything."[14] In a memoir, former White House chief of staff H. R. Haldeman wrote that Nixon had carefully scripted it all. According to Haldeman, Nixon told him, "I call it the Madman Theory. . . . I want the North Vietnamese to believe I've reached the point where I might do anything to stop the war. We'll just slip the word to them that, 'for God's sake, you know Nixon is obsessed about communism. We can't restrain him when he's

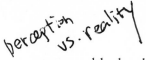

angry—and he has his hand on the nuclear button,' and Ho Chi Minh himself will be in Paris in two days begging for peace."[15]

In reality, Putin's goal in planting stories about himself is more complicated than Nixon's. He is not simply trying to project a specific image of himself or even to sow confusion about the "real" Putin. He also wants to track how the initial seeding of an idea is carried forward, and by whom. Putin wants to see how the original version is embellished and then how it ultimately is played back to him again. This is an exercise. It is Putin's own version of an American children's game, "telephone" (known in the United Kingdom as "Chinese whispers," where it was also called, in earlier versions, "Russian scandal"). In seeding intrigue, Putin wants to see how others interpret what he says and then how they react. The focus is on people's perceptions rather than reality. Figuring out how others think and act, when they know nothing about him or how he operates, gives Mr. Putin a tactical political advantage.

As we have concluded over the course of writing this book, for Vladimir Putin the main thing about information is not whether it is true or not. It is how words and deeds are perceived by others. Putin is less interested in presenting a particular version of reality than in seeing how others react to the information. For him, others are participants in a game he directs. He chooses inputs, they react. He judges. Their responses to his input tell him who they think he is—but by responding they also tell him who *they* are, what *they* want, what *they* care about. For his part, Vladimir Putin reveals very little in return. Indeed, he goes to great, often elaborate, lengths to throw other participants off track. As president and prime minister, he has presented himself as a myriad of different personas. Since 2000, Mr. Putin has been the ultimate international political performance artist.

THE KREMLIN SPECIAL PROPS DEPARTMENT: STAGING THE PRESIDENT

Over the last several years, Vladimir Putin's public relations team has pushed his image in a multiplicity of directions, pitching him as everything from big game hunter and conservationist to scuba diver to biker—even nightclub crooner. Leaders of other countries have gained notoriety for their flamboyant or patriotic style of dressing to appeal to and rally the masses—like Fidel Castro's and Hugo Chávez's military fatigues, Yasser Arafat's ubiquitous keffiyeh scarf, Muammar Qaddafi's robes (and tent), Hamid Karzai's carefully calculated blend of traditional Afghan tribal dress, and Yulia Tymoshenko's ultra-chic Ukrainian-peasant blonde braids—but Vladimir Putin has out-dressed them all. He has appeared in an endless number of guises for encounters with the press or Russian special interest groups, or at times of crisis, as during raging peat bog fires around Moscow in 2010, when he was transformed into a fire-fighting airplane pilot. All this theatricality is done with the assistance, it would seem, of the Kremlin's inexhaustible wardrobe and special props department.

On the surface, Mr. Putin's antics are reminiscent of a much-beloved children's book and animated cartoon series in the United Kingdom, "Mr. Benn." Each morning, Mr. Benn, a nondescript British man in a standard issue bowler hat and business suit, strolls down his street and is beckoned into a mysterious costume shop by a mustachioed, fez-wearing shopkeeper. The shopkeeper whisks Mr. Benn into a changing room. Mr. Benn puts on a costume that has already been laid out by the shopkeeper, walks out a secret door, and assumes a new costume-appropriate identity, as if by magic. In every episode, Mr. Benn solves a problem for the people he encounters during his adventure, until summoned back to reality by the shopkeeper.[16] Like his cartoon analogue, Mr. Putin, with the assistance of his press secretary, Dmitry Peskov (mustachioed but without the fez), and a coterie of press people, as if by magic embarks on a series of adventures (some of which oddly enough overlap with Mr. Benn's). In the course of his adventures, Mr. Putin pulls off every costume and performance with aplomb, a straight face, and a demonstration of skill.

Vladimir Putin and his PR team—which closely monitors the public reactions to the Mr. Putin episodes—are aware that these performances lack universal appeal and have sparked amusement at home and abroad because of their elaborate and very obvious staging. This has led people to depict him as a shallow, cartoonish figure, or a man with no face, no substance, no soul. Putin is often seen as a "man from nowhere," who can appear to be anybody to anyone.[17]

But Russian intellectual elites, the Russian political opposition to Mr. Putin, and overseas commentators are not his target audiences. Each episode of Mr. Putin has a specific purpose. They are all based on feedback from opinion polls suggesting the Kremlin needs to reach out and create a direct personal connection to a particular group among the Russian population. Press Secretary Peskov admitted this directly in a meeting with the press in August 2011 after Mr. Putin dove to the bottom of the Black Sea to retrieve some suspiciously immaculate amphorae.[18] Putin himself has asserted in biographical interviews that one of his main skills is to get people—in this case the Russian people, his audience(s)—to see him as what *they* want him to be, not what he really is. These performances portray Putin as the ultimate Russian action man, capable of dealing with every eventuality.

THE SERIOUS SIDE: SHOWING RESPECT

It is important to realize that there is something deeper, more complicated, at work beneath the façade of the "Mr. Putin" performances, something that an outside observer will always find hard to grasp. Each of the guises that Putin adopts, and the actions he undertakes, pays a degree of respect to a certain group and validates that group's place in Russian society. If the Russian president pulls on a leather jacket and rides off on a motorcycle with Russia's equivalent of the "Hell's Angels" or dresses up in a white suit to fly a microlight aircraft directing the migration of endangered birds, Russian bikers and Russian conservationists both get their time in the spotlight. Bikers and conservationists can believe they are equally worthy of presidential attention. They have inspired presidential action. They have their role to play in Russian society, just like everyone else. The performances create a sense of commonality and unity.

Western politicians routinely set out to convince voters that they are one of them, downing beers and snacks they would never normally eat in bars and restaurants they would not otherwise frequent. But Putin is not out to win votes. He is running a country. His actions have more in common with the leaders of traditional societies than Western leaders. Hamid Karzai, when leader of Afghanistan from 2004 to 2014, for example, frequently told his Western interlocutors that contrary to their interpretations of democracy, he understood democracy to be rule by consensus, not by majority. Without consensus, Afghan society would quickly descend into fragmentation, conflict, and violent strife. To bring reform to Afghanistan there had to be a broad consensus. Consensus created unity. Traditional Afghan methods of forging consensus, like the *shura,* a formalized consultation with societal leaders and elders, were more effective in reaching consensus, Karzai argued, than Western parliamentary innovations. The most important element of a *shura,* a consultation, Karzai emphasized, was not reaching some kind of decision, but showing respect in a credible way and validating the views of others. Karzai's adoption of traditional dress was one way of establishing credibility. Showing up in person and sitting for hours at a *shura,* or inviting Afghan tribal leaders to meetings in his own home, and simply listening to the discussions were important ways of showing respect. In Afghanistan, societal leaders wanted to feel they had been listened to by the Afghan president, not just informed of executive decisions after the fact.[19]

Similarly, Putin has stressed on several occasions that he considers listening to the Russian people and hearing what they have to say in person as part of his duty as head of the Russian state.[20] He has traveled extensively to Russia's far-flung regions over the course of his presidencies and during his time as prime minister and devised an array of forums for meeting with and hearing from the public. In an impromptu 2012 meeting with Russian-American journalist and author Masha Gessen, Putin also claimed that most of the costumed stunts were his own idea and not his staff's. He wanted personally to draw attention to certain people and places and issues that he thought were being neglected or, in other words, not given sufficient respect by the rest of society.[21] Collectively, these small but elaborately staged and highly publicized acts of respect have been one of the reasons why Vladimir Putin has consistently polled as Russia's most popular politician for a decade and a half.

Putin's stage performances have the double advantage not only of ensuring his domestic popularity but also of keeping outside analysts confused about his true identity. He benefits from leaving people guessing about how accurately his various PR versions reflect his real persona. But if we do not accept these stage performances as even partly reflecting his identity, then the question remains: Who is Mr. Putin? In fact, Putin hints that he is like Russia itself in the famous poem of Fyodor Tyutchev:

With the mind alone Russia cannot be understood,
No ordinary yardstick spans her greatness:
She stands alone, unique –
In Russia one can only believe.[22]

THE REAL MR. PUTINS

In this book, we pick up the idea of a multiplicity of Mr. Putins from his PR stunts in creating a portrait that attempts to provide some answers to the question "Who is Mr. Putin?" We argue that uncovering the multiple "real Putins" requires looking beyond the staged performances and the deliberately assumed guises that constitute the Putin political brand. For most of the first decade of the 2000s, Putin displayed remarkable strength as a political actor in the Russian context. This strength was derived from the combination of six individual identities we discuss and highlight in this book, not from his staged performances. We term these identities the Statist, the History Man, the Survivalist, the Outsider, the Free Marketeer, and the Case Officer. In Part I of this book, which focuses on the period up until 2012, we discuss each of the identities in detail, looking at their central elements and evolution, and their roots in Russian history, culture, and politics. We then explain how Russia's current political system can be seen as a logical result of the combination of Putin's six identities, along with the set of personal and professional relationships he formed over several decades in St. Petersburg and Moscow.

We begin Part I with an initial set of three identities: the Statist, the History Man, and the Survivalist. These are the most generic, in the sense that they characterize a larger group of Russians than just Mr. Putin, especially Russian politicians in Putin's general age cohort who began their careers during the Soviet period and launched themselves onto the national political stage in the 1990s. These first three identities provide the foundation for Mr. Putin's views about the Russian state, his political philosophy, and his conception of his first presidential terms in the 2000s. The decade of the 1990s—the Russian Federation's first decade as a stand-alone, independent country after the dissolution of the USSR—is a central element in the Statist, History Man, and Survivalist identities. This was the decade when Russia fell into economic and political crisis, and Moscow lost its direct authority over the rest of the former Soviet republics, including lands that had previously been part of the Russian Empire. This period also provides the overarching context for the identities as well as for Vladimir Putin's personal political narrative. Putin began his tenure as acting Russian president by publishing a December 1999 treatise, which we refer to as his "Millennium Message," on the lessons from Russia's experience in the 1990s and how he would address them. During his 2012 presidential election campaign, Putin returned to the themes of this earlier treatise. He made frequent explicit reference to what he described as the chaos of Russia in the 1990s under President Boris Yeltsin. He sharply contrasted this to the decade of political and economic stability he believes that he, personally, brought to the country after taking office in 1999. Putin essentially ran his 2012 campaign against the past, specifically the 1990s, rather than against another candidate. Mr. Putin clearly sees his presidency as the product of, as well as the answer to, the Russia of the 1990s.

The first three identities help explain Mr. Putin's goals, while the next three—the Outsider, the Free Marketeer, and the Case Officer—are more personal. They are primarily about the means he has been able to employ to achieve his ends. Putin's childhood experiences in a working class neighborhood of Leningrad, his years in the KGB at home and abroad, and his activities in the local government of post-Soviet St. Petersburg and then in a series of below-the-radar positions in the Kremlin in the late 1990s, all left him with a unique combination of skills and experience that helped propel him into the presidency in 1999–2000. They allowed him to build up and maintain the political and economic system that has been in place in Russia ever since.

That system, and Mr. Putin personally, has faced major challenges, both at home and abroad, in recent years. Part II of the book attempts to explain Putin's responses to those challenges in terms of the framework developed in Part I. At home, beginning with a political crisis in 2011–12, it seemed that some of Mr. Putin's core identities had ceased being strengths and had become sources of weakness for him, as well as a fundamental vulnerability for the personalized system of governance he had created within the Kremlin. As we will show, key elements of his identities prevented Mr. Putin from relating and connecting to thousands of Russian citizens who took to the streets in protest after Russia's 2011 parliamentary and 2012 presidential elections. In the end, however, Putin prevailed over the protesters. We will argue that he did so by going back to his core identities.

Our final chapters in Part II examine Mr. Putin in the context of his views of and interactions with the outside world, culminating with the crisis in Ukraine in 2013–14. Our objective is to understand Putin's motivations and his behavior by again drawing upon the insights of Part I. We first trace the evolution of his thinking about Russia's relations with the outside world and then show how Mr. Putin, the Operative in the Kremlin, translated that thinking into action as the Operative Abroad.

A CONTEXTUAL PORTRAIT

The ultimate purpose of our analysis is to provide a portrait of Mr. Putin's mental outlook, his worldview, and the individual aspects, or identities, that comprise this worldview. Like everyone else, Putin is an amalgam, a composite, of his life experiences. Putin's identities are parallel, not sequential. They blend into each other and are not mutually exclusive. In many respects they could be packaged differently from the way we present them. The most generic identities—the Statist, the History Man, and the Survivalist—could be merged together. They overlap in some obvious ways and have some themes in common. Nonetheless, there are key distinctions in each of them that we seek to tease out. Putin's outlook has been shaped by many influences: a combination of the Soviet and Russian contexts in which he grew up, lived and worked; a personal interest in Russian history and literature; his legal studies at Leningrad State University (LGU); his KGB training; his KGB service in Dresden in East Germany; his experiences in 1990s St. Petersburg; his early days in Moscow in 1996–99; and his time at the helm of the Russian state since 2000. Instead of trying to track down all the Putin stories to fit with these experiences, we have built a contextual narrative based on the known parts of Putin's biography, a close examination of his public pronouncements over more than a decade, and, not least, our own personal encounters with Mr. Putin.[23]

Just as we do not know who exactly selected Mr. Putin to be Boris Yeltsin's successor in 1999, we do not know specifically what Putin did during his 16 years in the KGB. We do, however, know the context of the KGB during the period when Vladimir Putin operated in it. So, for example, we have examined the careers, published writings, and memoirs of leading KGB officials such as Yury Andropov and Filipp Bobkov—the people who shaped the institution and thus Putin's role in it. Similarly, Putin constantly refers to Russia's "time of troubles" in the 1990s as the negative reference point for his presidency and premiership.

Although we do not know exactly what Putin was thinking about in the 1990s, we know a great deal about the events and debates of this decade in which people around him were closely involved. We also have ample evidence in Mr. Putin's own writings and speeches from 1999 to 2014, of his appropriation of the core concepts and language of an identifiable body of political and legal thought from the 1990s. In short, we know what others around Mr. Putin said or did in a certain timeframe, even if we cannot always prove what Putin himself was up to. We focus on what seems the most credible in a particular context to draw out information relevant to Putin's specific identities.

But before we turn to Mr. Putin's six identities, we begin with the context of his emergence onto the political scene—Russia of the 1990s. Putin did not appear out of the blue or from "nowhere" when he arrived in Moscow in 1996 to take up a position in the Russian presidential administration. He most demonstrably came from St. Petersburg. He also came from a group around Mayor Anatoly Sobchak to whom he had first gravitated in the 1970s when he was a student in LGU's law faculty and Sobchak was a lecturer there. Vladimir Putin's KGB superiors later assigned him to work at LGU in 1990, bringing him back into Anatoly Sobchak's orbit. Features of Mr. Putin's personality then drew him into the center of Sobchak's team as the former law professor campaigned to become mayor of St. Petersburg. Because of his real identities—and particular (often unsavory) skills associated with his role as a former KGB case officer—Vladimir Putin was subsequently determined by the St. Petersburg mayor and his close circle of associates to be uniquely well-suited for the task of enforcing informal rules and making corrupt businesses deliver in the freewheeling days of the 1990s. Putin became widely known as "Sobchak's fixer," and some of the activities he engaged in while in St. Petersburg helped pave his way to power in Moscow.

CHAPTER TWO

BORIS YELTSIN AND THE TIME OF TROUBLES

SOME COMMENTATORS HAVE DEPICTED THE story of how Mr. Putin came to be prime minster and then president of Russia as something akin to a tragedy that ruptured what appeared to be a generally positive trajectory of post-Soviet Russia in the 1990s toward the development of a more pluralistic democratic state and market economy. Vladimir Putin views the trajectory of 1990s in a very different way. For him, the Russian state was in a downward spiral. His elevation to the presidency at the end of 1999 was the logical culmination of, as well as the response to, a series of sometimes fatal (not just fateful) mistakes made by Russian political figures over the course of this tumultuous decade. The agenda of his presidency was an explicit response to the 1990s. His goal, as he himself often states, was to address the mistakes that were made and put Russia back on track.

The early part of the 1990s was framed by the great upheaval of the Soviet collapse, attempts at radical economic reform, and a declaration of hostilities between an ambitious Russian parliament and a weak presidency. In the years before Mr. Putin came to Moscow, factional squabbling within the Russian leadership, and endless changes in top personnel and the composition of the Russian government, created a strong sense that President Boris Yeltsin had allowed events to spin out of control. In 1993, President Yeltsin laid siege to the Russian parliamentary building to force a recalcitrant legislature to its knees and back into line with the executive branch, thus inaugurating a period of rule by presidential decree that would last for several years. In 1994, Yeltsin launched a brutal and unsuccessful domestic war to suppress an independence drive in the republic of Chechnya, sparking two decades of brutal conflict and ongoing insurgency in Russia's North Caucasus region. In 1996, Yeltsin's team ran a dirty election campaign to keep their, by now, ailing and unpopular leader in the Kremlin. They made a deal for political support with the oligarchs—the leading figures in Russia's new private business sectors—that resulted in the supposed pioneers of Russia's market economy manipulating politics and fighting among themselves over the purchase of former state assets. In the same timeframe, repeated setbacks to Russia's foreign policy goals in the Balkans and elsewhere in the former Soviet space compounded a public perception of disorder verging on chaos.

One narrative among the Russian political and intellectual elite in this period—both inside and outside government—was that the Russian state had fallen into another time of troubles (*smutnoye vremya*). This is the narrative that Putin adopted when he embarked on his presidency in 1999–2000. Russia's infamous *smutnoye vremya* was the historical period that marked the end of the sixteenth and beginning of the seventeenth century. The death of the last tsar of the Rurikid dynasty was followed by uprisings, invasions, and widespread famine before the establishment and consolidation of the new Romanov dynasty. Boris Yeltsin's critics compared him unfavorably with Boris Godunov, the notorious de facto Russian regent during the time of troubles. Similar evocations were made to other historical periods of insurgency and uncertainty in the eighteenth century under Peter the Great and Catherine the Great, to the aftermath of the Decembrist revolt in the 1820s–30s, and to the long span of episodic revolutionary turmoil from the 1860s up to World War I that culminated in the Revolution of 1917.[1]

On January 1, 1992, President Yeltsin launched an ambitious economic reform program intended to transform Russia's inherited Soviet economy into a modern market economy. The approach, labeled "shock therapy," was modeled on the recent experience of transition in Poland and other former communist countries. The key steps included the abolition of central planning for manufacturing and other production, the privatization of government enterprises, rapid liberalization of prices, and stark budget cuts aimed at restoring fiscal balance. For a Russian population that for decades had known only fixed prices, lifetime employment guarantees, and a cradle-to-grave welfare system, there was no doubt about the shock. Since virtually all prices were deregulated at the same time, they predictably jumped to unprecedented levels in one single leap. Accumulated household savings were rendered worthless. There were no provisions for compensation by the government. Enterprises were left without government orders. Their directors had neither the time nor the skills to find alternative customers before they had to simply shut down production.[2] Unemployment soared.

The austerity measures did not lead to any immediate improvement in government finances. Deficits ballooned while government services collapsed. Yeltsin's team of academic policymakers, headed by Yegor Gaidar, reassured the president and the public that all this had been expected but that the painful period would be brief. Recovery was around the corner. The result would be much greater prosperity than ever before under the Soviet system. The recovery—the therapy part of shock therapy—did not come. Inflation raged: prices rose on average by 20 percent a month throughout 1993.[3] Unemployment continued to grow. The economy as a whole shifted from a growth and development orientation to pure survival. On a private level, Russian households did the same. But publicly there was outrage.

From the outset, Gaidar and his group of young economists bore the brunt of the criticism for the economic and political consequences of the program. They became the target of conservative factions in the Russian parliament and industrial circles who had vested interests in Soviet-style business as usual. By the end of 1992, they were out of the cabinet and Boris Yeltsin had appointed Viktor Chernomyrdin, former head of the Russian gas industry and a member of the industrial lobby, as prime minister. Although parliament viewed Chernomyrdin as a proponent of a slower pace of reform, the conservative factions maintained their pressure on President Yeltsin. With Gaidar no longer overseeing economic policy, the Russian parliament moved to challenge Yeltsin on other political issues, including the process for passing a new Russian constitution. Both the parliament and the presidential administration set about creating their own competing drafts to replace the defunct Soviet-era constitution.

PRESIDENT VERSUS PARLIAMENT

The political standoff between the Russian legislative and executive branches degenerated to the point where effective governance was virtually impossible. In September 1993, Yeltsin abolished the existing parliament and announced that there would be elections for a new lower house in December 1993. He declared that the new lower house would now be called the State Duma, the name of the late imperial Russian legislature. The Russian parliament countered by naming its own acting president—Vice President Alexander Rutskoi, who had moved into open political opposition to Yeltsin. Rutskoi set up an alternative cabinet in the "White House," the Russian parliamentary building. The confrontation came to a bloody end on October 3–4, 1993. Supporters of the parliament marched on Ostankino, the Moscow television tower, and a number of protesters were killed in a skirmish with interior ministry forces. On the morning of October 4, Yeltsin ordered Russian military tanks to fire on the White House to force his erstwhile vice president and the deputies to surrender. One hundred forty-five people were killed and 800 wounded in the assault and associated street fighting, according to official statements.

The events of October 1993 were (at that point) the most violent political confrontation in the Russian capital since the Revolution of 1917.[4] They left their mark on many Russian political figures of the period, including Mr. Putin. After the fighting was over and new elections were held, President Yeltsin stripped the new State Duma of many legislative oversight functions. He relocated parliament from the charred remnants of the White House to an old Soviet building symbolically in the shadow of the Kremlin walls. The scorch marks on the White House were washed off, the building was cleaned up and renovated, and it was handed off to become the seat of the Russian government. In a January 2012 interview with the British newspaper *The Guardian*, Gleb Pavlovsky—a former Kremlin adviser and political strategist who worked closely with Putin during his tenure as president and prime minister before being fired in 2011—observed that the 1993 standoff between Yeltsin and the parliament had a profound effect on Vladimir Putin. The assault on the White House shaped Putin's views about what tended to happen when the balance of power shifted in Russia. The losers in a political confrontation would be put against the wall and shot. "Putin always said, we know ourselves . . . we know that as soon as we move aside, you will destroy us. He said that directly, you'll put us to the wall and execute us. And we don't want to go to the wall . . . that was a very deep belief and was based on [the] very tough confrontations of 1993 when Yeltsin fired on the Supreme Soviet [parliament] and killed a lot more people—Putin knows—than was officially announced. . . ."[5]

A NEW PRESIDENTIAL CONSTITUTION

Fortunately for Putin, he was nowhere near either the Kremlin or the White House walls in 1993. He was a bystander to Yeltsin's showdown with the parliament, sitting on the sidelines in the mayor's office in St. Petersburg. Putin's then boss, Anatoly Sobchak, however, was one of the key drafters of the new Russian constitution.[6] This would prove to be one of the most consequential documents for defining Putin's future presidency. Having shelled the parliament into submission, Yeltsin pushed through a draft of the constitution that granted the Russian president and the executive branch extensive powers over domestic and foreign policy. In effect, Yeltsin's new constitution retroactively legitimized many of the steps he had taken (excluding the military action) to curb the powers of parliament. It was a potentially powerful tool for any president, like Mr. Putin, trying to secure the preeminent position in Russian political life.

The 1993 Russian constitutional process was deeply rooted in earlier historical attempts to create a constitution. Although there was a good deal of discussion of other international conceptual sources and constitutional models, the document that emerged drew heavily from ideas put forward in Russia's late tsarist era. One of the creators of the 1993 Russian constitution, Sergei Shakhrai, would later claim that it was a "myth" that the Russian constitution had drawn any inspiration whatsoever from any Western constitutional models—except, perhaps, for the fact that the Russian president was conceived as the "Russian equivalent of the British Queen."[7] (Great Britain, of course, does not have a constitution in the modern sense of a single written document, nor does the British monarch have real political power.) The Russian presidency enshrined in the constitution far exceeded even the U.S. and French equivalents in its sweep of authority.

DEBACLE IN THE DUMA

In spite of the bloodletting and his new quasi-monarchical powers, President Yeltsin found the Russian State Duma no easier to work with than the old parliament. The 1993 December elections produced a parliament split between generally anti-reform parties, including the nationalist Liberal Democratic Party (LDPR) and the Communist Party of the Russian Federation (CPRF), and pro-reform parties such as Russia's Choice and the Russian United Democratic Party, *Yabloko* ("apple"). Among the parties, the nationalist LDPR secured almost a quarter (22.9 percent) of the popular vote, outstripping the second-place Russia's Choice with 15 percent.[8] The Duma subsequently fell upon itself in a series of factional and personal squabbles. Parties and blocs formed and reformed with dizzying frequency, and some parliamentary sessions were disrupted by fistfights.[9] Similar scenes played out in regional legislatures, including in St. Petersburg. A decade later, Putin would refer to the legislative rough and tumble with considerable distaste, noting that the repeated brawls had given him a very low opinion of politics.[10]

In spring 1995, after much debate, a new election law was passed setting parliamentary elections for December 1995 and presidential elections for June 1996. As would happen again in 2011, the Kremlin had an unpleasant "December surprise" in the 1995 parliamentary election. The opposition Communist Party trounced the ruling party of the period, *Nash dom Rossiya* (NDR), or Our Home Is Russia, which had been formed under the leadership of Prime Minister Viktor Chernomyrdin to try to unify the range of pro-reform or "democratic" parties.[11] As we will discuss later, Putin had his own role to play in this debacle, leading NDR's local campaign in St. Petersburg, an experience that put him off electoral politics even further.

YELTSIN, THE OLIGARCHS, AND THE JUNE 1996 ELECTION

The subsequent 1996 presidential election—which like other Russian presidential elections consisted of two rounds to reduce the pool of candidates to two if no one got a clear majority of the vote—was transformed into an apparent head-to-head contest between Yeltsin and Gennady Zyuganov, the Communist Party leader. Zyuganov made it clear that he would end Yeltsin's economic reforms and return to a modified Soviet-style system if he won the presidency. At this fateful juncture, Yeltsin was undergoing his own personal time of troubles. The Russian president was in poor health. He would in fact have a serious heart attack between the electoral rounds and disappear from public view for a substantial period of time. These troubles compounded his government's political difficulties. They also set the scene for Putin's subsequent move to Moscow. Just before the presidential election, Yeltsin's approval ratings fell to an all-time low of 3 percent. Yeltsin risked forfeiting the election to Zyuganov unless the team around him could pull off a political miracle, but the team lacked the resources for a full-scale national electoral campaign. The Kremlin's coffers were empty, and new independent media outlets had eclipsed the stale programming and content of the old state television, newspapers, and radio.[12]

Yeltsin's team reached out to a set of business people who had benefitted directly from the government's reform program. They had amassed fortunes in new financial institutions and acquired stakes in the new media. Among them were Boris Berezovsky, head of Logovaz, one of Russia's largest holding companies, which had controlling shares or interests in media outlets, including the Russian television station ORT, the newspaper *Nezavisimaya gazeta,* and the weekly magazine *Ogonyok*; Vladimir Potanin, the president of Uneximbank, Russia's third-largest bank in terms of assets; Mikhail Khodorkovsky, head of the Menatep-Rosprom financial industrial group; Vladimir Gusinsky, the founder of the Most Bank and media group; Pyotr Aven, a former Russian minister turned banker; Mikhail Fridman, the president of Alfa Bank; and Alexander Smolensky, the head of Stolichny Savings Bank.[13] In return for campaign contributions on a massive scale and preferential media access, Yeltsin promised this group of seven oligarchs privileged bidding positions for controlling shares in some of Russia's most important state companies in the oil and gas, metallurgy, and other industrial sectors when they were privatized. This notorious "loans-for-shares" agreement has been thoroughly parsed and widely documented.[14] It brought the titans of Russian business, the oligarchs, who bankrolled the campaign into the business of deciding who would run Russia. It also laid the ground for clashes between the Yeltsin "Family" (Boris Yeltsin's family members and his closest associates) and some of the businessmen—with serious political consequences for Russia in the period leading up to 1999—as their respective sets of interests inevitably diverged.[15]

The 1996 Russian presidential campaign prefigured the political tools, components, and principal actors of the Putin era in the 2000s. The heavy use of Western-style PR, the negative campaigning, discrediting of opponents, the rise of both independent reformed communist and Russian nationalist political movements, and massive infusions of campaign capital from vested private business interests paved the way for the politics of the subsequent decade. Gennady Zyuganov became the main political pretender to the Russian presidency. He was also Putin's primary putative opponent in the March 2012 presidential election, reprising his 1996 role. Russian general and Afghan war hero Alexander Lebed, a strong nationalist candidate who came in third place in the first round of the 1996 election, died in a helicopter crash in April 2002. He was succeeded on the national stage at various points by his colleague and co-founder of the Congress of Russian Communities (KRO) nationalist movement, Dmitry Rogozin.[16] Other political figures—like nationalist politician Vladimir Zhirinovsky, head of the LDPR, which Yeltsin's team in 1996 portrayed in the domestic and international media as the stalking horse for fascism— also became permanent fixtures of the Russian political scene. After that election, some of the "magnificent seven" oligarchs were given positions in the Russian government, including Boris Berezovsky as deputy secretary of the Russian Security Council and Vladimir Potanin as first deputy prime minister. Berezovsky, along with Vladimir Gusinsky and Mikhail Khodorkovsky, would later become the dramatis personae of Putin's clashes with the oligarchs in the early 2000s. Berezovsky and Gusinsky ended up in exile and Khodorkovsky was dispatched to a Siberian jail.[17]

WAR IN CHECHNYA: DOUBLE-DEALING WITH RUSSIA'S REGIONS

In the midst of the political machinations around the parliament and the presidency, Yeltsin was embroiled in another struggle to forge a new political relationship between Moscow and the individual regions of the Russian Federation. This struggle unleashed a war in the Russian North Caucasus that would also prove instrumental in Putin's rise to the presidency in 1999. Like its dealings with parliament, the Yeltsin government's engagement with the regions was ad hoc and contradictory. It vacillated among legislative measures, police action, military intervention, repression, and conciliatory bilateral treaties that granted different regions varying concessions. The policies Yeltsin initiated provided the frame for contentious center-periphery relations that have dogged Vladimir Putin's time in office.

Protests against central government policies—including changes in internal administrative borders and Moscow's high-level political appointments at the regional and local level—had been an enduring feature of politics in the Soviet periphery since the late 1950s.[18] After the dissolution of the Soviet Union and the establishment of the Russian Federation, Russia's own regions continued to demand territorial and political changes. The Russian North Caucasus republic of Chechnya declared its independence and seceded, even before the end of the USSR, in November 1991. In February 1992, Yeltsin tried to push through a new Federal Treaty to resolve all the contested issues. Chechnya and the republic of Tatarstan in the Russian Volga region rejected it—raising fears that Russia would unravel like the USSR. Tatarstan and a number of other Russian regions then rejected the provisions in the new 1993 Russian constitution that delineated regional powers. As a stop-gap effort, the Yeltsin government concluded a bilateral treaty with Tatarstan in February 1994. As far as Chechnya was concerned, Yeltsin made a half-hearted effort to negotiate the republic's return to the Federation. He then threw Moscow's support behind forces opposed to the independent Chechen government. A botched effort in summer 1994 to overthrow the Chechen government ended with Chechen government forces capturing Russian operatives, who were paraded in front of the media to humiliate Moscow and Yeltsin.

In December 1994, the Russian government launched a full-scale military assault on Chechnya. The assault became the largest military campaign on Russian soil since World War II, with mass civilian and military casualties and the almost complete destruction of Chechnya's principal city, Grozny. In August 1996, just after the presidential election and simultaneous with Putin's arrival in Moscow, the over-extended Russian military essentially collapsed as an effective fighting force. The military's morale was sapped by high casualties, as well as by shortages of critical armaments that forced commanders to dip into stocks of vintage World War II ordnance. Even some of the most basic supplies for the predominantly conscript soldiers ran out—with appeals sent out during one part of the winter campaign for the Russian population to knit thick socks for Russian forces fighting in the cold and unforgiving mountainous regions of Chechnya. The war in Chechnya resulted in Russia's most significant military defeat since Afghanistan the previous decade, but this time on its own territory.[19] Partly at the instigation of General Lebed—who was now a power to be reckoned with in Russian politics after his strong showing in the June presidential election—the Yeltsin government was forced to conclude a truce with the Chechen government. In a subsequent peace agreement, Moscow agreed to end the military intervention and then conclude a bilateral treaty on future relations with Chechnya. Many prominent figures in the Russian political and military elite bristled at this humiliation and stressed that the arrangements hammered out with Chechnya in 1996–97 would be temporary.[20]

The war between Moscow and Chechnya emboldened other regions to demand bilateral treaties. Instead of a stopgap measure, the treaties became the primary mechanism for regulating Moscow's relations with its entire periphery.[21] Over a two-year period, the Yeltsin government was forced to negotiate agreements with Bashkortorstan, a major oil-producing region next to Tatarstan; republics neighboring Chechnya in the North Caucasus; Nizhny Novgorod, Yekaterinburg, Perm, and Irkutsk, all predominantly ethnic Russian regions stretching from Russia's heartland into the Urals and the Lake Baikal region of Siberia; the Siberian republic of Sakha-Yakutiya, which is the heart of Russia's diamond industry; the exclave of Kaliningrad on the Baltic Sea; and even St. Petersburg and the surrounding Leningrad oblast.[22] The treaties proved a useful tool for avoiding further ruinous conflict. They also resulted in the piecemeal, asymmetric decentralization of the Russian state and a confounding set of overlapping responsibilities.

The bilateral treaties were extremely unpopular in central government and parliamentary circles. By the end of the 1990s, as Putin rose to the top of the Russian government, they had become one of the most enduring symbols of the administrative chaos and weakness of the Russian state. Politicians in Moscow demanded they be overturned. With the treaties in place, leaders of republics vaulted from the status of regional functionaries to presidents and national-level political figures. Regional politicians reinterpreted Moscow's decrees to suit local concerns. They refused to implement Russian federal legislation. They created their own economic associations. They withheld tax revenues from the federal government. They openly criticized central government policy.[23] Beyond Chechnya, this weakness found perhaps its best expression in the Russian far east, in Primorsky Krai. There, at the furthest edge of the Russian Federation, Moscow engaged in what seemed like a never-ending political battle with the region's obstinate governor, Yevgeny Nazdratenko. From his political perch in Vladivostok, the governor assailed the Yeltsin government's attempts to reach a border agreement with China. He accused Moscow of cutting off Primorsky Krai's access to the Pacific Ocean. He stationed his own paramilitary Cossack forces on the border, diverted federal funds for his personal pet projects, and generally harangued Yeltsin for creating the region's chronic economic problems.[24] Putin would later find a creative way of dealing with Governor Nazdratenko that would become a hallmark of his efforts to deal with other difficult personalities in the 2000s.

THWARTED ABROAD

In the meantime, as the Yeltsin government waged war with Chechnya and engaged in a tug-of-war with Primorsky Krai, Moscow's foreign policy faltered. Russia's internecine conflicts and economic weakness constrained its ability to exert influence on consequential developments abroad. In the late 1980s USSR, Soviet leader Mikhail Gorbachev and Foreign Minister Eduard Shevardnadze had drawn a direct link between domestic and foreign policy. To secure international financial support for restructuring and revitalizing the Soviet economy, they abandoned the USSR's traditional confrontational posture toward the West and focused instead on reducing international tensions.[25] Boris Yeltsin initially continued the same foreign policy line with Foreign Minister Andrei Kozyrev. During the early stages of shock therapy, relations with international financial and political institutions and the United States were prioritized. On February 1, 1992, President Yeltsin and U.S. president George Herbert Walker Bush issued a joint declaration that Russia and the United States were no longer adversaries. They proclaimed a new era of strategic partnership.

Optimism for this partnership rapidly faded as Russia's relations with the West became mired in a series of international crises. After the breakup of Yugoslavia, full-scale fighting erupted in Sarajevo, the capital of the new state of Bosnia-Herzegovina. United Nations (UN) sanctions were slapped against Serbia—Yugoslavia's primary successor state and one of imperial Russia's traditional regional allies—which openly supported ethnic Serbian forces in what soon became a civil war. In July 1992, UN and other international peacekeeping forces intervened, provoking a backlash from Moscow. Conservative and nationalist factions in the Russian parliament protested that Russia had not been suitably consulted in spite of its historic interests in the Balkans. Russia's relations with its neighborhood immediately took on a harsher tone.

The term "near abroad" was introduced by Foreign Minister Kozyrev and other Russian officials to describe the former Soviet states on Russia's borders. Government reports were produced on ways of safeguarding Russian interests in these states.[26] At an Organization for Security and Cooperation in Europe (OSCE) meeting in Stockholm in December 1992, Kozyrev offered a version of a speech to his counterparts that clearly captured a new mood in Moscow. He outlined an assertive Russian foreign policy, reaffirming Russia's traditional support for Serbia, laying claim to the entire former Soviet space, and reserving Russia's right to exert influence through military as well as economic means.[27] By this time, the Russian parliament's backlash to shock therapy was in full swing. There was a general perception, in both the Yeltsin government and parliament, that Russia was being treated as a developing or second-tier country by the West. Despite repeated promises of substantial financial aid, the United States and international financial institutions had been unable to provide sufficient assistance to alleviate the most severe effects of Russia's economic reforms.[28] The disillusioned Yeltsin government increasingly turned its foreign policy attention away from the West and toward the new states of the former Soviet Union—trying to salvage what was left of Moscow's previous regional authority.

REBUFFED IN THE NEAR ABROAD

Yeltsin's overtures for closer relations were soon rebuffed in the near abroad. After the collapse of the USSR, the Yeltsin team thought it had created a mechanism for some form of post-Soviet regional reintegration under Russian leadership through the creation of the Commonwealth of Independent States (CIS). Nothing went quite according to plan. Most

CIS member states saw the organization either as a means for heading off nasty Yugoslav-style conflicts, or as the beginning of a mutual civilized divorce. The Baltic states of Estonia, Latvia, and Lithuania—which the USSR had annexed during World War II in an act that the UN declared illegal—refused to join the CIS. They set their sights instead on membership in the European Union (EU) and North Atlantic Treaty Organization (NATO). Georgia also initially refused. Moldova and Azerbaijan agreed only to associate membership. Ukraine, the most important of the other former Soviet republics, joined the CIS but clashed with Russia over dividing the former Soviet Black Sea Fleet—based in Sevastopol on Ukraine's Crimea Peninsula.[29]

Then fighting broke out between several new states and various separatist territorial entities, pulling Moscow into the fray. Armed clashes flared between Azerbaijan and the ethnic Armenian population in Nagorno-Karabakh. Across the border from Azerbaijan, Georgia fought with two of its autonomous regions, South Ossetia and Abkhazia. In Moldova, violence erupted between forces loyal to the new government and the secessionist Transnistria region. Troops from the Soviet 14th Army stationed in Transnistria intervened. General Alexander Lebed, commander of the 14th Army, burst into the national spotlight with his efforts to separate the sides and secure Russian military installations and weapons stockpiles. Further afield, in Central Asia, Tajikistan fell into civil war.[30]

The ethno-political violence in the Soviet successor states was exacerbated by Moscow's confrontation with Estonia and Latvia over the status of post-war Russian-speaking immigrants. Both states introduced legislation demanding that those immigrants fulfill residence and language requirements before they could apply for citizenship. In November 1992, the UN adopted a resolution calling for Moscow to withdraw all former Soviet troops from the Baltic states, given their illegal annexation. The Yeltsin government tried to link the troop withdrawal demanded by the UN to its dispute with the Baltic states. If the immigrants were given citizenship, the troops would be withdrawn; otherwise they would stay until the issue was resolved. In September 1993 at the United Nations General Assembly, Foreign Minister Kozyrev dug in Moscow's heels even further. He declared Russia's "special responsibility" for protecting Russian language speakers (including in Transnistria and the Baltic states) and demanded the UN grant Russia primacy in future peacekeeping missions sent into former Soviet republics.[31] These efforts were to no avail. Sustained Western pressure, including specific threats to withhold loans vital for Russia's economic reform program, ultimately forced Moscow's hand. The last former Soviet soldier was out of the Baltic states by August 31, 1994.[32]

Elsewhere in the former Soviet Union, Moscow did its best to retain whatever leverage it could. In the Caucasus, Russian operatives and weaponry were used in conflicts and coups against perceived anti-Russian leaders. Economic pressure was deployed against Ukraine and the Central Asian states in a variety of disputes. A Moscow-encouraged Crimean independence movement impinged on Ukraine's claims to the Black Sea Fleet. By September 1995, the CIS and the near abroad had become the priority area for Russian foreign policy and the focal point of its principal vital interests. President Yeltsin signed a decree on the integration of the CIS, which set ambitious goals for enhancing economic, political, and military ties.[33] When he came into office in 1999–2000, Putin would continue to emphasize the importance of Russia's relations with the former Soviet republics and of maintaining Moscow's grip on the various levers of influence over them. He also took away some critical lessons from Russia's experience of being ousted (in his view) ignominiously from the Baltic states in August 1994.

VEERING FROM WEST TO EAST

At the time, none of the Yeltsin government's actions were seen by the political and military elite in Moscow to have appreciably improved Russia's international standing. The conflicts dominated Russia's domestic and foreign policy agenda. Relations with the United States and the West degenerated. In 1994, the civil war in Bosnia-Herzegovina escalated, culminating in punitive actions against Serbia by the EU and the United States, and then NATO air strikes. The Russian Ministry of Foreign Affairs and President Yeltsin were informed of the air attacks after the NATO allies had already made the decision. Although NATO later worked out an arrangement for Russian troops to serve in a NATO peacekeeping contingent in Bosnia under their own command, Russia's parliament was, once again, infuriated. Concurrent with the action in the Balkans, NATO's 1994 decision to expand the alliance to the new democracies of Eastern Europe, and by extension to former Soviet republics such as the Baltic states, was protested by all Russian political factions. Between 1994 and 1997, the expansion of NATO dominated Russia's interactions with the West.

In an interview in the *Moscow News* in September 1995, former Soviet President Mikhail Gorbachev summed up the general elite consensus in Moscow.[34] The West had taken advantage of Russia's weakness. The West's policy in Europe, the Balkans, and within the former Soviet Union, he asserted, "is marked by a clear disrespect for Russia, as is shown by its failure to consult Russia on the issue of NATO bombings [in Yugoslavia]. . . . All this proves that some Western politicians would have liked to see Russia play second fiddle in world politics. . . . Whatever Russia's domestic problems, it will never reconcile itself to such a humiliating position."[35]

Gorbachev insisted that Russia "badly need[ed] a meaningful policy on the international scene, a policy aimed at restoring the security system in Europe and Russia's role as a top player in world politics." He also urged a change in Western policies in Russia's former spheres of influence, warning that "an arrogant attitude towards Russia and her interests is deeply insulting to the Russian people, and that is fraught with grave consequences."[36]

Not long after Gorbachev's interview, President Yeltsin replaced Foreign Minister Kozyrev in January 1996 with the former head of Russian foreign intelligence and Middle East specialist Yevgeny Primakov. Humiliated and insulted in the West, Moscow made foreign policy overtures toward former Soviet allies in Asia and the Middle East—again with the urging of factions within the parliament and government. Primakov's appointment marked the beginning of initiatives aimed at rebuilding Russia's relations with China, India, Iraq, Iran, and other powers the USSR had previously courted. There was little further talk of partnership with the United States.

MOUNTING DEMANDS FOR THE RESTORATION OF THE STATE: PUTIN COMES TO MOSCOW

This is when Putin came to Moscow to join the Russian presidential administration. Between 1991 and 1996, Russian domestic and foreign policy had endured a long series of humiliating setbacks. Russian politicians were at each other's throats. Yeltsin had shelled the Russian parliament but had not forced it into complete submission. New political opposition forces and the oligarchs had been emboldened by their roles in the June 1996 presidential election campaign. The government's progressive economic reform program was in tatters, and its team of economic reformers was in disarray. The economy was in full-blown recession. Tens of thousands had taken to the streets to demand unpaid wages and pensions and to protest rising prices. War had ravaged Chechnya and pulled it even further away from Moscow's orbit. Regional leaders were picking apart the Russian Federation, treaty by treaty. NATO had denied Russia its traditional role in the Balkan conflicts. The West had pushed Russia out of the Baltic states. Ukraine and other putative allies in the near abroad were fighting over the Soviet spoils—with Moscow and among themselves. Relations with the United States were on a downward trajectory.

CHAPTER THREE
_____

THE STATIST

WHEN PUTIN ARRIVED IN MOSCOW in August 1996, few in Russian elite circles had any illusions about the depth of the state's domestic crisis and the loss of its previous great-power status internationally. Many internal observers feared Russia was in danger of total collapse. They bristled at Western commentators constantly regurgitating a description of the country during the late Soviet period as "Upper Volta with missiles."[1] Russian politics was focused on preserving what was left and avoiding further humiliations. Practically every political group and party across the Russian political spectrum, from right to left, felt that the post-Soviet dismantling of the state had gone too far and advocated the restoration of Russian "state power." Even some of the liberal economists around Yegor Gaidar who were at the forefront of pulling apart the old Soviet economy in 1992–93 had moved in this direction.[2]

Everything Putin has said on the subject of saving Russia from chaos since he came to power is consistent with the general elite consensus in the late 1990s on the importance of restoring order. Most of the Russian domestic and foreign policy priorities that Putin would adopt when he became president were already identified by the Russian political elite in the same period. All Vladimir Putin had to do in the 2000s was to channel and synthesize the various ideas percolating through newspaper columns and political manifestos about how to address Russia's crisis of statehood to produce what has loosely been referred to as "Putinism." This included the re-creation of a more authoritative centralized state apparatus—the so-called *vertikal vlasti* or "vertical of power"—and greater assertiveness in foreign policy, especially in the near abroad and other areas where Russia had experienced its greatest setbacks under Boris Yeltsin.[3] Although Putin was short on the specifics of what he would actually do at the outset of his presidency, he would ultimately derive most of his ideas for action from some of the more conservative factions in the 1990s political debates.

THE "MILLENNIUM MESSAGE"

The first key to Vladimir Putin's personality is his view of himself as a man of the state, his identity as a statist (*gosudarstvennik* in Russian). Putin sees himself as someone who belongs to a large cohort of people demanding the restoration of the state. Vladimir Putin publicly presented himself as a statist and offered his vision for the restoration of the Russian state in one of his first major political statements and presentations just before he became acting Russian president. This statement sets the scene for Putin's time as both president and prime minister. As a result, we need to examine the specific connotations of being a statist in the Russian context of the 1990s.

On December 29, 1999, the website of the Russian government posted a 5,000-word treatise under the signature of then Prime Minister Vladimir Putin. Its title was "Russia on the Threshold of the New Millennium." Two days later, the president of Russia, Boris Yeltsin, appeared on national television to declare that he was resigning and handing over power to Putin. The Internet treatise became known as the "Millennium Message." It was Vladimir Putin's political mission statement or manifesto for the beginning of his presidency, and it provides the overall framework for understanding the system of governance he has created around him.

One of Putin's main points in his manifesto was that throughout history, the Russian state lost its status when its people were divided, when Russians lost sight of the common values that united them and distinguished them from all others. Since the fall of communism, Putin asserted, Russians had embraced personal rights and freedoms, freedom of personal expression, freedom to travel abroad. These universal values were fine, but they were not "Russian." Nor would they be enough to ensure Russia's survival. There were other, distinctly Russian values that were at the core of what Putin called the "Russian Idea." Those values were patriotism, collectivism, solidarity, *derzhavnost'*—the belief that

Russia is destined always to be a great power (*derzhava*) exerting its influence abroad—and the untranslatable *gosudarstvennichestvo*.

Russia is not America or Britain with their historical liberal traditions, Putin went on:

> For us, the state and its institutions and structures have always played an exceptionally important role in the life of the country and the people. For Russians, a strong state is not an anomaly to fight against. Quite the contrary, it is the source and guarantor of order, the initiator and the main driving force of any change. . . . Society desires the restoration of the guiding and regulating role of the state.[4]

Putin promised to restore that role. He declared himself to be a *gosudarstvennik,* a builder of the state, a servant of the state. A *gosudarstvennik,* a person who believes that Russia must be and must have a strong state, has a particular resonance in Russia. It does not imply someone who engages in politics. A *gosudarstvennik* is not a politician driven by a set of distinct beliefs who represents a certain group or constituency and jumps into the fray to run for political office. Instead, the term refers to someone who is selected or self-selects to serve the country on a permanent basis and who believes only in the state itself.

Similarly, the state, or *gosudarstvo,* has a very specific meaning. In Russia, the relationship between the state—Mother Russia, the motherland, *Mat' Rossiya,* or *Rodina*—and the individual is different from that in most Western countries. In the United States, the state exists to protect the rights of the individual. The twist in Russia is that while Mother Russia must be protected, she does not necessarily protect her own citizens. In Russia, the state is primary. The state is a stand-alone entity—sometimes rendered in a capitalized form as the "State." The individual and society are, and must be, subordinate to the state and its interests. This is the essence of *gosudarstvennichestvo* as Putin conceived of it in the Millennium Message.

"STATE PEOPLE" AND THE KGB

Given his KGB background, Putin's designation of himself as a *gosudarstvennik* seems rather obvious. The KGB (now FSB) and other agencies focused on the security of the Russian state and the projection of the state's power abroad, including the interior and defense ministries, are viewed as the central elements in the Russian state apparatus or bureaucracy. In Russia, they are collectively known as the *silovyye struktury*, the "force" or the "power structures"—which could be rendered in English as the "power ministries." Russians, like Vladimir Putin, whose careers originated in these ministries, are commonly known as the *siloviki*. In the KGB/FSB, many individuals have cultivated a myth about themselves and their institution as being the ultimate Russian patriots and proponents of a strong state. They even claim a role that stretches back over several centuries of Russian history and tradition.[5]

This myth is perfectly encapsulated in a May 2001 interview in *Spetsnaz Rossii,* a journal closely linked with the intelligence services. The interview features retired KGB general Nikolai Leonov, who was a top figure in the KGB's First Main Directorate in the 1970s–80s, heading up operations in North and South America.[6] Leonov was asked about the sudden appearance at the top of government of a number of the "younger generation that entered the KGB in the 1970s." These included, in addition to Vladimir Putin, Sergei Ivanov (secretary of the Russian Security Council in 2001 and later defense minister and a deputy prime minister, and now chief of staff of the presidential administration); Viktor Cherkesov (a former head of the KGB directorate in St. Petersburg, before becoming first deputy director of the FSB, and then in 2001 the presidential envoy to the Russian Northwest Federal District covering St. Petersburg); and Nikolai Patrushev (director of the FSB from 1999 to 2008, and then secretary of the Russian Security Council). Leonov responded:

> First of all, the demand today is precisely for such tough, pragmatically thinking politicians. They are in command of operative information. . . . But at the same time, they are patriots and proponents of a strong state grounded in centuries-old tradition. History recruited them to carry out a special operation for the resurrection of our Great Power [*Derzhava*], because there has to be balance in the world, and without a strong Russia the geopolitical turbulence will begin. . . . [W]hat is a KGB officer? He is, above all, a servant of the state. . . . Experience, loyalty to the state . . . an iron will—where else are you going to find cadres? . . . The only people that can bring order to the state are state people [*gosudarstvennyye lyudi*].[7]

"SOCIETY" AND THE RUSSIAN ELITE

Vladimir Putin is thus hardly unique among his KGB cohort in present-ing himself as a servant of the state. The ideas he expresses about the state, as well as the society subordinated to it, belong to a clearly identifi-able and long-established body of Russian conservative political thought. These ideas were prevalent among those who considered themselves to be part of the Russian elite in the 1990s when the concept of restoring the state became an obsession. Putin speaks directly to them, from the very beginning of his tenure, in the Millennium Message.

When Putin says in the Millennium Message, "*Society* desires the restoration of the guiding and regulating role of the state," he does not mean the whole of Russian society, the Russian population. Putin means the politically and socially active segment of society—the people with a vested interest in how the state is structured and functions. In other words, these are the elite groups in Russian society that he, Vladimir Putin, has been associated with during his career, including groups who previously worked directly for the Soviet state in the power ministries. Gleb Pavlovsky, the former Kremlin adviser and political strategist, summed up this idea in his interview with *The Guardian* in January 2012:

> Putin belongs to a very extensive but completely politically untrans-parent [sic], unseen, unrepresented layer of people who after the end of the 1980s were looking for [a] *revanche* in connection with the fall of the Soviet Union. I was also one of them. . . . My people and my friends were people who couldn't accept what had hap-pened. . . . There were hundreds, thousands of people like that in the elite, who were not [all] communists—I was never a member of the Communist Party. They were people who just didn't like how things had been done in 1991. It was very different people with different ideas of freedom. Putin was one of the people who until the end of the 1990s was passively waiting for the moment for *revanche*. . . . By *revanche* I mean the resurrection of the great state, in which we lived, which we became used to. Not a totalitar-ian one, of course, but a state that could be respected. And the state of the 1990s was impossible to respect.[8]

Just like the state, "the elite" has a set of connotations for Russians that often differs from views of the elite in the United States or Europe. The idea of a Russian elite with a specific role or function in Russian politics has been around since the nineteenth century. Over time it became synonymous with the Russian concept of the intelligentsia—a term that educated Russians in the nascent revolutionary movements of the 1890s used to describe themselves.[9] Nineteenth-century Russian "intelligents" saw themselves as the only group truly committed to the improvement of public welfare. In their opinion, they were the representatives of Russian society in opposition to the tsarist economic and political system.[10] In some respects, they also considered themselves to be statists, but they were pushing to reform the state and its institutions from below, not from the top.[11]

In the Soviet period, the intelligentsia was officially used as a collective term for professional or white collar groups that defied Marxian social classification: doctors, engineers, teachers, scientists, researchers, writers, and artists.[12] In the 1960s and 1970s, the term assumed more anti-establishment connotations with the emergence of the dissident human rights movement among disaffected Soviet intellectuals (often engaged in white collar professions). In the 1990s, the concept persisted as a reference point for an educated group of Russians acting—more at their own behest than anyone else's—in the name of society and channeling public opinion. The intelligentsia, and thus the elite, adopted a permanently critical posture toward the prevailing economic and political system.

ACCORD IN THE NAME OF RUSSIA

One of the most pertinent expressions of the elite sentiment Putin would pick up on in his Millennium Message came in early 1994. Shortly after the new Russian constitution had been passed in the wake of the shelling of parliament, a number of conservative Russian politicians formed a political organization—*Soglasiye vo imya Rossii* (Accord in the Name of Russia) or *Soglasiye*. In an "Address to the citizens of Russia," the organizers of the Soglasiye movement promised "to restore the capacity of Russian statehood (*gosudarstvennost'*), protect the national market and national wealth, provide conditions for Russia to make a breakthrough into a post-industrial future, combat crime, overcome unemployment and hunger, and give every citizen a decent standard of living."[13]

The politicians who created Soglasiye all remained active well into Putin's presidency. The leading members were Sergei Glazyev, a former minister for external economic relations, who became a member of the Russian parliament in 1993 and would in 2003 become one of the founders of the nationalist Rodina ("motherland") party; Communist Party leader Gennady Zyuganov; and Valery Zorkin, the former head of the Russian Constitutional Court who had resigned from his position as chairman after openly and vocally opposing Yeltsin's assault on the Russian parliament.[14] Other high-profile members of the Russian elite endorsed the movement. These included Russian film director Nikita Mikhalkov (who would later become a strong supporter of President Putin), former Vice President Alexander Rutskoi (who survived the bombardment of parliament), Alexander Tsipko (a Soviet political philosopher and adviser to Mikhail Gorbachev, who became director of programs at the Gorbachev Foundation), and former Soviet film director Stanislav Govorukhin (who became a prominent conservative member of the Russian Duma).[15] As the movement consisted of disparate political groups and individuals with a range of policy perspectives, it soon lost cohesion and momentum. The themes of reviving a strong Russian state nonetheless continued to reverberate, along with Soglasiye's core idea of creating some kind of all-encompassing movement to rally the elite behind the cause of restoration.[16] In many respects, Putin's December 29, 1999, Millennium Message could be viewed as an echo of this movement's principal ideas.

Over the next several years, the elite debate about pulling Russia out of its crisis settled on the concept of finding a national idea to bring the country's political factions together. The concept of a Russian Idea had many prominent proponents before Putin featured it in the Millennium Message. One of the first was Andrei Kokoshin, a leading academic arms control specialist who served as first deputy defense minister from 1992 to 1997. Kokoshin circulated a treatise on Russia's national security and "military might" in 1995 that argued that Russia could not revive unless it came up with a new national idea.[17] Kokoshin asserted in this treatise and in subsequent publications that the importance of creating this idea had "already been acknowledged by the most active part of our *society*—politicians, scholars, journalists, public servants, party leaders, union activists, entrepreneurs, and of particular importance by leaders of industry and regular workers."[18] This was exactly the same reference Vladimir Putin would make in December 1999 in the Millennium Message, when he asserted, "*Society* desires the restoration of the guiding and regulating role of the state."

General Alexander Lebed chose the same theme as a focal point for his political program during and after the 1996 Russian presidential election. In a series of speeches, interviews, and articles, Lebed stressed the importance of establishing "powerful authority" in Russia by formulating a unifying national idea.[19] The Russian Communist Party presented itself as the "party of the restoration of Russia's great-power status" in the 1995 parliamentary elections and then continued to emphasize restoration as a key political goal.[20] Gennady Zyuganov's 1997 report to the annual Congress of the Communist Party of the Russian Federation, for example, declared that "the restoration of the people's power and the rebirth of the ruined state . . . is the basis for a true national consensus." Zyuganov also argued that "during its thousand-year existence [the Russian] people have discovered the ideals of Spirituality and State Strength, Justice and Collectivism. The history of Russia testifies that none of these qualities can be neglected without the risk of causing the greatest upheavals. . . . We are confident—Russia will be Great and Socialist."[21] With the exception of the reference to a "Socialist" Russia, Zyuganov's 1997 report could have been given by Vladimir Putin at any point on or after December 29, 1999.

YELTSIN'S SEARCH FOR A NEW RUSSIAN IDEA

In July 1996, Boris Yeltsin's weak, crisis-ridden government concluded that with so many of its supporters and opponents obsessing about a national idea, it would have to jump into the fray. Yeltsin designated a presidential aide and prominent political thinker, Georgy Satarov, to chair a group of scholars and analysts that would sift through all the material on the issue. Yeltsin directed the group to roll out prescriptions for creating a new Russian Idea before 2000 and the new millennium.[22] In a speech justifying his decision, Yeltsin noted, "In Russian history during the 20th century, there have been various periods—monarchism, totalitarianism, perestroika and finally a democratic path of development. Each stage has its own ideology . . . [but now] . . . we have none."[23]

Unfortunately, the group did not make much progress in coming up with a Russian Idea. At the end of 1996, Georgy Satarov came out with a few vague parameters and some strong cautions for the new national idea. He recommended that it should be neither "intellectually abstract" nor politically, ethnically, and religiously exclusive.[24] Given the multiethnic and diverse nature of the Russian Federation, he also advocated something for everyone—communists and liberals, ethnic Russians and nonethnic Russians, Orthodox believers, Muslims, Jews, and others. Satarov's group then disappeared from view. In August 1997, it announced that it was essentially admitting defeat. Instead of offering prescriptions for a new Russian Idea, the group would produce a compendium of articles on the general subject.[25]

IGOR CHUBAIS AND THE IDEA OF A NEW RUSSIA

Although the Satarov group did not succeed in synthesizing the national idea in 1996–97, one book in the same timeframe had a notable impact on the debate. This was the book of Russian philosopher Igor Chubais, *Ot russkoy idei k ideye novoy Rossii* (From the Russian idea to the idea of a new Russia).[26] Igor Chubais was the elder brother of liberal economic reformer Anatoly Chubais, who was then serving as chief of the Russian presidential administration. This relationship partly explained the considerable attention the book received in the Russian media. Igor Chubais reread and synthesized the classics of Russian history and Russian philosophical thought as well as all the other publications that had been produced on the theme of a national idea between 1992 and 1996. He then wrote a "one stop shop" for the Russian Idea, which he asserted would have to pull together "the vectors of the past, present and future."[27] Igor Chubais proposed that a new Russian Idea must be a system of values rooted in Russia's culture and past. Chubais put a great deal of emphasis on historical continuity, pointing out that post-Soviet Russia was in fact the third version of a Russian state created on the same territory. The other two were pre-revolutionary Russia and the USSR. The new Russian state could not be a repetition or duplication of imperial or Soviet Russia, but it would need to incorporate elements of both.[28] Chubais also rejected the notion of creating a new Soviet-style state ideology. He argued instead for a *commonly* held Russian Idea that could draw together and unify "all healthy-thinking forces of society."[29]

Even though there is no direct evidence that this book is the progenitor of some of the core ideas about the state and the Russian Idea in Putin's Millennium Message, the conceptual and substantive overlap is striking. Like the Satarov report, Chubais's book was published during Putin's first year in the Russian capital in 1996. Three issues that Igor Chubais identified as critical to the creation of a Russian Idea as well as a new Russian state—Russian history, the Russian language, and religion—are also themes that Putin repeatedly embraced in the 2000s. History, language, and religion are the core elements in Russian conservative political thought in both the 1990s and the 2000s.

EXTOLLING RUSSIAN VIRTUES

In October 1996, not long after Chubais's book was published, the Russian Duma's Committee on Geopolitics initiated hearings on enshrining the Russian Idea (*Russkaya ideya*) in state law.[30] The Duma committee's use of the term *Russkaya ideya* had a very specific resonance in the debate about a national idea. It underscored the ethnic Russian elements of the concept, not its more neutral attributes, which would have come under the rubric of a *Rossiyskaya ideya*. *Russkiy* is the adjective associated with ethnic Russianness, while *rossiyskiy* is derived from *Rossiya*, or Russia, the name of the state. While most Americans and Europeans might find these distinctions somewhat too fine and even ponderous, they are important in the Russian context. They are also distinctions that Vladimir Putin has been carefully attuned to since he came into office in 1999–2000. They featured prominently in his 2012 presidential campaign.

At the 1996 Duma hearings, Russian nationalists, such as Vladimir Zhirinovsky and Dmitry Rogozin—then leader of the Congress of Russian Communities (KRO)—gave testimony calling for the protection and promotion of "ethnic Russianness" (*russkost'*) through Russian law. In the years following these hearings, Zhirinovsky and Rogozin continued to advocate an exclusive embrace of the ethnic Russian elements in the Russian Idea, demanding the institution of laws on the Russian language, Russian culture, Russian education, Russian schools, and Russian spiritual values. In January 1997, a similar meeting on the Russian Idea between representatives of the Russian Orthodox Church and the interior ministry produced one of the first (of many) public appeals for the reestablishment of Orthodoxy as an official ideology and instrument of state policy. Church representatives spoke of Orthodoxy as the essential core of the Russian Idea and of the religion's ability to fill the spiritual and ideological vacuum in Russian society. Interior ministry officials discussed Orthodoxy's potential to combat alcoholism and crime. Only film director Nikita Mikhalkov, who was present at this meeting (as he notably was at many other similar gatherings in the 1990s and 2000s), pointed out that if the Orthodox religion was turned into a state doctrine or policy it would quickly be rendered spiritually meaningless.[31]

Not surprisingly, the KGB, not just the interior ministry, was heavily involved in the debates and interpretations of the Russian Idea in this period. Embracing the Orthodox Church became very popular in KGB circles in the 1990s. In 1995, several years after his retirement from the KGB, General Nikolai Leonov, for example, became a political commentator for a popular Russian TV program, *Russian House* (*Russkiy dom*). [32] The TV program also published a magazine of the same name. It was widely seen as "an Orthodox, nationalist program," and Leonov was viewed as a strong advocate of the more exclusive, ethnic Russian version of the Russian Idea championed by Zhirinovsky and Rogozin. Leonov even sought election to the Russian parliament in 1999 as part of the Russian Popular Union (*Rossiyskiy obshchenarodnyy soyuz* or ROS), a nationalist party then headed by Sergei Baburin, vice speaker of the Russian Duma. In his May 2001 interview with *Spetsnaz Rossii*, Leonov claimed that Vladimir Putin was in fact "a pupil of . . . I'd say, *Russkiy dom*, in the broad sense of that word." He described Putin as "the president of our hopes," for Russian "professional" patriots like himself.[33]

Putin, however, has consistently proved more circumspect on the issue of *russkost'* and *russkiy* than General Leonov and the other professional patriots in Russian nationalist circles. While their hopes may have offered a broader frame of reference for the Millennium Message, Vladimir Putin explicitly talked about a *Rossiyskaya ideya,* not a *Russkaya ideya* in his manifesto. Putin's concern as Russian president, as we will discuss later in more detail, has been to create a sense of unity in his Russian Idea—something inclusive for everyone, as Georgy Satarov recommended—not to be exclusive and sow disunity. In the Millennium Message, Putin explicitly warned against the danger of creating another schism (*raskol*) in society with the creation of a new state ideology. He also took direct issue with politicians, publicists, and scholars who demanded it: "I am against the creation in Russia of a state, official ideology in any form."[34] He went on to note that societal consolidation could only be accomplished on a voluntary basis with the majority of Russian citizens (*rossiyane*)—not just ethnic Russians—firmly on board with the general ideas underpinning the state. In many respects, this section of the Millennium Message was the rollout of the prescriptions for a national idea that President Yeltsin had called for in July 1996. The prescriptions had been produced in advance of the 2000 presidential election as Yeltsin had requested, but it was the soon-to-be new president of Russia, Vladimir Putin, who produced them, not the Satarov group, nor the Yeltsin government.

YELTSIN'S *POSLANIYE* AND RESTORING STATE AUTHORITY (*VLAST'*)

Although the Yeltsin government failed to come up with a new Russian Idea, it did produce a major pronouncement on the issue of state power or authority that would also shape Putin's thinking in the 2000s. This was the so-called *poslaniye,* or annual presidential message to parliament in March 1997. Yeltsin's *poslaniye* outlined the importance and means of restoring order to the Russian state and strengthening state capacity. This document, like Igor Chubais's 1996 book, is an important precursor to Putin's later policy statements—although Putin gives a much more conservative spin to the concepts in the *poslaniye* on the role of law and order in contributing to the development of a strong state. The *poslaniye* and a series of other official documents associated with it also played a significant role in putting Putin on his path to power in the period between 1997 and 1999.

The *poslaniye* was written by the second Chubais—Igor's brother Anatoly, who at the time was essentially standing at and steadying the helm of the Russian state, although not always officially.[35] After his heart attack between the two rounds of the presidential election, Boris Yeltsin was in precarious health. In fall 1996 he underwent heart bypass surgery and was then incapacitated for several months as he recuperated.[36] In

March 1997, when he reemerged from his convalescence, the first thing Boris Yeltsin did was deliver the *poslaniye*. It was a very unusual address to the nation. It contained nothing about the government's accomplishments. Nor did it offer a broader vision for the state in spite of all the machinations on this topic and the official creation of the Satarov group. It did not say much about foreign and defense policy, apart from a few short final paragraphs mostly condemning the expansion of NATO. The *poslaniye* was a nuts-and-bolts speech that honed in on the importance of restoring government control over the country's political disarray. Its main message was that the greatest danger facing Russia in 1997 was the excessive weakness of state authority (*vlast'*). "One lesson is already clear," the address asserted, "Russia needs order. But it is necessary to answer two not-so-simple questions: what kind of order and how to introduce it?" Yeltsin went on: "One reason for the current situation is that we had such political disagreements that we needed to compromise to avoid clashes. Now the situation has changed, and we can return to complete the reforms. . . . The most effective way to establish order on the construction site is to complete the construction."

The president's address concluded:

> The main obstacle to establishing a new economic order and a new political system is the low effectiveness of the government authorities [*vlasti*] . . . order in the country begins only by establishing order in the state organism itself. . . . Only a strong government authority [*vlast'*] which makes reasonable decisions and is capable of ensuring their effective implementation is in a condition for fulfilling its obligations: to give guarantees for the activity of the strong and of supporting the weak with dignity. . . .[37]

The reference to *vlast'* (government authority) instead of *gosudarstvo* (the state) was particularly significant. Anatoly Chubais, Yegor Gaidar, and the other liberal economic reformers had focused in the early 1990s on dismantling and deregulating the defunct Soviet state so they could unleash the forces of the free market. They were not adherents to the *gosudarstvennik* myth of the enduring stand-alone power and permanence of the "State." Faced with institutional chaos and attempts on every front by individual interests, like the oligarchs and regional leaders, to capture bits of the Russian state, they could not press ahead with their reforms. The liberal reformers recognized the state was now too weak. They needed to restore some capacity to the apparatus of the state, to the *vlast'*, even if they intended only for the state to play a more instrumental or caretaker role until the reforms could take hold. The primary key to restoring this version of a strong state was to ensure, first, that the team administering the state apparatus—the Russian leadership and the Russian government—was strengthened. This is what the *poslaniye* laid out.

The *poslaniye* also claimed (as Putin would later in his Millennium Message) that Russian society was crying out for order. The best way to achieve order was to complete the reforms that the government had begun. Order in the government and the implementation of reforms would lead to order in the country. The *poslaniye* went on to discuss the role of the state in the economy in some detail: "An effective market economy is not merely freedom of private initiative but also a strict legal order, [with] uniform, stable, and universally observed rules of economic activity. The state's task is to establish those rules and ensure that they are followed." Finally, the *poslaniye* criticized the state's supervisory agencies in charge of making sure rules were obeyed. They were essentially toothless: "Authority [*vlast'*] not constrained by law [*pravo*] is dangerous. Law not backed up by authority is powerless. The former truth has been confirmed many times in our history. The latter truth is becoming obvious today."[38]

ANATOLY SOBCHAK AND THE LAW-GOVERNED STATE

The reference to the law (*pravo*) in the *poslaniye* is another important element. Anatoly Chubais and his team wanted the law to set the new rules of the market economy and provide the means to enforce them. They wanted to get everything back on the right track of reform again (their track). Putin, after becoming acting president in 2000, would also emphasize the importance of the law. He would emphasize it as an instrument—as a means of controlling, proscribing, and constraining economic, as well as political, reform. Putin's concept of the law as a means of control draws upon ideas he became well-versed in during his long association with Anatoly Sobchak, first as his student and then as his aide and deputy. Although Sobchak was seen as a leading Russian democrat in the 1990s, his legal views were much less liberal than his political reputation might have suggested.[39] In his legal writings in the Soviet period and the 1990s, Sobchak presented the establishment of a "law-based state" (*pravovoye gosudarstvo*) as a form of conservative rebellion against the Communist Party, which he described as "substitut[ing] itself for all government institutions."[40] The concept of a *pravovoye gosudarstvo,* standing above any party or other institutional entity, with rights guaranteed by the state itself, was an idea to which Putin would frequently return during his presidency.

On January 13, 2000, for example, Putin received an honorary degree from St. Petersburg State University, where he had studied law under Sobchak when it was Leningrad State University. In his speech, Putin underscored the influence of his legal training at the university, noting, "For people like me who are now engaged in the construction of a new Russian state, we know that this project must be founded on the principles that have for decades developed within the walls of the Faculty of Law of the University of St. Petersburg."[41] Later in January 2000—his very first month in power—Putin emphasized the importance of implementing the tenets of the 1993 constitution, which Sobchak played a key role in drafting. In a series of speeches, which took place against the backdrop of a spate of terrorist attacks and a renewed war with Chechnya, Putin placed the Russian constitution right at the center of Russia's war on terror. He also presented the constitution as the core instrument for recentralizing state power as well as for developing the Russian economy. In one speech, to the Russian justice ministry, Putin stated that there was only one way to create a *pravovoye gosudarstvo*—by "making Russia strong."[42]

On February 20, 2000, Anatoly Sobchak died suddenly of a massive heart attack while on a campaign trip to Kaliningrad in support of Putin's official candidacy in the 2000 Russian presidential election.[43] Putin was shaken by Sobchak's death. It was a personal blow. Putin had initially been assigned to work with Sobchak by the KGB, but his relationship with the mayor long preceded this arrangement. Sobchak had been an important figure in Putin's life, a close confidant and mentor as well as his professor and boss.[44] A few days after Sobchak's death, Putin turned to elaborate again on Sobchak's, and his, core idea of the importance of a law-based state in an open letter to Russian voters. The letter laid out Putin's view of the law and democracy, and the idea of the Russian people being governed by and abiding by the laws of the state: "but democracy—this is a dictatorship of the law (*diktatura zakona*), not a dictatorship of those whose jobs oblige them to uphold the law. . . . The police and the prosecutors should serve the law, and not try to 'privatize' the powers given to them and use them for their own benefit."[45] This letter marked the beginning of Putin's efforts to deploy the law as an instrument to strengthen the state. In doing so, Putin would enlist the assistance of Russia's leading legal *gosudarstvenniki*, who, like Anatoly Sobchak, saw a powerful law-governed state as critical to Russia's future development. The key person in this cohort was Valery Zorkin, the chairman of the Russian Constitutional Court, and the central figure—along with Sergei Glazyev and Gennady Zyuganov—in the 1994 Soglasiye movement for the restoration of the Russian state.

PUTINISM AND THE CONSTITUTION

Valery Zorkin belongs to a group of Russian legal scholars who have been heavily influenced by the "statist school" of the tsarist-era "liberal conservative" movement.[46] The intellectual father of this movement is Boris Chicherin, a nineteenth-century Russian lawyer and political philosopher who argued that the law-based state (*pravovoye gosudarstvo*) should be the anchor for the gradual reform of the tsarist political system. Chicherin famously advised Tsar Alexander II to follow a policy of "liberal measures and a strong state" when Alexander abolished serfdom during the era of Russia's Great Reforms in the 1860s–70s.[47] Members of this movement in the tsarist era promoted the creation of a constitutional monarchy as defensive liberalism against the revolutionary ideas of the Russian socialist movement. Constitutionalism was a classic third way.[48] Its proponents hoped it would gradually constrain the authority of the autocrat, the tsar, which was deemed lawless and arbitrary in its absolutism. The movement did not succeed. No fully law-based constitutional monarchy was introduced in Russia. The project was ultimately swept away by the Revolution in 1917, along with the last tsar, Nicholas II. Its proponents were forced into exile.

Zorkin resurrected the idea of liberal conservatism in the late Soviet period. Publishing extensively in Soviet legal journals, Zorkin landed a prestigious job teaching constitutional law at the Academy of the Russian Ministry of Internal Affairs, where he quickly rose to prominence.[49] In 1991, Zorkin received by far the most votes to become chairman of the newly created Constitutional Court. Initially a proponent of a strong presidential republic, Zorkin clashed with Yeltsin after opposing the president's bloody move against the parliament in 1993. He was forced to step down from the chairmanship. Despite this personal opposition to Yeltsin, and his flirtation with politics as part of Soglasiye, Zorkin remained on the Constitutional Court through the 1990s and was reelected chairman in 2003. [50] Since then, Zorkin has adapted the ideas of the late tsarist liberal conservatives to fit the present day. In many respects, he has continued to refine the nineteenth-century idea of introducing a constitutional monarchy for Russia, but with the president effectively replacing the tsar as the monarch at the heart of the Russian constitution.[51]

Like Zorkin, Putin has underscored the intimate connection between the Russian presidency and the Russian constitution. The constitution is the embodiment of the concept of *gosudarstvennichestvo* that Putin first rolled out in the Millennium Message. It strengthens and unifies the Russian state. It is the primary building block of the *pravovoye gosudarstvo*. The constitution enshrines the president as the guarantor of the constitution. The president is elected by the entire Russian people and stands above the system of separated executive, legislative, and judicial powers. As a result, the Russian presidency is the only office that represents the unity of the state. The Russian president also guarantees the constitution's grant of individual rights to the Russian population.[52]

In the words of the Millennium Message, the Russian president is required to ensure the "constitutional security of the *gosudarstvo*." Thus, in keeping with the constitution's prohibition against three *consecutive* presidential terms, Putin stepped away from the presidency in 2008 and into the role of Russian prime minister. Putin was explicit in his assertion that he did this to ensure the constitutional security of the *gosudarstvo*. "I will not change the constitution and in line with the constitution, you cannot run for president three times in a row," Putin said repeatedly in the years leading up to the end of his second term.[53] Similarly, in April 2012, just before leaving the premiership to reassume the presidency on May 7, 2012, Putin resigned from his leadership of the United Russia party, putting Dmitry Medvedev in charge. Mr. Putin stated that "the president should be a non-party figure . . . a consolidating figure for all the political forces in the country, for all its citizens."[54]

These ideas about the Russian constitution and the presidency, and many other concepts espoused by Valery Zorkin since the 1990s, infuse Putin's official publications. In a January 16, 2012, presidential campaign article in *Izvestiya,* for example, reviewing the challenges Russia faced, Putin proclaimed that the Russian state would not allow itself to be swept up by the growing forces of instability. Instead it would seek to control these forces by actively "setting the rules of the game." Putin continued with an analysis that echoed the language of the tsarist statist school, noting that Russia will "muscle up" by "being open to change" through state-sanctioned procedures and rules.[55] In a subsequent article in *Kommersant,* on February 6, 2012, entitled "Democracy and the quality of the state," Putin directly cited one of the tsarist-era liberal conservatives embraced by Valery Zorkin, Pavel Novgordtsev, who was a law professor at Moscow State University. The quote reflected Novgordtsev's (and Putin's) antirevolutionary, statist beliefs: "People often think proclaiming various freedoms and universal suffrage will in and of itself have some miraculous strength to direct life onto a new course. In actual fact, in such instances in life, what happens usually turns out not to be democracy, but depending on the turn events take, either oligarchy or anarchy."[56]

THE COLLAPSE OF THE USSR: CREATING THE STATE AGAIN

In sum, by the end of the 1990s, the Russian elite had drawn a range of conclusions about the Russian state and the need to restore the rule of law as well as order to the Russian government. They had also identified the need to create some kind of Russian Idea to mobilize the population and to give some coherence to the imperative for economic and political reforms. Vladimir Putin's 1999 Millennium Message, his political mission statement, was a product of this very specific Russian context. It neither marked a break with the past nor broke any new conceptual ground. It was entirely derivative of a particular set of philosophical and legal ideas about the state emanating from conservative circles within the Russian elite.

What the Millennium Message did was to lay out how Vladimir Putin himself viewed and approached issues of order and the state. Putin emphasized what he believed were distinctly Russian values and his concept of what a strong state (*sil'noye gosudarstvo*) should be. Putin's Millennium Message was also an emotional appeal. In addition to evoking the almost mystical, historically rooted conception of Russian *gosudarstvennichestvo,* it was loaded with references to the Russian state (*gosudarstvo*) and the idea of Russia as a great power (*derzhava*). Putin's manifesto called for Russia to overcome its crisis and recreate the state—by rediscovering and taking back its fundamental values, reenergizing its historical traditions, and abandoning the desire to blindly copy abstract Western models. Following on from the Millennium Message, Putin's subsequent elaborations on issues like stability, unity, and the importance of gradual, evolutionary reform or change also take a long look back on Russian history. They are shaped by his interpretations, and those of others in the conservative elite, of the danger of repeated times of troubles to the survival of the Russian state. Because of these times of troubles, these great social and political upheavals, Russia was a state that had collapsed and been created and recreated three times over the centuries.

Vladimir Putin felt the collapse of the second iteration of the Russian state, the USSR, very keenly. He made this clear in an often misquoted line in his annual address to the nation in April 2005. In the address, Putin declared the demise of the Soviet Union to be "the greatest geopolitical catastrophe of the [twentieth] century."[57] Most references to this line have suggested that Putin was bemoaning the loss of the communist economic and political system, but Putin has since frequently underscored that he was talking about the collapse of the Russian state itself. Indeed, in October 2011, in a prime-time Russian TV interview shortly after he announced his intention to return to the presidency, Putin revisited the issue during a discussion about the series of crises Russia experienced in the 1990s:

We went essentially through the breakup of a state: the Soviet Union broke up. And what is the Soviet Union? It is Russia, only it had a different name. We went through a very difficult period in the 1990s and only started getting on our feet in the 2000s, established peace inside the country, stabilized the situation. And, of course, we need this period of stable development.[58]

Fears of the collapse, *raspad,* and disintegration or break-up, *razval,* of the Russian state dominated debates among the Russian elite during the 1990s. The terms *raspad* and *razval*—along with *raskol* (schism)— are staples of Putin's speeches. They even feature prominently in the works of Russian political figures and experts more closely associ- ated with the liberal reformers' efforts to open up Russia's politics and economy than with Putin's restoration of the vertical of power (*vertikal vlasti*). For example, Yegor Gaidar, the father of shock therapy, in his last book—*Collapse of an Empire: Lessons for Modern Russia,* which was published in Russian in 2006 and in English in 2007—focused on the issue of state collapse.[59] Gaidar looked closely at the economic roots of the collapse of the Soviet Union, couching his explanations and conclu- sions in a sweeping historical context. While Gaidar certainly did not see himself as a *gosudarstvennik,* he was a Russian patriot and his family had a long history of state service.[60] Gaidar had a different view from Putin of what needed to be done to reform the Russian economy and polity. This included dismantling the old Soviet state structures. At the same time, Gaidar's ultimate goal was to revive Russia after the collapse of the USSR. He sought to build a new prosperous Russian state that would regain its old place as a leading international actor.

SEEKING *REVANCHE*

Gaidar firmly believed that in spite of all the criticisms about the ruinous effects of shock therapy on individual Russians' savings and of a priva- tization program that essentially handed state assets to a new class of corrupt oligarchs, he had saved the country from bankruptcy and starva- tion. He had done what was absolutely necessary to turn things around in an impossibly difficult situation. As Gaidar noted during presentations and private discussions of his book (including with the authors), many of the mistakes and miscalculations of over-centralized Soviet political and economic policy were being repeated in Russia in the 2000s.[61] Gaidar wanted to ensure that Putin and those around him would pay atten- tion to his conclusions and recommendations. Essentially, Gaidar wrote

Collapse of an Empire for President Putin and his team. He wanted to pass on the lessons that he had internalized from his own personal experience in state service in the 1990s and his analysis of Russian and Soviet history. For Gaidar, like Putin, the Soviet Union was simply another historical and political manifestation of the Russian state. It was not a separate entity.

In the early 1990s, Gaidar saw his mission as trying to "shock" the state into reviving, thus reversing the domestic catastrophe created by the demise of the Soviet Union. In 1999, Putin set out to restore the state's guiding and regulating role in society by bringing an end to shocks and creating stability. Former presidential adviser Gleb Pavlovsky in his January 2012 interview with *The Guardian* gave Putin credit for doing this over the course of the 2000s:

> Putin in fact achieved the task of *revanche*. The risk of collapse of the country was averted. Despite all the corruption there, the [North] Caucasus no longer has a threat of separatism and a consensus appeared around a united state which didn't exist before in the 1990s. No one in the regions wanted to break away and create a separate state. That disappeared. Putin created a legitimate presidency, there was stabilization. . . . People no longer had the desire to rebuild the Soviet Union. Although, of course, I think Putin wanted to create a great state, and he continues to want that.[62]

The idea of a united state that Pavlovsky cites is a key one for Putin. It runs as both a thread and a theme through several of Putin's identities. In his writings and speeches, Vladimir Putin is obsessed with the general idea of unity and unifying, or rallying forces and closing ranks (*splotit'*)—the very opposite of and antidote to collapse and disintegration. In a February 2001 interview with a Vietnamese newspaper on the eve of a trip to Asia, for example, Putin asserted that his major accomplishment at the very beginning of his presidency was to get everyone to unite around the idea of a strong state: "In the political sphere we managed to get all the main political forces in society to unite (*ob'yedinilis'*) around the idea of restoring a normal and viable state. I think that has been the basis of our success. It was precisely lack of unity (fragmentation, *razobshchennost'*) that hindered us throughout the 1990s."[63]

THE UNIFIED (*YEDINOYE*) STATE

Overcoming fragmentation by diluting and reversing the pernicious political effects of the bilateral treaties Moscow had been forced to conclude
with Russia's regions since 1994, for example, became one of the top
priorities for Putin once he became president. Having amassed sufficient
authority to override regional leaders, Putin appropriated another set of
ideas from the 1990s to address the issue. Many prominent Russians—
including Defense Minister Pavel Grachev, former Vice President Alexander Rutskoi, and nationalist leader Vladimir Zhirinovsky, as well as the
heads of ministries and members of President Yeltsin's administration—
had advocated the abolition of both the bilateral treaties and Russia's
autonomous republics. They proposed a return to the traditional Russian
provinces of the tsarist era (*guberniya* in the Russian singular form). [64]

Instead of abolishing the republics, Mr. Putin modified a concept that
had been floated by Yegor Gaidar, constitutional drafter Sergei Shakhrai,
and Yabloko party leader Grigory Yavlinsky, among others. This concept
opted for the creation of new Russian administrative units on the basis of
territorial size and economic principles, not simply historical origin, with
the units having similar sets of privileges. [65] Beginning with a presidential
ukaz or decree in May 2000, Putin set out to subsume all of Russia's
existing republics and regions under seven large federal districts.[66] A
presidential *polpred* or plenipotentiary envoy (essentially a viceroy) was
put in charge to reassert Moscow's and the Kremlin's authority. This
became another cornerstone of Putinism—the return to the semblance of
a *yedinoye,* or unified, *gosudarstvo* rather than a federal, divided, state.[67]

In September 2007, on the eve of Putin's fifty-fifth birthday, film
director Nikita Mikhalkov went to extraordinary lengths to highlight
and credit Putin's efforts to unify Russia by producing a documentary
film tribute to the Russian president: *55*.[68] Mikhalkov, like many other
gosudarstvenniki, has a long family history of cultural achievement and
service to the Russian state. His father, Sergei Mikhalkov, was a children's writer as well as the author of lyrics to the Soviet and Russian
national anthems. His great grandfather was the tsarist-era governor of
Russia's Yaroslavl province. Other ancestors were poets and artists—
including Vasily Surikov, one of Russia's most famous painters of historical subjects—and aristocrats close to the Romanov dynasty. The tone

and content of Mikhalkov's 55 film tribute suggested that as Russian president, Putin had been nothing less than a savior. Putin had fulfilled a mission to reunify and restore the state—the very mission laid out in the original Soglasiye manifesto that Mikhalkov had signed on to in 1994. [69]

Mikhalkov's emphasis on the mission to unify Russia also echoed a much earlier treatise by one of the top figures from the KGB, General Filipp Bobkov, founder of the KGB 5th Directorate. Next to KGB leader Yury Andropov, Bobkov was the key official in the creation of the "New KGB" that recruited Putin's cohort of young officers into the institution. In 1995, Bobkov produced a memoir, *KGB i vlast'* (The KGB and the regime), to draw "from the KGB's past those lessons that are important for the modern day."[70] The bulk of Bobkov's memoir was clearly completed well before the 1995 publication date, perhaps as early as 1991, when he retired from the KGB. The brief final chapter, however, was probably added closer to 1995, when the Russian elite debates about the state were reaching their peak and just before Putin arrived in Moscow.

Bobkov's book presented an extremely idealized view of the future of the Russian state, including his personal musings on the necessity of finding new ways to unify (*splotit'*) Russian society. He offered his own thesis for the conceptualization of some kind of new national idea. In the last chapter, "Looking to the Future," Bobkov noted that there was no longer "a unified idea of what Russia we're talking about," which was natural, "since 'Russia' is associated with two time periods: the Russian Empire, and the USSR. Thus the ideas about regenerating Russia will naturally follow two distinct paths, not likely to converge." Bobkov went on to assert that the crisis Russia was experiencing in the 1990s was the "crisis of a destroyed state," which had lost not only its political and economic order but also its territory:

For Russia . . . the highest priority task is not rebirth but the construction of a new state. The idea of creating a new state and its economic foundations would perhaps help us to find a way out of the dead-end and to unify the disparate forces of society. Unify [*splotit'*] in order to build; unify in order not to destroy what is left. . . . It will not be possible to elaborate the conceptual foundations and programs of construction of the new state without drawing in all healthy-thinking forces of society and unifying them on a new basis. On the basis of the slogan: "We are for a new Russia!"[71]

The ideas in the final pages of Bobkov's memoir, including drawing on Russia's own internal resources to rebuild the state; trying to find common elements in various programs to achieve unity; looking for compromises wherever possible on economic and political issues to solve the tasks of constructing the new state; and responding to the desire of the Russian population to be the citizens of a great power (*velikaya derzhava*) again, are all elements of Putin's and many others' expositions on the state after 1999.[72] In his Millennium Message, when addressing his conception of the *Rossiyskaya ideya,* Putin talks of the need for a new Russian Idea to emerge like an "amalgam" or *splav* (from the same root as to unify or *splotit'*), to bring everything together again stronger than before. Putin calls for an "organic binding element" that can combine "the universal values, common to all mankind, with the primordial Russian values that have survived the test of time."[73] Putin concluded his 1999 address with a final observation that the state must mobilize all Russia's resources to avoid becoming a third-rate power:

Russia has [just] experienced one of the most difficult periods in its many centuries of history. Perhaps for the first time in 200–300 years, she faces the real danger of becoming not just a second but even a third tier country. To prevent this from happening, we need an immense effort from all the nation's intellectual, physical, and moral forces. We need well-coordinated, constructive work. No-one will do this for us. Everything now depends entirely on our own ability to recognize the level of danger, to unify and rally ourselves [*splotit'sya*] and get ourselves ready for prolonged and difficult labor.[74]

After December 1999, with the assistance of his deputy chief of staff, Vladislav Surkov, and others in the Kremlin, Vladimir Putin set out to create a slogan for a new Russia, a *splav* to unify the disparate forces of society.[75] He and Surkov dealt with all the inherent contradictions that bedeviled Georgy Satarov's group in its search for a new Russian Idea by simply papering over them. In essence, Putin created a pastiche Russian Idea in the 2000s. He ripped some ideas from the headlines of the debates during his first year in Moscow in 1996–97. He lifted other ideas on how to achieve national or societal unity—as we will discuss in the next chapter—directly from Russian history, including from an earlier time of troubles in the 1830s and from the decades of the 1890s and 1900s. He appropriated yet more ideas from the period after the 1917 Russian Revolution and collapse of the Russian Empire—from the so-called émigré writings of White Russians. Putin's efforts have often had a documentary, if not exactly cinematic, quality reminiscent of a production by the most prominent film director of his presidency, Nikita Mikhalkov. They have not, however, done a great deal to create a Russian Idea that has unified and strengthened the Russian state.

CHAPTER FOUR

THE HISTORY MAN

PUTIN'S FORAYS INTO THE DEBATES over the Russian Idea underscore the second set of central elements to Putin's persona—his firm conviction that his personal destiny is intertwined with that of the Russian state and its past.[1] Vladimir Putin is a self-designated student of history. He claims it was his favorite subject in school, and he remains an avid reader today. He also presents himself as man of history with a special relationship to the subject. Throughout his time in office, Putin has actively deployed his own and his team's interpretations of Russian history to reinforce policy positions and frame key events. Putin recognizes the power of history both to accomplish his and the state's goals and to cloak himself and the Russian state with an additional mantle of legitimacy.[2]

At the outset of Putin's presidency, his personal attachment to history was featured prominently in biographical materials, clearly with his encouragement. In chapter 8 of volume 1 of his 2002 book, *Vladimir Putin: istoriya zhizni* (Vladimir Putin: history of a life), for example, Oleg Blotsky relates a set of personal (and glowing) accounts by a certain Viktor Borisenko, who attended the same schools in Leningrad as Putin from first grade through ninth, and apparently also knew Putin at university. Borisenko tells Blotsky:

My comrade really impressed me one time. It must have been in the seventh or eighth grade. We were in history class. The teacher asked a question and all of a sudden Volodya, who before that had taken pains to remain completely unnoticed, suddenly stood up and gave an answer. And his answer was logical: these are all secondary causes, here is the real explanation of this historical event. I could see how the history teacher's jaw dropped. She had suddenly discovered who this young man was, and at that moment I too discovered who my friend was. I saw a completely different side of him.[3]

Decades later, in October 2011, Putin's press secretary, Dmitry Peskov, stressed that "Putin [still] reads all the time, mostly about the history of Russia. He reads memoirs, the memoirs of Russian historical state figures."[4] Putin, like many other Russian and Soviet leaders, appreciates the role of "useful history" in policy—the manipulation of the past and its application as a policy tool. History is a social and political organizing force that can help shape group identities and foster coalitions.[5] For Putin, history and the lessons it teaches reinforce the importance of serving the state. History underscores the eternal nature of the Russian state versus the ephemeral nature of the individual *gosudarstvennik*. However, individual *gosudarstvenniki* plucked from the pages of Russian history have proven very important to Putin in his pursuit of restoring the state in the 2000s.[6]

In the January 1997 meeting in Moscow between representatives of the Russian Orthodox Church and the interior ministry, explicit reference was made by the participants to the so-called Uvarov doctrine of the Russian imperial idea—or "Official Nationality." This doctrine, which was based on the trinity of "Orthodoxy, Autocracy, Nationality" (*Pravoslaviye, Samoderzhaviye, Narodnost'*), was first propounded by Nicholas I's minister of education, Sergei Uvarov, in 1833. It was supposed to be a simple formula, or appeal, to rally teachers throughout the Russian Empire to the imperial cause.[7] It was in essence an early version of a slogan—à la Filipp Bobkov—to unify society, but behind old, traditional Russia rather than a new Russia. With his appeal, Uvarov offered the first explicit definition of what many have since viewed as the three pillars of the Russian state: the Orthodox Christian religion and the institution of the Russian Orthodox Church; the tsarist regime in the person of the tsar, the autocrat; and the Russian nation loyal to the tsar. At the January 1997 session, participants referred to the Uvarov doctrine as a possible justification for reestablishing Orthodoxy as both an official Russian state ideology and an instrument of government policy.

Uvarov's last formulation in the trinity, nationality, is an awkward translation from the Russian word *narodnost'*, which is rooted in *narod* or "the people"—the collective Russian people. There is no real counterpart in English, although *narod* is somewhat similar to the idea of "das Volk" in German. In this period, in the 1830s, the word *narod* denoted the peasantry. Uvarov meant *narodnost'* to convey everything from the spirit and essence of the Russian people to the collective rural life of the peasant. The term was also supposed to provide a link to Russia's native Slavic traditions and to evoke the perceived historic bonds between the people and the tsar as well as between the "land" and the state. *Narodnost'* was a heavily loaded, and uniquely Russian, idea.

The period of the Uvarov doctrine was another time of troubles in Russian history, when the Russian Empire faced social and national unrest at home and abroad. In 1825, St. Petersburg had been roiled by the Decembrist revolt, in which tsarist officers—many of whom had pursued the remnants of Napoleon's invading armies back into Europe and Paris a decade before—staged a rebellion to demand the creation of a Russian constitutional monarchy. The officers' mutiny was followed in 1830–31 by an uprising among the Polish population in the empire's western provinces. Abroad, other European monarchies had taken a beating, with the 1830 July Days revolution in Paris, the Belgian insurrection against the Netherlands, and a spate of rebellions against Ottoman rule in the Near East. Autocratic rule was growing increasingly unpopular. The tsarist government was under considerable pressure to consolidate support. Uvarov rose to the occasion with his slogan. He emphasized the importance of the autocratic system and appealed to the system's core constituencies—Orthodox Russians and the rural peasant population—to rally around the tsar.

The Uvarov doctrine was frequently revisited in the nineteenth century and again in the early 1900s to mobilize support for the last tsar of the Romanov dynasty, Nicholas II. It was not so surprising that Russian nationalists would try to reprise it in the 1990s for the same purpose. There were striking historical parallels between the 1990s and the decade just prior to the First World War—both in terms of political and economic developments and the issues that gripped the political debates in

Russia's capital city (St. Petersburg in the early 1900s and Moscow in the 1990s). For many in the Russian elite, the debate in 1990s Moscow about Russia's present and future was even the continuation of the same debate in St. Petersburg that had been interrupted by war and revolution in 1914–17. As Russian literary historian Konstantin Azadovsky pointed out in a 1995 anthology of Russian cultural and political thought:

> Today at the end of the [twentieth] century, just as at its very beginning, Russia's "eternal" questions are once again being discussed on the pages of our journals: the country's true path, its identity, the people [*narod*], the intelligentsia, the Slavophiles and the Westernizers. The arguments broken off during the fateful years of the Revolution and the "triumphant procession of Soviet power" have been resumed. Who is to blame? Why did Russia allow itself to be drawn into the abyss? Can Russia be "renewed"?[8]

For Russia, the early 1900s and the 1990s represent more than just the century's bookends. They also are twin periods of transition in Russian history. Both decades were marked by defeat in war, imperial and economic collapse, and attempts at dramatic reform. Both were infused with nostalgia for a past. In the 1900s and the 1990s, the state and the Russian government revisited history, looking for what might be a "golden" or at least a "silver age" that could be referred to, to give some substance and legitimacy to the present. Again, a quote from Konstantin Azadovsky: "We are infected with nostalgia for pre-revolutionary Russia. We want to immerse ourselves in the age of 1910 . . . to transport it to our troubled days. It is precisely there, in the past, that we stubbornly seek the answers to the burning questions of the day. We are restoring the pillars of that life—the nobility, the Cossacks, Orthodoxy, Autocracy."[9]

THE SEARCH FOR USEFUL HISTORY

In the 2000s, Putin took a number of steps to establish physical links to Russia's past—its imperial and, to a lesser extent, Soviet pasts. Putin's antechamber in the Kremlin was adorned with busts and portraits of the most celebrated Russian tsars, including the famous reformers Peter the Great, Catherine the Great, and Alexander II.[10] Sergei Mironov, then the chairman of the upper house of the Russian parliament, the Federation Council, called for the creation of a portrait gallery of all the chairmen of the Federation Council extending back to the imperial State Council to emphasize the historical continuity of both the upper house and Russia's parliamentary traditions.[11] Statues of military heroes from famous battles across the centuries were returned to the pedestals from which they had been removed during the Soviet era. Churches destroyed by the Bolsheviks in Moscow, such as the massive Cathedral of Christ the Savior, were rebuilt from scratch. Soviet luminaries toppled in the heady early days of the 1990s were quietly put back on their plinths, sometimes with Putin in ceremonial attendance.[12] Lenin was left in his mausoleum on Red Square.

Key individuals from Putin's inner circle played an important role in these cultural restoration projects. Vladimir Yakunin, for example—a former Soviet official, neighbor of Putin's in a dacha (country home) community in Leningrad oblast, and since 2005 the CEO of Russian Railways (one of the most important Russian state monopolies)—became the head of a number of organizations devoted to the restoration and celebration of Russia's Orthodox heritage.[13] In this capacity, Yakunin personally oversaw the refurbishment of historic monasteries and churches. He also traveled (mostly by rail) to the furthest reaches of the far-flung Russian countryside to display long-lost Orthodox icons newly returned from abroad. Similarly, oligarchs like Viktor Vekselberg, who built up a fabulous collection of imperial Fabergé eggs, now housed again in Russia, brought back other Russian artifacts for the state. In 2008, Vekselberg secured from Harvard University a complete set of pre-revolutionary bells that had originally hung in Moscow's Danilov Monastery, the seat of the Russian Orthodox patriarch. He had them shipped from the United States and restored to their original location.[14]

PUTIN'S REFORMULATION OF OFFICIAL NATIONALITY

In a sense that is more metaphysical than physical, Putin also returned to historical precedent and the Uvarov formulation of "Orthodoxy, Autocracy, Nationality." Given his rejection of an official ideology of any kind in the Millennium Message, he did so in a less explicit, but still obvious, way. Putin personally and openly reembraced Russian Orthodoxy and the Orthodox Church in the 2000s. He continually stressed the importance of rediscovering his Orthodox faith, pointedly discussing his beliefs with prominent international interlocutors like President George W. Bush—to whom he told a story about finding a cross his mother had given him intact after a devastating fire at a family dacha.[15] He also made sure that his appearances at church services (often with Yakunin in the background) were well publicized. He allowed information to circulate about his personal connections with Orthodox clergy.[16]

Instead of autocracy, Putin's reformulation of the Uvarov doctrine settled upon "sovereign democracy," a term first championed by Deputy Chief of Staff Vladislav Surkov. Sovereign democracy captures the singular importance and independence of the Russian state and its unique culture and history. Russia is accountable and answerable to no one (certainly no outside power) apart from the opinion of the majority of its population.[17] Sovereign democracy à la Surkov is the epitome of a strong and powerful state, just as autocracy was in the tsarist era. Sovereign democracy also picks up on the historical reasoning of Putin's Millennium Message, which posits that universal norms of democracy are not Russian and have in fact damaged Russia's political development. Russia must, therefore, return to a political system that is uniquely its own, that is sovereign and historically rooted.[18]

In terms of nationality or *narodnost'*, Putin has made frequent reference to the *narod,* the collective people of Russia, in speeches and presentations, including emphasizing his own efforts to commune with and reach out to the *narod*.[19] At one of the Valdai Discussion Club meetings in September 2010, where the group met with Putin for dinner in Sochi, Putin had just returned from a road trip to Siberia and the Russian Far East to inaugurate the opening of the final section of a new cross-country highway.[20] He spent considerable time extolling the virtues of the Russian *narod* (a term he used repeatedly), as personified by the people he encountered along the way. Putin picked up further on this concept in sponsoring the creation of the *Obshcherossiyskiy narodnyy front,* or the All-Russian People's Front, in May 2011. The *Narodnyy front* was intended as an umbrella entity to pull together and mobilize a range of Russian civil society organizations to provide fresh ideas for the United Russia party in advance of the December 2011 parliamentary elections.[21]

Until the Ukraine crisis of 2014, Putin was very careful, however, to avoid the conservative and exclusionary elements of the original Uvarov formulation, to distinguish himself from Russian nationalists like Zhirinovsky and Rogozin, and in keeping with his own admonitions in the Millennium Message. He set out to create something for the diverse population of modern Russia—not the old Russia of the 1830s or early 1900s. In this regard, Putin seemed to have picked up again on the ideas of the KGB's Filipp Bobkov who, in his 1995 book, cautioned against championing the cause of ethnic Russians or of Russian-speakers in building a new Russian state and urged a more inclusive approach.[22] In the Millennium Message, in his section entitled "Lessons for Russia" (*Uroki dlya Rossii*), Putin noted:

> Russia has reached its limits of political, and socio-economic earthquakes, cataclysms, radical transformations. Only fanatics or those political forces who are deeply disinterested in the fate of Russia or the people [*narod*] are calling for another revolution. The state and the people will not support the idea of returning to yet another cycle of completely breaking with everything, no matter what slogan this comes under—communist, national-patriotic, or radical-liberal. . . . Responsible societal-political forces must offer the people a strategy for Russia's revival and renaissance, which will be based on all the positive things that were created during the economic and democratic reforms [of the 1990s], and which will be achieved exclusively through evolutionary, gradual, well-considered methods. This will be achieved in conditions of political stability and without worsening the Russian people's living standards, no matter what strata or group [they belong to].[23]

In this formulation in the Millennium Message, Putin's conception of the *narod* is not confined to the ethnic Russian population of the Russian Federation or any particular political or social group. Putin's later emphasis on the "*All-Russian* people's front" also makes this clear. Putin's *narod* is all-encompassing and inclusive in a way that Uvarov's was not. In one of his speeches to the conference of the United Russia party on November 27, 2011, just before the 2011 Russian parliamentary elections, for example, Putin proclaimed:

We will do everything to uphold civil peace and harmony. At stake is the future of our statehood, the well-being of our citizens, the things that we will cherish and uphold. Let those who proclaim the slogans of social and ethnic intolerance, and are smuggling in all kinds of populist and provocative ideas that actually lead to national betrayal and ultimately to the breakup of our country, know that: we are a multinational society but we are a single Russian nation, a united and indivisible Russia.[24]

RECONCILING WITH RUSSIAN HISTORY

In addition to stressing Putin's communion with the united and indivisible Russian *narod*, the 2010 Valdai Discussion Club conference took up the theme of "Russia's History and Future Development." It featured a group trip around the so-called Gulag Archipelago in the Lake Ladoga and Karelian regions near St. Petersburg before the meeting with Putin in Sochi. Some of the top contemporary international historians of Russia, including Richard Pipes and Dominic Lieven, were invited to attend along with prominent Russian counterparts. The purpose of the discussions was to examine the historical tendency of strong central power in Russia, the conception of the state both before and after the 1917 Revolution, and Russia's long experience of attempts at reform and modernization.[25]

The setting of the 2010 Valdai Discussion Club meeting, and its focus on the tragic history of the tsarist and Soviet penal systems and the tradition of internal exile for political dissenters, led to a number of pointed and revealing exchanges with Putin on September 6 in Sochi. At one point, Putin was asked by a British journalist in the group if he ever planned on removing Vladimir Lenin from the mausoleum on Red Square as a signal to the broader Russian population that the Soviet era of political purges was finally over. Putin retorted that there was still a statue of England's seventeenth-century revolutionary leader Oliver Cromwell outside the Houses of Parliament in London. The questions of history had to be addressed, but in their own time, Putin asserted. Who killed more people, he asked, Cromwell or Lenin? Was Stalin worse than Lenin? They all did dreadful things, but they also helped build a great country.

Putin's overarching message was that just as Cromwell was part of British heritage, warts and all, Lenin and Stalin were part of Russia's and Russians' common history. All should reconcile themselves with their histories. There was nothing to be ashamed of. Lenin could be kept in his mausoleum. The tsars and Soviet leaders could all return to their pedestals and stay there, just like Cromwell still stood outside Parliament in London.[26] Film director Nikita Mikhalkov, who published his own "Manifesto of enlightened conservatism" around the same time as the 2010 Valdai meeting, makes almost exactly the same point: "In each period of Russian history there are white and black pages. We cannot and we do not want to divide them up and associate with some while we repudiate others [*delit' ikh na svoi i chuzhiye*]. This is our history! Its victories—are our victories, its defeats are our defeats."[27]

During other Valdai Club meetings, and in public speeches, Putin has made reference to his personal history and the deep roots of his family, stretching back to the early seventeenth century, in Russia's Ryazan province southeast of Moscow.[28] Given the destruction of records during Russia's revolutionary and Soviet upheavals, it is unusual for Russians to know their family history in detail, and it is difficult to verify Putin's assertions. Nonetheless, Putin clearly believes that these claims of long, almost uninterrupted, historical family roots in the Russian heartland give him a unique personal connection to the Russian state and to the Russian *narod*. They are frequently referred to and used to further legitimate his position as Russia's preeminent leader.

MANIPULATING HISTORY: PUTIN AND STOLYPIN

In his pronouncements about Russian history over the course of his tenure as president and prime minister, Vladimir Putin has made it clear that he is obsessed with averting social upheaval and revolution, and thus with maintaining the unity of the Russian state. One of Putin's favorite quotes in 2011 was: "We do not need great upheavals. We need a great Russia."[29] This is a paraphrase of Pyotr Stolypin—prime minister under Nicholas II— in his famous rebuke to his fellow Duma deputies in 1907: "You, gentlemen, are in need of great upheaval; we are in need of Great Russia." In 2011, Stolypin became Putin's "go to" *gosudarstvennik*, facilitated by the neat historic parallelism of the centenary of Stolypin's death by assassination in September 1911. Pyotr Stolypin's latter-day rise to public prominence was blatantly manipulated by Putin and the Kremlin.

In 2008, the Kremlin and Russian government conducted a national contest in which Russian citizens chose "the most important persons in Russian history." The contest unfolded according to an elimination-round format in which each round's highest vote-getters would be pitted against one another in subsequent rounds. The top designee turned out to be Alexander Nevsky, thirteenth-century Grand Prince of Vladimir and one of the most significant early Russian rulers, who was declared a saint by the Russian Orthodox Church. Number 2 was Stolypin. As a number of prominent Russian commentators pointed out at the time of this contest, it had all been fixed. Independent polls showed that few Russians would have actually placed these two figures even in the top 25. The regime manufactured their popularity for its own purposes.[30] Stolypin, a central protagonist in a complicated period in Russian history from 1904 to 1914, had been denigrated in the Soviet era. He was depicted as a failed reformer who was also a brutal repressor of the people. Putin, however, embraced Stolypin as the model for his premiership and future presidency because Stolypin tried to accomplish a great transformation of Russia through non-revolutionary means. Stolypin was also the ultimate *gosudarstvennik*. He sacrificed himself, or was sacrificed, in the service of the state.

A MAN FOR ALL OCCASIONS

Pyotr Stolypin is a *gosudarstvennik* whose biography, along with the developments and events that defined him, can be tailored to suit all occasions. Putin has highlighted a number of elements of historical resonance, while glossing over others that point in more complicated directions. Stolypin emerged on Russia's central stage after the country's 1905 defeat in a war with Japan led to economic collapse and provoked social unrest. The winter of 1905–06 was marked by widespread peasant rioting and arson in Russia's rural areas. Swift action was required to prevent the unraveling of the tsarist regime and the Russian Empire. In 1906, a series of laws were passed creating a qualified constitutional monarchy with Pyotr Stolypin as its premier and a new legislative institution, the State Duma. Stolypin saw that Russia's revolutionary upheavals had far deeper causes than reaction to the Russo-Japanese war. Repression to stem violence would have to go hand in hand with addressing its roots through a comprehensive program of reform.[31] Once the situation in the countryside was brought under control, between 1906 and 1910, Stolypin pushed through a series of agrarian reform measures aimed at creating a prosperous and independent peasant farming class, which would then become the backbone of a new rural economy.[32]

Stolypin governed in his premiership as Boris Chicherin had advised Alexander II in the 1860s—by pursuing liberal reforms and a strong state simultaneously.[33] Stolypin was a firm believer in the Russian monarchy and in the capacity of the tsarist system to adapt. While he saw the new Duma as an important innovation in state governance, "he would not accept the Duma as a loyal opposition: he expected it to cooperate with the government."[34] This is almost exactly the same view that Vladimir Putin expressed about the role of the modern Russian State Duma in the 2000s. On numerous occasions, including before his assumption of the role of prime minister in 2008, Putin referred to the Duma as assisting the presidency in the governing of the Russian state. He saw the Duma embarking on its legislative functions within the context of a "division of labor" with the executive branch.[35]

Stolypin's reforms were cut short by his assassination in 1911. By this juncture, however, as in the case of shock therapy in the 1990s, the success of Stolypin's reforms was in dispute. There was no significant improvement in the efficiency of Russian agriculture. Russian yields were still the lowest in Europe.[36] Across the economy as a whole—in spite of a seeming boom in 1913, which indicated dramatic strides in industrialization—an expanding proletariat was living in appalling conditions in equally expanding cities. Russia's per capita income in 1913 was the lowest among the contemporary great powers and made it one of the poorest countries in Europe.[37] With the constancy of economic and social crisis in the background, the relationship between Tsar Nicholas II and the Duma was as difficult a relationship as that between President Yeltsin and his parliament.

Putin does not delve into these difficulties when he resurrects Stolypin in speeches. Instead, he emphasizes that although Stolypin presided over a time of troubles, he had a far-reaching plan to restore and reform the Russian state. He was also the first Russian prime minister rooted in a Russian parliament that drew upon the popular support of a swathe of the Russian population—even if he still served at the pleasure of the tsar.

In April 2012, as Putin wrapped up his tenure as prime minister and prepared to return to the presidency, he made an explicit reference to the link to the first Russian Duma. In the opening section of his last presentation to parliament as prime minister, Putin exclaimed: "Dear Colleagues! In December of next year we will commemorate the twentieth anniversary of the [Russian] constitution and the modern parliament of [our] country. However, we must not forget about the fact that today's State Duma is already the tenth in our national history, if we take as our starting point the first Russian Duma of 1906."[38]

For Mr. Putin the History Man, the past, and the length of that past, confers legitimacy on the much shorter, and perhaps not so glorious, present. In the 1900s, Pyotr Stolypin never got the chance to finish what he set out to do as Russia's prime minister. He was cut down in 1911, at the beginning of his second decade in office. His endeavors were swept away by the Revolution of 1917. In contrast, in the 2000s, Mr. Putin has specifically said that he wants to finish what he set out to do—as both prime minister and president of Russia. He and his team are sticking to the plan that he put together at the beginning of his first presidential term to set the state on a multi-decade course of recovery.

In 2010–12, Putin openly stated that he saw his work as incomplete. He also asserted that he, Vladimir Putin, was the only person who could really guarantee that the reforms he set in motion would be fulfilled. During his time as prime minister, Putin created a series of task forces to draw up "Russia 2020," a strategy for promoting economic growth, improving living standards, bringing in new technology, and reindustrializing the Russian economy. Russia 2020 set out a series of prescriptive goals for the Russian government to achieve—all by 2018, which would mark the end of Putin's new, third term back in the presidency.[39] In several meetings, in which he referred to this strategy and his general plans for the future, Putin used the term *dostroika* (finishing up the construction or completing the project).[40] Here, however, there was a sharp difference with the *gosudarstvennik* of the early 1900s. In 1909, in an interview with a foreign journalist, Pyotr Stolypin said: "Give *the state* twenty years of internal and external peace and you will not recognize Russia."[41] In 2011–12, Putin instead seemed to be demanding in his speeches and interviews: "Give *me* 20 years and you will not recognize Russia."

Ultimately, Putin's uses of history and his synthesis of ideas are part of a carefully calculated policy. Drawing on his personal interest in Russian history, Putin has weighed up the political debates of the 1990s about Russia's future and the restoration of the state. He has then carefully mined Russia's past for what he deems to be appropriate parallels and concepts. Since his 1999 Millennium Message, Vladimir Putin has channeled, manipulated, and ultimately used these parallels and concepts to his own ends in forging and legitimizing his system of governance, "Putinism," in the 2000s. Putin has also, as a result of intertwining himself with *gosudarstvenniki* across the centuries like Pyotr Stolypin, transformed himself into a protagonist in Russian history.

As he moved into his third presidential term in May 2012, Vladimir Putin presented himself as the modern standard bearer of a program of all-encompassing reforms for the Russian state that stretched far back into imperial history. During the presidential campaign, Putin frequently asserted that he was *the* leader who personally saved the state from the disastrous condition of contradiction and conflict in the 1990s. In his final address as prime minister to the Russian parliament in April 2012, Putin congratulated himself for having "restored the country after all the upheavals, which have been the lot of our people [*narod*] on the threshold of centuries. . . . We," he went on—clearly meaning I, Vladimir Putin personally—"have, in fact, completed the post-Soviet period. A new stage in the development of Russia stands before us—the stage of creating a state, economic, and social order and a viable societal structure that is capable of guaranteeing the prosperity of the citizens of our country for the decades ahead."[42] In 2012, Mr. Putin, Statist, History Man, savior, restorer, and reformer stood in very sharp contrast to the behind-the-scenes operative he was when he first came to Moscow from St. Petersburg in August 1996.

CHAPTER FIVE

THE SURVIVALIST

HISTORY FOR PUTIN IS VERY personal and immediate as well as a source of material for his own political use. More significant than the Putin family's deep roots in Ryazan province is the fact that Vladimir Putin is the child of survivors of one of the blackest periods in Russian history during the Second World War. This personal history of survival is the third element in providing the context for Putin's worldview. It has multiple dimensions and has produced a series of clearly identifiable personal and policy responses.

In World War II, Putin's father, also called Vladimir, served in a so-called destruction battalion set up by the NKVD (*Narodnyy komissariat vnutrennikh del*)—the People's Commissariat for Internal Affairs, a forerunner of the KGB. The battalion was sent behind enemy lines, into Nazi-occupied territory, to carry out a scorched earth policy and destroy critical infrastructure. In this case, Vladimir Putin senior was deployed to territory that is now part of modern Estonia. He was among only 4 of 28 commandos who returned alive from one operation outside Leningrad.[1] Severe wounds suffered early in 1942 disqualified him from further active duty. Out of the hospital, Putin senior remained in Leningrad with his wife and son. At least 670,000 of the Putins' fellow Leningraders died during the subsequent Nazi blockade of the city from September 1941 to January 1944, from artillery barrages, bombings, starvation, or disease (some estimates put the number of casualties at 1.5 million).[2] The Putin family's five-year-old son, Vladimir's older brother, was among them.

This personal story of death and survival during the siege of Leningrad fits neatly into the general context of Russia's national historical narrative. In this narrative, Russia constantly battles for survival against a hostile outside world. Through times of troubles, frequent invasions, and wars, Russia is always put to the test by God, fate, or history. The one critical lesson from history is that Russia, the state, always survives in one form or another. Every survived calamity reaffirms the special status of Russia in history. Vladimir Putin, and almost every other Russian politician, refers to this in public presentations. Just as Russia is put to the test, so are the Russian people, individually and collectively. Some individuals and their families perish, while others survive against the odds—without much protection from the state, but for the sake of the state. Those individuals who make it through are survivors. Their collective experience has turned the Russian population into survivalists, people who constantly think of and prepare for the worst.

The Survivalist as a mentality, or mindset, may be the one that is the most widespread among Russians of nearly all backgrounds and ages, given their shared experiences of war and privation. It is reflected even today, in possibly the most prosperous period in Russian history, in the overwhelming prevalence of the potato and other staple crops grown on private dacha plots. Leningraders or St. Petersburgers like Putin demonstrate this trait more than most. Every Leningrad family was deeply scarred by that terrible time. Vladimir Putin, born soon after the war, knew everything about the sufferings of his family and their fellow citizens, including his older brother who did not survive the blockade. Putin understood that had there been enough food in the city, his brother and others might have survived in spite of the Nazi onslaught. As a child and young man, Putin was aware of the dangers that food shortages can pose and of the ultimate vulnerability of cities. Thus, for Putin, his family, and for all Leningraders, the notion of food security became an essential element in the functioning of their native city. Indeed, in a June 2003 Kremlin press conference, Putin even made reference to the fact that he had his own personal experience of growing his family's food to ensure their basic security. Putin noted, "My own parents in their time worked hard keeping up their garden, labored away from morning till night and made me do the same. So I know very well what it's all about."[3]

For Putin, history is focused on individuals and their actions more than on political, social, and economic forces. It is a source of lessons to apply to contemporary circumstances. Vladimir Putin derives lessons not just from big history or national history, but also from small history, from his own personal history. In this case, Mr. Putin has a number of instances of personal survival in a variety of forms—including surviving by his wits during childhood and political survival in St. Petersburg in the 1990s. His career as a deputy mayor was almost derailed by a major scandal in the midst of another period of privation and food shortages in his home city. His experiences of state-level survival through the crises of the 1990s, and again in the economic crisis of 2008–10, provide additional lessons.

A TALE OF POLITICAL SURVIVAL:
PUTIN AND THE ST. PETERSBURG FOOD CRISIS

Putin's lessons of survival from his family's history of the Leningrad blockade were compounded by his personal experiences in post-Soviet St. Petersburg. The test of how well Putin had learned the importance of basic food security came unexpectedly with the breakup of the Soviet Union, itself an unexpected event. The winter of 1991–92 was Russia's first under the free market. It marked the end of the Soviet-era practice of requisitioning food from the countryside to supply Russian cities. Links between the countryside and cities that had been maintained in the Soviet command economy failed. Collective farms kept food for themselves. They deprived the industrial and administrative centers of the supplies they had grown accustomed to in the post-war decades. Russia's large cities, especially Moscow and St. Petersburg, found themselves on the brink of hunger that winter.

The weakened Russian state was of no help. In the three previous years, as Yegor Gaidar described in considerable detail in *Collapse of an Empire,* the Soviet government had run out of hard currency. It was torn between using its limited remaining funds to import grain or to stabilize the supply of consumer goods. Even before the Soviet Union finally disintegrated, there were chronic shortages of everything from meat, baked goods, sugar and tea, flour, grain, vegetables, fruit, and fish, to fabric, shoes, children's clothes, construction materials, and matches.[4]

By the fall of 1990, the supply of food and consumer goods across the entire country was in a precarious position. Regional leaders, observing "lines of a hundred, a thousand people" outside stores, feared imminent revolution and that they would not "be able to save the country."[5]

In May 1991, Anatoly Sobchak, who was then chairman of the Leningrad Soviet, or city council, wrote a desperate letter to Soviet prime minister Valentin Pavlov pointing out that "the supply of basic foodstuffs is continuing to worsen in Leningrad" and bemoaning the fact that his "numerous appeals to the central government organs of the RSFSR [Russian Federation] and the USSR and direct contacts with the leadership of the Union republics [were] not producing the necessary results."[6] By November 1991, Sobchak, who was now mayor of newly renamed St. Petersburg, was writing more letters calling the food shortages for the general population of St. Petersburg "critical" and stressing that "the remaining meat supply in refrigeration is [only] enough for three or four days for the city . . . [and] [s]teady supplies for December and early 1992 are not expected." Sobchak predicted, "This could lead to a dangerous social and political situation in St. Petersburg."[7] An article in *Izvestiya* recorded the fact that over the course of 1991 the Russian people had returned en masse to growing their own food: "People realize that they have to rely on themselves. So after work and on weekends they work their allotments with shovels and rakes. Of course, this is not a complete solution to the food problem, but rather an aid in the event of disruption in the food supply."[8]

Indeed, the internal food supply was soon completely disrupted. Once the USSR finally collapsed, inflation then destroyed the purchasing power of the Soviet ruble even further. The only option left for cities like St. Petersburg and Moscow was to obtain food from outside Russia through barter schemes—using the only product of real value the country had to offer: natural resources. In Leningrad in early 1991, the person designated by the mayor's office to negotiate agreements to barter resources for food was Vladimir Putin, who became chairman of the city's Committee for External Relations. The city lacked its own independent mechanisms to execute the barter schemes, so Putin designated several private trading companies to serve as middlemen in facilitating the deals. Putin's scheme became a spectacular failure, and a political scandal. The companies delivered only a fraction of the initially agreed quantities of food, and in some cases vital food products from abroad were delivered to Moscow instead.

In her book *The Man without a Face,* Russian American journalist and writer Masha Gessen relates in detail the story of Marina Salye, the chairwoman of the Leningrad City Council's Committee on Food Supplies, who traveled to Berlin in May 1991 to negotiate a contract for importing meat and potatoes to Leningrad. Salye discovered upon her arrival that the negotiations had already been completed by Vladimir Putin on behalf of the city administration (rather than the council) and a Leningrad trading company, Kontinent. It was Salye who later determined that the deliveries from Germany had been sent to Moscow rather than Leningrad.[9] Leningrad ultimately survived the crisis, but only because the winter turned out not to be as severe as feared. In addition, and perhaps most important, the population's food stocks from their allotments—the traditional, almost instinctive, survival mechanism that Putin's parents had instilled in him and that people had turned to in the 1991 growing season—helped relieve the very worst of the shortages. Putin was also personally bailed out of his predicament by an old veteran of the Soviet agricultural elite—Viktor Zubkov. The man with the necessary set of relationships with the Leningrad regional food producers (rather than with private companies), Zubkov was brought into Putin's team in January 1992. As we will discuss later, Viktor Zubkov has since proven to be one of the most important figures in Mr. Putin's inner circle.

In retrospect, this early failure in his public career seems to have taught Vladimir Putin two lessons that would influence his model for approaching economic management, a model he would eventually apply to the entire country as Russian president. First, during cataclysmic events, Russia's ultimate guarantee of survival—and of the country's wealth and development—is its natural resources. They should, therefore, always be kept in strategic reserve. The second lesson Putin drew from his mismanagement of the resources-for-food schemes was that private companies cannot be trusted, even if (and especially if) there is a lot of money to be made. In an unstable and unpredictable environment, private companies will disregard their obligations to society and act exclusively for their own narrow interest. Consequently, the state—and the person at the top in charge of the state—must always reserve the power to exercise some degree of control. These are both "lessons learned" for survival to which we will return later.

World War II and the Leningrad blockade were the primary existential threat for a generation of Russians. They put an emphasis on survival and created the tendency to think in terms of worst-case scenarios and insurance. The lesson of the Leningrad blockade was repeated in the early 1990s in the St. Petersburg city government. Again, insurance was needed in case something went wrong due to internal miscalculations or a dramatic change in external circumstances. In a meeting with the heads of Russia's media outlets in January 2012, during the presidential election campaign, Putin picked up this theme as he turned to the issue of governing and developing the Russian state. He asserted:

> I think our task is to create a viable organism—a state organism in Russia that would be vital and adapted to a changing world. And in the world in which this organism is developing today the threats are many—so that it is prepared for these external shocks, so that it can completely guarantee our sovereignty, it must be stable as well as developing and capable of ensuring the growth of the citizens of Russia's wellbeing for the decades ahead.[10]

Surviving in a hostile and competitive world means thinking about the worst thing or things that could happen, and having something to rely upon to assure yourself, and the state, when the external shocks come along. These ideas have governed Putin's policies as Russia's preeminent leader since 2000. Putin applies his worst-case scenario thinking to the state level. Do not make any irreversible commitments that will trap you when things go wrong. Always have a Plan B. The key for a Plan B is to emphasize reserves, like the private dacha food stores—potatoes in the family plot—but on a massive scale. As president and prime minister, Putin has engaged in a concerted policy to create and protect Russia's reserves, including by prioritizing the Russian government's budget stabilization fund and building up foreign exchange reserves.

STRATEGIC PLANNING: BUILDING UP RESERVES

The idea of building up Russia's reserves may also have been reinforced for Putin by an American textbook on strategic planning that he most likely read in the KGB academy (the Red Banner Institute) in 1984–85—and which he used extensively when writing his dissertation in the mid-1990s.[11] The main theme of the textbook, by University of Pittsburgh professors William King and David Cleland, was "how to plan in an uncertain environment." King was in business administration and Cleland in engineering ("systems management engineering"). Their work, *Strategic Planning and Policy,* was first published in 1978 as a business school textbook.[12] We cannot be certain that Putin actually read King and Cleland in the 1980s and, if so, when exactly, but the Russian-language edition of the book was published in 1982 in a very limited edition by the USA-Canada Institute in Moscow. It was almost certainly published on behalf of the intelligence services, and it may well have been used, or at least available, at the Red Banner Institute.

The key point King and Cleland made was that the essence of true *strategic* planning is not long-range planning but "planning for contingencies," for the unexpected. The question is how best to be prepared, and if not, how to adapt to the worst-case scenario when there are uncontrollable, unpredictable changes in the environment. The authors focused on the role of strategic planning in the management of a corporation. They went into great detail on the concept of strategic intelligence, with chapters on strategic corporate intelligence, including financial intelligence. King and Cleland also concluded that the key to strategic planning was to set up a hierarchy of goals and objectives. Anyone doing the strategic planning for a corporation would have to identify, define, and explain what is a constant objective and what can be adapted or even sacrificed. A planner would have to distinguish the overarching from the temporal; and then, from that, see what needs to be made precise and what not. The goal was to separate the truly important, the strategic, from the lower-level, shorter-term concerns.[13]

As Russian president, Vladimir Putin certainly seems to have applied King and Cleland's conclusions in his planning and management of the Russian state—as we will discuss further in chapter 9. Immediately on entering office, Putin began setting goals along the lines that King and Cleland prefigured, including creating strategic state reserves to deal with a range of contingencies. Indeed, Putin's first goal was to address the issue of the strategic material reserves that had been depleted in the final years of the USSR as the Soviet state grappled with chronic shortages and its food crisis. In July 2001, Putin assigned a close KGB colleague from St. Petersburg, Alexander Grigoriev, to take charge of this project. Grigoriev was named the head of *Gosrezerv,* the Agency for State Reserves tasked with maintaining the reserves. One Russian biographical work on Putin provides details on Grigoriev and his career in the KGB—as well as his relationship with Putin, complete with a photograph of the two as young men at a dacha. It notes that "under B. N. Yel'tsin the strategic reserves were almost completely stolen."[14]

These state reserves were built up and consolidated in secrecy during both the Soviet and the post-Soviet periods. They were intended to tide the country over a period of war, catastrophic emergencies, and exceptionally harsh winters. The general idea of state reserves was a very old one, dating back to a decree by Tsar Peter the Great in 1700. As he set about expanding and transforming the Russian Empire, Peter wanted to ensure that he could adequately supply his forces as he sent them into battle.[15] The system of reserves that Putin inherited, however, was primarily put in place by Josef Stalin in the 1930s. It was intended, on the basis of a 1931 decree, to become a "state within a state."[16] Autarky—ensuring the USSR could survive almost entirely on its own material and industrial resources—was at that time a critical concern of the Soviet leadership, given the hostility of neighboring countries to the communist regime. Since the 1930s, the structure of the reserves has been "carried forward to the present day practically unchanged."[17]

Gosrezerv's activities and scale are difficult to penetrate and conceptualize, as the authors of an August 2000 article in *Izvestiya* noted. The agency was deliberately mysterious, with "no sign at the entrance, no press office and no internet site." The agency, however, had hundreds of well-protected and guarded installations across the whole of Russia. These included giant warehouses, one of which the *Izvestiya* authors visited, and "in the event of a global catastrophe only on the basis of [these reserves] could we [Russians] expect to survive for any length of time."[18] The exact contents of the warehouses and the volumes of commodities and products they contained were a state secret, as was the budget of the agency. The reserves covered, along with foodstuffs for the entire population, many of the products that Yegor Gaidar discusses in *Collapse of an Empire* as being in chronic short supply in the late 1980s–90s. They included livestock feed, uniforms and clothing for the military, tents, basic medicines, body bags, construction equipment, heavy machinery, generators, water and air filters, firefighting equipment, and grain, uranium, oil and gas, refined petroleum products, and other primary commodities.[19] It was these commodity reserves that were dipped into by Leningrad/St. Petersburg, Moscow, and other Russian cities in their barter schemes in the fateful period of 1991–92.

In addition to tiding Russia, or any part of Russia, through a repetition of the kind of experience of the Leningrad blockade, Putin's strategic reserves were intended to help stabilize Russia's domestic markets. Part of their purpose was to help revive the price of a critical commodity in the event of a crisis (in a manner similar to the United States' strategic petroleum reserve). In March 2004, *Gosrezerv* was renamed *Rosrezerv*—to emphasize the all-Russian nature of the vast state reserves. As one journalist investigating the work of the agency in 2006—which marked the peak of Putin's efforts to restore the Russian state's strategic reserves—put it: "In essence, *Rosrezerv* is a guarantee of the stability of the country. And as long as this is the case, no-one will be capable of bringing us to our knees."[20] In 2006, Putin's colleague and agency head Alexander Grigoriev gave a series of interviews outlining his work on consolidating the state reserves. Grigoriev asserted that *Rosrezerv* had amassed enough food to supply the entire country for up to three months, as well as sufficient fuel, clothing, medications, and other products and equipment for a similarly lengthy period. Based on the prices for these commodities in 2006, this would have amounted to around $100 billion worth of strategic reserves.[21]

Grigoriev boasted that no other country in the world had created such massive or wide-ranging strategic reserves. He stressed that *Rosrezerv* was as important to ensuring the security of the Russian state as the Ministry of Defense, Ministry of Internal Affairs, FSB (KGB), and the Agency for Emergency Situations. It was a vital part of this network of security agencies (the so-called power ministries) even if it was not as well known to the public as the others. This assertion was underscored by the location of Grigoriev's office close to the Kremlin, within immediate hailing distance of Vladimir Putin.[22] Indeed, Grigoriev summed up the entire ethos behind the creation of this vast, costly system of material reserves in these interviews in a manner entirely in keeping with President Putin's pronouncements on the issue:

The situation in the world is developing so dynamically that it is not possible to make some unambiguous forecasts of a cloudless future either for mankind as a whole or for the Russian Federation. . . . The state materials reserve is a universal instrument in the hands of the leaders of the country for the purpose of overcoming resource constraints in various circumstances. But the stocks of the state reserve are not only an important element of the system of ensuring national security. They are also a stabilizing factor for the development of the economy. Underappreciating the state reserve has always led to serious consequences. In 1917 one of the reasons for the collapse of the Russian Empire was the exhaustion of the state reserves. In contrast, the state material reserves that were created [by Stalin] before the Great Patriotic War allowed us to withstand and win, and then to rebuild the economy.[23]

DEPLOYING RUSSIA'S FINANCIAL RESERVES

This link between the state reserves and the economy is a critical one for Putin. In the same period of 2000–06, he extended the concept of amassing reserves from the material to the financial arena. Putin assigned another close St. Petersburg colleague to spearhead this task: Alexei Kudrin, an economist who had previously been deputy mayor in charge of finances in Sobchak's administration. Kudrin moved to Moscow as deputy chief of the presidential administration in 1996 and then became Russia's first deputy finance minister in March 1997. He helped to bring Putin to Moscow in 1996 by recommending him for a position in the presidential administration. In May 2000, Putin appointed him finance minister, and Kudrin went on to play the same role for President Putin and Russia as he had played for Mayor Sobchak in St. Petersburg, managing the finances at the macrolevel. Kudrin's and Putin's shared goals were to reduce the state's debt burden, reduce Russia's exposure to the volatility of the global economy, and to build financial reserves sufficient to weather a major economic downturn. This would ensure not just the physical survival of the state but Russia's survival as an independent state. One of the lessons Putin, Kudrin, and others around them had learned from the Soviet experience was the connection between a country's financial and fiscal health and its sovereignty.

The fall of the USSR, as Yegor Gaidar clearly spelled out in his book *Collapse of an Empire,* showed that military power alone could not guarantee sovereignty if the state then lost its financial independence.[24] Surviving without being sovereign, without being able to autonomously shape your own destiny free from outside pressure or control, was essentially meaningless. The late Soviet regime had enjoyed a period of high resource rents—that is, the value of its oil, gas, and other natural resources—and national wealth followed by a period of very low rents. But it had managed the rents poorly. It had become so deeply indebted to Western governments that it sacrificed its financial—and ultimately its political—sovereignty, its independence. Putin, Kudrin, and their colleagues were very aware of how the United States and the West had been able to leverage post-Soviet Russia's indebtedness and dependence on International Monetary Fund (IMF) bailouts and World Bank loans in the early 1990s. The withdrawal of former Soviet troops from the Baltic states in 1994 was one glaring instance where Moscow had been forced to acquiesce on foreign policy issues.[25]

Between 1999 and 2008, the first decade of Vladimir Putin's tenure as president, Russia had one of the fastest growing economies in the world. This was in stark contrast to the late Soviet period. As we will discuss again later (when we consider Putin's perspectives on capitalism), this was largely thanks to rising prices for Russia's oil and gas. The rents generated by oil and gas were leveraged to other Russian economic sectors. Demand by oil and gas producers for inputs such as steel and machinery bolstered the manufacturing industry. Strong growth in personal incomes boosted the retail, construction, and real estate sectors. Putin, along with Kudrin, made it a priority to use the unexpected period of high rents from the oil price windfall to pay off the country's foreign debt and to build up Russia's foreign exchange reserves for the future. When Putin first assumed the post of prime minister in August 1999, Russian foreign-currency reserves were close to rock bottom and still falling. By January 2000, as Putin moved into the position of acting president, the reserves were down to $8.5 billion and the government's external debt was $133 billion. The debt to the IMF alone was $16.6 billion. By the end of 2007, with government foreign debt down to $37 billion, Russia had one of the lowest debt-to-GDP ratios in the world. Its foreign exchange reserves had grown to over $600 billion by mid-2008—the third largest in the world.[26]

The decade spent building up reserves helped Russia, and Putin, weather the global financial crisis of 2008–10. This stood in stark contrast to Russia's performance in 1998 when, in the aftermath of the Asian financial crisis of 1997, Russia defaulted on its debt and devalued the ruble. The 2008 global crisis, and especially the accompanying oil price collapse, did hit Russia hard. From June 2008 to January 2009, the stock market lost nearly 80 percent of its value. In 2009, GDP dropped by 7.9 percent and industrial output by 10.8 percent from the previous year. Yet, thanks to a substantial package of bailouts and stimulus measures, households were largely protected. Real incomes continued to grow, albeit modestly, and job losses were less than nearly anywhere else in Europe. Russia's ability to ride out the crisis reasonably well was due to Putin's and Kudrin's prudent fiscal and financial management during the oil boom period as well as a rebound in oil prices after early 2009. In contrast with the 1990s, Russia's reserves played the critical role in protecting Russia's financial sovereignty and the welfare of its citizens.[27]

In Putin's view, the 2008–10 crisis vindicated and reinforced his and Kudrin's policy of fiscal conservatism and extreme self-insurance to enhance Russia's resiliency to short-term shocks. Putin referred to this directly and very clearly in his last annual address to parliament as prime minister in April 2012. The speech also underscored his plans to continue on the same course once he was again inaugurated as Russian president the following month. Putin asserted in the address, "In assessing the results of the last four years, we can state—with full justification—that Russia has not only overcome the [economic] crisis, but we have made a serious, significant, notable step forward, we have become stronger than we were before." The reserves were central to this achievement: "Where can we turn to [if there is a crisis]? Well Greece can go to Brussels for money, and will get it. But who will give us money? Someone could also give it to us, but with what conditions attached? I remember this situation very well after 2000, when we were overburdened with debts and when people forced conditions on us. . . . In Russia we have a very specific set of circumstances—being without reserves is very dangerous." The contrast with the 1990s could not be greater, he argued: "If at the beginning of the 1990s and in 1998 the economic blows turned into such a shock for millions of our people, then during the crisis period from 2008 to 2010, the government [*vlast'*] demonstrated its solvency [*sostoyatel'nost'*] when put to the test."[28]

In the 1990s, the insolvent Russian state failed the test. In the 2000s, the very much solvent Russian state passed with flying colors. In an April 2012 address to the staff of the finance ministry, in another of his final presentations as prime minister, Putin was clear in his praise for the ministry and for Alexei Kudrin's role as finance minister in this critical period (by this point Kudrin had resigned from his ministerial position). Putin noted that thanks to the farsighted work of the ministry, the country had been well prepared to deal with the 2008 economic crisis. Russia and the finance ministry had built up a solid financial capacity through the creation of two sovereign wealth funds, the Reserve Fund (*Rezervnyy fond*) and the National Welfare Fund (*Fond natsional'nogo blagosostoyaniya*). He directly thanked the staff of the ministry and "its former, long-serving, director—Alexei Leonidovich Kudrin—for [their] professionalism, firmness, sense of responsibility, and sticking to [their] principles in carrying out the country's chosen financial strategy and tactics."[29]

In all of these instances of building up reserves, both material and financial, there is a notable difference between being a survivor and having the outlook of a survivalist. The former is passive; the latter is active. The survivor makes it through the catastrophe largely thanks to good fortune. The survivalist takes measures to increase the chances of survival. In Putin's case, his family experiences, his first-hand observations and knowledge of the basic survival responses and mechanisms of the population at the grassroots level, his close reading of the lessons of Russian history from early imperial times through to the 1990s, and his studies of Western and other textbooks on the importance and essence of strategic planning further developed and deepened this outlook. Putin clearly believes that allowing Russia to be materially, financially, or politically vulnerable is dangerous. So even at a cost—a high cost in many cases—it is better for Russia to rely on itself. For Putin this national-level concept translates to the personal level.

PREVAILING IN "THE 'SANDPIT' STREETS" AND CHECHNYA

Putin frequently tells personal stories of learning how to survive by relying on his own resources when growing up in Leningrad—stories that he presents as shaping his general approach to his role as Russian prime minister or president. For example, in Oleg Blotsky's interview-based biography of Putin, there is a sharply rendered episode where Putin talks about his early childhood in the back streets and courtyards of Leningrad. A chapter entitled "The 'Sandpit' Streets" relates the story of a fight Putin had when he was little—possibly around seven years old.[30] Putin explains in the interview that he was a rebellious kid in school because he came from a tough neighborhood. He claims he was rejected by the Young Pioneers—the Soviet organization for children—because of this background. He "hooked up" with the neighborhood boys, who ran around in packs, or gangs, and got into fights. Putin goes on to enumerate all the lessons he learned from the experience of his first fight:

> The first time I got beat up, it was a disgrace. . . . That incident was my first serious street "university." . . . I drew four conclusions. Number one. I was wrong. I don't remember the exact details of the conflict, but . . . [b]asically I insulted him for no good reason. So he immediately beat me up, and I deserved it. . . . Conclusion number two . . . I understood that you shouldn't act like that to anybody, that you need to respect everybody. That was a nice "hands-on" lesson! Number three. I realized that in every situation—whether I was right or wrong—I had to be strong. I had to be able to answer back. . . . And number four. I learned that I always had to be ready to instantly respond to an offense or insult. Instantly! . . . I just understood that if you want to win, then you have to fight to the finish in every fight, as if it was the last and decisive battle . . . you need to assume that there is no retreat and that you'll have to fight to the end. In principle, that's a well-known rule that they later taught me in the KGB, but I learned it much earlier—in those fights as a kid.[31]

Over time, Putin's childhood fights morphed into something more formal, which took him off the streets when he was around 10 or 11. First he took up boxing, then sambo, a combination of judo and wrestling; then he moved to judo itself. The discipline of the sport provided him with more serious lessons about respecting his opponent, building inner strength, and preparing himself for competition.[32] Putin seems to have applied all these lessons to another political challenge, the second war in

Chechnya that marked his entry into office in 1999–2000. In the wake of the 1996–97 ceasefire and peace accords in Chechnya, the republic descended into political chaos. There was a continual cycle of internecine violence, high-profile abductions, killings, and terrorist attacks. In 1998–99, when Putin was head of the FSB, the situation careened out of control. Then Chechen separatist leader Aslan Maskhadov survived a number of assassination attempts. He declared a state of emergency in Grozny, prompting calls in Russian security circles for Moscow to intervene again.

In March 1999, Russia's envoy to Chechnya, interior ministry General Gennady Shpigun, was kidnapped (and later killed). In August 1999—just around the time Vladimir Putin was first appointed prime minister—violence spilled over Chechnya's borders into the rest of Russia. A group of Chechen insurgents led by notorious warlord Shamil Basaev, who had carried out a series of brazen hostage-taking assaults outside of Chechnya in the first war, now raided neighboring Dagestan in alleged support of a group of Islamist militants. The insurgents engaged in an intense standoff with local authorities. Basaev's incursion into Dagestan was immediately followed by a series of bombings of soldiers' residences and civilian apartment buildings, including in Moscow, which were blamed on the Chechens. Several hundred people were killed and injured. In late August–September 1999, President Boris Yeltsin launched a massive air offensive against Chechnya, subsequently followed by a ground assault. By the time Putin took over as acting president in December 1999, Russian forces had blockaded Grozny and were in the process of reducing it to rubble for a second time. They were also engaged in open warfare in Chechnya's mountainous south.[33]

Putin's association with the renewal of the brutal, destructive war in Chechnya is close and personal. For many analysts and commentators it is viewed as "Putin's War"—"the sole undertaking associated with Putin's name and begun on his initiative."[34] Some observers also contended that the inner circles around Vladimir Putin and Boris Yeltsin were the actual instigators of the conflict. According to this argument, top Kremlin officials wanted to use the war as a justification for moving Putin—a former head of one of the key security services—into the presidency.[35] Whether or not this was the case, as Russian president, Putin certainly made it clear that (in the words of his interview with Blotsky) he would conduct this round of the conflict as a no-holds-barred "fight to the end." There would be "no retreat" like in 1996–97, when Moscow essentially sued Chechnya for peace. Putin would make sure things were done differently, whatever the cost and however long it took.

Putin famously claimed, in an early speech as prime minister in September 1999, his willingness to pursue Chechen rebels and terrorists into their outhouses (he used crude phrasing in Russian) if necessary to "answer back"—again as he put it in the biographical interview—to the Chechens' "offense."[36] In other interviews for his mass-edition "campaign biography," *Ot pervogo litsa,* from the year 2000, Putin even went so far as to state that he had decided that "my mission, my historical mission—it sounds bombastic, but this is true—would be to resolve this situation in the North Caucasus. At that time, it was completely uncertain how everything would turn out, but it was clear to me, and no doubt not only to me, that in the North Caucasus 'this kid was going to get his head kicked in.' That is how I approached this. I told myself: to heck with it! I have a certain amount of time—two, three, four months—to bang these bandits about."[37]

RESERVES AND SACRIFICES

In keeping with Putin's survivalist approach, he drew on the state's strategic material reserves. He used them to supply the military—to ensure that the deprivations the Russian armed forces faced in the first war, including shortages of warm clothing in the winter, would not undermine their fighting capacity. Putin also used them to guarantee that the government had the wherewithal to deal with the aftermath of terrorist attacks.[38] There were many sacrifices, and not just on the part of the Russian military or Chechen forces. As in the Leningrad blockade, individuals, civilians, perished on a massive scale—in Chechnya itself and in the spillover of the conflict into the rest of the North Caucasus and other parts of Russia, including Moscow. Before President Putin could complete his self-declared mission, there were multiple, devastating, and high-profile terrorist attacks on the capital and other vulnerable targets. Often masterminded by Shamil Basaev (who was killed in July 2006), these included the taking of around 850 hostages in a Moscow theater in 2002; several bombings of passenger trains and the Moscow metro, as well as the downing of commercial Russian airplanes in 2003–04; and the seizure of more than a thousand children in a school in Beslan in North Ossetia in 2004. Russian analyst Lilia Shevtsova, in her book on *Putin's Russia,* notes that Chechnya became a "round-the-clock slaughterhouse."[39]

Given the fact that the interviews with Blotsky took place against the backdrop of the war, the parallels between Chechnya and Putin's tale of his boyhood fight in "The 'Sandpit' Streets" were inescapable for Russians reading the book in this period. Putin's reference in *Ot pervogo litsa* to himself as the "kid" about to "get his head kicked in" in the North Caucasus echoes the core theme of his Blotsky interview. With these pointed, personalized references, Putin was clearly signaling to the Chechens, as well as to the rest of Russia, that he was not to be underestimated. He would not back down. He had the personal reserves and resources to fight this fight. He was the tough, self-reliant survivor. He was a survivalist who knew how to make the right preparations for a long conflict. He would prevail. Over the course of the 2000s, Putin doggedly pursued the war to an uneasy, and incomplete, conclusion. In April 2002, Putin and the Russian government made a controversial decision to declare military victory in Chechnya. They transformed the war into a peacekeeping and counterinsurgency operation—an operation that was declared officially at an end seven years later in April 2009.[40]

In 2012, as Putin entered the presidency once more, and in spite of all the declarations of victory, Moscow was still struggling on a daily basis with Islamic militant groups, insurgents, and terrorist attacks in the Russian North Caucasus. From Putin's point of view there had been some successes. The Russian state was bloodied by the two cycles of war in Chechnya, but ultimately it survived. By the end of the 2000s, almost all of the Chechen secessionists who led the region in the 1990s had, literally, been physically wiped out. Chechnya's secession of 1991 had been reversed, and the republic was back as part of the Russian Federation. Nonetheless, Vladimir Putin was very conscious of the fact that Chechnya almost tore Russia apart and that war in the North Caucasus could do this again. Early in the second war, in his interviews for *Ot pervogo litsa*—in the same discussion of the need to "bang [the Chechen] bandits about"—Putin noted that if the war in Chechnya was not brought to an end, the Russian state could collapse:

Believe me, even back in 1990–91 I knew very clearly . . . that the country would very quickly find itself on the edge of collapse. Now, about the Caucasus. What is the essence of the current situation in the North Caucasus and in Chechnya? It is the continuation of the collapse [*raspad*] of the USSR. It is clear this has to stop at some point. Yes, at one time I hoped that with economic growth and the development of democratic institutions this process would begin to slow down. But life and experience showed that this was not happening. . . . If we did not quickly do something to stop it, Russia as a state in its current form would cease to exist. At that juncture the discussion was about how to stop the disintegration [*razval*] of the state. I realized that I might have to do this at the cost of my political career. It was a minimal cost that I was ready to pay. . . . I reckoned I had a few months to consolidate the armed forces, the MVD [Ministry of Internal Affairs] and the FSB, and to find public support. . . . I was convinced that if we did not immediately stop the extremists, then in no time at all we would be facing a second Yugoslavia across the entire territory of the Russian Federation—the Yugoslavization of Russia.[41]

This response is replete with a number of classic Putin references and themes that infuse all three of his broader Statist, History Man, and Survivalist identities. The danger of state collapse, the importance of paying whatever cost is necessary to prevent this, and the imperative of ensuring unity are core, overlapping elements in these identities and bind them together. In the context of his Survivalist identity, Putin's reference to "the extremists" is significant. Extremists are a threat to the state's survival. Here, he does not simply have in mind the Chechen Islamists or separatists. Putin is acutely aware that the rise of competing nationalist and separatist movements—including Russian extremism— was instrumental in the break-up of both the Russian Empire and the Soviet Union. These movements severely weakened the integrity of the Russian Federation, including helping to provoke the war in Chechnya.[42] Having fought the fight with the Chechens to the bitter end, Putin would need a different strategy for moving beyond the battlefield. This is where another lesson from "The 'Sandpit' Streets"—that you need to respect everyone—comes in.

SURVIVING THROUGH UNITY: RECONCILING WITH CHECHNYA

Chechnya's drive for independence, and Moscow's particularly vicious retaliation, created a crisis that has, since the 1990s, symbolically pitted Russia's indigenous Muslim groups, and other nonethnic Russian citizens, against its Orthodox Slavs. This imperils Putin's concept of a united and indivisible Russian *narod,* which he sees as essential to Russia's survival as a unified multiethnic state.[43] The war in Chechnya and the counterinsurgency operations across the region left the ruined economies of Chechnya and its neighboring North Caucasus republics almost completely dependent on direct transfers and subsidies from Moscow. Against the backdrop of the 2008 economic crisis, this sparked a backlash from Russian nationalist groups.

In the late 2000s, clashes between ethnic Russians and representatives of North Caucasus ethnic groups who lived in Moscow and other cities outside the North Caucasus became a frequent and often fatal occurrence. In one prominent incident in December 2010, on Moscow's central Manezh Square just beyond the Kremlin walls, a memorial rally for an ethnic Russian soccer fan killed in an altercation with a youth from one of the North Caucasus republics turned into a violent brawl. A crowd of several thousand clashed with police. The incident was widely portrayed in the media as a sign that inter-ethnic violence in Russia was increasing and that European or U.S.-style race riots would soon become a fact of Russian political life.[44] One of the Russian nationalist slogans— "stop feeding the Caucasus"—also featured in the December 2011 protests after the Russian parliamentary elections. Inflammatory appeals for policies favoring ethnic Russians and ridding the Russian heartland of Chechens and others were revived as staple elements in the stump speeches of Vladimir Zhirinovsky and other nationalist politicians.[45]

In his own speeches, like his November 2011 address to the United Russia party conference, Putin made a public virtue of countering separatism and extremism of all kinds.[46] At the same time, Putin championed the ideas of Russian nationalists about the importance of a strong state and flirted with national-patriotic groups, including the government's own youth movement, *Nashi* (Ours).[47] Nashi is less known by its longer official name—the Youth Democratic Anti-Fascist Movement. This was clearly intended to give it an all-encompassing, anti-extremist profile even though the movement's primary focus was on stirring up a sense of Russian patriotism among students and young professionals, and thus mobilizing them to support Kremlin policies.

In addition to countering extremism with rhetoric, Putin began in the late 2000s to reference the importance of reconciling with the Chechens and reintegrating Chechnya into the body politic of the Russian Federation. At the Valdai Discussion Club meeting in Moscow in November 2011, just before the parliamentary elections, for example, Putin pointedly stressed the need to show appropriate respect to the Chechens in response to a question from one of the participants about the persistence of violence in the North Caucasus.[48] The idea of reconciliation with individual Chechens and Chechnya itself was also the central theme in *gosudarstvennik* film director Nikita Mikhalkov's 2007 movie, *12,* a remake of American director Sidney Lumet's courtroom drama *Twelve Angry Men.* In the film, Mikhalkov (who is also a renowned actor) plays the role of the jury chairman. In an evident nod to Mr. Putin, the chairman was rescripted from the original as a tough yet compassionate former KGB officer. Mikhalkov, playing the simultaneous jury chairman and Mr. Putin, persuades the rest of his fellow jurors to acquit the defendant. The defendant is a Chechen youth accused of murdering his stepfather, a Russian military officer. The youth has clearly suffered a great deal and was likely framed for the murder by a group of criminals. In a "Putinesque" moment at the end of the film, the chairman vows to track down the real perpetrators himself.[49]

In the same timeframe as Mikhalkov's film, Putin was conspicuously befriending Ramzan Kadyrov, the controversial young leader of Chechnya, who eventually succeeded his father, Akhmad Kadyrov, as president of the republic. Kadyrov senior had been the Mufti or religious leader of Chechnya in the 1990s. After the first Chechen war, Kadyrov fell out with other separatist leaders and switched his allegiance to Moscow. He brought with him a large swathe of the armed groups who had fought the Russian military. The *Kadyrovtsy,* the former fighters who agreed to stay loyal to Moscow, were granted a blanket amnesty for their actions in the first war. They were then essentially given a mandate to go after the remaining militant groups that refused to surrender and reconcile with Moscow, as well as their domestic political opponents. The older Kadyrov was assassinated in May 2004 only a year into his presidency.

Ramzan Kadyrov, a teenage militia leader during the first Chechen war, was still in his twenties and too young to succeed his father when Akhmad Kadyrov was killed. The junior Kadyrov held a series of deputy and acting prime minister positions in the Chechen government until becoming president when he turned thirty in 2007. After assuming the position he garnered equal measure of praise from Putin for rebuilding Grozny (with ample funds from Moscow) and condemnation from Russian and international human rights organizations for his violent power struggles and brutal suppression of dissent.[50] This tactic of the top Russian leader personally engaging and joining forces with a local warlord in the Caucasus to pacify the region dates back to the tsarist-era Circassian Wars of the 1800s—another example of Putin mining the past for applicable lessons and useful history.[51]

THE MOST REASONABLE MAN

In all of these forays into the territory of Chechnya and the North Caucasus, ethnicity, religion, and Russian nationalism, Putin and the team around him painted a portrait of Mr. Putin as the most reasonable statesman in Russia—the only person capable of ensuring Russia's survival. Putin's PR team depicted him as standing above the fray and holding back reactionary forces, like Zhirinovsky, who would otherwise upend or rip apart the Russian state. A frequent refrain of Russian officials and Kremlin-connected commentators was that "Vladimir Putin is more reasonable than 99 percent of Russians," with the clear inference that, as one independent Russian journalist remarked, "The Russian *narod* [people] would elect a 'new Hitler' if Vladimir Putin did not exist."[52] This is one of many tools in Putin's political arsenal. It is also another tactic tried and tested in the 1990s and with the same stock cast of characters. Boris Yeltsin and his political team often conjured the idea of *après moi le déluge* with explicit reference to Vladimir Zhirinovsky and other nationalist politicians—suggesting that if Yeltsin were swept from office, a fascist regime in Russia would be only a step away.[53]

In his December 15, 2011, televised call-in show, in which he directly responded to questions from a select audience as well as from carefully screened callers from around the country, Putin took issue with the idea that Chechnya and the North Caucasus were the major source of strife for Russia. Responding to a question from a woman whose son had been beaten up by someone from the North Caucasus, Putin noted: "I want to say that, believe me, guys [*rebyata*] from the Caucasus may show the very best human qualities. As for hooligans, they can be from the Caucasus, from Moscow, and, unfortunately, from my hometown of Leningrad, St. Petersburg, from anywhere at all."[54] In a January 2012 article in *Nezavisimaya gazeta* on ethnicity issues, "Russia: the national question," Putin also directly criticized the calls to "stop feeding the Caucasus":

> I am convinced that the attempts to preach the idea of a "national" or monoethnic Russian state contradict our thousand-year history. Moreover, this is a shortcut to destroying the Russian people and Russian statehood, and for that matter any viable, sovereign statehood on the planet. When they start shouting, "Stop feeding the Caucasus," tomorrow their rallying cry will be: "Stop feeding Siberia, the Far East, the Urals, the Volga region, or the Moscow Region." This was the formula used by those who paved the way to the collapse of the Soviet Union. As for the notorious concept of self-determination, a slogan used by all kinds of politicians who have fought for power and geopolitical dividends, from Vladimir Lenin to Woodrow Wilson, the Russian people made their choice long ago. The self-determination of the Russian people is to be a multiethnic civilization with Russian culture at its core. The Russian people have confirmed their choice time and again during their thousand-year history—with their blood, not through plebiscites or referendums.[55]

This Putin article is particularly significant in that it stresses the importance of ensuring the survival of the Russian state and tying that survival (which millions have died for) to protecting Russia's multiethnicity. As is the case with so many of Vladimir Putin's writings and pronouncements on the Russian state, the article reflects the ideas of other Russian thinkers, primarily from the 1990s. In this instance, some of the key ideas are those of Valery Tishkov, the director of the Institute of Ethnology and Anthropology at the Russian Academy of Sciences. In 1992, Tishkov set up Russia's first ministry of nationalities for Boris Yeltsin to address and avert the threat of the Russian Federation's disintegration. He served in the position of minister for only a year before returning to the Academy of Sciences.[56] The ministry was most active during the period when Moscow was forced to conclude bilateral treaties with Tatarstan and other regions. It then expanded its mission to deal with migration issues. It was dismantled by Putin in 2001 when he began to stress the importance of a unified Russian state.[57]

Tishkov, in his many scholarly writings on the issues of nationality and ethnicity in Russia, continually criticized the brutality of Moscow's treatment of Chechnya and the Chechens. He stressed the importance of reengaging with Chechnya to bring it back into the Russian body politic and of effecting a reconciliation between Moscow and the Chechen people.[58] Tishkov was also a major proponent of the idea of inculcating a civic, or "post-nationalist," idea of being a Russian—a *rossiyanin* rather than a *russkiy* citizen. In all of his books and articles, he insisted on the use of the neutral word *rossiyskiy* whenever there was an official reference to anything "Russian" to overcome any ethnic Russian particularism that might be rooted in the idea of the Russian state or the concept of the *narod*.[59] Yeltsin carefully adhered to all of this in his public pronouncements in the 1990s, just as Putin embraced the same idea in his references to a *Rossiyskaya ideya* and *rossiyane* in the Millennium Message.

In Putin's view, disunity, like revolutionary change or not having sufficient reserves or resources, is a prime threat to the survival of the Russian state. Preserving unity and stability at almost any cost—even by reducing Grozny to the ground and killing thousands of Russian citizens—is necessary to ensure the survival of the state. In the siege of Leningrad, with its personal ramifications for the Putin family through the death of a son, a million perished so the city would not fall. Many more millions perished in World War II so the state would survive the Nazi invasion and prevail. Indeed, in this particularly dark period, Josef Stalin, the wartime Soviet leader, broke with his own practice of denigrating the tsarist past to reach back into history to find potent symbols of unity for the Soviet population to rally around in its struggle to survive.

Mother Russia superseded the USSR. The image of a woman in a kerchief urged people to fight for the survival of the country in propaganda posters of the era—"Mother needs you" as the equivalent to "Uncle Sam needs you" in the United States.[60] Ancient Russian heroes such as

Alexander Nevsky (resurrected again by Putin and his team in 2008) featured in similar posters exhorting the Russian people, for example, to battle against Nazi Germany in 1942, just as Nevsky had battled the invading Teutonic Knights across some of the same territory 700 years before, in 1242.[61] Stalin also looked for national heroes from other ethnic groups across the Soviet Union, including from the peoples of Central Asia and the Caucasus, to pull the multiethnic Soviet population together. World War II became the Great Patriotic War and provided the ultimate narrative of survival for Vladimir Putin and the many others born during and shortly after WWII.

UNITY, RECONCILIATION, AND THE LEGACY
OF WHITE RUSSIAN SURVIVORS

Stalin mined Russia's pre-Soviet history for heroes who could create unity in the 1940s and help the state survive the Second World War. Putin continued to do the same in the 2000s. Another group that Putin turned to in framing his quest for unity was the so-called White Russian émigrés. Many of these were *gosudarstvenniki,* former servitors of the tsar, or intellectual supporters of the tsarist order, who fled the country when the Russian Empire collapsed and thus survived the 1917 Revolution. In Europe, and occasionally in the United States, they kept the idea of the Russian state alive even as they rejected the ideology of the USSR. Among this group were a large number of writers who spent their time in exile trying to figure out a new ideological basis for reviving Russia should the Soviet Union ever collapse—as it did in 1991. In the 1930s, 1940s, and even into the 1980s, these writers engaged in the traditional debate "What is Russia?" untainted by the Soviet experience. In essence, they formed a strategic reserve and repository of Russian thought. Their ideas came back into modern Russia in the 1990s and provided a bridge from the late imperial period across the 70 years of communism to post-Soviet Russia.[62] Among the émigré writers, two in particular stand out: the religious philosopher Ivan Ilyin (1883–1954) and linguist Nikolai Trubetskoi (1890–1938). Along with Soviet historian, ethnographer, and geographer Lev Gumilev (1912–92), they made considerable contributions to shaping the ideas of Russia's revival with which Mr. Putin associated himself in the 2000s.

Ivan Ilyin joined Pyotr Stolypin as a favored reference point for Vladimir Putin during his presidency and premiership. Like Stolypin, Ilyin had a great deal to say about the restoration of the state and patriotism. In his writings, Ivan Ilyin stressed the importance of forging a new Russian national identity to respond to times of crisis and to guide the governance of the state. Ilyin wrote that the search for this identity would be led by a politically, culturally, and spiritually renewed elite. He suggested that Russia's identity should be based primarily on its religious faith and "the love of one's country." Ilyin charged the Russian elite both with the "Christianization" of the Russian government and with aiding the "free creativity" of the Russian people. He cautioned the elite not to overestimate the power of government and advocated the creation of a strong Russian middle class, a free and prosperous peasantry, and a "fraternal" working class to support the operations of government. Ilyin was opposed to government activity in the spheres of private and corporate life. Although he was in favor of the progressive Christianization of Russia, Ilyin specifically urged the separation of church and state and broad religious tolerance.[63] Finally, Ilyin was a firm believer in the importance of a strong law-based state.[64] Putin has paid lip service to all these concepts.

A number of analysts have pointed to Putin's (or his Kremlin team's) apparent interest in Ilyin and his writings—especially Putin's references to Ilyin in his national addresses in 2005, 2006, and 2007.[65] In 2005, partly at the instigation of film director Nikita Mikhalkov (again playing a central role on these issues), Ilyin's remains were repatriated from Switzerland. They were reinterred in Moscow along with a number of other leading White Russian émigré figures.[66] The public rationale for the reinterment—which came against the backdrop of the restoration of toppled statues, churches, and icons in the 2000s—was explicit. Ilyin's return was the ultimate expression of reconciliation and of healing the rifts between imperial and Soviet Russia. Just as Ilyin's body was reunited with Russian soil, two eras of Russian history were symbolically brought together again. In May 2009, Putin made a well-publicized pilgrimage to Ilyin's new gravesite at Moscow's Donskoi Monastery to underscore and reinforce the point.[67]

For their part, the other two writers, Trubetskoi and Gumilev, have not enjoyed quite so much prominence in Putin's speeches as Ilyin.

However, their work emphasized Russia's dual heritage in Europe and in the fusion of Slavic and Turkic cultures in the Asian steppe. Technically the Eurasian steppe, or vast grasslands, stretches from the southern reaches of Ukraine in the west, through southern Russia, into Kazakhstan and Central Asia, and further east into southern Siberia. Based on the unique nature of Russia's heritage in the heart of the steppe lands, the two writers promoted the idea of a specifically Eurasian path of development for Russia, which would always distinguish it from the countries of Europe.[68] In the 1990s, Trubetskoi and Gumilev were credited with inspiring a revival of so-called Eurasianist thought in post-Soviet Russia.[69] Putin embraced these ideas, including in 2011–14, in his promotion of the idea of creating a new Eurasian Union. Putin's Eurasian Union, often called the Eurasian Economic Union, was presented as a new economic and political association that would cover Ukraine and Kazakhstan, among other lands of the former Russian Empire and USSR. It was also intended to supersede the now largely defunct CIS.[70]

As a philosophy, Eurasianism bridges the gap between an exclusive ethnic Russian concept of Russia and the reality of the state's multiethnicity. It allows for the concept of a unique Slavic, Orthodox Russia to survive and coexist with an embrace of the non-Russian Asian peoples of the steppe—and by extension Chechnya and the North Caucasus. It restores the idea of a multiethnic, multiracial, multinational, and multireligious Russia.[71] Lev Gumilev, the son of two noted Russian poets, Nikolai Gumilev and Anna Akhmatova, who opposed the obscurantism of the Bolshevik regime, was persecuted for his family associations. He was also a survivor of the darkest periods in Soviet history and spent long periods confined in the gulag. Gumilev lived until 1992 and remained a prolific writer throughout his life. Although banned for decades, his scholarly writings were revived at the end of the Gorbachev era and became bestsellers in the 1990s.[72]

PUTINISM = "KOMAROVISM"

As his speeches and presentations make abundantly clear, splintering and fracturing in society and politics are anathema to Vladimir Putin, as well as threats to the Russian state. After the contradictions and chaos of the 1990s, the Putin of the 1999 Millennium Message, as well as the Putin of his 2012 presidential campaign essay on the national question, called on Russians to put aside their famous historical conflicts if they wanted to continue to survive and see the state survive. No more Slavophiles versus Westernizers, Whites versus Reds, Left versus Right, or liberals versus fascists. No KGB pitted against ordinary Russians, the perpetrators against the victims of the purges and the gulag. Certainly no ethnic Russians clashing with Russia's indigenous minorities. In this regard Putin resembles the Komarovs, the colorful and eccentric couple conjured by the celebrated Russian American émigré writer Vladimir Nabokov, in his novel *Pnin*.[73]

In his novel, Nabokov describes the Komarovs, whom Pnin (aka Nabokov) meets when he first moves to the United States. Timofey Pnin is a professor of Russian at a small American college and encounters another Russian émigré, Oleg Komarov, at the college, in the Fine Arts Department. Nabokov writes of Komarov and his wife, Serafima: "Only another Russian could understand the reactionary and Sovietophile blend presented by the pseudo-colorful Komarovs, for whom an ideal Russia consisted of the Red Army, an anointed monarch, collective farms, anthroposophy, the Russian Church and the Hydro-Electric Dam."[74] The Komarovs' "reactionary and Sovietophile" blend would be completely understood by Vladimir Putin and all Russians who emerged from the confusion of the 1990s. Like the Komarovs, Putin's view of an "ideal Russia" attempts to reconcile the entire span of the country's national history, with ideas plucked from the imperial and Soviet versions of the Russian state. Where Georgy Satarov's group in 1996–97 got bogged down in the inherent contradictions of the Russian Idea, Putin simply embraced them all.

In the 2000s, in addition to reinterring dead émigrés and restoring their reputations, Putin repeatedly reached out to the living: to the descendants and the survivors of the White Russian *gosudarstvenniki* across Europe and the United States. He also extended his embrace to other groups from disparate waves of emigration from the Russian Empire and Soviet Union. Sessions of the Valdai Discussion Club from 2004 to 2011, for example, frequently featured prominent scholars with Russian heritage. These included Alexander (Sasha) Rahr, one of Germany's top Russian experts, biographer of Putin, but also the son of exiled Russian journalist and church historian Gleb Rahr; Hélène Carrère d'Encausse (née Zourabichvili), France's leading Russian historian and secretary of the French Academy, whose parents fled the Russian Empire after the Revolution; Anatol Lieven, British journalist and academic, and the descendant of one of the most famous political families of the tsarist era; and Serge Schmemann, American journalist and descendant of a Russian aristocratic family with long roots in the provinces around Moscow.[75] In one incident, during his December 15, 2011, call-in TV show to address questions from viewers across the country, Valdai Club participants Sasha Rahr and Nikolai (Kolya) Zlobin—a Russian academic who was based for extensive periods in the United States before returning to Russia to become a prominent foreign policy commentator—were placed in the front row of the audience. They were referenced directly by Putin for the important role they played in "representing" Russia abroad.[76]

At certain junctures, official representatives of overseas Slavic and émigré organizations were also invited to participate in the Valdai Club sessions—most notably in September 2010. At this session, participants in the group met with Putin in Sochi just after he had concluded a high-level visit and discussion with Israeli defense minister Ehud Barak. In addition to stressing the importance of reaching out to Russian émigrés, Putin talked wistfully of bringing back "our Jews" (*nashi yevrei*) who had emigrated to Israel, and he stressed the importance of the new Russia's blossoming ties with Israel. He rejected the idea that former Jewish citizens of the Russian Empire and Soviet Union might not want to come back to Russia, given past experiences of pogroms in the imperial era and the purges and consistent discrimination in the Soviet period.[77] In line with these comments, Putin made considerable effort during the 2000s to reach out to the Russian Jewish communities in exile and in Moscow. He also encouraged Russian oligarchs—irrespective of their ethnic or religious origin—to fund the restoration of synagogues and mosques, not just churches and monasteries. For Putin, this was all part of Russia's multiethnic, indigenous culture, which must be preserved and actively maintained for the state to survive. In Putin's view, the Bolsheviks made a serious mistake in destroying these cultural artifacts. They got rid of what could otherwise be useful history for binding all the different groups together and creating a common heritage. In pulling down churches, synagogues, and mosques, the Bolsheviks destroyed some of the basic underpinnings of the Russian state. In doing so, they ultimately undercut the legitimacy of the communist regime. They pitted people and peoples against each other. Those internecine conflicts helped tear the USSR apart.

Putin's final major address as prime minister to parliament in April 2012 hammered home this point—the dangers of dividing and thus destroying. It came in the form of an answer to a suggestion from a member of the Russian Duma that the preamble to the Russian constitution be changed from beginning with "We the multinational people [*narod*] of Russia," to "We the [ethnic] Russian [*russkiy*] people and the people who have joined with it." Putin retorted:

> Do you understand what we would do [if we did that]? Part of our society would consist of first class people and part would be second class. We must not do that if you and I want to have a strong single [*yedinaya*] nation, a single people [*narod*], if we want each person who lives on the territory of the country to feel that this is their homeland, and that there is no other homeland, nor can there be one. And if we want each person to feel like that, then we have to be equal. This is the principal question. The fact that the [ethnic] Russian [*russkiy*] people are—without a doubt—the backbone, the fundament, the cement of the multinational Russian [*rossiyskiy*] people cannot be questioned. . . . But to divide everyone up into first, second, third categories, you know, this is a very dangerous path. You and I, all of us, must not do this.[78]

With this retort, Putin underscored his view that the issue of ethnicity in Russia is neither a moral nor an ideological one. On a purely practical level, dividing the country into groups or allowing people to divide the country into groups weakens it. This was a mistake made in both Russia's imperial and Soviet pasts. To keep Russia, the state, intact—as he is determined to do—this mistake should not be repeated. This is the hallmark of Mr. Putin, the Survivalist. The survivalist mentality is based on an exaggerated notion that if you don't learn from past mistakes—your own as well as larger, national-level mistakes—then you personally, and the country, will continue to suffer from them. To survive, you must also learn by observing the mistakes that others make. Ultimately, this mentality is also rooted in distrust and in the necessity of relying on one's own means. The person best suited to observe the mistakes and to build up the resources and capacity to take appropriate action avoiding similar mistakes in the future is an "outsider." As we will discuss in the next chapter, this is one of the identities very specific to Mr. Putin. He was an outsider to the national political system when he came to Moscow, and he has cultivated an image of himself as the Outsider since his youth. The Outsider is not part of the existing system and is not burdened by vested interests in the status quo. He is detached and not responsible for any particular failure, so he has no reason to ignore the truth. He can defy conventional wisdom and learn how to do things better in similar circumstances. When you are the Outsider, watching people make decisions that may affect you but which you are not a part of, you can be much more critical. You can think outside the box.

Here again, tsarist prime minister Pyotr Stolypin in the early 1900s provides a historical path for Vladimir Putin as the Outsider moving to the center in the 1990s. Before he stepped into the inner circles of St. Petersburg, Stolypin was a provincial governor, first in Grodno in what is now Belarus and then in Saratov in Russia's southern Volga region. Stolypin was even born outside Russia in the very place where Putin himself was sent in the 1980s—Dresden—in what during Stolypin's time was the German Kingdom of Saxony. He grew up in what is now Lithuania. In 1907, Stolypin argued that in spite of serving as a Russian governor, he was not a bureaucrat: "I am a stranger to the Petersburg official world; I have no past there, no career ties, no links with the court."[79] By the end of the twentieth century, the St. Petersburg that had been the center of the Russian government for Pyotr Stolypin was now the periphery, the second city, the provinces for Vladimir Putin. In the 1990s, Moscow was the focal point of power and political activity, and St. Petersburgers were on the outside, looking in.

CHAPTER SIX

THE OUTSIDER

IN 1996, VLADIMIR PUTIN AND a group of friends and acquaintances from St. Petersburg would gather in an idyllic lakeside setting—barely an hour and a half north of the metropolis of St. Petersburg. The location, on the Karelian Isthmus between the Gulf of Finland and Lake Ladoga, was only an hour and 20 minute car drive to the Finnish border, in an area that has variously been part of the Swedish Empire, the tsarist Russian empire, independent Finland, the Soviet Union, and now Russia. This was a wonderful place for Mr. Putin the History Man to reflect on the twists and turns of fate and Russia's evolving borders over the centuries. It also put Mr. Putin the Outsider far away from the center, Moscow. Putin had built a dacha, a weekend house, in this locale not long after his return to Leningrad from Dresden, but it had burned down in 1996.[1] He had a new one built identical to the original and was joined by a group of seven friends who built dachas beside his. Later in the fall of 1996, the group formally registered their fraternity, calling it *Ozero* (Lake) and turning it into a gated community of houses. Reportedly, the group members were so close that they often car-pooled out from St. Petersburg to the dachas.[2]

As close as they seem to have been in 1996, Putin was also an outsider to this group. Of the eight founders of Ozero, seven were businessmen and one was a civil servant. Seven had degrees in physics or engineering, and one had a law degree. The odd man out was Vladimir Putin. What they had in common was the archetypical Petersburg mentality that they were outsiders to the Russian capital. They were the outsiders looking from afar, seeing all the mistakes made by Russian politicians in Moscow in the 1990s, yet generally powerless to change things. It is not hard to imagine that at least some of their vodka-infused conversations on the porches or in the saunas at Ozero that summer ran something like: "Think how much better off this country would be if people like us were running it! Don't 'they' see how they're taking us to the brink of ruin and collapse?"

All St. Petersburgers are by definition outsiders to the established center of power in Moscow. Many in this particular group had, like Putin, spent periods of time outside Russia and the USSR, where they were able to detach themselves from the ongoing events and form a more dispassionate analysis of the state of affairs. In contrast to the usual men from "the provinces" (*glubinka* in Russian), St. Petersburgers do not really accept the role of being second-class citizens. The city's downgrade in the Soviet period, and the Bolshevik decision to rename it Leningrad, created a sense of resentment, a grudge against Moscow. St. Petersburg was supposed to be important. It was built as the political capital and the center of high culture for Peter the Great's new Russian Empire, but its citizens were abruptly designated second rank.

Putin, with his humble family origins, was a double or even triple outsider in the St. Petersburg Ozero group and the Soviet *nomenklatura* (those who occupied state administrative positions). His family was never part of the intelligentsia. Putin was not part of the traditional structures of the Communist Party of the Soviet Union (CPSU). In many respects he was an outsider even within the KGB. He was not a KGB "golden boy" like his contemporary Sergei Ivanov—who later served as defense minister and deputy prime minister under Mr. Putin and was then appointed head of the presidential administration. The latter enjoyed early postings to Helsinki and London and always seemed to be on a fast track to somewhere as he rose through the academies and ranks of the KGB. In contrast, Vladimir Putin did not reach the upper echelons of the institution until he suddenly secured a political appointment to head the Federal Security Service (FSB) in 1998. Putin was an outsider even to Mikhail Gorbachev's perestroika (restructuring or transformation). He was posted to Dresden in East Germany during the critical period when Gorbachev took the helm of the USSR. Gorbachev was elected head of the CPSU in May 1985. Putin received his orders to relocate to Dresden that August. He remained there until after the fall of the Berlin Wall in 1989 and his return to Soviet Leningrad early in 1990. After his tenure as a deputy mayor of St. Petersburg, Putin was specifically brought into Moscow in summer 1996 as an outsider. As we will discuss, he was an operative on a mission to collect information on, monitor, and ultimately help the Kremlin rein in Russia's unruly oligarchs.

Putin's perception of himself and his Leningrad/St. Petersburg cohort as outsiders narrows the circle of individuals who share similar life experiences with Mr. Putin. All Russians are survivors or even survivalists by virtue of the tumultuous history of the Russian state. Many Russians come from families with long historical roots in the Russian heartland and are steeped in Russian history—although they do not necessarily see themselves as protagonists in Russian history in the same way Mr. Putin does. Many Russian political figures strongly identify themselves as statists, those who seek the restoration of a strong and capable Russian state and apparatus, at least nominally. Fewer Russians, and even fewer Russian political figures, are outsiders to a system or an organization who then come in and take charge. Indeed, a nominal member of an organization who is really an outsider to that organization may have a more tense relationship with the organization's insiders than with people who have had no association with it at all.

In an interview she gave shortly after Putin was appointed prime minister in 1999, Russian analyst Lilia Shevtsova described him as "an outsider who previously served in St. Petersburg. . . . He has not had the time to develop the personal relationships and the network of allies within the bureaucracy of the security services that is necessary to establish firm control." Shevtsova and many others cautioned in 1999 against seeing Putin "as some kind of superman" based on his previous, and brief, position as head of the FSB, the successor to the KGB. They concluded—as observers of Pyotr Stolypin's appointment a century earlier had also concluded—that "he [Putin] will be greatly limited in what he is able to do."[3]

ANDROPOV'S KGB

The group of outsiders, who watched what the insiders did and critiqued it (and probably begrudged them for their arrogance and incompetence), defines the brotherhood Putin identifies with. Most of his inner circle falls one way or another into the outsider category. In particular, Putin has a very ambiguous relationship with the so-called *siloviki* that he is often associated with—the insiders from the KGB/FSB and other security or power ministries like the ministry of defense and the interior ministry, which includes the police and Russia's paramilitary forces. This is not his fraternity. Apart from a very short period spent heading the FSB as a political appointee, Putin never served in the central apparatus of any of these entities and he never rose to the KGB's highest ranks during his official service. His formal positions in the KGB were always on the periphery—in Leningrad and in Dresden.

Putin was one of a generation of young recruits, a cohort of outsiders, brought into the KGB by its chairman Yury Andropov in the 1970s. Andropov himself had come into the KGB as an outsider. His career had been made in the CPSU, not the security services. He had spent a considerable period of time as first secretary of the Communist Party youth organization, the *Komsomol*, in Karelia. Andropov also served as Soviet ambassador to Budapest during the fateful Hungarian uprising of 1956 (an experience that in some respects mirrors Vladimir Putin's own time in Dresden as the German Democratic Republic fell apart). On his return to Moscow, Andropov was put in charge of relations with other Communist Party representatives in socialist countries. He also became the head of the International Department of the Central Committee of the CPSU Secretariat. He was appointed to head the KGB in 1967 just before another uprising in the communist bloc, in Czechoslovakia—the Prague Spring of 1968. During his time at the head of the KGB, from 1967 to 1982, these firsthand observations of political unrest (which were followed by revolts in Afghanistan and Poland toward the end of his tenure in 1979–81) shaped Andropov's approach to running the institution. In the late 1960s, he was closely associated with spearheading the KGB's efforts to crush political dissent and with creating the notorious network of psychiatric hospitals that prominent dissidents were often dispatched to "for treatment."[4]

Andropov was also aware, however, that the entrenched and increasingly enfeebled Soviet system was in dire need of reform. In an effort to bring some new perspectives into the KGB and by extension to create an atmosphere conducive to finding new ideas for dealing with the state's myriad problems, Andropov implemented a policy to expand the institution's recruitment of young officers from different societal groups, including the *Komsomol*. The idea was to bring in a cohort of critical-minded recruits to change things. Andropov moved on from the KGB to become leader of the USSR in 1982. Tensions between this group of recruits, which was widely referred to as the Andropov levy (or Andropov draft), and older KGB insiders increased after Andropov's sudden death in February 1984. Vladimir Putin's recruitment to the KGB in 1975 as part of this general group compounded his sense of being an outsider.

Putin's assignment to Dresden, after he completed his training at the KGB academy in Moscow, the Red Banner Institute, put him even further outside mainstream structures and the state. He was also now outside the USSR. During the crucial years of perestroika from 1985 to 1989, Putin could only look in from afar. Those who were back home, including people who would later end up in Putin's inner circle, like erstwhile president Dmitry Medvedev, were caught up in the heat of the dramatic political as well as social and cultural events of this period, especially in Moscow. While Putin today uses the 1990s as the touchstone for his presidency and spends an inordinate amount of time talking about Russia in the 1990s and channeling the debates and ideas of this decade, he has remarkably little to say about the 1980s. Putin probably also has a very different, much more uniformly negative, version of events of the late 1980s than his peers in St. Petersburg or Moscow.

OUTSIDER IN DRESDEN

As a foreigner in Dresden from 1985 to 1989, Putin was also an outsider to the system and events in East Germany. This must have been a strange position for Mr. Putin because it undoubtedly reinforced his view of his identity and role as the critical outsider learning from the mistakes of others. When Putin was posted to Dresden, the GDR was supposedly a Soviet ally, but in fact it was also a country where the leadership of Eric Honecker sometimes acted as if its counterparts in Moscow were as much the enemy as the West.

Honecker's regime was ideologically hardline, inflexible, not in the least bit pragmatic, and very much out of touch with the grassroots politics of East Germany—as well as out of step with the political changes under way in the Soviet Union. In 1985–89, the GDR's economy was also dysfunctional. Putin's years in Dresden made him privy to the ultimate controlled experiment in competing economic systems, between East and West Germany—an experience that he directly referred to, much later on, in his final address to parliament as prime minister in April 2012. Honecker was adamant that the GDR would pursue its own economic and political policies. He avoided public references to Gorbachev's policies of perestroika and glasnost (openness) as well as "new thinking" (novoye myshleniye) in foreign policy.[5] The feeling in the USSR leadership was mutual. There was no love lost between the East German leader and Mikhail Gorbachev. The Soviet leader used every occasion, including a public toast to Honecker marking the opening of an East German exhibition in Moscow in September 1988, to remind his German counterpart of the need for political change.[6]

The accepted story about Putin's KGB service is that Dresden—which was the third-largest city in the GDR with a population of about 500,000—was an unimportant backwater. Putin's work there has also routinely been described as unimportant and even unsuccessful.[7] There is no official version of what Putin was doing in Dresden, and he has not offered much personal detail. Nor is there any concrete information about which directorate of the KGB Putin worked for. One suggestion is that he was in an operation, "Operation Luch" ("beam" or "ray"), to steal technological secrets. Another says that while he was indeed part of Operation Luch, the mission was not to steal secrets at all. It was an undercover operation to recruit top officials in the East German Communist Party and secret police (Stasi). The goal was to secure their support for the reformist, perestroika, line of the Soviet leadership in Moscow against opposition from Honecker and his hardline East German leadership.[8] A third says simply that the goal of the KGB in Dresden was to contact, entrap, compromise, and generally recruit Westerners who happened to be in Dresden studying and doing business. Other versions suggest that the KGB was focused on recruiting East Germans who had relatives in the West. Some versions of the story have said Putin himself traveled undercover to West Germany on occasion.[9]

The most likely answer to which of these was Putin's actual mission in Dresden is: "all of the above." Not only is it likely that Putin engaged in some or all of these activities, it is virtually inconceivable that he did not. The KGB was stealing technological secrets everywhere it could. If there were some to be stolen in Dresden, rest assured Putin and his colleagues would be on the case. As for entrapping, compromising, and recruiting Westerners, or people with connections to the West, that, too, was a permanent assignment for anyone in the KGB. Regardless of what exactly Putin did in Dresden, which we will revisit in subsequent chapters, one thing is certain—Dresden was not a political backwater in East Germany. While Putin was far outside political events in the Soviet Union in the second half of the 1980s, he was not outside politics or world events in Dresden. The GDR was imploding. Dresden was one of the centers of opposition within the German Communist Party to the retrograde Honecker regime—an intra-party opposition in which Hans Modrow, the party's Dresden leader, was an active participant.

Given the ferment at home, Putin's KGB counterparts back in the USSR were unlikely to be paying a great deal of attention to what was happening in East Germany. But if Putin had even the slightest interest in political developments in the GDR, there could hardly have been a much better place to be than Dresden in those years of 1985–89. In Dresden, Putin was close enough to the ground that he could observe the activities of the East German opposition at first hand, just as Andropov observed the Hungarian opposition in the mid-1950s—albeit from a loftier vantage point in the Soviet Embassy—during his posting to Budapest. Putin was also low enough on the KGB totem pole in Dresden that part of his job could have been to monitor and to try to understand the opposition, its motivations, its strengths, and weaknesses.[10]

LESSONS FROM DRESDEN

Based on the proposition that Putin learns lessons from history in general and from his own personal history, Dresden would have become his first laboratory for political lessons, after his life lessons from his "university of the Sandpit Streets." St. Petersburg and the mayor's office in the 1990s would be the second. Indeed, in the book *Ot pervogo litsa*, when talking about the general impact and effect of his Dresden experience on his thinking, Putin noted:

When you come [home] with nine months between two trips you don't have time to get back into our life. And when you have returned from [serving] abroad it's hard at the beginning to get used to reality, seeing what's been done at home. . . . And we, the younger guys, would talk to our older colleagues. I am not talking here about the elderly who had gone through the Stalin period, but about the people with experience on the job, let's say. They were already a completely different generation, with different views, assessment, and attitudes. . . . After conversations like that, you start to think and rethink things. . . . In intelligence at that time, we permitted ourselves to think differently and to say things that few others could permit themselves.[11]

In the GDR, Putin was given the chance to witness the classic tension inherent in attempts to reform a complex system without losing control. This was also the dominant theme at home. Putin was, however, much closer to the action than he ever would have been in the USSR in this period. In *Ot pervogo litsa*, Putin concedes that Dresden, as well as Leningrad/St. Petersburg, was "a province," but he also boasts that "in these provinces everything was always successful for me."[12] In Dresden, Putin was in some ways a big(ish) fish in a small pond—at least a lot bigger fish than he would have been in Berlin, the East German capital, or at home at KGB headquarters. Arguably, in thinking about what was happening around him, and in talking to other, more seasoned observers, Vladimir Putin may have gained more insights about the fall of a totalitarian system than did many others in Moscow. He certainly gained very different insights. In *Ot pervogo litsa*, Mr. Putin muses on this point, admitting that "the GDR in many respects was an eye-opener for me. I thought that I was going to an East European country, to the center of Europe. Outside it was already the end of the 1980s . . . [but] in dealing with the people who worked for the MGB [Ministry of State Security, or *Stasi*], I realized that they themselves and the GDR were in a situation which we had gone through many years ago already in the Soviet Union. It was a harsh totalitarian country, similar to our model, but 30 years earlier. And the tragedy is that many people sincerely believed in all those communist ideals. I thought at the time: if we begin some changes at home, how will it affect the fates of these people?"[13]

Meanwhile, at a distance, Putin also learned that the changes afoot in the USSR, under Mikhail Gorbachev, were not working, either. In principle, Putin was for perestroika. Andropov, the long-serving head of the KGB before he became Soviet leader, had helped sponsor Gorbachev's rise within the Soviet politburo. Gorbachev's perestroika was intended to carry forward reform ideas that Andropov himself had advocated. But things were not playing out the way Andropov and others had wanted or planned. Gorbachev was unable to control the forces that he had unleashed at home and that he ultimately unleashed abroad in the GDR and elsewhere in the countries of the Soviet bloc. If you could remove ideological blinders, it was all perfectly clear. The Soviet system in general did not work. As Putin ruefully concluded after crowds descended on his workplace during the eventual political upheavals in Dresden and East Germany, and there was no immediate response from Moscow: "It was clear the Union was ailing. And it had a terminal, incurable illness under the title of paralysis. A paralysis of power."[14]

Probably no personal experience other than his time in Dresden could have done more to convince Vladimir Putin that his future activity, in the KGB or otherwise, could not be guided by blind loyalty to an ideology or to specific political leaders. His loyalty had to be to the state itself rather than to a specific system of governance. The ambiguities of the GDR in the second half of the 1980s were perfect training for Putin's move to the center of government in Moscow a decade later in 1996. The GDR experience forced him to confront some important issues. Whose side was he really on? What were the sides? Whose interests were being served? How could you be sure that your efforts were not undertaken in vain, or were not carried out in the interest of people whose values you did not share or who you might even regard as enemies? How could you ensure that you were not just being used as a tool of a narrow group? For Putin, the answer seems to have been that you need to decide for yourself what the "truth" is and what the highest value is, and serve those above all else. Never trust any individual institution or any specific idea, and certainly not any person or narrow group completely, even if you were closely associated with them. Watch and wait to see how things will turn out. Try not to preclude future paths of action for the sake of expediency today, but try to remain on the outside for as long as possible. Putin saw that the collapse of the

GDR "was inevitable." What he "really regretted," when the Berlin Wall and everything else came crashing down, he said, was "that the Soviet Union had lost its position in Europe, although intellectually I understood that a position based on walls and water barriers cannot exist forever. But I wanted something different to rise in its place. And nothing different was proposed. That's what hurt." Putin was shocked that, as the Soviet bloc crumbled away in Eastern Europe, "they [the group around Gorbachev in Moscow] just threw everything away and left."[15] A decade after this experience, Putin would set about trying to put something different, more durable in place in Moscow, something that would reassert Russia's lost position.

MR. PUTIN IN "THE VALLEY OF THE CLUELESS"

Disenchanted with his final set of experiences in Dresden, Putin returned to the USSR in early 1990, initially to work at Leningrad State University (LGU) and also to pursue his doctoral dissertation.[16] A lot had happened in Leningrad while Putin was in Dresden. In fact, unbeknownst to Putin, while he had learned a great deal in the GDR, he had also missed out on a whole set of life lessons that those who had remained in the Soviet Union had absorbed. As Putin's wife, Lyudmila, put it in interviews conducted as part of the *Ot pervogo litsa* project, which intersperses Vladimir Putin's own observations in the book: "Perestroika, and everything that happened between 1986 and 1988, we, in Germany, saw only on the television. Because of that, I know only of the enthusiasm and the lifting of spirits that people had during those years through the stories others told me."[17]

The late 1980s were a time of intellectual and cultural ferment and creativity in the USSR, as well as political upheaval. When the Putins came home, instead of appreciating the spirit of the period, they only noticed that they were returning to a country in its death throes, where "everything, including the law-enforcement agencies, was in a state of decay."[18] Lyudmila Putina pointed out that "the long lines, ration cards, coupons and empty shelves were still [t]here." In contrast with the availability of goods in the GDR, Lyudmila "found it quite horrifying [*strashno*] to even walk through stores. Unlike many, I could not run around searching for the cheapest goods and wait in the lines. I would just go straight to the nearest shop, purchase only the most necessary things and return home. The impression I got was terrible."[19]

If Putin had not been posted to Dresden in 1985, but had joined the KGB at a lower level in Moscow, stayed in Leningrad, or been posted to another Russian province, he would most certainly have had a very different set of experiences and impressions, as well as real-time discussions with colleagues and friends about the unfolding events. Putin's service in the GDR had a very specific, and quite negative, impact on his world view. Service in the Soviet Union might well have changed his outlook in other appreciable ways. It might conceivably have given him a somewhat more positive perspective on the Russia of the 1990s, which came out of the ferment of the 1980s, not simply out of the decay of the USSR. Russian American scholar Leon Aron—in *Roads to the Temple,* his in-depth intellectual and political history of this critical period in the USSR—describes how much the country changed in the late 1980s under Mikhail Gorbachev.[20] Gorbachev's championing of the policy of glasnost or political openness turned Soviet political thought and high culture on their heads. Formerly taboo issues, including the myriad state crimes and abuses of individual and human rights in the Soviet period, were given a thorough airing at the urging of the Kremlin and the Soviet leadership. This was an elite project at the very highest levels that took the rest of the population into uncharted territory. Soviet ideological touchstones and myths were widely debunked. Newspapers, magazines, TV screens, and cinemas were filled with often shocking revelations. New publications proliferated.[21]

As Leon Aron writes: "Millions of people read about subjects that as recently as three years before," when Putin would still have been in the country, "would have qualified as a crime. . . . Lines to newspaper kiosks—sometimes 'huge crowds' around the block—formed at six in the morning and the daily allotments were often sold out in two hours."[22] Aron goes on to recount how Soviet publications, like the newspaper *Argumenti i fakty,* became sources of critical commentary and saw their subscriptions increase exponentially in a three-year period. While Vladimir Putin was pouring over German newspapers and sources in Dresden, scouring them for nuggets of intelligence and insight into the inner workings of the GDR, more than 20 million people in the USSR were reading *Argumenti i fakty.* Even literary journals, illustrated weekly magazines, and old stalwarts like *Izvestiya* and *Komsomolskaya pravda* attracted millions of new readers.[23] Famous books and articles that had been suppressed by Soviet censors were published and widely read, like Mikhail Bulgakov's *Master and Margarita* and Boris Pasternak's *Doctor Zhivago*. Films like Georgian director Tengiz Abuladze's *Pokoyaniye* (Repentance), with its thinly veiled criticism of the Stalinist era, were shown in Soviet cinemas. They were critically acclaimed in the West as well as in the USSR.[24]

In the GDR, however, it is unlikely that Putin, even if he had any burning desire to, was able to keep up with the pace of information and the surge of political, literary, and cultural output at home. Indeed, while Putin was in Dresden, the GDR banned the Soviet magazine *Ogonyok*, one of the pioneers of glasnost, for being subversive, putting it and other publications out of general reach.[25] In Dresden, Putin was also subject to very different fare than his friends and colleagues at home on East German TV and radio, which were still under the strictures of Eric Honecker's censorship and propaganda. Furthermore, although most East Germans could watch West German TV given the proximity, this was not actually the case in Dresden. In the area around Dresden there was no reception for any of the West German television stations and only limited reception of Western radio broadcasts. For that reason Dresden was satirically referred to inside the GDR as *Tal der Ahnungslosen* (Valley of the clueless).[26]

In *Ot pervogo litsa*, Vladimir Putin had stated that those in the intelligence services permitted themselves to think differently and say things that few normal citizens could. But while Putin was in Dresden, glasnost suddenly allowed *everyone* in the Soviet Union to think differently. Saying things that were not previously permitted became normal. Aron describes how debating clubs sprang up in schools and factories, not just in colleges and scientific institutes, and how factory workers were bowled over by the unexpected freedom of debate. One metalworker talked about how "I was simply unused to a free exchange of opinions. Now I see freedom of thought as something natural."[27] Other observers commented that even people sitting passively in front of their TV screens were witness to programs "utterly unimaginable in [their] openness, frankness, and the heat of political passions."[28]

Putin is not a protagonist in Leon Aron's detailed history of this period. He hardly features in the book at all. Putin appears only fleetingly at the very end, in the epilogue, when Aron discusses the imperial nostalgia and themes of restoration in the 1990s that overturned the spirit of glasnost. Putin is referenced as the president who puts back the plaques and statues to Andropov and other KGB luminaries.[29] Vladimir Putin is not in Leon Aron's book in part because he simply was not there on the "road to the temple." Putin was an outsider to perestroika. He played no role in glasnost. He did not participate in the debates. He may not even have read all that much about them. While he was a witness to revolution in the GDR, Vladimir Putin was barely even a bystander to what many referred to as a "spiritual revolution" at home in Russia and the Soviet Union.[30]

OUTSIDE THE LENINGRAD *TUSOVKI*

Out in Dresden, Putin was clearly aware of the changes and developments at home, but he did not live through and absorb them like other ordinary Russians. For ordinary Russians and especially for younger Russians, like Dmitry Medvedev for example, who was in his early twenties in this period, there was also a lot happening in "low brow" or popular culture. Medvedev has famously spoken of his love of Western rock groups such as the British band Deep Purple, which were widely listened to by Soviet youth in the late 1980s as cultural barriers to the outside world fell away. But Russia and the USSR were also producing their own rock bands and icons, as well as youth movies, all with an entirely new popular lexicon. One film, *Assa,* a break-out sensation in 1987, brought some of the USSR's most famous new bands and actors together with Soviet stalwarts like Stanislav Govorukhin—the actor and director who would go on to join the Soglasiye movement in his political incarnation in the 1990s—in startling scenes of generational dissonance.

New cult figures like Viktor Tsoi, the charismatic front man of the rock band Kino (Cinema), featured prominently in *Assa* with his rock anthem *Khochu peremen!* (I want change!)—an anthem that significantly was reprised during the 2011–12 protests against Putin's political system. Tsoi went on to star in a number of gritty independent films and seemed set to topple Soviet-era music and screen heroes. His untimely death in a car accident in 1990 caused an unprecedented outpouring of grief among Soviet youth. It was seen by contemporary commentators as an event similar to the death of Hollywood movie icon James Dean in 1955. Dean's role in *Rebel without a Cause* also marked the emergence of a new era of youth culture in the United States. Leningrad, Tsoi's birthplace, was in the thick of this pioneering phase in popular culture in the late 1980s. It was the center of a counter-cultural scene that openly criticized and mocked old Soviet mores. Young people, fans of the new Soviet rock groups, in striking Western-style clothing with their own twists, turned heads as they strutted along the main streets. They collected to hang out in mass *tusovki* (gatherings) in city squares.[31]

Because Vladimir Putin did not evolve through all the stages of late Soviet and Russian development from the 1980s through 2000s that would have otherwise linked him to his peers, part of his "Russian DNA" was, and still is, missing. He could not have recaptured this lost time in Dresden's "valley of the clueless." This is notable in Putin's cultural and political references. The 1970s and early 1980s feature heavily in his allusions to Soviet movies and humor—especially the period when he was in his twenties and still a civilian, going to the cinema, watching TV, and sharing and telling jokes. Lyudmila Putina notes in *Ot pervogo litsa,* when talking about their time socializing in Dresden, that "Volodya" (Vladimir) always liked and knew how to tell a good joke.[32] The 1990s are the constant touchstone for Putin's political discussions, although much less a source of jokes than the 1970s. The pluralistic, creative part of the late 1980s, the Gorbachev era of optimism, is the missing link.

Vladimir Putin generally has a black view of the late USSR, of Gorbachev's Soviet Union. When he returned to Leningrad, the state and the Soviet system immediately plunged off the precipice into the abyss. As he noted at the time, this meant that "all the ideals, all the goals that I had had when I went to work for the KGB, collapsed." The situation "tore my life apart."[33] This great personal rupture with the collapse of the Soviet Union was followed by what was, in Putin's view, the unseemly chaos of Yeltsin's Russia and the 1990s. Mr. Putin's outlook is not tempered in any way by the more positive developments, the signs of a new and different Russia that could have emerged in the late 1980s—the Russia that Leon Aron recounts in his book. Others in Putin's inner circle, including most obviously Dmitry Medvedev, would have experienced and seen this period differently. This experience may have colored their own outlook on the future restoration of the state. Medvedev, during his presidency from 2008 to 2012, certainly appeared open to promoting a more pluralistic public debate about Russia's future and hinted at the possibility that the government would embark upon a new period of perestroika.[34] Putin, the outsider to the late 1980s, is much more concerned with personally setting the agenda for debate, and with *dostroika*—finishing what he, Mr. Putin, set out to do when he came into office in 2000.[35]

CULTIVATING THE OUTSIDER PERSONA: "THE THUG"

Since he first became Russian prime minister and president, Vladimir Putin has spent a great deal of time stressing his origins as an outsider. He has also actively cultivated key aspects of that personality. His public image is that of "the first person" who always stands outside politics, and above the fray, observing the action to determine if and when he might have to intervene to put things right. Documentary films in the period around the 2012 election stressed Putin's position as the lone, if not lonely, figure at the top of the Russian power structure. They showed him entirely focused on his work wherever it might take him across the vastness of the Russian Federation, practically single-handedly managing all issues of state, and concentrated on the welfare of the Russian people.[36]

It is clear from all of these depictions that while Vladimir Putin does not want to appear to be directly involved in politics, he actually controls the situation—or he wants the Russian elite and public to understand and think that he controls it. The Russian word *kontrol'* is like the German and French equivalents. It means to "monitor," or to "check"—as opposed to the primary English language definition of actively being in charge and making things happen. This idea of standing to one side and monitoring everything that is going on crops up repeatedly in Putin's childhood stories of himself as the scrappy little street fighter—"the kid" and "the outside contender." The quotes in Oleg Blotsky's book from Putin's putative schoolmate Viktor Borisenko, for example, stress the fact that, even as a boy, Vladimir Putin would strive not to be noticed until he decided to reveal himself to make a point—as he did during a memorable history class.[37]

Borisenko notes that both in school and at university, Putin "somehow seemed to be part of the group, yet always a little off to the side [*no chut'-chut' v storone*]. He would take part in whatever was going on, but he would still look at it as if from the outside [*no tem ne meneye smotrit na nego kak by so storony*]."[38] Other commentators who have encountered Putin in action at different points in his life and career have noted the same tendency. Putin was there but not there. This tendency was reinforced by the fact that Putin's passion for judo, both as a teenager and a student, consumed a lot of his time. He was often outside the crowd at school and university, working out at his judo club with his fellow teammates. Instead of partying with other students, he was focused on his training. His judo teammates were an alternative, tight-knit peer group in which he could anchor himself. Indeed, Putin noted in his biographical interviews at the beginning of his presidency, "I am still friends with those same people whom I trained with back then."[39] At Leningrad State University, Vladimir Putin was described as always having one foot in and one outside the various groups that congregated in the university's inner courtyard or *dvor* for a smoke during recess. He didn't smoke like the others because of his training.[40] Instead, he always seemed to be watching and thinking. Those around Vladimir Putin noted that he appeared quietly on top of everything—the ubiquitous, mysterious "Volodya."[41] Until he shot to the top of the Russian political system, Vladimir Putin was "the man who could vanish in a crowd of two."[42]

In her book *The Man without a Face,* journalist Masha Gessen devotes an entire chapter ("Autobiography of a Thug") to Putin's fixation with the "courtyard culture" of his youth as well as his "outcast status." She notes Putin's efforts to contrive the image of himself as a "little thug" from the streets precisely for public consumption.[43] Since he first threatened to "wipe out" Chechen terrorists in their outhouses in 1999, the image of the "thug," or the tough guy, has been central to Putin's public persona, drawing a line between him and the Moscow elite. Throughout his time as president and prime minister, whenever he engaged with the Russian *narod*, Putin built up the idea that he was a man of the people, a real *muzhik* in Russian. The message running through many of his televised publicity stunts and public encounters across the country was: "I'm like you. I'm not like those privileged types in Moscow." Indeed, following on from a series of protests in Moscow and other cities in the wake of the December 2011 parliamentary elections and then during the subsequent 2012 presidential campaign, Putin stressed this explicitly. He rhetorically put himself outside of Moscow elites at meetings and rallies, including during the question and answer session of his December 15, 2011, call-in TV show.[44]

During the call-in show, Mr. Putin engaged in an exchange with Igor Kholmanskikh, a foreman at the Uralvagonzavod (Urals Railcar Factory) in Nizhny Tagil. Kholmanskikh offered to come to help Putin restabilize the situation in Moscow given all the street protests in this period, and to "sort things out"—clearly with a show of manly or workerly muscle. The foreman indicated it was the least he and his colleagues could do given all Mr. Putin's help dealing with the problems of the regular guy. Mr. Putin, although appreciative, demurred—only to, a few months later, confound most internal and external observers by elevating this same Igor Kholmanskikh to the appointed position of regional *polpred,* the president's authorized representative to the Urals Federal District. Kholmanskikh was instructed by the president to "defend people's interests." A representative of the loyal *narod* from the Urals was thus put into the national spotlight to provide a stark contrast with the disloyal protesters in Moscow.[45]

THE *NACHAL'NIK* (THE BOSS) AND THE GOOD TSAR

The idea that Putin—after 12 years at the very center of Russian power— could still portray himself as an outsider and not as part of the privileged elite in Moscow seems absurd. Yet Vladimir Putin did begin his career as an outsider in several dimensions. That status as outsider is part of the explanation for his ability to rise to power by casting off his ideological baggage, thinking differently, and watching and waiting to seize his moment. The cultivated image of Mr. Putin the tough man—the scrappy survivor who lives by his knuckles, his wits, and his carefully marshaled reserves and who comes in from the outside to get things done—was part of the strength of his political brand in the 2000s. It was one of the reasons Putin was known as the *nachal'nik* (the boss, the man in charge) in Russian government circles for most of the period up until 2011, even during the years when he was prime minister and not sitting as president in the Kremlin.

As the *nachal'nik,* among Mr. Putin's most celebrated performances were the regular public dressing downs of his subordinates, various bureaucratic miscreants, or greedy oligarchs—on TV and at public meetings. These staged exercises in ritual humiliation occur at especially critical moments of public discontent on specific issues. They give Mr. Putin the boss the chance to show he is personally in charge (although not to blame) and that he can and will get things done, no matter how large or small the issue. In each of these instances, Mr. Putin makes it clear that he has personally monitored the situation and has then stepped in, just when he is needed, at the twelfth hour. As Russian analyst Maria Lipman has pointed out, the fact that Putin "is the boss" legitimates and enhances his role as Russia's top leader in the eyes of the broader public.[46]

There are multiple examples of Mr. Putin playing the boss. One of the best documented is an incident in 2009, in a so-called factory monotown, Pikalyovo, near St. Petersburg on Putin's home turf. In the midst of the period when Russia was reeling from the effects of the global economic crisis, hundreds of Pikalyovo's residents were laid off from the town's cement works, which was part of the massive Russian conglomerate Basic Element. The town was completely paralyzed when protesters, demanding restitution, blocked a major road and created traffic jams that extended for hundreds of kilometers. After local authorities proved incapable of resolving the situation, Vladimir Putin and an entourage from Moscow swept into town to dress down the nominal factory owner: high-profile oligarch and Basic Element chairman Oleg Deripaska. Putin's antics, which included calling Deripaska and factory managers "cockroaches" and ordering the cement factory to start production again, brought an end to a set of events that had dominated TV and newspapers and gripped Russia's attention.[47]

Putin's PR handlers have determined that the public loves to see him admonishing figures they do not like in the same language that they would use if they had the opportunity. In keeping with Mr. Putin's mining of historical parallels, these performances as the tough boss, the *nachal'nik,* pick up on the traditional Russian idea of the Good Tsar.[48] In the imperial era, there was a general popular belief that the tsar was always ready and willing to fix any range of large or small things for the *narod.* He was stopped from doing so by the bad boyars around him. These were the aristocrats (historical versions of Russia's modern oligarchs), advisers, and functionaries who refused to bring burning issues to his attention. As Russian commentators frequently note, "the idea that only the head of state can solve your personal problems is genetically ingrained."[49] In his PR performances, Mr. Putin pushes the bad boyars aside so he can get to the crux of every issue. An April 2012 editorial in the Russian newspaper *Vedomosti* suggested, however, that Mr. Putin had begun to take his outside interventions too far.[50] The editorial relayed a complaint from a prominent Russian actress, Chulpan Khamatova, who had set up a charity to help Russian children. During an interview with the BBC, Khamatova asserted that all her efforts had repeatedly run into stumbling blocks. In each case it seemed that the only person who could remove a specific bureaucratic or legal obstacle was Vladimir Putin himself.

The *Vedomosti* editors noted that for every organization in Russia—from charities, to the police, the courts, or electoral commissions—there had to be some kind of stimulus or pressure from the very top of the political system for them to do their work. With Russia's judicial and legislative branches tightly linked to the executive, even straightforward questions had to be channeled up to Vladimir Putin. They also referred to Mr. Putin's PR stunts. The editors reviewed his 2009 appearance at Pikalyovo to force Deripaska to sort things out, his response to August 2010 Moscow forest fires to spur the emergency services into action, and his frequent visits to far-flung Russian regions in 2011–12 to dole out funds from the federal budget to relieve local economic pressures. The editors concluded that only one Russian politician, only one person—"the first person" (*pervoye litso*)—could make the final decision on any important issue in Russia in 2012. Vladimir Putin was Russia's only Mr. Fix-It.[51]

The public humiliations of subordinates and the tough boss or action performances are, in fact, an innovation for Putin since he became Russia's predominant leader. Although Putin was always renowned as the fixer (dating back to his days in St. Petersburg with Sobchak and his team in the mayor's office), many of the stories from his earlier periods show that he often deployed a softer, quieter, more subtle behind-the-scenes approach to get results. Before he became prime minister and president—even when he was engaging in outright coercion—Putin was known for doing small, and sometimes larger, favors for people with whom he came into contact, including strangers. He related his rationale directly to one prominent Russian opposition figure, who once had been astounded to learn that Putin—who was then head of the FSB and had no personal connection to him whatsoever—had bailed him out of a potential corruption scandal by quietly defying a direct order from a higher official to gather compromising material. When this political figure later had a chance to thank Putin, he also asked him why he took the risk of doing such a thing. Putin merely shrugged and replied: "You never know who people might turn out to be."[52] Putin wants to have various means of making people feel beholden to him.

PUTIN'S POPULIST LANGUAGE

One personal story from Vladimir Putin's days in the LGU *dvor,* or courtyard, during recess links both to the idea of Putin being in control by standing to one side and to his propensity for doing favors. The manner in which the favor was extended also ties to another feature of Mr. Putin's thuggish image—his constant use of populist language and crude popular culture references to convey a message or win people over. Language and jokes are deployed by Putin as a point of connection with his contemporaries and the average Russian. They consistently distinguish him as an outsider from the so-called intelligentsia and other more privileged elites in both Soviet times and in contemporary Russia.

One of Putin's contemporaries at LGU, who was studying in another faculty but frequented the same *dvor* to smoke a cigarette, recounted a story about a personal encounter with Vladimir Putin in the early 1970s. The contemporary, who hailed from one of Russia's North Caucasus republics, talked about this ubiquitous "Volodya"—who always hung around the edges of the *dvor* and knew everyone, even if he was not part of the in group of every *tusovka* or clique. One day, the weather was particularly windy and the LGU courtyard especially crowded. The student from the North Caucasus could not find a good place to light his cigarette without the wind blowing out his match or someone knocking into him. Suddenly he heard a voice, "Volodya's": "Hey guys! The *dzhigit* here needs some space to smoke." The next thing he knew, everyone had moved out of the way to open up some space for him. He was surprised and grateful, but at the same time he felt offended. *Dzhigit* is an ethnic reference. He wondered how he should react. Then he noticed that "Volodya" was smiling warmly. "Volodya" had done him a favor. So he accepted it. "I've never forgotten it," he told us several decades later.[53]

Why *dzhigit*? Putin never uses words casually. There is always a calculation. Many of the words Putin uses, the jokes or the specific references he makes, link back to something quintessentially Soviet, as well as to the classics of Russian literature that were part of the Soviet curriculum Putin and his cohort were steeped in at school. *Dzhigit* is the native horseman from the Caucasus Mountains who fought against the expansion of the Russian empire into the region. The word crops up in the works of famous Russian authors like Leo Tolstoy and Mikhail Lermontov, who wrote stories of the Circassian Wars of the nineteenth century. It also features in a classic Soviet comedy film, whose title is partly inspired by one of Tolstoy's stories: *Prisoner of the Caucasus, or Shurik's New Adventures.*[54] The film was first released in 1967, when Putin would have been 14 years old, but it was endlessly replayed on Soviet and Russian TV in the 1970s. For someone of Putin's and his university colleagues' age at LGU in this period, the common frame for the *dzhigit* reference would have been the Shurik film. It was one of two in which Shurik, a hapless and naive student, has a series of farcical misadventures. A famous segment from the film features Shurik's first encounter with a trio of Three Stooges–like characters from the Caucasus in a restaurant.

In 2008, this famous segment was brilliantly dubbed by a group of young satirical filmmakers from the Russian city of Perm to create a YouTube masterpiece, "How Medvedev Happened."[55] In the satirical film, Shurik was artfully transformed into Dmitry Medvedev with a dubbed dialogue that mocked Medvedev's selection as Putin's successor and the orchestration of the 2008 Russian presidential election with its cast of stock opposition characters. The Three Stooges became Gennady Zyuganov and Vladimir Zhirinovsky, along with an out-of-left-field presidential candidate, Andrei Bogdanov, who 'Medvedev's' restaurant interlocutor cannot remember when he tries to introduce them. In 2008, Bogdanov, the leader of the Democratic Party of Russia, won just over one percent of the popular vote.

For Putin's fellow student from the Caucasus in the LGU *dvor*, and for the other students around him, *dzhigit* was clearly a slur. It was not especially egregious and was amusing in the context of the Shurik film. It was even slightly complementary or respectful. In Tolstoy and Lermontov there is a degree of admiration expressed for the fighting prowess and horsemanship of the Caucasus *dzhigit*. The slur also was conspicuously neutral in its ethnicity. The Caucasus is a complicated place, as Putin would find out when dealing with Chechnya after 1999. "Volodya" could not have been entirely sure which bit of the vast mountainous region his interlocutor came from, and if it was definitely from the North or perhaps even from the South Caucasus (from the then Soviet republics of Armenia, Azerbaijan, or Georgia). Putin's reference was the American cultural equivalent of saying "Hey guys, 'Tonto' here [from the extremely popular 1950s TV series *The Lone Ranger*] needs some space to have a smoke." He was doing a favor, but at the same time he was making an inside, Soviet-era joke—so as not to, or at least not too closely, associate himself with the student from the Caucasus.

THE ART OF THE SOVIET JOKE

As Russian leader, Putin has carefully deployed populist language and jokes like this to embellish his thuggish image and his position as an outsider to the Moscow elite. The use has often been offensive, in multiple senses—especially when he resorted to his crudest references like "wiping out" Chechen terrorists in the outhouse, or suggesting, in an exchange with French president Nicolas Sarkozy during the 2008 war with Georgia, that he would hang Georgian president Mikheil Saakashvili "by the balls."[56] The vulgar language underscores that Putin will be ruthless in pursuing someone else's "offense" or "insult." The references and the jokes are directed at those around him. They are, in many respects, a recruitment tool to forge a personal link, emphasize and illustrate a point, and bring people around to his way of thinking. This is a tactic Mr. Putin learned as a case officer in the KGB, an issue we will return to later in the book. However, it is clear from many of the jokes, which are steeped in Soviet popular culture, that they resonate most forcefully with Putin's immediate gender and age cohort—his generation of men now in their 50s and 60s.

In one memorable moment during the November 2011 Valdai Club dinner, Putin laughingly caught himself using the punch line of a dirty Russian joke in response to a question as to whether he would become a "new Putin," or "Putin 2.0," after the 2012 presidential election. He wanted to emphasize that he was just "one, single, person" like everyone else in the room. "Vladimir Putin," he said, referring to himself in the third person, "cannot be divided into two pieces." The Russian word he used for split into two was *razdvoyayetsya,* a perfectly acceptable word—were it not for its connection to a crude ethnic joke, again with Caucasus connotations. If slightly mispronounced in a manner attributed by Russian joke culture to a Georgian, say, or another native of the Caucasus, it becomes "raz-dva-yaytsa." That literally means "one-two-eggs," but in the Russian vernacular it actually means two balls (testicles again).

The original anecdote belongs to a well-known Soviet genre of irreverent and crude jokes—*Chapaev-Petka*—replete with colorful and unprintable (in this book at least) Russian words for the male and female genitals. Chapaev (Vasily Chapaev) was a Red Army commander during the Russian Civil War of 1917–22, who was portrayed as a great hero in Soviet literature and films. For that reason, he was frequently lampooned in Soviet joke culture. In one version of the joke, Chapaev learns of a village somewhere that has problems with its traffic. He sends his sidekick Petka to take action. After a while, Chapaev comes to inspect the progress. Petka takes him out in a car. As they drive down the road, Petka points out all the new signs he has put in place to warn of various traffic hazards. The signs have a series of increasingly vulgar symbols on them, all of which, Petka explains, indicate that the roads are really bad up ahead. Finally, they come to a sign that looks innocent enough—but still puzzling. It has nothing but two large circles on it. "How about that one?" Chapaev asks. "Why, it means the road splits into two—"raz-dva-yaytsa," Petka replies.[57]

At the dinner with Putin, the reference was lost to everyone but the older Russian participants at the table and those in his entourage standing around (and even they might not have caught it had it not been for Putin's own chuckle). They snickered and looked at each other. In the official transcript of the Valdai dinner exchange, Putin's answer is included, and the word *razdvoyayetsya* is put in quotes. It makes the association with the joke clear for anyone who is familiar with it.[58] For the younger Russians in the PR team, this was a joke from another era. Like the non-native Russian speakers they didn't get it, as they readily admitted after the dinner.

Just as he missed personal experiences back home in the late 1980s, Putin seems to have missed out on a more contemporary set of Russian jokes while he has been at the very center of Russian power structures. These jokes are more likely to be circulating on the Internet than in printed anthologies of Soviet jokes.[59] As we will discuss more in the second section of the book, this may be one of the reasons why Putin found it so hard to connect with a younger generation of protesters who took to city streets in 2011–12. Instead of winning them over, Putin ended up insulting them with jocular references to them as the "Bandarlogi" or "Monkey People," the anarchic band of primates from Rudyard Kipling's *The Jungle Book* who famously have no king. Kipling's book was another stalwart of the Soviet school literature curriculum, and Putin noted in interviews that he had loved the book since childhood. He also referred to the demonstrators' protest ribbons as "condoms," alienating his intended interlocutors even further.[60]

In his final speech to the Russian parliament as prime minister in April 2012, Putin told another old Soviet joke at a critical point in the question and answer period, creating a stir in the auditorium. The joke was also probably entirely lost on younger people listening, but it resonated with the older cohort of parliamentarians he was addressing. In response to a Communist Party deputy's contention that the agricultural sector had performed better in the Soviet period than under the current regime, Putin retorted: "Long, green, smells of meat. What is it? A Moscow *elektrichka* [commuter train]." This joke harks back to the late Soviet period and its chronic meat shortages, when *kolbasa* or sausage, a staple of Soviet diets, was especially hard to come by. Because Moscow as the capital had privileged access to the limited supplies, people from other regions would head in on the train to stand in line, often for hours, to purchase sausage and other products that were unavailable in their towns and cities. They would stagger home on the train again, laden down with as much as they could carry. As Putin noted in his speech, there was always a shortage of meat in the Soviet period, because the Soviet economy and the meat production sector simply did not function effectively.[61] He then went on to debunk the central idea of the Communist Party deputy and the Communist Party ideology that central planning is superior to the market economy.

Moving on from the initial joke, having illustrated his point, Putin referred the parliamentary audience to the more distant past. He took them to the era of Lenin and the early Bolsheviks' rule in the 1920s, when the Bolsheviks' proposed planned economy could not quite get itself off the ground. Putin noted that "Vladimir Ilyich [Lenin] intro-duced elements of a market economy. He himself [the father of com-munism] did this. So then . . . to say that: 'everything is bad in a market economy'—is simply not true. Even the Communist Party introduced elements of market regulation, when other elements did not function. It was only later that Josef Vissaronovich [Stalin] liquidated all these market instruments." Putin conceded that a planned economy ulti-mately enabled Russia, over time, to "concentrate state resources for the purposes of accomplishing the most important, critical elements of the national agenda, like defense and security." But "overall," he argued, the planned economy was "much less effective than the market economy."[62]

In this final presentation to parliament, with his joke and these com-ments, Putin offered the classic view of the Outsider. The Outsider is pragmatic. He has no vested interest in policies or in ideologies. In a system so burdened by ideology, only an outsider could clearly see the flaws of the system. This is what allowed Putin himself, in looking at the functioning, or the non-functioning, of the Soviet system, to abandon the strongest element of Communist Party ideology, the myth of state ownership and central planning. He could admit that private property, free enterprise, and the market were superior on the basis of hard facts and empirical evidence. In his response to the Communist Party ques-tioner, Putin pointed out that he had no intention of making a political statement nor engaging in ideological debates. His comments were based on practical considerations, first-hand observations, and the lessons of history. He referred his audience to this, using the example he knew best of all from his KGB service outside the USSR in Dresden and another contemporary example that everyone else would be familiar with:

There are two absolutely very well-known historical experiments in the world—East Germany and West Germany, and North Korea and South Korea. Now these are cases that everyone can see! But this does not mean that everything is all right in a market economy. If we would introduce so-called wild capitalism, it would not lead to anything good, it would never produce anything beneficial. So what are we aiming for? A market economy, but a socially oriented market economy. Together we have to look for these golden means in our practical work.[63]

Putin's polemics against the Russian communists' nostalgia for a centrally planned economy underscore another key feature of his personal worldview. He appears—on the surface at least—to believe in the free market. In his rejoinder in the Russian parliament, and on many other occasions, Putin has made a point of praising private ownership and criticizing too much government interference in the economy. Furthermore, during his tenures as both Russian president and prime minister from 2000 to 2012, he pursued some undeniably sensible economic policies in close coordination with Finance Minister Alexei Kudrin. This raises the questions of what views Putin really holds about the market economy and where he derived his knowledge of basic economics. In the next chapter we will consider some of the likely sources of Putin's thinking about the Russian economy and his model of economic management.

CHAPTER SEVEN

THE FREE MARKETEER

PUTIN SEEMS TO HAVE GAINED some grounding in general economic issues during the 1970s and 1980s. As a student at Leningrad State University (LGU) in the 1970s, studying under Anatoly Sobchak, Putin wrote an undergraduate thesis on international trade law. In the 1980s, at the KGB's Red Banner Institute, American business school textbooks were likely on the curriculum, and Yury Andropov had put reforming the Soviet economic system as one of the top items on the KGB's agenda. In the German Democratic Republic (GDR), as he made clear in his April 2012 remarks to the Russian Duma, Putin had been exposed to the controlled experiment that the economic development of the two Germanys presented during the Cold War—one that produced a clearly superior result for the Western, capitalist, version. In 1996, Putin wrote a graduate thesis in "economics," which was one of his goals when he returned to Leningrad from Dresden in 1990. Most of this was, however, in a Soviet context. Vladimir Putin's only real understanding of market economics would have come later, from his practical activity as deputy mayor of St. Petersburg, working with actual businesses, both Russian and foreign, in the 1990s.

In 1990s St. Petersburg, the capitalism and business practices Putin was exposed to did not have an emphasis on entrepreneurship, nor were they in the critical areas of production, management, and marketing. St. Petersburg capitalism was all about making deals. Personal connections with the St. Petersburg city government were more important for doing business than were relations between workers and customers. The focus was on finding and using leverage.[1] Putin seems to have emerged from his St. Petersburg experience with, first, the conviction that the only way Russia could survive in the modern world was with a market economic system. Second, he had the view that the winners in the market system were not necessarily those who were most skilled at providing goods and services at the best prices. Instead, the winners were those best at exploiting others' vulnerabilities. Those vulnerabilities were greed and an often flagrant disregard for legal niceties. Ultimately, as we will discuss later in the book, the wheeling and dealing Free Marketeer perspective would prove a very dangerous outlook on which to base the policies of a great power in a globalized world economy.

RUSSIA'S ECONOMIC PERFORMANCE UNDER PUTIN

By most objective measures, the performance of the Russian economy during Vladimir Putin's tenures as president and prime minister was outstanding—something Putin has frequently pointed out himself. In his report to the Russian parliament in April 2012, shortly before assuming the Russian presidency for the third time, Putin boasted about Russia's economic condition almost four years after the outset of the global financial crisis. While the crisis "was a trial for us," he noted, "we recovered much faster than many other countries. Today we have the highest economic growth rates in the G-8 (Group of Eight) and one of the highest among the world's major economies. For comparison's sake, the growth rate in the United States is 1.7 percent, in the Eurozone 1.5 percent, in India 7.4 percent, in China 9.2 percent and in Russia 4.3 percent. We are third among major economies."[2] Putin's entire speech was replete with similar claims of success. Like any politician, Putin was, of course, selective in choosing which statistics to highlight. But his case was still a strong one.

Russia's story over the decade since Putin's Millennium Message in December 1999 is one of the most dramatic reversals of fate in recent economic history. Russia was essentially bankrupt and practically in receivership when Putin first stepped into his top leadership roles. Yet within five years after Putin took power, practically all of Russia's foreign debt had been repaid and its foreign exchange reserves had been built back up. Putin made Russia's debt to the International Monetary Fund a particular priority. It was paid off three-and-a-half years ahead of schedule.[3] Equally important for Putin, Russia's share of the world economy grew rapidly in his first two presidential terms. Measured in dollars at the market exchange rate, Russia grew between 1999 and 2008 from the twenty-third-largest economy to the ninth largest. Its growth rate over this period was twice that of China.[4]

If performance alone were sufficient to gauge Putin's understanding of economics and his skill in management, he would deserve high marks. However, in the case of Russia it is very difficult to distinguish the results of Putin's policies from the effects of another variable—the increase in oil prices that coincided with his term in office. As noted earlier, thanks to higher oil prices, the country's wealth—the natural resource rent represented by Russia's oil and gas—soared.[5] Virtually all measures of Russia's economic performance also moved in lockstep with oil prices during the Putin era, climbing steadily from 1999 to 2008, dropping sharply in mid-2008 with the global economic crisis, and then rebounding in 2010–11 as oil prices recovered.[6] This does not mean, however, that government economic policy in this period was inconsequential. It would have been extremely easy to squander this wealth and to forfeit the opportunity to make the most of the oil price windfall. To what extent, then, did Putin's policies contribute to economic success from 1999 to 2008? And if they did contribute, what were the important elements of those policies and where did they originate? Was it Putin's Survivalist identity that made the critical difference, including the lessons he learned over his career about basic self-reliance and the importance of ensuring that the Russian state had sufficient reserves to withstand any eventuality? Or did Putin draw upon some other deeper understanding of the fundamentals of a market economy in shaping government policy?

THE PUTIN ECONOMIC PUZZLE

Vladimir Putin's attitude toward the market economy has often surprised and sometimes confounded Western observers. Putin's fierce defense of the market economy in his debate with the Communist Party members of the Russian Duma in April 2012—declaring a planned economy to be "less efficient than a market economy" and asserting that "nothing good" would come of a reversion to state property—attracted considerable attention in the international media.[7] In the early days of Putin's first presidency, the Russian government also adopted a number of reforms that were widely described as progressive. Russia's flat tax reform in 2001, for example, was even lauded as a model for the world by U.S. free market champions at the Heritage Foundation.[8] These reforms created a narrative of an early, "liberal" Putin, who was then somehow replaced by a crypto-communist Putin when further reforms did not materialize.[9] This image shifted again after the global financial crisis. Observers could not help but notice that Putin took the tone of the lecturer, with a provocative "I-told-you-so" attitude, when making public pronouncements on the crisis. In writing of Putin's appearance in early 2009 at the Davos conference of world economic leaders, *Washington Post* columnist David Ignatius described a Putin who "talked like a born-again capitalist, saying that Russia had seen the damage caused by too much government control of the economy and that it would never go back to the policies of the Soviet Union." "The former communist," Ignatius said, was "now a true believer in free market discipline."[10]

In contrast, however, to the perception of Mr. Putin as having flip-flopped from communist to capitalist, and then back again to advocate of state control, there has been a good deal of consistency in Putin's general views on economics—at least during his tenure as head of state and leader of the Russian government. Putin has always preached an orthodox version of fiscal policies. For 12 years, he both empowered and protected one of the most fiscally conservative finance ministers in the world, his close colleague Alexei Kudrin. More important, in spite of having every opportunity to renationalize critical assets, Putin did not reverse the course of Russia's 1990s privatization process. The most controversial and largest set of deals that transferred Russian state property into private hands—the so-called loans-for-shares agreements already mentioned—was overwhelmingly regarded by the Russian population as illegitimate. This arrangement, which effectively created the much-hated oligarchs, was concluded by the Yeltsin administration. Putin could have reaped huge political dividends by reversing this scheme.[11]

By Putin's account he made a similarly critical choice in favor of private business in 2008–09, in the wake of the global financial crisis. He claims that some of the oligarchs came to him and begged him to take over their private property. He refused. In light of the widespread notion that Putin is a forceful advocate of state ownership, it is worth quoting his remarks on this subject at length. Speaking to a meeting of leading oligarchs in April 2011, he said:

> During the acute phase of the crisis, some colleagues, including some who are in this room right now, asked whether they shouldn't fully transfer their business to the state. They were ready to do that and themselves even proposed it.
>
> Let me point out, dear colleagues: we did not go down that road. We chose a different path. We supported the private entrepreneur, we backed you up, gave you loans, helped you refinance from Western banks, put up collateral. . . . But we did not proceed towards nationalization of our economy. This is a fundamental choice of the Government: we don't want to create a system of state capitalism—we want to create a system of socially oriented market economy and, of course, we strive towards this, including using the tools of privatization. Here we must act carefully, but this is the way we will go.
>
> . . . *It would have been easy back then to take over, to seize, private business (and we could have done it on the cheap). It was more difficult to preserve private business* [emphasis added]. . . .[12]

The fact that Vladimir Putin did not reverse the fundamental pro-market reforms of the 1990s is, for many people, a genuine puzzle. There are several explanations for why he did not, each of which derives from the Putin identities we have discussed so far in the book. First, as a student of Russian and Soviet history, Putin saw that the Soviet system of economic management had failed. During his time in the KGB in the 1980s, even before the collapse of the USSR, Putin understood that this put the Soviet Union at a huge disadvantage. At various points, including during his exchange with the Communist Party deputies in the Russian Duma in April 2012, Putin has acknowledged that there may have been a historical rationale for the Stalin-era system of industrialization, which began in the late 1920s and laid the foundation for the modern Soviet Union. But he has also underscored—including in the same exchange—that history showed the reform of that system to be long overdue.

The second explanation is that, as a dedicated *gosudarstvennik* (statist) with a pronounced survivalist perspective, Mr. Putin has been focused on protecting the Russian state. As an outsider to the prevailing system, he was able to slough off the burden of ideology and assess what worked and did not work. Vladimir Putin's most successful economic policies have thus been based on what one might call intelligent pragmatism. Instead of adhering (or not adhering) to liberal or free-market economic principles, Putin has approached macroeconomic and fiscal discipline as the means to ensure state survival. The goals of building the state (with efficient tax collection) and protecting it (by reducing debt and building reserves) are not signs of economic liberalism. Perhaps the best support for this thesis is the fact that the most forceful advocate of similar macroeconomic policies in Russian history before Vladimir Putin was none other than Josef Stalin. In his report to the 14th Congress of the Bolshevik Party in December 1925, Stalin argued for the need to balance the budget, maintain a stable currency, keep inflation low, avoid dependence on Western loans, and build up financial reserves.[13] In addition, the actual introduction of the flat rate tax that was part of Putin's early tax reform package was far less important than the fact that Putin, and only Putin, proved capable of actually *collecting* taxes. Putin's 2001 innovation came after years of widespread tax evasion at all levels of the Russian economy and population. Putin also collected taxes using intimidation and force, including sending masked operatives armed with Kalashnikovs storming into the head offices of major corporations to seize their financial records.[14]

SOURCES OF PUTIN'S ECONOMIC THINKING: FROM THE USSR TO THE KGB

Lessons from history helped Putin understand that the market economy and capitalism worked. His Outsider pragmatism allowed him to accept history's verdict without the constraint of ideology. The problem, however, is that history did not necessarily impart information on *how* capitalism worked. What remains unclear, including from his many pronouncements on the issue, is the extent of Putin's real understanding of the market economy. As already stated, on three occasions in his past, Vladimir Putin was exposed to topics nominally described as economics in a more or less academic setting. These could, at the very least, have planted some theoretical seeds. During his law studies at Leningrad State University from 1970 to 1975, Putin took at least one course in international trade law. He then wrote a senior thesis on law relating to the most favored nation regime in international trade.

In the mid-1980s, when he returned to the classroom, this time under the auspices of the KGB as a student at the Red Banner Institute, Putin had courses in economics and management. Finally, in 1996, he wrote a dissertation for a graduate degree in economics at the St. Petersburg Mining Institute. In addition, he had his personal experience, the day-to-day activity in his two careers before coming to Moscow to work in the Russian presidential administration in 1996. These experiences cover his career activities as a KGB officer in Leningrad, Moscow, and Dresden, and his tenure as deputy mayor of St. Petersburg in the 1990s. These lessons from his personal history and his daily reality of dealing with real-life businessmen likely complemented the big lessons of history he absorbed—all before he rose to his positions of power.

It is not likely that Putin developed any notion of capitalism in his childhood. For someone outside the USSR, it is hard to appreciate how little anyone growing up in the Soviet Union of the 1960s or 1970s would know about business or business people. Parents, relatives, or neighbors provided no role models or even examples. Putin's father was a factory worker and his mother worked in various low-level positions as a janitor, a cleaner, and an assistant in a Soviet bakery. There was no corner grocer, no local butcher, no neighborhood bookseller that operated on a private, commercial basis. Soviet children and young adults generally did not deliver newspapers, shine shoes, mow lawns, walk dogs, babysit, or wait tables to generate their own income, although they could engage in summer jobs as they got older. The only place someone in this era would come in contact with entrepreneurial activity was in the so-called second economy. Actors in the second economy *were* entrepreneurial. They were innovative. They were also risk-takers, because their activity was either directly illegal or at best only quasi-legal (hence the alternative name of the "shadow economy"). Virtually every form of such activity involved using government property for private gain. Consequently, even though almost every Soviet citizen availed him—or her—self of the goods and services that were available in the shadow economy, few would have openly defended it.[15]

The second economy was a necessary evil in the USSR Vladimir Putin grew up in. The people from whom a Soviet citizen obtained the unofficial goods or services were deemed unpalatable. Especially for a family of industrial wage workers like Putin's, the image was unlikely to be one to emulate. However, there was one aspect of the shadow economy that came to affect nearly everyone, including, apparently, Putin. It taught citizens that money did matter, and prices mattered. This was not true in the official economy, where the goods simply were not available. Time— specifically the time to stand in line for hours for some small everyday items or to wait for months or years on an official list for a big-ticket item like a TV or a refrigerator or a car—was far more important than money. In the parallel shadow economy, all of the goods otherwise in short supply might be available, for enough money. Because money mattered in the shadow economy, most citizens were eager to get it. There is evidence that the young Vladimir Putin was among them.[16]

In this sense, at the micro level, Putin's direct personal relationship to the economy probably did not differ from that of most Soviet citizens of his age. At the macro level, during Putin's youth, the Soviet national economy actually looked fairly good. Beyond the difficulties experienced by the average Soviet citizen in trying to cope with procuring life's necessities and its luxuries on a day-to-day basis, the USSR was a superpower in the 1960s and 1970s. It was on a par with the United States in terms of military strength. The Soviet Union was also the second-largest economy in the world, although its economy was still far smaller than that of the United States.[17] The USSR emerged from World War II with an economy that was only about one-third the size of America's, but it had been narrowing the gap ever since—a fact that was much touted in Soviet propaganda of the era.[18]

In short, as Putin began his university studies at LGU in the fall of 1970, he was preparing himself to enter the service of a superpower that appeared to be gaining on its arch rival. During Putin's years at Leningrad State University, this general trend would continue. The Middle East oil crisis of 1973 led to a seven-fold increase in the world price of oil. The oil crisis, in turn, led to a recession in the West. The USSR, in contrast, benefited. The Soviet Union's big oilfields in western Siberia were brought on line at this very juncture. In 1974, the USSR even surpassed the United States as an oil producer for the first time.[19] All of this would have reinforced the impression for Putin and his contemporaries that the USSR was a rising power and the United States a declining one.

We cannot be certain that the young Vladimir Putin of the 1970s regarded the Soviet economy in these specific terms. We do not know what he thought about the national economy and how the Soviet economic system worked. Putin's only concerns could well have been about his own personal circumstances, his future career, his family's prospects, and all the other issues that tend to preoccupy most citizens of any country when they think about economics.[20] However, if there was any organization that would have given Putin the opportunity, or might even have forced him, to think about these big issues, it was the KGB. The KGB and its predecessor organizations had a long, but uneven, history of involvement with the economy. The secret police in Russia always had the task of monitoring economic activity and the economy's main actors. They were assigned to uncover economic crimes, whether they be misdeeds and abuse within the official Soviet economy or activity outside it, in the second economy. There were also periods when the security services were directly involved in economic policymaking and management.[21]

THE KGB AND THE ECONOMY

In the 1920s, the first head of the Bolsheviks' secret police, Felix Dzerzhinsky, was in charge of major economic decisions.[22] Later, under Stalin, the KGB's forerunners were direct and critical economic actors by virtue of their role as managers of the gigantic forced labor system known as the gulag.[23] At its peak, the gulag accounted for as much as 15 to 18 percent of total industrial output and employment in Russia.[24] But since the early 1950s, no KGB leader had been given direct responsibility for economic policy. The last leader with this assignment was Lavrenty Beria, head of the security police from 1938 to 1953. Whatever his other characteristics, Beria was, in the Soviet context, an economic liberal. Beria started the first de-Stalinization effort. He proposed the de-collectivization of agriculture. He disbanded the gulag because it was "inefficient." He proposed rapprochement with the West. But Beria lost the factional struggle after Stalin's death. He was executed, and his name and his policies became anathema in KGB lore.[25]

The KGB to which Putin was recruited was not particularly oriented toward economics. There were, however, two things about the Western economy that preoccupied the KGB. The first concern was that the West was capitalist, and therefore axiomatically and ideologically opposed to the Soviet economic system. It was the antithesis of all the USSR and the Communist Party represented. As the "Sword and Shield" of the Party, the KGB's main task was "revolutionary vigilance."[26] Its role was to combat subversive activities and ideas from the West. High on the list of such dangerous ideas was anything that could be construed as favoring capitalist economic principles and methods. The second fixation was with the scientific and technological achievements of the Western market economy—particularly anything with a military application. The KGB had a special section designed only to steal the advanced products of the Western system that Communist Party ideologists insisted was doomed to destruction.

In the years after Putin joined the KGB, serious new challenges to the Soviet economy caused the intelligence service to change the focus of its interest in Western economies. Although the USSR benefited from the oil price shock of the 1970s, this benefit proved short-lived. It masked an array of fundamental problems in the economic system. While revenues and rents went up, the physical performance of the rest of Soviet industry was dropping rapidly. Between 1977 and 1981, the increase in Soviet oil production suddenly slowed, after growing at an average annual rate of about 7.6 percent through 1976.[27] By 1981, Soviet oil production became flat, just as global oil prices collapsed. All Soviet economic plans and projections were upset. Behind the image of abundance and wealth, a crisis was looming. The title of the book by renowned American energy expert Thane Gustafson about the Soviet oil industry of this period aptly sums up the situation—*Crisis amid Plenty.*[28]

There is an irony here that becomes an important element in the future story of the USSR and Russia. While the 1973 oil price shock gave Russia added wealth and initially dealt a huge blow to the capitalist economies, it turned out to have a longer-term salutary effect for the West. After 1979, for example, the United States cut its crude oil imports by half in just four to five years.[29] Western economies eventually became more efficient by moving to new technologies, computerization, microelectronics, new materials, and new industrial processes. The

Soviet Union went in the opposite direction. Much of its oil windfall was spent to support the satellite countries of Eastern Europe and to expand production in defense industries and other manufacturing sectors inside the USSR. These industrial plants became even more energy inefficient than they had been in the past. So while the United States and most of the other Western economies came out of the 1970s crisis leaner and tougher, the Soviet Union emerged bigger but flabbier.

STEALING AND SQUANDERING TECHNOLOGICAL SECRETS

On the part of the Soviet leaders, the predominant response to this reality of falling behind in the technological race was a combination of denying the weaknesses of their own system and trying to stay in the game by simply stealing more of the technology the rival capitalist system had invented and produced. There were, however, more enlightened parts of the Soviet leadership, most notably in the military, that came to realize that the problem could not be solved by theft. The Soviet system itself had to change, but its denizens were trapped by an inherent dilemma. An innovative economy required more freedom for individuals. Such freedom was incompatible with the Soviet system of political control. This was the general message the Soviet Union's leading military innovator, Chief of the Soviet General Staff Marshal Nikolai Ogarkov, imparted to U.S. journalist Leslie Gelb in private remarks as early as 1983. Years later, Gelb recounted the conversation in an article in the *New York Times:*

> I began that afternoon by attacking Moscow for amassing forces that far exceeded defensive needs. [Ogarkov] waved me off with a tolerant smile. Then he proceeded to make the most astonishing argument I had ever heard from a Soviet official. . . . "We will never be able to catch up with you in modern arms until we have an economic revolution. And the question is whether we can have an economic revolution without a political revolution."[30]

Marshal Ogarkov, wrote Gelb, was admitting to him that "the communist system was not working and could not work. . . . [T]he Soviet Union without radical change was incapable of competing with the U.S."

But since a political revolution was clearly impermissible, Gelb concluded, what Ogarkov was really saying was that "the Cold War was already essentially over, if not finally won by the West."

To what extent that kind of fatalism, defeatism, and frustration permeated broader layers of the elites in the early 1980s is not clear. If it had percolated through the system, someone in Putin's position was bound to have sensed it sooner or later, even if the sentiments were not made explicit.[31] Meanwhile, for those in the KGB who were responsible for technology theft, to be pressured to do even more in the support of a losing cause could only produce resentment. This was something Putin himself expressed in public, albeit after a decade at the center of power. In May 2010, at a meeting with the Russian Academy of Sciences, Putin suggested how frustrated he and his KGB colleagues were—later in the 1980s—that the Soviet economic system was incapable of using the technology stolen from the West:

You know, when I served in a different agency, when I was still in my previous life, we encountered a moment, and I remember it very well, it was sometime at the end of the 1980s, I think—and I am sure that many of you here in the audience will back me up on this, as you doubtlessly also experienced this—when the results of our own research, and the results of your foreign colleagues' research that were obtained by "special means," were not actually introduced into the Soviet Union's economy. We did not even have the equipment to introduce them. And so there we [in the KGB] were, working away, gathering away, essentially for nothing. We would ask, so where [are the results]? Where [are they] in the economy? There weren't any, because it was impossible to utilize them.[32]

In conjunction with the KGB's preoccupation with stealing technological secrets from the West, foreign trade also fell within the special purview of the Soviet KGB. All foreign businesses operating in the USSR were carefully monitored (and infiltrated) by the secret police. Every Soviet foreign trade official was working directly or indirectly for the foreign department of the KGB. This fact is worthy of special note as it relates to Putin, who may have been thinking ahead when he took a course in international trade law with his future boss, Anatoly Sobchak, at Leningrad State University.[33] Whether Putin had a genuine interest in international trade, or whether taking the Sobchak course was a calculated step for career enhancement after he graduated, this item on his resume did prove a particularly useful asset after he left the KGB. When Mr. Putin returned to Leningrad from East Germany in 1990, he was employed as an expert in international economic relations, first at LGU and then in the mayor's office. We will return to this issue later.

PUTIN AT THE RED BANNER INSTITUTE, FALL 1984–JULY 1985

Shortly after Marshal Ogarkov made his startling admission to Leslie Gelb, in the fall of 1984, Vladimir Putin moved from Leningrad to Moscow to train at the KGB's Red Banner Institute. In the ensuing academic year, he would be a first-hand witness to critical changes in the Soviet Union that foreshadowed its history for decades to come. Putin arrived in the midst of a period not only of rapid transition from one Soviet leader to another—four within the span of less than thirty months—but also one in which the weight of the KGB in domestic politics was being greatly increased given the personal histories and connections of key people in the institution with the Communist Party's ruling body, the politburo. In November 1982, Yury Andropov, who until shortly before had been head of the KGB (the longest-serving head of the secret police ever in the USSR), had been chosen general secretary of the Communist Party of the Soviet Union to replace Leonid Brezhnev. In December 1982, the new head of the KGB—and thus Putin's titular boss—Viktor Chebrikov, was named a candidate member of the politburo.[34]

By the time Putin arrived at the Red Banner Institute, Andropov had died suddenly in office (in February 1984) and had, in turn, been succeeded by Konstantin Chernenko. Andropov's hand-picked successor, politburo member Mikhail Gorbachev, however, was already on the doorstep to the Kremlin. Putin would have read about—possibly even heard or watched—Gorbachev's speech in December 1984 at a scientific conference. In his speech, Gorbachev introduced his soon-to be-famous catchwords—perestroika and glasnost. Gorbachev also declared that the primary focus for Soviet analysts and experts should be to study economics and economic theory, including management theory.[35] Presumably those being exhorted to study included KGB analysts like Vladimir Putin.

THE GDR AS A LABORATORY OF REFORM

After his courses at the Red Banner Institute, Putin was immediately posted to the GDR. We have referred to the paucity of information about his actual mission in East Germany and some of his formative experiences there. He was undoubtedly involved in the enduring tasks of any Soviet agent stationed abroad: espionage and recruitment of agents directed against the West, and technology theft. In the GDR he was also likely tasked with monitoring East German political and security officials and identifying where they stood in the Eastern bloc–wide factional struggles for and against perestroika. It is in the performance of this last task that it is at least possible that Putin may have posed questions about the prospects for the future of communist economies and the Soviet system as a whole.

Stationed in Dresden, Putin was one of few Soviets, inside or outside the KGB, who had the advantage of seeing what he later described as a unique historical experiment at close range. The GDR economic system was an extreme example of failure. East Germany had many advantages that the USSR lacked. Its human capital was more advanced. It had a recent and relatively long memory of capitalism and entrepreneurship prior to the great rupture of World War II. It enjoyed considerable benefits from its location in the heartland of Europe, with access to Baltic Sea ports and other transportation nodes connecting it to European and global markets. It still had the basic infrastructure of an advanced manufacturing sector. Yet, it failed. Putin took note of some of the discrepancies. As he himself indicated, he seems to have learned from this close observation of the GDR case that reform in a communist system is both difficult and fraught with danger.

The Soviet Union and its satellites had been through cycles of reform efforts and regression almost ever since Stalin's death in 1953. But more often than not, East Germany had been out of sync with the cycles of other countries, including the dominant USSR. For example, after an initial Eastern bloc–wide reform effort in the mid-1960s, the Soviet leadership turned hyper-conservative again after the shock of the Prague Spring in 1968. The GDR, however, stuck to its reform program and even had to defend its reforms against Soviet opposition. Moscow's attempt to force the East German leadership to toe the new line by squeezing the GDR economically backfired. East Berlin defiantly turned to West Germany for loans. In 1971, Moscow engineered the removal of East German Communist Party boss Walter Ulbricht and replaced him with Erich Honecker. For a while, Honecker dutifully followed the Soviet line of focusing on welfare and consumption in the short term instead of on potentially disruptive economic reforms. This was the era of so-called Gulasch Communism in the GDR, but it could only be sustained with subsidies from the Soviet Union, especially oil.[36]

Throughout the 1970s, the USSR exported crude oil to the Eastern bloc at a nominal price. The Soviet Union's satellite countries then reexported this oil to international markets at the higher world price. The practice created conditions of significant dependency on the part of the East Germans. The GDR's leadership committed itself to providing a level of welfare for its citizens that it could not finance on its own. When global oil prices dropped in the early 1980s, removing the preferential differential between the subsidized and world price, the GDR had no ability to adjust.[37] It faced de facto bankruptcy as early as 1982, three years before Putin was posted to Dresden. In dire need of hard currency, East Germany was forced to choose "liquidity before profitability."[38] Cannibalizing its entire economy, East Berlin exported whatever it could to the rest of Europe and further afield, even at a loss. By the time Gorbachev proclaimed perestroika as the new party line for the Soviet camp in the mid-1980s, the last thing the GDR wanted were destabilizing and costly reforms. This was the GDR that Putin entered. It was a nest of hardliners opposed to any liberalizing reforms, fearful of contagion from the radical ideas of Gorbachev's Soviet Union, and completely focused on regime survival. It was almost like being posted into enemy territory.

If Vladimir Putin was indeed a serious enough student of history to see the pattern of development in the GDR, he would have been able to make a number of observations about how relations had developed between society and the rulers within East Germany, as well as between the GDR and the USSR. In both of these cases, clear cycles were evident. A crisis emerged. This led to experiments in reform. The reform experiments tended to fail, provoking protests and dissatisfaction. The leadership reacted to the protests by backing away from reform. Leaders then tried to quell the protests by buying off the population—emphasizing consumer goods, stability, and jobs. This, in turn, led to stagnation, a new crisis, a new push for reform, and so on.[39] This is the classic reform dilemma. It is especially piquant in the Soviet context where elites undertake reforms to preserve their control. But because control, rather than reform, is their actual top priority, they cannot free the economy to unleash its potential. The reforms, as a result, are half-measures at best, and usually end up being worse than no reform at all. Disappointment at both the elite and popular levels turns to frustration and then cynicism. In a system in which the only successes traditionally come from mobilization and moral exhortation, this period of cynicism is a particularly dangerous phase.

Putin would have had to have been extraordinarily perceptive to see all of this in real time in Dresden. He probably was not. But perhaps later, in standing back and mulling over the experience, he could have reflected on this and drawn some conclusions. Even if he was somewhat less perceptive, Putin would have been able to see in the GDR that an obsession with stability can lead to collapse. There was no flexibility at all in the Honecker regime—as Putin's own comments in the various interviews with his biographers in the early days of his presidency underscore. Later, however, back at home in the 1990s, under both Gorbachev and Yeltsin, Putin would see the opposite danger. Too much laxity also can lead to collapse. To succeed both in reforming a system like the Soviet Union's or post-Soviet Russia's and retaining control of the process, a balance somehow had to be struck between stability and flexibility. It is not an easy task by any means.

FROM DRESDEN TO BUSINESS DEVELOPER IN ST. PETERSBURG

In early 1990, Vladimir Putin—still on active duty with the KGB—returned to his hometown of Leningrad. Now, KGB leaders were no longer interested in tweaking the Soviet system. It was too late for that. They wanted to save themselves, individually as much as institutionally. Here, Putin's bosses had clear tasks in mind for him. In the final months of the USSR, KGB chairman Vladimir Kryuchkov had persuaded Mikhail Gorbachev to give the KGB far-reaching authority to run various economic and foreign trade operations. In May 1990, Kryuchkov summoned the Soviet Union's cohort of ambassadors to Moscow. He informed the assembled foreign envoys that the KGB "had at its disposal highly qualified economic experts who were particularly well-suited to represent the interests of major Western corporations on the Soviet market." He asked the ambassadors to understand that the KGB would also be giving support and advice to new and inexperienced Soviet firms as they made tentative forays into European and other markets.[40]

At the same time, Kryuchkov had a less public agenda for his agency. He issued orders for the KGB to infiltrate and co-opt Russia's democratic movements, to "create an artificially manipulated opposition."[41] One of the up-and-coming politicians the KGB was interested in was Anatoly Sobchak, Vladimir Putin's former academic supervisor and still a professor of law at Leningrad State University. The KGB arranged a job for Putin at LGU, as deputy to the university's vice rector for international relations, where he would be able to monitor Sobchak.[42] In May 1990, around the same time that Kryuchkov was giving his instructions to the Soviet ambassadors, Sobchak became head of the Leningrad City Council. He appointed Putin as his adviser for international affairs.

Nominally, within a few weeks or months of his return to Leningrad, Putin underwent a complete change—from spy to quasi public official. Yet he was still technically a KGB officer.[43] His formal assignment from the KGB was to liaise with foreign businesses wishing to enter the Russian market and with Russians looking to do business abroad. Given the prevailing circumstances in 1990, Anatoly Sobchak could not have been naïve enough to think that either Putin's work at the university or his advisory role could be divorced from his KGB service.[44] However, Putin's German language skills, experience living abroad, and personal contacts in Germany would have been considered genuine qualifications that few other Russians could claim. Furthermore, he had written his thesis on international trade with Sobchak at LGU. Putin was a de facto deputy to Mayor Sobchak from the beginning of Sobchak's time at the helm of the city. He was soon given the formal title. Under Sobchak, the St. Petersburg economy was run by a triumvirate of deputy mayors—Vladimir Putin, Alexei Kudrin, and Vladimir Yakovlev. Mayor Sobchak himself had virtually nothing to do with the economy. Alexei Kudrin was in charge of the fiscal side of the economy—the city budget and taxes. That is, Kudrin oversaw the local macro economy as he would later oversee Russia's macro economy. Yakovlev concentrated on St. Petersburg's old Soviet economy. That meant, above all, the defense enterprises. The city's military industrial sector was huge. More than 300,000 Leningraders worked in defense plants, more than in any other city in the USSR.[45] Putin, meanwhile, was chairman of the Committee for External Relations, a position that has been described as "foreign trade minister" at the city level. He was the person who promoted economic relations. His functions were thoroughly in line with the program outlined in Kryuchkov's speech to the ambassadors. Putin was to serve as the go-to person for every foreign company that wished to set up business in St. Petersburg or any local Russian business that wanted to export. More realistically, Putin was a broker, or fixer, which was the moniker given to him by those who interacted with him in this timeframe.[46]

Putin himself described his role in similar terms: "Under then-mayor of St. Petersburg Anatoly Alexandrovich Sobchak, I held what rather quickly became, if not the key position, then at least a position that made it possible to solve a fairly large number of problems and tasks of interest to various business structures."[47] There is no doubt that he did indeed help solve some of these "problems of interest to various business structures." But Putin was not a passive broker matching Russian and foreign businessmen. Nor was he merely a fixer who could help companies navigate the Russian bureaucracy. As deputy mayor, Mr. Putin was the main enabler. He was the individual who decided whether or not businesses could legally operate in the city. He issued licenses to tens of thousands of businesses. He may have helped create hundreds, if not thousands, of businesses himself, because the city of St. Petersburg would also usually function as a co-founder—with the city's contribution to the particular business coming in the form of real estate, an office, or warehousing space.

THE COMING OF CAPITALISM: WHEELING AND DEALING

One of Putin's most important licensing deals in this early period was in fact the food scandal that developed in late 1991. As mentioned in chapter 5, Putin selected a number of private firms, gave them access to minerals and commodities of various kinds, and licensed them to barter these goods abroad for food for the city. This episode nearly resulted in Putin's dismissal from office as the result of an inquiry launched by a group of politicians led by Marina Salye on the city council. Whatever impact the experience may have had on Putin's attitude toward politicians in general and elected legislators in particular, it shaped his view of capitalism. Capitalism, in Putin's understanding, is not production, management, and marketing. It is wheeling and dealing. It is not about workers and customers. It is about personal connections with regulators. It is finding and using loopholes in the law, or creating loopholes. That view, of course, is not entirely wrong. It is simply very one-sided and limited.

Putin's view of capitalism in this vein was quite widely shared in the emerging Russian business circles of the 1990s. In 1992, for example, Mikhail Khodorkovsky and Leonid Nevzlin, the oligarchs who would go on to found the ill-fated Russian oil company YUKOS, wrote a book entitled *Chelovek s rublyom* (Man with a ruble). The book explained the purpose of their original financial holding company, MENATEP, and their own personal philosophy. It was simple: "MENATEP is the realization of the right to riches. MENATEP is the path to riches." As for their personal philosophy: "Our compass is Profit. . . . Our idol is His Financial Highness, Capital." [48] In his January 2012 interview with *The Guardian*, former Kremlin adviser Gleb Pavlovsky offered similar corroborating insight into Putin's and other contemporaries' views on capitalism and capitalists:

Putin is a Soviet person who understood the coming [*prishestviye*] of capitalism in a Soviet way. That is, we were all taught [that capitalism is]: a kingdom of demagogues, behind whom stands big money . . . capitalism is a game with money, behind which stands that military machine which aspires to control the whole world. It's a very clear, simple picture and I think that Putin had [this] in his head—not as an official ideology, but as a form of common sense: that is, of course, we were idiots; we [in the USSR] tried to build a fair society when we should have been making money. And if we had made more money than the Western capitalists then we could have just bought them up. Or we could have created a weapon which they didn't have yet. And that's it. It's a game and we lost, but we lost because we didn't do several simple things: we didn't create our [own] class of capitalists, we didn't give the capitalist predators which were described to us a chance to appear and eat up their capitalist predators. These were Putin's thoughts and I don't think they've changed significantly since [the 1990s]. . . . So Putin's model is that you need to be bigger and better [*umeliye*] capitalists than the capitalists.[49]

THE ST. PETERSBURG BALANCE SHEET

For some six years (1990–96), Vladimir Putin played a key role in the economy of Russia's second-largest city. But in stark contrast with the performance of the Russian economy that he later oversaw, St. Petersburg's performance was very poor in this period. Every city and town in Russia suffered in the 1990s, but few places had lost as much in relative status as St. Petersburg. When the Soviet Union collapsed, St. Petersburg was nearly on a par with Moscow in terms of per capita measures of economic performance. Six years later, it was far behind in incomes, households, corporate sector, profits, and investment. St. Petersburg's per capita gross regional product (GRP) was only 60 percent of Moscow's, while its per capita income was only 35 percent of the capital city's. St. Petersburg outpaced Moscow primarily on negative indices. Its unemployment rate was 23 percent higher; the outmigration rate was 86 percent higher; and suicides among working-age males were 70 percent higher.[50]

The area of the economy that was Vladimir Putin's specific responsibility—trade and investment—was one where it had been expected that the transition to a market economy would benefit St. Petersburg because of its proximity to Western Europe. But, again, by the end of Putin's tenure, this was also a terrible failure. On a per capita basis, foreign trade was 26 percent of Moscow's, foreign investment was 55 percent, the number of small businesses set up with foreign participation was 38 percent, and the number of people employed by foreign-owned small businesses was 30 percent of the capital's.[51]

In short, judging by the abysmal economic record of St. Petersburg, Putin's credentials as an economic policymaker were not good. His credentials as a political manager, especially in light of the food scandal, were equally poor. Yet, in August 1996, Putin was given a job in the administration of the president of the Russian Federation, by people who had worked closely with him and knew how questionable his performance had been. On what basis did they appoint him if it was not on the balance of his record as deputy mayor in St. Petersburg? Why was Putin brought into Moscow in 1996?

The people who brought Vladimir Putin from St. Petersburg to Moscow never cared about his credentials as a specialist in *developing* business. For them he was an expert in *controlling* business. All the time Putin worked in St. Petersburg, he played an official role as deputy mayor and chairman of the Committee for External Relations, but behind the scenes, Mr. Putin operated in his most important identity—the Case Officer. In St. Petersburg, Vladimir Putin was an "operative." Businessmen were not partners but targets. Once he came to Moscow, Putin eventually began to target another set of businessmen, the Russian oligarchs. His goal was to make sure that Russia's own new class of capitalists did not predate on each other and on the Russian state. He was to try to harness them to be "bigger and better" and make more money in the service of Russia—not just for themselves.

CHAPTER EIGHT

THE CASE OFFICER

VLADIMIR PUTIN MANAGED TO KEEP a remarkably low public profile during his time as deputy mayor of St. Petersburg. But this was nothing compared to his obscurity during his first few years in Moscow. Mr. Putin was, as the clichés have it, a nobody when he arrived in Moscow in August 1996. Other than the man who seemed directly responsible for recommending him for a job in the capital, his St. Petersburg colleague Alexei Kudrin, Putin apparently had no solid contacts there. Only three years later, he was tapped to be Boris Yeltsin's successor as president of the Russian Federation. His rise to power in this relatively short timeframe thus seems remarkable. Some commentators accept this stage of Putin's career as a mystery and play it down. Masha Gessen, for instance, writes that Putin came to Moscow "as though airlifted by an invisible hand." His posting may have been due to "secret-police design [or] providence," but in any event the background is "probably unimportant."[1]

Providence may have played something of a role in Mr. Putin's meteoric rise, but the forces that brought him to Moscow were neither invisible nor unknown. Vladimir Putin was not sent into Moscow by the so-called *siloviki* of the KGB secret police or the other power ministries. Nor was he dispatched by his friends and neighbors from the Ozero group—the men with their dachas on a lake. The KGB may have instructed Putin to work for Anatoly Sobchak in St. Petersburg in the early 1990s, but it was a different group from St. Petersburg, from within the circles of the Yeltsin-era liberal economic reformers, who then moved Mr. Putin to

Moscow. They knew who he was, even if few others did. They ultimately had a mission for Putin, a very specific task. Putin was not brought in because he somehow had proved himself to be a good organizer of the local economy in St. Petersburg. Rather, he was expected to use on their behalf the skills he had acquired as an active officer of the KGB in Leningrad and Dresden and which he then personally adapted to the peculiar new market economy in *Banditskiy Piterburg*.[2]

Putin's earliest days of dealing with businesses in St. Petersburg of the 1990s, the fallout from the food scandal, and Putin's reaction to it were particularly pertinent elements. The 1992 food scandal was a major blemish on Putin's political record. More important, however, this event arguably marked the beginning of Putin's efforts to develop an approach to dealing with private businesses that would distinguish him enough to help bring him to Moscow in 1996. It would also help propel him to the post of Russian president in 2000. In the wake of the food scandal, Mr. Putin drew directly on the lessons he learned from his training and work as a KGB case officer to ensure he would never find himself in a similar situation again. The food scandal fuses together the identities of Free Marketeer and Case Officer.

THE FOOD SCANDAL REVISITED

In 1992, Marina Salye, the former chairwoman of the city council committee who had been in charge of securing food supplies during the critical period of the St. Petersburg food crisis, launched an official investigation into the deals Vladimir Putin had concluded on behalf of the mayor's office. She found major discrepancies in every contract. Salye determined that even though St. Petersburg had not received its promised foodstuffs, the exchanged commodities had in fact been exported. The intermediary companies had secured significant commissions. On the basis of Salye's report, the city council recommended that the city prosecutor's office press a case against Putin. The city council called for Mayor Sobchak to dismiss him. Salye also wrote a letter to President Yeltsin and conferred directly with Yury Boldyrev, the Yeltsin government's deputy chief auditor at the Russian Account Chamber, who was originally from St. Petersburg. Boldyrev—who would later in the 1990s become a founding member of the Yabloko opposition party—pressed forward with investigating the case. He even summoned Sobchak to Moscow to discuss the findings. The case was subsequently dropped. According to Marina Salye, this was at Anatoly Sobchak's direct behest.[3]

This whole episode remains as murky now as it was over two decades ago. The original versions of the documents that Marina Salye gathered on the case have vanished.[4] Salye herself is now deceased. This means that much of the story of the food scandal, like so many other crucial events and facets of Putin's life, is history told not on the basis of concrete evidence but from facsimile copies, second-hand accounts, and rumor.

According to Salye, the total value of the various commodities for which Putin's office issued export licenses was at least $92 million.[5] These metals, petroleum products, and other resources came from inside Russia and were to have been shipped abroad in barter deals with foreign food suppliers. At first glance, this aspect of the deals was not especially strange. Barter was widespread in transactions of all kinds inside Russia in the 1990s, motivated by a wide variety of reasons.[6] Barter in foreign trade was less common, however. Generally, sellers of the relatively narrow range of Russian goods that were marketable outside the country wanted to receive cash—dollars or some other hard currency. In a normal market economy, that is what would have happened. The owner of these valuable commodities, whether the government or a private company, would have exported them for dollars, or deutschmarks, or pounds sterling, and then used that currency to import the particular products it wanted from any supplier it chose.

As Putin describes it, and as the facsimile copies of the actual contracts show, what happened here was different. The commodities-for-food deals seem to have been something designed at the local level, but not by officials in either the city's legislature or executive branch. They came strictly at the initiative of private businessmen. In a letter that Putin, as chairman of the Committee for External Relations, wrote to his federal counterpart, Pyotr Aven, on December 4, 1991, Putin does not request any allocation of money, food, or natural resources to St. Petersburg from the federal government. He claims that since the city is not receiving the food shipments from inside Russia that it is due, "the only possible source of food to the region in January-February 1992" is imports. He lists what foods the city needs. He then says that some "enterprises and organizations" in the city have exportable commodities and asks for authorization to export them in the types and quantities he proceeds to list in the letter.[7] In other words, Putin is asking that the federal body merely rubber-stamp deals that had already been arranged. Private businessmen had come to Putin with proposals of what they had already lined up: this amount of these specific metals in exchange for these foods. The letter to Aven does not indicate where the commodities came from, where the foodstuffs will come from, or, most important, who the people are who devised this scheme.

Although the provenance of the commodities was not specified, judging by the fact that they included things like aluminum, copper, and rare earth metals—Putin listed "tantalum, niobium, gadolinium, cerium, zirconium, yttrium, scandium, and ytterbium"—they in all likelihood came from old Soviet defense sector enterprises that were desperate for cash. The traders who approached Putin were involved in what would become a classic survival mechanism in the post-Soviet Russian economy.

Typically, a state enterprise, often a defense enterprise, would find itself sitting on large stockpiles of valuable metals and other material inputs. (Some of these stockpiles would be part of the mobilization reserves or strategic materials the enterprise was supposed to use in an emergency or during wartime.) At the same time, the enterprise would have no commercial orders for its finished products in the new Russian market economy and thus no cash to cover its payroll and other ongoing expenses. So the enterprise director would try to sell off the stockpiles to generate some revenue. There were limited prospects of making a lucrative sale on the thoroughly depressed domestic market. The key to making the scheme work was to find a way to export the goods for hard currency. This required someone with a network of foreign contacts as well as the means and access to the infrastructure to ship the commodity abroad. In addition, of course, the enterprise or the middleman needed to have the legal right (in the form of an export license) to carry out the required transaction. The sellers at the enterprise typically sold the stockpiled commodities at a fraction of the international market value. But given the chronic cash shortages they were usually satisfied with the price.

Thus, what Putin was offering was an opportunity to profit from the discrepancy between Russia's asset-rich but market infrastructure–poor economy. Physically, the country was flush with valuable assets controlled by sellers who were desperate but had only very limited pos-sibilities to realize the market value of what they owned. The sellers were happy to sell off their commodities at a mere fraction of their true market value because they had no other option. For someone who had the know-how and contacts and who could arrange the transportation infrastructure to ship those commodities abroad, the profit potential was enormous. For such a person, receiving a contract to carry out the deal—and obtaining a legal license to export the commodities—would be valuable indeed. If everything had gone according to what Putin alleged the plan to be, it would have been "win-win-win." The middle-men profit, Putin gets more food for the city, and the defense or other enterprises that controlled the commodities also ended up with cash to help them survive for another day.

The problem, of course, was that somewhere along the line, things did not work as they should have. Again, as the Salye commission's inves-tigation found, it is hard to find anything that *did* work. The contracts were poorly drawn up. Whether that was intentional or not was unclear. Who ended up with the oil and other commodities was also not clear. In any event, the ultimate goal of all the complex transactions—food—did not wind up in St. Petersburg. (At least some of it appears to have been shipped to Moscow.) And then there was the critical issue of the export licenses. They had been issued illegally—before Putin had actually received authorization from Moscow to issue them.

Almost a decade later, in his own interviews on the subject of the food scandal and Salye's investigation, Vladimir Putin denied there had been a "criminal offense." He stated only that "some of the firms did not uphold the main condition of the contract—they didn't deliver food from abroad, or at least they didn't import the full amounts. They reneged on their commitments to the city." Putin brushed off the charges of personal corruption that had been thrown at him by Salye but conceded that "the city didn't do everything it could have done." He continued:

We needed to work more closely with law enforcement and use a stick to beat those firms until they delivered what had been prom-ised. But it was pointless to take them to court. They just vanished into thin air. . . . You remember those days. Phony offices were pop-ping up everywhere, financial pyramid schemes. . . . We just didn't expect that. . . . But you have to understand, we [in the mayor's office] weren't involved in trade. The Committee for External Relations didn't do any trading itself. It didn't buy anything. It didn't sell anything. It wasn't a foreign trade organization. . . . We didn't have the right to grant licenses.[8]

This is a set of truly remarkable statements. To take the last point first: The fact that Putin's committee did not have the authority to issue licenses but did so nevertheless was one of the principal charges brought against him by Marina Salye and the city council. More important is his overall reaction to the episode. Putin claims that private businessmen cheated him and the citizens of the city and that the city was powerless to do anything about it. Many in Russia at that time who were warning of the dire consequences for Russia of a market economy used such incidents as grist for their mill. Putin, however, did not react by rejecting private enterprise. But he also did not draw the conclusion that this episode showed how important it was to strengthen the formal legal system so that it might not be "pointless to take them to court." Instead, his words about "working more closely with law enforcement"—who could use the "stick"—without going to court suggest he saw the answer in *informal* methods, the kind of methods his KGB case officer training had schooled him in. Indeed, his subsequent actions confirm that that was exactly the direction he would take.

The food scandal was perhaps the most profound experience of Putin's career, even if it has never been fully explored. People had made money, this was evident. Putin and his schemes also had not delivered on an important matter for his city, St. Petersburg, at a time of crisis. This was also evident. Even in the most charitable of scenarios, Mr. Putin, the future Russian president, had been duped. In the most uncharitable assessment of Marina Salye and her colleagues, Mr. Putin was nothing but a crook who had used his official position to benefit a set of private interests including (in their view) his own. The food scandal affected Putin in multiple dimensions in a remarkably short period of time. It resulted in a huge political crisis for the mayor's office—underscored by Anatoly Sobchak being summoned to Moscow to explain the situation. Mr. Putin escaped being fired and disgraced only by the intervention and direct assistance of people to whom he would be indebted, and closely tied, for the rest of his political career. It also reinforced core elements of some of his identities.

Mayor Sobchak stopped the federal auditor Yury Boldyrev from pursuing the matter further in Moscow. Dmitry Medvedev, the future Russian president and then a young St. Petersburg lawyer, helped to create a legal defense for Putin to refute the accusations of corruption by the city council.[9] Pyotr Aven, another native of St. Petersburg, wrote a letter from the Russian federal government stating, after the fact, that Putin had the authority to issue the necessary foreign trade licenses to cover the transactions.[10] Aven subsequently left the Russian government to embark on a high-profile career in banking. He would quickly become one of Russia's richest, as well as best-connected, men.[11] In addition, Putin reportedly received assistance from three other well-connected St. Petersburg officials. These officials asserted that they had reviewed the Salye report, as well as the documentation prepared and provided by the St. Petersburg mayor's office, and could find no sign of impropriety in Putin's activities. They were Sergei Stepashin, who was then in charge of the St. Petersburg city and Leningrad oblast branch of the Russian Ministry of Security and Internal Affairs; Stepashin's deputy Viktor Cherkesov; and Nikolai Patrushev, who was then an official in the St. Petersburg security ministry. Stepashin would go on to serve as both the Russian justice and interior minister, as well as prime minister in the brief interlude in 1999 between Yevgeny Primakov and Vladimir Putin. Sergei Stepashin is now the chairman of the Russian Accounts Chamber, the same federal audit agency where Yury Boldyrev worked in the early 1990s and which first investigated the food scandal case.[12] Cherkesov would later work directly for Putin when Putin headed the FSB in 1998. He then became President Putin's plenipotentiary to the Northwest Federal District, the larger regional administrative entity that includes St. Petersburg. Cherkesov has since headed the Russian counter-narcotics agency. Patrushev became head of the FSB after Putin and then the secretary of the Russian Security Council.

At this point in his career, dealing with St. Petersburg's food crisis was by far the most significant personal responsibility Mr. Putin had held. Only facing down a mob that was trying to storm the building where he worked, during his KGB service in Dresden in 1989, comes close to this experience. Given the very personal as well as the broader

historical memory of mass starvation in Leningrad during the war, securing food supplies for St. Petersburg was a significant responsibility, which
he should have felt particularly keenly. Mr. Putin the Survivalist knew the
importance of Russia's natural resources. The country had no money in
the early 1990s. Its strategic stockpiles and financial reserves had been
depleted. But Russia always had commodities; the real challenge was to
figure out how to realize their value. The food scandal taught Putin a very
important lesson in this regard. Putin learned from his dealings with the
feckless middlemen that the mere physical presence of resources or access
to resources was not enough. If they were no longer owned by the state,
or if the state was not strong enough to commandeer them, then the revenues they generated could easily be diverted. To turn commodities into
real value for a specifically defined purpose, you had to have direct control
over them in some meaningful way. The key to handling resources was
not control of their physical existence, but control over their purchase,
transportation and sale, and the routing of the resulting revenue streams.

Ultimately, the commodities-for-food deal that lay behind the food
scandal was Putin's first real encounter with private business. It inevitably shaped his attitude toward the business sector and business people.
In spite of his KGB background, Putin was still a virtual novice in his
position of broker and fixer for businesses in the city. He clearly thought
he could make things happen quickly and get results through direct
deals. He had the money. He had some educational and theoretical background in foreign trade from Leningrad State University and his time in
the KGB. He obviously knew men who claimed to have access to the
resources as well as the knowledge of international markets to conduct
barter deals, again possibly through his KGB foreign trade connections.
Making these kinds of deals would have been extremely difficult, even
impossible, if he had operated only through the city government's channels. But the entire endeavor failed. Putin had made a serious mistake.
Putin's German biographer Alexander Rahr notes that after the failure
of the food deals, Putin realized he had been "overly trustful" of private
businessmen.[13] To this day, Putin seems to think that he suffers from a
tendency to trust other people "too easily." In 2009, when asked by a
Bloomberg journalist what he considered his main character flaw, Putin
immediately replied with a single word—*doverchivost'*, "a tendency to
be overly trustful."[14]

POLITICS AND BUSINESS IN ST. PETERSBURG

The food deal was not the only incident in which Putin felt betrayed by private business. At the same time that Putin acted as an operative on behalf of the KGB inside the Sobchak camp, Sobchak himself was deploying Putin on various missions—including political tasks. As early as 1993, Sobchak began assigning Putin to manage various political campaigns. Most of these were unsuccessful, and to such an extent that some of the failures seem to have been intentional; or the intent did not seem entirely in synch with their outcomes. For example, Sobchak instructed Putin to join Yegor Gaidar's party, *Vybor Rossii* (Russia's Choice), and to manage its campaign in the city for the December 1993 Russian Duma elections. Meanwhile, Sobchak had his own political party, resulting in the somewhat absurd situation where Putin and Sobchak, who were ostensibly part of the same team, simultaneously led two different liberal-democratic electoral campaigns. It is not clear what Sobchak really intended Putin to do with Vybor Rossii. Whatever the intended purpose, Gaidar's party got around 27 percent of the vote, but Sobchak's own party did not make the five-percent cutoff in the election.[15]

Putin's string of failures and dubious successes as a political manager in St. Petersburg continued in the next round of Russian Duma elections. In December 1995, Sobchak instructed Putin to join the party Nash dom Rossiya (NDR), which was led by incumbent Russian prime minister Viktor Chernomyrdin and was deemed Russia's "party of power." Putin became its regional head for St. Petersburg, and Chernomyrdin subsequently appointed Putin to NDR's politburo—or national political council. In St. Petersburg, however, NDR came in a disappointing third in the parliamentary elections, behind the Yabloko party and Vybor Rossii.[16] Putin's lack of success in his initial forays into Russian politics did not stop Sobchak from turning to him again. The 1995 Duma elections were barely over when the next political contest came along—the St. Petersburg mayoral elections, which were scheduled for June 1996, the same time as the Russian presidential election.

By all accounts, including his own, Sobchak seemed set on retaining the mayor's office.[17] He appointed Vladimir Putin head of his reelection committee. According to Alexander Rahr, it was Putin who came up with the idea of holding the election four weeks earlier than originally scheduled, on the basis that this would reduce the time for opponents to organize. Putin got Moscow's approval to shift the election date and, with much greater effort, persuaded local St. Petersburg politicians to agree. In the end, however, Putin bungled the campaign. He thought the main threat to Sobchak would come from "radical" democrats like Yury Boldyrev—the former Russian deputy auditor who had investigated the St. Petersburg food scandal before helping to create the Yabloko party. Boldyrev was presenting himself as an anticorruption candidate in the St. Petersburg election. It would clearly have been particularly damaging for Putin personally if Boldyrev, who had inside knowledge of the food scandal, succeeded Anatoly Sobchak and decided to clean house. Whatever the primary motivation was, Putin focused the Sobchak campaign's efforts against Boldyrev. He ignored the candidate who eventually won: former first deputy mayor of St. Petersburg Vladimir Yakovlev.[18]

In retrospect, it is hard to imagine how Putin could have ignored Yakovlev even if he were fixated on the potential threat from Boldyrev. Yakovlev was a former close associate of Putin's and co-member of Sobchak's team. He had shared responsibility for the economy with Putin and Alexei Kudrin. He also had the backing of a group of influential Russian political figures in the mayoral race. Although Prime Minister Chernomyrdin officially backed Sobchak, as a favor in return for Sobchak's help with the December 1995 Duma election, other Moscow power elites opposed his reelection. A trio of Kremlin insiders—Alexander Korzhakov, a former KGB general and head of Boris Yeltsin's Presidential Security Service, along with former First Deputy Prime Minister Oleg Soskovets, who was heading up Yeltsin's 1996 reelection campaign, and then FSB head Mikhail Barsukov—were conspiring to find an eventual successor to the ailing Yeltsin. They would need support in Russia's regions for their anointed candidate when the time came. St. Petersburg, the second city, was crucial. The trio knew they would never win Sobchak over to their side. Indeed, Sobchak was likely to be a strong presidential candidate himself if he won reelection in St. Petersburg. So these three backed Yakovlev. In addition to the Korzhakov-Soskovets-Barsukov clique, Sobchak was opposed by another man with his own presidential ambitions, Yury Luzhkov, Moscow's powerful mayor. Luzhkov, too, saw Yakovlev as a man who might support rather than challenge him when the time came.[19]

Yakovlev secured money as well as political support from Moscow. Sobchak's campaign ran out of money two months before the election. The Sobchak camp was desperate. Alexander Rahr writes that "Putin became noticeably more nervous" as the campaign progressed. "In an agitated discussion with Sobchak, he promised his mentor: 'I will force all the key businessmen in the city, who have profited from our support in the privatization of city property, to publicly declare their loyalty to us!'"[20] Putin then summoned those businessmen to the city government's official dacha, where he made his pitch for them to donate to Sobchak's campaign. They declined. Having failed to bring in support from the St. Petersburg business elite, Putin turned to smaller fry. He scheduled a fundraiser with owners of small and medium-size businesses. Again, this ended in a fiasco when Sobchak forgot the time of the meeting and did not make it to the event at all.

Putin went on to suffer the humiliation of watching a well-known St. Petersburg mafioso succeed in fundraising for the mayor where he had failed. The mobster invited all the small businessmen to donate $2,000 each to his "Foundation for the Support of the Mayor." They did not refuse the gangster's offer.[21] The real *Banditskiy Piterburg* prevailed over the KGB campaign chief and the mayor's fixer. Perhaps Putin was so embarrassed by the Sobchak no-show that he did not dare to make any further pitches on the mayor's behalf. Whatever the case may be, Putin ignored all of these dimensions to the story of the 1996 St. Petersburg election in his autobiographical interviews. The lesson from all of this, however, must have sunk in deeply. The next time that Putin sat down with a group of big businessmen, he would not simply depend on their good will for past favors. He would have leverage, significant, real leverage. He would be like that mafioso. They would not be able to refuse, and if they tried, there would be consequences.

THE "ZUBKOV SCHEME"

What is puzzling about this episode is that Putin actually did have leverage against the leading St. Petersburg businessmen. After the food scandal, Putin had set up a system that would give him the means to enforce future deals with private businessmen and even to exert control over them. This method was to gather information about firms' and individual businessmen's financial and tax transactions and to guard that information very closely. In his capacity as deputy mayor, Putin ordered all enterprises in the city to register directly with the Committee for External Relations, and "with the assistance of the local tax inspectorate, headed by his former deputy [Viktor] Zubkov," Putin then officially checked out the companies' finances.[22] To what extent Putin and Zubkov tried to conceal their scheme is not clear, but it did not go unnoticed. St. Petersburg City Council member Alexander Belyaev is on the record as accusing Putin of using "secret service methods" to control the city's businesses.[23]

The key question is, what exactly was the mechanism Putin and Zubkov used to exert leverage? The various accounts suggest that it involved a degree of blackmail. To the extent that Putin and Zubkov collected financial data that clearly indicated non-payment of taxes and other misdeeds, they had an ideal weapon with which to enforce business deals between private companies and the city as defined by the mayor's office. They had only to let the companies know that they were in possession of the incriminating information but that they had not turned it over to the law enforcement agencies and would not turn it over as long as the businessmen behaved properly. This was the type of classic "secret service method" that council member Belyaev was referring to. It was precisely the approach Putin would have been taught, and would have practiced, in the KGB.

There is undoubtedly much more behind Vladimir Putin's dealings with the St. Petersburg business circles in the 1990s than we will ever know. As obscure as these facts and events may be, they nonetheless foreshadow what Putin would be doing a few years later when he came to Moscow. The scheme Putin and Zubkov devised would have gone into operation by late 1993 or early 1994, although the plan itself was likely hatched earlier. The key element was Viktor Zubkov's appointment to head the local St. Petersburg tax administration. This is a remarkable story that has never been fully explained in any of the Putin biographies, in spite of Zubkov's very close and continued association with Putin over two decades in both St. Petersburg and Moscow.

In September 2007, Putin took the first public steps to orchestrate what came to be known as the tandem—that is, moving himself to the post of prime minister while allowing Dmitry Medvedev to serve as president. Putin needed an absolutely trustworthy individual to occupy the prime minister's office during the sensitive period when he transferred key powers from the presidency to the prime minister's office in anticipation of his assumption of that post. The one man Putin knew he could trust as caretaker of such extraordinary powers was Viktor Zubkov. During the September 2007 Valdai Discussion Club dinner session, Putin was effusive in his praise for Viktor Zubkov and eager to explain—at length—why he had chosen him to step in as interim prime minister. Zubkov, Putin explained, running through his entire biography, was "a man with great professional and life experience. Essentially, he's a true professional, an effective administrator with good character, but at the same time someone with a great deal of experience in production." Viktor Zubkov, he said, is an "exceptionally honest man." In all the positions he served, Putin stressed, Viktor Zubkov was chosen "for his personal qualities—he is an exceptionally decent man. . . . Not once, I would like to emphasize, did Viktor Zubkov abuse this trust."[24]

Zubkov—a generation older than Putin—was initially trained as a farm manager in the Soviet agricultural sector. He rose to a high level in the technocracy of the centrally planned economy in the Leningrad region. He appears to have been originally brought on to the St. Petersburg mayor's team in 1992 as a deputy to Putin in connection with the food crisis. Zubkov was able to use his contacts in the regional farming sector to get food to the city after the private businessmen reneged on their deals. (Another version of Zubkov's usefulness for the mayor's office was that he was in charge of arranging farmsteads for Soviet Red Army officers returning from East Germany.) Then, in November 1993, Viktor Zubkov, a man who had spent his entire career in the Soviet bureaucracy as a manager and administrator in the farm sector, suddenly vaulted from being "the deputy of a deputy" (Putin) to become head of the St. Petersburg department of the Federal Tax Inspectorate and deputy head of the State Tax Service for St. Petersburg. In other words, a third-rank local official with no background whatsoever in taxes or finance became the top tax official in St. Petersburg. Perhaps equally remarkable, despite the curious background to his appointment, Zubkov quickly established a reputation in St. Petersburg for efficiency and incorruptibility in tax collection. He was famous for his no-nonsense approach. His nickname was "Hand-Over-a-Million-Vic." According to one journalist,

Zubkov was known for his motto: "It's really very simple. Just pay your taxes and sleep well at night."[25]

With Viktor Zubkov's help, Putin collected damning information on companies and individuals and kept it safe. As a result, Vladimir Putin now had the possibility of offering businessmen protection against the tax authorities, who were . . . Zubkov himself. This paradigmatic protection scheme would become a hallmark of Putin's approach when he moved to Moscow and had to deal with another set of businessmen, the Russian oligarchs. The incorruptibility of the ultimate enforcer would be crucial to cutting and keeping any special deal with Putin. Only days before Vladimir Putin was named prime minister in August 1999, Zubkov was called to Moscow to serve as a deputy finance minister. When Putin moved up the leadership ladder from prime minister to president, Zubkov went on to help him establish the Russian Financial Monitoring Agency (*Rosfinmonitoring*, RFM), the monopoly national-level repository for the most sensitive financial information about Russia's businesses.[26]

RETURN TO THE ROOTS: "THE MOST COMPLICATED WORK"

The overarching context for all of these schemes in St. Petersburg is the set of skills Putin acquired in his first real job in the KGB. Although at various times throughout his 15-year KGB career he may have engaged in espionage and conducted some analysis, Vladimir Putin's principal function was neither spy nor analyst. Until the early 1990s when he began government administrative service in the mayor's office of St. Petersburg (at the behest of the KGB), Putin primarily served as a case officer. The practical skills he possessed all derived from that basic occupation. Those skills were best described by Putin himself in a revealing interview early in his presidency. In June 2001, President Putin held a special press conference for the heads of U.S. news bureaus in Moscow. The head of *Newsweek*'s Moscow bureau at the time, Christian Caryl, asked the final question in the session. Noting that Putin had himself talked about his pride in working for the KGB, Caryl asked what it was about his professional training in the KGB that had proved most useful for him as the leader of Russia. Putin replied and highlighted two critical skills:

[The] main thing is the experience of working with people. . . .
To be able to work with people effectively, you have to be able to
establish a dialogue, contact; you have to activate everything that
is the best in your partner. If you want to achieve results, you have
to respect your partner. You need to make that person an ally; you
have to make that person feel that you and he have something
that unites you, that you have common goals. That is the skill, if
you will, which is the most important—and, of course, one that
is not so removed from the first order of business in international
affairs, [as well as] one that is first of all a skill for working inside
the country. . . . [The second skill is] the ability to work with a
large amount of information. That's a skill that is cultivated in the
analytical services and special services, the skill of selecting what
is most important from a huge flood of information, of processing
information and being able to use it.[27]

The ability to "work with people" and "work with information" was
and would remain key to Putin's career. This was also not Putin's first
reference to the skills in which he took such pride. In *Ot pervogo litsa*,
in 2000, Putin encouraged the authors to include some comments from
his close personal friend from his early Leningrad days, Sergei Roldugin.
The interviewers asked Roldugin whether he knew his friend Vladimir's
true occupation. Not exactly, Roldugin replied:

Vovka told me right away that he worked for the KGB. Practically
from the beginning. Maybe he shouldn't have done that. He used
to tell some people that he worked for the police. . . . I never asked
Volodya anything about his work. Of course I was interested: what
was it like? But I do remember very clearly: there was one time
when I, in spite of myself, decided to find out what was going on
with some special operation. I couldn't get a word out. . . . So then I
asked him: "I am a cellist. I play the cello. I could never be a surgeon.
But I'm a good cellist. So what's your occupation? I know you're an
intelligence officer. I don't know what that means. Who are you?
What do you know how to do?" . . . And he replied: "I'm a specialist in communicating with people [*Ya—spetsialist po obshcheniyu s
lyud'mi*]." And that was the end of our conversation.[28]

"Communicating with people," or also "working with people," has a dual meaning in KGB jargon. On the one hand, it covers the effort to monitor the sentiments of the population at large, in order to preempt and accommodate discontent. This is the "focus-group" approach, first famously suggested to Tsar Nicholas I in the 1820s by the founder and most famous head of the tsarist secret police, General Count Alexander Khristoforovich von Benckendorff, who was trying to head off a repetition of the 1825 Decembrist revolt.[29] Von Benckendorff told the tsar that he and his colleagues would find out what was on people's minds—*izuchat' sostoyaniye umov lyudey*—and thus they would determine what they might have to do to keep the people content.

For the intelligence officer the most important function of "working with people" is to study the psychology of one's counterparts. For the case officer, this is also a necessary step in recruiting and running an individual agent. It means studying the minds of the targets, finding their vulnerabilities, and figuring out how to use them. For Putin and his KGB mentors, and his entire cohort in the KGB in the 1970s and 1980s, the dual meaning of *rabota s lyud'mi* (working with people) was not a problem. Everyone, from the concrete individual to the masses, was a target of the operative.

ANDROPOV'S NEW KGB:
WORKING WITH THE CONCRETE INDIVIDUAL

"Working with people" was the hallmark of the KGB under Yury Andropov. The key question for Andropov's KGB was: Would their targets simply be repressed, imprisoned, or destroyed; or would they be cultivated and recruited? The former approach was fairly straightforward and required no special skill, just brutality. It was also, according to Andropov and others, short-sighted. The latter approach offered much greater potential rewards—but it was a difficult task requiring skill, delicacy, patience, and, importantly, leverage. "Working with people is the most complicated work on the face of the earth," Putin once said in a meeting with young Russian law enforcement officials in 2003.[30]

Soon after taking over the KGB, Andropov announced plans to create an entirely new department, to be designated the "Directorate for the Struggle against Subversive Ideological Activity"—the 5th Directorate. The 5th Directorate set the tone for the KGB that Putin joined as part of the Andropov levy of the 1970s.[31] Putin also may have worked in the 5th Directorate for at least part of his career. Filipp Bobkov, head of the new department, described the background to the new approach in his 1995 memoir.[32] According to Bobkov, the liberalization of the Soviet system that had followed Stalin's death in 1953, and especially the revelations of Stalin-era crimes that came in Nikita Khrushchev's famous "secret speech" of 1956, created a different context for the KGB's work. Pure repression was now seen as counterproductive. By the time Andropov took over the KGB, spontaneous protests had erupted throughout the Soviet Union in response to repression as well other failings of the system. Andropov himself, who had been the Soviet ambassador to Hungary during the revolt of 1956, knew all too well how far things could go and how difficult they were to stop once protests picked up momentum.

Andropov's more proactive approach to working with people was frequently put to the test. Bobkov relates one incident that took place in the city of Rubtsovsk in Siberia's Altai Krai in 1969. A truck driver who had been jailed, apparently for drunken driving, died in custody. Practically the entire town turned out to protest his death. A colonel, I. T. Tsupak, from the KGB 5th Directorate was immediately dispatched to Rubtsovsk to address the situation. By the time Tsupak arrived more than 10,000 people had assembled in the main square, with agitators whipping them up into an increasingly emotional state. Colonel Tsupak went straight to the middle of the crowd. He announced that he had been sent by Andropov to hear their complaints and communicate them to Moscow. He succeeded in calming the mob. Bobkov wrote: "You might ask, was this [that is, going out and responding to complaints] really a job for the KGB? No, not really. But no one else was doing it." He continued: "[Whenever these protests erupted] Andropov recommended that we pursue a very cautious and flexible policy. Meanwhile, there were many people who were calling for harsh repressive measures. . . . But Andropov . . . tried to restrain his people from taking risky steps and to refrain from the use of extreme measures."[33] The Rubtsovsk incident and the intervention of Colonel Tsupak are reminiscent of Putin's 2009 personal intervention in the factory monotown of Pikalyovo near St. Petersburg to address the local complaints and calm things down.

More fundamentally, Andropov advocated preemptive action directed at prominent individuals, not just the masses. The so-called intelligentsia—artists, writers, engineers and white collar professionals—were also key. What was needed in the USSR in this critical post-Stalinist period, wrote Bobkov, was "broad-ranging communication with people [*obshcheniye s lyud'mi*]."[34] Here, Andropov's "new" KGB and the 5th Directorate were at odds not only with the hardliners elsewhere in the agency but also with the Communist Party leadership. Bobkov describes the clash between this self-described enlightened wing of the KGB and the party leadership over the issue of banning certain writers, including famous émigrés like Vladimir Nabokov. Andropov tried to bring up this subject in a report to the Soviet politburo but was told that this was not in the purview of the KGB. Bobkov writes:

> But we understood perfectly well: sooner or later we'd have to deal with this all the same, since the more prohibitions you introduce, the sharper would be the reaction of the intelligentsia. And in the end, there was no doubt that there would be people who would be prepared to break the law. So it was inevitable that we would have to get involved.[35]

In his book, Bobkov provided what he considered to be a particularly successful example of the preemptive approach in which he got personally involved. This was the case of dissident historian Roy Medvedev. Medvedev's articles were being published in the West by anticommunist publishers. Medvedev had already been kicked out of the Communist Party. KGB officers had talked to him and warned him of the consequences of going too far in his criticisms of the system and his foreign publications—but to no avail. When Medvedev began to slander Soviet leader and Communist Party general secretary Leonid Brezhnev personally, the party pushed the KGB to act. The party started a whispering campaign that Andropov was actually protecting Roy Medvedev personally and using him against Brezhnev in the pursuit of some internal power struggle. So Bobkov (by his account) had no choice but to take matters into his own hands. He invited himself to Medvedev's apartment and, over tea, had a long talk with the dissident:

> [During the course of that conversation] I saw both the weaknesses and the strengths of my interlocutor's logic. I understood where he

was right and where he was mistaken. For me it was very useful to know that. I was happy with the result of the meeting: Medvedev stopped his collaboration with publishers who were not linked to [Western] Communist parties. He stopped publishing his journal, *Political Diary,* altogether. Henceforth, Medvedev dealt only with the Communist Party press and began to lean noticeably towards "pluralism within the framework of socialism." . . . For me the most important thing of all was that Medvedev began working with Western Communists. Now we had other channels through which we could influence his undesirable attacks.[36]

The Medvedev affair, wrote Bobkov, was a prime example of how critical it was to be able "to work with people [*rabotat' s lyud'mi*] and use their potential in ideological work."[37] Bobkov's description of his intervention with Roy Medvedev is a classic illustration of the work of an "enlightened" secret service like the Andropov-era KGB. In theory, the goal was to persuade the target, in one-on-one exchanges, to give loyalty to your cause. In practice, the persuasion could almost never work without the threat of coercion or some other unpleasant consequences. The actual realization of the coercive threat was generally not desired— just as in the case of Putin and Zubkov's repository of St. Petersburg financial information and the Russian Financial Monitoring Agency, the preference was to keep damaging information closely held in reserve.

The ideal recruitment outcome for the KGB recruiter or case officer was essentially the conclusion of a mutually advantageous deal. The deal was enforced by the threat—a threat that, if carried out, would completely destroy the recruit. The case officer had to have a monopoly on this threat. The deal could not work if the target could turn to someone else for protection. It is possible that during at least part of his KGB career, Vladimir Putin may also have been involved in the recruitment of double agents, which added an extra dimension of complexity. For the most part, people who became double agents were not inclined to support the recruiter's cause or were even indifferent or opposed to it. If Putin was engaged in any of this activity, the most likely venue would have been in East Germany from 1985 to 1990, in Operation Luch if that was indeed one of its primary purposes.[38] Recruiting and running double agents is a much more difficult task than that faced by the ordinary case officer. It requires even more patience and subtlety, but also stronger threats and more ruthlessness.[39]

THE KGB—"A PLUS FOR A POLITICIAN"

There are other references to the work of Andropov's KGB that relate more directly to Putin's activities during his period of service, as well as to his time in the "active reserve" when he was assigned by the KGB to work with and infiltrate the Sobchak camp in St. Petersburg in the 1990s. In a 2000 interview, the deputy governor of Perm oblast in the Russian Urals, Valery Alexandrovich Shchukin, talked of his own career in the KGB.[40] He also stressed (as the title of the article suggested) that KGB service was "a plus for a politician."

Shchukin, a couple of years older than Putin, was a career KGB agent who then served as an "officer in the active reserve" as deputy governor of Perm, just as Putin served as deputy mayor under Anatoly Sobchak. Like Putin, Shchukin was brought into the KGB as part of the Andropov levy. He also attended the KGB academy at about the same time as Mr. Putin. In the local Perm newspaper, *Zvezda*, Shchukin explained what the Andropov levy was:

[M]y initial profession and education are not typical [for being recruited by the KGB]. But my brother had been serving in the agency for a long time by then, and thus my application was examined from cover to cover. Besides, not only metallurgists and miners encourage family dynasties. The fact that it all was happening in the Andropov period, when we had another one of the Party-*Komsomol* 'levies' into the KGB, was also important. The priority task of this levy was not to allow the secret services to gain supremacy over the Party. That is why another dozen or so other high-ranking *Komsomol* activists studied with me at the Higher School of the KGB.[41]

Shchukin said that he had been offered his position as Perm's deputy governor in 1996 while he was still active in the KGB. This was at the initiative of the governor himself, not the KGB. His superiors at the agency had then moved him into the "active reserve," although he had resigned from the reserve after a year. The newspaper asked Shchukin what it meant to be an "officer of the active reserve"—noting that "Putin also had that status for one year, when he was working for the St. Petersburg mayor's office. . . ." Shchukin responded: "It means that a person, while not on the KGB payroll nevertheless remains on the staff list, has access to operative information, is eligible for promotion, and is obligated to carry out assignments and orders from headquarters, including secret, confidential orders, but does not have the right to inform his superiors at his civilian workplace about such orders."[42]

The interviewer suggested that this arrangement seemed to put the reserve officer into the position of "infiltrator." That, said Shchukin, was "a bit too crude," but he allowed "that there are a lot of legal and ethical problems involved." Putin, on the other hand, does not seem to have expressed any particular discomfort with these aspects of his work as both an operative and a deputy mayor in St. Petersburg in the same period.[43] Indeed, Mr. Putin has repeatedly stressed—like Shchukin—the very positive role his intelligence career played in his life and the way it prepared him for his political positions. In one early interview on the topic in December 2000, for example, just a few months after Shchukin's own interview with the Perm newspaper, Putin was asked by journalists from the Canadian CBC and CTV channels, the Canadian *Globe and Mail* newspaper, and Russia's RTR TV channel if he was "annoyed" by being asked about his previous work in the KGB as a case officer. Putin responded by referring to former U.S. Secretary of State Henry Kissinger:

Why do you think I am annoyed? I have never said I was annoyed. I don't know if it is appropriate to recall my first meeting with Mr. Kissinger for whom I have great respect. When I told him that I started my career as an intelligence officer, he paused and then said: "All decent people started their careers with the intelligence. Me too." I am ashamed to say that was something I hadn't known before. . . . So what? There is nothing you can do about it. I know that some leaders in other countries, even U.S. presidents, once worked with the intelligence. I served my country and I did it honestly and I have nothing to repent about. And I must say that, strange though it may sound, I have never broken the laws of other countries. It was an interesting and a highly professional job. It played a positive role in my life. It was interesting work.[44]

Identifying, recruiting, and running agents is done on a very intimate, one-to-one basis. But as Russian president, Vladimir Putin has had to apply his case officer tradecraft and skill set to an entire country, to secure loyalty to the cause and to enlist every Russian in the service of the state. How can that possibly work? Mr. Putin cannot hope to co-opt every single Russian individually. As the recruiter and Case Officer for an entire nation, Mr. Putin has had to have different tools at his disposal. As we have already discussed, defining history has been one powerful instrument in Vladimir Putin's toolbox along with the adoption of his various fake guises in his PR stunts as president and prime minister.

Using history and public relations, Putin has scaled his role as Case Officer for the individual up to the national level to recruit specific groups to his cause. In speeches and writings, beginning with the December 1999 Millennium Message, Putin has set out to determine which groups' history will be part of the inclusive Russian myth and which groups risk finding themselves outside the collective history if they do not conform or withdraw their support for his ideas or policies. The ultimate implicit threat is the risk of groups (like opposition protesters during the 2012 presidential election campaign) finding themselves designated as "them"—*chuzhiye* (aliens)—rather than "us," *nashi* (ours). Putin's various performance pieces as a biker, an outdoorsman, a fireman, and his meetings with workers on factory floors or in factory monotowns simultaneously embrace different Russian groups and social classes as *nashi* and appeal directly to them for political support.

PUTIN AS PRESIDENT:
WORKING THE MASSES THROUGH THE *HOT LINE*

One of the most specific features of Mr. Putin's mass Case Officer approach has been his propensity for engaging one-on-one with the Russian people in televised or recorded public settings. These include lengthy press conferences and the so-called *Hot Line*, the annual TV call-in show where the Russian masses can listen to President or Prime Minister Putin respond and tailor his answers to the questions of a specific individual.[45] The initial question and answer portions of the annual Valdai Discussion Club meeting between foreign experts and Putin have also been televised since 2004, with the resulting Russian and English transcripts generally made available on official websites.

These sessions give a whole new definition and dimension to von Benckendorff's early concept of focus groups. Instead of Fidel Castro–style speeches and monologues before a mass audience, Putin takes the Case Officer approach. He interacts directly and engages in a dialogue with individuals for hours on end. Putin approaches each of these interactions as a hands-on recruiter. He views other individuals as sources of raw intelligence—information. The questions they ask are the information. They provide insight into their state of mind and their concerns. His answers are intended to address the issues people raise and win them over to his point of view. As Putin told *Newsweek*'s Christian Caryl in June 2001, he takes great pride in selecting the key elements from a huge flood of information, then processing them and using them.[46]

Putin has, in fact, been explicit about the purpose of these sessions right from the outset of his presidency. During his first official *Hot Line* in December 2001 he personally identified this format of interacting with the Russian population as the prime example of "communicating with people" and soliciting information. In the course of the December 2001 session one of the callers praised the format of the *Hot Line* and asked him to comment on it. Putin said:

Indeed, this form of dialogue between the head of state and the population is unprecedented. . . . But, knowing the demand for dialogue, I believe this form of communication is an acceptable form of communication with the people, and the head of state is duty-bound to communicate with his people, to listen to them and hear them, and there should be feedback. I often go to the regions and I see that people have such a need. . . . I must tell you that this is just as important to me as to those who ask these questions, because I can get a feel for what's happening, get a feel for what is on people's minds. And I should tell you that our analysis of the incoming information shows that priorities are changing: yesterday or the day before there were one set of priorities, and today they are changing. Of course, I won't be able to answer all the questions: there are more than half a million of them. When the meeting was announced, 300,000 telephone calls were coming in every day.

So it's hard to answer all the questions. But I would like to thank all those who are taking part because it provides a good sociological base which will be processed 100 percent and will be taken into account in our work.[47]

Putin assured the caller that he would "try to see to it that this is not the last such event," and he has since continued with the *Hot Line* format every year. In each case, as Putin underscored, the telephone lines have been flooded with calls in advance of the event. The Kremlin has deployed veritable armies of receptionists and analysts to take the calls, record the questions, and distill and categorize them to determine what people are thinking. In engaging with a select, representative number of the questions in the live format, Putin assures people that he and the state can solve their problems at the individual as well as the larger group level. The implicit message is that Putin and his team are on top of all the issues. There is no need for people to self-organize to solve their own problems, or to take to the streets to protest. Just call Putin and he will fix it.

The *Hot Line* format encapsulates the dual aspect of *rabota s lyud'mi* that Filipp Bobkov explains in his book. *Rabota s lyud'mi* is about engaging with the masses, like Colonel Tsupak in Rubtsovsk, and engaging one-on-one with individuals, like Bobkov inviting himself for tea with Medvedev. With the *Hot Line,* Putin engages with the mass audiences in the television studio who have been brought there to witness and participate in the session, and with the even larger mass audience of the Russian population watching from home or the workplace. He also engages one-on-one with the individual callers and their questions, and with the individual sitting in his or her living room, perhaps with a cup of tea, in front of the television set.

It is important to note that Filipp Bobkov's stories—just like many of Putin's autobiographical statements—are mainly after-the-fact anecdotes, and possibly even myths. We cannot know for sure if any of the events Bobkov relates actually happened, or happened the way Bobkov says they did. But these are the kinds of stories that Bobkov, as the head of the 5th Directorate, would have passed on to his young KGB recruits in the 1970s and that a young officer like Vladimir Putin would have internalized. There are traces of these same kinds of stories throughout Putin's own remarks and references. Another key aspect of the Bobkov stories and of Putin's own stories is that they are very much one-sided. The stories stress the skills of the KGB recruiter, the Case Officer, as a communicator and persuader. They deliberately and most obviously omit the fact that none of these alleged skills would be effective without the person on the other side of the dialogue—the target of the recruiter—knowing that the alternative to an amicable arrangement with the recruiter could be an extended period in the cellar of KGB headquarters, the Lubyanka, or in one of the KGB prison camps like Perm-36, or in the psychiatric hospital, a favorite KGB destination under Andropov.[48]

Bobkov's and Putin's self-appraisals of success in any individual case would likely be in large part based on the extent to which they could achieve their goals with the target without having to resort overtly to the ultimate threat. A successful recruitment was all about how well the threat was conveyed in disguised form. The target would get the message perfectly clearly, but the KGB case officer could pretend he did a masterful job of persuasion. This is part of the essence of "working with people." One of the advantages of the one-on-one approach is that it works with targets of any category and at any stage of the recruitment process. It can be applied to those who might be friendly to begin with, to neutrals who offer something of value, to those like Roy Medvedev who might potentially do damage, and to outright foes who could be recruited as double agents. Depending on the category, the process may be longer or shorter, and the kind of leverage becomes critical.

DEALING WITH THE MADDENED CROWD

The major disadvantage of scaling up to the mass level and dealing with large numbers of people is that it is very difficult to apply the one-on-one approach to an overtly hostile crowd. In this regard, the Tsupak story seems an extraordinary one—and, frankly, hard to believe. Masses or mobs are not easily calmed by quiet, extortionary techniques. Indeed, in the case of Pikalyovo, Putin did not wade into the midst of the crowd to calm the situation. He went to Pikalyovo, but headed to a conference room to berate oligarch Oleg Deripaska and other factory officials. It was a public dressing down, on TV, that addressed the grievances of the Pikalyovo protesters, but it was conducted well away from the maddened crowd. It was also a heavily controlled and staged intervention.

Presumably, Putin could have "worked with people" on a mass basis if he had chosen to do so at Pikalyovo. He could have gone out to the streets to meet with the protesters. Instead he focused on a small group. According to Russian media and PR specialists, some of whom had first-hand knowledge of the event, the dressing down was even prearranged by Putin and his PR team with Deripaska, the Pikalyovo plant director, and a representative of the workers' union.[49] Prime Minister Putin was filmed landing in a helicopter in the town, striding out, and marching into the meeting room, looking tough and businesslike. He presented Deripaska with an agreement that the oligarch had already seen, along with a pen to sign it, in what played out as a dramatic TV scene.[50]

As a result of one-to-one approaches behind the scenes, "working" successfully with Deripaska and the other key protagonists, Putin and his PR staff were then able to portray Mr. Putin, the prime minister, flying into Pikalyovo as the pro-worker man of the people. Putin's solution to the difficulty of applying "working with people" to masses is thus first to work with key people individually to arrange things and then to let the PR team portray the meeting, or on-the-spot appearance, as a spontaneous working with the masses. Another episode in this vein occurred when Putin traveled to the Siberian city of Novosibirsk in October 2008 for a meeting with oligarch Pyotr Aven at a branch of Aven's Alfa Bank. The next morning, Putin met with activists from the United Russia party. At this meeting a local party member, who also was a small businessman and construction contractor, Sergei Alexandrovich Shchapov, approached Putin to complain that he was having difficulty securing loans for his company. Putin essentially responds, "Really? Well, I was actually just in a bank. Let me see if I can get the head of the bank to come here so we can talk to him." He then tells an aide to find Pyotr Aven, who after a few minutes materializes at the meeting. Putin says: "Come and sit down. I guess I'm just bumping in to you everywhere. . . . You and I were just talking about bank operations . . . and this is Sergei Alexandrovich. . . . He is a concrete example [of exactly what we were talking about]." From there Putin, Aven, and Shchapov engage in an exchange on the assistance banks can provide to small businesses—another seemingly successful intervention by Putin.[51]

There is, however, another more telling and more troubling episode that illustrates how interventions can go wrong for Putin when they are not prearranged. This incident was captured by smartphone video and played out in a short clip on You Tube, not on official Russian television channels.[52] During the height of the summer peat bog and forest fires across the Russian heartland in July 2010, Prime Minister Putin went out to meet with people in one of the most affected regions near the city of Nizhny Novgorod. In the preamble to the You Tube clip, the individual who posted it notes that about 22,000 individual fires were raging across Russia at this particular juncture. On July 29, in one of the worst incidents, every house—340 in total—was destroyed in the village of Verkhnyaya Vereya, with tens of people killed and hundreds made homeless. According to the preamble, the fire had burned for almost two weeks in the surrounding countryside, gradually encroaching on the village. The villagers had repeatedly appealed for outside assistance in extinguishing the blaze, including the dispatch of a firefighting plane. Nizhny Novgorod governor Valery Shantsev had rebuffed their pleas and, reportedly, informed "Moscow" that everything was under control in the region.

Putin was dispatched to the scene immediately after the catastrophe, just like Colonel Tsupak to Rubtsovsk. He was surrounded by a group of angry men and women from Verkhnyaya Vereya—mostly women—furious at the lack of action by the local and central government authorities to tackle the fire as their houses burned to the ground and family members and neighbors perished. Putin's attempts to calm the crowd down and to respond to their issues, by saying that he and the government would take action to restore their property, were rebuffed. In the video, people in the crowd appear more, rather than less, enraged by the direct engagement with the prime minister, who personifies the authorities in this context. A visibly uncomfortable Putin moves off with several women still shouting after him about the poor performance of the authorities. The author of the video clip, or at least the narrator who posted it, observes that on this occasion Putin's "PR action clearly did not work: people reacted in disbelief at the premier's promises. Moreover, some even screamed: 'You wanted us to burn alive! Our administration functions very badly! They should be put on trial and hung up by the balls.'" (The favorite phrase of Mr. Putin, the boss, thrown right back at him.) Others shouted that there was not much point appearing now the damage was done: "This should have been thought of before! If you'd thought about this [the fire risk], then this wouldn't have happened."[53]

In her book, Masha Gessen describes a very similar interaction with a hostile crowd during what was essentially Putin's first experience of dealing with a crisis and major public relations disaster as president—the so-called *Kursk* incident.[54] In August 2000, one of Russia's nuclear submarines, the *Kursk,* caught fire after an explosion and sank with all hands on board in the northern Barents Sea. Survivors of the blast were trapped underwater for several days as Russia rebuffed international offers of assistance in attempting a rescue. By the time rescuers reached and penetrated the submarine, the group of survivors were long dead. Throughout what became a very public Russian and international vigil for the *Kursk* sailors, Putin was conspicuously absent. Initially he was on vacation, then he resisted entreaties to go to the site of the disaster. Gessen recounts the story, as told by Russian journalist Andrei Kolesnikov in his book on Putin, *Ya Putina videl!* (I saw Putin!).[55] Quoting from Kolesnikov, Gessen notes that Putin's then presidential chief of staff, Alexander Voloshin, and others had to work extremely hard to persuade Putin to travel to the Barents region to meet with the *Kursk* wives, mothers, and families. He finally traveled there ten days after the accident and also arrived four hours late to the designated meeting.[56] Using Kolesnikov's first-hand account, Gessen relates—just as the narrator posting the July 2010 YouTube video did—that people were screaming at Putin, telling him to "Shut up!" and asking why he took so long to ask for help.[57] Gessen writes: "Putin emerged from the meeting battered and bitter, and unwilling ever again to expose himself to such an audience. After no other disaster—and there would be many in his tenure as president—would Putin allow himself to be pitted publicly against the suffering."[58]

There may have been other incidents since the *Kursk* debacle where Putin found himself in the same situation, but they are hard to find in official records. Putin's foray into the Verkhnyaya Vereya crowd was a smaller-scale and much-less-public rerun of his bitter experience with a hostile and very emotional crowd, dominated by women, a decade before. It escaped the purview of Mr. Putin and his PR team because it was captured on a smartphone video and immediately uploaded to YouTube. It must also have been a very unwelcome reminder of the dangers of wading into unknown and uncharted waters. In stark contrast, Pikalyovo, like the *Hot Line,* is Putin's preferred method of engaging with larger audiences—in controlled, prearranged formats where his Case Officer one-to-one methods can be more readily and easily applied.

As is so often the case, Vladimir Putin's first lesson on this issue came from earlier events in his personal history, during his KGB service in Dresden in the 1990s. In Dresden, Mr. Putin the KGB case officer, who may have been trying to recruit agents or even double agents, had a very unfortunate encounter with an angry mob as East Germany fell apart.

DRESDEN: FACING DOWN A HOSTILE MOB

As already underscored, there is virtually no concrete information about any of the real activity Vladimir Putin performed in the KGB, in Leningrad, Moscow, and then Dresden. He does not seem to have told anyone, including one of his closest friends, Sergei Roldugin, anything specific about those years. There are, however, a few snippets of information about Putin's time in Dresden, some of which have been related in earlier chapters. In both *Ot pervogo litsa* and the interviews for Blotsky's biography, Putin recalled a group of angry Germans massing around the Stasi's headquarters in Dresden about the time of the fall of the Berlin Wall.[59] Putin had been feeding valuable KGB records into the furnace in his building's basement, including lists of German contacts and agent networks at the time, and he was worried that the crowds were going to "come for us, too."[60] They did.

As an angry crowd began to form around his building, Putin came out, accompanied by bodyguards. The Germans surrounded him, barraging him with questions about what really went on in the building, which was identified as a Soviet cultural center. They asked Putin why his car had a German license plate and why his German was so fluent. He came out prepared to use violence in self-defense if the crowd tried to break in. He does not say precisely how he intended to do this. In the end, nothing more dramatic happened that day. But the hours when the building was surrounded—the crowd outside, the KGB officers inside—were a trauma for Putin. He told his interviewers this directly. When he called a nearby Soviet military base for backup, he was told they could not help without orders from Moscow, and "Moscow is silent."[61] He felt bitterly abandoned by Moscow—"nobody lifted a finger to protect us."[62]

Putin clearly had no experience with, and no idea of how to deal with, large crowds. During the years of perestroika and glasnost in the USSR, protests were everywhere, from all sectors of society. If he had been living in Russia during the turbulent perestroika era, Putin would have been surrounded by crowds in this period—but he was in Dresden. Until 1989, there was no perestroika and glasnost in the GDR. The East German Communist Party was led by the last great holdout against reform in the communist world, Erich Honecker. In Dresden, Putin operated in the shadows. His encounter with the street protesters—the crowd, the mob, gathered around the Stasi building and Putin's own liaison office—came at the very end of his service there.

In Oleg Blotsky's biography, Putin gives a very emotional, blow-by-blow account of how he had to decide whether to follow the rules and defend the building, with all its secret files on informants, with the armed guard, or try to talk the crowd out of taking action. He was, he asserts, actually in charge because his superior was not in Dresden at the time. Talking to an aggressive crowd was against the rules of operation. If his initiative failed, he would have been tried and convicted by a military court. As Putin tells the story:

> Therefore as I went out to the people on the street, I understood perfectly well that I was risking not only my career but my family's future. But I calculated that saving the lives of the people whose files were lying on my desk, and the lives of those planning to storm the building, was worth more than my career. At that moment I firmly decided in my own mind that I had to sacrifice my career. No career is worth more than a single human life.[63]

Once he was out on the street, face-to-face with the Dresden crowd, Putin diverted them not with artful persuasion but by a blatant lie. The crowd was obviously looking for members of the *Stasi,* and Putin seemed to speak German very well, almost too well. When they aggressively asked who he really was, Putin responded that he was "a translator."[64] Instead of playing Colonel Tsupak in Dresden, Putin lied his way out of trouble.

The fact that Vladimir Putin was not good with hostile crowds, which would prove difficult for him as a mass politician, was of no consequence at this juncture. His rise to the presidency was still in the future. The KGB may have assigned Putin to Sobchak's office based on his one-to-one skills as a case officer, his general KGB background in foreign trade, his foreign service, and his linguistic skills (as well as his prior connections with Sobchak at Leningrad State University). The lessons Putin then learned during his time in St. Petersburg in dealing with businesses propelled him to Moscow in 1996. He came to Moscow and embarked on a mission that did not require the application of his limited economic or political skills. He was not supposed to provide input into policy or deal with mobs. He was called up almost as a "sleeper operative" to work for people in the Kremlin and eventually deal with businesses and businessmen, as he had done in St. Petersburg. The methods for exerting leverage he had developed in St. Petersburg were his key strengths. The other tools at his disposal would become relevant later when he began to move rapidly up the leadership ladder in Moscow. Only when he got to the top would some of his weaknesses—like dealing with hostile crowds—prove problematic.

MR. PUTIN'S MISSION TO MOSCOW

One of the most immediate causes of the weakness of the Russian state in the 1990s was its inability to collect taxes. This created a vicious circle. In the Soviet years, when all factories were owned by the state, the director of a large enterprise was effectively the mayor of a small town. After privatization in the early 1990s, the so-called nonproduction assets on the books of a factory that had been set up to cater to the social needs of the workers—the daycare centers, clinics, recreation facilities, summer camps, and so on—were supposed to be handed over to the local municipal governments. Instead of the enterprises paying directly for these services, their operations were supposed to be financed by local government budgets out of the tax revenues paid by the enterprises and local workers and residents. In theory, this would be both more efficient and more equitable than the old Soviet system. With economies of scale, the town or city could manage the facilities more cheaply, and all citizens, not just those who worked at a big plant, could use them.

The weak link was the assumption that tax revenues would pay for everything. There was no tradition of individuals or companies paying real taxes. There was also no administrative framework for assessing and collecting the taxes. The state, at both the local and national level, was broke and unable to perform the functions and services previously provided by the enterprises. As a result, a bottom-up system for survival developed—without government funding. Tax evasion became the norm. The team of liberal economic reformers around Anatoly Chubais in the Yeltsin government correctly concluded that the vicious circle of a weak state unable to collect taxes and no taxes leading to a weak state had to be broken. The critical step was to enforce tax compliance.

Chubais made repeated efforts to enforce tax discipline during his time in office. They all failed because the wealthiest new business owners used their money to suborn and collude with government officials to evade taxes. They purchased influence over tax legislation and enforcement at the very highest as well as lower levels of government. This problem was compounded when the Yeltsin team chose to make a Faustian bargain to secure enough money from top businessmen to win reelection in the 1996 presidential election. The critical step in this bargain was taken just weeks before Vladimir Putin came to Moscow from St. Petersburg in August. The businessmen who gave Yeltsin their financial and media support expected that, in return, they would get full title to some of the most valuable companies in the Russian resource sector. In the immediate wake of the election, they also began to fight over the initial distribution of property.[65]

From 1996 to 1999, the alliance Chubais and the Yeltsin team had forged between the government and the oligarchs steadily unraveled. Chubais wanted to reinstitute the rule of law, as indicated in the 1997 *poslaniye,* and level the playing field again in the Russian economy. With the emergency of the 1996 presidential election campaign in the past, the sweetheart deals with Russian business were over. Privatization would continue, but the process would now be open and transparent. Chubais hoped that a proliferation of new owners in the economy would prevent the kind of collusion among a handful of the wealthiest owners that had marred Russia's early privatization process, and would mark progress toward realizing his and others' goal of competitive capitalism. The oligarchs, however, were now at the peak of their power, and they had to be disciplined so rules could be enforced again.

Days after Yeltsin's election victory, Chubais penned a confidential memorandum outlining some proposed next steps. The Russian Communist Party, which had been defeated in the presidential race, would have to be eliminated as a political force. Chubais advised against direct repression, which was likely to be counterproductive, and recommended instead fomenting division within the Communist Party. Chubais also proposed creating a more streamlined and unified team around President Yeltsin by purging top presidential administration officials whose loyalty was questionable. However, if he was to deal with the oligarchs, Chubais would need muscle. His team was made up almost exclusively of academic economists. They were young and had no experience dealing with seasoned Soviet-era politicians and officials or with the ruthless businessmen who now owned most of Russia's wealth. Chubais realized that something more was needed. He turned to his former St. Petersburg colleague, Alexei Kudrin.[66]

Chubais's memo specifically recommended bringing Kudrin in from St. Petersburg. It did not mention Vladimir Putin, but Putin nonetheless came along with Alexei Kudrin. Chubais assigned Kudrin to take charge of the GKU, the presidential administration's Main Control Directorate. The GKU was the government's financial inspectorate, and an agency Chubais had previously strengthened through an *ukaz* (presidential decree) on March 16, 1996. The decree gave the GKU new logistical support from the Presidential Property Management Department. At the same time that Alexei Kudrin was appointed head of the GKU (in August 1996), Vladimir Putin was made deputy head of the property management agency.[67] In November 1996, another decree gave the GKU even more power, enabling Kudrin to deploy inspectors all across Russia to probe the finances of government and federal agencies and uncover acts of corruption, embezzlement, and misuse of funds.[68]

In March 1997, only a short time after Boris Yeltsin delivered the *poslaniye* to the Russian parliament about the importance of cracking down and reestablishing order, Chubais appointed Kudrin deputy finance minister. He also, at Kudrin's recommendation, named Putin head of the GKU on March 26. When Kudrin handed over the reins to Putin in 1997, Russian journalist Andrei Kolesnikov described the GKU as a "menacing structure."[69] On April 3, 1997, another presidential decree gave the GKU primary responsibility for issuing edicts to implement the crackdown necessary to reestablish order, including oversight of Russian financial and business sectors and authority to collect financial and other company information.

Yeltsin's March 1997 *poslaniye* and the April *ukaz* set the GKU's operations and thus Putin in motion, along with some of his closest associates. Across the country, the GKU took the lead in organizing special meetings of top local officials in law enforcement, as well as in the tax and customs authorities, to urge action in establishing the "order" called for in Yeltsin's *poslaniye*. One meeting in St. Petersburg on May 20, 1997, brought together a particularly weighty group. Putin himself (and most likely his close associate at the GKU, Igor Sechin) had come in from Moscow. The locals included the city's head tax man, Viktor Zubkov, and Vladimir Yakunin, Putin's neighbor in the Ozero dacha cooperative, whom Putin had appointed regional head of the GKU and would later promote to be head of Russian Railways.[70]

Unfortunately for Chubais, just as Putin was positioned and poised to tackle the misuse of funds, Chubais's plans were upended. In summer 1997, Chubais and his team prepared to put a major telecommunications company, Svyazinvest, up for bid and to enforce new rules with the oligarchs. He intended to use the telecommunications privatization to create an impartial system with transparency. Chubais, however, miscalculated. The Svyazinvest privatization led instead to a split within the group of oligarchs, resulting in the so-called Bankers' War—with Chubais and his team ending up as collateral damage. They were set up on charges in the media of corruption just before the bidding for the company could take place.[71] Cash advances for a book project, received by Alfred Kokh, a close associate of Chubais and the former head of the Russian privatization agency, were portrayed as bribes from Uneximbank, one of the banks in the running to acquire Svyazinvest.[72] Chubais leapt to Kokh's defense, putting his credibility on the line. The *kompromat,* or smear attack, succeeded, however. Chubais was ousted from the government, and the rest of his team was purged. Only Kudrin, Putin, and the GKU group were left in place. Putin still had a mission to accomplish. To his great fortune, the oligarchs, had also created a dilemma for themselves by launching a war. They would end up having to turn to him for the solution.[73]

THE OLIGARCHS' DILEMMA: MR. PUTIN'S SOLUTION

Despite their vast wealth, Russia's oligarchs in the 1990s were constantly at risk from the public, which almost universally regarded their ownership of the country's largest corporations as illegitimate. At the same time, the oligarchs were individually at risk from one another. They were constantly predating on each other's businesses and could not trust each other. Thanks to their own efforts to reduce any power of the government to control them, they had also undermined the state as the one institution that could protect all their property rights. As a result, they were reduced to trying to protect themselves individually. The biggest vulnerability each of them had was the information about their financial status and their financial operations.[74] In such circumstances, the only protection the oligarchs had was to make everyone equally vulnerable. They focused on digging up potentially damaging information about each other. The threats and counter-threats deterred aggression. The result was a mutual and perpetual state of blackmail—what is known as a "mutual conflict equilibrium" in game theory. In other words, delicate balance is better than war, but only barely so.

To maintain the equilibrium, the oligarchs had to expend a huge amount of effort and resources that they could otherwise have used to manage their companies and generate more wealth. They also ran the constant risk that the balance would tip, that the infighting would get out of control, and the whole system would come crashing down around them. For their own sake, the oligarchs needed an outside arbiter. They needed a completely and clearly impartial agent who would be strong enough to enforce the peace in a credible and sustainable way—and who, most important for them, would never become a rival, another oligarch. This arbiter would, in effect, have to hold them all hostage so that each of them would have the opportunity to disarm and conclude a non-aggression pact. If the state could not do this, by enforcing the rule of law, then something or someone else would have to step in.[75]

The oligarchs could hardly appoint someone themselves, but someone was out there in the wings waiting for them. At the GKU, Putin was amassing inside information about the oligarchs' financial and business dealings. By May 1998, Putin had become deputy head of the presidential administration for work with Russia's regions as well as overseeing the GKU. Later in 1998, when Putin became the head of the FSB, he purged the leadership of the FSB's economic crimes department and appointed his close associate Nikolai Patrushev as head of a new Directorate of Economic Security. Putin went on to replace the head of the tax police with an associate of his from the GKU, Vyacheslav Soltaganov, who had previously made a career in the Ministry of Internal Affairs.

By April 1999, Putin had established a monopoly on financial information. When he became president, he established a new agency to oversee this in November 2001, the Russian Financial Monitoring Agency (RFM), and put Viktor Zubkov in charge. Zubkov remained head of the agency until September 2007 and even afterwards, as he served as interim prime minister between September 2007 and May 2008. As first deputy prime minister under Putin until 2012, Zubkov continued to have special responsibility for the RFM. Throughout that entire time, the RFM reported ultimately to Putin. In May 2012, when Putin moved from the prime minister's office back to the Kremlin, he brought the RFM with him.

When he was propelled into the highest Russian offices in 1999–2000, Putin first offered himself to the oligarchs as a protector. He reassured them that he would not dispossess them. He would recognize the basic parameters of their 1996 deal with Yeltsin in acquiring their business assets. He also reminded the oligarchs that few others in Russia saw their ownership as legitimate. He used this reminder, in February 2000, to announce that Russia's businesses would now be "equidistant from power."[76] They could not use any of their old levers to buy influence and cultivate goodwill across the Russian Federation. They would have to start from scratch. Their only key relationship would be with Putin's Kremlin, and this would be for their protection, from disappropriation, not for their influence.[77]

In an televised meeting in July 2000, Putin laid down the ground rules with the oligarchs.[78] Putin sketched out a scheme that essentially resembled a "protection racket." It was the kind of deal he might have forged as a KGB case officer trying to recruit a double agent in Dresden. The oligarchs would be allowed to continue to pursue their businesses and increase their wealth, but they would have to agree to a new tax regime that would give the federal government more resources. They must not try to change this regime as they had in the past, or there would clearly be consequences. They must also actively consider Russian national interests, as defined by Putin and the state, when engaging in economic activities abroad. This was private enterprise with strings attached. Their property rights were ultimately dependent on the good will of the Kremlin. The logic of this approach—keeping the oligarchs in place, but pulling them close—was explained by presidential aide

Vladislav Surkov to a Russian journalist. Surkov told Yelena Tregubova that Putin and his team understood that they could not just dispossess the oligarchs and find another group of businessmen to take over their companies. There were simply not enough capable entrepreneurs in Russia in 2000. The group of businessmen was "very thin and very precious . . . they are the bearers of capital, of intellect, of technologies." In many respects Russia's oligarchs, like their assets, had to be treated carefully. "The oil men," Surkov opined, "are no less important than the oil; the state has to make the most of them both."[79]

The new scheme for dealing with the oligarchs was complex, but it suited Putin's training as a KGB case officer and also grew out of his Case Officer identity. In the KGB, Mr. Putin had learned how to identify, recruit, and run agents, and how to acquire the patience to cultivate sources. He had also learned how to collect, synthesize, and use information. He had come to Moscow in 1996 to apply those skills. As a result of monopolizing information at the GKU he had also acquired a great deal of power and leverage. He had maneuvered and moved his way up to the top of the Russian state. He would now try to apply his Case Officer skills on a larger, grander scale than he might possibly have imagined when he was first posted to Dresden.

CHAPTER NINE

THE SYSTEM

PUTIN'S JULY 2000 TELEVISED MEETING with the oligarchs, which laid out the terms of his deal with them, is emblematic of his style and system of governance. All the evidence from Putin's words and actions since 1999–2000, when he first moved from the shadows into the position of prime minister and then acting president, indicates that there is nothing contrived or secret about his goals and his policies. Putin's practice has been to state them directly. On the other hand, there has been a significant discrepancy between the transparency of Putin's goals and the nontransparency of the means by which he intends to achieve them. How he goes about implementing his policies has been mostly off-limits for general discussion. Politics and the political system—how Putin rules Russia in order to achieve the goals he has laid out—are supposed to be unquestioned by those outside (and perhaps even many inside) the inner circle.

Nonetheless, Putin does have a mode, a system of governance that he has developed over more than a decade. It is, in many respects, a tiered system—or perhaps better, a series of concentric circles. Putin's special arrangement with the oligarchs who own the key companies that produce and distribute the economy's natural resource wealth lies at the very core. This arrangement, as we have described, is based on a particular kind of protection. Putin protects the oligarchs from having their assets appropriated by the state; he also protects them from one another. In creating the arrangement, Putin applied his skills in "working with people." He developed leverage over the oligarchs by creating a monopoly on financial information, including incriminating information about corruption and malfeasance.

Beyond this protection scheme at the core of the system, Mr. Putin plays the role of the chief executive officer, the CEO, of the "corporation" that is Russia—the sum of all the assets managed either by the oligarchs or by the appointed stewards of state enterprises. In carrying out these functions, Putin is assisted by a very small group of trusted aides—in essence, the staff of the CEO's office. Outside this small group lies the larger, vast sphere of the state apparatus of Russia, which includes officials of both the federal (central) and regional governments. In Putin's idealized version, this is the sphere of governance that is supposed to function like a "Swiss watch." It is not supposed to require his personal attention—although, to his evident frustration, it constantly does. Finally, beyond the circles of governance are the governed, the Russian populace. They have no voice in the operation of the corporation or the system.

The disconnect between the *what* of political goals and the *how* to achieve or implement them is evident in Putin's Millennium Message, the programmatic statement he issued on December 29, 1999, to inaugurate his reign over Russia. To a remarkable degree, the goals he outlined in the Millennium Message remain the priority today, more than 15 years later. They were straightforward, although colored with emotion and fraught with historic and cultural symbolism. In December 1999, Putin pledged to rebuild the Russian state, protect Russia's sovereignty, preserve domestic stability and unity, and ensure national security. He did not state in the Millennium Message *how* he would rebuild, protect, preserve, and ensure. In fact, this discrepancy became, over time, the key part of a deal he struck with the population to complement his deal with the oligarchs. Putin laid out what he would deliver. He told the Russian public they could hold him to this deal—that this would be his part of the bargain in becoming president. Once they had confirmed him in the office of president, the Russian people's part of the bargain was then not to ask questions about his methods. Nor should they ask for a voice in deciding the nuts and bolts of policy or of governing.

A PROHIBITORY SYSTEM

Former Kremlin adviser Gleb Pavlovsky, in his January 2012 interview with *The Guardian*, makes many of the same points about the deal Putin concluded with the Russian population in 2000:

We are talking about managed democracy, but I think that maybe you in the West have forgotten that this concept was widespread in the 1950s in Europe in countries where there had been totalitarianism. . . . In Germany, for example, there was the same idea: that German people have a tendency to totalitarianism and they must not be allowed near politics. So they must have the possibility to choose, (vote) freely, but the people who control real politics must be the same, they must not yield. So a prohibitory system [*zapretitel'naya sistema*] must be created. . . . Is it cynical from the point of view of the theory of democracy? Probably yes, but here it didn't look like cynicism. . . . What we need to note here is that a certain "Putin consensus" existed. . . . A consensus of the people and the elite. . . . No ideology is necessary. . . . It will be a state without ideas oriented on common sense and on the average man, the citizen. Nonetheless, the masses must not be given access to power.[1]

The fact that Putin did not describe any particular design for governance beyond a series of basic deals in the Millennium Message or elsewhere is not strange. When he began his presidency in 2000, he was not proposing to overthrow the institutional order that he inherited. He was actually promising to fulfill it. Putin was and remains a restorationist, a conservative reformer. He was not, and is not, a revolutionary. Putin's mission, as he repeatedly stated in 1999 and throughout the 2000s, was to put an end to the process of undermining the existing state institutions—just as, he claimed in the Millennium Message, *society* (the Russian elite) had demanded. Putin wanted to make *vlast'*, the state institutions, work. This was part of his goal of strengthening the state and the authority of its governing structures.

As Gleb Pavlovsky's comments also underscore, Putin is a pragmatist, not an ideologue. In setting up his system of governance, he did not follow a model that can be captured by a description in the abstract. Although we use the term "system," what Vladimir Putin and the inner circle around him have created is in fact not as simple as the term might suggest. It is not an intentionally designed, well-formulated system. Rather, it is piecemeal and ad hoc. It is shaped by Putin's own skills and experience. It has evolved to fit circumstances, as we will discuss in

Part II. The system is both concrete and personalized. The ideas it draws upon are fluid and flexible, as we have described throughout this book. The fact that Putin has synthesized a whole range of concepts and not tried to twist some fixed orthodoxy of ideas or ideology to pursue his goals has proven to be an advantage of the system.

The synthetic nature of the system comes in part from the fact that Mr. Putin began operating in Moscow as the Outsider, the man without a vested interest in a particular ideology or structure. Whatever he needs to do in the service of the ends he has laid out, he does. He feels no need to justify the means. This is both good news and bad. It is bad because it leaves room for arbitrary decisions in response to what he decides is uniquely demanded by the particular circumstances. The political system can thus be turned on its head if need be, and seemingly on a whim. This happened in 2008 when Putin first announced the creation of the tandem arrangement with Dmitry Medvedev that would enable him to move smoothly from the position of president to that of prime minister. It happened again in September 2011, when he announced he would be moving back to the presidency (whether people liked it or not).[2] As we will discuss, this arbitrary element reinforces Russian public cynicism about the political system and the concept of democracy.

On the other hand, the official Russian state institutions (the parliament, the courts, and others), which were created by more genuine democrats in the 1990s, still remain in place. The formal structure of the institutions and the separation of powers have been preserved even if their functioning has been altered over the past decade. In theory, this offers the possibility of restoring a more institutionalized form of governance in the future. Unfortunately, because the functioning of Russian state institutions is now so connected to Putin personally, the institutions, in and of themselves, cannot necessarily be used by another individual to put Russia on a different trajectory of political development. The tandem experiment with Dmitry Medvedev as the Russian president underscores this point. Many observers anticipated that the constitutional authority of the Russian presidency, the power of the institution itself, would convey directly to Medvedev and enable him to make his own mark on the governing of the state.[3] As Medvedev's presidential term progressed, there was even considerable speculation that he would use the institutional prerogatives of the presidency to keep himself in the position for a second term—even by possibly going so far as to "sack" Prime Minister Putin and his team.[4]

In fact, the institution of the Russian presidency under Dmitry Medvedev was not quite what it was under Vladimir Putin. There was a greater degree of openness. Medvedev brought some people into the Kremlin more closely associated with him personally than with Putin. A larger group beyond the inner circle became engaged in the discussion about Russia's future and was even allowed to challenge the how of governance as well as the what.[5] Medvedev also used the president's prerogative to sack or, at least, remove a number of officials who tested the Kremlin's patience from powerful perches they had occupied since the more permissive 1990s. The most prominent of these was Moscow mayor Yury Luzkhkov, who enjoyed reminding Kremlin officials that he, not they, ran the city of Moscow. Medvedev replaced Luzhkov in 2010 with Sergei Sobyanin, who had previously served as head of the presidential administration and, before that, governor of the oil-rich Tyumen region in Siberia.[6]

Medvedev, however, discovered that serving as president did not mean that he could claim all of the presidential powers that Putin had exercised. Medvedev had clearly been put in the position of president by Putin. He remained beholden to him and dependent on his good will. As Gleb Pavlovsky again notes in his revealing January 2012 interview, Putin had decided in 2007–08 to engage in an experiment to "expand the consensus" on the governance of the system he had developed and to "modernize" it. Putin had decided that his presidential "successor [in 2008] need[ed] to be someone who is not similar to me. Or there will be stagnation."[7] Nonetheless, Putin still saw himself, and only himself, as the guarantor of the system.[8] When he moved to the prime minister's office, Vladimir Putin retained certain key powers for himself—especially control over the deal with the oligarchs and the monopoly of financial information.

As two former Kremlin insiders described to us in private interviews, Dmitry Medvedev was entrusted with the "keys" to the presidency and the Kremlin, but he was not allowed to "open all of the doors" nor to "go into all of the rooms."[9] The "prohibitory system" described by Gleb Pavlovsky was applied to Dmitry Medvedev as well as to the Russian population at large. Medvedev was ultimately the caretaker president, not the owner of the house, the Russian *khozyayn*. The same is true of other formal institutions like the prime minister's office, which Putin claimed and adapted in his own inimitable way. It is not likely that any other successor, even one who does not have a Putin looking over his shoulder, will be able to make of the presidency or premiership what Vladimir Putin did from 2000 until at least 2014.

CEO . . . OR TSAR?

Even though Putin's system of governance is not formal, there is evidence, including from his own direct statements, that Putin does have an internalized version of what his system is. As idealized as it may be—like the KGB myths of "working with people"—this version is important for what it reflects about Vladimir Putin. The system begins with his own role in it. Mr. Putin envisions his task in ruling Russia as that of the CEO of a corporation. This concept of CEO allows him to resolve the apparent contradiction between "working with people" on a very small scale and ruling an entire state, a nation of people. In spite of his propensity for PR stunts and for playing the role of the boss in Pikalyovo and other settings, Putin is not interested in micromanaging the apparatus of the Russian state, nor the private business sector, and certainly not the lives of 140 million citizens. For Mr. Putin, the CEO is the strategic planner. His task is to issue general guidelines and then supervise and monitor the way the guidelines are followed. The key to making such a system work is to identify the smallest possible part of the entire governance mechanism that requires his personal attention and make sure that this is managed closely. As for the rest, as much as possible needs to work on its own, as long as it does not stray beyond the boundaries of the strategic course that CEO Putin has chosen.

Putin has repeatedly used metaphors that sum up how he thinks the system should operate. One is that the machinery of the state needs to "operate on automatic." Another is that it needs to work like a Swiss watch. In other words, everyone in the Russian government should be working like the cogs in a precision clockwork, so Mr. Putin will not have to step in to sort things out. Or, as Putin puts it, there will be no need for him to have his hand constantly on the steering wheel of the machinery of state, no need for "manual operation" (*ruchnoy kontrol'* or *ruchnoye upravleniye*).[10] In this case, the law and its use and application have an important role in the system. In Putin's view, making law work is critical in creating a system in which the top executive does not have to intervene; this is the concept of the law-abiding state, the *pravovoye gosudarstvo* that we discussed earlier. The law lays down rules of the game. Abiding by the law means that things run according to plan. The first step is to ensure that the laws are consistent.

In the Millennium Message, Putin emphasized the importance of "constitutionalizing" the Russian state by bringing all of its laws into line. He asserted that this process would ensure the "constitutional safety of the state, enabling [or empowering] the federal center and [thus] preserving the integrity of the country."[11] Since 2000, Putin has made it a priority to direct and control the passage of legislation in the Duma and in the higher parliamentary chamber, the Federation Council, so that it is coordinated with his broader long-term goals. Strong courts also play an important role. They help systematize the state by sorting out the mess left behind by the Yeltsin-era of endless decrees, proliferating bilateral treaties between Moscow and Russia's regions, and regional legislative innovation. Under Putin, Russia's courts have been instructed to strike down regional laws that contradict federal statutes as well as the Soviet laws that remain on the books. The courts also help keep the tiers of governance in order and act as a kind of release valve for pressures building up in the lower levels of the system. For example, Putin has repeatedly insisted that electoral complaints must be referred to the courts rather than taken to the streets.[12] The situation has been similar for business and other political disputes.[13]

The constitution remains the key document in this context. Officially, Putin subscribes and adheres to the 1993 Russian constitution. While people often say he has emasculated it, or turned it into a charade, in fact the constitution accords substantial and sweeping powers to the president, as we have already outlined.[14] Putin has simply taken complete advantage of the ample provisions for presidential power that Boris Yeltsin pushed through in the 1990s. Constitutional drafter Sergei Shakhrai quipped then that the constitution turned the Russian president into the "British Queen." Putin has made sure that the enshrined monarch is not the Queen but rather her distant and more autocratic old cousin—the Russian tsar.[15] The constitution and the law mean something to Putin—so do the courts, and even institutions such as elections and legislative assemblies. To the extent that they do mean something, they constrain him and they provide a tempo and a timetable for his rule. The constitution forbade three consecutive presidential terms. So Putin had to step aside in 2008 and create a new arrangement, the leadership tandem with Dmitry Medvedev, before he could return legally to the presidency in May 2012. The formal institutions cannot be ignored in analyzing how Russia is ruled. Nevertheless, there is no doubt that the important decisions, the real decisions, are made outside the formal institutions.

BLUEPRINT FOR A SYSTEM

Over the course of the 2000s, it has become commonplace to speak of Russia as a corporation, as "Russia, Inc.," or "Kremlin, Inc." But, in fact, the meanings differ. Most typical is the idea that Russia, Inc. is a corporate empire in which the interests of the Russian state are intertwined with the private commercial interests of wealthy oligarchs linked personally to Putin, Putin's own family and close associates, and, of course, Putin himself.[16] There are also some who use the notion to signify that Putin operates the economy of the entire country as a single, superpowerful business enterprise (not necessarily for his personal gain) that is designed to outcompete the biggest of the multinational corporations. "GE on steroids," for example, is the way Putin's Russia has actually been described by top managers of the multinational General Electric corporation, who have directly dealt with and operated inside Russia over the last decade.[17] Our usage of the idea of Russia, Inc. or Russia as a corporation is more limited. It is related to what appears to be Putin's own understanding of organizational management and, specifically, the role of the CEO or the strategic planner of an organization—in this case the CEO/president of Russia. As in so many other instances, it is most likely that Vladimir Putin first encountered the idea of the CEO as the ultimate strategic planner during his KGB training.

The section on strategic planning in Putin's dissertation (see box on pp. 198–99) drew on one principal source: the Russian-language edition of the American business-school textbook by William King and David Cleland, *Strategic Planning and Policy*. As we have already noted, this book appears to have been instrumental in shaping Putin's views of the

DR. PUTIN AND THE PH.D.

One of many manifestations of the Putin enigma is the graduate degree in economics that he earned in the 1990s. Putin was awarded the degree from an institution that he never attended, the St. Petersburg Mining Institute. He also wrote the dissertation for a degree on a topic—raw materials—in which he appears never to have been directly involved. Putin has, on a couple of occasions, mentioned the degree or the dissertation in passing, and it is listed as part of his official biography on the presidential website. However, he has not explained his motives for writing the dissertation on this particular topic, nor has he discussed how he managed to write it during the period when he was presumably deputy mayor of St. Petersburg and also moving to take up his new positions in Moscow. No biographer, neither Russian nor foreign, has adequately described the circumstances of the dissertation. Instead, in the 2000s, there were numerous accounts of the alleged inaccessibility of the text of the dissertation, which only added to the overall "mystery" of the topic. The mystery was compounded by some of the key figures involved in the dissertation's production.

The head of the St. Petersburg Mining Institute, Vladimir Litvinenko, claims responsibility for supervising Putin's degree work and has vigorously defended Putin against charges of plagiarism in the thesis.[a] Litvinenko subsequently saw his star rise under Putin's presidency. He served as Putin's St. Petersburg campaign chairman for both the 2000 and 2004 presidential elections and then again in 2012. In 2010, he was elected to the board of directors of PhosAgro, one of the world's largest producers of phosphate fertilizers. His shareholdings in the company are worth more than half a billion dollars.[b]

a. For more details on the dissertation, its availability, and evidence of plagiarism in the work, see the presentations by Igor Danchenko and Clifford Gaddy at the Brookings Institution panel discussion "The Mystery of Vladimir Putin's Dissertation," March 30, 2006, Washington, D.C., at www.brookings.edu/events/2006/03/30putin-dissertation.

b. As of 2014, Litvinenko owns nearly 15 percent of PhosAgro. The company's total market capitalization as of November 24, 2014, was $4.18 billion. For more background on Litvinenko and PhosAgro, see Andrew E. Kramer and David M. Herszenhorn, "Midas Touch in St. Petersburg: Friends of Putin Glow Brightly," *New York Times,* March 1, 2012, and Yuliya Fedorinova, "Putin Campaigner Buys $269 Million Phosagro Stake From Guryevs," at www.bloomberg.com/news/2014-04-28/putin-campaigner-buys-269-million-phosagro-stake-from-guryevs.html.

Putin's degree—*kandidat ekonomicheskikh nauk* (candidate of economic science)—is a postgraduate degree sometimes considered to be the equivalent of a Western Ph.D., although in Putin's case it would be much closer to an MBA. The candidate degree was awarded on the basis of a dissertation entitled "Strategic Planning of the Reproduction of the Mineral Resource Base of a Region under Conditions of the Formation of Market Relations (St. Petersburg and Leningrad oblast)," which is dated 1997. Its convoluted title poorly reflects the actual content. The issue of reproduction of the reserves of a resource is an important one, especially in the case of oil and gas. But neither of those commodities is found in the Leningrad region, so they are not addressed in the dissertation. Nor is the policy for replacing the reserves for *any* resource actually discussed. This part of the title seems to have been chosen independently of the content of the thesis. Putin does discuss the concept of "strategic planning" at great length, and has applied that concept throughout his presidency, as we point out in the book. It is the most important theme of the dissertation. The discussion is also taken, with little modification and without proper academic citation, from a single source, the Russian version of the King and Cleland textbook *Strategic Planning and Policy*.[c] Meanwhile, the second most important theme of Putin's dissertation is not mentioned in the title. This is the subject of chapter three of his dissertation, Russia's strategic need for expanded export-import infrastructure, specifically for what Putin refers to in his text as "integrated transportation and production port complexes."

c. King and Cleland (1978).

importance of planning for contingencies and thus building up Russia's strategic material and financial reserves during his presidency.[18] It is likely that the Russian edition of this book was produced as part of the KGB effort of the 1980s to develop expertise about Western economic management methods, when the KGB was looking for ways to reform the Soviet system, which it knew to be failing. The idea of strategic planning was also used at various points to tweak the KGB's and the Communist Party's staid notions of *central* planning. In the late 1980s, during the effort led by KGB head Vladimir Kryuchkov to run economic and foreign trade operations, the KGB may have used King and Cleland's text to develop the internal expertise to start up and/or infiltrate new business ventures in the USSR.[19] In Vladimir Putin's dissertation, some of the most relevant theses of the American text are summarized fairly well.

In addition to setting up a hierarchy of goals for strategic planning, the King and Cleland text provides a blueprint for the way an ideal corporation should operate, viewed through the prism of planning. Planning occurs at all levels, but the key point, the authors write, is to distinguish between strategic plans and operational plans.[20] King and Cleland also use a very specific set of terms. First comes the most fundamental concept of all: the basic purpose of the organization, the *mission*. The mission statement "tells what the organization is, why it exists, and the unique contribution it can make." The mission needs to be consciously chosen and continually reviewed. It is the common thread that binds everything together. Next come the *objectives*. These are "broad and timeless statements." Only then come the concrete *goals,* which are quantitative and time-based. King and Cleland note that the goals should be implemented through *programs* and *projects*.

The hierarchy of priorities that the organization lays out determines what King and Cleland refer to as a natural dichotomy in the activity of members of the organization, between strategic considerations and activities, and operating ones. The "strategic-operating dichotomy" in turn defines two categories of managerial decisionmaking. Establishing the organization's mission and its objectives is on the level of strategic planning. Strategic choices concern "the basic purpose of the organization, the objectives to be sought, as well as the general way in which they will be sought."[21] Operational decisionmaking, by contrast, does not involve defining objectives. They have already been set. Operational activity is about implementation—getting things done. It is not hard to see how this model of corporate governance could be interpreted to suit Vladimir Putin's needs when he became the Russian president. If one assumes that strategic planning is the purview of a single individual, the head of the organization, the CEO, then that one individual alone must make all the big decisions. He or she defines the goals and strategies and stakes out the general course. Other individuals implement decisions. They devise tactics. They have clearly delineated responsibilities. They report to the head of the organization and are monitored by him.

How Putin has applied this to Russia is obvious. Putin makes the strategic decisions for Russia, Inc. The juridical owners of Russia's big resource companies (the oligarchs) at the core of the system are for him merely managers in the King and Cleland sense—operational managers or division managers. Their job is to figure out the best way to achieve specified goals.[22] Putin will decide which goals are best suited to the overall mission and purposes of the organization. The same applies to the division of labor within the Russian executive branch. The people immediately around the president and at the top levels of the cabinet are not there to set the goals. Mr. Putin sets the goals. They execute them.

The problem is, Putin's interpretation of the book he so liberally cites in his dissertation is a distorted one. King and Cleland expressly point out that while it *might appear* that the strategic-operating dichotomy implies that "different kinds of people, possessing different mixes of skills, should be assigned to strategic and operating responsibilities," in fact, modern organizations do not work that way. Rather, they operate on the principle that their "*managers should have both strategic and operating responsibilities* [emphasis in the original]."[23] Success does not come from having one individual arrogate all responsibility for strategic planning. Although there is a chief executive, *every* manager needs to be able to allocate time and effort to make both operational and strategic decisions. Vladimir Putin's interpretation was not King and Cleland's, but it came to shape the way he governed Russia. He made himself the all-powerful CEO of Russia, Inc. and took on all the responsibility for himself.

When he was prime minister from 2008 to 2012, Putin took the key strategic planning and goal-setting functions along with him. As president, Dmitry Medvedev executed and carried out some of the main goals. He did not get to set the national agenda on his own, although he was allowed to make a few tweaks here and there and exert some influence.[24] The basic mission statement for Russia, Inc. was already laid out in Mr. Putin's December 1999 Millennium Message. It was refined again in the set of goals encapsulated in the Russia 2020 strategy, which government task forces produced and Putin oversaw during his time as prime minister. Medvedev was at best a version of a COO, chief operating officer, as president, not the CEO or strategic planner in Putin's conception of that role.

The key to applying the corporate management model as envisioned by Putin is to have a small number of key players. This is where the peculiarities of modern Russia proved to be a distinctive advantage for Putin. The first peculiarity is that a single sector, oil and gas, so thoroughly dominates the Russian economy and the politics of the country. Value creation in the economy is overwhelmingly concentrated in the energy sector. Most of the rest of the economy, including manufacturing, creates little added value. In some cases it is even net-value-subtracting—heavily dependent on direct government subsidies and other handouts, including under-priced energy and other material inputs. As a result, the two-fold challenge for Russia's economic management is to ensure that value continues to be created by the oil and gas sectors and that enough of this value is shared with the rest of Russian industry for other sectors to be able to survive.[25]

The second distinctive feature of the Russian economy is that there are so few companies in these critical value-creating oil and gas industries compared to other advanced industrial countries like the United States. Ten companies account for about 90 percent of Russia's oil output. Gazprom, Russia's massive natural gas company, produces nearly 80 percent of the country's natural gas.[26] Third, thanks to the 1996 "loans-for-shares" deal, several key oil companies, as well as other top commodity producers, were acquired by the group of oligarchs who became deeply beholden to Putin as a result of the protection deal he struck with them in 2000.[27] Such a high degree of concentration of ownership is a disadvantage from the perspective of pure economic performance. For Mr. Putin, the Case Officer who prefers "working with people" through informal arrangements in order to accomplish his goals as president, the degree of concentration is a clear advantage. There are only a small number of people to deal and make deals with.

THE IMPORTANCE OF OIL . . . AND TRANSPORTATION

Vladimir Putin was aware of the importance of oil and gas for his mission and goals as early as he knew what the goals themselves should be. As discussed in chapter 5 on Mr. Putin the Survivalist, and again in chapter 8 on the Case Officer, Putin knew that Russia's natural resources—its oil resources in particular—were a built-in reserve for surviving crises. Of all the resources in the food barter deals Putin oversaw in St. Petersburg in 1990–91, the most important one featured in the contracts was also oil.[28] One single contract, indentified in Marina Salye's report on the St. Petersburg food scandal case, involved the export to the United Kingdom of over a million barrels of refined oil products—fuel oil, diesel, and gasoline. As we noted earlier, the debacle of the St. Petersburg commodities-for-food deals also taught Mr. Putin the importance of establishing control not just over the actual resources, but also over the business networks and physical infrastructure needed to purchase, transport, and sell them.[29]

This lesson learned in the early 1990s makes one specific topic in Putin's 1996 dissertation—a topic that is not reflected in the title, but is delved into in detail in the text—particularly relevant to his management of Russia, Inc. Putin devotes an entire chapter of his dissertation to what he terms "the need for Russia's transportation independence on the strategic level." This is the idea that Russia must not allow itself to be dependent on any foreign country or countries for the infrastructure crucial to ensuring the export and import of key commodities and goods.[30] Putin describes, in great detail, a plan for the construction of a multifunctional oil refining and transportation complex. There is nothing especially original in Putin's thesis about the importance of transportation infrastructure, but it nonetheless underscores the significance of this issue for his presidency. Beyond the unfortunate experience of the food scandal, transportation was a general theme that Putin encountered on a regular basis during his time in St. Petersburg. As deputy mayor, his job was to deal with the domestic and foreign businesses moving oil and commodities, as well as other goods, in and out of Russia through St. Petersburg's vital Baltic Sea ports.

After the breakup of the Soviet Union, one of the earliest concerns of the Russian leadership at both the federal and regional levels in the

1990s was how to build enough new port capacity on Russian shores to replace the former Soviet Baltic, Black Sea, and Caspian ports, lost to what now were foreign countries.[31] The St. Petersburg mayor's office was involved in these discussions about ports from the beginning. Putin used materials from the various government committees as sources and references in his dissertation. Similar concerns were expressed about how to contend with the loss of the Soviet rail and oil and gas pipeline networks, which had linked producers in the USSR, and thus Russia, to global commodities markets. These now extended out from Russia over the territories of foreign countries like Belarus, Ukraine, the Baltic states, or Kazakhstan and other Central Asian states. As president, Putin has prioritized upgrading Russia's rail network, as well as constructing new energy pipelines directly to key consumers in Europe, bypassing countries like Ukraine.[32]

In sum, the importance of oil and gas as the main sources of value for Russia, and the significance of transportation infrastructure as a means of ensuring control over the physical flows of oil and gas, have helped Putin to define which companies needed to be in the core of his Russia, Inc.[33] In this context, the juridical ownership of the core Russian companies has proven almost irrelevant. Some of the companies are owned by the Russian state. Many others are privately owned. In all cases, Mr. Putin, informed by his Survivalist and Free Marketeer identities, has seen to it that these companies are inside his system and have been subject to his oversight in both formal and informal ways. This is where the top operational managers of Putin's Russia, Inc. come into play. The near-monopoly producer of natural gas, Gazprom, and the largest producer of oil, Rosneft, are owned by the state. They are also overseen by two individuals who could be described as indispensable in Mr. Putin's Russian management and governance system.[34] In 2012, Viktor Zubkov was the chairman of Gazprom and Igor Sechin was the president and CEO of Rosneft.[35] Putin's relationships with these two are among the oldest of all his close associates. One or the other, or both, have featured in virtually every important episode in Putin's career over the past two or more decades. The linkages between them extend in multiple directions. For example, only one year after Putin produced his dissertation, Igor Sechin also wrote his dissertation under the auspices of Vladimir Litvinenko's St. Petersburg Mining Institute, on the same theme: transportation infrastructure for oil. The title of Sechin's thesis was the "Economic Evaluation of Investment Projects in Transportation of Oil and Oil Products." It was a cost-benefit analysis of a project to build a pipeline from Russia's largest oil refinery at Kirishi in Leningrad oblast to the loading terminal in Batareynaya (Battery) Bay on the Gulf of Finland.[36] In 2000, Viktor Zubkov also received his degree from the very same Mining Institute. True to form, Zubkov's dissertation was on "Improving the Taxation Mechanism of the Mineral Resource Complex."[37]

Apart from Rosneft and Gazprom, most of the rest of the oil and gas industry was in private hands during Putin's presidency and premiership but with highly diverse structures and ties that extended back to Vladimir Putin himself. The number two oil producer, Lukoil, was a private company controlled by a former Soviet oil industry insider, Vagit Alekperov (an ethnic Azeri from Baku, but a Russian citizen). TNK-BP, a close number three in terms of oil production and number two in reserves, was half-owned by a group of Russian financial oligarchs (including Pyotr Aven and his Alfa Bank partner, Mikhail Fridman) and half by a foreign partner, BP, until 2013, when it was required by Rosneft. The fourth-largest oil company, Surgutneftegaz, one of the most opaque companies in Russia, has never revealed its ownership.

The companies that transport oil and gas—given their importance in the equation and the prominence of this issue in both Putin's and Sechin's dissertations—were also under control of trusted Putin associates. All of Russia's natural gas pipelines were owned by Gazprom. The crude oil pipeline system was a state monopoly, Transneft, headed by Nikolai Tokarev, an associate of Putin's from his arrival in Moscow in 1996, and possibly earlier.[38] All pipelines for refined oil products were owned by a Transneft subsidiary, Transnefteprodukt. Both crude and refined products can also be transported by rail.[39] The Russian rail system, another state monopoly, was led by Vladimir Yakunin, Putin's Ozero dacha neighbor as well as the head of organizations devoted to restoring Russia's Orthodox heritage.[40] Leningrad native Yakunin served in an official capacity as a member of the Soviet delegation to the United Nations in New York in the 1980s and was then involved in private business ventures in St. Petersburg in the 1990s. He re-entered the government apparatus in 1997, when Putin named him as regional head of the Main Control Directorate (GKU).[41] Putin appointed him to head the rail monopoly in 2005.[42] Likewise, Russia's key ports and terminals also seem to fall under the ownership of Putin associates or under the direct purview of the state, given the importance of sea transportation for Russian exports (and Putin's and Sechin's dissertations).[43] For example, in 2007, President Putin established Russia's United Shipbuilding Company to consolidate the bulk of Russia's shipbuilding capacity.[44] Igor Sechin was the company's first chairman.

The mixture of ownership structures across these key companies and sectors underscores the point that juridical ownership—whether the companies are private or not—is not the key issue for Putin. It is rather whether the structures give him the ability to interact with the individuals who head the companies—either as owners or as appointed managers. As the CEO/president, Mr. Putin needs to ensure that the activity of the business owners is not detrimental to national interests, as he has defined them. Otherwise, the owners and managers are expected to act independently on behalf of the general guidelines Putin has laid down in his strategic plans. They should maximize performance, pay their taxes, and support the economically backward but politically important sectors of the Russian economy by placing orders with Russia's heavy manufacturing plants where large numbers of jobs are concentrated.[45]

THE APPARATUS

Outside Russia, Inc. is the next concentric circle of Mr. Putin's and Russia's system. This is the apparatus, the bureaucracy of the Russian state, where a whole range of officials serve at various levels. This, in many respects, is the Swiss watch level. Here, everyone is supposed to know his or her place and what to do. The apparatus has a hierarchy of its own. At its top are the ministers and other designated officials who run the government. They are disparagingly referred to as *apparatchiki* by most Russians, using the old Soviet term for the state bureaucracy or *apparat*. Mr. Putin, however, proudly calls them *chinovniki*—which has more historical resonance. This picks up on Peter the Great's creation of the Table of Ranks (*chin*) to formalize the positions in the Russian imperial bureaucracy in the 1700s. The system lasted until the Russian Revolution of 1917 and essentially created a professional class of state servitors.

Putin has also referred to himself, in this context, as a *chinovnik*—in interviews in November 1999, when he was successor-designate.[46] In fact, of course, at this juncture he most likely did not see himself quite on a par with the tens and hundreds of thousands of officials in the government apparatus in Moscow or the rest of Russia's regions. He was not a *chinovnik*. He was a *gosudarstvennik* as he declared himself only a month later in the Millennium Message. His identity was not defined by where he happened to work but by his vision for the state. Nonetheless, in keeping with his repeated attempts to create "in-groups" and co-opt key constituencies, especially through the deployment of historical references and analogies, Mr. Putin put himself in the guise of the *chinovnik*. His purpose was to make common cause with the huge numbers of people who would soon be working for and under him in Russia's vast state bureaucracy.

In Putin's system, tables of ranks, formal hierarchies, and organization charts are not particularly important. Positions in the inner circle as well as in the outer concentric circles of the government are *made* important by the individuals who hold them, not the other way around. The most obvious example was the post of prime minister when Putin occupied it.[47] In sum, the people who Putin has chosen to run the system are important—often entirely by virtue of his connections with them, as he made clear from the outset of his presidency in early interviews. These people are not really *siloviki,* representatives or former officials of the KGB or other power ministries, although some have worked within these agencies as Putin himself did. In one of his early interviews as acting Russian president, with ABC News' Ted Koppel in 2000, Putin stressed that KGB connections were less important than people's "professional qualities and personal relationships."[48] Igor Sechin has links with the security services through prior work as a military translator.[49] Viktor Zubkov's ties are with the Soviet Communist Party apparatus and agricultural sector. Dmitry Medvedev was trained as a lawyer and taught law at his alma mater, Leningrad State University, before joining Anatoly Sobchak's 1990 mayoral campaign.

Once within the system, at the core of the inner circle, people's "professional qualities" on the job supersede the "personal relationships." If they are to stay at the very top of the hierarchy, they have to perform in their assigned roles as well as consistently prove their loyalty to Putin.

The people Putin has chosen as his operational managers for Russia, Inc., as well as for running key parts of the state apparatus, are the people who can *deliver*.[50] They are charged with ensuring the smooth operation and a high level of performance for critical corporate elements or sectors. In the case of Sechin, it is the vital oil industry. In the case of Zubkov, the collection and protection of financial information, and, in the case of Medvedev from 2008 to 2012, the constitutionally crucial post of the presidency.

Others play somewhat different roles. They are the "ombudsmen" or intermediate representatives for the system.[51] As we shall discuss in more detail below, their job is to provide vital linkages between the CEO/president, the inner circle, and other important groups. They channel information and create a feedback mechanism to ensure that everything functions as it should. Igor Shuvalov, one of Russia's deputy prime ministers, for example, played this role as the "sherpa" to the Group of Eight (G-8) and the Group of Twenty (G-20). He was Russia, Inc.'s, as well as the Russian state's, interface with international financial institutions and international business circles.[52] As president, Dmitry Medvedev played a similar role with world leaders, conducting all the requisite regular meetings with global counterparts, while Prime Minister Putin could strategically pick and choose which encounters he wanted, or had, to take as CEO and strategic planner.[53]

PRESENTING ALTERNATIVES TO THE PRESIDENT/CEO

Within the upper levels of the system, and especially in the inner circle of operative management, Putin avoids assigning overlapping spheres of authority. He does not want conflict among his operational managers and deputies. People can disagree with each other—perhaps even directly with Putin—in initial phases before decisions are made on certain policy issues. Once Putin has made a decision, especially one that relates to the fulfillment of an explicit strategic goal, others should not openly act against it. Since Putin makes all critical decisions related to the state's mission, the vital issue within the system is: Who has access to Putin? Who can transmit an idea, a proposal, or a message to Putin? Weight in the system is not just who executes, who carries things out, but who transmits—who can convey information that might change or affect a decision on an important question by Mr. Putin in his role as the CEO/president.

As a number of Russian analysts and Kremlin insiders have pointed out, where there are unavoidable divergent interests on critical issues, Putin expects his close associates to present their cases (or synthesize and present the positions of other larger groups and interests outside the inner circle) and let him decide on the trade-offs. There is thus freedom of expression not only at the private level of close associates, but remarkably high up the system at a public level.[54] Individuals outside the inner circle as well as within can disagree openly with official proposals for policies. They can present alternatives and generally make contributions to policy as long as they work within the system, do not question its legitimacy, or question Putin and his team's competence, and then get on board with the leadership's policies once final decisions are made.

This explains why, over the past decade, there appeared to be considerable disagreement at the top of the Russian state apparatus on critical economic and other political issues, which was often aired in the press or in public statements. The differences became especially acute during the period of the tandem and the Medvedev presidency from 2008 to 2012. Two different teams—one around Medvedev and the other around Putin—aggressively competed to get their ideas and proposals into prime time consideration.[55] This period also overlapped with the most difficult phase of the economic crisis in Russia, when the Kremlin actively solicited outside ideas on how to tackle it. In many respects, this is a variation of what was called democratic centralism in the Soviet period—but in Putin's Russia it was played out in public instead of entirely behind the Kremlin walls.[56]

THE IRRESPONSIBLE OFFICIAL AND OTHER CAUTIONARY TALES FROM A VERTICAL SYSTEM

Everybody knowing what they have to do and when they have to do it—as well as knowing that they will be accountable to the man at the top—is the idealized essence of Putin's system. This is the key element of the *vertikal vlasti* (vertical of power), which Putin tried to create in centralizing the state apparatus in the 2000s. The man at the top lays out the mission and sets the goals. Everyone else from the top to the bottom of the federal state apparatus has a larger or smaller set of responsibilities for trying to achieve those goals. The same happens at the regional level. The *polpred,* the presidential envoy for one of the large federal districts, is charged with ensuring that the state's goals are met outside of Moscow. The presidential envoys must monitor the performance and compliance of the group of regions within their larger district. Regional governors report back to the *polpred,* and thus back to the Russian president. They must likewise ensure that every level of the regional state apparatus is working away on its respective set of responsibilities.

Getting the state machinery in motion in this way was Vladimir Putin's policy innovation after the school siege by Chechen terrorists in Beslan in the Russian North Caucasus in September 2004. The ideas certainly preceded the Beslan tragedy—having originated in the 1997 *poslaniye* and in many other documents—but Putin was waiting for an excuse and a coherent rationale to introduce them. Beslan provided one.[57] During the siege, no one on the scene took decisive action to deal with the standoff with the terrorists. They waited for instructions from the top (or even outright refused to respond to the situation) as everything got progressively out of hand. In what seemed like another rerun of the August 2000 *Kursk* tragedy, the lack of action was captured by Russian as well as international media outlets and widely documented.[58] Putin had to step in to dispatch negotiators and counter-terrorism SWAT teams from Moscow to the North Caucasus to tackle the crisis. For several agonizing days, the world watched as hundreds of children, parents, and teachers suffered, and then ultimately perished in the eventual assault on the school. Putin had been forced to assume manual control.

In the *vertikal vlasti* that Putin rolled out after Beslan, he announced that he would force the Swiss watch mechanism into proper, orderly, automatic operation again. Everyone who was appointed to a position within the mechanism of the state apparatus, at the federal, regional, or local level, would know what his or her job was and would have to answer for it. Putin declared that he would end elections for crucial positions in the regions and appoint people directly so that they would be personally accountable to him for their performance and actions. The Russian word for responsibility or accountability, *otvetstvennost',* has the same root as the word answer: *otvet.* In Russian this concept is thus quite powerful. In American parlance, having personal *otvetstvennost'* for something means that problems cannot be kicked upstairs. The "buck stops" with the particular individual. In creating the vertical of power, Putin wanted to make sure that the "buck" for most things would stop at a level much lower than him, than the presidency.

Since introducing the vertical of power, Putin and members of his inner circle have relished telling tales to illustrate why the system is in place. A particular favorite has been the "tale of the irresponsible elected official" in some remote (usually Siberian) locality. Putin has made this his stock anecdote for creating the vertical of power, including for ending the election of regional governors and other key officials after 2004. He has brought it up in press interviews and rolled it out twice at Valdai Discussion Club dinners. Both Valentina Matvienko, who was then governor of St. Petersburg, and Igor Shuvalov have repeated the same tale (with a few variations of their own) in meetings with the Valdai group. The tale usually begins as related to Putin or others directly by then Emergencies Minister Sergei Shoigu:[59]

A Siberian locality is plunged into an icy and potentially deadly blackout in the depths of winter. The local elected official has not realized he is responsible for dealing with potential winter fuel shortages in his region. He has failed to make the necessary advance provisions to stash away reserves. The population protests. Appeals are made to Moscow for assistance. Sergei Shoigu and a crisis response team are dispatched to take charge. Shoigu tries to persuade the hapless official to go out to address the crowds clamoring for action. The official demurs and excuses himself for a moment (ostensibly to go to the toilet in one of Putin's versions—another of his favorite references to outhouses) "never to be seen again." Putin concludes, after retelling this tale, that only people who are appointed and told what to do, and then made fully accountable to him and to Moscow, will take charge. If they know they have to answer to the top, they take responsibility and do what is necessary. If they are elected, and have no boss but the people, they simply take off.[60]

In the years since Beslan, Putin has found the vertical of power wanting. In spite of relishing his role as the boss, and the PR benefits it accrues, Putin has had to take action himself over and over again. Either he has had to send someone from Moscow out to Russia's regions, or he has had to intervene in person, like in Pikalyovo or during the 2010 fires. Instead of standing on the sidelines and monitoring the mechanism of the state, or formulating and providing the strategic vision from the top like the CEO, Putin has been increasingly diverted from his task. He has plunged into ad hoc tactical improvisations to fix the mechanism. Appointed officials still seem to have the same affliction as the irresponsible elected official who vanished from the scene in Siberia. They have a propensity to look for guidance and instruction—if not an outright bailout—from the top. They do not seem to realize that they are part of the mechanism of a Swiss watch all working in synchrony. They do not know that the buck stops with them. This clearly frustrates Mr. Putin, based on his numerous public complaints in interviews and in discussions about officials' general and specific lack of responsibility.[61]

A SYSTEM BASED ON DISTRUST

The failure of Putin's vertical of power shows that the corporate management model he envisages cannot work on the scale of the entire state apparatus. The apparatus is too large. The system he has created has too many peculiarities. There are no clear lines of responsibility within the system as a whole. Even if the formal institutions of the state are still in place, the entire system is in many respects completely unstructured. The corporate model appears to have worked in the 2000s for the purpose of controlling the oligarchs and monitoring their activity in service of the mission Putin has laid out. Beyond that, Putin's actual practice has not lived up to the blueprint. In a properly functioning corporation, there is delegation of responsibility and accountability up and down the entire chain of command. There is also reward and merit at every level. In Putin's virtual corporation there are no clear chains of authority because there can be no authority that does not come from Putin personally. Personal relationships trump professional resumes, apart from in a handful of cases, and rewards are concentrated at the very top of the system.[62]

There are three main reasons why Putin's system cannot match up to the corporate governance ideal. The first and most obvious reason is that Russia is a state not a corporation. At the top of Putin's system, the CEO is accountable to no one. Putin has claimed on occasion that he is just a "hired manager," but the reality is much different. He is officially Russia's president, not its CEO. Since he was formally elected president in 2000, no one has hired him, and in reality no one can fire him. There is no overriding institution that can oust Putin from his constitutionally guaranteed terms as Russian president. As a result, Putin's system operates in two parallel universes. There is the political, legal, constitutional environment of the state, which ordinary people as well as those working in the state apparatus have to live under. Beside it, and intertwined with it, is the informal, unofficial system Vladimir Putin has created.[63] This is the "special world" of the original oligarchs who Putin brought into his July 2000 deal. It also includes what one might call a set of crony oligarchs who have risen to prominence since 2000, all of whom have ties one way or another to Putin; and it includes the network of close associates who work with him in the inner circle.[64] In the special world, the oligarchs can make strategic decisions related to their business holdings. In this regard, their formal ownership of economic assets delineates a sphere of authority. This is not true in the government apparatus.

The so-called crony oligarchs have some important distinctions from the original oligarchs who emerged from the "loans-for-shares" deal of the Yeltsin era. These distinctions underscore some of the finer points of the system and Putin's efforts to create a sense of accountability. Putin did not inherit the cronies. They have become extremely wealthy under his presidency. Even if their personal associations with Putin are more tenuous than some of the reporting on their connections might suggest, they play an important role in the system he has created, and they occupy extremely responsible positions in the Russian economy. They are all predominantly involved in oil and gas transportation and trading and are thus key to Putin retaining ultimate control over Russia's economically and politically vital oil and gas sector. They are the active, mobile, adaptive intermediaries between massive and clumsy behemoths like Gazprom, Rosneft, and Transneft and the global markets. Their existence is the difference between a bureaucracy that does not, and cannot, get things done (like the Soviet, and now the Russian, state apparatus) and a group of individuals who can get things done and profit in doing so.

In Putin's conceptualization of the system, the crony oligarchs are accountable to him personally. The state-owned firms are not really accountable, because accountability to the public is no accountability at all (as the tale of the irresponsible Siberian official makes clear). The crony oligarchs, like the original oligarchs, are a small, limited group. This makes it easier to deal with them directly. The personal enrichment of the group is related to Putin's goal of ensuring control, accountability, predictability, security, and stability in all transactions involving oil and gas. Group members become wealthy because they deliver results, not simply because they are friends with Mr. Putin. They are rewarded and protected by Putin and his system on the basis of their performance.[65]

The second and third reasons why Putin's system does not match up to its ideals are interrelated: the massive distrust that permeates the relationships among the key players in the special world and the extreme, even hyper-personalization of the system. Putin personally distrusts most people. This fact comes out repeatedly in his interviews and in the various biographical works. Only a few people, including Viktor Zubkov, Dmitry Medvedev, Alexei Kudrin, and Igor Sechin, have ever been publicly singled out as deserving of Putin's trust.[66] They have clearly worked hard to earn it over their long associations with him. If you do not know people personally, how can you know whether they can be trusted to do something? If you do not trust people, you do not give them real responsibility. If people cannot be trusted, they also cannot be held accountable, in the Russian sense of *otvetstvennost'*. Those who knew Putin back in his St. Petersburg days underscore in interviews that loyalty and trust are always closely interlinked for him. Putin's former judo trainer, Anatoly Rakhlin, in a 2007 interview with the Russian newspaper *Izvestiya* stressed that Putin "doesn't take the St. Petersburg boys to work with him because of their pretty eyes, but because he trusts people who are tried and true."[67] There is ample evidence to suggest that while incompetence may be forgiven, breaking deals and personal disloyalty will merit the most extreme punishment.[68]

Distrust also means that the special world, the closed informal system around Putin and Russia, Inc., requires hands-on direction at all times. There must be some kind of hook to guarantee loyalty, even with the crony oligarchs and others who seem to be the most closely linked to him. Here again, Putin has applied his KGB case officer training and experience to create the same kind of arrangement with the inner circle that he made with the original oligarchs in July 2000. As he can fully trust only himself, Putin applies extortionary methods to everyone else— basically mutually assured incrimination to ensure loyalty.

A great deal has been written about corruption at the top levels of the informal Russian system, with much speculation about the inner circle's personal wealth, including Putin's.[69] The role of money in this system is important but commonly misunderstood. Money is ever-present in the system, but it is not money that guarantees loyalty or holds the top level together. Instead, it is the fact that the money derives from activity that is or could be found to be illegal. Participants in the system are not bought off in the classic sense of that term. They are compromised; they are made vulnerable to threats. Enforcement of group cohesion in the special world is achieved not by positive incentives but by implicit threats. Putin used threats as a case officer in the KGB. This was the essence of the system Putin put in place with Viktor Zubkov's assistance during his time as deputy mayor in St. Petersburg. Loyalty is ensured through blackmail. Corrupt, even illegal, activity will be kept secret as long as the individual continues to play the game.

People are rewarded with money and other perks for working for and within the system and for performing well in the tasks that Mr. Putin has set out for them.[70] But, as Putin learned in the KGB, there is always the risk that someone else will bid higher, or that one of the inner group might some day decide that honor or conscience are worth forgoing the monetary rewards. Therefore, as an enforcement mechanism, the risk of *loss* is more important than any reward. And, as in the most effective blackmail schemes, it is not the threat of loss of money or property that frightens most people. It is loss of reputation, loss of one's standing in the eyes of family, friends, and peers—loss of one's identity. (When confronted with a blackmail threat, the instinctive reaction of every victim is the proverbial plea to "take everything I have, just don't tell X.") Often the threat is made officially and publicly to underscore the risks. For example, in 2002, Viktor Zubkov, as head of *Rosfinmonitoring,* asked Russian journalists to "pass on" this message to tax evaders: "Anyone still involved in criminal business should cease immediately. We're going to find them and make them answer for their crimes. They'll end up as paupers and bring shame to their families."[71] Key oligarchs and others who have made a deal with the Kremlin and have responsibilities within the informal system are not allowed the option of cashing out. If all they stand to lose is the cash flow, then they *are* like hired managers. But they cannot have that independence. A very few have been allowed to leave, but they are still expected to adhere to the rules of the game and refrain from meddling in Kremlin business.[72]

In short, corruption (as viewed from a Western perspective) is the glue that helps keep Putin's informal system together. In the special world, everyone's wealth is deliberately tainted. Rumors or stories in the press about corruption can be used to bring people to heel, to curb their political or personal ambitions, and to remind everyone else of how much they have to lose. Everyone in the system is depicted as dirty. There are rumors of corruption about everyone, rumors that may or may not be true. No one passes unscathed. Everyone must be vulnerable. This binds the inner circle even more tightly together and makes it impossible for anyone to leave or betray the system. Criminal charges and the effects on families are the more powerful threats, as Zubkov outlined in 2002, than simply losing money. It is no surprise that many people within the inner circle of Putin's system, from oligarchs to government officials, have property, capital, and close family members living abroad. This is also a hedge against the risk of losing everything in Russia when the next person comes along and decides to disappropriate and reallocate.[73]

PERSONALIZATION: THE "ONE-BOY NETWORK"

Threats and extortion may address one set of systemic issues, but they will not solve everything. Since 2004, Putin has had to face the dilemma that distrust and the personalized nature of the system he has created also undermine his general concept of the vertical of power. The fact that the particular person in a specific position, or carrying out a discrete function, is crucially important has weakened the vertical of power from the top to the bottom. Some people are more powerful than others by virtue of who they are and their connections rather than their positions—especially if they have close personal ties to Putin. Most Russians working in the state apparatus are well aware of the existence of the parallel universe of the informal, unofficial, special world of privilege and access to Putin.

Putin himself underscored the personalization by taking back the presidency from Dmitry Medvedev in 2011–12. The so-called *rokirovka* (castling) or Medvedev-Putin job swap, was seen by many Russian analysts as undermining the institution and position of the Russian presidency.[74] When he left the presidency in 2008, Vladimir Putin reportedly commended the staff of the presidential administration for their efforts in rebuilding the institution since the 1990s. He often, in the same period, made public reference to his pride in strengthening the "one institution that works" in the Russian state. Putin instructed his staff to continue to serve the presidency and keep it strong. He noted that he was taking it upon himself to similarly strengthen the position of prime minister and thus the role of the government and cabinet of ministers to complement the institutional work he had done in the Kremlin.[75] Four years later, Vladimir Putin reclaimed the presidency as a personal sinecure. The *rokirovka* restored Putin the person but damaged a decade of efforts to restore the integrity of the Russian presidency as the position at the top of the vertical of power.

Furthermore, throughout his tenures as president and prime minister, Putin has undermined the value of other key institutional positions, either by moving the same set of close associates from job to job at the very top of the system, or conversely by keeping others further down firmly and unassailably in place. Again, the people count, rather than the positions they hold. Unlike Dmitry Medvedev during his presidency, Putin does not generally sack people within the system, even for clear incompetence—he gives them another chance to do better (or do something else). While some of the highest profile people move around in search of the ideal opportunity, or because Putin has reassigned them to undertake a particularly crucial task, people at other levels stay in their offices. Putin explained his motivations for keeping long-serving ministers and others in place in his December 15, 2011, call-in show:

> These are qualified people. . . . We can dispute with them or reproach them for something, but the worst thing we can do is to start shuffling them from position to position. . . . I have some experience with this work, and I know what constant reshuffling means and what it leads to. . . . If people are making the wrong decisions, our task is to organize the work in a way that will avoid these mistakes.[76]

From his time as a KGB case officer, Putin knows it is very costly to build up the levers to "identify, recruit, and run" an agent. When he contemplated dealing with the oligarchs in 2000, he also knew that Russia had a very limited number of its own capitalists who could run huge corporations and make them competitive internationally.[77] Likewise, when you fire a minister, you lose all that investment. Even a dull, incompetent team member who is loyal and fully under control is better than a new and competent one who might not understand the rules of the game and the workings of the special world, the parallel universe. This is why you keep people in place rather than fire them. If they are a real problem, you try to find something creative for them to do hidden in the depths of the system where they can do no harm.

The classic example of the latter is Yevgeny Nazdratenko, the former governor of Primorsky Krai and the bane of President Yeltsin's regional policies in the 1990s. Early in his term, Putin took action against Nazdratenko as one of the first moves in his policy to rein in Russia's regions. Rather than repress Nazdratenko, Putin carefully moved him away from the regional capital, Vladivostok, and gave him a lucrative chairmanship in Moscow in the Russian State Commission for Fisheries. One journalist, puzzled why Putin did not deal with such an obvious opponent more harshly, posed that question to Anatoly Chubais. Chubais replied:

This [the treatment of Nazdratenko] is the way that our president was demonstratively explaining the new rules of the game to the elite. . . . Putin was showing that those who play by the rules [and Nazdratenko did play by the rules, because in the end he agreed to voluntarily retire from Primorsky Krai] will be treated as one of ours, and we will not touch them. But those who do not agree to play by the rules will be dealt with, with the full severity of the law.[78]

In short, as a consequence of his Case Officer identity, Mr. Putin cannot simply abandon an "asset." Looking at all in the inner circle as assets is another reason the team around Putin always remains small. The fact that Putin sees himself as the person who has identified and recruited people to the team, the inner circle, and is responsible for running them, dictates a limit. His corporate model reinforces this. As a result, however, Russia, Inc. has no strategic reserve in terms of personnel, even if it has an enormous amount of material and financial reserves. It has very weak capacity for renewal by bringing in new faces and no mechanism for mobility at the top unless it comes through Putin. Everything is limited by relations with Vladimir Putin.[79] With the Communist Party of the Soviet Union long gone, and United Russia never having graduated to the position of fully institutionalized ruling party, Putin has no mechanism except personal connections to select people for key positions and responsibilities. The old Soviet and Russian establishment has been replaced by the ultimate old boy network—a *one*-boy network—where Vladimir Putin functions as the primary recruiter.[80]

Everyone's relationship at the top of Russia, Inc. is with Putin. The terminology of the inner circle reflects this. During the 2010 Valdai Discussion Club meetings, for example, top officials in the government and the region repeatedly referred to Putin and to doing things in tandem with him—*My s Putinom* (Putin and I) was a constant refrain.[81] There are only vertical links up to Putin, even within the informal system, and no real horizontal ties. Everyone, no matter who, needs to check back with Putin or refer back to Putin to legitimate his own position, ideas, or general standing. The most exaggerated example of the one-way relationship with Putin is Chechen President Ramzan Kadyrov. The Kadyrov-Putin relationship is an extreme case of personal fealty in both the informal and the formal state systems. Ramzan Kadyrov makes it clear that he considers he has a personal bond with Vladimir Putin and owes allegiance only to Putin, not to the Russian state.[82]

"WHO CAN TRANSMIT TO VLADIMIR?"

Putin is aware of the difficulties posed both by the hyper-personalization of the system and the coexistence of the informal and formal state systems. In fact, he has tried to create a solution. Bridging the gap between the two parallel universes is a set of intermediaries, the ombudsmen. As we noted earlier, the role of the ombudsmen is to reach out to interest groups beyond the informal system who have stakes in specific decisions the system makes. They channel information and afford outside stakeholders a limited degree of access to Russia, Inc. and to the personage of Mr. Putin. The nominal power and position of these ombudsmen is based solely on their access to Putin. Can they transmit?

Gleb Pavlovsky in his interview with *The Guardian* in January 2012 described the ruling party, United Russia (UR), as performing an ombudsman function. He noted that the party had been designed solely as a transmitter for the more formal state structures, so they could reach the top and the informal echelons around Putin, and the top could reach them:

> United Russia is a telephone system from the Kremlin to the bottom through the regional apparatus. *A transmission of the signal.* It has absolutely no independence and cannot act on its own, in contrast to the KPSS [Soviet Communist Party]. It cannot fulfill political directives. It needs full instructions, 1, 2, 3, 4 and 5. If 3 and 4 are missing it stops and waits for instructions. UR has nothing in common with the KPSS. It has just been useful as an important element.[83]

In his book covering Putin's presidency and premiership from 2000 to 2011, British journalist Angus Roxburgh describes a similar role for Putin's press secretary, Dmitry Peskov. Roxburgh spent three years as a consultant for the Moscow office of the Ketchum public relations company working as a media and communications adviser for Peskov and his team. Peskov was the interface between the Kremlin and international press, passing requests for interviews up to Putin and other key figures and transmitting information back again. As Putin's spokesman, he also played a key role in conveying Putin's views across the political system and to key international interlocutors as Roxburgh and other Ketchum colleagues described—including making phone calls to congratulate influential people on their birthdays.[84] Getting Putin and the Kremlin to open up and broaden access for the media was, however, a very hard slog for the Ketchum group—one they never pulled off. The system relied far too heavily on controlled transmissions and limited access to the top.[85]

Perhaps the best illustration of this point was still President Medvedev's statement "I will transmit this information to Vladimir," captured by a live microphone during his meeting with U.S. president Barack Obama in Seoul, South Korea, in March 2012.[86] President Obama was caught explaining to Medvedev that he could not make much progress on critical issues during the U.S. presidential election season but hoped to have more flexibility in a second presidential term. Medvedev nodded in sympathy and patted Obama's arm, reassuring him that he would tell this to

"Vladimir."[87] Over the four years of his premiership, Vladimir Putin studiously avoided meetings with world leaders, including Barack Obama who met with him only once, on July 7, 2009.[88] German chancellor Angela Merkel, French president Nicholas Sarkozy, and British prime ministers Gordon Brown and David Cameron all had the same limited interactions—one meeting (none in Brown's case) and some occasional phone calls.[89] From time to time, Putin would deign to meet with U.S. Secretary of State Hillary Clinton and other envoys when a critical issue needed his attention, but mostly the relationships at the state level were focused on Dmitry Medvedev. The assumption was that if Putin needed or wanted to know something, Medvedev would let him know. Otherwise there was no really good, or reliable, way of speaking directly to the man who still dominated Russian politics in 2008–12.

In this way, by limiting access to himself, Mr. Putin managed to transform himself back into the Outsider after 12 years at the very center of power in Russia. He played this to great advantage. Access to Putin remains one of the most valuable currencies in Russia. For the four years of his premiership, Putin kept everyone guessing about his intentions, inside and outside Russia. Just as he had back in the days of the Leningrad State University *dvor,* he stood to one side, monitoring the situation, saying little. Using the tandem structure with Medvedev, as in the words of Russia analyst Pavel Baev, Putin really did "vanish in a crowd of two."[90] As a result of Putin's aloofness, at all levels of interaction with the Russian state over the period from 2008 to 2012 (including in international government circles) there was a veritable obsession with the need to identify a reliable mode of transmission to Vladimir. If would-be interlocutors could not get the ear of President Medvedev, the ultimate "transmitter" to Vladimir, then they would latch onto others in the Kremlin orbit in the hope they could transmit up the vertical of power.[91]

At the same time that Prime Minister Putin was avoiding meetings with his state counterparts, he did continue to meet with international CEOs, as the head of Russia, Inc. This was especially the case in the vital oil industry, where Putin's meetings with global oil titans were publicly and frequently recorded as well as noted in private.[92] Similarly, Putin's meetings with former U.S. Secretary of State Henry Kissinger, who had become a trusted adviser to U.S. and other international strategic businesses, were publicized. In this way, Putin emphasized where his priorities lay as the CEO and strategic planner. He was making sure that Russia's economic assets were secure and international investment would continue to flow into the most critical sectors. While Dmitry Medvedev became the reliable ombudsman for statesmen, Putin created several ombudsmen for the world's top businessmen, to supplement the one-on-one meetings with him, with Vladimir himself.

In a June 2012 article during the St. Petersburg Economic Forum, for example, the Russian newspaper *Vedomosti* related how major international companies represented at the forum had stressed the importance of Igor Shuvalov's role as the ombudsman for business and investment in resolving a number of critical issues behind the scenes. International CEOs commended Vladimir Putin for creating the position.[93] *Vedomosti*, however, also highlighted the general mystery of the "investment ombudsman" position for most people operating outside the informal system in Russia, remarking that there was not much information on what exactly Shuvalov was doing in this role.[94] Beyond Shuvalov, another key figure who has played the ombudsman function is Matthias Warnig, a German businessman. Warnig's connections to Putin extend back at least to St. Petersburg and the 1990s, when Warnig opened up the St. Petersburg branch of Dresdner Bank.[95] In the 2000s, Putin appointed Warnig to a number of management and oversight positions in the Russian energy transportation sector. These included a leading role in the company constructing and operating the Nord Stream gas export pipeline under the Baltic Sea from Russia to Germany and senior board positions with Gazprom, Rosneft, Transneft, and other companies. Warnig is seen by international energy company executives as a crucial intermediary between them and these companies, as well as a direct interlocutor with Putin.[96]

The most important ombudsman of all for international and domestic interlocutors with interests in the Russian oil sector, however, is Igor Sechin, one of the closest of Mr. Putin's associates.[97] Putin reaffirmed Sechin's official ombudsman role in 2012 by creating a new presidential commission on the fuel and energy complex (the TEK Commission, to use the Russian acronym) with Sechin, the CEO of Rosneft, in charge.[98] Putin is technically the chairman of the commission as CEO of Russia, Inc., but Igor Sechin is the executive secretary. As the newspaper *Vedomosti* related, the commission was first set up when Putin was prime minister. There was a great deal of satisfaction with this arrangement among Russian oil executives, who as a result were able to meet regularly and secure access to Putin, as well as to Sechin. In 2012, Russia's oil executives assumed the commission would automatically migrate to the presidency along with Putin, given the importance of the oil sector and his traditional hands-on oversight. They waited patiently for an official announcement. In the interim, Sechin created an "oil club" with the same executives. It met totally off-the-record, informally and privately in Sechin's Rosneft office, once a week. To the executives' surprise, instead of an announcement from the Kremlin, Dmitry Medvedev's aide, Arkady Dvorkovich, suddenly revived the prime minister's TEK Commission, naming himself the head, and designating members. The oil executives apparently revolted. They wanted to retain their access to Putin through Igor Sechin. They appealed to Putin to set up a presidential TEK Commission and signed a formal letter with the request. This was transmitted to Putin via Sechin. Putin made no move to abolish the prime minister's TEK Commission, but he duly established a new presidential commission. The Kremlin commission appropriated all the language of the old commission Putin had overseen in the prime minister's office, along with some new key provisions. The oil executives were delighted. Their ombudsman facility to transmit directly to Vladimir had been restored.

A final example of this function is Alexei Kudrin, who left his position as Russian finance minister after the announcement that Putin and Medvedev would switch positions in the *rokirovka*.[99] There are other stakeholders in the system who would also like to transmit to Vladimir—mostly their displeasure. In 2011–12, Russia, Inc., the privately held company that sits astride the top of the Russian state found itself in trouble. Representatives of the population in whose name President Putin purports to rule demanded a say in how Russia, the state, is governed. They broke the deal Putin laid out in the Millennium Message in December 1999 of not questioning his methods. After the first demonstrations following the December 2011 Russian parliamentary elections, Alexei Kudrin in effect appointed himself as the ombudsman to the protesters—at least to the urban professional elites who constituted many of the protesters in Moscow. Kudrin might even have been encouraged to play that role by Putin.[100]

Alexei Kudrin is extremely well-regarded in Western economic circles, especially in Washington D.C., and is closely connected with everyone else in the Russian political spectrum given his long years of service as Russia's finance minister and as one of Russia's preeminent economic reformers. Like many others in the Russian system—and more so than most of them—Alexei Kudrin's primary claim to legitimacy, as he admits himself, is his relationship with Putin. Kudrin is one of the few from the inner circle who can genuinely claim that "Putin respects me," as Vladimir Putin has actually said he does. He has occupied positions both within the informal network and the official state apparatus. By virtue of their decades of working together, dating back to the St. Petersburg mayor's office, the two are closely linked. They know each other extremely well. As noted earlier, Alexei Kudrin brought Putin to Moscow in 1996 and recommended him for key positions, including heading the GKU. In 2012, Alexei Kudrin may have recommended himself for a mission, outside government, to figure out how to deal with a "stakeholders" revolt against Mr. Putin's system.[101]

PART TWO

THE OPERATIVE ENGAGES

CHAPTER TEN

THE STAKEHOLDERS' REVOLT

"DON'T GO PLANNING MY FUNERAL quite yet!" Mr. Putin interjected when one of us asked how he wanted his legacy to be viewed once he was no longer leader of Russia. On that occasion—at the Valdai Discussion Club dinner outside Moscow in November 2011—his response was meant to be a joke. But more than one guest around the table thought it interesting that Vladimir Putin so instinctively seemed to assume that only his own personal demise could bring an end to his rule.

Within just a few weeks of the dinner, discussion of the possible end of Putin's rule would become public. In a string of protest events beginning in December 2011 and extending into 2012, Russian citizens came out onto the streets in numbers not seen since the 1990s. The protests caught Putin, his associates, and outside observers by surprise. The reaction from much of the Western media was gleeful. "The beginning of the end of Putin," proclaimed the headline on the cover of *The Economist* on March 3, 2012.[1] But those who hoped that the end would come soon were disappointed. Mr. Putin the Survivalist weathered the protests and reemerged as Russian president in the March 2012 election. The street demonstrations of the winter of 2011–12 were not the end of Putin, nor of "Putinism," but they were the biggest domestic challenge he had faced in his tenure as Russia's leader. The story of how the protests emerged, how Putin viewed them, and how he then responded in 2012 and 2013 says much about him and his system.

As the previous chapter showed, even before the protests, Putin's frustration with the internal workings of Russia, Inc. was unmistakable. The

227

system was not running smoothly on automatic as he intended. Even his own repeated attempts to assume manual control were not producing the desired results. But as the December 2011 events were to underscore, the internal problems of Russia, Inc., as serious as they were, paled in comparison with the crisis emerging outside. Russia on a broader, societal, level now demanded Putin's personal attention.

There is, in the corporate world, the concept of non-market or secondary "stakeholders." These are the people and groups who are not themselves owners or shareholders in a company but who are nevertheless affected by the actions of the corporation. So while they have no formal legal rights as owners, they feel they do have rights because the business affects their lives. The stakeholders are workers, the general public, and the communities in which the corporations operate. Because they often have little or no formal voice, they may resort to informal, even extra-legal means of making their views heard. Putin's Russia, Inc. may have only a very small set of shareholders clustered around Mr. Putin and the Kremlin, but it has a nation full of stakeholders. In late 2011, some of them revolted.

Nominally, the protests that began on December 10, 2011, were a reaction to the previous week's parliamentary election. The Russian voters delivered what was broadly interpreted as a defeat for the ruling party, United Russia. The 49 percent of the vote the party received was less than the figure planned and predicted by the Kremlin spin doctors, as voters turned instead to the communists and the other "official" opposition parties. The protests were triggered by the belief of many ordinary Russians that the United Russia tally should have been even lower than the announced numbers, as well as by their outrage over evidence of extensive fraud in voting procedures and vote counting, especially in Moscow. More important still was the steadfast refusal of the electoral authorities to admit even the most egregious violations. Using all the available range of Russia's social media, individuals posted on the Internet blatant examples of vote tampering at the precinct level well ahead of official election reports. Then, every bumbling attempt by electoral officials to deny the problems was spread through the same media.

The role of the Internet in these developments was key. In the 2000s, Russians became some of the world's heaviest social networkers, with their own version of Facebook—*vKontakte* (also known as

VK.com)—and a profusion of blogs and YouTube postings. One of the many dimensions of Russia's flurry of social media activity was implicitly political. Blogs, for instance, became a popular way for ordinary Russians to mobilize community action. During the summer of 2010, when forest and peat bog fires spread around Moscow and throughout central Russia—taxing local authorities' fire-fighting abilities—many Russians used the Internet to organize emergency assistance and even to fight the fires themselves. Parallel with this grassroots mobilization, the Kremlin's response to public anger about the lack of government action to tackle the crisis was to stage Putin in the role of firefighter. The contrast could not have been greater—community organizers, using the Internet to accomplish something real, versus the performance artist, "Mr. Putin: Firefighter." As we noted earlier, YouTube video clips of Mr. Putin's visits to afflicted villages showed he was not as well received as the official images suggested. His staged antics were regarded not just as a charade but as an insult to those suffering from the fires. It was not surprising, then, that entering the election season in the winter of 2011–12, social media offered Russian voters an opportunity to create an information space beyond the state's control. Voters would have multiple sources for updates about the political campaign and then the vote itself. Even more dangerous for the Kremlin, social media offered a way for citizens to voice their sentiments about Putin and the system.

Although the Duma election was the immediate catalyst for the protests, public resentment at being taken for granted had already become palpable with the September 24, 2011, announcement that Putin would return as president.[2] The future suddenly looked a lot gloomier for many Russians. Immediately after the September announcement, a picture of an aged Putin morphed into the image of Leonid Brezhnev, the elderly Soviet leader associated with the USSR's period of semi-comfortable political and social stagnation in the 1970s, began to circulate on the Internet. It captured a growing popular mood.

In January 2012, journalist Michael Idov wrote an article in *The New Yorker* called "The New Decembrists."[3] Idov has roots in Russia and close ties to many young professional Russians who turned against Putin in the December 2011 street protests in Moscow. He related how his 20- and 30-something friends had sat around after September 24, calculating how old they might be when Putin finally decided to leave the political scene. They did not like the answer. They did not like what it said about them and their own prospects. They did not want to spend another six to twelve years of the most productive and creative period of their lives under the political shadow of one man—with all the implications of personal, not just national, stagnation.[4] Idov's friends wanted something else. Although they were not exactly sure what, they at least wanted a choice, a say in what would happen next in Russia. They wanted real, not fake, political alternatives. They certainly did not want a system hinged on one man, no matter how many guises or brands in which he might appear.

PUTIN FATIGUE SETS IN

In 2011, a portion of the Russian people had simply grown tired of the Putin brand. They had "Putin fatigue." Every month since Putin's first term as president had begun, pollsters at Russia's top independent public opinion agency, the Levada Center, had asked Russians whether they approved of Putin's activity. The results did not look good in 2011. Putin's ratings were in overall decline long before the September 2011 announcement that he would end the political tandem arrangement with Dmitry Medvedev. From May 2006 through December 2010—that is, for 56 straight months—Putin's approval rating had remained above 75 percent. Then, between December 2010 and March 2011, it dropped by 10 points.[5] The drop was striking and unprecedented. When Putin made the announcement that he would return to the presidency, his ratings were lower than at any time in the previous six years. While Putin's polling numbers were hardly dire in a normal democratic context, Russia's political scene was not normal. With no political competitor, and no political party officially backing him, Putin's popularity was tied to the public's appraisal of his current performance as compared to his past performances as president and prime minister.

The Kremlin spin doctors missed this growing mood. Or at least they misjudged it. They had to some extent sensed public dissatisfaction with the regime as they prepared for the election season. Their analysis, though, was that Putin could easily survive any negative outcomes in the parliamentary elections if they made United Russia the scapegoat for anything that went wrong. For that reason the Kremlin spin doctors tried to separate Putin from the party ahead of the parliamentary election. In fact, Putin was never a formal member of the party even though he was its de facto leader and enjoyed its support. Dmitry Medvedev was put in charge of the United Russia election campaign. The Kremlin also promoted the *Narodnyy front,* or Peoples' Front, as a putative citizens initiative to channel new political ideas from coalitions of nongovernmental organizations.[6] The *Narodnyy front* was targeted as an alternative base of support for Putin to stress his direct connections with the *narod,* the Russian people, beyond the confines of the party. Those maneuvers proved fruitless. Voters rejected the artificial distinction between Putin and the ruling party. After the Duma election the blame fell right where it had to in Putin's personalized system: on Mr. Putin. Everything that happened in December 2011—the disappointing vote totals for United Russia, the vote fraud, the leadership's failure to take responsibility for the fraud (much less to apologize for it), and then the public displays of discontent, including unprecedented disrespect for Putin himself—all served to tarnish Putin's political brand in the run-up to the March 2012 presidential election.[7]

The Kremlin was hard pressed to find the right next move. Putin and his team sought first of all to distance him even further from the discredited United Russia party. After the parliamentary election was over, they ran Putin as an independent candidate. However, this also meant they could not rely on the party's machinery, such as it was, to manage the presidential campaign and mobilize the voter base at the grass roots. Operating mainly on the media level, Putin's team had to pull out all the stops to boost his ratings, discredit his opponents, and get the electorate to the voting booths to avoid the specter of a second round of voting in the event that he did not receive the minimum 50 percent of the vote in the first round.[8] In spite of the money spent—not to mention the fact that he faced no real competition—Putin's eventual result was just under 64 percent of the vote.[9] While this would be an enviable result in other electoral settings, it was not what the Kremlin hoped for. Dmitry Medvedev's total in 2008 had been 71 percent. Putin himself received 72 percent in 2004.

Not only was the overall decline in Putin's support troubling. There were also disturbing trends in the geographical and socioeconomic breakdown of the vote. On the one hand, some of the regions where

Putin purportedly had strong support showed results so outrageous as to make any objective observer wonder whether the point was to underscore that the entire election was a sham. Five regions reported vote totals of over 90 percent for Putin. Those were regions run by clan structures tied to the Kremlin by personal fealty, money, and force—structures clearly able to deliver any number of votes asked of them. Chechnya, for example, produced a claimed tally of 99.76 percent for Putin. Meanwhile, in a series of Russia's largest cities stretching from European Russia in the west to Siberia in the east, Putin polled under 50 percent, or dangerously close to that margin. Moscow, Russia's richest and most powerful city, gave him the lowest percentage of votes in the country, under 47 percent.[10] In short, Putin regained his status as master of the Kremlin in March 2012, but his position in significant parts of the country, including right outside the Kremlin gates, in the nation's capital, was more tenuous.

Putin's relative unpopularity among Muscovites was a particular problem. Ironically, the one place where he was still viewed as an outsider in Russia was the city of Moscow. He came into Moscow in 1996 from the outside, from (as he put it) the provinces—from St. Petersburg, the nation's second city, with all its resentments at having been downgraded from imperial Russia's capital in the Soviet period. Putin came on a mission, essentially "to enemy territory," to rein in the oligarchs and restore the state. He remained in enemy territory. His Kremlin was at odds with Moscow, the city, throughout Mayor Yury Luzhkov's tenure. Moscow's urban population voted against Putin in large numbers in March 2012. Putin's bitterness was palpable in disdainful references he made to the protesters and to Moscow's privileges and sense of entitlement during the street demonstrations. In the case of Moscow, Putin was not detached; he was emotional. Moscow was not a source of strength for Putin's presidency as he entered his third term. Moscow had grown increasingly distrustful of the president and did not like his personalized system.

THE NEW URBAN MIDDLE CLASS

Underscoring the broader nature of the problem for Putin, many of the people who took to the streets in Moscow in December 2011 could easily be described as his *chinovniki*. Many of them were public sector workers, including professionals in government agencies, think tanks, Kremlin-sponsored task forces and committees, and in some of the companies owned by oligarchs close to the Kremlin. As even Dmitry Medvedev noted, some of the people on the streets were people who worked for him, or for the groups that had clustered around him, during the period of his presidency.[11] Putin's former finance minister, Alexei Kudrin, and many others connected to Kremlin circles who worked within the state apparatus, observed that people they knew personally were out on Moscow's streets.[12] The protesters on the streets of other regional cities had similar profiles.

The relative concentration of anti-Putin sentiment in Russia's bigger cities suggests a theme and an important contrast between the nature of protests in Russia and those in, say, Western Europe during a similar timeframe. The Russian election protests were not a reaction to unpopular economic policy or hardships wrought by the 2008 global financial crisis. If anything, they were the result of Russia's success. In an online interview a few days before the March 2012 presidential vote, Russian opposition leader Vladimir Ryzhkov described the kinds of people he saw on the streets in Moscow. They were not the modern-day counterparts of the starving peasants and disgruntled soldiers and sailors that had brought down the tsarist regime a century before. They were "programmers, managers, lawyers, engineers, journalists, and bankers."[13]

In other words, the demonstrators were the relatively privileged in economic and social status, not the economically disaffected and disadvantaged. They were people who consumed at the world level, traveled to neighboring countries in Europe for business and vacations, people who thought like Europeans and expected to be treated like them in all respects, including in politics. It was a social stratum that had emerged thanks to the prosperity and stability of the 2000–12 period—the Putin period. The protesters on Russian city streets were objecting to the incongruity of their improved economic status, on the one hand, and the way they were being treated politically by Putin and his system, on the other. In his interview, Ryzhkov made exactly this point: Russians in 2012, he said, were no longer the same naïve Soviet people they used to be—people who did not know what they wanted. Russian society is now very mature. It is European. "But," he added, "the regime is still *Chekist*-Soviet. And that's the main contradiction."[14]

Ryzhkov spoke of a "mass middle class" that had developed in Russia in the past 20 years. From somewhere inside that social grouping the protesters had emerged.[15] Exactly who they were was elusive, but the one attribute that was often used was "new." They were the *new* intelligentsia, Michael Idov's "*New* Decembrists," the *new* urban middle class. It was this newness that separated them, indeed alienated them, from Putin. In his January 2012 interview with *The Guardian,* Gleb Pavlovsky talked about the elite cohort that Putin seemed to belong to in the 1990s. The new elite were not the same people. The troubled times of the 1990s that Putin evoked in his speeches were not a major reference point for this cohort. Many of the protesters were only teenagers in the 1990s. They did not have the same dark memories of the period, and Putin had no connections to them. He was often out of his depth in dealing with them. He could not think like them. As we noted in discussing the Outsider identity, this was evident in Putin's language and references. He made crude jokes that harked back to Soviet times. His generation snickered, but the references flew over the heads of the new urban elite, who either did not get them or were offended when they did.

Consequently, when Putin was forced to attempt to engage in a dialogue with the protesting elements of society, he simply could not. He was not a sufficiently skilled contemporary politician. Mr. Putin was the Statist, the *gosudarstvennik* who had been selected for his political positions. He only engaged with his grassroots base and individual constituencies in the context of staged encounters. In all of his time at Russia's helm, Putin had been very consistent in professing the same goals he outlined in the December 1999 Millennium Message to restore the Russian state. He had not developed a new political program for a changing Russia.

During the 2011–12 parliamentary and presidential election campaigns, Putin stuck to his old script. He put heavy emphasis on his previous accomplishments. He drew a strong distinction between the period of stability and prosperity he had presided over since 2000 and the chaos of the 1990s.[16] He compared himself to long-serving world leaders and statesmen like President Franklin Delano Roosevelt who was elected to an unprecedented—and unrepeated—four terms that took the United States from the Great Depression through most of World War II.[17] In the Russian context, Mr. Putin repeatedly presented himself as the "hero-reformer" who had set out to bring to completion centuries of abortive or thwarted efforts at various state-level reforms.

For many, that message fell on deaf ears. Instead of praising Vladimir Putin for his past efforts and achievements, the protesters, the new urban middle class, questioned what he was actually doing today and what he planned to do tomorrow. They rejected Putin's History Man references to Russia's glorious past and traditions as a valid basis for a political program.[18] Vladimir Putin may have restored Russia's reputation abroad and Russians' sense of pride in the Russian state's ability to project its influence—*derzhavnost'*—but at home there was less sense that the state was functioning on behalf of the population. Putin did not offer any new answers for how he intended to address this issue apart from his promise to finish what he had begun—his *dostroika*.[19]

For Russia's growing urban professional classes, especially in Moscow, Mr. Putin was denying them individual dignity with his insistence that he should return to the presidency. The manipulation of politics and the media, his staged performance pieces, the falsification of the parliamentary election results in December 2011, were an affront to their desire to be treated like full-fledged citizens of a modern European country. Putin studiously rejected their demands. He portrayed their concerns as illegitimate. He claimed the protesters were driven either by fringe minorities and professional oppositionists, or by foreign funding and intervention. On several occasions, Putin asserted that the protests had either been incited or financed by the United States and Secretary of State Hillary Clinton—which resulted in some ironic responses from those on the streets. Some protesters even took to the streets with hand-held pieces of paper bearing the words in English: "Hillary, I'm still waiting for my money."[20] Even when he was not insulting the demonstrators—as he also did in a nationally televised remark that he mistook the protesters' white lapel ribbons for condoms—Putin could only say to them what he told those who worked in government circles, his *chinovniki*.[21] That is, in effect: You can have your say in the election campaign (this is the approved forum for dissent)—either by voting, supporting the campaigns of opposition candidates, or even by protesting publicly. But once the election is over and the final results are in, that's it. Rally behind the majority decision, get with the program. Dissent and disunity are not permissible once the course is set.

Putin spelled this out in a speech on April 18, 2012, marking his election and discussing his program following his May 7 inauguration as president:

The country has gone through a tense period of elections to the parliament and for the head of state, and, today, of course, we still feel the echoes from the aggravated emotions, the political battles; but the logic of a mature democracy resides in the fact that elections come to an end, and after them another much more important period of joint work always begins. We have one Russia, and its current advanced development must stand as the goal uniting all the political forces in the country that want to work constructively. [22]

The admonition to "forget about politics and get back to work" was not what the protesters wanted to hear. It was in fact the very reason they had been protesting.

Coming out of the 2012 presidential election, it might perhaps have seemed easy for Putin to think the new urban middle classes were inconsequential in the big picture of Russia. To the Kremlin, they were a minority and a fairly small one at that.[23] In Putin's view, he had received a 64 percent national approval rating from the presidential election. Putin thus chose to build his political support on Russia's "silent majority." These are the industrial workers, public sector employees, pensioners, and rural residents—bolstered by residents of monotowns like Pikalyovo, the North Caucasus, and other regions heavily dependent on subsidies from the state and thus on their leadership's strong personal ties with Putin. While the middle class protesters saw their glasses increasingly as half empty, Putin and his silent majority saw theirs as half full or even a lot better than half full.

Try as he would like to ignore the protesters, however, Putin was trapped by a dilemma that will persist as long as he remains president and tries to pursue a strategic long-term plan to rebuild and restore Russia. In the modern world, Russia's future success will depend critically on the new urban middle class, what some have called the "creative class." This notion was first developed by the American scholar Richard Florida in his 2002 book, *The Rise of the Creative Class,* to describe broad groups within the work forces of advanced economies whose professions require creativity, innovation, and problem solving. In Florida's conception, the creative class not only encompasses workers in the traditional artistic professions but also spans business, science, engineering, hi-tech industry and information technology, health care, the commercial and service sectors, education, media, and a range of other occupations. Although Florida's book was published in Russia as early as 2005, the concept received relatively little attention until it began to be used in discussions of the social groups protesting Putin's system in 2011.

As it turned out, Putin himself began using the very term during the protest wave, but he made clear that he had his own specific version of what this class is or should be. Putin noted: "In every country, teachers and doctors, scientists and cultural workers [*rabotniki kul'tury*] are not only the backbone of the 'creative class' [*kreativnyy klass*]. They are the people who make the development of society sustainable and who serve as the pillar of public morals."[24] Putin's notion is very different from Richard Florida's. In what he terms the "basic argument" of his creative capital theory, Florida asserts: "Economic growth is powered by creative people, who prefer places that are diverse, tolerant and open to new ideas." Cities, regions, and countries can be graded according to a special "diversity-tolerance-openness" index.[25] Vladimir Putin's Russia was not scoring very high on that scale in the eyes of Russia's new creative class. Putin—as he was to demonstrate in the aftermath of the winter's protests—did not particularly seem to care. He had other scores and ratings to pay attention to.

RUSSIA AND MR. PUTIN AT A CROSSROADS

In 2012, Russia appeared to be at the same kind of crossroads it encountered in the late 1970s and early 1980s, and again in the mid-1990s, where demands were mounting to reform the prevailing political system.[26] In the late 1970s, when the Soviet Union found itself over-stretched and social discontent began to increase, the demands for change first came from deep within the system itself, including from within Yury Andropov's KGB. The eventual response in the 1980s was perestroika and glasnost, which set the system on its head. Contrary to plan, the response led to the destruction of the state, the USSR, not its reform and restoration. In the 1990s, demands to restore the capacity of the apparatus of the state and its authority, *vlast'*—the re-creation of a strong state—facilitated Putin's ascent to the Kremlin. In the early 2010s, many of those who had benefitted from the restoration of the state, including some who had worked within it, wanted to democratize it. In many respects they wanted the same thing that people within the sclerotic Soviet system wanted in the 1980s—to pluralize and open up, to facilitate more public participation in politics and governance.

In the 1980s, prominent people in the KGB, the quintessential power institution, objected to the interests of the Soviet state being sacrificed to the ideological whims of the Communist Party. Legal scholars like Anatoly Sobchak and Valery Zorkin—mentors and supporters of Putin's— wanted to curb and constrain the party's powers. Soviet intellectuals and Soviet youth demanded that society, not just the Communist Party, should have a say in determining their country's future. The protesters of 2011–12 saw Mr. Putin as the contemporary personification of the old Soviet Communist Party. Their demands were focused on putting the state and society back above Mr. Putin by de-personalizing the presidency. The protesters wanted the top positions at the head of the state to mean more than the people who occupied them. Some of the same people who embraced Mikhail Gorbachev's perestroika in the 1980s, including former youth icons of Soviet popular culture, could be found among the protesters a quarter century later.

Given his work as a case officer who prided himself on his ability to "work with people," it seems an obvious question to ask: How could Mr. Putin have been so unaware of what his own people were thinking? How could he have failed to see the changes in Russian society and Russians' professional and political expectations? The explanation may be equally obvious—Putin simply had no direct personal experience with the kind of societal change then emerging in the country. The fact that many protesters had experienced the perestroika crossroads of the 1980s explains a great deal about why Putin seemed so out of touch with them. These years were a formative period in their lives, a positive political reference point. For Putin, they were not. He was outside the USSR, in Dresden.

Putin's reference points for the protests were more likely the mob outside the *Stasi* headquarters in Dresden, or the bloody confrontations of 1993 between Boris Yeltsin and parliament. In the German Democratic Republic, Putin had seen the difficulties of trying to reform a rigid authoritarian system without unleashing and empowering previously unseen forces from below and losing political control. When he got back to the Soviet Union in the waning days of perestroika, he found his own state overwhelmed by those same forces, teetering on the brink of collapse and disintegration. In his personal experience, there was nothing positive, no potential to harness, in protesters demanding political change. As Gleb Pavlovsky observed during his interview with *The Guardian*, Putin feared that political change in Russia would always lead to a situation where the losers of the political confrontation would literally be put against the wall and shot—or in the best case scenario sent off to rot in a Siberian jail.[27]

TRAPPED IN THE BUBBLE?

Another explanation for Putin's apparent blindness to the changes happening around him is that, in 2011–12, he seemed to live in a bubble of his own propaganda. Putin saw himself moving on a straight-line trajectory—on course to accomplish the strategic plan he set out years ago and had kept on refining. He saw change as evolution—a progression with him at its head. And he seemed genuinely to think that he had broad support among the population. As Gleb Pavlovsky further noted in *The Guardian* interview: In September 2011, when Putin publicly announced his intention to return to the presidency, he thought "he didn't need anything to run the country, he would do it himself—it was the idea of a personalized system. And that was a mistake because the system had already not been personalized for a long time. And it wasn't ready to love Putin. The tandem was at least a kind of pluralism. And people didn't want to return to a stereotypical single leader. And Putin thought that they did want that. I was surprised. He's normally cautious and has good instincts."[28] How did Putin miscalculate so badly? Partly it was the result of being in power for more than a decade and having had significant political success in the 2000s. Partly it was from having bought into some of his own phony public relations guises, rather than drawing on the strengths of his six identities, after playing the role of political performance artist for so long.[29]

Losing touch with the real world can affect anyone in positions of power. Yegor Gaidar frequently told the story of how, in December 1992, having been forced to step down as acting prime minister, he walked out of his office as a private citizen, down the hall and through the open doors of the elevator, where he stood waiting for it to take him down to the ground floor. The elevator didn't move. "I must have stood there for a full minute," Gaidar said, "trying to figure out what was wrong. Until it dawned on me that I hadn't pushed the button. Before, my security man had always pushed it." He then smiled and added: "It was that trivial incident that made me realize how the position influences the person."[30]

Yegor Gaidar held his position for only six months. By the end of 2011, Vladimir Putin had been the supreme leader of Russia for more than 12 years. It is not certain whether Putin, even privately, had come to the self-awareness of Gaidar. All the shameless, staged displays and his PR guises indicated that he probably had not. Even our own, very limited and infrequent contact with Mr. Putin through the Valdai Discussion Club meetings convinced us that over time he increasingly came to show signs of a different persona, one of privilege and entitlement. In Sochi in 2007 we first noticed a "new" Putin, tanned and bulked up. This was after a summer of excursions in Siberia with his friend, Prince Albert of Monaco, when photos of the bare-chested, horseback-riding Mr. Putin first appeared. Again, when we saw him in Sochi in September 2010 he had stepped up the level of elegance: "Putin appeared in the most beautiful linen suit, incredibly tailored, looking like he just came from a massage or a sauna or something because he looked so fresh and relaxed."[31]

A year later, at the November 2011 Valdai Club meeting, Putin entered the restaurant where the dinner was held in what Ellen Barry of the *New York Times* described as "a ritual worthy of a czar." "Prime Minister Vladimir V. Putin stopped in his tracks, eyes ahead, arms hovering at his sides. An aide materialized, silently whisked away Mr. Putin's parka, and vanished. A second aide appeared with a sport jacket and slipped it over his shoulders. Then Mr. Putin resumed walking without a word or a look, almost as if he had never stopped."[32]

AN INFLEXIBLE SYSTEM?

In his memoir, Filipp Bobkov, the former head of the KGB's 5th Directorate, took issue with the top leadership of the Communist Party and the USSR under Leonid Brezhnev for their inability to see the pressing need for change and democratization. With the wisdom that only comes from hindsight (his memoir appeared several years after the collapse of communism), Bobkov lambasted the party for ignoring all of the accumulating information and analyses on the Soviet Union's social, political, and economic crisis: "Their incompetence did not allow them to forecast events by drawing on data provided by serious scholars—sociologists, philosophers, political scientists, and historians."[33] Although it is not clear that he had actually realized everything in real time, Bobkov ran through the litany of mistakes the party made in the waning days of the Soviet Union. The Communist Party and leadership failed to address the grievances of its constituent ethnic groups in a forthright and timely manner.[34] They hounded the Soviet intelligentsia instead of trying to embrace, channel, and co-opt their ideas.[35] They rejected religion and the Russian Orthodox Church outright, even though Orthodoxy continued to be one of the mainstays of the Russian population as well as a major factor in generating support for the state.[36] Bobkov concluded that dissidence was normal and inevitable, and engaging in "broad-ranging communication with people [obshcheniye s lyud'mi]," including meeting with political opponents and engaging with different world views, was crucial.[37]

As we discussed earlier, Putin joined the KGB as part of the Andropov levy, when Bobkov was still there heading the 5th Directorate. In KGB training, he likely was exposed to these "enlightened" views in some form, and on various occasions in his post-Soviet political career, even in the heat of the protests, he paid lip service to the idea that opposition to the regime is normal and indeed something to be welcomed.[38] Yet, in practice, Putin seemed to have decided that the particular manifestation of dissent that emerged against his own rule in 2011–12 was not natural, and that he did not need to engage in direct communication with the individuals involved in it. In this, he violated the tenets not only of Bobkov but of the long tradition of enlightened secret police in Russia that dates back nearly 200 years. It was in response to the first Decembrist revolt in 1825 that one of Putin's favored historical personages, General Count Alexander von Benckendorff, set up the Third Section of His Majesty's Private Imperial Chancery (he called it the "Higher Police"). The mandate of the Third Section, which was effectively the predecessor to the 5th Directorate of the KGB, was to study popular sentiment by engaging with the groups in society that were most likely to dissent.

Von Benckendorff took society's demands seriously to figure out how to address grievances and preempt people from becoming revolutionaries.[39] The ultimate end, of course, was to preserve the state. Interacting with the opposition, learning its grievances, and then acting selectively to promote change and thus stave off revolution—these were the means to that end.

In 2012 Putin personally shunned his political opponents. Nevertheless, it is possible that he was also pursuing a Higher Police approach to the oppositionists at the same time—via intermediaries. In April 2012, Putin's close associate and erstwhile finance minister, Alexei Kudrin, set up the *Komitet grazhdanskikh initsiativ* [Committee for Citizens' Initiatives—or KGI]. KGI's purpose was to channel new ideas for resolving societal problems to the government and the Kremlin.[40] Kudrin made it clear in numerous speeches and presentations that, in response to the protests, he had set himself the task of finding a way of engaging with Russia's new professional groups: to harness their "great constructive potential" and to head off the further radicalization of the Russian opposition.[41] With the Committee for Citizens' Initiatives, Alexei Kudrin seemed to have established himself as another kind of ombudsman for the Putin system—playing the role of the outside adviser to Putin, as well as a mediator between Putin and the stakeholders' revolt in the outside world.[42] Even before he set up the committee, members of the Russian protest and opposition movement noted Kudrin's overtures toward them. They did not doubt Kudrin's access to Putin, nor his sincerity in seeking their views, but they wondered both about his motivations and his ultimate goals.[43] The most perceptive of them concluded that Kudrin's objective was to save the system, not overturn it, by reaching out to the opposition and stressing the need for reform of the system.[44] In other words, Kudrin was playing the role of von Benckendorff to Putin, the tsar. He had deliberately removed himself from inside the system in order to do what Putin inside the Kremlin could not do.

Kudrin was not the only person in this period who warned of the danger of clinging to an inflexible system that could not find ways to engage and accommodate critical societal groups. Some of the warnings came from individuals at some distance from the Kremlin. Prominent Russian sociologist Olga Kryshtanovskaya and pollster Mikhail Dmitriyev, whose work in 2010–12 focused on the changes within Russian elites and the emergence of the new professional classes, both spoke out increasingly forcefully on the need to address the emerging splits in Russian society.[45] Even stronger criticism came from an unlikely source, the Russian Orthodox Church. British journalist John Lloyd relates the criticism from the hierarchy of the Russian Orthodox Church—conveyed in an essay by Archpriest Vsevolod Chaplin—that "the government must respond to popular concerns or be 'slowly eaten alive.'"[46] Russian Orthodox Patriarch Kirill made similar comments in his Christmas interview on January 12, 2012. The patriarch pointed out that the protests after the December Duma elections were a legitimate form of expression and should lead to a correction in the political course. "If the authorities [*vlast'*] remain insensitive to the views of the protesters, then this is a very bad sign. . . . It is a sign of the inability of the authorities to recalibrate themselves. The authorities should recalibrate, including by grasping the signals from below."[47]

THE RETURN OF THE TSAR

Putin's victory in the March 2012 presidential election was perhaps not all he and his team had hoped for. But it was a victory. In spite of everything, there was no real question of his legitimacy. Whether the opposition and the protests had been manipulated by the West—as the Kremlin believed—or not, it was Putin who had prevailed. Putin proved overwhelmingly more popular than any alternative, and this must have been encouraging. But what worried Putin was "next time." There was sure to be a next time in future election cycles or during other times of crisis. So the Kremlin set to work to preempt the ability of any group from within or outside Putin's system to challenge and disrupt his presidency.

Putin's watchwords as he began his new presidential term were among those he had used so frequently in the past: unity, cohesion, consolidation. Unity, he had said many times before, was Russia's greatest strength throughout history. In the aftermath of the protests, Putin promised that he would forge greater cohesion in Russian society through a combination of exclusion of the "bad" elements and inclusion of the "good," by promoting ideas, values, and beliefs that could unite disparate groups and constituencies. To exclude the dissenting and the disaffected in order to preserve the cohesion of the collective is an old Russian practice. As we will discuss in the next chapter, it enabled the traditional Russian peasant commune, the *mir,* to survive for centuries.[48]

Putin took the classic police approach of "good cop, bad cop," pairing offers of cooperation with threats of coercion. The methods came straight out of Putin's KGB background. As head of the KGB's 5th Directorate, Filipp Bobkov extolled the advantages to the KGB of working with people and communicating with people. What he did not mention was the unstated incentive for people to work with the KGB. The alternative was the prospect of a stint in the cellars of the notorious Lubyanka Prison. Once the figurative smoke had cleared from the protests, and his victory in the election was clear, Putin made similar offers to Russia's disaffected intellectuals, government technocrats, and urban professionals to come back into the fold. He signaled that it was fine for them to propose alternatives to government policies—even if these might contradict the Kremlin's current position on an issue—as long as everything remained on the level of persuading through debate and ideas. Once Putin had taken a final decision, however, there should be no efforts to overturn it. Above all, there should be no attempts at political organization and popular mobilization to thwart Kremlin policies. Those who accepted the ground rules would be *nash*—"our people"—again. Those who did not would be declared *ne nash*—"not ours"—or worse, *chuzhoy*—"alien."

Once the grace period for coming back into the fold had expired, Putin's crackdown began. It was a delicate operation to balance the hard and soft methods. Putin had to remove the opposition ringleaders without alienating the broad groups that once had supported them. Meanwhile, lurking in the background were new challenges presented by Russia's economy.

PUTIN FATIGUE RETURNS

The propaganda machine the Kremlin mobilized to secure the presidential election in spring 2012 gave Putin a short-lived boost in his ratings. But after the intensity of the political battles, a clear sense of weariness permeated Russian politics by the time Putin was re-inaugurated as president in May. "Brand Putin" was once again flagging. Admittedly, Putin's ratings stayed far above those of any other Russian political figure, including former president and now, once again, Prime Minister Dmitry Medvedev. In a September 2013 poll, for example, asking Russians who, across a range of politicians, they would vote for if a presidential election were to be held within a week, only Putin scored above single digits.[49] But it was the downward trend over the longer term that was most worrying for the Kremlin spin doctors. By the end of 2013, Putin's ratings had fallen from a high of 87 percent in 2008 to just under 64 percent. Other polls showed that as many as 80 percent of respondents expressed a desire not to see Putin as Russia's president after the end of his 2012–18 term, even though they had no alternative candidate in mind.[50]

In 2013, in spite of the absence of any credible opposition figure on Russia's political horizon, Putin and the Kremlin focused closely on monitoring these opinion polls for the first hints of any real trouble. One concern was possible contagion from abroad. A decade before, major protests had erupted in Russia almost immediately after the Orange Revolution in Ukraine, one of a series of so-called color revolutions in Russia's neighborhood, where street protests led to a change in government.[51] In January 2005, Russian pensioners and their supporters spilled out into the streets in response to government efforts to replace some of their in-kind benefits and privileges with direct cash subsidies.[52] The Kremlin feared this was the beginning of Russia's own color revolution and adopted a watchful attitude. In 2011, when the protests against the Duma elections erupted against the backdrop of upheavals in the Arab world, the Kremlin went on alert again. The fact that the West seemed to embrace all these events as the sign of a new wave of democracy sweeping the globe, and that the United States and the EU accepted the premise that street demonstrations could produce political change in Egypt and elsewhere, made the Putin team very nervous. Russian demonstrators and the Western press continually drew linkages between the earlier color revolutions, the Arab Spring, and the 2011–12 protests.

It was not only the opposition movement among Russia's urban professionals that troubled Putin; other groups with more nationalistic and xenophobic agendas, which had occupied the political fringes in the 1990s, reemerged. Anti-immigrant and racist sentiments were increasingly expressed in street demonstrations and riots, including a mob attack on a Tajikistan-bound train in October 2013.[53] In November

2013, 73 percent of Russians, responding to a Levada Center poll, stated that they wanted the government to deport immigrants from other former Soviet states.[54] One prominent Russian opposition leader from the 2011–12 demonstrations, Alexei Navalny, embraced the popular nationalist slogan of "stop feeding the Caucasus," criticizing the Russian government for its continued heavy subsidization of Chechnya and other North Caucasus republics, and for adding Abkhazia and South Ossetia to the subsidization list after Moscow recognized their independence in 2008.[55] Navalny, a lawyer and blogger who popularized the epithet a "party of swindlers and thieves" [partiya zhulikov i vorov] as a label for the United Russia party during the Duma election campaign, also ran for the position of mayor of Moscow in September 2013. Navalny's platform of anticorruption and social justice, and his accusations that the government was mishandling immigration and internal migration, resonated with some voters. To the Kremlin's chagrin, he picked up more than 27 percent of the vote. Navalny's ability to garner support from different ends of the political spectrum gave him what in the marketing world is referred to as crossover appeal. He—or someone like him—had the potential to become dangerous in the future.[56]

THE CHALLENGE OF THE ECONOMY

The possibility of a tightening of the Russian economy raised the stakes for Putin and the Kremlin. Putin was always acutely aware of the importance of the economy for political stability. There is a strong case to be made that his September 2011 decision to return to the presidency was motivated by fear that Russia's economy was at risk and needed his firm hand back on the wheel. As noted in chapter 5, Russia recovered fairly quickly from the severe effects of the global financial crisis of 2008–09. But by 2011 something new was brewing. The Greek debt crisis that had started in late 2009 had by early 2011 spread to Ireland, Portugal, and Spain. The entire world was again being affected. The news Putin received from his economic experts in the summer of 2011, when he presumably made his decision to return to the presidency, was ominous. On August 5, 2011, Standard & Poor's downgraded the credit rating of the United States.[57] France and other countries feared the same would happen to them. The IMF estimated that European banks might be in danger of losing €200 billion through their exposure to the sovereign bonds of the most affected countries.[58] European stock markets collapsed in late summer 2011. Even Germany's DAX had dropped by over 30 percent in the two months before Putin announced he was coming back.[59]

Major decisions about the economy were put on hold during the course of the 2012 presidential campaign, but as he prepared his return to the office of president, Putin began to rethink previous economic policy, which had prioritized stimulating growth. The so-called euro zone crisis seemed to have convinced him that there was a strong likelihood that the international economic climate would be characterized not by stable growth but rather by repeated crises for some time to come. In 2013, across Russia's rural areas and small towns, polls picked up grumblings of discontent about the performance of the economy and personal economic prospects. The situation was not dire, but this trend line was moving in the wrong direction for Putin and the Kremlin. If jobs began to disappear in the Russian heartland in the years ahead, the existing political tensions might mesh with economic grievances—just as they had in Russia in the 1990s. The fact that the respondents in these opinion polls were not members of the disaffected creative class was particularly troubling. They were people who had *opposed* the protesters, the very Russians who provided Putin with his largest base of political support. Putin and his team would have to address their discontent in the next phase of his presidency.[60]

Putin's economic policy priority for his third presidential term was therefore to make Russia and his regime robust in the face of global challenges. Putin made it clear in a series of articles and speeches that he now thought of competitiveness in terms of survivability. The winners in the global economic competition would not be those that grew fast in normal times, but those that could best weather a crisis and emerge stable. This presented a real problem for Putin. Achieving economic growth in the absence of rising oil prices (the secret to Russia's growth between 2000 and 2008) was always difficult for Russia.[61] Growth in a stagnant global economy would pose an additional challenge. But if he had to focus on making the economy robust to external shocks, the growth task was virtually impossible. Reducing dependency on the global economy was costly and less efficient. But, in the trade-off between prosperity and survivability, Putin chose robustness and began to deemphasize GDP growth as a goal.[62]

Putin pursued a number of approaches to making Russia less vulnerable to external shocks. One was to encourage the development of domestically produced goods to replace imports. One powerful instrument to help achieve that goal was a policy of forcing foreign manufacturers that wanted to enter (or remain in) the large and lucrative Russian consumer goods market to start producing more of their products inside the country. Putin also put more emphasis on large state-financed projects, in particular, three gigantic transportation infrastructure projects—two railroads and one highway—and a massive defense industrial spending program designed to channel funds mainly to large cities in the Urals and Siberian regions. Other programs targeted the development of Eastern Siberia and the Russian Far East. But perhaps the most important project of all was the establishment of the Eurasian Economic Union. This was an idea that had been around for years and had, in fact, been partly operational for some time in the form of a Russian customs union with Belarus and Kazakhstan.[63] The goal now was to reintegrate the regional economies that had once been parts of a whole but drifted away after the collapse of the USSR.

The Eurasian Union project became a linchpin in Putin's effort to reduce the vulnerability of the Russian economy to external shocks. Combined with his programs inside Russia, the Eurasian Union would represent a guaranteed market for existing, basic products at home and abroad. Contrary to descriptions by some commentators that the Eurasian Union was Putin's attempt to challenge the European Union, in Putin's mind the program was primarily defensive, not offensive. It was a way to protect the vulnerable Russian economy and preserve political stability. The key to the success of the entire project was Ukraine, as Putin admitted to the members of the Valdai Discussion Club during their November 11, 2011, meeting.[64] Without Ukraine, given its population of more than 45 million, its industrial base, and its close ties to Russia, the Eurasian Union made little sense for Moscow. In this context, as we will discuss later in the book, when the European Union and Ukraine drew close to concluding an economic partnership agreement in 2013, Putin could only view the negotiation as an effort to derail the Eurasian Union and undermine Russia's economy.

THE STEEL FIST COMES OUT OF THE VELVET GLOVE

Spurred on by his mounting concerns about the economy, Putin faced down his political challenge from the emergent opposition movement with calculated efficiency and ruthlessness. Using the Case Officer tools he had honed in the KGB and during his career in Moscow, Putin essentially decapitated the movement. He singled out small, select groups of people to co-opt wherever possible and others to intimidate and punish when necessary. Putin turned the Russian legal system into a blunt instrument of repression. Anticorruption blogger Navalny, who first made his name by bringing corruption charges against the government and public officials, was tarred with his own brush. He and his close associates were accused of their own corruption, arrested, and put on trial.[65] Members of a young female punk rock group and art collective, Pussy Riot, who staged a "Punk Prayer" denouncing Putin at the altar of Moscow's Cathedral of Christ the Savior, were arrested and detained. So were over a dozen protesters from demonstrations in Moscow around the May 2012 presidential inauguration. They were all subjected to Soviet-style show trials in the full glare of the media spotlight. While several of the defendants were later acquitted—and some amnestied just before Russia hosted the February 2014 Sochi Winter Olympics—others were given suspended sentences or placed under house arrest. Two members of Pussy Riot—both young women, one with a small child—were sentenced to hard labor in penal colonies for their acts of "hooliganism."[66] The Kremlin also targeted figures beyond the creative class who had crossover appeal like Navalny. Two leftist opposition leaders, Sergei Udaltsov and Leonid Razvozzhayev, eventually received harsh sentences in summer 2014 for "organizing mass disorder" during and after the 2011–12 protests.[67]

Among the highest-profile figures targeted during the crackdown was Ksenia Sobchak, the daughter of Putin's old mentor and boss from his Leningrad/St. Petersburg days, Anatoly Sobchak. Ksenia Sobchak had become a popular and prominent Russian media commentator and the glamorous "it" girl of the 2000s. In 2011, she emerged as one of the surprise supporters of the protests, especially given her family's connections to Putin. She regularly spoke at public rallies and vocally expressed her dislike of the political system. She even began dating one of the opposition leaders, personalizing her links with the movement even further. In June 2012, just after Putin's inauguration, Sobchak was the target of a raid by the Russian interior ministry police. The police seized an estimated €1 million and $500,000 in cash from her home safe, and she was threatened with prosecution for tax evasion. Not long after, Ksenia's mother—Lyudmila Narusova, Anatoly Sobchak's widow and purported close friend of Putin—was unceremoniously booted from her seat on Russia's Federation Council, the upper chamber of the Russian parliament. Most Russian and international commentators assumed that the two women had been punished for having "betrayed" Vladimir Putin.[68]

As the crackdown against the opposition continued, Ksenia Sobchak noticeably and rather rapidly changed her tune in public. She muted her complaints about the system, broke up with her opposition boyfriend, married a film director nine years her senior, and got her money back in October 2012.[69] Like others close to the core of the system, Sobchak had been warned that personal disloyalty would merit the most extreme punishment. She would not be permitted to keep her social status and comfortable lifestyle if she persisted in railing against the regime. Ksenia Sobchak chose to return to the fold. She was co-opted back into the system and given a new deal. At the end of the crackdown, Sobchak kept her political talk show on the small independent television channel Dozhd'. She retained her oppositionist patina but could no longer cause any trouble for the president. In 2014, Dozhd's audience was dramatically cut after a poll the channel conducted on the siege of Leningrad touched Putin's historical nerve. The pollsters asked if the city should have surrendered to save the population—an impermissible proposition given Putin's survivalist national narrative. The Kremlin was outraged, and the channel's advertisers and supporters abandoned it in droves.[70]

With the exception of Ksenia Sobchak, the groups and social currents Putin chose to repress so dramatically did not necessarily have anything to do with Putin's personal preferences or connections. Individuals were selected for the purpose of sending a message. In the case of Pussy Riot, for instance, the group's arrest was a warning to the opposition in general. The trial made it clear that the Kremlin policy was zero tolerance: the law is the law. If you violate the law (any law) there will be no extenuating circumstances. Young mother or not, innocent-looking girl or not—you broke the law and challenged the unity of the Russian nation.

In keeping with this message, Putin refused to comment on individual cases in press interviews. He referred every issue to the jurisdiction of the police and the Russian legal system. As president he had nothing to do with any of the cases. Those on trial had been accused by others of breaking the law. The decision either to acquit or punish them, and how to punish them, was not Putin's; it lay with the courts.[71] Russian opinion polls in 2013 clearly showed that the Russian public had received Putin's message and understood that the Kremlin was raising the costs of acts of political protest to deter them from mobilizing again in the future.[72]

By fall 2013, the opposition movement that had brought tens of thousands of people out onto the streets of Moscow and other major cities had been crushed. Even Alexei Navalny's surprisingly strong showing in the September Moscow mayoral election reflected this. Voter turnout for the election was low. Only 32 percent of Moscow's eligible voters actually participated in the election, which meant that Navalny's active support was only in the range of 9 percent.[73] From the Kremlin's perspective, if less than 10 percent of voters had been bold enough to cast their ballots for Navalny, in the city where the opposition movement had its greatest impact and support, then the challenge to Putin's regime had been rolled back.

PLAYING THE NATIONALISM CARD

The "real" nationalists, however, were another matter. Russian nationalism and populist politics were always a feature of the 1990s. As we discussed earlier in chapter 3, Boris Yeltsin was never able to resolve the political contradictions that came into the open once the Soviet Union collapsed. It was nationalist politicians like former general Alexander Lebedev and conservative patriots like Communist Party leader Gennady Zyuganov, not "liberal" political figures like Yabloko party leader Grigory Yavlinsky, who became the serious contenders for the Russian presidency when Boris Yeltsin lost popularity. In his 1999 Millennium Message, Putin had cautioned against the destructive nature of ideologies. Yet, from the outset of his presidency in 2000, he was himself engaged in an ideological struggle with these nationalists and patriots to keep the Russian population united around him. His goal was to maintain the Kremlin's control over the conception of Russian national identity, which Yeltsin had all too often ceded to others. Putin was not wedded to a particular ideological approach, but others were. After 2012, Putin had to step up his game to mobilize his core supporters—who were prone to sympathize with populist sentiments—and to defang and deflect potential extremists. To do this, Putin turned back to the concept of the Russian Idea and set about usurping the nationalists' and patriots' agendas.

Russian nationalist/patriotic groups and their leaderships bled into each other in the 1990s and 2000s, but each embraced some form of political and social conservatism, along with nostalgia for the USSR, patriotic support for Great Russia, and the veneration of the precepts and values of the Russian Orthodox Church. Putin's task was to keep all the disparate currents together in what Americans might call a "big tent coalition." A revamped version of the Russian Idea had to be compelling enough to make sure that no one broke off from the coalition to challenge the Kremlin on the issue of Russian national identity and launch an ideological attack against Putin's presidency. The primary threat to Putin's big tent coalition was always posed by the "true" ethnic Russian nationalists with their potential to mobilize people from Putin's base constituency against Russia's ethnic minorities.

Since the beginning of his presidency, Putin had kept Russian nationalists in check by targeting the real and perceived leadership of all the political groups. Putin had created alternative leaders and muted or expropriated political agendas through selected social and economic policies. He had made his own populist appeals to the common working man—like appointing Igor Kholmanskikh, one of the foremen from the massive Uralvagonzavod, as the presidential envoy to the Urals region (see chapter 6). Up until 2012–13, Putin's "all Russia" and "all Russians" approach worked to rein in Russian nationalist movements. The Kremlin kept nationalist leaders and ideologues like Dmitry Rogozin and Vladimir Zhirinovsky on a short leash. Rogozin, for instance, was brought into the inner circles of government and appointed to senior political positions, including the deputy prime minister in charge of the Russian defense industry.[74] Nationalist leaders were not allowed to go too far in their rhetoric or actions in case their supporters ran amok. They were supposed to control and divert extremists. In early November 2013, Putin quickly pulled back Vladimir Zhirinovsky after he made some especially inflammatory statements about the volatile North Caucasus, saying that the region should be literally fenced off from the rest of Russia.[75]

Using the reins in such a visible manner presented some serious drawbacks for Putin and the Kremlin. The nationalist old guard, like Zhirinovsky, was a "special project" of the past. He was created by the Russian security services in the 1990s and became stale from his close association with the Kremlin. This was especially apparent in 2012, when Zhirinovsky essentially endorsed Putin's candidacy in the presidential election, even though he was supposed to be running himself.[76] Putin was most effective at restraining the extremists when he was able, in old KGB style, to recruit leaders who could do all the hard work themselves. Nationalist leaders were more genuinely popular, and effective, if they appeared to be fully outside of Kremlin circles as Dmitry Rogozin seemed to be when he led the Rodina party in 2003–06.[77] Creating leaders from scratch and then having to prop them up politically was hard work—another example of Putin having to resort to manual rather than automatic control.

HARNESSING THE POWER OF ORTHODOXY

Beyond politicians, parties, and movements, the Russian Orthodox Church was the sole organization in Russia with mass mobilizing potential for patriotic purposes. Religious events attracted hundreds of thousands of people, many of whom had some sympathies for nationalist political agendas. Putin had to ensure that the Church hierarchy and believers stayed focused on spiritual matters, not politics. During the Soviet period, the state and the KGB had been greatly concerned about the potential political appeal of Russian priests and religious activists. As British journalist Oliver Bullough recounts in *The Last Man in Russia*—which retraces the life of one of these figures, Father Dmitry Dudko—the state was always worried that a priest or a patriarch might make the leap from the spiritual realm to the realm of politics. Even when the activities of a religious figure were seemingly innocuous or even beneficial to society, as in the case of Father Dudko's mobilization of his congregation against alcohol abuse, the state feared that these activities might rally the public to further political action. Dissident priests were treated just as harshly by the KGB as political dissenters.[78]

In the wake of the 2011–12 protests, Putin and the Kremlin needed a unifying set of ideas that would appeal to the maximum number of people. Russian Orthodoxy offered both deep ideas and intensity. It also helped to provide a clear dividing line between *nash* and *chuzhoy*—between "us" and "them." It removed the gray zone. You were either a Russian Orthodox or religious believer, or you were not. The Kremlin's attack on Pussy Riot signaled the approach. The members of the group were "hooligans," and were convicted of hooliganism. They had not insulted Putin with their "Punk Prayer," they had insulted the Russian Orthodox Church. Their performance art had defiled the inner sanctum of one of the Church's most sacred places. Pussy Riot members were anarchists, but worse than this, they were atheists, nonbelievers. They and their kind—the Russian intelligentsia and others who embraced their cause—were *chuzhoy*. They were not part of the true Russian community. This viewpoint resonated in Russian opinion polls. Russian citizens were somewhat sympathetic to the plight of the young women as they faced trial, but they had no sympathy whatsoever with what Pussy Riot had done and thought some kind of punishment was deserved.[79]

Putin's overall conclusion from his observations of the 2011–12 protests was that Pussy Riot, the intelligentsia, and the urban professionals had all acted as a "fifth column" for foreign influence during the events. As we will discuss in more detail in chapter 14, he determined that whether they intended to be or not, they became conduits for Western attempts to undermine his presidency. In the wake of the protests, those who followed their example would be similarly extirpated, and they would be excommunicated. They would find themselves outside the big tent coalition and, instead, in the camp of the *chuzhoy*. In his address to the nation in December 2012, Putin marked out this new dividing line in Russian society:

> In society there are always some sort of bacilli that infect the organisms of society or the state. But they are only activated when immunity to them is lowered, when problems appear, when the masses begin to suffer. . . . I think it was Pushkin . . . who once said: "We have a lot of people who stand in opposition not to the government, but to Russia." Unfortunately, our intelligentsia has this tradition. This is of course because they always want to highlight how

civilized and learned they are. They want to follow the best models. And perhaps this is inevitable at a certain stage of development. But it is undeniable that this loss of self-identification with the state during the periods both of the collapse of the Russian Empire and the collapse of the Soviet Union was ruinous and destructive. We must understand this in advance and not allow the state to fall into such a condition as it did in the final phase of World War I or, for instance, in the last years of existence of the Soviet Union.[80]

Putin's punishment of the women from Pussy Riot and these harsh statements were all very logical from his point of view. He had a situation to deal with. He also had potent tools to deal with it—the Russian Orthodox Church and Russian nationalism. Putin had always criticized the Bolsheviks for destroying the Church and depriving the Russian government of using this important instrument. Russian nationalism was more risky to deploy, as Putin had concluded at the beginning of his presidency (see chapter 3), but it could also be used in certain circumstances *if* he exercised appropriate caution. Over the course of the 2000s, Putin had gradually begun to suggest in his speeches that "universal values," as argued by the United States and the West, were, by definition, anti-Russian. Instead of being universal, they were actually the West's own values, which it sought to impose on others. True "Russianness" (*russkost'*) was instead embodied in the Orthodox Church. In his annual address to the Russian parliament in December 2012, Putin called on the Russian people to turn inward to protect the Russian state. He asserted that the international system was entering a critical period that could be a "turning point" for Russia in terms of increasing risks and threats rather than opportunities. Russia should not reach out to the world under these circumstances. Instead, "real Russians" should look inward and even physically move inward, deep into the Russian provinces, where the repositories of *russkost'* could be found. Russians, Putin commanded, should look to their own patriotism, not Westernism; to solidarity, not individualism; to spirituality, not consumerism and moral decay.[81]

A year later, in his annual address of December 2013, Putin went even further in using language that he had previously avoided when sketching out the contours of the Russian Idea in the early 2000s (see chapter 3).

He told Russians that Russia would now have to go it alone. It should create its own model in world affairs and become a bastion and champion of political and social conservatism. The West was not a model for Russia, Putin argued. Its "allegedly more progressive model of development" was more likely to lead to "retrogression, barbarism, and much blood" than to global and regional stability. Putin's speech was replete with old Russian Orthodox Church terms and historical allusions. He invoked "Russia's historic responsibility" to "defend its value-based approaches . . . [i]ncluding in international relations." He denounced "the 'top down' destruction of traditional values" in the West, which was, in his view, implemented on the basis of "abstract ideas, against the will of the majority." Putin declared that "more and more people support our position on the defense of traditional values, which for millennia have constituted the spiritual and moral basis of civilization, of every nation: the values of the traditional family, of genuine human life, including religious life — not just material life but spiritual life as well. . . ." And Putin confirmed: "Of course, this is a conservative position. But . . . the meaning of conservatism is not that it prevents movement forward and upward, but that it prevents movement backward and downward, to the chaotic darkness, a return to a primitive condition."[82]

SOCHI: THE TRIUMPH OF HIS WILL

The year 2014 was intended to mark the beginning of a period of political consolidation for Putin and Russia after the upheavals of the previous two years. February 2014 saw the realization of a project that Putin had long championed: the staging of the Winter Olympics in Sochi. In 1980, the USSR had been humiliated by the U.S.-led boycott of the Moscow Summer Olympics to protest the Soviet invasion of Afghanistan. This was Putin's opportunity to put that episode behind the new Russia. For the Russian president, Sochi was designed as a triumphal moment, demonstrating the restoration of the Russian state. The USSR might be gone, but *Russia* was back—back in its rightful, historic position on the world stage.

The location of the games—Sochi, on the outskirts of the North Caucasus—was a crucial part of the story. Putin had ascended to his first presidency against the backdrop of Russia's second bloody war against separatists in Chechnya. Terrorist attacks had repeatedly shaken the country in subsequent years, and the casualties on both sides were high. At the beginning of his third presidency, Putin was now staging one of the world's largest and most famous spectacles, not far from Chechnya, on the slopes of the Caucasus Mountains in one of Russia's fabled Black Sea summer resorts. The timing gave this even more historic piquancy, as the 2014 Olympics coincided with the 150th anniversary of the expulsion of the Circassian peoples from the Russian Caucasus to the Ottoman Empire. That expulsion effectively marked the end of the nineteenth-century Circassian Wars and Russia's final conquest of the region.[83]

In the run-up to the games, Putin and his team were stung by a chorus of criticism in the Western media casting doubt on the readiness of the Olympic facilities and the suitability of the snow (given the subtropical climate). Commentators constantly raised the threat of terrorism from insurgent groups still active in the North Caucasus and still capable of carrying out suicide bombings against Russian civilian targets. A series of fatal bombings at the 2013 Boston Marathon perpetrated by two young immigrants to the United States—brothers whose family origins were in Chechnya and the North Caucasus—were widely depicted as a harbinger of similar terrorist acts in Sochi.[84] The critics also took the opportunity to highlight Putin's crackdown on the political opposition and a raft of punitive legislation targeted at various "nontraditional" social groups that was moving through the Russian Duma.

On the eve of the Olympic events, Putin moved quickly to quash the international backlash. The Russian government undertook a massive antiterrorist campaign, blanketing Sochi with troops to ensure that there could be no breach of an extensive security cordon established around the Olympic facilities and the Black Sea city.[85] And Putin stepped into the role of the Good Tsar. He pardoned and released oligarch Mikhail Khodorkovsky, who had languished in a series of penal colonies for 10 years, and did the same for the two young women from Pussy Riot, as well as 30 international Greenpeace activists who had been detained in September 2013 while protesting Russian drilling activities at an Arctic oil rig.[86] Putin had shown mercy, but he had also made it clear that he was not to be tested.

The opening and closing ceremonies of the Sochi Games celebrated the glories of Russian history and the richness of its culture. As created by the Putin-loyalist and television director Konstantin Ernst, all the world literally became the stage for a display of Russia's international significance, national vigor, and overall success.[87] *Time* journalist James Poniewozik wrote of the opening ceremony: "The ceremony . . . like this whole Olympics, felt like a story Russia was telling the world, but most of all a story it was telling itself, about a vital, proud, storied country on the rise."[88] As the Olympic Games wrapped up, Putin underscored these points. The Russian Olympic team had won more gold and overall medals in Sochi than at any other Winter Olympics, including during the Soviet era. The athletes' performance had been a resounding success, and Putin had personally proven the naysayers wrong. Russia had accomplished what the Soviet Union had tried to do with the Summer Olympics in 1980—but had been thwarted by the West.

Putin had offered the world a new vision of Russia. He held Olympic Winter Games—with snow—in a subtropical zone, and prevented the terror attacks that Western commentators had predicted with near certainty. Sochi was a proud statement that Russia could overcome seemingly insurmountable obstacles. Russia had finally risen from the ashes of all the humiliations of the early 1990s. In an interview with Russian television at the end of the Olympics, however, Putin wanted to have the last word on the subject. One of the interviewers, Alexander Lyubimov, asked Putin how he viewed the Western criticism of the Olympics, which seemed to have more to do with international politics and anti-Russia propaganda than sports. Putin replied that the criticism had

nothing to do with sports and I always take this calmly. Do you know why? Because I know exactly what this is, what it is worth, and I know that arguing with [such critics] is pointless. Whatever we say, whatever we do to convince people of the opposite, it is impossible because they have a different agenda. I would like to repeat that this is a competitive struggle in the sphere of international politics. In a way it is a geopolitical issue. Whenever a strong competitor appears, Russia in this case, there is always someone who does not like this, who starts working against it. However, they fail to understand how deep the changes are in Russian society, changes that have affected its very nature. . . . In this sense, the Olympics [were] very important for us, because I believe (and

I would like it to be so) that the Games opened the door not only to Russia, but also to the Russian soul, to the hearts of our people. Others could look and see that there is nothing to fear, that we are open for cooperation. This may have even had an effect on those unfriendly critics, though we cannot call them that—they have a different job altogether—but maybe even their fears have diminished. I strongly hope this is the case. And if it is, this is another one of our Olympic victories.[89]

Most significant for Putin's immediate reality, Sochi also marked the definitive end of the stakeholders' revolt. Putin fatigue seemed to be over. Putin scored his own success in public opinion polls. The Olympics coincided with the unfolding of another crisis for Russia in Ukraine, but this crisis would give a further boost to Putin's domestic ratings with the annexation of Crimea in March 2014. At the end of that month, Putin saw the greatest single increase in his performance approval since the Levada Center began to monitor his standing with the public in 2000. He shot up an unprecedented 20 points. It was his own peak performance—and a sharp contrast to how dire things had looked back in 2012.

CHAPTER ELEVEN

PUTIN'S WORLD

TRAPPED IN THE KREMLIN BUBBLE, Putin initially missed what was happening around him in Russia in 2011–12. He made a miscalculation about the popular mood in Moscow and other cities. He ultimately recognized that the stakeholders' revolt had domestic roots; but in trying to understand how it had developed and figuring out how to tackle it, he filtered the revolt through his own particular prism. In Putin's assessment, the opposition movement was encouraged and then exploited by the West—both by the United States and Europe. When he accused foreign funders of paying protesters, he meant it.[1] As far as Putin was concerned, when the walls came down around the Soviet bloc and the borders opened, the West had invaded Russia's cultural and political space. After 1991, in his judgment, the West had tried time and time again to impose its norms on Russia, moving in its operatives (its nongovernmental agencies and human rights organizations) and recruiting segments of Russian civil society to carry this out. Putin took the measure of these "foreign agents" in 2011–12 and then moved against them himself.[2]

In Putin's view, since the early 2000s, Ukraine and the other former borderlands of the old Russian Empire had become the *platsdarm,* the staging ground, for Western intervention. For him, the so-called color revolutions were dry runs for similar operations planned by the West in Russia.[3] As Putin saw things, the Orange Revolution in Ukraine in 2004–05 and the events in Ukraine in 2013–14 surrounding Kyiv's decision to negotiate an association agreement with the European Union were all the result of Western efforts to drag Ukraine away from the Russian sphere. Putin concluded that the West wanted to prevent Russia, Ukraine, and Eurasia more broadly from integrating.[4] It wanted to do so by creating problems on the domestic front, by provoking social discontent, by creating fifth columns and opposition movements, and then, by taking advantage of periods of public unrest.[5] The West was the cause of Russia's new times of troubles.

Putin and his inner circle of security associates saw this very clearly. After all, this was what the West had been doing for centuries—fomenting and exploiting civil strife in Russia. In a July 2010 speech to a group of U.S. security analysts, one of Russia's top military historians, General Makhmud Gareyev, made this very point in explaining the threat perception in Moscow.[6] He asserted that, in most cases, domestic insurgencies were fueled by foreign manipulation and financing. In the nineteenth century, for example, when Russia was trying to secure its position in the Caucasus Mountains, the tsar's top emissaries went to France to tell the Europeans to stop sending weapons to the local fighters. Once the flow of weapons ended, so did the Circassian Wars. During Moscow's two wars with Chechnya in the 1990s, the internal conflict was fed from the outside until the external funding was cut off. There were endless "territorial pretensions" against Russia, Gareyev complained, and only Russia's nuclear arsenal kept them at bay. At times of domestic troubles, Russia had to be prepared to mobilize against and deal with threats raised by local conflicts on its borders, which could quickly escalate into full-scale wars.[7] Russia was always having to protect itself against a hostile outside world and fend off those who, in the words of President Putin, "wanted to tear off from us as juicy a piece as possible" (*odni khotyat otorvat' ot nas kusok pozhirneye*).[8]

REWRITING THE POST–COLD WAR NARRATIVE

In 2013–14, what Putin saw through his prism propelled him toward a political and military confrontation with Kyiv—and the United States and Europe—over Ukraine's future geopolitical trajectory. He saw a clear threat from NATO enlargement in the 2000s and Ukraine's efforts to conclude an agreement with the EU. Putin's perceptions about the risks to Russia put him on a collision course with the West and its post–Cold

War narrative about the course of relations with Russia. For most Western scholars of international relations, the period from 1990 to 2010 was essentially one of unprecedented great-power cooperation. In their view, until the outbreak of war between Russia and Georgia in August 2008, Russia was largely integrated into the international system. The international system was a "unipolar concert," where states accepted the rules of the road laid down by the United States and practiced restraint for the sake of everyone else. Russia, they concluded, and rising powers like China, did not see the United States as threatening in this period. Although Russia disagreed with the West on NATO's intervention in the Balkans in the 1990s, and was consistently unhappy about NATO enlargement, "it did not see NATO as a threat that would invade Russia."[9]

Putin's depiction of the two decades since the collapse of the USSR made a stark contrast. In his speech marking the annexation of Crimea on March 18, 2014, Putin underscored (as he had on many other occasions) that, *no*, NATO *did* pose a threat to Russian territory. It was a military alliance. It *could* invade.[10] And, for the historical record, he stressed that in the 1990s, Russia had not accepted the rules of an international order created by the United States and its European allies. Russia had simply endured a series of humiliations. It had "hung down its head" and "resigned itself to the situation." It had "swallowed the insult" of the loss of its territory and population. It had been forced to do so, Putin lamented, because the "country was then in such a severe condition that it simply could not realistically defend its interests."[11] It did not have the capacity, the ability, or the strength to do anything else. But the desire to change that unacceptable situation never faded.

Twenty-five years after the collapse of the Berlin Wall—which marked the loss of the Soviet Union's position in Europe that Putin regretted so much in his early interviews—the Russian president savored a moment of personal triumph. Russia's capacity for action and its international position had been restored. *Today,* Putin emphasized in his speech, in March 2014, Russia was a very different country. In his statements surrounding Crimea's annexation, Putin underscored the fact that although Russia might still be interested in cooperating with the West in the future, it would do so only on its own terms. Russia was not in a transition to become a Western European–style liberal democracy and market economy, as many Western analysts had assumed (or hoped) in the 1990s.

Russia was not going to join or create some kind of strategic partnership with the two major institutional pillars of the post–Cold War Euro-Atlantic order, NATO and the European Union. Even if Europe was its center of gravity, Russia was not some ordinary European state. Russia was Russia, and it was going to stay that way. Russia was no longer in retreat; it had taken back Crimea. It was going to chart its own course in the world. A few months later, in a speech to an audience of Russia's ambassadors, Putin declared that the unipolar world, the unipolar moment, was finally over. The rest of the world was moving on from a post–Cold War period defined by the United States.[12]

"HE LIVES IN ANOTHER WORLD"

Russia's actions in Ukraine, and Putin's March 18, 2014, speech sent shock waves around Western foreign policy and security circles. Putin's interpretation of events, his criticisms of NATO, the United States, and Europe, were all seen as a blatant act of revisionism.[13] The annexation of Crimea was a jolt, and yet Russia had engaged in a similar military conflict with Georgia in August 2008. It had launched strikes deep into Georgian territory and recognized the independence of Abkhazia and South Ossetia. Before, during, and after the Russo-Georgian war, Putin had made many of the same assertions about NATO and threats from the West, and had rejected the concept of a unipolar world order led by the United States. Putin's March 2014 speech in the Kremlin was consistent in content and tone with statements dating back to the early days of his presidency. In fact, it echoed the grievances of many Russian political figures from the 1990s even before Putin moved to Moscow. It picked up on themes favored by conservative and nationalist politicians, like Sergei Glazyev and Gennady Zyuganov, who had banded together in the *Soglasiye vo imya Rossii* movement 20 years before (see chapter 3). Glazyev and Zyuganov, and many others from that era, had prominent supporting roles to play during the crisis in Ukraine.[14] Putin was not charting new territory in March 2014. He was circling around familiar territory.

Vladimir Putin's views of developments in Ukraine in 2014 and in the world at large were just as much the product of his past personal and professional experiences in the USSR and post-Soviet Russia as his approach to governing the modern state. The six identities outlined in

Part I of this book help explain the origins of Putin's thinking on these issues. In the 2000s, Putin extended his goals and priorities for Russian domestic policy into the foreign policy arena. He adapted the methods he used to become CEO of Russia, Inc. to deal with the outside world. In his overall approach to foreign policy, Vladimir Putin's primary identity has been that of the Statist. Putin's goal since December 1999 and the Millennium Message has been to restore Russia's position as a great power and world civilization. In the Millennium Message, Putin promised he would entirely devote himself to putting Russia back on its feet again.[15] In his 2012 annual address to the Russian parliament, after returning to the presidency, Putin reaffirmed this goal. He also promised to ensure that Russia would be in "geopolitical demand" in the years ahead.[16]

Since 1999, Putin has played the History Man internationally, not just at home. He has staked out a place for Russia and the Russian people in the great sweep of global history. At times, including when he formally annexed Crimea for Russia, he has literally rewritten the narrative of Russia's interactions with the outside world. He has put himself in charge, in control, of the definitive history. Putin has validated and defended Russia's international position by selecting and manipulating key events. He has acted as the Survivalist who sets out to ensure Russia can protect itself against all external threats, by preparing and deploying every reserve or resource—even history itself—in the state's defense. The Operative in the Kremlin has projected himself abroad by drawing on his personal experiences and insights as the Outsider and the Free Marketeer, and by applying the professional tools of the Case Officer.

In March 2014, Germany's chancellor Angela Merkel reportedly told President Barack Obama that Putin "lives in another world."[17] If by that Merkel meant that Putin saw things in a fundamentally different way than his European and U.S. counterparts, then Putin would essentially agree. That was in fact a point he made in his speech marking the Crimean annexation, as he demanded that his European neighbors, the United States, and other international actors try to understand *his* world, the historical and political context in which he operated. "Russia," Putin declared, ". . . has, just like other states, national interests, which must be taken into consideration and respected."[18] In Putin's world—a world refracted through his personal reading of Russian history—"they" (Western leaders) were "always trying to drive [Russia] into some kind of corner," even when

Russians have had the best of intentions. Why? Because "we" have always had and continue to have "an independent position."

In Putin's view, the situation that unfolded in Ukraine in 2013–14 reflected, as if in a mirror (*kak v zerkale otrazilos'*), what was going on in the world as a whole. Developments in Ukraine, and the efforts of the European Union to create a new relationship with Ukraine, were simply a continuation, if not the culmination, of several decades of efforts by the West to put pressure on Russia and thwart its foreign policy priorities. Indeed, as he considered the situation in greater detail, Putin concluded that Russians had "every basis for thinking that the notorious [*preslovutaya*] policy of containing Russia that was conducted in the eighteenth, the nineteenth, and the twentieth centuries is also being continued today [in the twenty-first century]." In the case of Ukraine, as many times before in the history of Russia's interactions with the outside world, Putin asserted, limits had been reached. The West—"our Western partners," as he called them—had crossed a line (*nashi zapadnyye partnery pereshli chertu*) by pushing Ukraine toward the European Union, just as it had crossed a line in 2008 by promising eventual NATO membership to both Ukraine and Georgia. The EU was nothing more than a stalking horse for NATO enlargement for countries that signed association agreements. Russia had been put in an untenable position. In one of Putin's usual colorful turns of phrase: Russia was a spring that had been pushed back to its absolute limits. It had inevitably sprung back into place again with considerable force. As Putin explained it, annexing Crimea was a completely reasonable act of self-defense.[19] The West, he complained, should have understood what Russia's reaction was going to be. "They" knew only too well that millions of Russians lived in Ukraine and in Crimea. Those Russians were clearly not going to become part of the West. "They" must have totally lost their political instincts and sense of proportion if they didn't foresee what was going to happen.

THE RUSSIAN WORLD

Just a week after his March 18 speech, at another ceremony in the Kremlin, Putin announced that he had commissioned an official report on "The Fundamentals of State Cultural Politics" that would inform and underpin public discussions of Russia's history and traditions.[20] Presidential adviser Vladimir Tolstoy subsequently informed the press that the report would underscore that "Russia is not Europe," and is instead a "unique and distinctive civilization belonging neither to the 'West' nor the 'East.'"[21] This insistent embrace of the idea of an independent Russia that stands apart from the rest of Europe and the West, under constant pressure and facing the threat of some kind of external assault, is not simply a concoction of Putin and his inner circle. As historian Marshall Poe writes in *The Russian Moment in World History,* for Russia's leaders and elite "the Europeans were always coming, even though a neutral observer would think otherwise."[22]

In his book, which surveys the major trends in Russia's interactions with the outside world, Poe describes Russia as essentially a "start-up" state.[23] Russia, he argues, emerged in a territory where no earlier civilizations had been established given the vast distances from open coastline and the harsh northern climate with its impenetrable forests and endless steppe. For most of the period up until the eighteenth century, when Putin claims that the West's policy of containment began, Russia was culturally, politically, and geographically distinct. Russia's political system and religion developed in tandem in a remote space. A broader sense of Russianness [*russkost'*] and of living in "their own world"—the *russkiy mir* or Russian world—evolved for the people living there in a great degree of isolation.

Just as the idea of the state (*gosudarstvo*) has a very specific meaning for Russians (see chapter 3), so does the idea of the world, or *mir*. In fact, the word *mir* in Russian has a multitiered meaning. *Mir* is the outside world and the infinitely larger world of the universe. It is also peace and, in various verbal forms, the idea of making peace and reconciliation. At the same time, *mir* refers to the micro-world of the mass of inhabitants of the Russian world, the basic village community: the peasant commune. This smallest unit of the *russkiy mir* had to work together to provide for itself and protect its members. "Making peace" or putting the micro-world back together after some internal dissent or conflict was a survival mechanism. Disunity could result literally in catastrophe in the marginal lands of Russia with their poor soils, short growing seasons, and scattered agricultural settlements. Everyone worked together or they died apart. Before the advent of urbanization, being expelled from the community (literally ex-communication) was a death sentence for any member who persistently refused to follow the *mir*'s internal rules. No matter how rugged the individual, chances of surviving on one's own were slim.

This concept of the commune where internal cohesion is essential for protection and survival provides the frame for Mr. Putin's world. It is a very different historical frame from Angela Merkel's world, where the infrastructure for modern European states was created on the basis of building blocks inherited from the Roman Empire. As Poe and many other historians of Russia have pointed out, in their isolation Russians did not develop European-style feudal systems or networks of prosperous independent cities. Instead, intermittent trading posts along river networks became small towns, their size and activities constrained by the meager agricultural surplus of the vast hinterland. When a group of Viking raiders—the Rus', who gave their name to the territory—sailed down the rivers sometime in the tenth century, they took over the towns by giving the inhabitants "offers of 'protection' they could not refuse."[24] The early empire the Rus' and their successors created was under constant assault from the east rather than the west. Successive waves of horsemen invaded from the Eurasian steppe to despoil local populations. Adopting Christianity from distant Byzantium and arranging political marriages with princesses from far-off lands were ways of doing deals to ensure protection and establish rules of interaction with the outside world.[25]

In this historical context, the system Vladimir Putin created around him and that Russia's new urban middle classes revolted against in 2011–12 is recognizably *Russian*. Putin's system was created in a piecemeal, ad hoc fashion, using the skills he acquired in the KGB; but his protection scheme and his one-boy network fit with ideas about the structure and methods of governance that have evolved over several centuries along with the development of the Russian state (see chapter 9). The country has been ruled since first recorded times by a tiny number of princes and their tightly bound inner circles of close associates. In one of the most celebrated and cogent essays on the persistence of political patterns from medieval to modern Russia, "Muscovite Political Folkways," Harvard University historian Edward Keenan explains:

The "power structure" of the Muscovite court can best be visualized [as an] atom, with a fixed nucleus encircled by a number of concentric rings, each of which is composed of particles that may move from ring to ring, from lower to higher energy level, while maintaining the basically stable structure of the atom itself. At the center of this system, alone and immobile, stood the grand prince (later tsar, emperor, etc.). Around him in the innermost ring . . . were the most important clan leaders, the boyars, typically his maternal uncles, cousins or in-laws.[26]

Putin's system has its antecedents in early Muscovite history. Indeed, when Anatoly Sobchak and his colleagues drafted the new post-Soviet Russian constitution in 1993, with the president at its center, they drew heavily on ideas from the late tsarist period (see chapter 3). As he promised in the Millennium Message, Putin picked up the basic contours of a political system that is historically appropriate for Russia in the same way that he and Vladislav Surkov reformulated Sergei Uvarov's nineteenth-century doctrine of official nationality as sovereign democracy (see chapter 4). The tsarist autocratic order emerged in response to the realities of the physical geographic space it occupied and the many hostile interactions between the rulers and inhabitants of this space and their neighbors. Similarly, Putin has constantly adapted the core of his system, as well as the Russian state apparatus, in response to his understanding of Russia's environment and how he perceives the outside world has changed over time.

From the Mongol invasions in the thirteenth century to the "rise" of Muscovy in the sixteenth century that marks the beginning of the premodern Russian state, the political and administrative system developed as the direct consequence of ensuring protection.[27] The Mongols had no desire to settle in the harsh north and moved on south to Central Asia. They empowered the princes of Moscow to collect their taxes and send the tribute on to them. The princes prospered by serving the Mongols well and keeping some of the money for themselves. When circumstances changed and the Mongol-Moscow arrangement needed to be adjusted, brief wars raised the stakes for both sides if diplomacy failed. Once the terms and the amount of tribute were agreed again, the wars stopped. Eventually the Mongols' successors fell into disarray and Moscow's princes took advantage. They took over the Mongols' protection racket and coerced the princes of other Russian territories and the inhabitants of trading cities to accept "Moscow's protection." They validated their actions by writing their own historical narratives, chronicling their "gathering of the Russian lands."[28]

From the fifteenth to the seventeenth century, the early Russian state organized on its own terms with very limited interaction with the outside world.[29] The Russian Orthodox Church viewed the Europeans to the west as heretics. The Church encouraged the state to keep its distance. Russia stood apart from Europe and its agricultural, economic, political, cultural, and military developments in this period. Marshall Poe relates how Russia was "mauled" by the Swedes and then the Poles who invaded from the northwest in the sixteenth and seventeenth centuries because the Russian military class had not adopted gunpowder.[30] Only Russia's vast, inhospitable territory prevented the Swedes, the Poles, and later invaders like the French under Napoleon from holding Moscow or other Russian lands for long.[31]

MODERNIZING FOR PROTECTION

Putin invoked many of these invasions and battles, including the Crimean War of the 1850s, in his March 18, 2014, speech. He used the historical fact of that war to justify Russia's claim to the peninsula and to Sevastopol, the "city of Russian military glory." Historians have noted that European invasions and military disasters like the Crimean War shaped Russia's approach to system modernization. Defeat in the Crimean War resulted in an intense period of top-down reforms by Russian tsars in the latter half of the nineteenth century to shore up the autocracy and reduce its vulnerability to Western pressure.[32] Every time Russia was threatened or invaded by Europeans, its rulers pushed through military, economic, political, and cultural innovations to fend off future invaders. Russia's borders were closed, but small numbers of foreign mercenaries and specialists were invited in to pass on their technical skills.[33] European culture and politics were kept at bay by placing all foreigners and their activities under the close supervision of the state. By borrowing from but limiting interaction with the outside world, Moscow protected and reformed itself to protect itself even better.

In short, the kind of top-down reforms that Putin undertook in Russia after 1999 can be understood as part of a long historical pattern that was laid down several centuries before the Pyotr Stolypin reforms of the early 1900s to which Putin has referred. At every major historical juncture, Russia's leaders have tried to modernize the state in reaction and response to a perceived external threat. The Russian world at home has been forged anew because of interactions with the world outside. The objective has been to produce a better, stronger version of Russia, not a Western European version of Russia. After every burst of reforms, the basic features of the Russian world tended to remain constant—including during the Soviet period, when the collective farm replaced the peasant world in the countryside, and the Soviet general secretary with the politburo around him substituted for the tsar and his boyars at the core of the system. Like old Muscovy, the USSR closed its borders, restricted the movement of foreigners, and implemented reforms when threatened. Mikhail Gorbachev's perestroika was essentially an old-style effort at top-down reforms to save the Soviet state and communist system as they weakened in Cold War competition with the West, just as Stolypin's efforts aimed to shore up and save the Russian Empire and tsarist order after the debacle of the Russo-Japanese War.

THE UNIPOLAR LEADER

Marshall Poe also identifies in his book several salient features of autocracy, many of which have parallels in Putin's system. One of the most important is the fact that autocracy is "the unconditional rule of one," but with a group of very close associates to assist the autocrat in his duties, as "absolute rulers never rule alone but rather in cooperation with other elites."[34] Poe underscores the historical point made by many other historians that tsarist Russia never developed the features of an oligarchy. Political power did not reside with the boyars or aristocrats, or even with an extended royal family. It always remained concentrated with the tsar. So did economic power. The aristocrats' lands and property were all concessions. They were granted by the tsar in return for personal service. This is the essence of the "patrimonial state" in Russia, analyzed and described in great detail by historians like Richard Pipes.[35]

Unlike in Europe during the same rough historical periods, there was no private property in Russia to generate independent, feudal interests that could then collectively challenge the tsar and impose constraints on his rule.[36] The tsar stood above a tiny warrior elite, a tiny urban population, and the mass of peasants (the *narod*), bound together and organized at the most micro level in their *mir*. The "tsar's elite servitors enjoyed privileges, power and wealth," but they were "under the strict control" of the tsar.[37] The elite servitors got the personal protection of the tsar. This close relationship defined and underpinned their property and their position in society: "the more powerful one's protector, the higher one's status."[38] Edward Keenan emphasizes the "informal, inter-personal, and conspiratorial" nature of this relationship. Even as the tsarist bureaucratic system got more complex, "the official institutions and offices of the state did not in fact determine or regulate the game of politics, but were, rather, its prizes." In the tsarist system, as in Putin's, individual positions in the inner circle and government "depended ulti-mately upon the 'confidence,' i.e., personal choice of the tsar."[39]

The tsar came in a political and spiritual package with the Russian Orthodox Church. His own position was "unlimited by any but divine law."[40] This essentially unassailable position of the tsar created a "uni-polar political context."[41] The tsar enjoyed a unity of command, which enabled the autocracy to overcome systemic and popular resistance to modernizing reforms.[42] Representative institutions in tsarist Russia devel-oped from the top down to facilitate the transmission of orders from the tsar and his inner circle down to the level of the *narod*. These institutions were intended to be a "staff meeting, not a parliament."[43] This is entirely in keeping with Pyotr Stolypin's idea that the role of the first Russian Duma was to work directly with the tsar's government to help implement reforms. Stolypin did not believe that the Duma should provide alterna-tive input or impose any kind of check on his activities. Representative institutions were also one way of showing respect to those far beneath the tsar and his inner circle. They provided a semblance of consultation within the system. By giving a hearing to different voices, they helped to foster a sense of unity and consensus between the tsar and his people.

As a student of Russian history, Putin has internalized and adapted these basic Russian political patterns to modern times. The special closed world of the oligarchs at the core of Putin's informal system echoes the relationship between the tsar and his elite servitors. Neither the current crony oligarchs nor the original post-Soviet oligarchs are oligarchs in the Western sense. They are not a single group or even a set of groups with an independent base of power. They are all part of Putin's one-boy network. They do not jockey for power with Putin, although they do clearly try to get access to the person of the president to transmit their views and concerns and have some influence over his decisions. As in earlier, historical versions of this system, their positions and status are entirely dependent on Putin. So is the oligarchs' property—it is a privilege that flows from their relationship with the president. As president, Putin protects the oligarchs and his inner circle. The oligarchs steward and manage the key sectors of the Russian economy. They pay formal taxes and also deliver tribute to Putin and the state through the informal systems of taxation. They prosper because they deliver and precisely because they have Putin's protection.

Putin's informal, unofficial system *and* the formal world of the state apparatus both depend on unity of command. Putin may have rejected the idea of a unipolar world dominated by the rules and institutions of the United States and its Western allies, but he is very much a unipolar president. Others can bring ideas to the table and criticize the president during the deliberative part of the policy process, but his word is final. What he says goes once the decision is made. As related in chapter 9, in Putin's conceptualization of himself as the CEO of Russia, Inc. and in his conceptualization of the *vertikal vlasti,* everyone beneath him is an operational manager. They implement, they do not set the strategic direction. There are rituals of consultation with the Russian people at different levels—through mechanisms like opinion polls and Putin's annual *Hot Line* show, and representative institutions like the Russian Duma. Regular elections are also a transmission belt up and down the system. But as Putin underscored through his treatment of the opposition after the stakeholders' revolt, once the population has made its voice heard in these formats, and a conclusion has been reached, the *narod,* the population, has no role whatsoever in governance. Managed democracy and forms of social engineering are not a recent invention; they have been a Russian practice for centuries.

All of this is laid down and circumscribed by Russian law. Rather than the divine right of the tsar, Putin is bound by the secular law of the 1993 Russian constitution—and only by the constitution. The Orthodox Church still comes in a package with Putin and the state, even if the modern presidential base of power is secular. In Putin's system and formulation, it is *Rus'* (Russia) that is divine (*svyataya* or holy). The president is certainly not divine or holy. The stress on *svyataya Rus'* picks up on another older Russian Orthodox and tsarist tradition, where Rus' refers to something larger than the idea of the Russian state and people and encompasses the entire Russian Orthodox religious community. Before the Russian Revolution, citizens of the empire who were baptized as Russian Orthodox Christians were seen to be Orthodox (*pravoslavnyy*), and therefore Russian (*russkiy*), no matter where they lived or what their specific ethnic origins. Tatar nobility, Baltic German aristocrats, Georgian princes and princesses, and their subjects, all became *pravoslavnyy* on conversion. Religion and language became the primary identifying markers of a Russian, even if an individual did not russify his last name. The overarching *pravoslavnyy* identity was one of the mainstays of loyalty to the tsar and to the Russian state. This idea was captured in an interview in July 2014 by the *New York Times*'s Moscow correspondent, Neil MacFarquhar, of a Russian believer participating in a pilgrimage to the monastery founded by Russia's most important saint, Sergey (or Sergius) of Radonezh, in commemoration of the 700th anniversary of the saint's birth. The pilgrim told MacFarquhar, "We are all one people, we are all part of Holy Rus'. . . . Any person, regardless of where he lives, if he is Russian in spirit, he must be defended by his president, by his country, because he is an indivisible part of the nation."[44]

Putin and the Russian Orthodox patriarch repeatedly underscored the idea of *svyataya Rus'* in speeches about the annexation of Crimea. For example, in his March 18, 2014, speech in the Kremlin, Putin spoke of Crimea as a territory filled with places that are holy for Russia. These included "symbols of Russian military glory and unprecedented valor," and the site of the baptism of *svyatoy knyaz' Vladimir* (holy Prince Vladimir), the grand prince of Kyiv who assumed Christianity on behalf of all Russia in 988. Putin dropped the usual Russian reference to Vladimir as prince of Kyiv (*velikiy knyaz' kievskiy Vladimir*) in his speech, a reformulation that was immediately remarked on in Russian opposition circles.[45]

Vladimir Putin would essentially share Marshall Poe's analysis of the sweep of Russian history and what Poe calls "the cold, hard historical facts of Russian-European relations."[46] As a History Man with his own selection and narrative version of events, Putin might not agree with all of Poe's reinterpretations of Russia's early Muscovite history. But Putin *would* agree that it was Russia's unique autocratic system that enabled the state to survive for so long in such hostile and uncertain climatic and geopolitical conditions. The constant variations on the autocratic system and its unity of command provided a means to protect Russia from the West. Russia was the "first sustainable society capable of resisting the challenge of Europe."[47] Russia has been, in one form or another, a permanent fixture on the globe for centuries. Putin's goal for Russia, as he outlined it in the 1999 Millennium Message, was the same goal that successive Russian tsars and Soviet leaders embraced over the previous thousand years: the establishment of a strong state that would guarantee political stability and produce no cleavages and infighting for the outside world, the West, to exploit. As Putin noted after the 2004 terrorist attack against the school in Beslan, Russians could not afford to show any divisions, any weakness: "Because the weak—they get beaten" (*A slabykh—b'yut*).[48]

GERMANY–PUTIN'S PORTAL TO THE WEST

Putin stated bluntly in 2014 that he saw a clear threat to Russia from the West; but what does Putin really know personally about the West, about Europe, and the United States, beyond his reading and interpretations of Russian history? When compared with the line of Soviet leaders stretching from Stalin through Yeltsin, Putin seems the most Western of Russia's modern rulers. He speaks a European language, German, fluently. He is the only Russian leader to have lived abroad since Vladimir Lenin and the early Bolsheviks.[49] Most Soviet and Russian leaders only visited the West through the usual episodic routine of official visits. But Putin lived in East Germany for nearly five years. He has admitted in his biographical interviews that his time in Dresden in the late 1980s played a critical role in shaping his views on international developments. Germany is Vladimir Putin's portal to the West and the outside world.

Putin has frequently emphasized how much he turns to his own past personal and professional experiences as reference points and guides for present action. Until 1990, everything Putin knew about the outside world was through his professional KGB role. In the KGB he was likely in two directorates, both focused on foreigners. In Putin's case, "foreigners" meant Germans and German-speakers. Given Putin's personal history, he was already linked to Germany through the prism of World War II—his parents' and his home city's terrible ordeal during the siege of Leningrad and his father's wartime exploits in the NKVD destruction battalion behind enemy lines (see chapter 5). Growing up as the child of two wartime survivors in Leningrad, Putin would have heard a great deal about the Soviet Union's struggle with Nazi Germany. But in the Soviet Union of the 1950s and subsequent decades, the government was also trying to shift the population's memories and the national narrative away from the horrors of war. Part of Germany—East Germany, the GDR— was now in the Soviet bloc. It was under the occupation of Soviet troops and the governance of a Communist Party that wanted to put as much distance as possible between it and the Nazi past.[50]

During the Cold War, forging solidarity and a sense of unity across the Soviet bloc against the capitalist West required creating a new narrative of shared suffering and common cause. The blame for the wartime atrocities—the mass slaughter of the Soviet Union's Russian, Jewish, and other populations—was shifted to West Germany, the Federal Republic of German (FRG), part of which was occupied by the United States. U.S. efforts to root out the remnants of the Nazi Party, and to promote a long period of national debate in the FRG over the sins of the past, assisted the Soviets in shifting their narrative. West Germans took responsibility for the war and Nazi crimes. East Germans were embraced by the broader band of communists from Eastern Europe to the Soviet Union who had battled against the most monstrous forces of the capitalist West. Museums and monuments were erected in East Berlin and across the GDR honoring the exploits of the Soviet army and their liberation of East Germany. Many Russians were stationed in, or moved to, the GDR. Some married Germans, creating blended Russian-German families and tightening the new bonds. Russian and German language classes became staples of the respective school systems.

This backdrop produced a kind of "love-hate" relationship with Germany in Soviet popular culture. World War II was a staple of Soviet film and literature. And while the context of these books and movies was, by necessity, the war between Germany and the Soviet Union (the Western allies were rarely mentioned), the writers and producers had to find a way to present the heroism of the Soviet struggle without demonizing all Germans. As a result, there were few, if any, films that fell into the genre of pure revenge fantasy. The war's outcome—with Russia in East Germany— was the revenge. In 1945, Soviet forces had pushed deep into Germany and taken Berlin. Today, the Reichstag, the parliament building in Berlin, still has Russian graffiti on the walls, along with bullet holes and shrapnel scars. Most of the graffiti is from Soviet soldiers, some just marking their names, others chronicling the catharsis of revenge: "They've paid the price in full for Leningrad" (*Za Leningrad zaplatili polnost'yu*), scrawled one. "We went out today and looked at Berlin in ruins. We feel good," wrote a couple of other Red Army soldiers, identifying themselves with their first names and hometowns in Russia.[51]

The World War II literature and films that targeted Putin's generation in the 1960s and 1970s shifted the narrative about the war and about Germans. Some of the most popular books in the late 1960s, when Putin was in school and embarking on his German language studies, were novels about deep-cover Soviet intelligence officers operating in the innermost ranks of the Nazi military command. One characteristic feature of these works was the way some of the Germans, even high-ranking officials, were portrayed as "normal" and human. One of the books, *Seventeen Moments of Spring,* was made into the most successful TV series ever in the Soviet Union, airing almost nightly for two weeks in August 1973. The series relates the exploits of deep-cover Soviet operative Maksim Isayev, who passes himself off as a German aristocrat, Max Otto von Stirlitz, to infiltrate and eventually rise to the highest ranks of the SS. The plot unfolds in the spring of 1945. Nazi Germany is on the verge of defeat, and in a last desperate move, insiders in the Nazi hierarchy attempt to broker a separate peace with the Americans, in order to allow the Germans to turn their full attention to defeating the USSR. Stirlitz is assigned to subvert that effort. So, in effect, for Stirlitz, although he is operating in Germany, the "main adversary" is the United States.

It is not hard to imagine how the then 20-year-old Vladimir Putin, already determined to join the KGB on graduating from the university and knowing German, would have identified with Isayev/Stirlitz. This was a Russian hero who was able to infiltrate the Nazi command thanks to his fluency in German and his cold-blooded patience and persistence. Later, after Putin had joined the KGB, the idea of the Soviet operative cleverly manipulating Germans in order to thwart the Americans perhaps would have even greater resonance.[52] Indeed, in his first years in the KGB, Putin was in counterespionage in Leningrad, and Germans were KGB targets. Putin's work would have involved monitoring German-speaking tourists and business people in Leningrad and looking for ways to entrap them. This was done, more often than not, through networks of informers in the Soviet "shadow economy"—informers who were engaged in illegal foreign currency deals and hard-currency prostitution.

Konstantin Simis, a former senior researcher at the Moscow Law Institute, exiled to the United States in 1978, describes a typical KGB operation to target a foreigner in his seminal 1982 book on USSR corruption. A KGB informer in one of the black market syndicates would be instructed to contact the foreigner to

> entrap him into agreeing to sell foreign currency (which is a heinous crime under Soviet law), and set a time and place for concluding the deal so that the KGB might catch the foreigner red-handed. As the result of such an operation the KGB would be able either to recruit the victim as a full-time spy or to obtain specific information from him by threatening him with scandalous exposure and expulsion from the country (if he had diplomatic immunity) or with arrest and many years of imprisonment in the camps.[53]

Simis notes in conjunction with this point that in the 1970s, Soviet criminal syndicates "headed in fact by secret agents" had cornered the black market in major Soviet cities. They had squeezed out the competition all in the service of compromising and recruiting foreigners. The mafia and the KGB were operationally fused together by the time Putin joined the agency.

These kinds of entrapment operations were the frame for Putin's interactions with Germans until 1985, when he was posted to Dresden by the KGB to work directly with his counterparts in the *Stasi*. Germans were now his colleagues, not just his targets. Putin moved from the Soviet and Russian world into the German world. But the GDR was not part of the

West. Putin lived and worked in the East, which had been cut off from the rest of its German *and* European roots by the political and physical barriers of the Cold War. Putin himself made this observation in *Ot pervogo litsa,* when he talked about the fact that in 1985 he initially thought he was heading off to live in an East European country in the center of Europe. When he got there, he realized this was not the case at all. The GDR was more like the USSR than anywhere else. It was not even as politically advanced as Gorbachev's Soviet Union.[54] The world of Dresden and East Germany was a special, distorted one. So was Putin's time there in the KGB.

In the West, we find it hard to believe that Putin lived and still lives in another world, as German chancellor Merkel reportedly put it in March 2014. We assume that Putin's time in the KGB provided him with something more than just a window on the outside world. We presume that when Putin does not see or describe events as we do, he is either "delusional" or deliberately distorting the facts. He is making things up for some nefarious "KGB purpose."[55] When Chancellor Merkel's comment was first reported in the U.S. and Western press there were a flurry of articles suggesting, and then agreeing, that the Russian president was "out of his mind" when he said he saw a threat from the West in events in Ukraine.[56] Similarly, during previous periods of conflict with Russia, such as in 2008 around the war with Georgia, senior U.S. government officials repeatedly questioned the validity of Putin's perspective on the war, which was frequently at odds with the Western narrative.[57]

It does not occur to those of us in the West that the reason Putin does not think like we do is because he simply *cannot* think like we do. He was an operative in the KGB where blatant lies, disinformation, and dissimulation were part of the tool box. As president, he has deliberately distorted narratives for his own political purposes on many, documented, occasions. But even if he had not served in the KGB and internalized its methods, Vladimir Putin would still not have the necessary educational and practical framework to put things in a "European" or "Western" or "U.S." perspective. Vladimir Putin did not grow up, go to school, live, or work in the same cultural, economic, political, and historical environment as Western leaders. He was far away on the other side of the wall during the Cold War. Throughout Putin's long stretch as the head of the Russian state, the only Western counterpart who shared some of his background was, in fact, German chancellor Angela Merkel, who came into office in 2005.

MIRROR IMAGES?

Angela Merkel is only two years younger than Vladimir Putin. They come from the same post–World War II generation. She was born in West Germany but grew up in East Germany. Her father was a Lutheran minister and her mother a school teacher. She learned Russian in school and studied at Leipzig University (close to Dresden) around the same time in the 1970s that Putin was enrolled in the law faculty at Leningrad State University and beginning his career in the KGB. While Vladimir Putin was posted with the KGB in Dresden, however, Angela Merkel was studying and working at the Academy of Sciences in East Berlin. She joined the nascent East German democratic movement after the fall of the Berlin Wall in 1989. Merkel then embarked on a political career that eventually took her from the grassroots to the upper echelons of the German Christian Democratic Union (the CDU) after the reunification of Germany.

As Chancellor Merkel and her circle of advisers note in interviews, the general background and similar experiences she shares with Putin provide her with insights into Putin's world.[58] One of her biographers observed that they "have followed similar paths in life, almost as if they were mirror images."[59] The German chancellor understands how the Russian president thinks, and why he thinks the way he does about certain issues, but Angela Merkel does not think *like* Vladimir Putin. She is not *of* his world of the KGB and the *Stasi*. This point was made abundantly clear during Merkel's early official visits to Russia in 2006–07 to meet with Putin. The chancellor has an aversion to dogs, having reportedly been attacked by one in 1995. On two occasions, Putin played with this information, including allowing his black Labrador, Koni, to sniff around Merkel and lie at her feet during a meeting in his Sochi residence.[60] Observers of the scene understood that this was Putin's attempt to intimidate the chancellor. It was an act straight out of the KGB handbook for dealing with foreigners—target their weaknesses and play on their vulnerabilities. It was not the kind of official welcome that a diplomatic protocol officer would have recommended.[61]

Beyond his time in the KGB, Vladimir Putin has no firsthand experience of Western society. To assume that he does, and that he should think like us or even understand how we think, is an example of what U.S. scholar Zachary Shore—in his 2014 book, *A Sense of the Enemy: The High-Stakes History of Reading Your Rival's Mind*—describes as "simulation theory." We ask ourselves what we would do in another person's position, but this is "unfortunately, the worst approach to empathy because it assumes that others will think and act as we do, and too often they don't."[62] As we have pointed out in earlier chapters, Putin's understanding—in the Russian context—of how the free market works or should work is very different from a U.S. or European perspective. It was informed by his experience growing up in the Soviet Union and working in St. Petersburg as deputy mayor, as well as by his studies in the KGB and life in Dresden when the East German economy was in shambles. Putin's conception of democratic politics, or at least what he views as democratic politics, was filtered by his experience in the German Democratic Republic, and then in the rough-and-tumble of post-Soviet Russian politics in St. Petersburg and later in Moscow.

Unlike other Soviet and Russian leaders, Putin does not seem especially keen on getting any real insight into Western societies or how their political systems work. Judging by the accounts in *Ot pervogo litsa* and other biographical interviews, Putin became friendly with German intelligence colleagues and polished his language skills while he was in Dresden. Otherwise, his interactions with ordinary Germans were quite limited, as were his travels to other parts of East Germany. The head of the Dresden office of the German newspaper *Die Zeit,* for example, could not identify any ordinary Dresdener who had befriended Putin during his time there, in spite of extensive investigative work by the paper's staff. They had been able to pinpoint a few beer halls that Putin had frequented from time to time, and some passing encounters, but Vladimir Putin otherwise left very little trace of his presence in the city.[63]

PUTIN'S GERMAN PATRIARCHS

In interacting with Germany and the rest of the world outside the *russkiy mir,* Putin has adopted the same approach he uses to run Russia, Inc. He deals with the smallest number of people possible. Just as he relies on formal and informal ombudsmen to channel information to various interest groups inside Russia and to manage connections with international business, Putin uses a network of intermediaries as his connections with the West. They are usually at a very high level. In the case of Germany, apart from businessman Matthias Warnig (see chapter 9), Putin has famously befriended Angela Merkel's predecessor, Gerhard Schröder, chancellor of Germany from 1998 to 2005. Putin and Schröder bonded over a common hardscrabble background, some similar professional experiences, and a shared interest in creating an economic partnership between Russia and Germany, based on Russia's and Gazprom's huge natural gas reserves and Germany's status as Europe's largest gas consumer.

Schröder, who is more than a decade older that Putin, lost his father in World War II when he was an infant. He grew up in an impoverished household, and worked his way up from the bottom of society. Schröder trained as a lawyer in West Germany before entering politics and then steadily progressed through positions in regional politics to the top of the German state. As chancellor, he spearheaded a tough set of economic reforms and laid the groundwork for a set of long-term contracts and pipeline projects to bring Russian gas to Germany. Energy issues were among Schröder's top priorities in government, and, like Putin, most of his closest political advisers were linked to energy companies. Schröder's aides observed that the German chancellor and Russian president were like "brothers in biography."[64] They became much more. Three months after Schröder left the German chancellery, Putin appointed him to the board of the Nord Stream company, operating a new gas pipeline under the Baltic Sea from Russia to Germany, in which Gazprom had the majority share. Putin also paved the way for the former chancellor and his wife to adopt two children from St. Petersburg. In 2004, Putin was the only foreign guest at Schröder's sixtieth birthday party at his home in Hannover. Ten years later, in April 2014, at the height of Russia's stand-off with Germany and Europe over Ukraine, Putin hosted a seventieth birthday party for Schröder in St. Petersburg (much to the irritation of Angela Merkel).[65]

Putin has courted other prominent German politicians, including former West German chancellor (1974–82), and elder statesman, Helmut Schmidt, who is also the copublisher of *Die Zeit,* Germany's most prominent newspaper. Putin hosted Schmidt, for example, in his dacha outside Moscow in December 2013, calling Schmidt "not only the patriarch of European politics but of global politics as well."[66] In these orchestrated settings, Putin's "patriarchs," his high-level interlocutors, transmit information to him and offer their assessments of German and international developments. In effect, they are crucial assets and sources. They translate the outside world for Putin. As the Case Officer, Putin still does some direct collection of information of his own—at summits in foreign countries and on state visits. He welcomes foreign leaders, CEOs, and various foreign delegations to Russia. He listens to what they have to say. But he rarely asks probing questions of them or takes things further in discussions. When he does, his probes are targeted—to collect specific information.

Germans certainly seem to be Putin's preferred interlocutors in the West. Only a small number of European countries have long histories of dealing with Russia—including the Baltic states, Finland, and Poland, which were part of the Russian Empire in the past, and Norway and Sweden, which have had various territorial disputes with their neighbor as well as close trade relations. The Netherlands and the United Kingdom also have several centuries of trade and diplomatic relations with Russia. Germany's size, its role in Europe, and its deep connections and proximity to Russia give it, perhaps, a unique position among European countries. In addition to playing a role in Putin's personal history, Germany gave Russia one of its most famous rulers in the eighteenth century, Catherine the Great, formerly Princess Sophie of Anhalt-Zerbst, a minor principality in Germany's eastern lands.[67] The Russian Federation also now includes a historic slice of German territory as part of the post–World War II division of the state: Königsberg, birthplace of German eighteenth-century philosopher Immanuel Kant. Stripped of its original German inhabitants, this ancient East Prussian city is now Kaliningrad, an exclave of the Russian Federation on the Baltic coast, sandwiched between Poland and Lithuania. In July 2005, Vladimir Putin and Gerhard Schröder met in the city for a joint celebration of its 750th anniversary. They announced together that Kaliningrad University (formerly Königsberg University) would henceforth be renamed in honor of Immanuel Kant.

In the 1990s, Germans provided Putin with portals for engaging with issues of foreign policy even before he became president. When he assumed his post as deputy mayor of St. Petersburg, Putin engaged with Germans at the individual and small group level, alone and with his boss, St. Petersburg mayor Anatoly Sobchak. In 1994, for example, at a roundtable in St. Petersburg organized by the German Körber Stiftung, Putin sat with Sobchak and a host of other prominent Russian and German political figures and commentators to discuss relations between Russia and the West. The transcript from the meeting records Deputy Mayor Putin listening intently to the discussion and monitoring its flow. He intervened to correct a point and set the record straight on a critical issue. Putin noted that Gorbachev and the Central Committee of the CPSU never intended to dismantle the USSR. They wanted to preserve it along with Communist Party rule. Unfortunately, Gorbachev and his team mishandled the situation. In his intervention, Putin then presciently moved on to stress the risks posed to European security by having 25 million ethnic Russians and Russian speakers left stranded outside of Russia's borders.[68]

In his March 2014 speech in the Kremlin, reflecting back on his interactions with his German counterparts in the 1990s, Putin made a personal appeal to Germans and Germany. He asked them to understand his actions in annexing Crimea: "I believe that even Europeans will understand me, and first and foremost Germans. I remember how during the political consultations for the unification of the FRG and the GDR—at, putting it mildly, the expert (but at a very high) level—representatives of not all the countries that then were, or appeared to be, allies of Germany, had their own ideas about unification. But our country, in contrast, unequivocally supported the sincere, irrepressible striving of Germans for national unity. I am certain that you [Germans] have not forgotten this, and I consider that the citizens of Germany likewise support the struggle of the Russian world, of historical Russia for the restoration of unity."[69] In other words, many of Germany's allies opposed its reunification in 1990, but Russia did not. Putin did not. Germany, therefore, should not oppose Russia's reunification with Crimea in 2014.

In sum, Putin knows German and he knows some high-level Germans, including former chancellors such as Gerhard Schröder and Helmut Schmidt, who are clearly representatives of their country on a political level. Soviet popular culture in the 1960s and 1970s helped to transform Germans (in the GDR at least) from the World War II enemy into

Cold War–era allies. Germans were humanized in popular culture. They became real people. When Putin lived in Germany as a KGB officer, Germans from the *Stasi* were his colleagues. Dresden and Putin's personal interactions with Germans cannot, however, substitute for a deeper understanding of German society or Europe as a whole. Germany has been only a partial portal through which Putin looks out at the West. Putin has continually asserted that despite Germany's importance, the United States is the leader of and dominates the West. It remains the most important Western interlocutor for Russia. In the Cold War, the United States was the USSR's "main adversary" (*glavnyy protivnik*). By the end of the popular Stirlitz TV series, the Americans had become the bad guys. They betrayed their Soviet allies and set the division of Europe between East and West in motion. And they continue to play that role in Putin's real-life scenario.

CHAPTER TWELVE

THE AMERICAN EDUCATION OF MR. PUTIN

BECAUSE OF HIS KGB HISTORY, Vladimir Putin is typically accused in U.S. media of still harboring an anti-American, Cold War view of the United States, and of blaming the United States for undermining and bringing down the Soviet Union. In fact, there is little evidence of any anti-American view in the early phases of Putin's public life. In the 1990s, when Putin was in the company of Anatoly Sobchak and the St. Petersburg reformers like Alexei Kudrin and Anatoly Chubais, who later brought him to work in the Kremlin, his positions were mainstream. He did not accuse the United States of destroying the Soviet Union. In his comments at the 1994 Körber Stiftung roundtable, Putin put the blame for the collapse of the USSR on the miscalculations of Soviet leaders and their mishandling of reforms in the 1980s. Putin also subscribed to the Chubais view—laid down in Yeltsin's 1997 presidential message, or *poslaniye*—that the most important task for Russia's leaders was to restore order to the state. As he asserted in the Millennium Message in December 1999, if Russia got its own house in order, and the state was strong again, its international position would be reaffirmed. Putin's more negative views about the United States, and the perceived threat the United States poses to Russia, seem to have hardened later in the 2000s, over the course of his interactions and relationships with two American presidents, George W. Bush and Barack Obama.[1]

Putin's general view of the United States appears very pragmatic. As president, he has shown no particular interest or curiosity about America beyond its top leaders and their actions. There is no sign on Putin's part of anything more than a passing interest in American literature, music, or films, or the way Americans live their lives. Germany is concrete, real for Putin. The United States is abstract. A former senior Russian Foreign Ministry, and later Kremlin, protocol officer noted in interviews that during trips to the United States, Putin rejected proposals for informal visits with Americans.[2] He accepted the "at-home" meetings with the U.S. president, but he asked few background questions about American society, values, and issues.[3] Notably, it was Dmitry Medvedev, during his tenure as president, who engaged in more informal encounters on his state visits to the United States and went to visit California's Silicon Valley.[4] Instead, like most of his Soviet predecessors, Putin always kept close to the official program. In fact, only two Soviet leaders— Nikita Khrushchev in 1959 and Mikhail Gorbachev, who first visited in 1987—made trips across the United States, taking in the Midwest and California in addition to Washington, D.C., and the East Coast.[5] In 1989, Boris Yeltsin visited a number of U.S. cities when he was a Moscow city representative in the Soviet Congress of People's Deputies and then seemed to relish his later visits as Russia's president. But the idea of a Khrushchev- or Gorbachev- or Yeltsin-like tour of the United States seems unthinkable for Vladimir Putin.

There is no reliable record of Putin's interactions with Americans or his thoughts on the United States during the key phases of his life: his youth in Leningrad, his KGB service, his time in Dresden, his period in the St. Petersburg mayor's office, and his prepresidential years in Moscow. When Putin went to Leningrad State University in the early 1970s, only a small number of American exchange students were there. But Putin did not study English, and he would have had limited opportunity to socialize with the American students outside the university, especially given the focus on his judo training. During his early KGB service in Leningrad in the late 1970s and early 1980s, the United States was filtered through the world of counterespionage and global developments of the time. At this juncture, Americans seemed dangerous and unpredictable.

The early 1980s were years of heightened Cold War confrontation. After a period of détente in the late 1960s and 1970s, the United States had become a clear and present danger for the Soviet Union. Based on their analysis of U.S. defense budgets, global U.S. military exercises, American and NATO air probes near sensitive Soviet borders, statements by top White House and Pentagon officials, and increased operations by the CIA in Afghanistan and elsewhere, the Kremlin leadership was thoroughly convinced that the United States posed a real military threat. By 1983, Kremlin leaders believed nuclear war was imminent.[6]

In 1981, the KGB went on full alert to look for any indications of U.S. intent to initiate a first strike against the USSR. According to Markus Wolf, head of the civilian foreign intelligence agency, the Hauptverwaltung Aufklärung (HVA), in the German Democratic Republic (GDR), the Soviet Union instructed its German allies—who essentially manned the Soviet bloc's frontlines with the West—to set up special task forces to monitor a "catalogue" of political and military indicators, including Pershing II and cruise missile sites in the Federal Republic of Germany (FRG), for any evidence of an impending U.S. attack.[7] In a top secret KGB cable from February 1983, entitled "The Problem of Discovering Preparation for a Nuclear Missile Attack on the USSR," the KGB fretted about "the so-called period of anticipation essential for the Soviet Union to take retaliatory measures." The agency worried that if it did not uncover the "process of preparation by the adversary to take the decision for a nuclear attack," and take "subsequent measures to prepare the country for a nuclear war," then "reprisal time would be extremely limited."[8]

LESSONS FROM 1983

March 1983 brought a full-scale war scare, just after U.S. president Ronald Reagan announced the proposed development of the Strategic Defense Initiative (SDI), or "Star Wars"—a land-based antiballistic missile defense system to shield the United States from a Soviet nuclear strike. Yury Andropov, who had moved from leading the KGB to helming the Soviet state in late 1982, lashed out against the Reagan administration's plans and raised the specter of a nuclear holocaust. The tension was palpable in Europe and the United States, not only in the Soviet Union. During a British war game to test NATO's preparations for a Soviet nuclear strike, a draft "World War III" speech was prepared for Queen Elizabeth II to give to the nation once war was declared.[9] The Queen's address, urging Britons to stay united and resolute during the "madness of war," was drafted almost at the very same time Reagan made his famous "Evil Empire" speech on March 8, 1983, about the dangers posed to the United States and its way of life by the Soviet Union. In an address to an evangelical Christian convention, President Reagan rejected calls from Western nongovernmental organizations for a U.S. nuclear weapons freeze and called on Americans to meet "the test of moral will and faith."[10] In September 1983, the situation deteriorated even further when Soviet warplanes intercepted and shot down a civilian South Korean Airlines plane, KAL 007, in the mistaken belief that it was a U.S. spy plane. The plane had strayed off-course into Soviet airspace while flying from Alaska to Seoul.

The idea of an impending nuclear World War III reverberated well beyond government circles. It permeated and dominated Western popular culture in 1983–84, particularly in countries like the United Kingdom, where the government of Prime Minister Margaret Thatcher was seen as the United States' most committed NATO ally. The war alarm spawned TV films and miniseries like "The Day After" in the United States and "Threads" in the United Kingdom, which focused on the attempts of ordinary Americans and Britons to survive and deal with the horrifying aftermath of a U.S.-Soviet nuclear exchange.[11] In this vein, one of the most popular posters in the United Kingdom evoking the idea and image of a global nuclear conflagration was a satirical take on the movie poster from "Gone with the Wind." Ronald Reagan as Rhett Butler held Margaret Thatcher as Scarlett O'Hara in his arms against the background of a nuclear mushroom cloud. The poster was captioned: "The Film to End All Films. The most EXPLOSIVE love story ever. Gone with the Wind. She promised to follow him to the ends of the earth. He promised to organize it! Now showing world-wide."[12] Permanent peace camps sprang up around U.S. and NATO military bases in the United Kingdom and elsewhere in Europe in direct response to the war fears. Greenham Common Airbase in southern England became the focal point of massive blockades by women's groups in 1982 and 1983 protesting a 1979 NATO decision to station U.S. cruise missiles at the base. The Greenham Common Women's Peace Camp persisted in one form or another from 1982 until 2000.[13]

The never-delivered "Queen's speech" invoked personal memories of the outbreak of World War II. In the Soviet Union, the top leaders terrified themselves and their population with similar memories of World

War II and specifically of Operation Barbarossa, Adolf Hitler's surprise attack on the USSR in June 1941. As Benjamin Fischer, an analyst and scholar at the CIA's Center for the Study of Intelligence, who produced a major review of the materials from this period, noted: "For decades after the war, Soviet leaders seemed obsessed with the lessons of 1941, which were as much visceral as intellectual in Soviet thinking about war and peace." Fischer underscored that for people of Yury Andropov's generation, World War II was "the formative experience of their political lives." Andropov and his colleagues put the KGB on full alert in the early 1980s in response to the lessons they had learned from the Soviet intelligence failures of World War II. They wanted "to create a strategic warning system in response to new challenges [they] saw looming on the horizon. That response was panicky but not paranoid." Fischer pointed out that Andropov's thinking was shaped by "adverse trends, not just adversarial personalities" such as Ronald Reagan or Margaret Thatcher—that is, by the Soviet Union's own pessimistic assessment of the "correlation of forces" and the "ever-widening gap in the USSR's technological lag behind the West."[14]

Just as many Western observers viewed Putin's depiction of events in Ukraine in 2013–14 as irrational, U.S. and European officials and intelligence analysts—including Markus Wolf in the GDR—considered Soviet officials "out of touch with reality" in 1983–84.[15] Looking at all of the available source material from this period, Fischer concluded, however, that the Soviet leadership and its population did genuinely feel "vulnerable to the prospect of a U.S. attack." Outside observers, for their part, saw no objective U.S. threat to the USSR: "Reagan was not Hitler, and America does not do Pearl Harbors." They failed to see that the view was very different from the vantage point of the Soviet Union, and "even fear based on a false threat can create real dangers."[16] In August 1984, Ronald Reagan stoked those fears even further in one of the most infamous "hot mic" incidents in international affairs, when he joked to U.S. National Public Radio engineers just before a live broadcast from his California ranch, "My fellow Americans, I'm pleased to tell you today that I've signed legislation that will outlaw Russia forever. We begin bombing in five minutes."[17] In the USSR nobody got the joke.

During that fall of 1984, Putin moved from his position with the Leningrad KGB and entered the KGB Red Banner Institute in Moscow. Soviet paranoia about the United States and fears of a nuclear war had not abated. This undoubtedly framed the tone and content of his instruction. It was only after March 1985, when Mikhail Gorbachev came into power to replace Yury Andropov as the Soviet general secretary, that things began to calm down in Soviet relations with the "main adversary," the *glavnyy protivnik*. In fall 1985, when Putin was already posted in Dresden, the USSR and the United States embarked on the series of negotiations that would ultimately lead to the signing of the 1987 Intermediate Range Nuclear Forces (INF) Treaty. In November 1985 in Geneva, Mikhail Gorbachev and Ronald Reagan held the first meeting between a Soviet and an American leader in seven years. They began a process that would put the tensions and war scares of the early 1980s behind them.[18]

In Dresden from 1985 to 1990, the focus shifted from war games to spy games and counterintelligence conspiracies. KGB efforts to steal U.S. and Western technology were stepped up. In the absence of English, Putin's list of foreign targets—if he had one in the GDR—was still most likely all German. He was too low in the KGB rankings to have much interaction with any top level targets, which would have included Americans. Until he came back from Dresden in 1990, Vladimir Putin may never have met an American in any personal context.

ST. PETERSBURG AND PUTIN'S FAVORITE AMERICAN

In contrast with all of Putin's previous experiences, St. Petersburg in the 1990s offered many opportunities for interactions with Americans through his official position as the deputy mayor in charge of external relations. The atmosphere also was very different from the 1980s. On December 25, 1991, the Soviet Union was gone and the United States was trying to figure out a whole new relationship with the Russian Federation. The threat perceptions and confrontations of the Cold War seemed to be a thing of the past. In 1990s St. Petersburg, Putin and the rest of the mayor's team were trying to get their house in order and figure out how to run the city and make its economy competitive again in a completely new environment. As the first democratically elected mayor, and an icon of the Russian reform movement, Anatoly Sobchak was openly courted by American and other Western politicians and technical specialists. Their approach and proposals were constructive on the surface, and they genuinely appeared willing to assist the mayor in his endeavors. Putin, the pragmatist, seemed to respond well to the overtures.

U.S. businesses and businessmen moved into St. Petersburg along with German, Finnish, Dutch, and other European private sector representatives. The U.S. Consulate in St. Petersburg reached out to Mayor Sobchak's office to assist its constituents. All Western businesses had to deal directly with Deputy Mayor Putin given the role of his office in issuing licenses and providing real estate for foreign joint ventures with Russian partners (see chapter 7). In his book *Russian Tide,* which described Proctor & Gamble's (P&G) entry into Russia, former CEO John Pepper wrote about the crucial role that the St. Petersburg Committee on External Relations played in helping the company establish itself in Russia.[19] P&G opened its first joint venture in Leningrad even before the dissolution of the Soviet Union, in 1990. Initially it worked with representatives from Leningrad State University, where Putin had first ended up after returning from Dresden. It was Putin who later signed the official registration documents for P&G's joint venture in his capacity as chairman of the Committee on External Relations.[20]

John Evans, who served as consul general in the U.S. Consulate in St. Petersburg from 1994 to 1997, had many encounters with Deputy Mayor Putin during his time there, often in response to mafia threats against American investors and contract disputes between U.S. and Russian businesses. Evans described Putin as always very helpful and approaching every issue in a "very legal, legalistic way." Putin would ask to see every contract and would refer to domestic and international law when looking for a solution to the problem. The legal cases might drag on for some time, but they would usually be resolved. Putin attended consulate receptions (usually spending most of his time talking in German to the German consul general) and was solicitous in dealing with the St. Petersburg diplomatic corps. Within the city's U.S. and Western business community, Putin was seen as "pro-business." He gave no impression whatsoever of any anti-American or anti-Western views.[21]

The St. Petersburg and Proctor & Gamble connection gave Putin a very important entry point into the United States. In 1992, P&G helped set up the International Action Commission for St. Petersburg with the Center for Strategic and International Studies (CSIS) in Washington, D.C.[22] The International Action Commission introduced Putin to an influential American, former Secretary of State Henry Kissinger, who was appointed as co-chair alongside Mayor Anatoly Sobchak.[23] It is not clear how much actual direct contact Putin and Kissinger had in the context of the bilateral commission.[24] However, it is clear that Henry Kissinger, like the German "patriarchs" Helmut Schmidt and Gerhard Schröder, became one of Putin's favorite interlocutors once he was president.

Putin admitted that the source of his initial interest in Kissinger as an interlocutor was the former secretary of state's early professional career in intelligence—in military intelligence in World War II (see chapter 8). More important, Henry Kissinger—like Helmut Schmidt—was an elder statesman, another patriarch. He was someone with a huge international reputation who offered a physical connection to an important set of key episodes that shaped global affairs. Kissinger was also a real History Man. He was a renowned scholar, with an academic career and numerous books to his name—just as Schmidt was a publicist. Kissinger was not *just* an American. He was originally from Germany. For Putin, Kissinger was literally the German in the White House. By straddling both the German and the American worlds, Henry Kissinger was an ideal ombudsman for Putin. Kissinger could provide a sounding board for ideas about geopolitics. He could interpret the United States and the West for Putin. He could transmit messages and information back to Washington, D.C. Henry Kissinger could explain Vladimir Putin to other influential Americans.

Another element in Henry Kissinger's personal biography that appears to have appealed to Putin was the fact that Kissinger was Jewish and fled Germany to escape anti-Semitism and Nazi persecution. Putin has a rather curious professional and personal history when it comes to anti-Semitism. In 1998–99, during at least one key step in his rise to the presidency, Putin seems to have cynically exploited deep currents of popular and political anti-Semitism in Russia as part of his operation to establish a kind of "protection racket" over Russia's oligarchs.[25] Other evidence suggests that while Putin has been willing to use anti-Semitism at times as a political instrument, he has seen Russia's relationship with Israel and the broader Jewish diaspora (including in the United States) as important elements in his domestic and foreign policy. In various speeches and meetings, Putin has made it clear that Russian Jews are as much *nash* (ours), part of the fabric of the Russian state, as Orthodox

Christians (see chapter 5). Putin also seems to have genuine regard for some individual Jews dating back to his childhood. In *Ot pervogo litsa,* for example, Putin talked with affection about an elderly Jewish couple and their middle-aged daughter who looked after him as a boy growing up in his Leningrad communal apartment.[26] And he has often emphasized the common suffering of Russians and Jews at the hands of the Nazis during World War II.

WOOING ISRAEL

Scaling up from the home front to the international arena, Putin has actively drawn on personal contacts in Israel's large Russian-speaking émigré population and frequent bilateral visits to cultivate an entirely new relationship with the Jewish state.[27] During a 2005 visit to Israel, for example, Putin met with his former high school German teacher who had emigrated in 1973. He reportedly bought her an apartment after learning she was struggling financially. The former teacher related the story with considerable pride to an Israeli newspaper, and showed the journalists a book the president later sent through the Russian Embassy. A photograph of the book, accompanying the article, revealed that—in a rare burst of personal and public affection—Putin had dedicated it "with love."[28]

In November 2012, in a further manifestation of how much Russia's relationship with Israel had changed since the Soviet period, Putin invited Israeli president Shimon Peres to Moscow to dedicate the opening of a new Jewish Museum and Center of Tolerance.[29] In exchanges of mutual admiration and gratitude that accompanied the ceremony, President Putin made some striking statements. A few months earlier, in June 2012, he had traveled to Israel for the dedication of a monument to the Red Army soldiers. Putin reminded Peres of this event and that the Soviet military had "made *the greatest sacrifices* [*zhertvy*] on the altar of [our] common victory over Nazism."[30] Putin went on: "We in the Soviet Union, in Russia, you know, had enormous sacrifices during the Second World War, and the greatest number of those who perished was precisely among the Russian people. But we will never forget the sacrifices made by the Jewish people in the fight against Nazism, and we will never forget the Holocaust." President Peres thanked Putin and Russia not just for defeating Nazism during World War II, but "for giving Jews the possibility to live here over the course of a thousand years and for making it possible for our people to have not just a past but also a future."[31]

At the press conference following the dedication, Peres noted: "There is no other museum in the world that retells the development over history of the relations between two peoples: a big people—the Russian people, and a small people— the Jewish people." Peres alluded to the "shadows and difficult times" in that common history, but stressed nonetheless the Russian people's "greatness of soul" and the deep debt the entire world owed "to the Russian people for their superhuman efforts in destroying the Nazi threat."[32] Vladimir Putin himself in many respects represents a microcosm of the complexities of that Russian-Jewish relationship. The agency that launched his career, the secret police, was notorious for its manipulation of anti-Semitism in Russia.[33] He has personal connections with the Soviet Union's and Russia's Jewish community. He first learned German from a Soviet Jew, now living in Israel. And he has learned something about America from a German Jewish émigré to the United States, who has a deep connection to World War II, the Holocaust, and the fight against Nazism.

A NARROW AMERICAN VANTAGE POINT

Beyond Henry Kissinger, Putin has had few representative Americans to fall back on if he wants insights into how the United States political system works and how Americans and their leaders think. As president, Putin has tended to focus on gleaning information from his official interactions with U.S. leaders—a set of usually formal encounters that he ceded almost entirely to Dmitry Medvedev in 2008–12—and presumably from the various reports produced for him by the Russian intelligence agencies, government ministries, and the presidential administration. In the Kremlin, for most of the 2000s and the early phases of Putin's presidency, these reports were produced by staff reporting to senior presidential aide Sergei Prikhodko and his deputy, Alexander Manzhosin.[34] Although they spoke English, to our knowledge neither Prikhodko nor Manzhosin had any experience of living or working in the United States. They were nonetheless in charge of overseeing critical aspects of relations between Moscow and Washington, D.C.[35] Otherwise, Putin's "go-to guys" for the United States within the Russian government and the Kremlin have been Sergei Lavrov, Russia's foreign minister and former representative to the UN in New York, who speaks fluent English, and Yury Ushakov, a personal presidential adviser and former Russian ambassador to the United States. As in the case of Germany, this offers a very narrow vantage point.

Since the 1990s, only a tiny sliver of Russian and American elites have interacted with each other. Putin's lack of fluency in English has limited his own ability to have direct contacts except through interpreters or others who can act as connectors and conduits. The 1994 transcript from the Körber Stiftung's roundtable in St. Petersburg underscores this point. At that session, Putin was likely the only Russian who could speak directly in German to the German participants. The other Russian participants, like First Deputy Defense Minister Andrei Kokoshin, if they had second-language skills, were mostly English-speaking specialists who started their professional careers in the Soviet Institute on the United States and Canada. Kokoshin might have spoken in Russian with translation into German during this particular roundtable session; but in other meetings he could listen to the Americans in their native language and talk to them and other English speakers informally during breaks. Putin would always have to rely on Germans or translators for his American education.

The biggest concern expressed by everyone in the 1994 Körber roundtable was the future of NATO. Five years later, the issue of NATO and NATO enlargement came to play a significant role in Putin's professional life and in his ascent to the presidency. By 1994, the USSR's military alliance, the Warsaw Treaty Organization, had collapsed along with the rest of the Soviet bloc, but NATO was still going strong. East European countries were knocking on NATO's door seeking new security arrangements. In January 1994 at the NATO summit in Brussels, the alliance began the process of enlargement with the creation of the Partnership for Peace Program (PfP). This was intended to facilitate military and political cooperation between NATO and former members of the defunct Warsaw Pact—including Russia and all the other new states that had emerged from the Soviet Union. Many Russian political figures saw PfP as a way for the United States and NATO to draw new exclusionary borders in Europe. At the Körber roundtable, Anatoly Sobchak and his

Petersburg reformers, along with Andrei Kokoshin and others, fretted about the impact NATO enlargement would budding relationships between Russian elites and their Western counterparts. They feared that NATO's activities would be seen as extremely provocative by the Russian public.

NATO AND THE "COLD PEACE"

In their seminal 2003 analysis of U.S. policy toward Russia from 1991 to 2001, U.S. scholars James Goldgeier and Michael McFaul relate numerous interviews with American and Russian policymakers that convey their thinking about NATO in this period.[36] While American principals in the Clinton administration sought ways to satisfy demands to join the alliance from countries like Poland, they were also mindful of undermining the administration's "policy of supporting Boris Yeltsin, their man in Moscow."[37] Clinton administration officials were frequently told by the reformers around Yeltsin, including Anatoly Chubais, that NATO enlargement was a major mistake. Chubais's "resistance to NATO enlargement stemmed not from his worries about a NATO attack on Russia but from the problems created by the enlargement debate for liberal reformers in Russia." It created a backlash against the Yeltsin team from Russian nationalists and communists and undermined the Russian government's efforts to pursue a "more Western friendly" foreign policy.[38] Yeltsin himself warned President Clinton in December 1994 that NATO expansion risked creating "a cold peace" if it went ahead.[39]

The Clinton administration also had to contend with pressure from constituencies within the United States who believed that expanding the NATO alliance was the key to long-term European security—a necessary hedge against the risk of a more belligerent Russia down the road. In their view, the United States had only a limited window of opportunity to press ahead. As former George H. W. Bush administration official and Harvard professor Robert Blackwill remarked at a 1995 Körber Stiftung roundtable in Poland: "If we [in the U.S. and the West] postpone NATO expansion until we've persuaded the Russians that it's good for them, too, we'll have to wait a long time. We should instead draw up a strategy that tries to minimize the damage that will be done to Russian-American relations as a result of the NATO expansion that we *should* carry out [emphasis added]."[40]

From 1994 to 1996, the Clinton administration tried to pursue a two-track approach. It pushed forward with the process of enlargement and tried to formulate a NATO-Russia accord that would reduce Moscow's threat perceptions. But the Clinton team never really succeeded in reducing those perceptions. As Goldgeier and McFaul underscore, NATO remained the ultimate "four-letter word" for Russians. For the Yeltsin team, which included Putin after 1996, the challenge was how could team members explain to Russian opposition forces that NATO was no longer a threat if it expanded? If NATO was still a military alliance and a mechanism for ensuring collective defense, who was that alliance against? If it was not Russia, then NATO would have to be very specific about its intentions. Members of the Russian elite who spoke German or English could be persuaded that the relationship with the West had really changed in a significant way since the 1980s. Their regular in-person discussions with influential Germans and Americans gave them a deeper perspective. Even if they did not like NATO's decision, they could look their counterparts in the eye and judge the sincerity of their words. But how could they then persuade the average Russian who had grown up seeing NATO and the United States as the enemy?

Explaining and persuading became even more difficult after Yeltsin's reelection in 1996. Once the election was out of the way, the Clinton administration put NATO enlargement into higher gear. Poland, Hungary, and the Czech Republic were slated to join NATO in 1999. The Clinton administration still believed it could secure a deal with Yeltsin on some kind of arrangement that would provide for "consultation and joint action between Russia and the alliance" but would not give Russia a veto.[41] At first, U.S. discussions with Russian counterparts seemed to suggest that Moscow's strong opposition could be overcome. Michael Haltzel, who was then the senior adviser to Senator Joseph Biden (later Vice President Biden), the ranking Democrat on the Senate Foreign Relations Committee, traveled with the senator on a fact-finding trip to Russia in early 1997. Biden was a skeptic on NATO enlargement, but as Haltzel relates, no one among the leading political figures they met in Russia, or on Yeltsin's national security team, "believed that NATO enlargement posed a security threat to Russia." Haltzel conceded, "None of the Russian leaders was happy about the prospect of enlargement," but there was no "paranoia on the subject," and "in the evening meeting in the Kremlin we even discussed the possibility of eventual Russian membership in NATO."[42] Biden was persuaded that the United States should press ahead. Shortly thereafter, in Paris on May 27, 1997, Yeltsin signed the NATO-Russian Founding Act on Mutual Relations. The Founding Act laid out the basic political framework for Russia and the alliance to work together. Unfortunately, as Goldgeier and McFaul relate, the U.S.-Russian relationship quickly went "into a downward spiral" after Paris. August 1998 saw the Russian financial collapse, followed by the spring 1999 outbreak of war in Kosovo, and Russia's renewed war in Chechnya in summer 1999.[43]

NATO AT WAR

In 1999, "NATO went to war for the first time in its history" in response to Yugoslav military atrocities against ethnic Albanian civilians in Kosovo, which was still part of Yugoslavia.[44] The war came only two weeks after the alliance had admitted Poland, Hungary, and the Czech Republic. The United States did not secure the usual authority from the United Nations to intervene, and the operation was spearheaded by NATO with the United States in clear command. NATO warplanes bombed Belgrade. NATO forces, with American troops in the lead, then moved into Kosovo to secure the territory and roll back the Yugoslav military. NATO's intervention shook the Russian establishment to the core.[45] As Vladimir Putin put it in his March 18, 2014, speech 15 years later, no one in Russia could believe that NATO had attacked Yugoslavia: "It was hard to believe, even seeing it with my own eyes, that at the end of the 20th century, one of Europe's capitals, Belgrade, was under missile attack for several weeks, and then came the real [military] intervention."[46] Yeltsin was barely consulted by his American counterparts on the NATO decision and felt that all the international rules of the game had been thrown out the window. Moscow could do very little to change the facts on the ground. "NATO's campaign against Yugoslavia brought Russia's international impotence into painfully sharp focus."[47]

NATO's Kosovo campaign was a turning point for Moscow and for Putin personally. The fears of Russia's opposition about NATO's intentions seemed to have been realized, and the Yeltsin team's assumptions were upended. Russian officials interpreted the intervention as a means of expanding NATO's influence in the Balkans, not as an effort to deal with a humanitarian crisis. They began to revise their previous conclusions about the prospects for cooperating with NATO as well as with the United States as the leader of the alliance.[48] This was the juncture at which Vladimir Putin entered center stage in Moscow.

In 1999, Putin found himself in a very different position from his time in St. Petersburg. Americans were no longer constructive colleagues working on the common cause of developing new businesses in his home city. They were back to being the *glavnyy protivnik*, trying to push through their own policies at the expense of Russia's national interests. The United States and NATO had taken action in Kosovo without referring the issue to the United Nations. As Putin noted, again in his speech of March 18, 2014, the experience left him with a rather harsh view of Americans, who"prefer in their practical politics to be guided not by international law, but by the law of force. They believe in their exceptionalism and exclusivity, in the fact that they are permitted to decide the fate of the world, that only they can ever be right." The Americans had, as they would on numerous occasions, "taken decisions behind our backs, presented us with accomplished facts."[49]

PUTIN'S DASH TO PRISTINA

In 1999, Putin, who was then head of the Federal Security Service (FSB), had been vaulted up to chair the Russian Security Council. He was on the front lines of dealing with NATO and the United States in June, when Russian forces engaged in a risky standoff with NATO troops in Kosovo. The Clinton administration had tried to persuade Russia to take part in the next phase of the NATO operation to create a Kosovo peacekeeping force, KFOR. This was something that Moscow had agreed to a couple of years earlier in Bosnia, and Russian troops were still serving there. In the wake of the Belgrade bombing, Russia chafed at the idea of its forces being under any kind of NATO command. Moscow also demanded a decisionmaking role in KFOR. U.S. military commanders were concerned that this time around, Russia might attempt to create a "Russian sector" in Kosovo (with shades of post–World War II Berlin perhaps).[50] While the issue was being thrashed out between Moscow and Washington, Russian general Leonid Ivashov ordered the redeployment of a Russian troop contingent from Bosnia to Kosovo.

The Russian forces secured the main airport in Kosovo's capital Pristina and tried to dig in. Unfortunately, they soon found themselves isolated and out of food, water, and fuel. New NATO member Hungary, along with NATO aspirants Bulgaria and Romania—all former Soviet satellites—denied Russian planes access to their airspace to resupply the troops. The top American commander in Europe, Wesley Clark, tried to up the ante and ordered the NATO commander in Kosovo, British general Michael Jackson, to send in some of his own forces to block the runways at the airport. Jackson refused, telling Clark, "Sir, I'm not starting World War III for you."[51] The British did seal off the roads leading to the airport and informed the Russians that NATO did not accept the situation, but they also provided the beleaguered Russian troops with food and water.[52] The result was another humiliation for the Yeltsin administration and Moscow, which tried to cast the whole debacle as a rogue military operation. It seemed to many observers that it was more than that. Russia was trying to head the United States and NATO off at the pass in Pristina, and Vladimir Putin was right in the middle of this effort in his first public role in the Russian Security Council. NATO's intervention in Kosovo was one of the defining moments of Putin's career.[53] Six months later, Putin was Russia's acting president.

"WHY WE MUST ACT" IN CHECHNYA

In August 1999, Yeltsin appointed Putin as prime minister. The NATO bombing and events in Kosovo were critical learning moments for Putin in his education about America. As prime minister, Putin's immediate concern was Chechnya. Several Russian officials had raised the specter of a NATO or U.S. strike against Moscow—a fear that seemed irrational to most external observers but was stoked by considerable high-level Western attention to and criticism of the second outbreak of war in Chechnya.[54] In the United States, for example, Zbigniew Brzezinski, former national security adviser in the Carter administration, and retired general Alexander Haig, a former secretary of state in the Reagan administration who had also served in top positions in the U.S. military and in NATO, helped to set up an advocacy group, the American Committee for Peace in Chechnya.[55] The committee demanded a diplomatic solution to the war and policies to protect civilians caught in the conflict. Given the Soviet leadership's neuralgia about officials like Brzezinski and Haig in the 1970s and 1980s, this group was viewed with alarm in Moscow. Their paranoia was not entirely far-fetched; the committee helped establish a Chechen representation in the United States. Chechnya's wartime leader, Aslan Maskhadov, also made frequent efforts to reach out to Brzezinski as well as to U.S. official representatives and agencies for concrete assistance.[56] Just as they did in the case of Yugoslavia, and during the 1983 war scare, Russian political figures saw what their threat perceptions led them to see—the risk of the Americans and NATO intervening in Chechnya to protect civilians just as they had intervened in Kosovo. They sought ways to reduce the threat.

Putin's response was to write an op-ed, in the *New York Times* in November 1999, to appeal to the American public. It was an early foray into international PR. Putin explained to the United States in "Why We Must Act" that Moscow had launched the second military campaign in Chechnya to respond to acts of terrorism. Putin attempted in this piece to make common cause with Americans. He praised the United States for its own strikes against terrorists. He noted that "when a society's core interests are besieged by violent elements, responsible leaders must respond." He called for the "understanding of our friends abroad" for Russia's action in Chechnya.[57] The prose was careful. The general message was conciliatory. Putin clearly hoped that the constructive atmosphere that had framed his interactions with Americans in St. Petersburg could be restored in some way.

In September 2001, the 9/11 terrorist attacks gave Putin a new opportunity to frame Russia's interactions with the United States. Putin immediately reached out to President George W. Bush to express his sympathy and offer his assistance in combating the shared problem of terrorism.[58] The first official meeting between Putin and Bush in Slovenia in July 2001 had gone relatively well, and a few days before September 11, Putin had called Bush to warn him about a looming terrorist threat from Afghanistan that Russian intelligence had picked up.[59] Putin was convinced after September 11 that Washington would come to see things from Moscow's perspective and would recognize linkages between al Qaeda in Afghanistan and terrorists in Chechnya. In a press conference in Brussels on October 2, 2001, Putin called terrorism a "bacterium" that quickly parasitizes its host. Terrorists, he asserted, took advantage of "Western institutions and Western conceptions of human rights and the protection of the civilian population for their own ends." Terrorists did this, Putin warned, "not in order to defend Western values and Western institutions, but rather they do so in a struggle against them. Their final goal is annihilation."[60] All states would have to clamp down politically at home, as well as improve military postures abroad, to deal with this problem. Based on Russia's experience in Afghanistan and Chechnya, Putin offered the United States concrete assistance in rooting out al Qaeda.[61] He expected that the United States would duly drop its objections to the way Russia was conducting the assault against its secessionist republic.

Putin's expectations for a shift in Russia's relationship with the United States were never fulfilled. As most analysts generally conclude, they could not be, because "U.S. and Russian expectations were mismatched."[62] Chechnya remained a bone of contention between Russia and the United States. After 9/11, Putin and the Kremlin hoped that they might be able to convince Washington to create an "anti-terrorist international coalition like the anti-Nazi coalition" that would give Russia an equal say with the United States in a new multipolar world order.[63] As Georgetown professor and former U.S. government official Angela Stent points out in her comprehensive analysis of 20 years of ups and downs in the U.S.-Russian relationship: "When countries form partnerships forged out of exigencies such as the 9/11 attacks, the shelf life for these alliances is usually short because they have a specific and limited focus—defeating a common enemy. After all, the wartime U.S.-Soviet partnership—which the Russians invoked as a model for the post 9/11 partnership—was formed with one sole aim, defeating Hitler. Once Germany was on the way to defeat, the alliance began to fray as the victors disagreed about what would happen after Germany surrendered, and the Cold War began."[64]

Neither George W. Bush nor Barack Obama saw Putin and Russia as an equal partner in Washington's global endeavors. They wanted to have good cooperation in areas and on issues where U.S. and Russian interests overlapped, but they did not necessarily have the same view of the terrorist threat or any other major issue. The United States saw itself engaged in a global war on terrorism after 9/11 and openly described it that way. The United States was under direct assault. Chechnya, from the U.S. perspective, was not a front in this global war. There was no threat to the United States from Chechnya. It was an internal conflict, and the terrorist acts that emanated from Chechnya and the North Caucasus were directed against Moscow and Russian targets. In the prevailing U.S. view, Chechnya had morphed from an ethnopolitical dispute into a magnet for terrorists with links to al Qaeda because of Russia's misman-agement of the original conflict.[65]

THE UNITED STATES: SEEN AS THROUGH A GLASS, DARKLY

In the aftermath of 9/11, Putin was mystified by this view and by the actions of his U.S. counterparts. He also failed to see that the United States was operating on the basis of a different worldview and its own set of assumptions—and he had no trusted American interlocutor, no patri-arch, to offer any real insight into why this was the case.[66] In the absence of countervailing information, Putin initially saw American failure to respond to his warnings about the common threat of terrorism as a sign of dangerous incompetence. In a series of speeches just after the Septem-ber 11 events, Putin underscored that he had tried to warn the Clinton administration that a terrorist plot was brewing in Afghanistan, but to no avail: "I spoke with the previous U.S. administration and pointed out the problem of bin Laden to them. I was astonished by their [lack of] reaction," Putin said. In a speech on September 15, 2001, he lamented: "I feel that I personally am to blame for what happened. Yes, I spoke a great deal about that threat, but it appears not to have been enough. Apparently, I didn't say enough. I didn't find the words that could rouse people [in the U.S.] to the required system of defense."[67]

As General Gareyev, who had been Afghan president Najibullah's chief military adviser from 1989 to 1991, told American security analysts in Washington, D.C., in 2010, Russian military intelligence had watched al Qaeda leader Osama bin Laden in action for a long time in Afghani-stan. Gareyev talked of encountering bin Laden in Jalalabad in the 1980s and seeing the huge sums of money flowing to him from Saudi Arabia to fund his private army. Gareyev asserted that the United States and the CIA had made a major error of judgment in supporting individuals like bin Laden and the *mujahiddeen* in their struggle against the Soviets in Afghanistan. It had been clear to Moscow since the 1980s that transna-tional forces like these, without any government formally behind them to impose checks and balances, would eventually make their own common cause and menace every major state. Russia had repeatedly tried to warn the United States, and the United States had failed to heed the warnings.[68]

In December 2001, Washington announced it was pulling out of the 1972 Anti-Ballistic Missile (ABM) Treaty and would move ahead with creating a new missile defense system to counter threats from "rogue states." Although Putin's initial response was relatively muted, all the old fears and suspicions about the Reagan Star Wars program, which had caused such a crisis in Moscow in the 1980s, were revived. Putin and other Russian officials made numerous statements expressing skepticism about the new U.S. rationale for the system. As did Andropov before him, Putin saw, from his perspective, that American missile defense was more about diminishing Russia's nuclear second strike capability than about countering errant missiles from places like North Korea. Putin and those around him in the Kremlin believed the U.S. rationale was a far-fetched ruse.[69]

The 2003 U.S. intervention in Iraq convinced Putin even further that the United States must be up to no good on the world stage and was looking for pretexts to intervene against hostile regimes and leaders to enhance its geopolitical position. Putin and his intelligence officials knew that Iraqi leader Saddam Hussein was bluffing about his possession of chemical and other weapons of mass destruction (WMD). Indeed, they stated this bluntly to U.S. officials on numerous occasions. In a meeting in the Kremlin in February 2003, for example, Putin aide Alexander Manzhosin told a visiting group of U.S. experts from the Brookings Institution, including former Clinton administration deputy national security adviser James Steinberg, that Hussein had no such weapons. "Why," he asked, "do you not see that he is bluffing? Our intelligence professionals know this, don't yours?"[70] After the invasion of Iraq, and the U.S. failure to find any WMD, a comment attributed to Putin was passed around European diplomatic circles: "Pity about the WMD. I would have found some."[71] In other words, the U.S. intelligence services and government were beyond incompetent—if you're going to use a pretext, do your homework; make it a good one. Similar comments were made by Russian defense minister Sergei Ivanov and other Russian officials in discussions with members of the Valdai Discussion Club during meetings in September 2004. In their view, Americans were driven by emotion and hubris.[72]

THE UNITED STATES BECOMES A THREAT

Ten years later in 2013–14, Putin and his security team had come to the conclusion that the United States was not just incompetent (which was bad enough in their view)—it was dangerous and malicious, and intent on inflicting harm on Russia. This was an opinion at striking odds with the conclusion in the United States that until the 2008 war with Georgia, at least, the longstanding "major military threat emerging from a hostile regime in the heart of Eurasia" had disappeared with "the collapse of Soviet communism and the emergence of a quasi-democratic, market-oriented Russia."[73] Russia was not perceived to be a threat to the United States, and—as in the 1980s—U.S. officials had a hard time believing that Russia could genuinely see the United States as a threat. As a result, Washington made a series of policy decisions in pursuit of its own priorities that were consistently misinterpreted in Moscow.[74]

NATO remained the focal point of Putin's perceptions. Just as he thought he had made some progress with the United States and NATO on the establishment of a new NATO-Russia Council at the NATO Rome summit in May 2002, Putin was forced to think again with the second major tranche of NATO enlargement in March 2004. This brought in seven new members: Bulgaria, Estonia, Latvia, Lithuania, Romania, Slovakia, and Slovenia. From Moscow's perspective, the inclusion of Estonia, Latvia, and Lithuania in the group was the most galling because they had been part of the Russian Empire and the USSR.[75] The three Baltic states, along with the Czech Republic, Hungary, Poland, Slovakia, and Slovenia, were also admitted to the European Union in May of that same year (Bulgaria and Romania had to wait a little longer, until 2007). With this so-called big bang enlargement of both major Euro-Atlantic institutions, Putin and Moscow began to see their convergence—although it was not until 2013 that the European Union became completely conflated with NATO as far as Putin was concerned.

FEARS FROM COLOR REVOLUTIONS

The color revolutions in Georgia in 2003 and Ukraine in 2004, along with NATO's 2004 enlargement, darkened Putin's view of U.S. activities even further. For Moscow, Georgia was a tiny failed state under

Eduard Shevardnadze, but Ukraine was a smaller version of Russia. In Putin's view the Orange Revolution demonstrations in Ukraine in 2004, and their scale, could only have been orchestrated from the outside. The scenario of a disputed election, followed by a mass uprising, and U.S. and other international support for regime change from the street, rattled Moscow in this period.[76] This was especially the case when the color revolutions became conceptually tied to the Bush administration's "Freedom Agenda" and its efforts to support the development of civil society and the conduct of free elections in Afghanistan and Iraq—two countries that the United States had invaded and occupied.[77]

As we will discuss in more detail in chapter 14, Putin did not buy the sincerity of U.S. democracy-promotion efforts in the 1990s and 2000s. He saw U.S. funding for international and local nongovernmental organizations demanding greater transparency and accountability and engaged in election monitoring as a new version of the CIA's so-called active measures from the Cold War. He believes them aimed at undermining political systems like Russia's that were antithetical to the United States. Looking back, Putin was particularly scathing about the color revolutions in his March 18, 2014, speech—which by then encompassed the 2011 Arab Spring and its aftermath. The color revolutions, he purported, were not spontaneous. The West inflicted them on a whole array of countries and people. The West, Putin argued, tried to impose a set of "standards, which were in no way suitable for either the way of life, or the traditions, or the cultures of these peoples. As a result, instead of democracy and freedom—there was chaos and the outbreak of violence, a series of revolutions. The 'Arab Spring' was replaced by the 'Arab Winter.'"[78]

In the wake of the Georgian and Ukrainian color revolutions and having dismissed the precepts of the "Freedom Agenda" as another U.S. ploy, Putin and those around him in the Kremlin looked at U.S. support for the new Georgian government of Mikheil Saakashvili with a jaundiced eye. They could not understand Washington's fixation on Georgia as a major element in U.S. foreign policy in the period up to 2008 unless it was directed against Russia.[79] The accusation that the United States was seeking to use Georgia, and discussions of Georgia's prospective membership in NATO, as a means of constraining or containing Russia, was repeatedly thrown out by Russian foreign minister Sergei Lavrov and other officials in meetings with American counterparts. This dyspeptic view was fed by Moscow's interpretation of a number of speeches by Vice President Richard Cheney on behalf of the Bush administration in advance of the July 2006 G-8 conference in St. Petersburg. In visits to the Lithuanian capital, Vilnius, and to Kazakhstan, in May 2006, Cheney made strong statements about American support for Georgia and other new democracies and denounced Russia's position on these issues, including its actions in January 2006 to cut off energy supplies to Ukraine over a gas pricing dispute.[80] Putin was quick to accuse the vice president of still fighting the Cold War and of rhetorically misfiring. In an interview with the *Today* show on NBC News, Putin took several swipes at Cheney. In his classic style, the Russian president made a snide reference to Cheney's "unsuccessful hunting shot"—evoking the image of a much-publicized incident in February 2006 when the vice president accidentally shot a friend during a quail hunting expedition in Texas.[81]

PUTIN'S PATIENCE RUNS OUT

By 2007, Putin professed that his patience with the United States and with NATO had run out. He used his German portal and the February 2007 Munich Security Conference to talk directly to American officials and experts. His criticisms of the United States, the unipolar security system, and its decisions to use military force outside of the framework of the United Nations were scathing. His views of NATO enlargement were made crystal clear: "It turns out that NATO has put its frontline forces on our borders, and we continue to strictly fulfill the treaty obligations and do not react to these actions at all. I think it is obvious that NATO expansion does not have any relation with the modernization of the Alliance itself or with ensuring security in Europe. On the contrary, it represents a serious provocation that reduces the level of mutual trust. And we have the right to ask: against whom is this expansion intended?"[82] This was the first time that the Russian president had laid out all of his grievances against the United Sates in a major international forum. "Putin's broadside" was not well received in Munich or in Washington.[83]

A year later, Putin made almost identical remarks to the press on the sidelines of the April 2008 NATO summit in Bucharest, Romania. On this occasion, building on his remarks in Munich, Putin returned to what he saw as the fundamental questions posed by NATO's continued existence and seemingly inexorable expansion, even after the collapse of the Soviet Union. Putin stated:

> It is obvious that today there is no Soviet Union, no eastern bloc and no Warsaw Pact. So NATO exists to confront whom? We hear that it exists in order to solve today's problems and challenges. Which ones? What are the problems and challenges? . . . I think that many here in this room would agree with me that, in itself, the existence of the NATO bloc is not an effective answer to today's challenges and threats. But we recognize that it is nonetheless a factor in today's international life, a factor in international security, and that is why we cooperate with the bloc. With regard to expansion, I heard today that this expansion is not against Russia. You know, I have a great interest in and love for European history, including German history. Bismarck was an important German and European political leader. He said that in such matters what is important is not the intention but the capability. . . . We have withdrawn our troops deployed in eastern Europe, and withdrawn almost all large and heavy weapons from the European part of Russia. And what happened? A base in Romania, where we are now, one in Bulgaria, an American missile defense area in Poland and the Czech Republic. That all means moving military infrastructure to our borders.[84]

NATO's Bucharest summit had brought an unpleasant shock for Vladimir Putin. Although the alliance formally declined to offer the two former Soviet states the technical step of a NATO Membership Action Plan, it did not rule out the possibility of eventual entry. All in all, 2008 was a bad year for Putin in his relations with the United States, NATO, and the West. In February, the United States and a raft of European states recognized Kosovo against Russia's wishes, rubbing salt in the old wounds of 1999. Putin declared this "a harmful and dangerous precedent" and immediately raised the implications of Kosovo's independence for Georgia's secessionist republics of Abkhazia and South Ossetia.[85] In June 2008, Dmitry Medvedev, newly inaugurated as Russian president, headed to Berlin for his first major foreign policy visit and speech; there, he proposed the creation of a new European security arrangement and treaty. The overture was quickly rebuffed by the United States and its allies.[86] By August 2008, Russia was at war with Georgia—responding to Mikheil Saakashvili's decision to launch his own operation against separatists in South Ossetia. Georgian shelling killed Russian peacekeepers in the South Ossetian capital, Tskhinvali, provoking a full-scale Russian military invasion. Although Medvedev was now Russian president and nominally in charge, it was clear that Mr. Putin had taken off the gloves.[87]

GEORGIA AND THE BEGINNING OF THE END

The 2008 war with Georgia marked the end of Putin's relationship with George W. Bush and his administration. The Obama administration came into office shortly afterward intent on reassessing and resetting the relationship with Moscow, to try to defuse the obvious tensions over NATO enlargement, missile defense, Georgia, and a whole host of other issues.[88] The Obama administration's "reset" seemed to address Putin's main stated desire for Russia to be approached by the United States with pragmatism on issues of mutual interest and importance. But once again, Putin and the Kremlin took their policy cues from U.S. actions rather than words. As was the case in the immediate aftermath of 9/11, Putin assumed that the shock of Russia's war with Georgia would force a reassessment of U.S democracy-promotion policies and a recalculation in Washington about how far to go in pushing NATO membership for Georgia and Ukraine. Moscow initially interpreted the "reset" as implying this, but Washington was not entirely on the same page.

U.S. offers of modernization partnerships to boost bilateral trade and help secure Russia's accession to the World Trade Organization were combined with bilateral presidential commissions for human rights and civil society development. The repeal of the Cold War–era Jackson-Vanik congressional restrictions on U.S. trade with Russia was accompanied by the introduction of a new raft of sanctions in the form of the Sergei Magnitsky Act targeting a list of Russian officials who had been complicit in the death of a crusading Russian lawyer while in prison on trumped-up corruption charges. Disagreements with the United States and NATO over interventions in the civil wars that erupted in Libya and then Syria in the wake of the Arab Spring uprisings marred U.S. and Russian cooperation on negotiating with Iran over the future of its nuclear program.

Putin was especially angered by the violent and ignominious death of Libyan leader Muammar Qaddafi at the hands of rebels who found him hiding in a drainage pipe during an attempt to flee Tripoli following NATO's intervention in Libya.[89]

In Putin's interpretation, the 2011–12 Russian political protests were just part of this one long sequence of events, with the hand of the West barely concealed. On September 11, 2013, on the anniversary of the 9/11 terrorist attacks, Putin returned to a public format that he had not used since 1999. He again wrote an op-ed in the *New York Times,* directed at the American public and calling for U.S. caution as it contemplated a military strike on Syria. The tone was anything but conciliatory. The prose was bold, not cautious. The United States, Putin asserted, and its tendency to intervene militarily in international conflicts posed a major risk to global security and international law and order. Using language that he would later echo in his March 18, 2014, speech, Putin observed: "It is alarming that military intervention in internal conflicts in foreign countries has become commonplace for the United States. Is it in America's long-term interest? I doubt it. Millions around the world increasingly see America not as a model of democracy but as relying solely on brute force, cobbling coalitions together under the slogan 'you're either with us or against us.'" He accused the United States of failing in its interventions in Afghanistan, Iraq, and Libya, and of encouraging rather than curbing the proliferation of nuclear weapons and other weapons of mass destruction with its interventions. A "growing number of countries seek to acquire weapons of mass destruction. This is logical: if you have the bomb, no one will touch you. We are left with talk of the need to strengthen nonproliferation, when in reality this is being eroded." The United States was not an "exceptional" country, Putin warned: "We are all different, but when we ask for the Lord's blessings, we must not forget that God created us equal."[90]

With this op-ed, Putin effectively declared that his American education was complete. The game was up. He would still show a degree of pragmatic cooperation wherever he could on a case-by-case basis—for example, in disposing of Syria's chemical weapons arsenal, which was one of the subjects of the article and a headache for both Russia and the United States—but otherwise there was not much prospect of broader collaboration with the United States. As Angela Stent noted at the conclusion of her 2014 book, which was completed in the wake of Putin's fulminations against the United States over Syria: "Three U.S. presidents have tried to find the golden key that would unlock the door to a qualitatively better U.S.-Russian relationship since the Soviet collapse. So far no one has found the key. . . . Russia's worldview is significantly at odds with that of America and will remain so for the foreseeable future."[91]

By 2013, as the crisis in Ukraine first began to unfold, Putin's worldview and his view of America had become dark indeed. As he concluded in his March 18, 2014, speech: "Russia strived to engage in dialogue with our colleagues in the West. We constantly propose cooperation on every critical question, want to strengthen the level of trust, want our relations to be equal, open and honest. But we have not seen reciprocal steps [from the West]." Limited by lack of direct contacts with the United States, and driven by his threat perceptions, Putin believed that he had been rebuffed or deceived at every turn by the West. In response, the Operative in the Kremlin became the Operative Abroad.

CHAPTER THIRTEEN

RUSSIA RESURGENT

VLADIMIR PUTIN DISPLAYED NO BOLD ambitions for a Russian foreign policy program at the beginning of his presidency. Foreign policy was conspicuously absent from the December 1999 Millennium Message. It was discussed only tangentially in his 2000 presidential campaign biography, *Ot pervogo litsa.* The general thrust of Putin's statements in both the message and the book was that Russia's problems were the result of "Russians' own doing." Russians must solve the problems themselves, and get their house in order. If Russians did not get their house in order, as Putin stated in the Millennium Message, they risked being relegated to the status of a third-rate nation, "for the first time in 200–300 years."

At this juncture, in 1999–2000, Putin did not dismiss what the West calls "universal values" as alien, let alone dangerous to Russia, as he would in his presidential addresses after 2012. He did not reject Western concepts of democracy, individual liberties, and private property. These were ideas that could be embraced in some form alongside Russian values. Putin played down the conspiratorial thinking of the Russian communists and nationalists, who blamed the Soviet Union's downfall on the Cold War warriors of the West. Rejecting this and other ideological frames for foreign policy, Putin's initial concept for dealing with the outside world was based on the idea of a *peredyshka,* of carving out a breathing space for Russia to focus on its own affairs.[1] Here Putin picked up again on the idea propounded by his favored statist, Pyotr Stolypin, in the turbulent first decade of the 1900s: "Give the state 20 years of internal and external peace and you will not recognize Russia."[2] In Putin's view of the breathing space, Russia should put foreign entanglements aside while it concentrated on domestic restoration. Integration into the global economy would, of course, still be a priority given the link between economic transformation and domestic restoration.

Early in his presidency, Putin seemed generally and genuinely to have believed that if Russia focused on the economy and got its own house in order, then Russia would automatically be reinstated in and by the international community. A restored Russia would not provoke anyone and should not be seen as a threat to anyone. Nor would anyone else be a threat to Russia. It was Vladimir Putin's version of the "peaceful rise" adopted across the border in China. But problems with Putin's please-leave-us-alone approach were apparent from the beginning.

PUTIN'S PROGRESS AND RUSSIA'S RESURGENCE

As outlined in chapter 12, Putin's views of the United States, and of broader relations between the West and Russia, essentially evolved through three phases. At first, based on his relatively positive interactions with Americans in 1990s St. Petersburg, Putin gave the United States the benefit of the doubt. He certainly did not seek to provoke Washington at the beginning of his presidency—and he made considerable personal efforts to win over President George W. Bush in 2001.[3] Putin soon concluded in the second phase, however, that U.S. global behavior was destabilizing and had a negative impact on Russia's neighborhood and on Russia's domestic interests. In Putin's view, unilateral actions by the United States, its willful refusal to consult seriously with others, and its disregard of long-established UN procedures, caused risks to Russia even when the U.S. president or his administration did not seem to intend to do so. Putin pulled back from his personal relations with the president. Given the nature of American politics, with Congress and so many other political actors involved in the decisionmaking process, the executive branch's ability to "deliver" on key undertakings was constrained. What seemed to be a commitment made in a bilateral meeting by the president or a cabinet member would be walked back almost immediately after the U.S. principal presented the decision to other domestic stakeholders.

In stark contrast with the unipolar political system in Russia and its one-boy network, there were considerable checks and balances on the authority of the U.S. leader. Based on this assessment, there did not seem to be much point for Putin to deal in a substantive way with the man at the top.[4] By 2009, Dmitry Medvedev was put in charge of courting the new American president, Barack Obama, while Putin focused on haranguing Obama about U.S. policies, mostly from a distance. Nonetheless, it took some time before Putin came to his third and, so far, final conclusion that the United States was actively hostile—engaged, along with its European allies, in subversion and covert warfare against Russia.

Understanding the specific events that produced Putin's reactions and responses in these three phases is important. Even more important is to understand why Putin reacted to the events in the way he did. The interplay between Putin's perceptions and misperceptions of the United States and of the outside world's intentions toward Russia framed his reactions and policies at home *and* abroad. Over time, everything seemed to unfold for Putin like the episodic misadventures of a picaresque novel: "Putin's Progress on the Road to Russia's Resurgence."[5] Putin and Russia try to get back on track at home. Every time they succeed, or nearly do, the United States throws up an unexpected obstacle and the West tries to push them back. They resist and keep on going. The series of interactions results in Putin abandoning the idea of a breathing space, and moving from focusing primarily on domestic economic and political issues to engaging on foreign policy. Putin's early foreign policy moves were reactive and defensive. Over time, he became more proactive, more offensive.

The first chapter in Putin's progress toward Russia's resurgence began with Chechnya. As he focused on the task of domestic restoration, Putin needed calm on all fronts to succeed. The renewed war with Chechnya in 1999 put the whole enterprise at risk. Putin and his security team saw mounting risks from extremist elements moving closer to the home front. Threats had come from the combination of terrorism and Islam that Russia faced in Afghanistan in the 1980s. The disorder of Afghanistan in the 1990s had spilled over into Central Asia, with its extensive and porous borders with Russia. Russia's fears were heightened in particular by the brutal civil war in Tajikistan from 1992 to 1997.[6] The North Caucasus was clearly vulnerable to the same dynamic, especially after Moscow decimated the more secular nationalist element of the separatist leadership in Chechnya. Individuals on international terrorist watch lists with links to al Qaeda had begun probing the weaknesses in the North Caucasus toward the end of the first Chechen war in 1996.[7] Large numbers of Chechens and other peoples from the North Caucasus lived in Central Asia as a result of Stalin's decision to deport several Soviet ethnic groups en masse from strategically vulnerable border regions to the deep Soviet interior at the height of World War II.[8] Small numbers of ethnic Chechens kept popping up in militant circles in Central Asia and in Afghanistan. In Putin's view, the pacification of Chechnya and its reintegration with the Russian Federation was an imperative. He saw it as one of his early great accomplishments—but the foreign response was a serious setback.

Chechnya was the first big disappointment for Putin as president in dealing with the United States and the West. Putin built up his *vertikal vlasti* to centralize government functions and improve coordination among the security services to take charge of the war. From his perspective, Western officials and analysts only seemed to see and emphasize the negative aspects of his approach. His decisions to abolish regional and local elections in favor of appointing governors and mayors were depicted as examples of democratic backsliding. The United States and the West stepped up the pressure on him personally as the military and counterterrorism campaigns in Chechnya progressed, decrying the high civilian casualties and mass detentions of suspected terrorists and their families. Putin alluded to this criticism and noted his displeasure early on in his interviews for *Ot pervogo litsa*: Some unidentified forces were waging an "information war" against Russia over Chechnya. He also said this very sharply immediately after the Beslan terrorist attack in September 2004, and complained in speeches and interviews many times in between that a double standard was being applied to Russia in Chechnya. He was certain that the United States and other countries would adopt similar measures if they found themselves in Russia's predicament.[9] For Putin, his personal appeal to the American people and their leaders in the *New York Times* in November 1999 had fallen on deaf ears—and seemed to have no impact even after the 9/11 disaster inflicted on the United States two years later.

The U.S. failure to understand (even if it could not embrace) the Russian approach to terrorism in Chechnya was a turning point for Putin.

He began to talk differently about the United States and its role in the world—moving from giving the United States the benefit of the doubt to voicing doubt. In spring and summer 2001, on the sixtieth anniversary of Russia's entry into World War II, Putin warned that by trying to solve its own problems without considering how its actions might negatively affect other countries, the United States was putting Russia at risk. The problem was U.S. unilateralism—the unipolar world. In his view, when it took action without consulting with others or without seeking the authority of the United Nations, the United States was acting selfishly and irresponsibly. Its actions inevitably led to unpredictable consequences. "The entire experience of postwar history tells us: it is impossible to build a secure world only for yourself, and even less at the expense of others," he said at the May 9, 2001, military parade on Red Square commemorating the anniversary of victory over Nazi Germany.[10] The 2003 U.S. invasion of Iraq reinforced Putin's impression. Iraq made America even more of a problem. The decision to invade Iraq was incomprehensible on so many fronts for Putin and his team. He now saw the United States as irresponsible and incompetent—not just unchecked in its exercise of power.

It took some time before Putin came out and said this openly and bluntly, as he would in 2007 at the Munich Security Conference, or in his speech on the annexation of Crimea in 2014. For a while, Putin made his comments behind the scenes, passing them on and transmitting them to the outside world through intermediaries.[11] But his shift in a more forceful direction was easily anticipated. In a 2001 analysis of Putin (written and published before 9/11), two veteran U.S. analysts of Russia, Dale Herspring and Jacob Kipp, noted that eventually the Russian president would feel compelled to "stand up to Washington."[12] Based on a review of Putin's early presidential speeches and their own interviews with representatives of the Russian security services, they assessed that Putin would "take every opportunity both to undermine American influence and to project Russia's influence around the world."[13] Putin's intent, in their view, was to "do whatever he believes is necessary to keep the country moving in a positive direction. If he can do so without resorting to force and violating human rights, he will, for he understands that a democratic path (even as understood in the restrictive Russian context) is preferable to the blunt use of force. But the bottom line is to get the country moving again no matter what." Herspring and Kipp observed that Putin would actively resist "efforts [by the United States] to actually interfere in Russian affairs," and that the Russian president would "become a major nuisance" if "Washington decides not to work with [him]."[14] By 2007 and the Munich speech, it was Putin who had concluded that he could not work with Washington.[15] Once Putin drew this conclusion and decided that Washington was not just irresponsible, but hostile toward Russia, then he began to move from rhetoric to action. He became the Operative Abroad, even as he remained the Statist focused on restoration at home.

RUSSIA UNCHAINED

Putin's capacities for action changed dramatically in the summer of 2006, when Moscow finally paid off the last of its international debt to the so-called Paris Club, composed of the major creditor nations. Putin had paid off Russia's debt to the IMF in January 2005, but from Putin's perspective, summer 2006 was the point when Russia's resurgence really began. Russia was effectively unchained from its financial shackles to foreign countries and international financial institutions. The United States and the West could no longer exert pressure over Russia using debt in the way they did when Washington pushed Moscow to withdraw the last Soviet troops from the Baltic states in 1994. The Clinton administration had constantly reminded Yeltsin of how short his leash was whenever he pulled against it in the 1990s. Putin now had no leash. He had a new operational perspective.[16]

In summer 2006, Russia became fully *solvent* and *sovereign*. Financial solvency was a necessary condition of political sovereignty, and after 2006 Russia literally owed nothing to anyone.[17] The notion of sovereignty was central for Putin, as for all Russian statists. In Putin's conception, there were two categories of countries. First was a handful of genuinely sovereign countries—countries that were strong enough in terms of history, culture, and identity, as well as economically and militarily, to assert their own interests independently. Then there was everyone else. As Putin saw it, Russia was, of course, sovereign, and unequivocally so after 2006. China was sovereign, for certain. The United States was clearly sovereign, but it also had obligations, entanglements, and responsibilities that infringed on its sovereignty. Beyond Russia, China, and the United States, everyone else had more or less limited sovereignty.

Germany, France, and Britain, for instance—the big three of Europe—not only depended on the United States for their security as part of NATO, they had also sacrificed some sovereignty to the supranational European Union. Putin learned this during his interactions with Angela Merkel and Germany. In interviews, Chancellor Merkel's aides recount a vignette from the German leader's bilateral meeting with Putin in the Russian city of Samara in May 2007 during the annual EU-Russia summit. Germany held the presidency of the European Union in early 2007, and the summit was the culmination of Germany's chairmanship. Putin and Merkel had both participated in a series of meetings with the other EU leaders, but some of the agenda items had not been finalized before they moved to their bilateral meeting. As they sat down together, Putin turned to Merkel and essentially said, "So let's get down to business, and get these [EU] issues settled." Merkel responded in terms of "that was the business, back there in the other meeting. Germany does not command the EU. I am not the Queen of Europe. This meeting is about Germany and Russia." Putin seemed taken aback. Merkel's aides said they watched Putin visibly changing his assessment of Germany. One of the aides indicated that after the meeting in Samara, Putin seemed to view Germany as a diminished power. He did not take on board the message that the chancellor was trying to convey—that the power of the EU had been enhanced, not that Germany had been enfeebled.[18]

Putin concluded, on the basis of his own observations, that alliances did weaken countries. From Putin's perspective it was better for Russia not to be in alliances. Russia needed independence and freedom of maneuver. This was the essence of sovereignty. Russia had to have the prerogative to reject any stipulations in international affairs that impinged on its interests. If Russia needed institutional arrangements to bring other states into its orbit (or keep them there), then these arrangements should not entail much in the way of obligations for Moscow. This was the essence of the entities Russia created in its immediate neighborhood with other former Soviet states—like the Collective Security Organization with Armenia, Belarus, Kazakhstan, Kyrgyzstan, and Tajikistan, and the Customs Union with Belarus and Kazakhstan. Putin made this approach very clear in an address to the Russian Security Council on July

22, 2014: "Russia, thank god, has not entered any alliances. In this also lies, to a significant degree, the key to our sovereignty. Any country that enters an alliance immediately gives up part of its sovereignty."[19]

THE DIVERSIFICATION OF FOREIGN POLICY

In practice, Putin's aversion to alliances and giving up sovereignty translated, somewhat curiously, into Russia seeking entry into every organization, institution, and club that would admit it in the 2000s. The goal was foreign policy diversification. As challenges mounted in relations with the United States and the West, Putin wanted to make sure that Russia had plenty of alternatives if its relations soured with any critical country or group of countries. Just as he wanted to ensure economic robustness to withstand the shock of future global financial crises, Putin wanted geopolitical robustness. Freed from the burden of debts that had shackled Russia to the West and the international financial institutions, Putin steadily intensified the pursuit of multilateral and bilateral relationships that would maximize Russia's position and create a kind of geo-economic and geopolitical protective wall around Russia to secure the home front. Putin's attitudes toward global organizations and other foreign relationships evolved along with his view of the United States—moving first from doing little apart from seeking entry, then to exploring ways of using organizations and individual relationships to restrain or block U.S. action. Eventually, his focus became seeking ways of countering and undermining the United States.

For Putin, the top priority was the United Nations. Russia's privileged position on the UN Security Council gave it veto power over U.S. and other resolutions. Security Council membership was vital to Russia's security and sovereignty. The council set the paradigm for all other organizations. Putin would ensure that Russia was part of every international institutional arrangement that would give it real status and weight, and that would enable it either to participate in establishing global rules and norms of behavior or to monitor and influence what the United States and other major countries (including China) were doing. The World Trade Organization fell into that category. Organizations where Russia was "just one of the crowd" were a low priority, unless, like the Asia-Pacific Economic Cooperation organization, they offered mechanisms to protect Moscow's interests in one of the multiple regions spanned by Russia's vast territory. Institutions like the G-20 (the forum of leading economic powers that was established to consult on the global financial system) and the BRICS grouping of five of the fastest growing economies (Brazil, Russia, India, China, and South Africa) brought a degree of prestige by associating Russia with new rising powers, rather than with the old staid cohort of European countries with which it was usually bracketed. The G-20 and the BRICS, along with the Shanghai Cooperation Organization (established by Russia with China and the Central Asian states), also were not dominated by the United States.

Beyond these and other multilateral arrangements, Putin cultivated Russia's bilateral relationships selectively. While continually stressing in his speeches that "Russia has no enemies" and every country—including and especially the United States—was a "partner" and their leaders were "partners," Putin made it a priority to seek out and associate with countries that wanted to chip away at the unipolar system and dilute the influence of the United States regionally and globally. As in the case of working with people on the home front, personal relationships were Putin's preferred means for handling the countries he selected. Targeting key world leaders enabled him to work with the smallest number of people possible. Putin prioritized presidential visits and one-on-one meetings where he and the targeted leader could stand in the spotlight together. Putin began to revitalize old Soviet connections in Africa, Asia, and Latin America as well as in the Middle East. He nurtured personal relationships with leaders like Hugo Chávez of Venezuela who were seen as thorns in the side of the United States, not so much because he agreed with their policies, but because he viewed them as hedges against U.S. influence. Putin was often critical of Chávez and did not want to surround himself with leaders of lesser powers—which was how he viewed countries like Venezuela.[20] But he recognized that some of those powers played important roles within their regions.

In selecting other countries and targeting their leaders, Putin was often guided by Russia's economic interests. States in Eurasia, like Kazakhstan and Ukraine that were formerly part of the Soviet Union, had industries and infrastructure that still formed part of the production chains of key Russian economic sectors.[21] The largest number of personal Putin visits was always to these neighbors. They were a top priority. The home countries of international companies operating in the energy and manufacturing sectors that produced massive tax revenues or large numbers of Russian jobs, or both, also headed Putin's list. Putin would lay out all of these priorities in his national addresses on foreign policy and in his speeches to Russian ambassadors, making sure that they understood the significance to Russia's overall interests of the countries where they served.[22]

COURTING COMMUNIST CHINA

Of all the bilateral relationships, China became Putin's key to diversifying Russian foreign policy. During 2000–08, Russia's own economic growth was facilitated by China's increasing demand for Russian natural resources. In the Russian Far East, China's presence across the border far outstripped Russia's demographically and economically. Good relations between China and Russia immediately boosted the security of this region, where tensions and armed conflicts along the Sino-Russian border had been a major preoccupation for Moscow in the Soviet period.[23] Elsewhere, China helped Russia counterbalance the United States politically in the international sparring arena of the United Nations, and geopolitically in the Middle East and Central Asia by supporting the general thrust of Russian policies. Close association with the world's most dynamic country, and its surrounding region, allowed Putin to promote the idea of Russia serving as the geopolitical balancer or civilizational bridge between Europe and Asia.

At the same time, Putin found boosting relations with China and the Asia-Pacific region something of a heavy lift. Putin's informal style of leadership was out of synch with the more formal structures of collective leadership that ran the Chinese state. The juxtaposition of the Chinese Communist Party against Putin's one-boy network put limits on the relationship. Putin could not just recruit the top guy in Beijing and then manage affairs on a one-to-one basis. Putin and the Kremlin had to find a way of working directly with the different parts of the Chinese economic, political, and security systems if Moscow was to make any headway on critical agenda items—especially when the whole Chinese system overhauled itself every 10 years, while Putin and his network were still in power.[24]

In China and Asia, Putin and the Kremlin, along with the Russian Foreign Ministry, had few personal contacts and intermediaries to draw on. During the Cold War, the cream of the USSR's foreign policy, security, and intelligence personnel were directed toward the United States, Europe, and the Middle East. These Soviet-era biases continued in Russia during the 1990s. For their part, Chinese and other Asian elites regarded Russia neither as being the slightest bit "Asian" (in spite of all of Russia's stress on its "Eurasianism" or "Euro-Asianism"), nor did they view it as being a credible economic and political player in the region.[25] They saw Russia as still rooted in Europe, or, at best, partly extending into Central Asia, and as having little to contribute farther East except as a supplier of natural resources and arms.[26]

Putin did not waver publicly in touting the importance of Moscow's strategic partnership with Beijing. Courting China brought considerable short- to medium-term benefits for Russia, but over the longer term it was easy to see the downside. China was expanding its naval activities and had clear ambitions for projecting itself from the Pacific Ocean into the Arctic through waters that Russia had long considered part of its maritime domain. In 2012, for example, the *Snow Dragon*, a massive Chinese icebreaker, undertook a historic Arctic expedition and transpolar navigation, passing the Russian island of Sakhalin and through the Sea of Okhotsk on the first leg of its journey. A year later, five Chinese naval vessels startled Moscow by entering international waters in the Sea of Okhotsk for the very first time while heading home after a planned joint exercise with the Russian navy.[27] China also had a different perspective on the long-term development of Central Asia: where Moscow wanted to block independent political and economic actions by the former Soviet states, Beijing wanted to penetrate their markets and energy resources. Russia had many potential vulnerabilities in its relations with China. Even though things seemed to be going well, Putin would still have to keep Russia's options open in case the relationship soured. As he returned to the Kremlin in 2011–12, Putin moved to improve relations with Japan as a future hedge against China.

HEDGING ON JAPAN

For 75 years Russia and Japan have been unable to finalize a peace treaty for World War II—dogged by a territorial dispute over what Moscow calls the Kurils and Tokyo calls the Northern Territories.[28] In the 1990s, Boris Yeltsin famously promised (and failed) to settle the issue and sign a peace treaty before 2000. From 1993 to 1998, various bilateral and multilateral working groups put forward a series of proposals. They have remained on the table ever since. In 2009, during their tandem power share, Putin and Medvedev picked up the proposals again, indicating to Tokyo that Moscow was prepared to return to the negotiating table. Both Russian leaders engaged in a flurry of meetings and telegraphic speeches on the issue until then Japanese prime minister Taro Aso asserted in a press conference that Russia had illegally occupied the islands during World War II. By 2010, despite a visit to Tokyo by Putin in his temporary role as prime minister, relations had soured to such an extent that Dmitry Medvedev took the inflammatory step of paying the first Russian presidential visit to the disputed islands. In 2011, Russia indulged in a series of military exercises on and around the islands and declared it would enhance its military deployments there. Bilateral relations seemed to have reached an impasse.

In spite of all the posturing, Putin launched a quiet, behind-the-scenes "charm offensive." Shortly after his September 2011 announcement that he intended to return to the presidency, Putin indicated in meetings with senior Japanese officials that he would now prioritize Russia's relationship with Japan. Putin and a new Japanese prime minister, Shinzo Abe, met numerous times on the sidelines of other large international events, steadily stepping up their personal encounters and diplomatic engagement until the crisis in Ukraine.[29] Putin's overtures were embraced in Tokyo, where drawing closer to Moscow was its own hedge against an uncertain future. In 2013, fears of a military confrontation with China over islands in the East China Sea had become particularly acute in Japan. Senior Japanese officials privately described China as "the biggest existential threat to Japan since 1945."[30] Japan's relations with its other immediate neighbors were also marred by unresolved issues from World War II, and Japan needed foreign policy alternatives and options beyond its security treaty with the United States. In this context, even if wariness about China's regional ambitions was the primary impetus for a new bilateral relationship, Tokyo was enthusiastic at the prospect of better ties with Russia.

BUILDING ON THE BRICS

As he moved back into the presidency, Putin was able to capitalize on the desire of a range of other countries, not just Japan, to maximize their foreign policy options—particularly the members of the BRICS grouping. Brazil, Russia, India, China, and South Africa shared some common economic interests but not an overall perspective on international affairs. All had a degree of antipathy toward the United States and the unipolar system—and, most important, from Putin's perspective, they were a group of independent international players that were not part of the Euro-Atlantic system. None was a formal ally of the United States. Each country was a leader in its region.[31]

The BRICS grouping was an ideal organization for Putin. It had a great "brand" image—putting Russia in the company of China and other economic success stories. It was the perfect size—only five countries. And the goals were straightforward—all the countries sought to reduce U.S. and Western economic leverage in the global system. It was not an alliance. Instead of potentially dangerous obligations, it offered a kind of geopolitical safety net for the countries involved. Putin's efforts to embrace the BRICS and diversify Russia's foreign policy paid off in 2014. The BRICS helped to cushion the blow when Russia was axed from the G-8 in March 2014 just after its annexation of Crimea. Putin was due to host the G-8 meeting in Sochi as a finishing flourish to top off the successful Winter Olympics. He was able to shrug as the remaining G-7 leaders decamped to Brussels in June; and he left them far behind a few weeks later in July, when he headed off to Brazil for the BRICS summit, the 2014 World Cup final, and a six-day tour of Latin America.

PUTIN'S WAGER ON GERMANY

Over the course of his time in office, Putin came to realize that Russia could not rely on the constancy of any foreign relationship. He always had to hedge his bets. He needed contingencies and back-up plans in case things went wrong. In spite of his personal connections and all the time he had spent courting Gerhard Schröder and other German patriarchs, for example, Putin's wager on Germany seemed less likely to pay off after he returned to the presidency in 2012. In part this was due to the way he had handled his return. Just as Putin had disappointed Russia's urban professionals by abruptly dissolving the tandem with Dmitry Medvedev in September 2011, he irritated Western leaders who had built up close working relationships with Medvedev while he was president.[32]

Angela Merkel was particularly displeased with the way Putin seemed to jettison Medvedev—especially when Putin went on to suggest that they had planned to switch places all along.[33] In indicating that Medvedev's presidency had been a sham and simply a means for Putin to stay in power, Putin insulted the German chancellor and other world leaders who had taken Medvedev seriously and met with Medvedev frequently because he was the Russian president. In Merkel's view, Putin had duped the world, not just the Russian people. According to the German leader's aides, Putin had even hinted in discussions with Merkel in 2011 that he would keep the tandem in place. For her part the chancellor had made it clear to him that this was also her preference. It was a lot easier politically at home to make the case that Russia was modernizing and progressing with the younger, tech-savvy Dmitry Medvedev at the helm. Russia hardly looked like it was moving forward when Putin came back again.[34]

As Germany entered its own election season in 2013, German officials and parliamentarians were busy reassessing their strategy toward Russia. In addition to concerns that Putin had turned the Russian presidency into a personal sinecure, German industry was becoming less enthusiastic about the returns from its sizable investments in Russia and future prospects for sectors like the auto-manufacturing industry, where Moscow had pushed German companies to move assembly operations into Russian regions.[35] In October 2011, German intelligence had also found two sleeper Russian agents left over from the old Soviet "illegals program." The spies were a couple, Andreas and Heidrun Anschlag, who had been living in the western state of Hesse for more than 20 years—first setting down roots around the same time that Putin was posted to Dresden. Their discovery and trial came against the backdrop of other revelations about Russian intelligence operations in Germany. The case revived tensions and strains from the Soviet era.[36] In late 2012, the German intelligence agency, the BND, compiled a damning report about the role of Russian organized crime in Germany and Europe, pointing to a deep organizational presence in Cyprus and links to circles close to the Kremlin.[37]

German Foreign Ministry officials were particularly frustrated by the failure of the so-called Meseberg Initiative, which had begun in 2010 as a bilateral German-Russian effort to resolve the conflict between Moldova and its breakaway region of Transnistria.[38] The Organization for

Security and Cooperation in Europe, the EU, the United States, and many other entities had been heavily involved in conflict resolution in Moldova, but the German Foreign Ministry went out on a limb with the bilateral initiative, bypassing other arrangements. After months of negotiations, things went nowhere. The Meseberg Initiative ground to a halt.[39] By the end of 2012, the disillusionment with Russia had permeated from government, business, and intelligence circles into German public opinion, where polls reflected the lowest positive views of Russia in two decades.[40] Andreas Schockenhoff, one of the top German parliamentary officials from Merkel's party, the Christian Democratic Union (CDU), and the designated coordinator for Germany's broad-based relations with Russia, produced a scathing assessment of Russian political and economic activity and foreign policy.[41] Schockenhoff's report, along with the earlier report by the German intelligence agency, helped to shape Germany's decision to chart a new, less ambitious, and more sober path for the relationship with Moscow.[42]

The shift in Germany's position was a personal blow to Putin. He had seen Russia's relations with Germany as the model bilateral relationship—heavy on economics (especially trade and investment) and lighter on politics. He was also convinced that of all the Western and European countries, Germany understood Russia the most. The two countries were fatefully entangled, both positively and negatively. Their bloody clashes in the two great wars of the twentieth century had inflicted great harm on both states. Germany and Russia both grasped what it meant to lose power and status and to seek the restoration of the state. Germany had played and continued to play a vital role in modernizing the Russian economy, introducing new technology and techniques into Russian industry as well as purchasing massive volumes of Russian gas. But the changes in popular German attitudes signaled to Putin that, nevertheless, he would have to adapt to a new relationship and find different ways of handling Germany if he wanted to get back to the process of doing business with Berlin.[43]

"YEVROREMONT"

From the beginning of his presidency and the Millennium Message, Putin made it clear that he wanted to upgrade and modernize the Russian economy—on Russia's terms—to be a better Russia, not to become just another European country. The term commonly used to explain this in Russian political circles was that Russia did not want to be a second Poland in Europe. In this conceptualization, Poland was a big country, but it was a middle-tier country. It was a player in Europe, but not a decisive one. Russia was a big country, a first-tier country, a decisive player. This is what Putin's discussions of sovereignty and his foreign policy were all about: securing Russia's position in global affairs, a *dostoynyy* (worthy of respect) position. Europeans seemed to miss the distinction, but even Russia's opposition understood the point and sympathized with Putin when U.S. or European officials failed to pay Russia sufficient deference. As veteran Russian journalist Yevgeniya Albats and her guests highlighted in an April 2014 radio discussion:

> . . . whenever Putin went to the West, they would always tell him, no, you know, comrade President of Russia, we can only talk with you like we would talk with a second Poland. And of course, this offended him, and he tried to explain that Russia is not a second Poland and the President of Russia should not be spoken to like he was a second Poland. And they treated him exactly like in the thesis, where he actually had reasons to resent the West.[44]

To be fair, Putin often confused the issue for outsiders. There is a section in *Ot pervogo litsa,* for example, entitled "We Are Europeans."[45] It is quite short, but Putin makes the point (which begins with a question about Chechnya) that Russia does not need to seek out a special path for itself. "There is nothing to seek," he says, because "everything has already been found." Of course, Putin explains, Russia is a "diverse country," but it is more than that. It is "part of western European culture." This is where our values are, he says: "Wherever our people live—in the Far East or in the south—we are Europeans." Putin's interviewer asks if Europeans actually think this too. Putin responds that "we will try to establish ourselves in the place where we find ourselves geographically and spiritually. And if we are pushed out of there, then we will be forced to find allies to strengthen ourselves. And of course we will. We have to."[46] This is a very telling formulation. Russia *is* part of Europe. It is physically part of Europe. It has a European culture. It may need a little bit of work around the edges, but it is fundamentally just as good as any Western European state. And if anyone wants to try to tell Russia it is not European, or push Russia around or out of Europe politically, then there will be consequences, and Russia will always have other options.

There is an expression in Russian that also encapsulates this idea—*yevroremont*—a European style renovation of a house or a room. The *yevroremont* can be amazingly expensive and real, as far as appearance and functionality are concerned. But it is understood to be a superficial makeover. The house is still at its core a Russian house even if it has a fancy French baroque facade. The renovated room—the kitchen or bathroom that has been revamped in some generic Italian or Scandinavian style—is still in a Russian house. The appearance is "European," the core remains Russian. This is what Putin wanted to do with the country after 1999, a *yevroremont*. At the household and the national levels, Russians wanted the West to recognize that they were European with new clean, light, modern fixtures, great appliances, beautiful flooring. Putin and the Russian people were engaged in a renovation that upgraded but did not impinge on their Russianness.[47] Russia would be as modern as any other European or Western, first world country, but it was not planning on actually becoming a European country.

In short, one way or another, *yevroremont* was about sovereignty—enhancing sovereignty through modernization, and adapting to changing circumstances. As in the tsarist era, when the Russian military had to scramble to adopt gunpowder after its defeat by the Swedes, Russia had to keep up with the times and with appearances. It had to constantly adopt new appliances, new technologies, new techniques to maintain its freedom of maneuver. Adaptation was key—learning lessons and redirecting effort and resources to hedge against uncertainty and any eventuality, especially challenges from the West.

ADAPTING TO SURVIVE

Speaking to a group of his campaign activists in Moscow in the days before the March 2012 presidential election, Putin told a joke that sums up his concept of adaptation. It is a Jewish joke, widely available on the Internet.[48] Putin most likely heard the joke from Berl Lazar, the chief rabbi of Moscow. Lazar delivered the joke at Davos in 2009, when

Putin was in attendance. He may have told Putin the joke earlier, as the two have had frequent meetings—and Putin always enjoys a good joke. Lazar's Davos version of the joke was related by a journalist from the Israeli newspaper *Haaretz*: "Lazar told the joke about the rabbi, the priest, and the imam who receive a message from God. The message is that he's had it with mankind's sins once and for all, and plans to punish them with a flood, leaving no survivors this time. The priest goes to his people, reports on the oncoming inundation and suggests they take advantage of their last day to carouse and sin. The imam does the same. But the rabbi goes to his people and says, 'Jews, we have to learn to live under water.'"[49]

Putin's telling of the joke was identical to Lazar's at Davos. The punch line was the same: "Jews, we have to learn to live under water." But in Moscow in 2012, after the laughter quieted, Putin turned serious and said: "We Russians have to be like the Jews. We have to learn to live under water."[50] The point of the joke is the importance of adaptation if Russia is to survive. Survival is everything and you have to plan for it. You have to be able to change course and do something different if circumstances change.

Throughout his tenure at the top of the Russian political system, Putin has demonstrated great ability to adapt and to learn lessons from crises as well as by observing the actions of others in the international system, including the United States. Putin's approach to the 2011–12 protests in Moscow illustrates this point. Many in the West (ourselves included) nearly wrote him off in 2012, but Putin figured out how to decapitate the Russian opposition movement and consolidate his political system. A prominent German journalist, who had covered Putin extensively since the beginning of his presidency, privately sought us out in November 2013 to emphasize this specific point. The journalist had read the original version of *Mr. Putin* and its last chapter in which we questioned if Putin could change, as Russia had between 2000 and 2012. "He learns," said the journalist—who had conducted hours of one-on-one interviews with Putin directly in German. He went on that Putin doesn't necessarily change, but "he acts on what he learns." The journalist had met with Putin at the height of the protests against his return to the presidency. He asked if Putin was worried about the opposition and about its chances of creating a viable political movement that might eventually unseat him. Putin said, "Give them five years and then come back and ask me what I think or how they've done." Putin had probed the opposition; he had found their weaknesses. There was no unified leadership, no common platform beyond "Putin fatigue" and the desire for more political choices. So he moved to pick off the leaders one by one, and to deter the rank and file from taking to the streets again.[51]

As Putin learned from reading the William King and David Cleland textbook in the 1980s and 1990s, planning for uncertainty is the most important element of strategy. Chapter 3 of King and Cleland has a section devoted to contingency and adaptive planning:

> Effective planning requires an ability for the organization to adapt to a changing environment. If such adaptation is to be accomplished efficiently, contingency plans are required. . . . The purpose of a contingency plan is to prescribe what actions the organization should take in the event some of the key environmental assumptions on forecasts fail to hold or be sufficiently accurate. Every strategic plan is highly subjective in nature and is based on assumptions, judgments, and predictions, each having varying degrees of risk and uncertainty. The need to think through what should happen if the key assumptions and forecasts fail to hold is critical. This concept is well understood in the context of a military commander who prepares a plan for the retreat of his military forces if the campaign does not go as anticipated, but it has not been widely practiced in nonmilitary situations. . . .
>
> Contingency plans specifically deal with the [question]: What if things don't go as anticipated? . . . Without such contingency plans, environmental changes can create havoc and force the organization into an undesirable choice between doing nothing in the face of impending difficulty or taking major strategic actions on the basis of high-pressure crisis thinking and panic decision making.[52]

In short, there are always uncertainties. Nothing is preordained and nothing can be ruled out. Things always go wrong. There will be unexpected events and operational setbacks.[53] Being prepared is key. You need contingency plans. You have to diversify and maximize your positions, and keep all options open. You must not do anything irrevocable—make a decision or take actions that put yourself in a position you cannot get out of later. In this regard, the 2011–12 period was a tough one for Putin. It was not at all what he expected when he said he was coming back to the presidency. Things did not go according to plan. He believed that an assault had been launched against him on the Russian domestic front, and that the West was behind it. He had to adapt to the new circumstances. He had to make a series of operational shifts to regain control of the situation. In fact, he had also had to do this before in 2008, from behind the scenes, when Russia went to war against Georgia during Dmitry Medvedev's tenure as president.

OPERATION GEORGIA

Russia's war with Georgia in August 2008 was Putin's first major military operation after the war in Chechnya, and this time it was outside Russia's borders. The stage was set for the war by the U.S. and European decisions early in 2008 to recognize the independence of Kosovo and NATO's resolution at the April 2008 Bucharest summit that Ukraine and Georgia would eventually be admitted into the alliance. Georgian president Mikheil Saakashvili's decision to retaliate against separatist forces in South Ossetia tripped the wire. Russia's swift military response, sending troops first into South Ossetia to confront the Georgian forces and then deeper into Georgian territory, was a message directed at Georgia and any other former Soviet state that might decide to challenge Moscow's authority. Putin, along with other Kremlin officials, personally made the message clear in encounters with Georgian counterparts, effectively telling them: "You were warned about pushing for NATO membership and trying to regain Abkhazia and South Ossetia by force; you didn't listen. Your Western partners promised you protection and didn't deliver. We threatened you with consequences. We delivered."[54] But the message was also directed at the United States and at NATO.

The Georgia war was intended to be a restatement, but now in blunt and brutal fashion, of Putin's message in Munich in February the year before: We've had enough! As it turned out, this new amplified version of the message (delivered on this occasion by Dmitry Medvedev) was received in Washington and Brussels in the same way as the Munich speech had been.[55] Rather than convince the West that it had to respect Russia's security concerns, the war in Georgia reinforced the idea in Western capitals that Putin was the aggressor, not an aggrieved party. From Putin's perspective, Georgia was thus a repeat of the experience of the war in Chechnya: Russia attempts to remove threats to its own security; it signals what it is doing and why; the outside world brushes off or ignores Moscow's explanations and sees only the kind of bullying that warrants even greater integration of Russia's neighbors into the NATO sphere.[56] For Putin, Georgia became another example of the West's refusal to even try to understand Russia's perspective. He remained certain that this was all deliberate and that U.S. and NATO engagement with Georgia was intended to roll back Russia's influence in its own neighborhood.[57]

The war in Georgia failed as a message of warning to the West in the way Putin intended, but it proved decisive in how Putin would prepare operationally for future confrontations with the West. Putin and his circle scrutinized every aspect of the Georgia venture. It became a reference point not just for the Russian military and the Kremlin but also for how the outside world could be expected to react. The behavior of the United States confirmed for him what he likely already suspected: its actions did not always live up to its words (or at least how he interpreted its words). Before the war broke out, senior U.S. officials had publicly proclaimed "defiant support for Georgia," as one American newspaper account described it.[58] But when push came to shove, there was no support in military terms. After the hostilities had ended, there was a significant, but relatively brief, international political backlash— tempered by the sense in many government circles, including in the United States, that Saakashvili had mishandled Georgia's relationship with Russia at critical junctures and had provoked the war by taking military action in South Ossetia.[59] Moreover, the United States, NATO, Europe, and the UN had all reacted differently to the conflict. These differences were something that Putin and his team could exploit later if a similar set of circumstances arose.

THE IMPETUS FOR MILITARY REFORM

Most immediate, the Georgian war served as the impetus to step up the reform of Russia's military. Some of the initial assessments in the West of

Russia's performance in Georgia seemed positive. "This is not the Russian army from the humiliation of Afghanistan, and it's not the Russian military that had to flatten Chechnya to save it," observed one Pentagon official. "The Russian military is back. They are to be contended with," remarked another.[60] But, in fact, the Russian military did not acquit itself particularly well in Georgia. Although Russia had been training for contingencies with major exercises in the North Caucasus Military District just across the border with Georgia since around 2006, it was not yet ready for new operations in 2008. All it could do was fall back on its old, mass army approach.

In the wake of the war, Russian leaders exuded confidence in their public statements. President Dmitry Medvedev included a section about the "lessons of the conflict" in his annual message to the parliament just a few months later. Russia came out on top in Georgia, he said. It had delivered the message that Russia is back. Strongly suggesting that Russia was preparing some sort of demonstration of its new strength at perhaps a different time or place than Georgia in August, Medvedev explained: "The August crisis merely accelerated the arrival of the 'moment of truth.' We showed in reality—including to those who sponsored the current ruling regime in Georgia—that we're capable of defending our citizens. That we are also capable in deed of defending our national interests."[61]

Yet there was also a feeling that the performance of the military left much to be desired. In the same address, Medvedev spoke of "blunders" in the operation that needed to serve as "highly serious lessons" for the military leadership.[62] Real professionals in the West would not be impressed (and the real professionals in Russia knew that).[63] The Russian military's performance had at times been embarrassing. Communications broke down, forcing soldiers to resort to their personal mobile phones to get instructions. Russian army tanks did not have night sights for their guns, and the reactive armor designed to protect them from Georgian antitank weapons proved unreliable. "Russian forces entering South Ossetia lacked even basic intelligence regarding Georgian artillery positions and troop deployments, which led several of their leading units into costly ambushes. . . . In a desperate effort to get information, the Russians sent an electronic reconnaissance version of the Tupolev Tu-22M Backfire bomber over the battlefield, and it got shot down. In all, Russia lost four planes, including three Sukhoi Su-25 attack fighters, to unexpectedly effective Georgian air defenses."[64]

Operation Georgia was something of a bluff, and Russia was lucky the bluff was not called more seriously. Before the next military showdown, which Putin and his security team now deemed inevitable, something had to be done. Beginning literally days after the hostilities ceased in Georgia in 2008, and extending until 2013, Russia engaged in an across-the-board reassessment and reform of its military based on the lessons from Georgia. The process proceeded on two levels, one very public and designed for maximum attention, the other quiet and conducted almost entirely beneath the West's radar. It was the second, quiet level that came into play in Crimea and Ukraine.

REFORM AT THE PUBLIC LEVEL

It is particularly significant that Putin waited so long to get serious about military reform, which had been a major political preoccupation of the 1990s.[65] For Putin, as for any leader, national defense was necessarily an important consideration, but it was not a top priority for him in the first years of his presidency. Putin knew that Russia was weak in many dimensions, and other areas needed more urgent attention. Russia's fiscal strength and the imperative to rid itself of foreign debt, for instance, were most critical for Putin in the early 2000s. When Putin did turn to defense sector reform, he was initially motivated as much by the need to stop the hemorrhaging of state finances through the military budget as he was by concerns about military weakness.

In February 2007, Putin replaced Sergei Ivanov, who had served as his defense minister since 2001, with Anatoly Serdyukov. The new minister was a stark contrast to Ivanov. Ivanov had been a general in the KGB. Serdyukov's career was strictly civilian. His most recent position had been head of the Federal Tax Service, a ministerial level function. Ivanov was a close and long-time associate of Putin's. He was in the inner circle. Serdyukov, by contrast, had no direct personal relationship to Putin. But he did have power to instill fear among the military brass because he was seen essentially as an extension of his father-in-law, Viktor Zubkov.[66] Thus he was one of Putin's controllers of financial information.

Serdyukov's initial task was to stop corruption in the military sector and get its finances in order. With the launching of military reform post-Georgia, however, the mission shifted. Like nearly all previous reform plans, the 2008 military reform came with ample and lofty rhetoric. Much of it resembled discussions in the United States, and indeed, some of it came directly from the pages of various documents on U.S. military doctrine, which the Russians had studied carefully. Buzzwords such as "network-centric warfare," "cyber warfare," "information warfare," "joint operations," and "integrated command" abounded. But like all previous efforts, the reality of reform boiled down to one main issue: tackling the bloated and imbalanced manpower situation of the armed forces. Only once that had been resolved could other critical issues—such as replacing antiquated and poor-quality equipment—be addressed. In concrete terms, Serdyukov's job was to force the retirement of hundreds of thousands of officers and to convert the old Soviet-style, mass conscription–based army into a leaner, more mobile professional force. The smaller army could then get new weapons and modern training.

This part of the reform lasted three years. At the end there was relief that the culling of personnel and structural reorganization was over. Nikolai Makarov, chief of the general staff during the Serdyukov reforms, expressed a widespread sentiment among the Russian professional officers' corps, in a January 2012 speech, when he said that it was (finally) time to stop talking about the reform: now let's talk about weaponry.[67] In early 2012, Putin seemed to be on a similar wavelength, announcing during the election campaign for his third presidential term that he would be focusing on the modernization of Russia's defense industry.[68] In May 2012, Putin issued new decrees along these lines—on improving military service and developing and procuring new, modern, high-tech weapons.[69]

The 2008 military reform was generally recognized as Russia's most far reaching. But at its end in 2012, no one, inside or outside Russia, could credibly claim that it had produced a modern fighting force. The problems that existed at the beginning of the reforms remained, including corruption and procurement scandals, mismanaged budgets, low-quality weapons production, demographic imbalances, questionable quality of training, and labor market challenges. The general assessment was that the reform had still not produced a military that was capable of conducting much more than the Georgia operation.[70]

These opinions changed dramatically after March 2014 and the stealth military operation in Crimea. Suddenly, a flurry of articles quoted

Western experts' high opinions of Russia's "new" military, citing dramatic improvements over the past performance in Georgia: "It does seem to us that they are much more professional this time around. . . . It's impressive." Articles referred to new Russian capabilities but also to an entirely new mode of warfare that had been on display in Crimea. It was "special warfare," "non-linear warfare," "hybrid warfare."

THE QUIET CHANGES: MOVING TO AN OFFENSIVE DEFENSE

Some observers, like former Russian presidential economic adviser Andrei Illarionov, have argued that Putin planned to go to war in both Georgia and Ukraine long in advance of both events.[71] As always with Putin it is difficult to say definitively that he decided at a particular time to do something at a set date in the future, or to pinpoint a critical shift in his thinking at a specific juncture. Given his emphasis on contingency planning, Putin was always preparing responses to changing circumstances and measures to adapt to them. The Russian military engaged in regular training exercises in its North Caucasus and western military districts that included scenarios reminiscent of subsequent events in Georgia and Ukraine. But none of these, or other steps, suggested on the surface that Putin was planning for a new type of war. For most of 2012, Putin made no mention of a shift in Russia's defense doctrine. In his presidential election campaign article on military policy in February 2012, as well as in his two defense-related decrees in May 2012, he spoke in rather conventional military terms.[72] But in October that year he submitted amendments to Russia's Law on Defense that gave him, as president, more direct power over national defense. He essentially established a unity of command. In the same timeframe, Putin also asked for a whole set of new documents related to defense planning, but the language was vague.[73]

One critical event, in retrospect, was Putin's simultaneous replacement of Russia's defense minister, Anatoly Serdyukov, and the chief of general staff, Nikolai Makarov, in November 2012. For his new minister, Putin turned once again to a close associate, this time Sergei Shoigu, who had served for 11 years as head of Russia's Ministry for Emergency Situations, a quasi-military body, and held the rank of general. Most important, he was one of Putin's few personal friends in the government.

Shoigu, who was born in the southern Siberian republic of Tuva, served as companion and de facto host when Putin indulged in his highly publicized summer excursions of bare-chested fishing, hunting, and horseback riding in Siberia. For chief of the Russian general staff, Putin appointed Valery Gerasimov, an experienced former tank commander who had served in a high-level command position in Chechnya. While Shoigu was seen as "Putin's man," forging a close and personal connection between Putin and the defense ministry bureaucracy, Gerasimov was the transmission belt to the other men who counted: the uniformed military. Gerasimov was tasked with drawing up and implementing the new plans for Russian military defense and mobilization that would be displayed in Crimea. The new chief of general staff was also charged with rolling out the new approach, which he did—speaking before a semi-private audience—in January 2013. In his speech, Gerasimov declared that the Russian military needed to come to terms with the fact that across the globe in the twenty-first century a "new kind of war" was being fought, one that involved the greater use of "nonmilitary methods to achieve political and strategic goals":

> The emphasis in methods of struggle is shifting toward widespread use of political, economic, informational, humanitarian, and other nonmilitary measures, implemented through the involvement of the protest potential of the population. All this is supplemented by covert military measures, including implementation of measures of information struggle and the actions of special operations forces. Overt use of force, often under the guise of peacekeeping and crisis management, occurs only at a certain stage, primarily to achieve definitive success in the conflict.[74]

Post-Crimea, Gerasimov's words sound ominous. But, at the time, what he was saying was not new. For years, Russians—military and civilian—had asserted that the United States was conducting this kind of war against Russia, and they had listed and described these same measures.[75] But later in his speech, Gerasimov shifted to something that *was* new and different. Now *Russia* would begin to fight this kind of war. It would have to if it was to survive. It was the military equivalent of Putin's joke about learning to live underwater. Times had changed. The situation was acute. Russia would have to adapt. Gerasimov's message was that Russia could no longer stand on the sidelines and observe and complain about the "new typical twenty-first-century war." Russia needed to organize its military to fight with the same methods. And because of the asymmetry of military capabilities and economic strength between Russia and the United States and its allies, Russia would have to be better, more aggressive, and smarter at fighting the new war than its opponents.

There was no hint of Russia actually launching an offensive operation at this stage; Gerasimov's remarks were entirely framed in terms of what Russia needed to do for its own "territorial defense." But as British security expert Mark Galeotti pointed out in a July 2014 assessment, Gerasimov's rhetorical frame was deliberately misleading—"defense" was "used in Aesopian terms." Gerasimov's speech was the clear assertion of an offensive doctrine: a "new way of war" that required "the close coordination of military, intelligence and information operations."[76]

Looking back and analyzing Gerasimov's January 2013 speech in the wake of events a year later, Galeotti concluded that every element of the Russian state system had an assigned role in the operation Putin launched in Crimea and Ukraine in 2014. The GRU (Russia's military intelligence) first took the lead in Crimea. When the theater of operations shifted to eastern Ukraine, the Federal Security Service (FSB) was at the forefront, having "thoroughly penetrated the Ukrainian security apparatus . . . [and] . . . encouraged defections and monitored Kyiv's plans." For its part, the Russian Interior Ministry "used its contacts with its Ukrainian counterparts to identify potential agents and sources," while the task for the Russian military was "to rattle sabres loudly on the border" for maximum effect. The Russian media and Russian diplomats "kept up an incessant campaign to characterise the 'Banderite' government in Kyiv as illegitimate and brutal, while even cyberspace [was] not immune, as 'patriotic hackers' attack[ed] Ukrainian banks and government websites." Russia's operation in Ukraine was the very essence of the new "non-linear war," Galeotti stressed: "as Gerasimov says . . . the war is everywhere."[77]

Until Gerasimov's speech, no one at the very top of the Russian military had stated in such a fashion that Russia needed to conduct war using a broad range of military, intelligence and information methods. Gerasimov was, at least on the surface, the quintessential (and conventional) soldier's soldier, which underscored the radical nature of the speech and the doctrinal shift. For a Russian tank commander to state that the Russian military needed a comprehensive set of strategic deterrence measures in which *nonmilitary*, political, measures now dominated was nothing short of revolutionary.

Gerasimov's elaboration of the new Russian doctrine continued in 2014. In a speech at the Russian Academy of Military Sciences, the same venue as his January 2013 speech, he repeated the idea that twenty-first-century wars were first fought by nonmilitary means (political, information, supported by "international nongovernmental organizations") followed by a military phase. But, Gerasimov went on to ask, how then could Russia defend itself and deter the enemy from moving to the military phase?:

> To avert military conflict, our plan calls for a comprehensive set of strategic deterrence measures embracing the entire state apparatus [*obshchegosudarstvennyye mery*]. These will be based on political-diplomatic and foreign economic measures that are in turn closely interconnected with military, information, and other measures. Their general aim is to convince potential aggressors of the futility of any forms of pressure on the Russian Federation and its allies.[78]

UKRAINE AS A TRAINING EXERCISE

Russia's doctrinal approach was on full display in the crisis in Ukraine in 2013–14. Reflecting Gerasimov's words after Viktor Yanukovych's precipitous flight from Kyiv upended Ukrainian politics and put Russia's position in jeopardy, Putin had to deter the West from stepping in. He had to signal Russia's capability in twenty-first-century warfare through an offensive operation. The problem for Putin, as the crisis unfolded, was that Russia did not have all the capabilities it needed at the end of 2013. It was still developing them. As we will discuss in more detail, with every move Putin made after annexing Crimea in March 2014, the subsequent conflict essentially became a single giant training exercise in twenty-first-century warfare for Russia—combining real-world and simulation inputs to continue to develop those capabilities.

"Inputs," in this context, is a technical term from scenario-based war games and military exercises. The director of the exercise feeds new information into the overall scenario to test whether the participants are making the correct decisions, including whether their decisions are robust enough to adapt to changing circumstances. The evaluation aspect of the exercise focuses on how participants deal with these "new inputs." For Putin and his military, secret service, political, and economic command team, every event and development in the Ukraine crisis became a new scenario input. Military units and their commanders, whether involved in actual operations or formal training exercises, assume that what they are being deployed for is real. But exercise directors can look at both the real-world and simulation inputs and evaluate them separately and in the same way: How did the units, organizations, leaders, commanders, perform? How did they respond to these specific new inputs?

In fact, in his speeches responding to the Ukraine crisis, Putin's own language reflected the idea of war games. Meeting with representatives of Russia's defense industry and military leadership on May 14, 2014, Putin reminded the participants that at a similar gathering six months earlier, they had discussed the national defense procurement plan—the schedule for production and delivery of new weapons systems to the forces. Referring to the Western sanctions against the Russian defense industry, Putin said that the procurement plan would obviously have to be adjusted. "Today, we know that there are new scenario inputs, as the expression goes in such cases, connected to the necessity to solve issues of import substitution."[79] OK, now there's been something new, he seemed to say. Let's see how you handle it. Putin's subordinates were using the same language. On May 8, 2014, Putin's press spokesman, Dmitry Peskov, referred to reports that eastern Ukrainian separatists had decided to go ahead with a referendum on independence for the Donetsk region (despite Putin's nominal appeal to them to refrain from doing so) as "new inputs" into the situation. "They need to be analyzed," he added.[80] Furthermore, the Ukraine conflict was accompanied by continuous Russian military training exercises inside Russian territory—ranging from exercises with the space and missile forces, and nuclear forces, to special forces and conventional military units, to psychological operations teams and political operatives. These exercises pulled in all branches of the military and security services, as well as the civilian leadership. And Putin oversaw this giant war game outside Ukraine "in operational mode," as the Kremlin announced cryptically.[81]

It was only logical that Putin would have to treat Ukraine in 2014 as a training exercise and training ground. Gerasimov's new mode of twenty-first-century war fighting required new weapons. Most of these weapons were nonmilitary, but the cycle of development and deployment was similar to that for military weapons. There would have to be a development cycle that began with R&D, followed by limited production runs, and then testing, deployment to units, and further testing. The new weapons would next have to be integrated into an overall war-fighting strategy, adapted to varying circumstances, and further refined. And, given the fact that a war had begun in Ukraine before everything was fully in place (as it had in 2008 in Georgia), Russia would have to catch up in real time.

One way or another, all Russia's aggressive behavior in Ukraine in 2014 was linked to the development and deployment of the military, political, economic, and other weapons of new warfare. Putin was refining them in simulations as well as in a real-world operation to "convince potential aggressors of the futility of any forms of pressure on the Russian Federation and its allies," to use Gerasimov's words. Operation Ukraine was based on the premise that a good offensive defense, "based on political-diplomatic and foreign economic measures that are in turn closely interconnected with military, information, and other measures," would deter the West from moving to the military phase of war.[82]

CHAPTER FOURTEEN

THE OPERATIVE ABROAD

WITH HIS NEW TEAM OF Sergei Shoigu and Valery Gerasimov leading the Russian military, and unitary command in place, Putin was preparing Russia to engage in the new form of twenty-first-century warfare. Wars would be fought everywhere and with every means at a state's disposal. In a war that was everywhere, Putin had to be able to mobilize the population at home behind his decisions and actions. The Russian people, along with the Russian military, all sectors of the Russian economy, and the Russian state apparatus would have to prepare for contingencies, just as Putin the Survivalist did. Even the nuclear forces would be part of this since they were the umbrella (the ultimate strategic deterrent measure) under which nonmilitary weapons could be deployed.[1] Putin also had to be prepared to take the overall campaign outside Russia's and Ukraine's borders to cope with the inevitability of Western action in the international arena. Anticipating economic and political sanctions—which, as he noted in his March 18, 2014, speech, the West had repeatedly used against the USSR and Russia—Putin had to deploy Russia's own economic weapons against the West and try to use Russia's membership in major international institutions to block and undermine Western resolutions.

Once he had determined that Russia was under assault and he would have to take action, Putin's first task was to secure the home front to make sure it was robust enough to withstand the new kind of warfare. In this context and from his perspective, Putin's political clampdown in 2012–13 was the first phase in his preparations for a confrontation with the West.

As he looked at the protests against his return to the presidency, Putin saw the West trying to use (in Gerasimov's words) "political, economic, informational, humanitarian, and other nonmilitary measures" against Russia, all "implemented through the involvement of the protest potential of the population." This was a potential vulnerability he had to neutralize.

SHORING UP THE HOME FRONT DEFENSES

Since the color revolutions in Georgia and Ukraine, Putin had been alert to Western attempts to invade Russia's political space with democratization projects and election monitoring missions. At all turns, Putin saw U.S. and European institutions as actively fomenting dissent and encouraging protests to pull Russia's urban professionals and creative class away from his big-tent coalition and turn them into fifth columns that would be deployed against his system. In Putin's analysis of his experience in Dresden and the collapse of the Soviet bloc, the West had already successfully done this in Eastern Europe in the 1980s. Western governments had then done the same in the Baltic states in the 1990s. They had used their nongovernmental organizations (NGOs), democracy-promotion policies, and funding for local groups first to dismantle and then to transform the old Soviet systems. Eastern Europe and the Baltic countries had been brought into NATO and the EU. And then the West had turned its attention to Georgia and Ukraine. Russia was clearly in their sights. The United States and its allies had openly discussed their intent to transform the Russian political system since the 1990s.

The Western media reactions to the September 2011 announcement that Putin was returning to the presidency had made it crystal clear to Putin that the West did not want him back in office. The West wanted him gone. He was certain that Western leaders preferred Dmitry Medvedev—or perhaps anyone but Vladimir Putin. They wanted regime change. But Putin had no intention of going anywhere. He thus had to check Western activities. He had to eliminate the domestic fifth column and shore up faith in himself and his system.

For Putin, the old counterintelligence game with the Americans and the West was a key element in shaping his thinking on this particular issue. The United States had not pulled back its intelligence networks at the end of the Cold War; neither had Russia. There were plenty of spies still out there, still collecting material, still trying to recruit agents, still trying to undermine their opponents. Russia had its spies, so did all the others—as the constant spy scandals with the United States and other European countries in the 1990s and 2000s underscored. And, as far as Putin was concerned, some of those spies were so-called illegals. They were covert operatives living in the targeted country as citizens of that country, blending in with everyone else to penetrate secure systems and transmit operational information back to Moscow. The "sleeper couple," the Anschlags, whom the Germans uncovered in 2011, confirmed that Russia's intelligence services continued to operate this way; so did a similar discovery by the U.S. counterintelligence services.

The United States busted a larger sleeper cell of 10 agents in 2010.[2] Unlike in Germany where the Anschlags were put on trial, Washington promptly sent the U.S.-based illegals back to Moscow. Putin seemed to revel in their exposure, bristling with the professional pride of a fellow intelligence officer as he welcomed them back home. In a televised gathering with the operatives, Putin sang patriotic songs with them, including "From What the Motherland Begins," the theme to *Sword and Shield*, a 1968 film about Soviet spies who had infiltrated the Nazi SS and a film that Putin had mentioned in *Ot pervogo litsa*.[3] Putin publicly praised the spies for their bravery and patriotism, and their services to Russia, saying: "Just imagine, first you have to master a language as if it were your own, think in that language, talk in it, [then] fulfill the task set in the interests of your motherland over many years, suffering daily dangers for you and your loved ones, who don't even know who you are or for whom you work."[4]

Although Russian counterintelligence had not uncovered a similar U.S. or other Western network of illegals and covert operatives in Russia, Putin was convinced an equivalent had to be in place. Based on his experiences in the KGB, Putin assumed that Russian counterintelligence must not be looking hard enough. From Putin's perspective, if Russia had left its illegals in place in Germany and sent new ones to the United States after the Cold War, then the United States surely had done the same. Indeed, in public discussions, Putin repeatedly talked of plots and conspiracies. He spoke about "the fact" that many of the Americans who came to work in technical assistance projects in Russia during the 1990s had worked in the CIA or for other U.S. security agencies. He did not offer proof, he simply asserted it—often—to the consternation of some of his colleagues, like Anatoly Chubais, who had worked on those projects. Putin was particularly adamant that an extensive (and controversial) project related to the Yeltsin-era privatization program, and managed by Harvard University in conjunction with Chubais and his team, had been staffed by CIA operatives. In interviews, a somewhat embarrassed Chubais would note that he had no idea why Putin kept saying this.[5] It was, however, a classic example of mirror-imaging. As Putin himself had been assigned to work at Leningrad State University by the KGB after he returned from Dresden, it was a logical assumption on his part that the CIA would make similar assignments. From there it was an easy extrapolation to see foreign agents working in Russia under the guise of the new NGOs that had been established in the 1990s and 2000s. Russia's illegals in the U.S. cell had been instructed by Moscow to reach out to think tanks, universities, and NGOs, so Americans were obviously, in Putin's view, doing the same in Russia. For Putin, Western NGOs were front organizations for intelligence operations. They were recruiting fifth columns among those Russian citizens—particularly from Russian NGOs and the Russian intelligentsia—who were susceptible to being swayed and had questionable loyalties.

THE SNOWDEN COUP

If Putin had any lingering doubts whatsoever about the accuracy of his assessment, these were dispelled in late 2010 with the WikiLeaks affair, when Julian Assange and his team published reams of secret U.S. government cables on their website. From his perspective Putin was proved correct: the United States was still out gathering information on every front. Then, in June 2013, Putin got all the evidence he could ever want when a young U.S. National Security Agency (NSA) contractor, Edward Snowden, turned up at Moscow's Sheremetyevo airport. After deciding to blow the whistle on what he depicted as NSA surveillance overreach, Snowden fled the United States and released a huge cache of extremely sensitive intelligence data files to American and other international journalists. Aided and abetted by the WikiLeaks team, who wanted to be in on the action, Snowden flew first to Hong Kong and then to Moscow after the United States revoked his passport. The files Snowden handed over to the press revealed questionable domestic monitoring practices by the NSA and the existence of a highly classified program that penetrated international communications on a massive, almost unfathomable, scale. U.S. spies really were everywhere—at least electronically. The various newspaper articles on the Snowden files offered invaluable operational information for the Russian intelligence services (along with everyone else) about how the United States was approaching its intelligence gathering.

Snowden's appearance was both a public relations and a major intelligence coup for Putin. In granting Snowden asylum, and playing up the young contractor's whistleblower status, Putin presented himself as the protector and defender of civil liberties, free speech, and transparency of information. He even won cautious praise from some of Russia's most ardent human rights activists who only moments before had denounced his clampdown on the opposition.[6] He was able to tweak the U.S. government and intelligence services when Washington vehemently protested the asylum decision and demanded Russia send Snowden back to the United States. Snowden was a rogue NSA contractor, a spy, Putin retorted, and if a Russian spy had popped up suddenly in Washington, the United States would have granted him asylum too. The United States knew this was the case, which compounded Washington's frustration.[7]

Edward Snowden strengthened Putin's hand in a number of ways, including in countering some of the reversals in Russia's relationship with Germany. The Snowden files exposed the NSA's surveillance program in Germany, which included monitoring Chancellor Angela Merkel's cell phone. In spite of Germany's reunification and its status as a close ally, the United States did not seem to have pulled back its Cold War activity from the days when Germany was divided. The information that the United States "spied on its friends" was a major blow to German-U.S. relations. It consumed the German press and political elite. U.S. explanations, assurances, and entreaties were seen as inadequate. Popular German attitudes toward the United States took a nose dive. Germans were angry and disillusioned. Edward Snowden was hailed as a hero, a champion of liberty. Some members of the German parliament even talked about bringing him to Germany.[8]

Russia and Putin suddenly gained moral equivalency with the United States in German public opinion, even if opinions of Russia in general remained low. Russia and the United States both spied. In the case of Russia, the Germans expected it. Putin was always open about being a spy. He was proud of it. He never said that Russia had stopped spying. The United States, by contrast, lied about it and never apologized! The German government barely protested during the early months of the Ukraine crisis when the audiotape of a phone call between the U.S. assistant secretary of state for Europe and the U.S. ambassador to Ukraine was leaked and posted to YouTube.[9] German officials conceded that Russian intelligence had played some role in the affair, but the United States was the country that spied on its friends, not just its enemies. It was getting a taste of its own sauce.[10]

OPERATION FIFTH COLUMN

On the home front, the Snowden affair deflected attention away from how Putin had been targeting Russian groups and individuals along with Western NGOs. Putin treated all of them as if he were engaged in a counterintelligence operation—dealing especially harshly with Russians suspected of holding dual allegiances. In July 2012, the Duma passed a law requiring all organizations that took foreign money or grants to register with the government as "foreign agents." Government inspection and tax agencies raided civil society groups like GOLOS, which had monitored violations in both the 2011 parliamentary and 2012 presidential elections, looking for any signs of malfeasance.[11] Groups that did not register as foreign agents were subject to massive fines, as were individuals singled out for participating in demonstrations or marches that caused damage to property.[12]

A semester that opposition politician Alexei Navalny had spent at Yale University was cited as evidence that he was an American agent bent on shaming Russia with his accusations of institutional corruption.[13] The punk rock collective Pussy Riot and activists among Russia's homosexual community were depicted as being fifth column representatives of Western decadence bent on subverting Russian culture.[14] The United States Agency for International Development, which had given grants to democracy and human rights groups including GOLOS, was ousted in October 2012. Other American democracy-promotion groups like the International Republican Institute soon followed. European NGOs, including foundations linked to Germany's political parties, were raided by inspectors.[15] The message from Putin and the Kremlin was loud and clear: all foreigners trying to operate inside Russia to change the political system, no matter who they purported to be, would be exposed for what they were—agents of a foreign government. And Russian citizens for their part should keep away from foreigners if they didn't want trouble.[16]

THE POLITICAL KOMMISSARS . . .

In the course of targeting the fifth column and the foreign agents, Putin set about adapting old mechanisms to new tasks and developing new political tools to assist with the exercise. The Russian media were one of these. Over the course of the 2000s, the Kremlin had steadily taken control of the Russian information space. Heavy manipulation of the media, from television and newspapers to the Internet, was a key feature of Putin's system. Unlike in China, the Kremlin did not initially try to censor the Internet. Instead, it sought to fill the available political and public information space with its own content and to co-opt, or in some cases create, new media outlets. Oligarchs close to the Kremlin capitalized on this policy to become some of the richest men in the world, penetrating global social media markets.[17]

Like the political kommissars of the Bolshevik era, who were charged with ensuring politically correct reporting, the Kremlin's media team kept close tabs on critical commentators and prominent bloggers. They convened focus groups specifically intended to counter dissenters and critics (from abroad as well as at home) and set up training sessions for loyal bloggers. The Kremlin also hired leading Russian and international public relations firms, like Ketchum Inc. from the United States, which helped to set up the Valdai Discussion Club, to help improve its media strategy (see earlier discussion in chapter 9). At the beginning of his presidency, Putin had made it clear that controlling the mass media was an essential element in rebuilding the authority and strength of the state. He emphasized in early speeches that press freedom in Russia would not be unlimited and that the needs of the state would always take precedence. The mass media and the press—like the parliament and other institutions—were always viewed as tools by the Kremlin, instruments to be deployed in the service of the state to further its goals.[18]

The protests of 2011–12 appeared to be proof to Putin that he had been too lax in the information space. He had paid insufficient attention to the new social media. It had become a Trojan Horse, a transmission belt for Western political ideas, propaganda, and psychological operations. Most of the new social media networks originated in the West and the United States, and Putin called the Internet a "CIA project."[19] Social media, in Putin's view, were a means for foreign and domestic operatives to engage in stealth mobilization and subversion. The opposition had used them as the mechanism for bringing people out into the streets. Now, Putin squeezed social media along with the older media forms. Libel and slander were recriminalized in the Russian legal code.[20] Other laws were passed to blacklist and block websites. So-called liberal media outlets in print, radio and TV—which were previously tolerated by Kremlin watch dogs as long as they did not become too popular or provocative—suddenly found themselves under scrutiny and assault.[21] For Putin, after the protests, the role of the mass media at all levels was to rally the public "around the flag," to broadcast the strength of Russian politics, society, and culture, and to publicize the irreversible damage that Russia's enemies were doing to the country. The state media were one of the weapons put on the offensive, producing documentaries about foreign plots to subvert Russian domestic politics and foreign policy goals, showing films that glorified Russia's past, offering talk shows that framed issues as a Russia-against-the-world struggle.[22]

As part of the exercise, Putin created a new presidential directorate for "Social Projects" in October 2012. Its purview included providing "information, analytical, and organizational support for the fulfillment of the President of the Russian Federation's constitutional powers to determine the main direction of state policy in the field of patriotic education." The directorate was tasked with formulating "proposals to strengthen the spiritual and moral foundations of Russian society, improving the work of the patriotic education of youth, [and the] development and implementation of public projects in this field."[23] A year later, in October 2013, the directorate issued a public Request for Proposals (RFP) to solicit new ideas for "educational mechanisms" to inspire the younger generation of Russians. The directorate wanted to find ways of "using religious and values-based foundations" in the educational process, and to identify "key events and personalities that have symbolic consolidating potential."[24] Presenting values and framing history and events in ways that bolstered official positions and furthered Russian national interests would be formal elements of state policy.[25] The intent was clear: the Kremlin and Putin would deploy Russian values and Russian history as weapons in their conduct of new warfare.

. . . AND THE CONSERVATIVE INTERNATIONAL

Shortly after the Social Projects directorate's RFP, in December 2013, the Kremlin downgraded the status of the official Russian news agency, RIA Novosti, which was established in 1941 to coordinate all aspects of Soviet news coverage during World War II. The decision came as a considerable shock to the staff of the agency who had gained respect for their efforts to ensure balanced coverage of issues inside and outside Russia and been acclaimed for their international news reporting.[26] RIA Novosti was put under the umbrella of Russia's state-owned international television company, Rossiya Segodnya, the parent organization of the Russia Today channel, which had been renamed RT in 2011. Dmitry Kiselyov, a journalist renowned for his strident commentary and closely associated with the Kremlin, was named as head of the combined entity.[27] In announcing the decision, presidential chief of staff Sergei Ivanov stressed that "Russia pursues an independent policy and robustly defends its national interests. It's not easy to explain that to the world, but we can and must do this."[28] As General Gerasimov had indicated, information was a key component of the new warfare, and Rossiya Segodnya and RT would be important weapons in the arsenal. RT was well funded by the Kremlin. It had multiple foreign broadcasting outlets in several languages, including English; and it had established itself in international markets alongside other foreign news networks like Al Jazeera, China's CCTV, Deutsche Welle, and France 24.[29] The Kremlin promoted RT as Russia's version of the BBC and CNN.[30]

Dmitry Kiselyov was particularly notorious for his unrestrained comments on social issues, lambasting homosexuals and other minority groups.[31] Kiselyov and RT became part of a Kremlin effort to present Russia as the champion of conservative values globally—defending these from the predations of the United States and Europe. RT programming was heavily directed toward pointing out the nefarious activities, hypocrisy, moral failings, and decadence of the West. For every media article and report from the United States or a European country citing Russia for undermining human rights or violating some international norm, RT would present a counter-accusation and report.[32] RT would also reach out to pundits and politicians in the West who were skeptical about and critical of their own governments and political systems, giving mavericks like Julian Assange their own programs or enlisting them as their "go-to" commentators.[33]

The rise of a host of far-right, anti-EU, and antiglobalization parties in Europe greatly helped Putin's and RT's cause. In the May 2014 European parliamentary elections (which coincided with the May 25, 2014, Ukrainian presidential election), many of the "European Right" parties secured seats as voters expressed their deep dissatisfaction with the ruling establishment's handling of the ongoing political and economic fallout from the euro zone crisis.[34] Putin set out to make common cause with Europe's conservatives and populists. In launching his broadsides against the West for rejecting its traditional values and threatening a return to "chaotic darkness" with its ill-advised social policies, Putin presented Russia as the defender of what he considered true European values. Russia's conservative agenda, Putin asserted, was the real European agenda. It was not the mishmash of policies that gave the views and behaviors of marginal and minority groups a greater voice in society than they deserved under the guise of multiculturalism. Conservative religious and cultural values had made Europe great over the centuries. Bureaucrats in Brussels and feckless politicians in European capitals had undermined these achievements in a few decades. Europe's new "value-less" secular society was bringing the continent to ruin, Putin asserted.[35]

Populist and nationalist political leaders in Europe became a staple of RT programming (sometimes landing themselves in political hot water at home).[36] They were also courted by other Kremlin-backed groups in Russia in different formats. These included the expansion of the Valdai Discussion Club into a range of smaller meetings outside Russia with specially selected individuals; and conferences and seminars under the umbrella of the "Dialogue of Civilizations," an entity sponsored by Putin associate Vladimir Yakunin. Representatives of the Russian Orthodox Church, the ultimate repository of Russian values, played a role in many of these meetings, especially when members of other international religious groups were present and the faith-based aspect of conservative values was a prominent theme.[37] In a variant of the old Marxian slogan "workers of the world unite," the Kremlin, RT, the Orthodox Church, and other Russian groups urged "conservatives of the world to unite" behind Putin's conservative agenda.

In short, Western populist politicians, nationalist parties, and international conservative groups were being tested as potential weapons in the new warfare, even if they did not know they might be deployed in this way.[38] As one high-ranking German official noted, in analyzing this series of developments, Putin had identified key vulnerabilities in European politics: in the anti-establishment, anti-EU sentiment of populist and nationalist parties, and in the backlash by conservative and religious groups against policies that recognized the equal rights and freedoms of minorities, such as the legalization of gay marriage. Putin was determined to exploit this weakness if he needed to.[39] From Putin's perspective, if the West was going to try to create fifth columns in Russia, then he was going to do the same in Europe. Social values, nationalism, religion, language, history—everything could and would become part of the battlefield.

PROTECTING AGAINST ECONOMIC WARFARE

Putin's military reform, the development of the doctrine and capability for fighting a "twenty-first-century war," along with his operations at home against political fifth columns, and his efforts to create his own fifth columns abroad were essential elements in Russia's defense against the assaults Putin perceived to be coming from the West. At the same time, Putin was working on another front to develop the capability to resist and deter economic warfare. Stung by the memory of how Russia had been pushed from the Baltic states in 1994 under the threat of economic sanctions, and informed by aborted Western efforts to apply sanctions against Russia during and after the war in Georgia, Putin moved to reduce Russia's vulnerability to economic pressure from the West.

Putin pursued a two-track approach. He would reduce Russia's vulnerability, and he would create counter-leverage against the West. One step was obvious: wherever possible he would reduce the exposure of vital Russian economic sectors to potential Western attacks. After 2006, by paying off Russia's foreign debt and building up very large foreign exchange reserves, Putin had already accomplished a great deal. Doing more was not easy. Putin was well aware that Russia's integration into the global economy was unavoidable and necessary for the country's economic development. He could not pull the country back and hunker down behind economic barricades as the Soviet Union had done during the Cold War. Nevertheless, based on his assessment of the situation, Putin had to be prepared to make some trade-offs. As he had stated in his addresses to the Russian parliament, the world was an increasingly risky place. The global economic and euro zone crises had put an end to the halcyon days of high economic growth that Russia had enjoyed in the 2000s. Based on the Western response to his decision to return to the presidency, and on the EU and U.S. support for the protest movement, Russia's position could be undercut even further in the near future. Some economic hatches would have to be battened down.

Immediately after his presidential inauguration in May 2012, Putin commanded members of the Russian parliament and key business figures from his inner circle to "de-offshore." They should get rid of any foreign assets and bring their base of operations back home, to Moscow.[40] Some of those whom he addressed moved swiftly. In July 2012, Gennady Timchenko, one of Russia's top international business figures and one of Putin's closest associates, moved his "Ural Invest" holding company from Switzerland to Moscow.[41] (In March 2014, the day before U.S. sanctions were to be enacted, Timchenko would sell his share of the global natural resource trading company Gunvor to his Swedish business partner.)

In the area of trade, Putin took a different tack to reduce vulnerability. To pursue a policy of autarky—blindly eliminating foreign-made goods in favor of domestic products no matter what—would make Russia weaker, not stronger. Diversifying Russia's economic links was smarter. Here, Putin could build on his diversification of foreign policy and his outreach to China, the BRICS, and other countries by concluding new trade deals with all these partners. The economic diversification approach would pay off in 2014 when the EU and the United States actually did impose sanctions in response to the annexation of Crimea and Russia's resulting conflict with Ukraine. Putin had already created relationships for "import diversification" rather than import substitution. Foods that came from Europe could be sourced from Asia and Latin America or other countries that did not follow the EU and U.S. policies, as well as from suppliers that were closer, like Turkey and former Soviet states in Central Asia.[42] Diversification of trade and investment ties was part of contingency planning. It would help to keep Russia's economic options open for as long as possible.

Putin was just as wary of creating economic entanglements as he was of foreign alliances. To be able to adapt to changing circumstances, he had to avoid making permanent commitments that would tie his hands. At the same time, Putin had to be careful not to burn bridges or to sacrifice investments in prior relationships that he had spent considerable time cultivating. Those relationships were important on a number of fronts and should not be jettisoned at the first sign of trouble—they might prove extremely useful at some point. They should be handled carefully.

LEVERAGE AND COUNTER-LEVERAGE

Putin's behavior at the height of the Ukraine crisis in 2014 illustrated all of these points. As soon as the United States and Europe imposed sanctions on Russia in response to the annexation of Crimea, Putin moved to adopt explicit import substitution policies in sectors that he deemed critical—especially defense and food. He also made it clear that he remained open for business cooperation with all the foreign corporations that had invested in Russia. This included American companies, even in the face of, as Putin put it, the "difficult current political situation." In a ceremony to launch the first exploratory drilling rig in the joint venture between Rosneft and ExxonMobil in the Kara Sea in August 2014, for example, Putin stressed how vital international cooperation was for Russia's energy sector and how much he welcomed its continuation in spite of the Ukraine conflict:

> Practice shows that it is nearly impossible, or at least very difficult, to implement alone such large high-tech projects, projects of global scale and significance. Today commercial success is determined by effective international cooperation. . . . We . . . are open to expanding our cooperation with partners. . . . [Such cooperation] will benefit our national economies, contribute to improving the global

energy situation and will undoubtedly lead to the development of breakthrough technologies and job creation.[43]

The Rosneft-ExxonMobil cooperation was, itself, an example of another strategy for protecting the Russian economy: that of creating codependency with foreign businesses. This was a practice Putin had begun as deputy mayor in St. Petersburg. Codependency was a source of counter-leverage against the West. In addition to joint ventures, in the 2000s Putin sought to enlist foreign manufacturers to set up production inside Russia and require them to use Russian raw materials and other inputs. Not only would this create jobs for Russians and demand for products in upstream Russian sectors, it would make foreign companies more reliant on Russia in their international business operations. Foreign companies would not just see Russia as a lucrative market. They would have a direct stake in the Russian economy. When there were political tensions, their operations inside the country would convert them into advocates for economic cooperation with Russia.

Putin's approach was an old one. The communist leadership of the USSR had done the same on a grand scale in the 1960s and 1970s in its "gas for pipes" deals with various Western European countries.[44] Much later, even market reformer Anatoly Chubais, who headed the team Putin joined when he came to Moscow in 1996, espoused a similar idea. In 2003, Chubais expounded in a series of interviews his "liberal empire" thesis: Russian energy pipelines, electricity transmission lines, and Russian companies' purchases of major foreign economic assets like refineries would replace the Red Army as Russia's means of moving back into Europe, consolidating its ties with its old neighborhood, and winning new political support.[45]

The 2008–09 global financial crisis provided Russia with an unexpected opportunity to build this kind of leverage. As companies across the world suffered in the downturn, Putin openly pushed Russia's biggest corporations to buy up distressed assets in Russia's neighborhood, in Ukraine, in the West, and even in the United States.[46] Putin encouraged joint ventures with major Western companies and entities that were vulnerable themselves, companies such as British oil giant BP after the 2010 Deepwater Horizon oil spill in the Gulf of Mexico, and the French shipbuilder STX, which needed shipbuilding orders and jobs for its massive facility in St. Nazaire.[47] Russia's purchase of France's Mistral-class amphibious assault ship in 2009 was as much about securing political leverage in France as it was about Russia's military modernization and getting new hardware and technology packages. Beyond these kinds of deals, additional leverage was developed by offering lucrative positions on Russian corporate boards to former high-ranking Western politicians and grandees, who could then be enlisted as allies to make Russia's economic case if necessary.[48] All these measures helped create a new version of mutually assured destruction on the economic front in the advent of a political standoff. If the West was to contemplate pulling the economic sanctions trigger, it had to know that Western interests, too, would suffer badly. Sanctions were a double-edged sword.

RESORTING TO ECONOMIC COERCION

The idea of creating economic leverage and counter-leverage could have a directly sinister side as well. As deputy mayor in St. Petersburg, and later in dealing with his domestic opposition, Putin had used methods of coercion and blackmail. He deployed tax inspectors to collect damning information about businesses and individuals and then either dragged them into court to answer accusations of economic crimes (rarely) or simply let them know that this might happen if they did not behave (much more frequently). The foreign policy equivalents included turning off gas supplies to Ukraine in 2006 and again in 2009; imposing import bans against Ukrainian chocolate in 2013, along with Georgian and Moldovan wine and a whole raft of European and U.S. products at other junctures during political spats; and sending inspectors into the Russian offices of foreign corporations searching for violations of tax, environmental, or labor codes. Or Putin could let the threat of such cutoffs and embargoes, and potential inspections, court cases, and fines, hang over the foreign countries and companies.

All these coercive moves by Putin had a series of reinforcing factors—at least in terms of how *he* interpreted a series of decisions in the West. One of the earliest and most serious, from Putin's perspective, was the push by the European Union for a common energy strategy and the development of the EU's so-called Third Energy Package. The stated goal of the policy, adopted in September 2009, was to promote greater competition in the energy sector by forcing energy suppliers to separate their upstream and downstream operations and divest themselves from consumer distribution networks. While the EU insisted the policy was not discriminatory and was merely intended to subject all foreign energy companies to the same rules it applied to EU companies, Putin viewed the policy as targeted specifically against Gazprom.[49] Indeed, EU pressure on Gazprom intensified in the following months and years—including European inspection raids on the offices of Gazprom affiliates in Europe in 2011 and threats of formal antitrust action against Gazprom in October 2013.[50] Putin made it clear that these were threats he would not take lightly.[51]

In 2012–13, Putin's comments underscored the fact that he increasingly saw the global economy as a battlefield. He was a top-level operative on this battlefield tasked with defending Russia's interests. One of the clearest illustrations of this was the Cyprus banking crisis of 2013. Cyprus had long been a favored offshore banking center and tax haven for Russian banks and corporations. In Putin's eyes it was a vital entry point into the global economy. Most important, it was an entry point where Russia exerted control. Cyprus was ideal as a Russian financial haven: it was in the EU and was a member of the euro zone; it was a popular destination for Russian tourists and had a vibrant Russian ex-pat population; and its economy was small enough for Russia to thoroughly dominate. By 2012, Russians accounted for between one-third and one-half of all deposits in Cypriot banks.[52] Informal Russian influence in Cyprus was even more important. The interests of leading Cypriot businessmen and politicians were intertwined with those of Russian banks and companies. Cyprus was nothing less than a strategic bridgehead—"an advanced position seized in hostile territory as a foothold for further advance," as the dictionary definition has it—in the battle for Russia's financial and economic security. The "hostile" territory was the European Union.

In March 2013 the bridgehead was under assault. The ongoing reverberations from the euro zone crisis finally hit Cyprus. The Cypriot banking system collapsed. European financial institutions and the International Monetary Fund made a €10 billion bailout offer to Cyprus on the condition that it levy a heavy tax on depositors, a tax that would naturally fall heaviest on Russian investors. Putin and other Russian spokesmen blasted the deal, both for its provisions and because it had been concluded without consulting Russia first.[53] In Putin's view, what was happening was an act of aggression by the West against Russia in the global financial arena—and one in which Germany played a surprisingly (for Putin) hostile role. The damning Schockenhoff and BND reports on Russian activities (see chapter 13) encouraged Berlin to take a harder line on the terms of the deal. German parliamentarians were adamant that corrupt Russian activities in Cyprus should not be assisted in any way or benefit from a bailout. Russia should be ousted from Cyprus. But as it turned out in the wake of the crisis, Russia was not kicked out. Russia doubled down on its investment, pumping money into the Cypriot banks when everyone else pulled out. In military terms, Moscow left its "commandos behind" to secure the bridgehead. This bore dividends later when the initial rounds of Western sanctions against Russia were being discussed after the annexation of Crimea in 2014. Cypriot leaders told German, UK, and other Western counterparts pushing for financial sanctions that they could not count on Cyprus. The message, in so many words, was: "We can't do that. The Russians own us!"[54]

THE EURASIAN UNION VERSUS THE EUROPEAN UNION

Thanks to actions like the antitrust suit brought against Gazprom, and the sequence of events in the Cyprus crisis, Putin concluded that the EU had become a geopolitical actor on an entirely different level than before. The Kremlin's perceptions of the role of European NGOs and institutions in encouraging the 2011–12 protests in Russia intensified Putin's suspicions that the EU and its actions were an integral part of the West's war against Russia. Increasingly for Putin, the EU was as much of a threat to Russia's interests and international positions as the old Cold War nemesis, NATO. This shift in Putin's assessment became his frame for the crisis in Ukraine at the end of 2013. As described earlier (see chapter 10), the trigger for the crisis was Putin's plan to reintegrate Ukraine and other former Soviet economies into a Eurasian Union. This was a contingency effort to protect the Russian economy from external economic shocks by guaranteeing regional markets for otherwise non-competitive Russian products.[55] At the same time, however, the European Union was pursuing its own agreements with four former Soviet states: Georgia and Ukraine, along with Armenia and Moldova. Putin deemed Ukraine vital to his concept. The two initiatives collided in Kyiv.

Russia's own partnership agreement with the EU had expired in 2007, and the 2008 war with Georgia threw off negotiations for a follow-up. Despite the growing animosity in Moscow toward the EU, Putin and his economic team continued to hold out hope that they could thrash out a new economic "modernization partnership" with Brussels and reverse the EU's new energy policies. Late into 2013, Moscow and Brussels were still engaged in bilateral negotiations to expand trade and investment, as well as to secure visa-free travel for Russians with official or service passports.[56] As always, Putin was trying to keep Russia's options open. In his view, pursuing the Eurasian Union should not preclude Russia having new arrangements with the European Union. Unfortunately for Putin, the proposed EU agreements with Ukraine and the other states went far beyond the scope of Russia's negotiations with Europe. At their core was a "Deep and Comprehensive Free Trade Agreement" that would align the states' economic standards with those of the EU and give them access to the European single market.

The agreements would put the states on a path toward adopting and implementing critical provisions of European Union legislation that were assumed by full members. Most important of all, absent Russia's own arrangements with the European Union, the association agreements would pull Ukraine and the other three states, with their collective populations of 62 million consumers, away from the Russian economy. The European Union association agreements and arrangements with Putin's Eurasian Union were basically incompatible. This would ultimately be an either-or proposition. For Putin this was unacceptable. Given the imperative to protect Russia's economy, he wanted to make sure that Russia, and Russia's interests, was factored into the agreements. But there was no formal provision for this.[57]

Russia pressured the countries to forgo their agreements with the European Union, which were set to be formalized at a summit in Vilnius at the end of November 2013. Georgia and Moldova pressed ahead with the process, but Armenia withdrew and agreed to join the Eurasian Union instead. With days to go before the Vilnius summit, Ukraine's leadership requested that the final signature on its agreement be postponed. Ukrainian president Viktor Yanukovych cited Russian pressure as a precipitating factor, along with the perilous state of the Ukrainian economy, which could not withstand the consequences of implementing European fiscal requirements. Shortly after the Vilnius summit, in December 2013, the Ukrainian government accepted a Russian offer to purchase Ukrainian bonds and provide a lower price for gas exports to Ukraine. The street protests that led to political chaos, violence, and then Yanukovych's ouster at the end of February 2014 began in direct response to this sequence of events.

THE CASE OFFICER'S APPROACH TO UKRAINE

In many respects there is a direct path from the events of 2008 and the war in Georgia to those of 2013–14 and the war in Ukraine. The fact that the two conflicts erupted five years apart obscured the linkages, but they were there from the beginning. Putin made it very clear in 2008 that Ukraine was of vital interest to Russia. He emphasized that the mere prospect of any kind of formal relationship between Ukraine and NATO would be considered a direct threat to Russia. In April 2008 at the NATO summit in Bucharest, Putin reportedly told President George W. Bush quite bluntly when Bush tried to discuss Ukraine with him: "You don't understand, George, Ukraine is not even a state. What is Ukraine? Part of its territories is Eastern Europe, but the greater part is a gift from us."[58]

Ukraine was already in Putin's crosshairs after the 2004 Orange Revolution produced a leadership under President Viktor Yushchenko that began to push for NATO membership and closer relations with the European Union. After the Bucharest summit and then after the war with Georgia in August 2008, many observers inside and outside Ukraine worried that Kyiv would be next in Moscow's firing line.[59] But Ukraine's own political infighting, domestic tribulations, and corruption among the elite seemed to push its Euro-Atlantic institutional perspective far over the horizon. Viktor Yanukovych, who replaced Yushchenko as president in 2010, seemed much more interested in running Ukraine as a "family business" than in dealing with the business of economic and political reform laid out by the European Union in its stipulations for closer association. He also made it very clear that Ukraine would not renew its pursuit of NATO membership. Instead, he renewed Russia's lease on Crimea's ports as the home base for the Russian Black Sea Fleet.[60]

From Putin's perspective, the Ukrainian president's well-documented venality was a major vulnerability that Putin could use to his benefit.[61] It provided leverage. Yanukovych was similar to the foreign targets Putin and his KGB colleagues had set up back in Leningrad or Dresden in the 1970s and 1980s. His greed and transgressions opened him up to reputational risk at home and abroad. They also made him relatively easy to buy off. Putin did just that—negotiating opaque energy deals that always seemed to involve some member of Yanukovych's inner circle and encouraging Russian companies to place lucrative orders with industries closely connected to the Ukrainian president and his family.[62]

In addition to ensuring Russia's sovereignty and freedom of maneuver, Putin's basic foreign policy principles can best be summarized in the same terms as his principles for managing the political system at home: you have to find ways of working with people (as proxies for countries) so that they cannot harm you (Russia). As the protests of 2011–12 had demonstrated, Putin could not micromanage everything and dictate to everyone. The task of exerting control or influence over people abroad was even more difficult than at home. As we discussed in chapter 9, blackmail was a useful tool in Putin's system to get people to refrain from doing things. You could force people to work for you through blackmail. But, you could not necessarily force people to work *well* under these circumstances. In Ukraine, President Viktor Yanukovych became a shining example (if Putin needed one) of this very point.

Internationally and in Russia's immediate neighborhood, it was very difficult for Putin to get "good performance" out of other leaders, even after deploying all the Operative's methods, tools, and tactics at his disposal. Yanukovych was not appointed by Putin, as he would have been in the Soviet period when Moscow selected the heads of Ukraine and other Soviet republics. He was elected by the population of Ukraine, and there were other claimants and constituencies applying pressure on him. Putin had to be able to exert more coercive influence over Yanukovych than the others. In 2013, Putin succeeded in doing so and managed to stop Yanukovych from taking Ukraine toward the EU. Yanukovych took Putin's economic bailout and did not sign the association agreement at Vilnius. Then Yanukovych let things get out of hand. Unlike Putin, he had not made contingency plans. He did not know how to handle the protests that erupted in Kyiv. He could not figure how to decapitate them as Putin had done in Moscow in 2012.

What were, at first, small demonstrations against Yanukovych's mishandling of the association agreement with the EU became a mass protest movement against his government. Yanukovych's crowd management was poor, his policing was appalling. He lost control. Violence escalated and engendered more protests. The Ukrainian population was emboldened, not deterred. Then, just as it seemed Russia had helped to broker an agreement to calm things down and keep Yanukovych in place until new elections, the Ukrainian president literally fled the scene.[63] As Putin summed it up immediately afterward, Yanukovych might technically still be Ukraine's legal president, but he had proven he had "no political future."[64] He had also put Russia's future at risk.

LOSING A BUFFER

As he fleshed out his agenda for the Eurasian Union, Putin had come to describe it as a means of protecting Russia's national identity, not just as an economic mechanism.[65] If the Eurasian Union acquired a political dimension, it could act as a regional buffer against the advance of political ideas and cultural values from Europe and the West. Putin could encourage close trade relations between the Eurasian Union and the EU, but the Eurasian Union and its members would steer clear of adopting Europe's political norms. In this context, there were several elements of the Ukrainian protests that were particularly threatening to Russia's interests and needed to be addressed.

Over the course of 2013, as he worked on shaping his narrative about Russia rejecting the West as a model and heading off on its own path, Putin had increasingly turned toward the issue of Ukraine and its relations with Russia. In many respects this was inevitable. In the series of events that Putin had selected for his version of the Russian national narrative, the territory of post-Soviet Ukraine, including the Autonomous Republic of Crimea, played a key role. In a number of speeches, Putin depicted Ukraine as Kievan Rus', the birthplace of the Russian state, and Holy Rus' itself.[66] Harking back to the overarching *pravoslavnyy* (or Russian Orthodox) identity of the tsarist era, Putin declared that Ukrainians and Russians were not just fraternal peoples: they were one single, united people (*yedinyy narod*).[67] During the crisis in Ukraine, however, the Ukrainian branch of the Orthodox Church seemed to go out of its way to violate the concept of a unified Holy Rus' that Putin and the Russian patriarch had embraced. Priests from the Ukrainian Orthodox Church played a prominent role during the demonstrations. Ukrainian church leaders expressed their open support for the protesters as well as their own aspirations to draw closer to Europe. After Yanukovych absconded, some segments of the Ukrainian opposition even demanded that the new government curb the activities of the Moscow patriarchy in Ukraine.[68]

When Putin assessed developments in Ukraine and the protests in Kyiv's Maidan (Independence) Square, he looked at them through the lens of his experiences in Dresden and East Germany. In East Germany, not only did opposition movements and demonstrators bring down the Berlin Wall and then their own state, but the reverberations from their actions upended the Soviet Union's geopolitical position in Europe. With surprising speed, they destroyed the entire Soviet bloc, including the Soviet Union itself. If the Ukrainian protests succeeded in pushing Ukraine back toward Brussels, Moscow's leverage over Kyiv would be greatly reduced. The Eurasian Union would be rendered meaningless. Russia's position in Europe would, once again, be diminished by protesters. Indeed, with Yanukovych out of the picture, Ukraine's opposition leaders quickly pledged to return to negotiations with the European Union.[69]

Furthermore, Western and European leaders had tried to forge direct connections with the protesters and the opposition. Several European foreign ministers and the EU's high representative for foreign affairs, along with senior U.S. officials, had appeared in Kyiv's Maidan Square to show their solidarity. They had expressed clear preferences for the formation of a new government in Kyiv and for particular members of the opposition.[70] For Putin this simply confirmed what he had thought all along, based on his previous assessment of the 2011–12 protests in Moscow. The West was trying, at the very least, to manipulate the protesters—if it hadn't actually put them out there in the first place.[71] From Putin's perspective, all of the high-level appearances on the Maidan Square were further proof of the West's use of "twenty-first-century warfare" methods. Once again, in Ukraine, the United States and its EU allies had overthrown a regime without firing a shot.[72]

OPERATION UKRAINE

Yanukovych's flight from Kyiv and the opposition's return to the Ukraine-EU association agreement were the final straw for Putin. In launching his subsequent operation in Ukraine, Putin pulled out the entire arsenal of weapons he had developed to fight the new kind of warfare. He would deploy economic tools, legal instruments, Russian nationalism and history, and information warfare and propaganda—along with more conventional military force. As previously discussed, Putin probably was not expecting to have to move quite so quickly in Ukraine. The mounting demonstrations in December 2013 and Yanukovych's actions in February 2014 forced Putin's hand. In many respects though, Putin was ready. He had several key elements in place.

Gas price hikes and supply disruptions had proven effective with Ukraine in the past. Putin turned to them again—breaking off a deal he had made with Yanukovych for a gas price reduction when the Ukrainian president decided not to sign the EU agreement. Putin demanded that the new leaders in Kyiv now pay off all energy debts that Ukraine had racked up.[73] Russia also had hooks in important parts of Ukraine's industrial sector. Since the collapse of the Soviet Union, Russia had continued to support the Ukrainian economy through orders to Ukrainian heavy-manufacturing enterprises and defense industries, along with metals producers and the mining and power sectors. By 2013, Russia's orders to Ukrainian industry ran in the range of $5–$10 billion a year. Many sectors of Ukrainian industry depended almost entirely on demand from Russia, and all of them depended on Russian gas to generate electrical power. Ukraine's defense industries were highly concentrated geographically, in Kyiv and three other cities: Kharkiv, Dnipropetrovsk, and Mykolayiv. In these cities, a quarter of the labor force worked in the defense plants. Putin pulled the economic plug. He effectively shut down the plants.[74] From Putin's perspective, if Ukraine was going to join an economic agreement with the European Union, it would do so with its economy in ruins. The process of association would be painful both for Brussels and for Kyiv.

Beyond the economy, Putin was equally ruthless. He struck against the new government in Kyiv by scaling up the methods of legal manipulation, intimidation, and force he had deployed successfully against his domestic opposition. In March 2014, although Ukraine's parliament remained largely intact after the departure of Viktor Yanukovych, the new acting president and interim government had not been legitimized by elections. Putin moved swiftly to declare Ukraine's interim government illegal. In a series of carefully crafted speeches, Putin decried the violence of the protests and emphasized the activities of extreme right-wing elements. When some prominent right-wing protesters were appointed to the interim government, Putin denounced the temporary Ukrainian authorities as a band of xenophobic, anti-Semitic extremists, thugs, and terrorists who had carried out a coup.[75]

When the interim Ukrainian government made a major miscalculation by repealing the status of Russian as a second official language, Putin pulled out the weapon of Russian nationalism. Although the government quickly reversed its decision, Putin used the uproar to his advantage. He declared that the new authorities in Kyiv posed a threat to ethnic Russians, Russian speakers, and religious minorities in Ukraine—especially in Crimea and in the eastern and southern regions close to Russia's borders. These, Putin stated, were the historic lands of "New Russia" (*Novorossiya*).[76] Having essentially staked out a claim to a swath of Ukrainian territory on the basis of Russian language, identity, and history, Putin pulled out another weapon in his arsenal: the anniversaries of the two great wars of the twentieth century.

HISTORY AS A WEAPON: REFIGHTING THE SECOND WORLD WAR

For Putin, 2014 brought the mother lode of events to commemorate. The year marked the 100th anniversary of the outbreak of World War I, the 75th anniversary of the outbreak of World War II, and the 70th anniversary of some of the seminal events that brought World War II to an end—including the end of the siege of Leningrad and the D-Day landings. The pickings were rich. Putin had put himself at the center of the action in January 2014 when he laid a wreath during ceremonies commemorating the end of the siege of Leningrad. He stressed his personal connection to the siege—"I know this from my own family history"—and the sacrifices of Leningrad's citizens (like his parents).[77] Russian state television continuously ran films and documentaries about the Nazi invasion of the USSR. These commentaries provided the explanation for why Putin and the Kremlin needed to deal with a "renewed fascist" threat in Kyiv.[78]

Weaving a narrative justification for Operation Ukraine and the annexation of Crimea, based on the events of World War II, required refining some of Putin's tools. Where Putin had previously brought Ukrainians and Russians together as a single people, now he had to pull them apart. Through the prism of World War II, ethnic Ukrainians became a fifth column, an enemy people of the Russians and of the Russian state. Putin's March 18 speech on the annexation of Crimea reflected this—rhetorically linking Ukrainians to Russia's domestic fifth columns that had threatened the state during the 2011–12 protests.[79] During the war, the fifth columns were the national traitors. They were individuals and peoples of the Soviet Union who collaborated with the Nazis.[80] Here Putin deliberately played on two decades of extremely troubled Soviet history—between the Russian Revolution and the beginning of World War II—when Ukrainians were often pitted against Russians and Ukrainian nationalist groups organized in opposition to Soviet rule.[81] One of these groups, the Organization of Ukrainian Nationalists (OUN), based itself across the border in Poland. The OUN and its leader, Stepan Bandera, initially collaborated with the German forces as they invaded Poland and then Ukraine in 1939–41, in the (vain) hope that Germany would endorse an independent Ukraine.[82]

Putin used the documented fact of the OUN's collaboration to turn Stepan Bandera into Hitler's henchman (although the two never met, and Bandera was eventually persecuted by both the Nazis and the Soviets) and the new Ukrainian government into Stepan Bandera's political heir.[83] In multiple speeches and references, Putin retold the age-old story of Russia fighting for its survival and in defense of the *russkiy mir*. In 2014, in this most recent chapter of Russia's long-drawn-out struggle, Putin was trying to beat back a return to the horrors of World War II in "Stepan Bandera's" Ukraine. In a series of adroit rhetorical maneuvers Putin absolved Nazi Germany and Russia of complicity in the horrors of World War II. The 1939 Molotov-Ribbentrop Pact and Stalin's secret deal with Hitler that facilitated Germany's invasion of Poland in 1939 were defended as necessary for Russia's survival. Stepan Bandera and the Ukrainian nationalists were accused of slaughtering Jews in Ukraine in the service of the Nazis, driven by their own extremism and anti-Semitism. In Putin's narrative, which was deftly disseminated by his media machine, they had perpetrated the Holocaust. They had also attacked Russians in their Ukrainian nationalist zeal. And now, instead of standing alongside Russia in the face of this new fascist onslaught—as they did in wartime alliance of the 1940s, Putin suggested, the governments of the United States and the West were actually aiding and abetting Ukrainian extremists. In their desire to undermine Russia, the United States and its European allies were betraying the very principles they had stood for in World War II.[84]

Putin had tried out some of these particular tactics and rhetoric before in other political disputes. Chechens during the war with Moscow in the 2000s, Estonians during an April 2007 dispute over the removal of a war memorial to fallen Soviet soldiers in Tallinn, and Georgians during their war with Moscow in August 2008 also had their wartime pasts dug up. It was another variant of the Case Officer's blackmail. In each case, Putin's implication essentially was: "We know something from your dirty past that we all ignored as long as we were together in the Soviet Union. But seeing how you're acting, we need to talk about that now. Every commemoration of World War II can become an occasion to ask whose side you were on then, and whose side are you on now?"[85]

These themes of national and personal loyalty and betrayal have been a frequent part of Putin's discourse as president.[86] As discussed in chapter 5, during World War II, Putin's father was in an NKVD (*Narodnyy komissariat vnutrennikh del*) destruction battalion sent from Leningrad into Nazi-held territory. Putin senior went into what is today Estonia explicitly to kill collaborators and destroy anything that could be of use to the occupying forces. This was essentially a suicide mission. Putin's father was wounded, but he survived and returned home. President Putin has talked about his father's experience as well as his strong sense of who was a traitor to the USSR during the war, a category that includes Estonians and Ukrainians.[87] Putin finds their behavior inexcusable, even if there might have been some mitigating circumstances. In the case of Ukraine, the ravages of the Soviet policy of collectivization and a catastrophic famine in the 1930s shaped Ukrainian animosity toward Moscow. Soviet leader Nikita Khrushchev transferred Crimea to Ukraine's jurisdiction in 1954 partly in recognition of this suffering (not, of course, anticipating the future collapse of the Soviet state). But for Putin, none of this particular history was relevant to his narrative in 2013–14.

KRYM NASH!

Wielding history as a weapon, Putin stoked inter-ethnic tensions and fears in Ukraine. Then he invoked the right and the obligation of the Russian state to protect ethnic Russians and Russian speakers, wherever they might be, from attack. This right was first claimed under President Boris Yeltsin in the early 1990s and was later formally enshrined in Russia's military doctrine.[88] Putin used this obligation along with other legal levers at his disposal to get well ahead of the planned May 25, 2014, presidential election in Kyiv and take effective control of Crimea. Putin used Russia's bilateral agreements with Ukraine on the long-term basing of the Russian Black Sea Fleet in Crimea, appeals for Russian assistance from Ukrainian president Yanukovych and local authorities, and Russian parliamentary resolutions as tools.[89] They provided legal cover for the movement of security forces to protect key military and civilian buildings and infrastructure. The hastily arranged March 16 referendum on Crimea's unification with Russia added the final element of legitimacy.

On the surface, the incorporation of Crimea seemed to be the ultimate sop to Russian nationalists and to the Russian Orthodox Church. Putin made a deliberate, calculated break with Russia's Soviet past by recognizing Crimea's Russianness, including its deep resonance with the Russian Orthodox faithful as the site of the baptism of Grand Prince Vladimir. Crimea was brought back into the Russian Federation not simply because of its historic ties with Russia, but because it was an explicitly designated "ethnic Russian" (*russkiy*) entity. This was a major departure from Putin's formulations in the Millennium Message, when he had been very careful *not* to make explicit references to ethnic Russianness and had, instead, stressed the multiethnic nature and status of the Russian state. The word *russkiy* does not appear a single time in any variant in the Millennium Message. *Rossiyskiy*—the adjective that refers to the multiethnic Russian state and its citizens—by contrast, is frequently used, as we point out in chapter 5, including in reference to the *rossiyskiy narod* and the *rossiyskaya ideya*. Putin even refers to *rossiyskiye tsennosti,* to values shared by all citizens of Russia, not to values espoused by ethnic Russians alone. In the Crimea speech, Putin used *russkiy* more than at any other time before or since.

Operation Ukraine demanded different rhetorical responses from Putin than the Millennium Message. In 1999–2000, the renewed war in Chechnya threatened to rip apart the Russian Federation. Putin was trying to keep Russia together as a multiethnic state. He had to pull nonethnic Russians—Chechens—back into the Russian body politic. He could only do this by stressing the importance of Russia's diversity of peoples and religions and the civic nature of citizenship in the Russian Federation. He had to downplay the ethnic Russian and Russian Orthodox elements of statehood. In 2014, by contrast, Putin was trying to stop Ukraine from breaking out of Russia's orbit. One way of doing this was by regathering and reuniting the historically designated lands of the *russkiy mir,* the world of ethnic Russians, and of Holy Rus', the broader Orthodox confessional community.[90] This required Putin to jettison his earlier set of formulations, at least temporarily, for the duration of the operation.

Switching to *russkiy* was a calculated, tactical move for Putin. It was not a strategic shift. To justify the seizure of Crimea, Putin had to convey a clear message that would be understood inside and outside Russia. Crimea was Russia's. It was Russian territory in every respect—historically, culturally, linguistically. It had been put outside Russia and left in Ukraine by an accident of history (and some misguided Soviet leaders and bureaucrats). This had been tolerable while Ukraine and Russia were in the same institutional arrangements. But it was intolerable, unacceptable, when they were not—or not likely to be. Putin was forced to take action, as regrettable as this might be. Putin, the Kremlin, the Russian media, the Russian Foreign Ministry, and a panoply of Russian commentators hammered this message across at every opportunity. In Putin's view, this part of the operation succeeded. The annexation of Crimea was broadly popular in Russia.[91] Even outside Russia it resonated with groups who were still nostalgic for the old certainties and associations of the USSR. As a visitor to Dushanbe, the capital of Tajikistan, in March 2014 was surprised to discover, even nonethnic Russians, Tajiks, were shouting "*Krym nash!*" (Crimea is ours!) in the streets when Putin signed the reunification documents.[92] It also played somewhat well with national groups around the world whose own populations were divided by state borders.[93] From their vantage points a wrong was made right: an old order had been restored.

REINING IN THE NATIONALISTS: BACK TO UNITY

After all Putin's efforts in the 2000s to curb Russian nationalist extremism, including in the immediate aftermath of the 2011–12 protests, the annexation had the potential to be explosive at home. Russian nationalists were emboldened by the events of March 2014, and it was only natural that they would now be chomping at the bit for further international acts of restoration. Putin had unleashed them, but he now had to rein them in, keep them in check. The unity of Russia, the state, not just the ethnic Russian people, was still the most important issue for Putin. Only a few weeks after the annexation, on May 9, Putin gave his speeches on Victory Day to commemorate the end of World War II. Both at the ceremony and the Red Square parade, the Russian president was back to his careful use of language. Putin noted that the unity of Russia's (and the Soviet Union's) multiethnic and multiconfessional people was the greatest legacy of its World War II victory.[94]

Indeed, not long after Putin's Victory Day speeches, at the end of May, another signal of the importance of unity came from an unexpected quarter: the North Caucasus. A number of Chechen fighters turned up in Ukraine's Donetsk region to lend their fighting skills in support of pro-Russian separatist forces. In interviews with Western journalists, some of the Chechen fighters explicitly presented themselves as defending Russia's interests. They stressed that they too were patriots of the Russian state. One of the Chechen fighters, Zelimkhan, told a reporter that he had traveled to Donetsk with a group of fighters that comprised 33 Chechens from Grozny and another 16 from the neighboring republic of North Ossetia. When the reporter asked if there were also "Russian fighters" with them—clearly implying ethnic Russians from the Russian Federation—Zelimkhan retorted somewhat indignantly: "Am *I* not Russian?"[95]

Chechens were now fighting *for* Russia, not against it as they were in the 1990s and 2000s. They were the "proof" that Crimea was a matter of Russia's statehood, not just a narrow ethnic dispute for Russia and Russians (although Ukrainians were still clearly traitors to the cause). As one Russian commentator noted: "Russians' attitudes toward Chechens have evolved in the last few decades. . . . During the Chechen wars, Chechens fought against Russia. With Kadyrov in power now, Chechens are viewed as being on the Russians' side, and for those who support the cause of the pro-Russian separatists in eastern Ukraine, reports of Chechen fighters are perceived as good news."[96] The Chechens' presence was the epitome of the unity of Russia and all Russian citizens, standing and fighting together in the face of an attack on the interests of the state.

Putin used another occasion, just after the August 2014 centenary of the outbreak of World War I, to stress the point of unity of all Russians no matter what their background. In another break with past narratives, although entirely in keeping with some of his previous commentary on the issue, Putin took a swipe at the role of the Bolsheviks in the First World War.[97] On August 29, 2014, at a meeting with participants in an annual Russian youth forum at Lake Seliger in the Tver region, Putin rebuked the Bolsheviks for pursuing their own narrow political goals in carrying out a revolution irrespective of the impact on the Russian state. "Regardless of how hurtful it might be to hear, perhaps, even to some of this audience, people who hold leftist views," Putin stated, ". . . in the First World War, the Bolsheviks wished to see their Fatherland defeated. And while the heroic Russian soldiers and officers shed their blood on the fronts in World War I, some were shaking Russia from within and shook it to the point that Russia as a state collapsed and declared itself defeated by a country that had lost the war. It is nonsense, it is absurd, but it happened! This was a complete betrayal of national interests!"[98]

In his meeting at Seliger and all of his speeches on these issues, Putin wanted to make sure that he was in control of the overall narrative. This was essential both for ensuring unity at home and for conducting the informational aspects of the new warfare. Crisis communication was key. Not only did Putin have to make sure that no one muddied or confused the message at home, he needed to be able to counteract competing interpretations of events that would be presented by Russia's opponents abroad. Indeed, the figures who became the main public advocates of the Russian nationalist perspective in this crisis period—including Sergei Glazyev, Alexander Dugin, and Alexander Prokhanov—exemplified this. They became the apparent ideologues of the Russian nationalist movement in 2014, with their commentaries, articles, and other publications framing and shaping the debate in Russia about the Eurasian Union, Ukraine and Crimea, and the role of the West. Abroad, they gained prominence in the Western media and were featured in articles alongside commentary on Putin's courting of the "European Right."[99] None of the three, however, was the Russian nationalist he appeared to be; nor were they independent, or alternative, political leaders with a mass following.

Glazyev, Dugin, and Prokhanov defined themselves explicitly as patriots. They were well-established figures in Russian political circles, all from the same mold as Vladimir Zhirinovsky and Dmitry Rogozin. Glazyev had played a number of prominent roles in Russian politics in the past (as discussed in chapter 3), both in parliament and in the formation of political parties, but always with an emphasis on the unity of the state. He was an acknowledged public figure with a background in economics. He had family ties to Ukraine (his mother was Ukrainian and he was born in the Ukrainian city of Zaporizhzhya). Glazyev was given a formal role as a presidential adviser on the Ukraine crisis. Dugin and Prokhanov were pseudo-intellectuals and "imperialists" who usually inhabited the fringes of political commentary. They were now mobilized into action and given center stage.

Alexander Dugin, who had played a leading role in the 1990s in the revival of Russian Eurasianist thought (see chapter 5), was by definition an all-Russianist, a unifier. He was not a "great Russian" particularist or ethnic, chauvinist nationalist. Dugin's theories, like those of his predecessors in the émigré circles after the Russian Revolution who dabbled in Eurasianism, fused ethnography, history, geography, and geopolitics together as a justification for the Russian state holding sway over its vast territory. The book that launched Dugin's career in the 1990s—*The Foundations of Geopolitics: The Geopolitical Future of Russia*—took part of its inspiration from a famous 1904 essay by British geographer Sir Halford Mackinder, "The Geopolitical Pivot of History."[100] Mackinder put Russia and the Eurasian landmass at the center of a great "heartland state" that all world powers would always seek to dominate and control. Dugin dusted off this theory and added new dimensions to show how and why Russia was always the focus of predatory action by the outside world. In this context, Dugin's fury with the events in Ukraine was fueled by the idea that Ukrainian nationalists, in the service of the United States, were bent on tearing apart the fraternal Russian-Slavic-Turkic Eurasian peoples. They were plucking away a piece of the great heartland state. Ukraine was yet another example of the centuries of efforts by the West to dismember the Russian state and seize the Eurasian heartland.

For his part, Alexander Prokhanov was a pure great-power imperialist, not a narrow Russian nationalist. Prokhanov was very open about his views and his role in shaping opinion, both at home and abroad, in an interview with American journalist Simon Shuster in *Time* magazine in May 2014.[101] Prokhanov even discussed the rationale for Putin and the Kremlin courting the European Right and trying to put the conservative international into play. He also stressed the need to tread carefully to make sure that nationalism did not blow up in Russia's face: "We have to take a two-faced approach [on nationalism]. . . . So far we've been able to control it at home, carefully steering these ideas toward neo-imperialism, toward the idea of a resurgent Russia. . . . We welcome what's happening in Europe. In some ways we even need it. But we also secretly fear it. . . . these nationalist tendencies could become a contagion that afflicts Russia as well."[102]

In short, Dugin and Prokhanov were operational tools in the informational and psychological aspect of the new warfare that Putin waged in Ukraine. They were useful domestically and internationally. At home they helped mobilize nationalists behind the Kremlin's cause. Abroad, they intimidated and confused. Given all of Putin's past references to Russian religious philosopher Ivan Ilyin, and Eurasianism, and his championing of the Eurasian Union, Western journalists and analysts assumed that Putin must have embraced Dugin's and Prokhanov's ideologies all along. In this interpretation, Putin was a closet Russian nationalist, they were his advisers, and in 2014 he had launched some kind of messianic program of neo-imperial Eurasianism that would take back territories of the former Soviet Union and Russian Empire.[103]

But the reality was that events were being shaped by Putin and the Kremlin, not by Dugin's and Prokhanov's commentary.[104] Dugin and Prokhanov were political weapons put into the service of the state. The timing of their sudden rise or resurrection in the public domain was entirely coincident with the crisis in Ukraine and Crimea. Their general melded idea of the *russkiy mir* at the core of a greater Eurasian imperium was a useful one for mobilizing those with national patriot sentiments. But as Prokhanov himself noted, this had its limits as well as risks. The whole geopolitical idea of a Eurasian imperial project could easily be misunderstood (it was certainly convoluted—Dugin had needed a whole book to scope it out). The concept of *russkiy mir* could pit Russians against other ethnic groups in the Russian Federation and send the state back down into another spiral of civil conflict. Russian nationalism always had to be countered with something else. And Dugin and Prokhanov also had to be kept in close check in case they got any ideas about attempting their own independent political operations.[105] Putin and the Kremlin had turned up the volume on Dugin and Prokhanov. They had to be able to turn it down again when the time came and their part of the operation was over.

PLAYING THE JEWISH CARD—CAREFULLY

In dealing with Ukraine, Putin also tapped into deep and dangerous currents of historic anti-Semitism that Shimon Peres had alluded to during his speech at the inauguration of Russia's Jewish Museum.[106] When he talked about Ukraine, Putin stressed the pogroms and other atrocities perpetrated against the Russian Empire's Jewish communities in the tsarist-era "Pale of Settlement"—the belt of territory across modern-day Poland, Ukraine, Belarus, Lithuania, Moldova, and parts of western Russia that the tsars designated for Jewish settlement through the nineteenth century. He had blamed Ukrainians for these, as well as for the slaughter of Jews during World War II. But Putin had neglected to note that it was Russia's tsars who officially restricted Jewish settlement inside this territorial zone; and he did not acknowledge the persistence of anti-Semitism among Russian nationalists, including some with close links to his own inner circle.[107]

If he was to succeed in depicting Ukraine as the sole repository of anti-Semitism in the tsarist and Soviet past, as well as the new source, then Putin had to put considerable distance between himself and Ukrainian extremists. He also had to tamp down the evidence of anti-Semitism in modern Russia, even though it was also a useful mobilizing tool in some political circles. In this vein, Putin pulled out another weapon in his arsenal—his carefully cultivated personal relationships with Russia's Jewish community, international Jewish leaders, and with Israel. At several points as the crisis heated up in Ukraine and Crimea, Putin met publicly with domestic and international Jewish leaders to highlight the horrors across the border in Ukraine.[108] He offered his personal protection to Russia's Jewish population during an audience with a delegation of rabbis in Moscow. At all these meetings, Putin's message was: I have proven my credentials. I keep anti-Semitism and extremism in check. I am dealing with the political heirs of Stepan Bandera, in Kyiv.

Putin's instrumentalization of these relationships was underscored by the fact that at the same time, other prominent Russian political figures were playing with the traditional symbols of anti-Semitism, without any rebuke from the Kremlin. During the protests in Ukraine in January 2014, for example, communist leader Gennady Zyuganov published on the Communist Party website his official statement about the developments. The statement was replete with a curious mishmash of references to the Ukrainian protesters as "pogromists," "fascists," "Nazis," "Hitlerites," "anti-Semites," as well as claims that the protests were being directed by the puppet masters of the "global oligarchy" and "world financial capital," who had subjected Ukraine to "kabala bondage." For anyone who didn't quite piece together the message from Zyuganov's jumble of code words, his statement was accompanied by a cartoon. The cartoon was very clear. The "puppet master" was represented as an American "Uncle Sam" figure with stereotypical Jewish features. It was the kind of cartoon, in content and style, widely circulated in anti-Semitic diatribes and publications.[109] In the cartoon's depiction, "Uncle Sam," the Jew, was orchestrating anti-Semitism in Ukraine.

The idea of orchestration and an outside plot was a staple of Russian state-sponsored propaganda extending back to the tsarist era. Sometime in the late 1890s, the tsarist secret police, the *Okhrana,* produced—and then in 1903 published—*The Protocols of the Elders of Zion,* which purported to document a plot by a Jewish oligarchy to control global media and financial markets. The document was translated into a number of languages and broadly disseminated. Revealed to be a forgery in the 1920s, it is still in print, is available on the Internet, and remains the source of conspiracy theories.[110] *The Protocols of the Elders of Zion* was part of an effort by the tsarist secret police to convince Russians and others that the Russian Empire was being targeted by a well-financed and well-organized conspiratorial group. The document was presented as a genuine item, but it was a piece of fiction. Other modern fictional works played a similar role in shaping opinions with the narratives and images they presented in the case of Operation Ukraine.

DYSTOPIAN UKRAINE

In the late 1990s and 2000s, a series of dystopian novels gained a kind of cult status in Russia, beginning with a short story published in 1997,

"Distill Iron from Blood," by Nick Perumov. The story offered the stark picture of Russia's destruction, occupation, and subjugation by a UN-led international peacekeeping force and focused on the resistance of a tiny group of youths who finally rally the rest of the population. This theme of a Russia invaded by international organizations dominated by the United States, and the subsequent battles to restore Russia's independence, runs through other essays and novels. In one 2005 novel, by Russian author Oleg Kulagin, the United States and Europe bring down the Russian government and carve up the country using non-Russian mercenaries from inside the state. Russia devolves into the kind of chaotic darkness Putin invoked in his annual address.[111] In the span of five months in early 2014, Russia's largest publishing house, Eksmo, also released a set of seven books about Ukraine as the key battlefield in a similar struggle for the future of Russia. This fantasy "Battlefield Ukraine" series became a frequent reference point for both Ukrainian and Russian commentators as the real battles in Ukraine unfolded.[112] In effect, the disturbing space of the novels played a role in the psychological operations of the new warfare Putin waged in 2013–14. Along with all the other references to plots and conspiracies, the novels bolstered the images of Russia and the *russkiy mir* pitted against the West in a struggle for survival.[113]

On August 9, 2014—15 years to the day after Vladimir Putin assumed power in Russia as prime minister—dystopia was brought to life on stage in a remarkable televised extravaganza in Crimea, nominally sponsored by a biker group known as the Night Wolves.[114] In its scale and excess, the show rivaled the opening and closing ceremonies of the Winter Olympics five months earlier in Sochi. Those ceremonies and the entire Olympics, Putin had said at the time, were designed to present the face of the new Russia to the world. This performance in Crimea was not for the world. It was for Russians. It presented not Russia's world, but the new Russia's view of the outside world. In keeping with the plots of the dystopian novels, the Night Wolves' performance staged a re-creation of the events leading up to the annexation of Crimea, showing the outside orchestration of the protests in Kyiv and the invasion of external forces. Protesters goose-stepped around the arena in the formation of a swastika, with dollar signs, Masonic symbols, and other code images for the United States, making it clear where the origins of the protest lay. A rock group belted out a song loaded with *Kievskaya Rus'* and *russkiy mir* slogans. Toward the end of performance, after Russian forces had intervened with an impressive show of force (armored vehicles took to the stage emblazoned with Russian flags) to engage in battle and save Crimea, the head of the Night Wolves called out Putin's name—President of the Russian Federation Vladimir Putin. The howl of the wolf echoed around the crowd.

In the grand finale, church bells pealed, fireworks exploded above the audience's head, and Putin's idea of the blended state appeared in the spotlight. A triumphal arch was crowned with the old Soviet emblem gilded with winged victory and the double-headed eagle. The Black Sea Fleet choir sang the old Soviet national anthem, with the original words. The imagery summed up the concept of restoration embodied in the annexation of Crimea—or the return of Crimea as Putin coined it.[115] Soviet and tsarist symbols were brought together with the restored state. The message was that the new Russia is not the USSR again. It is something different. It is a blended, pastiche new Russia. It is Vladimir Nabokov's "Komarovism" (see chapter 5). There was something for everyone—for the communists who wanted the old Soviet national anthem and symbols back again, and for nationalists who wanted the pre-revolutionary tsarist symbols.[116] And perhaps for the "new" Russians who wanted a different perspective, it was all done with ultra-modern, avant-garde staging and sleekness. The Night Wolves' extravaganza was the symbolic culmination of all the debates of the 1990s about the Russian Idea and its iconography. It was also intended to be the closing ceremony for the Crimean phase of Operation Ukraine.

MAN ON A MISSION: PUTIN'S NEW YALTA

A few days later, on August 14, 2014, Putin engaged in another piece of political theater. In contrast to the extravaganza only a week before, this event was surprisingly low key. It was also not shown on Russian television as the Night Wolves performance had been. This time Putin conveyed another message to the outside world. Addressing deputies of the Russian State Duma assembled not in Moscow but in Yalta, in the newly annexed Russian Republic of Crimea, Vladimir Putin declared:

> Regardless of the international political and economic situation, the most important thing for us now is our domestic affairs, our

goals and tasks set for us by the people of Russia, the citizens of Russia. We should focus on solving our national problems and tasks. It is important to ensure the high quality of state administration and civic institutions. And the most important of all is a high quality of life for the citizens of Russia.

The job is to develop this country in a calm, honest and efficient manner, without shutting out the rest of the world, without breaking ties with partners, but also without allowing a dismissive attitude or mentoring. Russian society needs to consolidate and mobilize itself, but not for war or conflict, not for resistance, but for hard work for Russia and in the name of Russia.[117]

Putin had come full circle. He entered office as president of Russia in 2000 with a focus on domestic affairs and national issues, to "develop the country in a calm, honest, and efficient manner." But in Putin's view of the world, he and his fellow Russian citizens were never permitted that inward focus on national issues, that calm development. The *peredyshka,* the breathing space, disappeared almost immediately as Russia grappled with its domestic agenda and attempted to solve its own problems in its own way. From Putin's perspective, the response from the outside world was not approval, but criticism, continued interference, and outright threats and aggression. In 2013–14, Putin mobilized the country to meet that threat.[118] In Yalta, in August 2014, he declared that the mission had been accomplished.

What Putin set out to accomplish in Operation Ukraine was the notion of strategic deterrence elaborated by his top military commander, General Gerasimov. It was deterrence against a "twenty-first-century war" that Putin and his security team concluded was being waged against Russia by the United States and the West. In Putin's mind as he made his August 2014 speech in Yalta, he had gotten what he wanted. Russia could no longer be ignored. Its objections would have to be taken seriously. He had annexed ("returned") Crimea. He had sparked a war in Ukraine. Russia had already fought a war in Georgia for similar reasons. Moscow's threats could not be dismissed as mere bluster and bluff, as they were in the 1990s under Putin's predecessor, Boris Yeltsin. From now on, when the United States or the European Union decided to act in Russia's neighborhood, or one of Russia's neighbors decided to invite them in, they would all have to consider that Russia would react. Putin would respond, in a real way. The United States and its allies would have to factor in the cost of taking certain actions.

Putin's speech in Yalta represented how Putin saw Russia's relationship to the world. It was a familiar message, but now framed by Ukraine in flames: Leave us alone. Let us build our own world inside Russia. Do not threaten us or encroach on our interests in our neighborhood. Putin had clearly chosen Yalta deliberately, given its location as the famous site of the 1945 great-power conference that sketched out a settlement for the end of World War II. The Yalta Conference had outlined respective spheres of influence for the wartime allies. Now Putin was proposing a similar settlement with the West. It was, granted, a unilateral settlement. But from Putin's point of view, the United States had superseded the Cold War order, unilaterally, in 1991. Post-Soviet Russia agreed to the post–Cold War settlement of 1991 in the same way as post-tsarist Russia acceded to the Treaty of Brest-Litovsk in March 1918, ending Russia's involvement in World War I. For Lenin, Brest-Litovsk and its harsh terms were necessities dictated by the Russian weakness of the time. The treaty would inevitably be overturned when circumstances and capabilities changed—as they did in World War II. Brest-Litovsk was an armistice, not a peace treaty, and never a final settlement. Putin—and many other Russians—had viewed the events of 1991 in the same way: as a tactical necessity, waiting to be supplanted.

As the Operative Abroad, Putin was on a mission: to defend Russia and repel the expansion and intervention of the West (NATO, the EU, the United States). Within this larger mission, there were many individual operations that required different tactics and tools. War against Georgia was necessary in 2008, but war against Ukraine at that time was not because Kyiv had backed away from NATO. Yanukovych's ouster (or flight) as Moscow's essential proxy in Ukraine changed the situation in 2014. The underlying mission remained the same, but the nature of the operation in Ukraine shifted. Putin had to move from classic Case Officer tactics to deploy new weapons including the use of real military force.

Putin always thought in terms of missions for himself. He posed his first mission in 1999, before he was even elected president of Russia, and spoke about it in the interviews for *Ot pervogo litsa*. He would resolve the issue of Chechnya and the North Caucasus to prevent Russia from collapsing like the Soviet Union. Putin declared that he told himself that this was "my mission, [my] historical mission," and he was determined to accomplish it, even if it meant the end of his career as a politician. "That may sound like bombast," he told his biographers. "But it's the truth."[119] Then and now, for Putin, being "on a mission" means reconciling himself to the notion that it could (at least figuratively) be a suicide mission, as it had nearly been for his father fighting behind enemy lines in World War II. But if you planned ahead and prepared contingencies, then you might just survive.

A NEW NORMAL?

With one part of the mission behind him and Crimea wrested from enemy hands, Putin's speech in Yalta was a call to return to what he viewed as a normal condition for Russia. Russians would return to focusing on their domestic concerns; the outside world would leave Russia alone. But was that possible? Operation Ukraine had done considerable damage to Russia's domestic development and its relations with Ukraine as well as with the United States and Europe. Putin's actions in 2014 alienated the world outside Russia more than any other set of actions in the decades since the collapse of the USSR. They put Russia on a different and dangerous course. In contrast with the Georgia war in 2008, the United States and Europe imposed a raft of sanctions against Russia that were targeted at interests reaching deep into Putin's one-boy network. At its summit in Wales in September 2014, NATO proposed new defensive measures against Russia that would extend close to Russia's borders. Opinion polls in Ukraine showed deep animosity toward Putin and Russia that had not been previously observed and a heightened interest in a closer association with the EU and Western institutions.[120]

Acts of aggression against another country, no matter what the motivation, have lasting consequences. They create resentments and new grievances that persist for decades and shape the attitudes and policies of subsequent generations. This was something Putin knew well and had reflected on. In *Ot pervogo litsa,* Putin was asked whether the Soviet interventions into Hungary in 1956 and Czechoslovakia in 1968 were big mistakes. Yes, they were, he replied. "And you didn't even mention that we used force in East Germany in 1953. . . . They were all big mistakes, in my opinion. And the Russophobia that we have today in Eastern Europe, that's the result of those mistakes."[121]

Ukraine was now bristling with anti-Russian sentiment fueled by the relentless barrage of propaganda launched against the country, its government, and people. Inside Russia, the domestic front of Operation Ukraine, Putin had distorted the information space by manipulating history and blatantly fomenting Russian nationalism. These were operational weapons in his and Russia's "new warfare" arsenal. Fearsome and effective, they would, like traditional weapons, be laid aside once they were no longer needed. But this would not be so easy—as Alexander Prokhanov had told *Time* magazine in May 2014. Nationalist and populist ideas, along with stories and rumors, have lives of their own. For too many people the propaganda and the lie become the truth, not an expediency for temporary use. True believers and their deeply held myths cannot easily be contained, as the history of *The Protocols of the Elders of Zion* underscores. What the Operative in the Kremlin and abroad turned on in 2014 would not be turned off again for a long time.

In Operation Ukraine, outrageous stories and conspiracy theories proliferated and persisted in Russia. They were circulated as part of the Kremlin's information war, which depicted the West as waging war against Russia, and Putin as trying to keep Russia out of the bloody chaos. With his propaganda onslaught in 2013–14, Putin managed to move Russia psychologically back to where he began his own professional career in the 1980s, with perceptions of threats, fears of an American attack, and alarm over a possible nuclear war that reverberated across Europe and the Atlantic. By engaging in the same sort of worst-case thinking as Yury Andropov and his other KGB mentors had done, and because of his inability to understand the mindset of Americans and Europeans and their political dynamics, Putin moved toward a Russian worldview that was far closer to that of the Soviet world of the 1980s than outside observers realized. Putin's—Russia's—world was now very different from the world of the West.

CODA

THE OPERATIVE IN ACTION

CODA
THE OPERATIVE IN ACTION

WE HAVE TRIED TO ANSWER the question of who is Mr. Putin and what motivates him to do what he does. Here, in this coda, we put this understanding and these insights to the test. Based on what we have written, we consider what lessons we have learned and what advice we might offer on how to deal with him. The 2014 conflict between Russia and the West over Ukraine convinced us that some observers of the crisis have several, potentially very dangerous, misconceptions about Putin. These fall into the category of underestimating him in a couple of important respects, and then overestimating him—or failing to understand his limitations—in others. First, many in the West underestimate Putin's willingness to fight for as long and as hard (and as dirty) as necessary to achieve his goals. Vladimir Putin will use all methods available, and he will be ruthless. Second, Western observers misread his skill as a strategist. Putin is not, as some have said, a mere tactician. He thinks strategically, and he has great advantages over Western leaders in his ability to translate that thinking into action. What we often fail to appreciate, however, is how dangerously little Putin understands about *us*—our motives, our mentality, and, also, our values. Only by trying to appreciate how Putin sees us can we see the logic in his actions—the logic *he* follows—and thereby get some idea of what he wants, where he might be headed, in Ukraine and elsewhere in Europe and Eurasia.

With this in mind we offer some preliminary conclusions about the war in Ukraine that Putin sparked in 2014 and thoughts about what

Putin's endgame is in Russia's neighborhood. All of this is offered with the obvious caveat that the story of Mr. Putin and Ukraine, and of Russia's relations with the United States and Europe, was still progressing as this manuscript was completed.

First, Vladimir Putin needs to be taken seriously. He will make good on every promise or threat. If Putin says he will do something, then he is prepared to do it, and he will find a way of doing it, using *every* method at his disposal. From Putin's biographical materials—beginning with *Ot pervogo litsa* and his early interviews—Putin and his Kremlin team wanted domestic and international audiences to conceive of him as a scrappy little street fighter (a little thug in Masha Gessen's depiction in *The Man without a Face*). All the stories laid out in these early materials and the subsequent embellishments were framed by the outbreak of the second war in Chechnya; but they also were intended to have a shelf life for future events. Their purpose was to underscore that if Vladimir Putin gets into a fight, then he is prepared to fight to the end. He will keep on fighting, even if he gets beaten up (as a kid), or risks losing his position (as the official leader of Russia), or has to embark on a potential suicide mission (as his father did during World War II). Vladimir Putin may be an underdog—he's small in stature, he seems weaker than his opponents, he was always in secondary, never high-profile, positions until the late 1990s—but he uses these and other attributes to his advantage.

In short, Vladimir Putin is a fighter and he is a survivalist. He won't give up, and he will fight dirty if that's what it takes to win. He didn't give up as a kid in the Leningrad courtyards. He didn't give up in Chechnya. He won't give up in Ukraine or elsewhere in Russia's neighborhood. Vladimir Putin's rules for street fighting are essentially the same as his principles in domestic and foreign politics. Establish credibility and don't back down until the advantage is yours and you've made your point. Once your opponent has capitulated and you have established your turf and terms, then you can patch things up and move on—until the next showdown comes along. Whether the stories Putin and his team tell about his childhood fights are all true or not, Putin's martial arts training lends them some veracity. It also brings in another dimension. Putin began with judo and the somewhat rougher Russian variant called sambo at an early age. Judo gave Putin a more disciplined and ritualized approach to fighting. It helped him overcome his own weaknesses in terms of his size and strength relative to others. Judo moved the street kid from anything-goes scraps into formalized matches. It gave him insight and techniques to figure out ways of pushing bigger, stronger opponents to the mat while protecting himself.

In the domestic and foreign policy arenas, Putin constantly sizes up his opponents and probes for physical and psychological weaknesses. Putin's adaptation of Nixon's "Madman Theory" approach helps flush out these weaknesses—it helps gauge reactions: They think I'm dangerous and unpredictable. How do they respond to this? Have I got them unbalanced and on the back foot as a result? Then Putin tests his opponents to see if they mean what they say: Will they also be prepared to fight, and fight to the end? If they are not, then he will exploit their empty threats to show them up, intimidate, deter, and defeat them. If they are prepared to fight, and he is outweighed or outgunned by his adversaries, then he will look for unconventional moves that get around their defenses so that he can outmaneuver them. In judo you can win on points over the course of a series of matches even if you are far smaller than your opponent and lose some of the individual rounds.

Much of this is borne out by events since Putin became president. As we have shown in the book, all of Putin's tactics at home and abroad are geared toward gaining advantage against his opponents—be they oligarchs and opposition figures in Russia, or Western leaders and international organizations. To maximize the tactical advantage, Putin and the Kremlin work very hard at making him as inscrutable and unpredictable as possible. Access to Putin is strictly limited. His image is carefully branded and rebranded. Putin's appearances and public pronouncements are highly orchestrated and well prepared. They are timed for maximum effect so that his audiences will hang on his every word—looking for any indication of what he might think, or what he might do next. The Kremlin maintains an almost complete unity of silence and message. When messages seem to be transmitted without approval, they are accompanied by equal measure of dis/misinformation. All of this deliberately complicates the task of the political opponent (as well as the outside analyst or biographer). Vladimir Putin is, and is supposed to be, unknowable to the outsider. The goal is to keep everyone confused and off balance.

These points can be traced through some of the events we refer to in the book. In Georgia in 2008, for example, Putin called the West's bluff about standing by its friends—which is what U.S. secretary of state Condoleezza Rice told Georgian president Mikheil Saakashvili the West would do during a visit to Tbilisi shortly before the August war. From Putin's perspective, given all the emphasis the Bush administration put on Georgia in its foreign policy, he thought this meant that the United States was prepared to fight militarily, not just rhetorically, for Georgia. Moscow was steeled for a possible fight with NATO. Many Russian officials in private meetings with the authors related the tension in Moscow security circles in August 2008. They talked of the fear in the Russian military that the United States and NATO would strike back and that they might then have to face a NATO force in some form, not just the Georgian army. When the United States and NATO did not come to Georgia's aid militarily, and the European Union, with then French President Nicholas Sarkozy out in front, rushed to broker a ceasefire, there was a sigh of relief in Moscow. NATO was still a formidable conventional fighting force, of course, but it did not have the political will to fight for partners outside the alliance and the frame of Article 5—even if (as in the case of Georgia) those partners were fighting alongside NATO forces in coalitions in Afghanistan and Iraq. Putin understood that the United States' security priorities were focused elsewhere. The West wanted to contain Russia on the cheap in Europe and Eurasia. The United States, NATO, and the EU would do everything they could to head off another major military confrontation, a "World War III," in Europe.

However, from Putin's perspective, there might come a point in the future where those priorities would change for the United States and NATO. If so, he would have to think in terms of such a worst-case scenario. We are convinced that this is exactly how Putin thinks, because contrary to the prevailing external assessment, Putin is a strategic planner. The notion that Putin is an opportunist, at best an improviser, but not a strategist, is a dangerous misread. Putin thinks, plans, and acts strategically. But as we have stressed in the book, for Putin, strategic planning is contingency planning. There is no step-by-step blueprint. There are strategic objectives, and there are many ways to achieve those objectives. Exactly what Putin's next step will be toward his objectives depends on the circumstances. It also depends on how his adversary reacts.

Putin has the same priorities today that he laid out in December 1999 just before the beginning of his presidency. His larger strategic goal is ensuring the defense of Russia's interests—which are tightly fused with, and now largely inseparable from, his own and his system's interests. As Russia's president, Putin is the Statist set on restoring, consolidating, and defending Russia's position. As the CEO of Russia, Inc., Putin's task is to protect the core assets of the economic system that he controls and which is managed by his inner circle. In both guises, Putin has to figure out how to plan for the present and future under conditions of economic and political uncertainty. Putin knows unexpected events can and will blow things off course in domestic and foreign policy. The key to dealing with the unexpected is to anticipate that there *always* will be setbacks. This means he focuses on contingency and adaptive planning to deal with them. He needs back-up plans and resources ready whenever they come along. Having back-up plans means learning from past mistakes as well as successes. It means reducing risk and vulnerability for the future. Putin has consistently shown that he can learn from his own policy or tactical mistakes at home and abroad. In his pronouncements and actions, Putin has emphasized the importance of operational flexibility and of maximizing options so he can adapt to changes in Russia's internal and external environment as he goes along.

Another aspect of Putin's strategic approach is to simplify and streamline his leadership at home and his interactions abroad. By creating a system in which he has to deal with only a small number of actors, Putin frees himself from having to deal with details and messy dynamics. He identifies and recruits people who can deliver results and holds onto them. Inside Russia, Inc., Putin creates incentives, rewards, and rules to keep his core team together. He does not micromanage; he *monitors*. He checks in periodically to make sure everyone in his core team and at lower operational levels knows what they're doing; and he steps in only if things go wrong and he has to put things back on track. He insists on cohesion and consensus—keeping his challengers as much as possible in his "big tent." He shows them respect, gives their ideas a regular hearing, and gives them a stake in the system. But *anyone* who breaks the rules or terms he has laid down in domestic and foreign policy is punished severely—from Mikhail Khodorkovsky to Mikheil Saakashvili.

Again, this plays out in foreign policy events. As we discuss in the book, Putin clearly had decided sometime before the Munich Security Conference in 2007 that he eventually would have to confront the United

States on what he perceived to be its destabilizing behavior, with something more forceful than heightened rhetoric. In the case of Georgia, Putin knew that Mikheil Saakashvili was going to keep on pushing to reassert Georgia's control over the secessionist republics of Abkhazia and South Ossetia, including trying to retake them by force if he felt he had to or could. Saakashvili never hid this intention. He often spoke of it to outside interlocutors, including to the authors on two occasions several years apart. Saakashvili also made it clear that he would keep pressing for NATO membership. So Putin had contingency plans prepared, including the armed forces' annual summer exercises in the North Caucasus military district. Sure enough, Saakashvili tripped the wire in 2008. After the Georgia war, Putin and his team looked back over the conflict and examined what had gone wrong in detail. They looked at Russia's large-scale military operations first in Chechnya and then in Georgia and at the West's responses. They decided that they needed to do something different when the next time came along.

The next time was Ukraine. Putin first took the 2011–12 protests as a signal that the West had opened another front of attack, and he would need to take immediate preparatory action. Putin set Valery Gerasimov and Sergei Shoigu to work at the end of 2012 to mobilize Russia for fighting this new twenty-first-century war with the West. Putin's second signal was the European association agreements in 2013, combined with the EU's decision to initiate its Third Energy Package and the financial crisis in Cyprus in March 2013. All this revealed how negative attitudes toward Russia had become in Brussels and Berlin. Initially in Ukraine, Putin thought he had the situation under control with the venal and vulnerable Victor Yanukovych in place. But he had bet on the wrong horse. Yanukovych could be blackmailed, but he couldn't keep control of Ukraine. Once it became clear that Yanukovych had "no political future"—which may have been in December 2013, when the protests in Kyiv stepped up, or not until February 2014, when things really got out of hand—Putin had to make sure his backup plans were in place. Annexing Crimea and setting the rest of Ukraine on fire were contingency operations. They were prepared in advance, ready to be used if needed—but only if needed.

Unexpected future events would also have to be dealt with. The downing of Malaysian Airlines Flight MH17 in the midst of the fighting over eastern Ukraine in July 2014 was one of those: It was a particularly tragic example of events blowing plans off course. Until the Malaysian Airlines disaster, the European Union had been lukewarm on imposing sanctions on Russia in response to the annexation of Crimea. MH17 was a game changer for Europe. Most of the casualties were Europeans, citizens of one of Russia's closest trading partners, the Netherlands (and as it turned out as a result of all the bad press, the sometime home of one of Putin's daughters). However, this event was not a game changer for Putin. He would stick to his overall strategy. But he would adapt his tactics to the new circumstances, the new "input." Putin had already anticipated that there would be sanctions—they were a favored punitive foreign policy tool of the United States, even if the United States had been reluctant to apply them in Georgia in 2008. Putin had started to prepare for this inevitability in advance. He had tried to boost Russia's overall economic leverage with the West, and he had pushed to de-offshore and diversify trade once he was back in the presidency. Now Putin would have to find ways of dealing with an intensified level of sanctions—including through non-economic means. In the case of MH17, Putin hit back with Russia's own (asymmetric) sanctions accompanied by a barrage of propaganda and misinformation to confuse the issue, sow doubt, and deflect attention away from who might actually have shot down the plane and why. *And* he stepped up the military aspects of the conflict in eastern Ukraine. He did not back down in any meaningful way.

All of this is consistent with the identities that we describe in the first section of the book. As we have already stated, Putin is primarily the Statist and the Survivalist when it comes to foreign policy—his priority is the defense of Russia and his position. When Putin prepares for action abroad he falls back on his Case Officer identity and methods, including resorting to forms of blackmail, intimidation, punishment, and blatant distortion of the truth. Lies are part of the coin of the intelligence operative, and facts are fungible. Here, the History Man identity is fused with the Case Officer. History is a tool, and as a student of Russian history, Putin knows how to use narratives and symbolic events as weapons in waging information war. The Free Marketeer identity comes into play along with the Case Officer and History Man. Putin relies on wheeling and dealing and exploiting the economic vulnerabilities of others to gain additional leverage. He uses this to the same effect abroad as he does at home—pulling on strings tied to French shipbuilders, German business-men, and American oilmen.

The one identity that does not quite play out in foreign policy in the same way it does at home is the Outsider. For an individual's status as an Outsider to be a strength, the way it was for Putin as he rose to power, that person has to be outside the inner circle, the elite, the decisionmak-ers, *but close enough to observe and analyze them*. That is not Putin's position in relation to the United States and Europe. He *does* live and operate "in another world," as Chancellor Angela Merkel reportedly put it in March 2014. But the effective Outsider cannot live in a differ-ent world than those he observes. He has to live in the same world so that he can understand—and critique—how those "on the inside" think. Putin has only a handful of contacts with U.S. and European insiders and thus a very incomplete grasp of what motivates or drives Western leaders. Finding himself too far outside their political perspectives and interactions, Putin falls back on his (and Russia's) age-old threat percep-tions. He looks for, and finds, plots and conspiracies. The plots he finds are consistent with his logic. They make sense in terms of his frame of reference—as seen through his filters of the Cold War, the KGB, his time in Dresden, and the prevailing political views of conservative and patri-otic Russia circles. This does not mean that the plots exist or that his views are correct. Putin's "too-far-outside," other-world, perspective is a source of weakness in this respect, not strength. Vladimir Putin has spent a great deal of time in his professional life bending the truth, manipulat-ing facts, and playing with fictions. He is also, we conclude, not always able to distinguish one from the other; his tools for doing so often are inadequate. This is a source of danger in Russia's relations with the West.

The United States and Europe encourage political and economic change as a matter of course in their foreign policies. The essence of Western political systems extends to promoting democracy and liberal markets abroad. Western leaders and their populations see this as benign. From Vladimir Putin's perspective, it is not at all benign. Western-style democracy and open markets are a clear threat to a Russian political system that thrives as a closed one-boy network and an economic pro-tection racket. The United States and the EU have not set out, as Putin assumes, to overturn his regime in a color revolution. But many Western politicians and opinion leaders have made it very clear that they would like to see the political system in Russia changed and another leader with a more Western outlook take Putin's place. Given the frequent references in the Western press to the prospect of a Russia without Putin, and Putin's own mindset, it is unlikely that he will be convinced that the United States and Europe are not "out to get rid of him." The escalating sequence of events in Ukraine in 2014—with successive rounds of Western sanctions, NATO's stepped-up defenses, and calls for military assistance to Ukraine have further darkened Putin's views about the West and deepened his convictions about its malign intent.

As many scholars of international affairs and psychologists have pointed out, perceptions and misperceptions are as potent as actual facts. Once an erroneous set of views takes hold, it is hard to refute and change them. In the case of Putin, his mindset is deeply rooted. The West will find it hard to change his views. From his perspective, Putin has no reliable interlocutors in the West, only a handful of intermediaries. And he simply does not trust anyone. Any effort to persuade him that he has misread the situation in some definitive, black-and-white way will likely be seen as a ploy. Restoring a degree of trust is not impossible, but it will be extremely difficult. In the meantime, the West will have to deal with the reality of Putin's views: the fact that he *does* think differently from his U.S. and European counterparts. He *does* see the West as a threat to him and his system.

So what about the conflict in Ukraine that Putin sparked in 2014? What does he want; and what might he do next? As he laid out in his August 2014 speech in Crimea, Putin seeks a "New Yalta" with the West in political and security terms. As he defines Moscow's sphere of influence in this new arrangement, that sphere extends to all the space in Europe and Eurasia that once fell within the boundaries of the Russian Empire and the USSR. Within these vast contours, Putin and Russia have interests that need to be taken into account, interests that override those of all others. For Putin, Russia is the *only* sovereign state in this neighborhood. None of the other states, in his view, has truly independent standing—they all have contingent sovereignty. The only question for Putin is which of the real sovereign powers (Russia or the United States) prevails in deciding where the borders of the New Yalta finally end up after 2014.

Unlike the old Yalta of the post–World War II Soviet period, Putin's New Yalta does not extend to economics. Putin wants preferential, even protectionist, provisions for the Russian economy, but he does not espouse the creation of rigid opposing economic blocs or autarky. That simply will not work in today's global economy. Putin does not want to put Russia on a path to international isolation. He wants, as he says, economic and geopolitical "demand" for Russia. He does not want Russia to end up being a pariah state like North Korea. Putin has made sure Russia has foreign policy and trade options to avoid this fate. He has diversified foreign policy and forged new multilateral and bilateral relations outside the Euro-Atlantic system. At the same time, Putin does not want to completely jettison Russia's ties with the United States and Europe. This is neither practical nor possible, nor even desirable, given the past two decades of interaction and integration. Putin also still holds out hope for making good on his Germany wager—by persuading Germans that all is not lost and that Berlin can return to the close economic and political relations with Moscow that prevailed until the crisis in Ukraine.

In short, in spite of his decision to go to war in Georgia in 2008 and again in Ukraine in 2014, Putin still wants to do business with the West. In political terms, this means collaboration when security interests actually do overlap. He and Russia can work with the United States and the EU on dealing with issues like Iran and curbing its nuclear weapons systems, or dismantling Syrian chemical weapons, or containing the activities of militant Islamist extremists across the Middle East and in Afghanistan. In his view there is no need to cut off cooperation on issues where there is a mutual strategic interest. Indeed, it is only by having a place at the international diplomatic table on these and other issues that Putin can protect Russia's position. Putin will not cut off diplomatic ties if this will hurt Russia. But most of all, Putin is concerned about the economy. He literally wants to *do business*—trade and investment—with the West. In this case, he is an exaggerated version of his former self as deputy mayor of St. Petersburg in charge of external relations. He is still the Free Marketeer, presiding over Russian economic relations, wheeling and dealing. Putin eventually wants to put the war in Ukraine aside, separate it off—war is war, but business is business. Western politicians want to fight with me, Vladimir Putin, but their businessmen want to keep working with Russia.

In the meantime, until a New Yalta is thrashed out, Russia and the West will remain at war. They will be fighting a new war that is fought everywhere with nonmilitary as well as military means. Ultimately, in pursuing his goals as the Statist, Putin remains a pragmatist. In figuring out how to prevail in this war, Putin knows that Russia does not have the economic or military resources for the old Soviet (and Russian) mass-army, total mobilization approach to defending its interests. Given the contemporary balance of forces, Russia will always lose in such a conflict. The United States, NATO members, and other de facto U.S. allies have a collective GDP more than ten times that of Russia's as well as more conventional arms. Putin needs to avoid a good old-fashioned twentieth-century war (even a small one) and accomplish his goals without resorting to total mobilization. Twenty-first-century wars involve targeted non-military efforts. They are the least disruptive to the normal functioning of the Russian economy even though they can also be very damaging.

In Ukraine and elsewhere in Russia's neighborhood, Putin wants the West to sue for peace without jumping into the military war phase. The 2014 war is essentially a big (war) game of "chicken." Based on the West's past performance in Georgia, Putin anticipated that the West would blink first in Ukraine, balking at the high costs of the confrontation, which he had laid out very clearly with his offensive defense. Ukraine would burn in the east and the flames would fan out further and further. On the very occasion of their anniversaries, the conflagrations of the twentieth century would be reignited in the same territories in the twenty-first. The Cold War decades would end with another hot war, not a cold peace.

This game of chicken will be a long one. Putin's goal is security for Russia and his system. The means to achieve that goal is deterrence. As has often been pointed out, the Russian word for security, *bezopasnost'*, means literally "absence of danger or threat." As a result, there is no definitive endgame. Putin will keep on playing as long as he perceives the threat to last. Even if he does secure a New Yalta deal in some form, he has no intention of abandoning his new warfare, because it is his way of deterring threats. In his and his team's conception of the new twenty-first-century warfare, there are no real declarations of war, and thus no real peace settlements—only partial cease-fires. Putin will keep all options open. He will continue to enhance Russia's capabilities. He will calibrate and recalibrate his actions based on the responses and reactions of his opponents. Putin will make sure his threats of Russian military action remain credible. Vladimir Putin is not Boris Yeltsin, and Putin's Russia has not resembled Yeltsin's Russia or been run like Yeltsin's Russia for a very long time.

In the 1990s whenever Yeltsin did not take strong action on issues inimical to Russia's interests, U.S. and European leaders routinely assumed that this was because Yeltsin had made a strategic decision not to do so. When Yeltsin objected to NATO expansion or NATO's intervention in Yugoslavia, his verbal complaints were considered perfunctory. Yeltsin, Western leaders concluded, had made good relations with the West a priority, no matter what. But Yeltsin and Russia were heavily indebted to the West. The economy was in ruins, the political system was a shambles, the security structures were gutted. In many respects, Yeltsin could not act in the 1990s because Russia was constrained. If Yeltsin made a threat, it was empty. He did not have the resources or the capacity to back it up.

Vladimir Putin has no such constraints. Sanctions hurt, but they do not deter him as they deterred Yeltsin. Putin has the capacity to act, and he is willing to deter the West. Putin has even put the nuclear option on the table to "scare the hell out of" the West. Being the Case Officer, Putin knows he has to make the West think he *will* use nuclear weapons if the war moves to the military phase, not just that he *might* use them. This is the ultimate deterrent. Putin is not hell-bent on destroying Russia or his presidency and his system. He will have a contingency for deploying nuclear weapons if he feels he needs to, but he is still the Survivalist. Putin wants the Russian state to survive with him at its head, even as he wants to push the United States and Europe away from Russia and out of its neighborhood.

As far as what Vladimir Putin might do next, it seems rather clear: He will keep Ukraine boiling, and he will probe and poke, and prepare for contingency operations elsewhere in the neighborhood. Putin will rely on asymmetry and the element of tactical surprise, whenever and wherever he strikes next, for maximum effect. Beyond Ukraine, *all* of Eastern Europe, the former Soviet bloc, has vulnerabilities from the Case Officer's perspective. Baltic states such as Estonia have shaky border agreements with Russia; they also have many Russian speakers without citizenship, as well as economic ties to Russia. All can be used to good effect. Old Cold War methods can be deployed across the region that fall short of the threshold of triggering an armed response from NATO. Ships can be interdicted near Russian waters, air defenses can be penetrated, weapons systems and army maneuvers can move closer and closer to vulnerable land and sea borders. If sleeper agents were still operating in Germany as recently as 2011, the chances are that plenty of other Russian operatives are in place across the old Soviet bloc, collecting compromising and operational information and waiting to subvert governments, discredit individual leaders who challenge Russia, and block any actions that run counter to Russian interests. Across the rest of Europe, economic leverage can be applied, fifth columns can be activated, and foreign businessmen, journalists, regular citizens, activists, and operatives can all be detained on various charges of violating Russian borders or laws. These methods, and many more, are tools that Putin can apply if NATO or the EU keep on pressing forward in Ukraine, or take more escalatory measures against Russia, or start to contemplate further expansion.

Putin's operational aims will continue to be to find the weaknesses in Western defenses, to goad and intimidate Western leaders and publics, and to make sure everyone knows he will make good on his threats. The onus will now be on the West to shore up its own home defenses, reduce the economic and political vulnerabilities, and create its own contingency plans if it wants to counter Vladimir Putin's new twenty-first-century warfare.

CHRONOLOGY

1952
October 7: Vladimir Vladimirovich Putin is born in Leningrad, USSR

1953
March 5: Soviet leader Josef Stalin dies

1956
February: Nikita Khrushchev delivers "secret speech" at the Twentieth Congress of the Soviet Communist Party
October: Hungarian uprising begins

1964
October: Khrushchev deposed; Leonid Brezhnev becomes general secretary of the Communist Party

1967
May: Yury Andropov is appointed head of KGB

1973
October: Arab oil embargo

1975
Putin graduates from Leningrad State University with law degree and begins KGB career

1979–89
Soviet war in Afghanistan

1982
November: Brezhnev dies; succeeded by Yury Andropov

1983
July 28: Putin marries Lyudmila Shkrebneva

1984

February: Andropov dies; succeeded
by Konstantin Chernenko

Fall: Putin begins one-year course
at KGB Red Banner Institute in
Moscow

1985

March: Chernenko dies; succeeded
by Mikhail Gorbachev

August: Putin posted to Dresden,
East Germany

1987

January: Gorbachev declares
glasnost, perestroika, and
democratization

1989

July 6: Gorbachev gives "Europe as
a Common House" address at
Council of Europe

November 9: Berlin Wall falls

1990

January: Putin returns from
Dresden to Leningrad; serves
as assistant to vice rector of
Leningrad State University

—Gorbachev announces Soviet
republics have right to secede
from USSR

May: Anatoly Sobchak becomes
chairman of Leningrad City
Council; asks Putin to become
his adviser for international
affairs

—Boris Yeltsin elected chairman
(speaker) of Russian Supreme
Soviet (upper house of
parliament)

June: Russian Congress of People's
Deputies (lower house of
parliament) adopts "Declaration
on the Sovereignty of Russia"

1991

June 12: Boris Yeltsin elected
president of Russia

June: Sobchak becomes mayor of
St. Petersburg

August: Putin appointed head of
St. Petersburg's Committee for
External Relations

August 19–21: "August Putsch"—
failed attempted coup against
Gorbachev

August 24: Ukraine declares
independence

November: Yeltsin appoints Yegor
Gaidar as deputy prime minister

—Chechnya secedes from Soviet
Union

—Valery Zorkin becomes
chairman of Russian
Constitutional Court

December: Yeltsin and leaders
of Ukraine and Belarus sign
Belovezhsky Accord, effectively
dissolving USSR and creating
Commonwealth of Independent
States (CIS)

1991–92

Winter: St. Petersburg food scandal exposed, as is Putin's involvement in scheme

1992

January: Yeltsin launches Yegor Gaidar's "shock therapy" program

February: President Yeltsin and U.S. president George H. W. Bush issue joint declaration that Russia and United States are no longer enemies

May: Five-year-long civil war in Tajikstan begins

June: Gaidar named acting prime minister of Russia

July: UN and international peace-keeping forces intervene in Bosnia-Herzegovina

November: UN resolution calls for Russia to remove troops from Baltic states

December: Viktor Chernomyrdin replaces Gaidar as Russian prime minister

1993

March: Russian Congress of People's Deputies motion to impeach Yeltsin narrowly fails

September 21: Yeltsin dissolves Congress of People's Deputies and Supreme Soviet

October 4: Yeltsin orders shelling of "White House" (parliament building)

—Valery Zorkin forced to resign chairmanship of Constitutional Court

December: Parliamentary elections held; new Russian constitution approved by national referendum and goes into effect, giving increased powers to president

1994

January: NATO launches Partnership for Peace (PfP)

February: Russian Federation concludes bilateral treaty with constituent republic of Tatarstan

August: Final withdrawal of Russian troops from Baltic states

December: First Chechen war begins

1995

March: "Loans for shares" idea first floated by Vladimir Potanin at Russian cabinet meeting

August: Yeltsin signs decree authorizing "loans for shares" program

December: Russian Communist Party dominates elections to new lower house of parliament, Russian State Duma

1996

May: Moscow concludes cease-fire with Chechnya

June 16: Yeltsin fails to secure majority in first round of presidential election

July: Sobchak loses St. Petersburg
mayoral election
—Yeltsin defeats Communist
Party candidate Gennady
Zyuganov in second round
of presidential election and is
reelected president
—Yeltsin appoints Anatoly
Chubais as chief of staff
—Yeltsin instructs Satarov
group to come up with new
"Russian Idea"
August: Putin moves to Moscow;
named deputy in Kremlin
property department;
St. Petersburg associate Alexei
Kudrin named head of Main
Control Directorate (GKU)
—Vladimir Potanin appointed
deputy prime minister
—First Chechen war ends with
peace accords signed by
Alexander Lebed on behalf
of federal government
October: Boris Berezovsky
appointed deputy head of
Russian Security Council
November: Putin's Ozero dacha
collective formally registered
—Yeltsin undergoes multiple
bypass surgery for heart attack
suffered during presidential
election rounds in summer

1997
March: After recuperating from
heart attack, Yeltsin returns and
delivers his *poslaniye* (annual
message to parliament) on
restoring order to the state
—Kudrin named first deputy
finance minister; Putin
succeeds him as head of
GKU
May: Yeltsin signs final version of
peace treaty and related bilateral
agreements with Chechen
president in Moscow
June: Putin defends dissertation for
graduate degree in economics at
St. Petersburg Mining Institute
July: Russian government sells
Svyazinvest shares to Vladimir
Potanin, triggering "Bankers'
War"
August: Alfred Kokh resigns as
head of State Privatization
Committee after scandal over
relationship with Potanin
November: Kokh and other
members of Chubais team
accused of taking bribes as
"book fees"; Chubais allies fired
from government positions

1998
March: Chernomyrdin dismissed
as prime minister, replaced by
Sergei Kirienko
May: Putin appointed first deputy
director of presidential adminis-
tration in charge of work with
Russia's regions
July: Putin named head of FSB

August 17: Russia defaults on
sovereign debt; devalues ruble
August 23: Kirienko sacked as
prime minister
September 8: Yevgeny Primakov
confirmed as prime minister

1999

May: Primakov resigns and is
replaced by Sergei Stepashin
June: Serbian president Milosevic
agrees to withdraw Serbian
troops from Kosovo
—UN establishes Kosovo
Peace Implementation Force
(KFOR)
—Russian troops occupy Pristina
airport in Kosovo, resulting in
stand-off with NATO forces
August 2: Chechen separatists
invade Dagestan
August 9: Putin becomes prime
minister, replacing Stepashin
August–September: Series of
bombs explode in Moscow and
elsewhere in Russia
September 30: Russian federal
soldiers enter Chechnya,
launching second round of war
November 14: Putin's op-ed piece,
"Why We Must Act," published
in New York Times
December 19: In Duma election,
parties nominally aligned with
Putin do well
December 29: Putin issues
Millennium Message

December 31: Boris Yeltsin resigns
as president; names Putin acting
president

2000

January 1: Putin issues executive
order giving Yeltsin immunity
from prosecution
February 1: Anatoly Sobchak dies
of heart attack
March 26: Putin elected president
of Russia in first round of voting
May: Putin appoints Kudrin as
finance minister
May 7: Putin inaugurated as
Russian president
May 13: Putin issues decree creating
seven new overarching federal
regions
July: Televised meeting between
Putin and Russian oligarchs
August: Russian submarine Kursk
sinks in Barents Sea

2001

April 3: Gazprom takes control of
independent Russian TV station
NTV
September 11: Putin calls President
George W. Bush to offer assis-
tance after 9/11
October: Putin dismantles Ministry
of Nationalities
November: Putin establishes Russian
Financial Monitoring Service
December: Putin participates in first
official televised call-in show,
Hot Line

2002

April: Putin declares "military victory in Chechnya" and moves to counter-insurgency and peace-keeping operation
—Nationalist leader Lebed dies in helicopter crash
October 23: Chechen terrorists storm Moscow theater

2003

February 24: Valery Zorkin reelected chairman of Constitutional Court
March: United States invades Iraq
October 25: YUKOS head Mikhail Khodorkovsky arrested in Novosibirsk
November: Rose Revolution in Georgia
December: Orange Revolution in Ukraine begins

2004

March 14: Putin reelected president for second term
March 29: NATO expansion includes six former Soviet and Soviet bloc countries
May 1: EU enlargement includes seven former Soviet and Soviet bloc countries
May: EU launches European Neighborhood Policy (ENP)
May–September: Chechen president Akhmad Kadyrov assassinated; Chechen terrorists attack Russian commercial airplanes and elementary school in Beslan, North Ossetia

2005

January: Russia repays IMF debt three-and-a-half years ahead of schedule
April: Tulip Revolution in Kyrgyzstan
—Founding conference of Kremlin-sponsored youth group *Nashi*
May: Khodorkovsky sentenced to nine years in prison

2006

January: Russia cuts off gas supply to Ukraine
Summer: Russia pays off last of inherited Soviet debt
September: Russian social networking site "VKontakte" launched

2007

January: Romania and Bulgaria join EU
February: Ramzan Kadyrov becomes president of Chechnya
February 10: Putin delivers controversial speech at Munich Security Conference
December 10: Putin names Dmitry Medvedev as his preferred successor; lays out plan to serve as prime minister

2008

March 2: Dmitry Medvedev elected president in first round of elections

April 2–4: NATO summit in Bucharest, Romania, rebuffs Ukrainian, Georgian membership efforts

May: Medvedev inaugurated as Russian president; Putin confirmed as prime minister by Duma

August 7–16: Russo-Georgian War

2009

January: Russia again cuts off gas supply to Ukraine over payment disagreements

April: Counterinsurgency and peacekeeping operations in Chechnya declared at an end

May 1: EU launches Eastern Partnership at Prague summit

September: EU adopts Third Energy Package

2010

August: Wildfires scorch much of Russia

December: Arab Spring begins

2011

May: Creation of *Obshche-rossiyskiy narodnyy front*

September 24: Medvedev and Putin announce that Putin will return to presidency in 2012

—Alexei Kudrin subsequently resigns from post of finance minister

December 4: Russian parliamentary elections

December: Wave of protest rallies and marches follows Russian parliamentary elections

2012

March 4: Putin wins Russian presidential elections in first round

April: Putin resigns leadership of United Russia party

—Alexei Kudrin establishes KGI

May 7: Putin inaugurated as Russian president for third term

July: Duma passes "foreign agents" law for NGOs

October: USAID ousted from Russia

November: Putin replaces Defense Minister Anatoly Serdyukov with Sergei Shoigu and Chief of General Staff Nikolay Makarov with Valery Gerasimov

December 12: U.S. adopts Magnitsky Act, which punishes Russian officials guilty of human rights abuses

December 28: Putin signs Dima Yakovlev Act, which prohibits Americans from adopting Russian children

2013

January: Chief of General Staff Gerasimov calls for Russia to prepare for "21st-century war"

March: EU and IMF offer €10 billion bailout for Cyprus

June: Putin and his wife, Lyudmila, announce decision to divorce

—Putin announces Russian economic pivot to China and Asia-Pacific region at St. Petersburg Economic Forum

—Edward Snowden arrives in Moscow

November 21: Ukraine's Viktor Yanukovych declines to sign EU association agreement, sparking months of protests

December 20: Mikhail Khodorkovsky is released from prison after being pardoned by Putin

2014

February 7–23: Winter Olympics held in Sochi, Russia

February 21: Ukrainian president Yanukovych disappears from Kyiv and is impeached by Ukrainian parliament as protests in Kyiv escalate

February 27–28: Unmarked Russian special forces begin to take over government buildings and airports in Crimea

March 1: Russian parliament approves Putin's request to use force in Ukraine to protect ethnic Russians and Russian interests

March 16: Crimean officials hold referendum to declare independence from Ukraine and desire to join Russia

March 17: First U.S. sanctions on Russia announced, with increasingly strong sanctions following in April and June

March 18: Russia officially annexes Crimea; Putin gives key speech

March 24: Russia suspended from G-8

May 21: Russia signs 30-year gas deal with China worth $400 billion

May 25: Ukraine elects Petro Poroshenko as new president

June: Russia cuts off gas supply to Ukraine

June 26: Georgia, Moldova, and Ukraine sign Association Agreements with EU

July 17: Malaysian Airlines Flight 17 shot down over eastern Ukraine

Late August: Thousands of Russian troops enter eastern Ukraine; later withdraw

September 12: U.S. extends sanctions to further sections of Russian economy

NOTES ON TRANSLATION, TRANSLITERATION, NOMENCLATURE, STYLE, AND SOURCES

TRANSLATION

All the translations in the text from Russian and other foreign language sources are the authors' unless otherwise noted in the endnotes for each chapter. We frequently cite official Russian government websites, notably those for the offices of the president and prime minister. These websites have English translations for most, but not all, of Vladimir Putin's speeches and interviews. They are useful for the non-Russian reader. We, however, found them lacking when it comes to conveying certain nuances of Putin's language, which is an important element of discussion in the book. As a result, we used our own translations from the original Russian.

Likewise, throughout the book, we cite what is often described as Putin's autobiography or semi-autobiography. The Russian version of this book, published by Vagrius in Moscow in 2000, is *Ot pervogo litsa: razgovory s Vladimirom Putinom*. Its authors are three Russian journalists who based the book on interviews with Putin in connection with the Russian presidential election of that year: Nataliya Gevorkyan, Natalya Timakova, and Andrei Kolesnikov. Public Affairs in New York published an English-language version of the book, also in 2000: *First Person: An Astonishingly Frank Self-Portrait by Russia's President Vladimir Putin*. Its authors were listed as Vladimir Putin "with" the three Russian journalists. We prefer the Russian version and have used it in all of the citations in this book, using our own translations.

The term *Pervoye litso*, or "the first person," is also sometimes used to refer to Putin in spoken references and in newspaper articles by Russian analysts, journalists, and sometimes politicians.

TRANSLITERATION

Transliterating names and words from the Cyrillic alphabet (used in Russian) into the Latin alphabet (used in English) is unfortunately complicated by the existence of a number of different systems. No transliteration system is ideal from both the point of view of the non-Russian-speaking reader, who simply wants to see familiar words and names rendered in that familiar way, and the point of view of the scholar, who needs to be able to convert Russian names and words in the Latin alphabet back into Cyrillic in order to track sources. So we use two different systems for the main text and the source citations. In the main text and the expository part of the endnotes, we use a simplified system that presents names in the form used in most U.S. newspapers. This means that in the text we use Alexander, Alexei, Arkady, Basaev, Chubais, Dmitry, Gaidar, Valery, Yeltsin, Yury, Zorkin, for instance, instead of Aleksandr, Aleksey, Arkadiy, Basayev, Chubays, Dmitriy, Gaydar, Valeriy, Yel'tsin, Yuriy, Zor'kin.

In the source citations, we use the United States Board on Geographic Names standard (http://earth-info.nga.mil/gns/html/index.html) when we are referencing a Russian source. When citing English-language materials, we have preserved the transliteration from the original source. The United States Board on Geographic Names transliterates, for example, the Cyrillic letter *e* as *ye* initially after vowels and after the soft sign (ь) (which is ' in Latin script). Otherwise it is transliterated as *e*. The letter ё can either be rendered in the same manner as *e* or transliterated as *yo*. The letters ы and й are both transliterated as *y*. X is *kh*, and ц is *ts*, and ю is *yu*. The hard sign (ъ) is usually omitted but transliterated as " before a vowel.

Russian words that have entered into standard English usage in literature—like Duma, glasnost, intelligentsia, perestroika, tsar—are not italicized in the text and are treated as English words. So are other foreign language terms and phrases such as ad hoc and pro forma.

We apologize for errors and inconsistencies that we have overlooked.

PLACES AND NAMES

The fall of the Soviet Union brought about a rash of changes in place names. For example, Leningrad, Vladimir Putin's place of birth, voted in 1991 to return the name of the city to its pre–Bolshevik Revolution name, St. Petersburg. Thus, we have chosen to use the dividing line of 1991 when referring to the city. When we refer to Putin's childhood and early years as an adult, we mention that it took place in Leningrad. When Putin returned to Russia from his KGB service in Dresden, he initially returned to Leningrad, soon to be renamed St. Petersburg. Occasionally we will use Leningrad/St. Petersburg in the text when the discussion spans periods before and after 1991.

Similarly, the fall of the Soviet Union saw a change in the name of the Soviet Committee for State Security (*Komitet gosudarstvennoy bezopasnosti*), the KGB. The KGB was formally dissolved in December of 1991, but most of its functions and operations reemerged under the name Russian Federal Security Service (*Federal'naya sluzhba bezopasnosti*), FSB. It is that dividing line that has determined our use. Thus, the organization that Putin joined in the 1970s is referred to as the KGB, but the one that he led briefly in 1998–99 though extremely similar to its predecessor is called the FSB. Again, we sometimes refer to the KGB/FSB in a broader discussion.

When referring to places in eastern Europe that were once under Russian or Soviet rule, we have chosen to use the version of the place name that is favored by the country in which they are located. For instance, we have written a southern Ukrainian city as Mykolayiv rather than use the perhaps more common Russian-language Nikolayev.

STYLE

Russian titles of books, articles, institutions, newspaper names, and most everything else follow the simple rule of capitalizing only the first letter of the first word (plus other proper names). Russians do not capitalize every noun. So the Russian newspaper is *Komsomol'skaya pravda*—not *Komsomol'skaya Pravda,* and so on. Even institutions like government ministries and political parties follow this rule: *Ministerstvo transporta RF* (Ministry of Transport of the Russian Federation), *Obshcherossiyskiy narodnyy front* (All-Russian People's Front), and so on. We follow the lowercase style, unless there is a somewhat generally used English-language term, title, or proper name for the institution or entity like the Ministry of Foreign Affairs. We do not use capitalization when we refer to institutions in "shorthand," such as foreign ministry or interior ministry. The correct English-language title for the latter would be the Ministry of Internal Affairs as the Russian is the *Ministerstvo vnutrennykh del.* So we capitalize where we render the correct institutional name in English and not where we do it in a more shorthand fashion (the same with the foreign ministry or Ministry of Foreign Affairs and so forth).

SOURCES

The material in this book comes from existing biographies of Vladimir Putin; Russian and international press accounts; a close examination of Putin's public pronouncements over more than 15 years; off-the-record interviews with U.S. government and European officials; private discussions with Russian and international business leaders; private interviews with Russian analysts and a few Kremlin insiders with whom we have long-established contacts; interviews with U.S., European, and Russian journalists who have either worked for many years in Moscow or covered Putin directly; and our own personal encounters with Mr. Putin through the Valdai Discussion Club. For our interviews, we have only cited by name in the endnotes those respondents who agreed to waive anonymity and the off-the-record rule for their specific comments.

All of the sources specifically referred to in the main text are cited in the endnotes and/or the bibliography. In the case of newspaper articles, we poured through a huge number of Russian and international publications. We used subscription-based resources, including Nexis.com, Eastview, and ProQuest, extensively in tracking down some specific articles, and were also assisted by the daily issues and archives of Johnson's Russia List (JRL) at www.russia list.org in identifying pertinent material. As a result of the sheer volume of material we looked at, we have only referenced the individual items we cited from in full in the endnotes. We have not included all of the newspaper sources in the bibliography. Wherever the URL information was available, we have provided this for the reader. Otherwise we have indicated the resource used to access the article. In some cases, newspapers now require a fee to access articles from their archives. Note that some of the 1990s newspaper articles cited come from old, archived, hard copy files, not from websites.

Newspaper and web articles are listed with full information in the endnotes the first time they are cited, chapter by chapter. So chapter 1 will include a full cite, as will chapter 2, for instance. After the first full cite in a chapter the article will be abbreviated for the remainder of that chapter. Books and journal articles are referred to in the endnotes by the "last-name-of-author (year)" format. The full information is provided in the bibliography.

We also did not include in the bibliography all the films, TV shows, Internet videos, websites, speeches, presentations, interviews, and public appearances that we looked at during our research. Those we cited from are referenced in full in the endnotes. The majority of Vladimir Putin's speeches, presentations, interviews, and public appearances can be found on Kremlin websites, although these sites were revamped in 2009 and then in 2012 when Putin transitioned from the prime minister's office back to the presidency. The website http://archive.kremlin.ru/ carries some of the older material for Putin's 2000–08 presidencies, as well as for the first year (2008–09) of Dmitry Medvedev's 2008–12 presidency. Likewise, http://archive.premier.gov.ru/ carries material for Putin's time as prime minister, 2008–12. The website www.kremlin.ru/ is the portal for Putin's post–May 2012 presidency and also holds the material from the remainder of Dmitry Medvedev's presidency, 2009–12. The website http://government.ru/ contains material on his post-2012 government.

A last note here—some of the material that we accessed for the first edition of the book is no longer accessible on the Internet. We have retained hard copies of this material for reference purposes.

ABBREVIATIONS AND ACRONYMS

ABM	Anti-Ballistic Missile
BBC	British Broadcasting Company
BRICS	Group of emerging economy countries—Brazil, Russia, India, China, South Africa
CIA	Central Intelligence Agency (United States)
Cheka	Extraordinary Commission (*Chrezvychaynaya komissiya*)
CIS	Commonwealth of Independent States
CPSU (or KPSS)	Communist Party of the Soviet Union
CPRF	Communist Party of the Russian Federation
CSIS	Center for Strategic and International Studies
EU	European Union
FRG	Federal Republic of Germany (West Germany)
FSB	Russian Federal Security Service (*Federal'naya sluzhba bezopasnosti*)
G-7	Group of Seven
G-8	Group of Eight
G-20	Group of Twenty
GDP	Gross domestic product
GDR	German Democratic Republic (East Germany)

GKU	Main Control Directorate (*Glavnoye kontrol'noye upravleniye)*
GRU	Main Intelligence Directorate of the General Staff of the Armed Forces of the Russian Federation (*Glavnoye razvedyvatel'noye upravleniye*)
Gulag	Chief Administration of Corrective Labor Camps and Colonies (*Glavnoye upravlyeniye ispravityel'no-trudovikh lagerey i koloniy*)
Gosrezerv	Federal Agency for State Reserves (*Federal'noye agentstvo po gosudarstvennym rezervam*)
HVA	Main Directorate for Reconnaisance (*Hauptverwaltung Aufklärung,* East Germany)
IMF	International Monetary Fund
INSOR	Institute for Contemporary Development (*Institut sovremennogo razvitiya*)
KFOR	The "Kosovo Force," a NATO-led peacekeeping force in Kosovo
KGB	Committee for State Security (*Komitet gosudarstvennoy bezopasnosti*)
KGI	Committee for Citizens' Initiatives (*Komitet grazhdanskikh initsiativ*)
KRO	Congress of Russian Communities (*Kongress russkikh obschestv*)
LDPR	Liberal Democratic Party of Russia (*Liberal'no-demokraticheskaya partiya Rossii*)
LGU	Leningrad State University (*Leningradskiy gosudarstvennyy universitet*), later to become St. Petersburg State University
MAP	Membership Action Plan, a set of guidelines to prepare aspiring countries for NATO membership
MGB	Ministry for State Security, East Germany (Russian variant—*Ministerstvo gosudarstvennoy bezopasnosti*)

MVD	Ministry of Internal Affairs (*Ministerstvo vnutrennykh del*)
Nashi	Youth Democratic Anti-Fascist Movement "Ours!" (*Molodezhnoye demokraticheskoye antifashistskoye dvizheniye "Nashi"*)
NATO	North Atlantic Treaty Organization
NDR	Our Home Is Russia (*Nash dom Rossiya*)
NGO	Nongovernmental organization
NKVD	People's Commissariat for Internal Affairs (*Narodnyy komissariat vnutrennykh del*)
OSCE	Organization for Security and Cooperation in Europe
P&G	Procter and Gamble
PfP	Partnership for Peace Program
Politburo	Central decisionmaking organ of the Soviet Communist Party (*Politicheskoye byuro*)
PPMD	Presidential Property Management Department
ROS	Russian Popular Union (*Rossiyskiy obshchenarodnyy soyuz*)
Rosrezerv	Russian Federal Agency for State Reserves (*Federal'noye agentstvo po gosudarstvennym rezervam*) (see *Gosrezerv*)
RFM	Russian Financial Monitoring Agency (*Rosfinmonitoring*)
RSFSR	Russian Soviet Federative Socialist Republic
SDI	Strategic Defense Initiative, the proposed American missile defense system also known as Star Wars.
SED	Socialist Unity Party (*Sozialistische Einheitspartei Deutschlands*), the Communist Party of East Germany
Stasi	Ministry for State Security (*Ministerium für Staatssicherheit*, East Germany)

TEK Commission	Presidential Commission on the Fuel and Energy Complex (*Toplivo-energeticheskogo kompleksa*)
UN	United Nations
USAID	United States Agency for International Development
USSR	Union of Soviet Socialist Republics
WTO	World Trade Organization

NOTES

CHAPTER 1

1. See Vladimir Putin, "Obrashcheniye Prezidenta Rossiyskoy Federatsii" [Address by the President of the Russian Federation], March 18, 2014, available on the Kremlin's website archive (in Russian) at http://news.kremlin.ru/news/20603. An English translation is available at http://eng.news.kremlin.ru/news/6889.

2. Olga Rudenko and Jennifer Collins, "As Many as 100 Killed in New Ukraine Clashes," *USA Today*, February 21, 2014, at www.usatoday.com/story/news/world/2014/02/20/ukraine-protests-truce-eu-leaders/5634235/.

3. Shore (2014), pp. 5–6.

4. Gevorkyan, Timakova, and Kolesnikov (2000).

5. Rahr (2000).

6. Dawisha (2014) is a recent work on the topic.

7. Peter Baker, "Sanctions Revive Search for Secret Putin Fortune," *New York Times*, April 27, 2014: "For years, the suspicion that Mr. Putin has a secret fortune has intrigued scholars, industry analysts, opposition figures, journalists and intelligence agencies but defied their efforts to uncover it. Numbers are thrown around suggesting that Mr. Putin may control $40 billion or even $70 billion, in theory making him the richest head of state in world history. For all the rumors and speculation, though, there has been little if any hard evidence. . . ."

8. See van der Does de Willebois and others (2011).

9. See, for one example of many, Stephen Sestanovich, "Putin's Reckless Gamble," *New York Times*, March 29, 2014, at www.nytimes.com/2014/04/01/opinion/putins-reckless-gamble.html?_r=0.

10. The books are Gessen (2012) and Judah (2013). Judah never mentions the primary source for the story, Putin's *Ot pervogo litsa*, but rather cites his source as Gessen's book. Gessen does cite Putin, but does not question the story.

11. Gevorkyan, Timakova, and Kolesnikov (2000), p. 34.

12. Ibid., p. 188.

13. Ibid., p. 35.

14. James Rosen and Luke A. Nichter, "Madman in the White House: Why Looking Crazy Can Be an Asset When You're Staring down the Russians," *Foreign Policy*,

March 25, 2014, at www.foreignpolicy.com/articles/2014/03/25/madman_in_white_house_nixon_russia_obama.

15. Haldeman (1977), quoted in ibid. Rosen and Nichter relate that in expounding the Madman Theory, Nixon was actually playing back to Kissinger an idea—"the concept of the strategic potential of madness"—with which Kissinger was familiar from his academic days. Nixon's words to Kissinger were captured on the White House tapes: "Now, Henry, we must not miss this chance. We're going to do it. I'm going to destroy the goddamn country, believe me, I mean destroy it if necessary. And let me say, even the nuclear weapon if necessary. It isn't necessary. But, you know, what I mean is, that shows you the extent to which I'm willing to go. By a nuclear weapon, I mean that we will bomb the living bejeezus out of North Vietnam and then if anybody interferes we will threaten the nuclear weapon." *Foreign Relations of the United States, 1969–1976,* Vol. XIV, Soviet Union, October 1971–May 1972, Document 126. Conversation between President Nixon and His Assistant for National Security Affairs (Kissinger). Washington, April 19, 1972. Available at http://history.state.gov/historicaldocuments/frus1969-76v14/d126.

The manipulated image is also a stock character trait of key figures in dramatic and popular fiction. For instance, a central character in the immensely popular American HBO series *Game of Thrones,* Lord Petyr Baelish, summed up the entire approach in a line in one of the final episodes of season 4 of the series, which by odd coincidence premiered in April 2014 against the real-life backdrop of the crisis in Ukraine. Having just poisoned and killed King Joffrey, Lord Baelish tells another major character: "Always keep your foes confused. If they don't know who you are or what you want, they can't know what you plan to do next." Petyr Baelish to Sansa Stark, *Game of Thrones,* Season 4, "Oathkeeper," at http://gameofthrones.wikia.com/wiki/Petyr_Baelish#cite_note-26.

16. Mr. Benn episodes are available at www.clivebanks.co.uk/.

17. Gessen (2012).

18. The multiplicity of Mr. Putins over the years has spawned a veritable cottage industry of Russian and international spin-offs and spoofs, including laudatory music videos, calendars, video games, a comic strip with Putin as "Super Putin," and a children's coloring book, where two young boys, Vova (Vladimir Putin) and Dima (Dmitry Medvedev, 2008–12 president), work "in tandem" in big buildings on important issues. The book was published on the occasion of Putin's October 2011 birthday. See http://like-putin.ru/; http://superputin.ru/; and http://seansrussiablog.org/2011/10/10/vova-and-dima-coloring-book/.

19. Authors' notes from presentation by Kai Eide, the former UN special representative to the secretary general (UN SRG) for Afghanistan, at the Brookings Institution in Washington, D.C., on July 10, 2014. Eide noted that "during my ten years of traveling to Afghanistan and two years as the UN SRG, I never met any Afghan politician with the finger so much on the pulse of his own society."

20. See Putin's remark to this effect during his first presidential *Hot Line,* discussed in chapter 8.

21. The president personally summoned Masha Gessen to the Kremlin after learning that she had been sacked as the editor of one of Russia's leading popular science magazines for refusing to send a reporter to cover his Mr. Putin PR stunt piloting the microlight aircraft with a flock of endangered cranes. See Masha Gessen, "A Call from the Kremlin," September 16, 2012, at http://latitude.blogs.nytimes.com/2012/09/16/a-call-from-the-kremlin/.

22. There are many different translations of this untitled poem, but our version comes from Billington (1966), p. 320.

23. Between 2004 and 2014, one or both of the authors met with Mr. Putin as part of the so-called Valdai Discussion Club. The Valdai Club is a Russian government–sponsored exercise to bring foreign experts and journalists to Russia to engage with Russian policymakers and think-tankers in a focus-group format. For the official description of the club and its activities, see http://valdaiclub.com/.

CHAPTER 2

1. For a concise discussion of the Russian and international debate about Russia under Yeltsin in the 1990s, see "The End of the Yeltsin Era," in Shevtsova (2005), pp. 44–68. This chapter on the key developments in Russian domestic and foreign policy during the period from 1991 to 1996 is also adapted from material presented in Fiona Hill's Harvard history Ph.D. dissertation (1998).

2. Defense enterprises, the backbone of the huge manufacturing sector in Russia, saw the government procurement order for military hardware in 1992 cut by two-thirds. Gaddy (1996), p. 72.

3. Official annual consumer inflation was 2,500 percent in 1992, 840 percent in 1993, 215 percent in 1994, and 131 percent in 1995. These data and others in the text relating to the economic situation of the 1990s have been compiled by the authors from various official Russian government sources from this period.

4. The official casualty figures can be found in *Izvestiya,* December 25, 1993.

5. See Gleb Pavlovsky, political strategist and former Kremlin adviser, interview with David Hearst and Tom Parfitt, *The Guardian,* January 24, 2012. The authors are extremely grateful to *The Guardian* columnist David Hearst for providing them with the full, unedited English language transcript of this interview. The original interview was conducted by Hearst and *The Guardian* Moscow correspondent Tom Parfitt. Parfitt translated Pavlovsky's Russian language responses. Extracts from this interview are featured in David Hearst, "Will Putinism See the End of Putin?," *The Guardian,* February 27, 2012, at www.theguardian.com/world/2012/feb/27/vladimir-putin-profile-putinism; and David Hearst and Miriam Elder, "How Dmitry Medvedev's Mentor Turned Him into a Lame Duck," *The Guardian,* March 2, 2012, at www.guardian.co.uk/world/2012/mar/02/dmitry-medvedev-rivalry.

6. Celestine Bohlen, "A. A. Sobchak Dead at 62; Mentor to Putin," *New York Times,* February 21, 2000.

7. See Leonova (2012). The authors thank Brookings visiting fellow William Partlett for giving us access to his research on the 1993 Russian constitution and the set of Russian legal scholars who deliberated on and drafted the document. For a fuller description of how the 1993 Russian constitution rejected Western constitutional models, see Partlett (2012).

8. See McFaul (2001), pp. 273–78.

9. In September 1995, for example, Nikolai Lysenko, leader of the right-wing National Republican Party, engaged in a physical confrontation with Gleb Yakunin of the Democratic Party. Several other deputies intervened, and in the ensuing fray LDPR leader Vladimir Zhirinovsky hit a female deputy.

10. See, for example, Alexandra Odynova, "Putin Says He's Prepared for Runoff," *Moscow Times,* February 2, 2012, accessed through EastView at http://dlib.eastview.com/browse/doc/26540808.

11. See McFaul (2001), pp. 279–82. Boris Yeltsin offered a jaundiced view of this effort in his memoir, *Midnight Diaries,* with obvious implications for similar exercises under President Putin: "In 1995, Viktor Chernomyrdin headed up a new 'party of power' called Our Home Is Russia. It bet on centrism with a moderate-liberal ideology emphasizing the priorities of the state. Of course it relied on state people. . . . It was a complete failure. A political party that is called upon to reflect the interests of large social groups cannot be built so obviously on a government-style vertical chain of command. . . . The result was very bad for the authority of the government, the economy, and the entire system of civil society." Yeltsin (2000), p. 352.

12. Timothy Colton's biography of Boris Yeltsin has the best account of the 1996 presidential election season, including a discussion of Yeltsin's low ratings, the heart attack, and the difficulties of the campaign, in chapters 14 and 15 (pp. 345–406). See Colton (2008).

13. See David Filipov, "Russian Mogul Makes Politics His Latest Venture," *Boston Globe*, March 5, 1997.

14. See Freeland (2000); Hoffman (2003); and Treisman (March 2010).

15. See Bill Nichols, "Yeltsin's Latest Firing Is Seen as Self-Preservation, Experts: He Wants Someone Who Will Protect Him, Cronies," *USA Today*, August 10, 1999; David Filipov and Brian Whitmore, "Yeltsin's 'Family' Is Seen behind Latest Move," *Boston Globe*, August 10, 1999; Dmitri Simes, "Yeltsin's Goal Is to Protect Inner Circle," *Newsday*, August 11, 1999; and Jonathan Steele, "Keeping It in the Family: In Today's Russia, Politicians and Businessmen Are Carving up Power between Them—And That's How to See Yeltsin's Latest Manoeuvers," *The Guardian*, August 13, 1999. Tatiana Yumasheva, Yeltsin's daughter, is the central figure in the so-called Family. She was first married to Russian businessman Alexei Dyachenko and later married her father's former adviser Valentin Yumashev, another key figure, in 2001. Yumashev's daughter is married to Russian oligarch Oleg Deripaska. Others associated with the Family include Alexander Voloshin, who served as chief of staff to both Yeltsin and Putin, and oligarchs Boris Berezovsky and Roman Abramovich, former owner of the Russian oil company Sibneft along with Berezovsky. In his memoir, *Midnight Diaries,* Yeltsin describes Tatiana (Tanya), Yumashev, and Voloshin as his "inner circle." Yeltsin (2000), p. 332.

16. Dmitry Rogozin—Russia's ambassador to NATO before becoming deputy prime minister in charge of the defense industry—has had a colorful political career of increasingly deeper nationalist hues since the 1990s. He began his political life as one of the founders in 1990–91 of the new Constitutional Democratic Party (*Kadet* party), a revival of the tsarist-era party of Pavel Milyukov, a Russian historian and leading "liberal conservative" promoting the development of a constitutional monarchy, who served in the Russian Duma of the early 1900s. See Vladimir Gromov, "Dmitry Rogozin: The Man behind Major Political Figures in Congress of Russian Communities," *Moskovskiy komsomolets,* November 14, 1995, accessed in English through the Foreign Broadcast Information Service, FBIS, in 1995. In 1993, Rogozin cofounded the Congress of Russian Communities with General Alexander Lebed and became a member of parliament and subsequently chairman of the Duma's foreign relations committee. In 2003, he helped found the "national-patriotic" Rodina party before being side-lined by the Kremlin in 2006. He was pushed onto the political fringes until being named ambassador to NATO in 2008. Rogozin revived the Congress of Russian Communities again in 2006 as a "civil society" organization rather than as a political party and became part of Putin's *Narodnyy front* (People's Front) in 2011. Putin appointed Rogozin deputy prime minister in charge of the defense sector in December 2011 and again in May 2012. For a discussion of some of Putin's attempts to co-opt Dmitry Rogozin and his nationalist supporters, see Michael Bohm, "Putin Playing with Fire by Courting Rogozin," *Moscow Times,* September 23, 2011, at www.themoscowtimes.com/opinion/article/putin-playing-with-fire-by-courting-rogozin/444203.html#ixzz1lG7UuSja.

17. See Baker and Glasser (2005). Chapter 4, "The Takeover Will Be Televised," deals in part with Putin's wrangling with both Berezovsky and Gusinsky and Putin's efforts to bring NTV and Gusinsky's other media holdings firmly under the influence of the Kremlin (pp. 78–98). Chapter 14, "Twilight of the Oligarchs," covers Putin's showdown with Mikhail Khodorkovsky (pp. 272–92). Another detailed discussion of Khodorkovsky's clash with Putin and the circumstances surrounding the seizure and dismantling of the oil company YUKOS that Khodorkovsky set up in the 1990s is in Coll (2012). Coll, in chapter 12, describes the creation of YUKOS and Khodorkovsky's outreach to ExxonMobil to form a business venture with the American oil giant in 2002. See Coll (2012), pp. 250–79.

18. Under Mikhail Gorbachev, nationalist groups in the Caucasus and the Baltic states demanded the revision of Soviet internal borders, increased autonomy from the center, and eventually outright independence. Gorbachev's failed attempts to broker a new Union Treaty to keep the USSR's constituent pieces together was one of the precipitating factors for the August 1991 coup, or putsch, by conservative figures in the Soviet government and

military, which hastened the demise of the Union in December 1991. See Dunlop (1993) and Hajda and Beissinger (1990).

19. See, for example, Lieven (1998).

20. In a seminar at Harvard University's Kennedy School of Government in 1997, not long after the Russian government concluded its series of peace agreements with Chechnya, Alexei Arbatov—who was from 1994 to 2003 deputy chairman of the Russian Duma defense committee and a leading figure in the Yabloko party—stressed that no one in Russian official or military circles considered the war with Chechnya settled. He noted that "Moscow" would eventually subjugate Chechnya again. Similar comments were made by other officials in summer 1997 during meetings Fiona Hill conducted in Moscow in preparation for her 1998 Harvard Ph.D. dissertation.

21. Sergei Shakhrai, Yeltsin's key adviser on these issues and one of the drafters of the 1993 constitution, made it very clear after 1994 that the Tatarstan treaty and the other bilateral treaties that followed it were conceived as a stopgap measure rather than as building blocks for a new Russian federal structure. They were intended to placate the most troublesome of Russia's republics to prevent them from following Chechnya down the path to secession. See Sergei Shakhrai, "Official Memorandum to President Boris N. Yeltsin," No. 1576, March 1995, cited in Rafael Khakimov, "Federalization and Stability: A Path Forward for the Russian Federation," CMG *Bulletin*, June 1995, pp. 10–14 (citation on p. 11).

22. See James Hughes, "Moscow's Bilateral Treaties Add to Confusion," *Transition*, September 20, 1996, pp. 39–43.

23. See Jean-Robert Raviot, "Fédéralisme et Gouvernement Régional en Russie" [Federalism and regional government in Russia], *Politique Étrangère* (Paris), December 1996, pp. 803–12; and "Russia's Regions: Fiefs and Chiefs," *The Economist*, January 25, 1997.

24. Mark Whitehouse, "Nazdratenko Rules a Far East Fiefdom," *Moscow Times*, July 26, 1997.

25. See Brown (1996), pp. 212–51.

26. See Lough (March 12, 1993), pp. 21–29; and Lough (May 14, 1993), pp. 53–59. See also William Safire, "On Language: The Near Abroad," *New York Times Magazine*, May 22, 1994.

27. See "Foreign Minister Returns to Anti-West Ways—Not!" *New York Times*, December 15, 1992; and Hill and Jewett (1994). As one of the U.S. officials who attended the ministerial later recounted: "The meeting where Kozyrev gave his faux speech was the OSCE Ministerial Council [annual meeting of foreign ministers] at Stockholm in December 1992. The speech was entirely unexpected; [Secretary of State] Larry Eagleburger listened and exploded, wanting to know what was going on. In an anteroom, before he gave his second, real speech, Kozyrev explained that his first speech reflected the approach of a substantial portion of Moscow's political society and was intended to show us what we would get if we didn't support Yeltsin and him." Ambassador William Hill, who was then the OSCE coordinator for the U.S. Department of State, in written exchange with the authors, July 30, 2012.

28. In 1992, a total of $24 billion in Western assistance had been promised to Russia, but only a fraction had been delivered. See Jeffrey Sachs, "Toward *Glasnost* in the IMF: Russia's Democratization Policy and the International Monetary Fund," *Challenge*, May 1994; see also Sachs's testimony to the United States Senate Committee on Banking, Housing and Urban Affairs, February 5, 1994.

29. Roman Glebov, "Russia and Ukraine—Controversy over the Black Sea Fleet," *Kommersant Daily*, January 13, 1992 (accessed in English through FBIS in 1995).

30. For a discussion of the developments of this period, see Hill and Jewett (1994).

31. Andrei Kozyrev, *Moscow News*, October 22, 1993, cited in Hill and Jewett (1994), p. 6. Immediately after Kozyrev's speech, in November 1993, a new Russian Military Doctrine identified conflicts in the neighborhood as Russia's main security threat.

32. See Hill and Jewett (1994).

33. "RF-SNG: Strategicheskiy kurs. Ukaz Prezidenta Rossiyskoy Federatsii ob utverzh-denii strategicheskogo kursa Rossiyskoy Federatsii s gosudarstvami-uchastnikami Sodru-zhestva nezavisimykh gosudarstv" [RF-CIS: Strategic course. Decree of the president of the Russian Federation on establishing the strategic course of the Russian Federation with the state-participants in the Commonwealth of Independent States], No. 940, September 14, 1995, in *Dipkur'er*, No. 16/18, 1995.

34. Mikhail Gorbachev, "Russia Will Not Play Second Fiddle," *Moscow News*, No. 37, September 22–28, 1995.

35. Ibid.

36. Ibid.

CHAPTER 3

1. See, for example, Gerschaft (October 1995), p. 2; and Kokoshin (1997), p. 41. Material in this chapter, on the debates over the "Russian Idea" and how to restore the Russian state in the 1990s, is adapted from Fiona Hill's Harvard history Ph.D. dissertation (1998) and the accompanying sources and research notes. The dissertation involved inter-views with a large number of prominent Russian political figures and analysts in Moscow between 1994 and 1997, including with some of the individuals featured in this chapter.

2. Yavlinsky (1994). In an article in *Nezavisimaya gazeta* in December 1996, com-mentator Rustam Narzikulov noted that the entire Yeltsin administration and a broad swath of the Russian elite had become consumed with the idea of a strong Russian state. Narzikulov provided a list of the political elite who now supported a strong state approach to reform, including members of the so-called financial bloc such as oligarch and Deputy Prime Minister Vladimir Potanin and academic and Economics Minister Yevgeny Yasin, as well as Moscow mayor Yury Luzhkov, one of the most influential post-Soviet political figures, and Prime Minister Viktor Chernomyrdin. "It is surprising," Narzikulov declared, "that the idea of a strong state policy has now been embraced even by those people who, a few years ago, saw the institutions of power as the ultimate evil. It would have been diffi-cult to predict, say, that Anatoly Chubais would become an apologist for the 'supporters of extraordinary measures' and for the strict and rigorous observance of the rules of the game in the economy." See Rustam Narzikulov, "Ot resul'tata bor'by storonnikov i protivnikov sil'nogo gosudarstva" [From the results of the struggle between supporters and opponents of a strong state], *Nezavisimaya gazeta*, December 31, 1996. Anatoly Chubais was, along with Yegor Gaidar, one of Russia's leading economic and liberal reformers. When Gaidar was ousted from the Russian government in 1993, Chubais became the key figure in pro-moting Russia's transformation into a liberal democratic market economy. However, it should perhaps not have been so difficult to predict that Chubais might advocate "extraor-dinary measures." He had done so in the past by stressing the need, if necessary, to impose capitalism in Russia against the will of the people. See Reddaway and Glinski (2001). Chubais, who was a native of St. Petersburg, was also a protagonist in the events sur-rounding Vladimir Putin's move to Moscow in 1996, as we will discuss later in the book.

3. See Shevtsova (2005).

4. Putin, Millennium Message, December 29, 1999, available in Russian on the *Nezavisimaya gazeta* website at www.ng.ru/politics/1999-12-30/4_millenium.html.

5. For a detailed discussion of the distinct identity and sense of higher mission within the Russian intelligence services, including the KGB, the FSB, the Bolsheviks' *Cheka* (*Chrezvychaynaya komissiya*, or Extraordinary Commission) set up by Felix Dzerzhinsky, and the earlier pre-revolutionary predecessor organizations that defined themselves as a "Higher Police," see Murawiec and Gaddy, *The National Interest* (Spring 2002). The

founder and most famous head of the tsarist-era Higher Police was General Count Alexander Khristoforovich von Benckendorff (1783–1844), who Vladimir Putin referred to in his 2012 presidential election campaign article in the Russian newspaper *Kommersant*, on February 6, 2012, when discussing democracy and the quality of governance in Russia. See www.kommersant.ru/doc/1866753.

6. Pavel Yevdokimov, "Russkaya pravda Generala Leonova" [The Russian truth of General Leonov], *Spetsnaz Rossii* (May 2001).

7. Ibid. In a famous early address to a group of Russian intelligence officers on the anniversary of the founding of the original secret police, Vladimir Putin quipped that "as you can see the intelligence operatives planted inside the Russian government have successfully completed the first stage of the operation." Although he would later stress that this was simply a joke, Putin's reference to this specific audience underscored the idea and the KGB myth of the importance of the "real" servants of the state, taking over and restoring order to the state. See Vladimir Putin interview with Ted Koppel: "Vladimir Putin Arises from Murky Background of KGB to Become Acting President of Russia," *Nightline* (Friday Night Special), ABC News, March 24, 2000 (transcript, with Mr. Putin speaking through a translator), accessed through Nexis.com.

8. See Gleb Pavlovsky, political strategist and former Kremlin adviser, interview with *The Guardian* on January 24, 2012.

9. The term intelligentsia as a description of the politically and socially active Russian elite has its roots in Western Europe in the first half of the nineteenth century. A combination of the French *intelligence* and the German *Intelligenz*, it came into usage in Russia in the 1860s and 1870s with general reference to "that portion of the educated class which enjoys public prominence." For some political commentators of the era, the intelligentsia assumed the role in Russian society that the middle class or bourgeoisie played in other European states of the period. See Pipes (1974), p. 251.

10. In the early twentieth century, Vladimir Lenin's Bolsheviks appropriated this general idea of the intelligentsia as the elite representatives of society for themselves. They turned the Bolsheviks into "the vanguard of the proletariat."

11. See Milyukov (1906), pp. 560–61.

12. Pipes (1974), p. 252. Soviet estimates of the intelligentsia in the early 1980s often included all the population that was engaged in non-manual labor as well as all university students. See White, Rose, and McAllister (1997), p. 12; and Petro (1995), p. 99.

13. "Valeriy Zor'kin," *Lentapedia*, February 24, 2012, at http://lenta.ru/lib/14164180/full.htm#65.

14. Yan Ulanskiy, "Otstavka Valeriya Zor'kina" [The resignation of Valery Zorkin], *Kommersant*, October 7, 1993, at http://kommersant.ru/doc/61475. After his resignation, although he still remained a member of the Court, Zorkin joined other opposition politicians and parties, including Zyuganov and Oleg Rumyantsev, another parliamentary deputy and the head of the parliament's working group for preparing the draft 1993 Russian constitution, in publicly opposing the passing of the constitution just eight days before the official referendum on the issue. See "Bloki obsuzhdayut konstitutsiyu" [Blocs discuss the constitution], *Kommersant*, December 4, 1993, at http://kommersant.ru/doc/66482.

15. Maksim Sokolov, "Politicheskiy vektor: Yedinstvo i soglasiye: ot slovo mezhdometiya k slovo-parazitu" [Political vector: unity and accord: from the word of an interjection to the word of a parasite], *Kommersant vlast'*, March 22, 1993, at www.kommersant.ru/doc/9692.

16. Shortly after Putin arrived in Moscow in 1996, for example, Vladimir Medvedev, a member of the Duma's Russian Regions group, made another appeal in the Russian press for all political factions and the rest of the elite to join together—as those who had earlier joined the Soglasiye movement had done—to pull Russia out of its crisis. See Vladimir

Medvedev, "V chem prichina 'nesostoyavshikhsya pobed'?" [What is the reason for the 'incomplete victories'?], *Nezavisimaya gazeta*, November 16, 1996.

17. Andrey Kokoshin, "Natsional'naya bezopasnost' i voyennaya moshch' Rossii" [National security and Russia's military might]. Draft obtained directly from the author by Fiona Hill in 1995. A version of this treatise formed the final chapter of Kokoshin's book *Armiya i politika* [The army and politics] (Moscow: Mezhdunarodnyye otnosheniya, 1995), which was later edited and published in English as *Soviet Strategic Thought 1917–1991* (Cambridge, Mass.: Belfer Center for Science and International Affairs, John F. Kennedy School of Government, Harvard University, 1998). The English version of the treatise is chapter 4, "In Lieu of a Conclusion: Russia's National Security and Military Power," pp. 193–209.

18. Ibid., p. 255.

19. See, for example, Lebed (1995); "Lebed Sets Forth Russia's National Security Concept," *Interfax*, June 26, 1996; online interview with Alexander Lebed at www.Intellectual Capital.com, November 14, 1996; and Alexander Lebed presentation on "International Aspects of Russia's Development," at the German Society of Foreign Policy, Bonn, January 1997 (transcript obtained from the German Society of Foreign Policy). The title of Lebed's best-known (1995) publication on this issue, *Za derzhavu obidno* [It makes you ashamed of your homeland], is a famous line from an extremely popular 1970 Soviet film, *Beloye solntse pustyni* [White sun of the desert], relating the travails of a soldier in the Bolshevik Red Army fighting in Central Asia during the Russian Civil War in the 1920s. For a discussion of the specific Russian connotations of this line see Michele Berdy, "Eastern Tricks for Western Predicaments," *Moscow Times*, July 11, 2003, accessed through Nexis.com.

20. Gerschaft (1995), p. 5. See also, for example, RAU Corporation (1995); Aleksey Podberezkin, "Reserv ustupok so storony Rossii ischerpan" [Russia has exhausted its reserves for concessions], *Nezavisimaya gazeta*, June 4, 1996; Aleksey Podberezkin, "Russkiy put'" [The Russian path], *Avtograf*, May 22–June 6, 1997; and Zyuganov (1994); Gennady Zyuganov, "Junior Partner? No Way," *New York Times*, op-ed, February 1, 1996; Gennadiy Zyuganov, "Smuta" [Troubles], *Nezavisimaya gazeta*, October 17, 1996; David Hoffman, "Zyuganov's Goal is Russia's Glory," *Washington Post*, May 13, 1996; and John Thornhill, "Fears of National Socialism," *Financial Times*, April 11, 1996.

21. Gennady Zyuganov, Report to Congress of the Communist Party of the Russian Federation (CPRF), April 22, 1997.

22. Chinyaeva (1997), pp. 40–46.

23. Cited in James Rupert, "In Search of the Russian Meaning of Life: Yeltsin Asks a Bear of a Question of His Post-Soviet Nation, Wants Answer within a Year," *Washington Post*, August 4, 1996.

24. Cited in Chinyaeva (1997), p. 46.

25. Maria Balynina and Lyudmila Vanina, "Satarov Presents Book on Russia in Search of an Idea," RIA Novosti, August 8, 1997; Bronwyn McLaren, "Big Brains Bog down in Hunt for the Russian Idea," *St. Petersburg Times*, August 18–24, 1997.

26. Chubays (1996).

27. Fiona Hill, personal interview with Igor Chubais at the Journalists' Club in Moscow, May 28, 1997. The phrase in quotation marks is a reference to Russian philosopher Pyotr Chaadayev's famous *Philosophical Letters*, which were widely circulated in manuscript form among the nineteenth-century Russian elite and first published in the journal *Teleskope* in 1836. Chubais's text is full of these kinds of historical references and deliberate echoes.

28. Chubays (1996), p. 9.

29. Ibid., p. 10.

30. Yekaterina Sytaya, "Ocherednoy proyekt geopolitikov" [The latest geopolitical project], *Nezavisimaya gazeta*, October 18, 1996. The hearings were entitled "Russkaya

ideya na yazyke narodov Rossii (Kontseptsiya geopoliticheskoy i natsional'noy bezopasnosti)" [The Russian idea in the language of the peoples of Russia (a concept for geopolitical and national security)].

31. Cited in Paul Goble, "Orthodoxies Old and New," *RFE/RL Analysis from Washington*, January 23, 1997.

32. Yevdokimov, "Russkaya pravda Generala Leonova."

33. Ibid. "Professional" patriots is actually Yevdokimov's own term to refer to himself and General Leonov in the interview.

34. Putin, Millennium Message, December 29, 1999.

35. Chubais was the head of the presidential administration from July 1996 through March 1997 when he was appointed first deputy prime minister.

36. See Colton (2008).

37. "Poslaniye Prezidenta Rossiyskoy Federatsii Federal'nomu Sobraniyu. Poryadok vo vlasti–poryadok v strane (O polozhenii v strane i osnovnykh napravleniyakh politiki Rossiyskoy Federatsii)" [Message of the President of the Russian Federation to the Federal Assembly. Order in the state authority—order in the country (on the situation in the country and on the fundamental directions of politics in the Russian Federation)], March 6, 1997. See www.inpravo.ru/baza1/art4z/nm-8zbwxv/index.htm.

38. The concept of the state in the *poslaniye* is highly instrumental. The text is also written in a very dispassionate and terse manner—reflecting the group of technocrats and economists who had drafted it.

39. See *The Economist* obituary of Anatoly Sobchak: "Anatoly Sobchak, a Flawed Reformer, Died on February 20th, Aged 62," *The Economist*, February 24, 2000.

40. See Sobchak (1990), pp. 211–16.

41. Vladimir Putin, "Vstupleniye na tseremonii vrucheniya Vladimiru Putinu mantii pochetnogo doktora yuridicheskogo fakul'teta Sankt-Peterburgskogo gostudarstvennogo universiteta" [Speech at the ceremony granting Vladimir Putin an honorary doctorate from the law faculty of St. Petersburg State University], January 13, 2000, at http://archive.kremlin.ru/text/appears/2000/01/121198.shtml.

42. Vladimir Putin, "Vstupleniye na rasshirennom zasedanii kollegii Ministerstva yustitsii" [Speech to the full meeting of the Ministry of Justice], January 31, 2000, at http://archive.kremlin.ru/text/appears/2000/01/28883.shtml. Putin's opening words to this assembly sum up the centrality of law to his statist beliefs: "In this hall are gathered people whose work encompasses two key words: statism [*gosudarstvennost'*] and legality [*zakonnost'*]."

43. For a detailed review of Sobchak's biography and complex legacy, see *World Socialist* website, March 10, 2000, at www.wsws.org/articles/2000/mar2000/sobc-m10.shtml.

44. In *Ot pervogo litsa*, Putin has a section discussing how important a figure Anatoly Sobchak was to him: "He is a decent man with a flawless reputation. Moreover, he is very bright, open, and talented. I really like Anatoly Alexandrovich, even though we are entirely different. I sincerely like people like him. He's real. . . . Few people knew that Anatoly Alexandrovich and I had close, comradely, trustful relations. Very often we would talk on our trips abroad, when in fact the two of us were left together for several days. I think I can call him my mentor." See Gevorkyan, Timakova, and Kolesnikov (2000), pp. 112–13. Sobchak also had high words of praise for Putin and their relationship. See, for example, Sobchak's comment in his book about the travails of his failed 1996 reelection campaign, that ". . . V. Putin during this entire saga conducted himself as someone with the highest standards. Not only did he not betray me, as many others did, but he even sprang to my defense, writing a letter [of support] to the very highest authorities." Sobchak (1999).

45. Vladimir Putin, "Otkrytoye pis'mo izbiratelyam" [Open letter to voters], February 25, 2000. Originally published in *Izvestiya*, *Kommersant* and *Komsomol'skaya pravda*,

this is available on the Kremlin's website archive (in Russian) at http://archive.kremlin.
ru/appears/2000/02/25/0000_type63374type63382_122118.shtml. An English translation is available at http://archive.kremlin.ru/eng/speeches/2000/02/25/0000_type82912
type104017_124556.shtml.

46. The authors are grateful to former Brookings nonresident fellow William Partlett
for his assistance with this section of the book. See Partlett (2013). Zorkin also used the
term *diktatura zakona* in a 1996 interview fiercely criticizing Yeltsin for his policy of
signing bilateral treaties with Russia's regions. See Trochev (2008), p. 142. For another
detailed discussion of Putin's attraction to liberal conservatism, see Prozorov (2004).

47. In the late nineteenth and early twentieth centuries, Boris Chicherin's work attracted
a large group of self-declared liberal followers among the Russian intelligentsia. Members
of this elite group helped to create the Constitutional Democrats, or the *Kadets*, which
promoted the development of a law-based constitutional monarchy under the last tsar,
Nicholas II (1894–1917). This was the same party that Dmitry Rogozin revived in the early
1990s as he began his career as one of Russia's leading contemporary nationalist politicians.

48. The most in-depth discussion of Russian conservative political thought in the imperial era is in Pipes (2005).

49. Like Sobchak, Zorkin saw the Soviet Communist Party lurching into the territory
of arbitrary application of power. He sought a means to counteract this, without upend-
ing the basic state structures of the Soviet Union. Between 1960 and 1991, Valery Zorkin
steeped himself in the work of the statist school. He wrote biographies of Boris Chicherin
as well as Sergei Muromtsev, another prominent representative. Zorkin originally intended
to teach constitutional law at Moscow State University but was unable to defend his thesis
outlining the efforts of the late tsarist statists in developing a less ideological, sociological
theory of law. The Academy of the Ministry of Internal Affairs—which was looking for
more "liberals" under the leadership of Major General Sergei Krylov—recruited Zorkin to
continue his work. For more details on Zorkin's Soviet-era academic life, see Boris Vishnevskiy, "Eks-predsedatel' konstitutstionnogo suda" [Ex-chairman of the constitutional
court], *Nezavisimaya gazeta,* March 28, 1998. See also Zor'kin (1984).

50. Zorkin had many supporters in official Russian circles and in the 2000s became a
central figure in the efforts to restore Russian state power under Putin. In March 2000, Mr.
Putin awarded Zorkin a medal for his long service to the Russian state.

51. Valery Zorkin's articles in *Rossiyskaya gazeta* in December 2011 and January 2012
exemplify this application of late tsarist statism to the present day. See "Dukh zakona"
[Spirit of the law], *Rossiyskaya gazeta,* December 12, 2011, at www.rg.ru/2011/12/11/
zorkin-site.html; "Rossiya: dvizheniye k pravy ili khaosu?" [Russia: moving toward law
or chaos?], *Rossiyskaya gazeta,* January 26, 2012, at www.rg.ru/2012/01/26/zorkin.html.

52. In his comments to David Hearst and Tom Parfitt in the January 2012 interview
with *The Guardian,* Gleb Pavlovsky stresses the unique position of the Russian president
standing above absolutely everything in the Russian constitution: "The idea of presidential
power that stands higher than all three powers, that is in our constitution. The president
has a special kind of power which does not relate [even] to executive power . . . executive
power ends with the prime minister. . . . The president is above them all, like a tsar. And
for Putin that is a dogma. . . ."

53. See, for example, "Russia's Putin Won't Run for Re-Election in 2008," Reuters,
April 13, 2005.

54. Marc Bennetts, "Putin Quits United Russia Party," RIA Novosti, April 24, 2012,
at http://en.rian.ru/russia/20120424/173011431.html.

55. Putin, "Rossiya sosredotochivayetsya: vyzovy, na kotoryye my dolzhny otvetit'"
[Russia muscles up: the challenges we must respond to], January 16, 2012. Originally
printed in *Izvestiya,* at http://izvestia.ru/news/511884. See also William Partlett, "Vladimir
Putin and the Law," Brookings Institution, February 28, 2012, at www.brookings.edu/

opinions/2012/0228_putin_law_partlett.aspx. Mr. Putin also seems to have borrowed from Valery Zorkin in formulating some of his ideas on the "national question" seven days later. Compare Vladimir Putin, "Rossiya: natsional'nyy vopros" [Russia: the national question], January 23, 2012, originally printed in *Nezavisimaya gazeta*, at www.ng.ru/politics/2012-01-23/1_national.html, with Valery Zorkin, "Sovremennoye gosudarstvo v epokhu etnosotsial'nogo mnogoobraziya" [The modern state in an era of ethno-social diversity], *Rossiyskaya gazeta*, September 7, 2011, available on *Rossiyskaya gazeta*'s website at www.rg.ru/2011/09/07/zorkin-site.html.

56. See Putin, "Demokratiya i kachestvo gosudarstva" [Democracy and the quality of the state], *Kommersant*, February 6, 2012, at www.kommersant.ru/doc/1866753.

57. Vladimir Putin, Annual Address to the Federal Assembly of the Russian Federation, April 25, 2005. For an example of the misquotation see Mike Eckel, "Putin Calls Soviet Collapse a 'Geopolitical Catastrophe,'" Associated Press, April 26, 2005.

58. Quoted in "Putin Warns 'Mistakes' Could Bring Back '90s Woes," RFE/RL, October 17, 2011, at www.rferl.org/content/putin_mistakes_could_bring_back_1990s_woes/24362626.html.

59. Gaidar (2007).

60. Gaidar came from a prominent intellectual family with a long record of service to the state. His father, Timur Gaidar, was a Soviet naval officer and later a military correspondent for the Soviet flagship newspaper, *Pravda;* his grandfather, Arkady Gaidar, was a celebrated journalist and writer of popular Soviet-era children's stories; and his maternal grandfather, Pavel Bazhov, was the author of a famous collection of fairy and folk tales from Russia's Urals region.

61. Authors' personal notes from Yegor Gaidar presentations at the Brookings Institution's Hewett Forum on December 3, 2007, and April 14, 2009; and from research meetings with Yegor Gaidar at the Gaidar Institute in Moscow on September 6, 2005, and at the Brookings Institution in Washington on November 3, 2009.

62. Gleb Pavlovsky interview with *The Guardian*, January 24, 2012. A decade earlier, retired KGB general Nikolai Leonov, in his interview with *Spetsnaz Rossii* in 2001, described "the pile of rubble to which the [Russian] great power [*velikaya derzhava*] has been reduced" by Yeltsin, who "was broken down by the events in Chechnya . . . by the entire situation . . . and left the country in a state of de facto disintegration." Leonov also described Chechnya as part of a "terrible legacy" that Vladimir Putin inherited from Boris Yeltsin: "A cancerous tumor in the North Caucasus that was metastasizing throughout the country." See Yevdokimov, "Russkaya pravda Generala Leonova."

63. See "Pis'mennoye interv'yu v'etnamskoy gazeta 'Nyan zan'" [Written interview with Vietnamese newspaper "Nyan zan"], February 27, 2001, at http://archive.kremlin.ru/text/appears/2001/02/28489.shtml.

64. See Dunlop (1993), p. 13. Even Ramazan Abdulatipov, an ethnic Avar from the Russian North Caucasus and the deputy chairman of the Russian Council of the Federation, the upper house of the Russian parliament where the republics were represented, was sympathetic to this view—although he acknowledged that getting rid of the existing administrative structures would simply "provoke additional conflict." Ramazan Abdulatipov, "O federativnoy i natsional'noy politike Rossiyskogo gosudarstva" [On the federal and national policies of the Russian state], published in full in *CMG Bulletin,* June 1995, p. 8.

65. Sergei Shakhrai, Yegor Gaidar, Grigory Yavlinsky, and former Russian nationalities minister Valery Tishkov all favored the creation of new administrative units whose privileges would be similar to those given to the constituent states in Germany's *Länder* system. Gleb Pavlovsky, in his January 24, 2012, interview with *The Guardian*, notes that Putin simply appropriated all these ideas as soon as he got into office: "Yeltsin also dreamed about such an arrangement but he just had no chance to achieve it. It's a very popular idea in Russia."

66. An eighth district was introduced in 2010.

67. See Hill (2005).

68. For a discussion of Mikhalkov's career and controversial relationship with Vladimir Putin, see "Cannes Russia Director: Genius or Pro-Kremlin Opportunist," *Sydney Morning Herald,* May 19, 2010, at www.smh.com.au/entertainment/movies/cannes-russia-director-genius-or-prokremlin-opportunist-20100519-vdak.html.

69. In the wake of the film, Mikhalkov was outspoken in his support for Putin staying on in 2008 for what would have been a third consecutive, but unconstitutional, presidential term. See Georgy Bovt, "Putin's Plan for Higher Turnout," *Moscow Times,* November 1, 2007. Later, in October 2010, Mikhalkov put out his own manifesto on the Russian state entitled *Pravo i pravda: Manifest prosveshchennogo konservatizma* [Law and truth: a manifesto of enlightened conservatism]. He addressed his 2008 transgression by putting the Russian constitution back in its rightful place as the fundamental law of the state and the guarantor of Russian statehood. Mikhalkov declared himself to be like Putin, the representative of a larger group of *gosudarstvenniki.* He also laid out once more the core ideas of Putin's 1999 Millennium Message. Mikhalkov talked about restoring traditional Russian values, focusing on Russian history and culture. He extolled the importance of unity and revisited many of the concepts also propounded by Valery Zorkin in his discussions of a *pravovoye gosudarstvo*—including society's subordination to the state. See Mikhalkov (2010).

70. Bobkov (1995).

71. Ibid., pp. 376–77.

72. Ibid., pp. 378–79.

73. Putin, Millennium Message, December 29, 1999.

74. Ibid.

75. Vladislav Surkov, who served as the first deputy chief of the presidential administration from 1999 to 2011, as a first deputy prime minister from 2011 to 2013, and then as top aide to Putin, is widely viewed as the Kremlin's leading ideologue, or "gray cardinal," who has played a key role in formulating many of Putin's core ideas about the Russian state. See Pomerantsev (2011), pp. 3–6; and Vladimir Stepanov, "The Gray Cardinal Leaves the Kremlin," *Russia Beyond the Headlines,* December 28, 2011, at http://rbth.com/articles/2011/12/28/the_gray_cardinal_leaves_the_kremlin_14123.html. The source cited in the first edition, "Bespartiynyy ideolog Vladislav Surkov" [The partyless ideologue Vladislav Surkov], *Gazeta.ru,* May 16, 2007, has been removed from the Internet.

CHAPTER 4

1. The ideas elaborated on here were first published in Hill and Gaddy (2012).

2. This is essentially in keeping with George Orwell's observation: "Who controls the past, controls the future: who controls the present controls the past." Orwell (1949), p. 37. Indeed, in May 2012, Putin appointed as the new Russian minister of culture Vladimir Medinsky, a best-selling Russian author of a series of books on Russian history, "Myths about Russia," that take issue with negative depictions of Russia's past. In 2009, Medinsky had been appointed to a Russian presidential commission focused on combating the "falsification" of history in Russian publications and pronouncements. See Amy Knight, "Russia's Propaganda Man," *NYR* (blog), *New York Review of Books,* May 31, 2012, at www.nybooks.com/blogs/nyrblog/2012/may/31/putins-propaganda-man/.

3. Blotskiy (2002), p. 76. In two volumes, Blotsky weaves together biographical information and extracts from interviews with Putin and people who knew him at various stages in his career. Blotsky, interestingly and fittingly, does not actually call his book chapters "chapters" but "istorii" or "histories": "Istoriya pervaya" (First history), "Istoriya vtoraya" (Second history), and so on.

4. Cited in Guy Falconbridge and Gleb Bryanski, "Putin Invokes History's Lions for Return to Kremlin," Reuters, November 1, 2011, at http://in.reuters.com/article/2011/11/01/idINIndia-60243820111101.

5. For a detailed discussion of the references to and the uses of history by Putin and Boris Yeltsin in their speeches, see Malinova (2011), pp. 106–22. In his article on the Russian national question in *Nezavisimaya gazeta* in January 2012, for example, Putin makes a series of selective historical references that leap from eleventh-century Russian texts to the nineteenth century and then post-communist Russia but blatantly skips the Soviet period, in an effort to create a harmonious picture of inter-ethnic relations in Russia.

6. See Clifford Gaddy and Fiona Hill, "Vladimir Putin's League of Extraordinary Gentlemen," Valdai Discussion Club, January 30, 2012, at www.brookings.edu/opinions/2012/0130_putin_gaddy_hill.aspx.

7. Riasanovsky (1959), p. 74.

8. Konstantin Azadovsky, "Russia's Silver Age," in Isham (1995), pp. 79–90, p. 84.

9. Ibid., p. 89. The governments of both periods adopted strikingly similar strategies to create links with an earlier, purportedly glorious, Russian past. In 1913, for example, the Romanov dynasty celebrated 300 years of rule in Russia. The occasion itself, and the years immediately preceding it, was marked by the glorification of Russia's medieval roots in the Muscovite state. There were building projects, and Court balls and pageants with seventeenth-century themes. Although St. Petersburg was not founded until the eighteenth century, an old Muscovite-style church was built in the heart of the imperial capital. Some of the city's buildings were reconstructed in a neo-Byzantine manner, evocative of old Muscovy. For a comprehensive discussion of the importance of imperial myth, symbolism, and evocations of the past in tsarist Russia, see Wortman (2006). The parallels between the 1900s and the 1990s in terms of events, ideas and debates—the century's bookends—are also one of the key themes of Fiona Hill's 1998 Harvard history Ph.D. dissertation.

10. The authors personally observed these during a visit to the Kremlin for the September 2005 Valdai Discussion Club meeting with Vladimir Putin.

11. See "Vystupleniye Predsedatelya Soveta Federatsii S. M. Mironova na konferentsii 'Rol' Gosudarstvennogo soveta i Soveta Federatsii Federal'nogo Sobraniya Rossiyskoy Federatsii v istorii rossiyskogo parlamentarizma" [Speech by Chairman of the Federation Council S.M. Mironov at the conference on "The Role of the State Council and the Federation Council of the Federal Assembly of the Russian Federation in the history of Russian parliamentarianism"], December 18, 2006, at http://council.gov.ru/inf_ps/chronicle/2006/12/item5465.html.

12. Andrei Soldatov and Irina Borogan, in their book *The New Nobility*, about the rise of Russian officials with backgrounds in the KGB and FSB in the 2000s, recount in detail the efforts to reinstate and reinvigorate the reputation of former intelligence head and Soviet leader Yury Andropov after 1999. These included Putin's attendance at a December 20, 1999, ceremony for the reinstallation of a plaque at FSB headquarters honoring Andropov; the naming of a school and the erection of a 10-foot-tall statue to celebrate the ninetieth anniversary of Andropov's birth; and the publication of several books on Andropov's life and work. In 2005, a bust of Felix Dzerzhinsky, the founder of the first Soviet intelligence agency, the Bolshevik's secret police, or *Cheka*, which had been removed from the inner courtyard of the Moscow police headquarters, was put back in its original place. However, the more famous statue of Dzerzhinsky that stood a few streets away in Lubyanka (formerly Dzerzhinsky) Square outside FSB headquarters before being toppled in 1991 was not similarly resurrected, in spite of a proposal by then Moscow Mayor Yury Luzhkov to put it back on the square in 2002. See Soldatov and Borogan (2010), pp. 91–97; Brian Whitmore, "Andropov's Ghost," *The Power Vertical* (blog), RFE/RL, February 9, 2009, at www.rferl.org/content/Andropovs_Ghost/1467159.html; and Douglas Birch, "Russian Nostalgia Feeds Struggle Over Monument to KGB Founder," *Baltimore Sun*, November 30, 2002, at http://articles.baltimore

sun.com/2002-11-30/news/0211300276_1_statue-secret-police-monument. Similarly, Donald Rayfield in his work on Stalin notes that in 2002 the Russian post office issued a set of stamps, "The 80th Anniversary of Soviet Counterintelligence," depicting some of the most "dreaded" leaders of the secret services in the 1920s who had organized the killing of hundreds of thousands of Soviet citizens. See Rayfield (2004), pp. xii–xiii.

13. See Max Delany, "An Inside Track to President Putin's Kremlin. Profile: Vladimir Yakunin," *St. Petersburg Times,* October 2, 2007, at http://sptimes.ru/index.php?action_id=2&story_id=23175. See also the website for the Fond Andreya Pervozvannogo (St. Andrew's Fund), which Yakunin heads, at www.fap.ru/.

14. See Elif Batuman, "The Bells: How Harvard Helped Preserve a Russian Legacy," *The New Yorker,* April 27, 2009. Abstract at www.newyorker.com/reporting/2009/04/27/090427fa_fact_batuman.

15. See Bush (2010), p. 196; and Rice (2011), p. 63.

16. See, for example, Yakov Krotov, "Oni v svoikh korridorakh: Svyataya pustota–Vliyaniye dukhovnika prezidenta na sud'bu strani sil'no preuvelicheno" [In their corridors: A sacred nonentity—The influence of the president's confessor on the country's destiny is greatly exaggerated], *Obshchaya gazeta,* December 20, 2001. Translation by *Johnson's Russia List,* under the heading "Views of Putin's Priest Described," January 8, 2002, at www.cdi.org/russia/johnson/6009-10.cfm.

17. See Gvosdev (2009), pp. 347–59. Gvosdev reviews Vladislav Surkov's writings on Russian political culture between 1997–2007. The discussion of sovereign democracy is on p. 349.

18. This kind of reasoning also comes out in the work of Valery Zorkin and in a 2012 proposal by Putin associate Vladimir Yakunin and Moscow State University scholar Stepan Sulashkin to rewrite the Russian constitution in line with Russia's historical values of *obshchinnost'* (community), *kollektivizm* (collectivism), and *paternalizm* (paternalism). This would involve purging the current 1993 Russian constitution of the universal democratic values enshrined within it and returning to the basic concepts outlined by Putin in the 1999 Millennium Message. See http://kommersant.ru/doc/1939276.

19. Ellen Barry, then the *New York Times*'s Moscow bureau chief, related, for example, in an e-mail exchange with the authors in early February 2012 that during an interview she conducted with Putin's press secretary, Dmitry Peskov, during Putin's campaign for the March 4 presidential election, she asked Peskov how Putin keeps up with all of the changes in Russian society. Peskov responded that Putin does this by "speaking with ordinary Russians [the *narod*]." Putin believes that he understands the Russians more than anyone, by virtue of the communion achieved during his interactions with the *narod.* See also Ellen Barry, "Putin Aide Says Foreign Hands Are Behind Protests," *New York Times,* February 3, 2012, at http://www.nytimes.com/2012/02/04/world/europe/putin-aide-promises-significant-changes-in-russian-political-system.html?_r=0.

20. See Fiona Hill, "Dinner with Putin: Musings on the Politics of Modernization in Russia," Brookings Foreign Policy Trip Reports, No. 18, October 2010, at www.brookings.edu/reports/2010/10_russia_putin_hill.aspx.

21. See the official website of the *Narodnyy front* at http://narodfront.ru/organization/20110606/379742791.html.

22. Bobkov (1995), p. 381.

23. Putin, Millennium Message, December 29, 1999, available in Russian on the *Nezavisimaya gazeta* website at www.ng.ru/politics/1999-12-30/4_millenium.html.

24. "Predsedatel' Pravitel'stva Rossiyskoy Federatsii V.V. Putin prinyal uchastiye v rabote syezda Vserossiyskoy politicheskoy partii 'Yedinaya Rossiya'" [Prime Minister Vladimir Putin takes part in the conference of the "United Russia" Party], November 27, 2011, at http://archive.premier.gov.ru/events/news/17248/. The English version is at http://archive.premier.gov.ru/eng/events/news/17248/.

25. An overview of the August 31–September 7, 2010, Valdai Discussion Club meeting is available on the Valdai website at http://valdaiclub.com/event/22152.html.

26. Authors' personal notes from Valdai Discussion Club meeting with Vladimir Putin in the Rus' Sanatorium in Sochi, September 6, 2010.

27. Mikhalkov (2010). In the penultimate sentence of the citation, the Russian word *svoi* is equivalent to *nashi* or "ours," while *chuzhiye* is "alien" or "other." So Mikhalkov, here, is echoing Putin's frequent admonition against dividing everything up into "ours" and "not ours" or "us versus them."

28. In his last address to parliament as prime minister, on April 11, 2012, for example, Putin remarked, in response to a question from a Duma member, about the importance of having an all-encompassing idea of the Russian people: "You know, it's very easy for me to say this, I've already talked about this publicly, I was handed some church documents showing that from some year after 1600, extending right up to me here, all my relatives lived in one single village about 120 or 180 kilometers from Moscow, and for 300 and some years they went to one and the same church." See "Predsdatel' Pravitel'stva Rossiyskoy Federatsii V.V. vystupil v Gosudarstvennoy Dume s otchyotom o deyatel'nosti Pravitel'stva Rossiiskoy Federatsii za 2011 god" [Chairman of the Government of the Russian Federation V.V. Putin appeared before the State Duma with the report on the activity of the Government of the Russian Federation for 2011], April 11, 2012, at http://archive. premier.gov.ru/events/news/18671/. The English version is at http://archive.premier.gov.ru/eng/events/news/18671/.

29. See, for example, "United Russia—Racing to the 2012 Elections," *Nezavisimaya gazeta,* translated and published by RIA Novosti in *Russian Press—Behind the Headlines,* October 7, 2011, at http://en.ria.ru/papers/20111007/167471677.html.

30. The authors are grateful to Maria Lipman of the Carnegie Endowment's Moscow Center, and editor of *Pro et Contra,* for reminding them of this contest, along with its circumstances and peculiarities, when we were writing *The National Interest* article. See also Tom Parfitt, "Medieval warrior overcomes Stalin in poll to name greatest Russian," *The Guardian,* December 28, 2008, at www.guardian.co.uk/world/2008/dec/29/stalin-name-of-russia.

31. As part of his initial efforts to restore order, in August 1906, Stolypin decreed the establishment of military-run civilian field courts, which summarily convicted those who had already been deemed guilty. The nooses on the gallows that were used for executions—during what the Soviets' later portrayed as Stolypin's nine-month reign of terror—were known as "Stolypin's neckties." See Pipes (1990), pp. 170-71. For a discussion of Stolypin's views on the balance between repression and reform, see Pipes (2005), p. 175.

32. This was Stolypin's "wager on the strong," an attempt to create a natural conservative force in the countryside in support of the Russian monarchy. As a number of scholars have pointed out, this is one area where Putin has not taken the lessons of history to heart in his reading of Stolypin: "The lack of such a deliberate policy of creating a supporting base for Putinism is . . . one of its key failings—as the [2011–12] protests show, the 'new class' is . . . urban and frankly unsupportive. . . . [Vladimir Putin only] looks at elites and an unvariagated mass population [when he looks at Russian society]." Mark Galeotti, in written exchange with authors, July 24, 2012. See also Mark Galeotti, "Putin, Kudrin and the Real Stolypin," *In Moscow's Shadows* (blog), January 6, 2012, at http://inmoscows shadows.wordpress.com/2012/01/06/putin-kudrin-and-the-real-stolypin/. Galeotti's point was reinforced at the November 2011 Valdai Discussion Club meetings in Kaluga, when Kremlin sociologists and advisers repeatedly talked about the elite and the *narod.* In spite of being pressed by other participants on the issue, they failed to differentiate the emergence of new social and interest groups within these two sweeping categories and their roles in shaping public opinion. Authors' personal notes from meetings on "2011–12 Elections and the Future of Russia. Development Scenarios for the Next 5–8 Years," Kaluga, November 7–9, 2011.

33. See Pipes (1990), pp. 169–70 and pp. 177–78.

34. Pipes (2005), p. 177.

35. Authors' personal notes from Valdai Discussion Club meeting with Vladimir Putin at Bocharov Ruchey, the presidential dacha in Sochi, September 14, 2007.

36. See Pipes (1990), pp. 175–77.

37. Falkus (1972), pp. 83–84.

38. Putin address to State Duma, April 11, 2012 (cited in full in note 28).

39. One link to the Russia 2020 strategy report by the Russian Ministry of Economic Development, "Innovatsionnaya Rossiya–2020 (Strategiya innovatsiyonnogo razvitiya Rossiyskoy Federatsii na period do 2020 goda)" [Innovative Russia–2020 (a strategy for the innovative development of the Russian Federation in the period until 2020)], can be downloaded at at http://innovation.gov.ru/taxonomy/term/586.

40. This is also essentially the same idea that the Yeltsin team expressed in the 1997 *poslaniye,* that if his administration's reform program was left incomplete, order would never be fully restored to the Russian state. See Hill, "Dinner with Putin: Musings on the Politics of Modernization in Russia," Brookings Foreign Policy Trips Reports; and Fiona Hill and Clifford Gaddy, "Putin's Next Move in Russia: Observations from the 8th Annual Valdai International Discussion Club," December 12, 2011, at www.brookings.edu/interviews/2011/1212_putin_gaddy_hill. aspx. See also Putin's meeting with a group of Russian political scientists on February 6, 2012, in Moscow as reported by Fedor Lukyanov at http://ria.ru/vybor2012_analysis/20120207/559346082.html.

41. Cited in Figes (2003).

42. Putin address to State Duma, April 11, 2012.

CHAPTER 5

1. This story is recounted in Gevorkyan, Timakova, and Kolesnikov (2000), pp. 9–10.

2. See Moskoff (2002), p. 196.

3. Putin press conference with Russian and foreign media, June 20, 2003. Putin continued: "90 percent of the potatoes grown in the country are grown in these little private gardens. 90 percent! And these gardens produce 80 percent of the vegetables and 60 percent of the fruit." These percentages were only slightly less as late as 2011. That year Russian families privately grew one-third more potatoes than the entire U.S. farm sector. The Russian total of "personal" potatoes amounted to over 1,200 pounds per household. Authors' calculations from data from the Russian Federal State Statistics Service, *Statistical Yearbook for 2011.* Putin's comment about working on the family plot is cited in Ries (2009), p. 202. In her article, Ries talks about the potato's centrality to mechanisms of everyday survival and basic subsistence in Russia and how the humble vegetable also functions as a "complex system of knowledge embedded in historical memory." The full source for the press conference document is "Stenograficheskiy otchet o press-konferentsii dlya rossiyskikh i inostrannykh zhurnalistov" [Press conference with Russian and foreign media], June 20, 2003, at http://archive.kremlin.ru/appears/2003/06/20/1237_type63380 type63381type82634_47449.shtml. The English version is at http://archive.kremlin.ru/eng/text/speeches/2003/06/20/1712_type82915_47467.shtml.

4. Gaidar (2007), p. 145 (cited from a document produced by the Presidium of the Soviet Council of Ministers).

5. Ibid., p. 187 (the quotes are from Boris Gidaspov, first secretary of the Leningrad oblast Committee of the Soviet Communist Party at a Soviet politburo meeting on November 16, 1990).

6. Cited in ibid., p. 198.

7. Cited in ibid., p. 239.

8. Cited in ibid., pp. 198–99.

9. See Gessen (2012), pp. 104–05 and pp. 118–19.

10. See "Prime Minister Vladimir Putin Meets with Heads and Editors-in-Chief of Domestic Television and Radio Broadcasting Companies and Print Media," January 18, 2012, at http://archive.premier.gov.ru/eng/events/news/17798/.

11. See box in chapter 9 for a more detailed discussion of Putin's dissertation.

12. King and Cleland (1978).

13. Ibid., passim.

14. Zen'kovich (2006), p. 130. In March 2004, *Gosrezerv* was renamed the Russian Federal Agency for State Reserves, *Rosrezerv*.

15. Grigory Puganov and Yury Shtukin, "Zakroma Rodiny: Ne vse v Rossii plokho lezhit" [The granary of the Motherland: not everything is in a bad condition in Russia], *Izvestiya*, August 9, 2000, at http://dlib.eastview.com/browse/doc/3049287.

16. Andrey Sergeyev, "Vserossiyskaya zanachka" [The all-Russian stash], *Russkiy kur'er*, No. 11, March 20, 2006.

17. Ibid.

18. Puganov and Shtukin, *Izvestiya*, August 9, 2000.

19. Ibid.

20. Sergeyev, *Russkiy kur'er*, March 20, 2006.

21. Authors' calculations, based on information about the amount and types of commodities in the reserves described in Mikhail Falaleyev, "Veto na neprikosnovennyy zapas" [A veto on emergency stores], *Rossiyskaya gazeta*, May 19, 2006.

22. Yevgeniy Verlin, "Gosregulirovaniye. Aleksandr Grigor'ev: 'Polnykh analogov sistemy Rosrezerva v mire ne sushchestvuyet'" [Regulating the state. Alexander Grigoriev: "A complete analogue to the Rosrezerv system does not exist elsewhere in the world"], *Profil'*, July 17, 2006.

23. Cited in ibid.

24. Gaidar (2007), pp. 110–14.

25. See Gaddy and Ickes (2010), pp. 281–311, note 9.

26. See Gaddy and Ickes (2009).

27. See Gaddy and Ickes (2010).

28. Putin, address to State Duma, April 11, 2012. The Russian word *sostoyatel'nost'* has multiple meanings, which also encompass the idea of strength, fortitude, wealth, and wherewithal. See "Predsdatel' Pravitel'stva Rossiyskoy Federatsii V.V. vystupil v Gosudarstvennoy Dume s otchyotom o deyatel'nosti Pravitel'stva Rossiyskoy Federatsii za 2011 god" [Chairman of the Government of the Russian Federation V.V. Putin appeared before the State Duma with the report on the activity of the Government of the Russian Federation for 2011], April 11, 2012, at http://archive.premier.gov.ru/events/news/18671/. The English version is at http://archive.premier.gov.ru/eng/events/news/18671/.

29. Putin, address to the staff of the finance ministry, April 17, 2012, at www.newsru.com/russia/17apr2012/kudrin.html

30. Blotskiy (2002), pp. 59–62. The title of the chapter is an allusion to the Russian title of a 1971 American film that Putin cites in the book. In Russian it is *Generaly peschanykh kar'yerov*. The American original was *The Sandpit Generals*. The movie features the daily struggles of a street gang of homeless youths in Brazil. It became an iconic movie in the USSR. The newspaper *Komsomolskaya pravda* declared it its "best foreign film" in 1974, when Mr. Putin was in his early twenties. Soviet popular culture references are very typical of Putin—especially when trying to cast a spotlight on a particularly pertinent personal experience or in making an emphatic point.

31. Blotskiy (2002), pp. 60–61.

32. See Gevorkyan, Timakova, and Kolesnikov (2000), pp. 20–22; also Blotskiy (2002), pp. 125–36. Putin became particularly accomplished at judo, rising to the Leningrad City championship level and traveling frequently to out-of-town matches with his Leningrad City team.

33. See Evangelista (2002), pp. 46–86.

34. See, for example, Evangelista (2002), pp. 63–86; and Shevtsova (2005), pp. 134–62; citation is from p. 134.

35. See Gessen (2012). Her chapter "Rule of Terror," pp. 199–226, recounts the accusations of Putin's and the security service's alleged role in staging some of the terrorist attacks that led to war in 1999.

36. See, for example, "Chechnya and the North Caucasus. And They Call It Peace: Vladimir Putin's Presidency Began in Chechnya; the Region Is Restive as It Ends," *The Economist*, February 28, 2008.

37. Cited in Gevorkyan, Timakova, and Kolesnikov (2000), p. 133.

38. See references to Alexander Grigoriev's role in the North Caucasus and his award of a state medal for his services, in Zen'kovich (2006), p. 130; and references to the use of the state reserves to set up a medical response for the aftermath of the devastating school siege by Chechen terrorists in Beslan in North Ossetia, in Sergeyev, *Russkiy kur'er*, March 20, 2006.

39. Shevtsova (2005), p. 137.

40. Adrian Blomfield, "Russia Ends 10 Year War in Chechnya," *The Telegraph*, April 16, 2009, at www.telegraph.co.uk/news/worldnews/europe/russia/5165328/Russia-ends-10-year-war-in-Chechnya.html.

41. Cited in Gevorkyan, Timakova, and Kolesnikov (2000), pp. 133–35.

42. For a detailed discussion of the pernicious political and social impact of ethnic Russian nationalism and extremism see Lacquer (1993).

43. The number of Russian citizens associated with "culturally" or traditionally Muslim ethnic groups is often cited as between 15 and 20 million. Scholars of Islam in Russia, such as Mikhail Alekseev at the University of San Diego, argue, however, that the number of practicing Muslims in the Russian Federation is far lower, more in the range of 11 million and mostly concentrated in Russia's Volga region and the North Caucasus. See Alekseev, "Overcounting Russia's Muslims: Implications for Security and Society," PONARS Eurasia Policy Memo No. 27, August 2008, at www.gwu.edu/~ieresgwu/assets/docs/pepm_027.pdf.

44. See Anna Arutunyan and Lidia Okorokova, "Race Riot on Manezhnaya," *Moscow News*, December 13, 2010, at http://themoscownews.com/politics/20101213/188276816.html. Some Russian political commentators also saw it as a deliberate provocation to raise the specter of race riots and the risk of things spiraling out of control absent a strong, guiding hand from Vladimir Putin and the Russian government. Authors' personal notes from discussion with Russian journalist Oleg Kashin and analyst Pavel Baev, Brookings Institution, March 29, 2012.

45. Vladimir Zhirinovsky offered an anti-immigrant and anti-Chechen tirade to members of the Valdai Discussion Club at a meeting at the RIA Novosti headquarters in Moscow on November 10, 2011. Zhirinovsky's campaign posters for the 2011–12 electoral season touted a Russia for (ethnic) Russians.

46. Vladimir Putin, "Predsedatel' Pravitel'stva Rossiyskoy Federatsii V.V. Putin prinyal uchastiye v rabote syezda Vserossiyskoy politicheskoy partii 'Yedinaya Rossiya'" [Speech to the conference of the United Russia party], November 27, 2011. The link in Russian is at http://archive.premier.gov.ru/events/news/17248/. The English version is at http://archive.premier.gov.ru/eng/events/news/17248/.

47. Nashi is the largest of a set of pro-Kremlin youth groups created in the 2000s. It was founded in 2005, shortly after the Ukrainian Orange Revolution in which student activism and student groups played an important role. One Ukrainian student organization, PORA, followed consciously in the footsteps of youth groups that helped bring down

Slobodan Milosevic in Serbia in the 1990s. It created hundreds of branches and outposts around Ukraine, which were instrumental in uncovering and reporting the electoral fraud that sparked Ukraine's mass demonstrations from November 2004 to January 2005 and overturned the results of the presidential election. Putin and the Kremlin expropriated the Ukrainian PORA model and, in addition to Nashi, created groups like *Molodaya gvardiya* (Young guard) and *Stal'* (Steel). Nashi established a substantial Internet presence for organizational and promotional purposes and created an annual camp at Lake Seliger in Russia's Tver region, where Putin and other key Kremlin officials have come to engage with the campers. For a further discussion of Nashi activities see Lucas (2008), pp. 78–91. Nashi rallies and demonstrations in support of Putin were organized in December 2011 to counter the street protests in Moscow; see Miriam Elder, "Russian Election: Police, Troops and Youth Groups Stifle Anti-Putin Protests," *The Guardian*, December 6, 2011, at www. guardian.co.uk/world/2011/dec/06/russian-election-anti-putin-protests, and Simon Shuster, "The Empire Strikes Back: Putin Sends in the Storm Troopers," *Time*, December 7, 2011, at www.time.com/time/world/article/0,8599,2101741,00.html.

48. This discussion came right after the anti-Chechen diatribe by Vladimir Zhirinovsky to the group at the RIA Novosti headquarters, which was clearly intended to cast a contrasting spotlight on Putin's measured and "enlightened" position.

49. The official (Russian language) website for Milkhalkov's film, which won an award at the 2007 Venice Film Festival and was nominated for an Academy Award for "Best Foreign Language Film," is at www.trite.ru/projects_in.mhtml?PubID=124/.

50. See, for example, Gregory Fiefer, "The Price of Progress—Life in Kadyrov's Grozny Permeated by Fear," RFE/RL, August 11, 2009, at www.rferl.org/content/The_Price_Of_ Progress__Life_In_Kadyrovs_Grozny_Permeated_By_Fear/1797452.html; and the detailed profile of Ramzan Kadyrov in the *New York Times*, updated on October 6, 2011, at http:// topics.nytimes.com/top/reference/timestopics/people/k/ramzan_a_kadyrov/index.html.

51. For a discussion of the evolution of this general policy in the tsarist era, see Paul Henze, "Circassian Resistance to Russia," in Marie Bennigsen Broxup (1992). A PDF version of Henze's article is online at www.circassianworld.com/Circassian_Resistance.pdf.

52. Authors' personal notes from meeting with journalist Oleg Kashin at the Brookings Institution, March 29, 2012.

53. See, for example, "Press conference by Russia's Choice Leaders Yegor Gaidar and Sergei Kovalev," *Official Kremlin International News Broadcasts*, December 13, 1993— just after the 1993 Russian parliamentary elections—in which Gaidar notes that "the threat of fascism [in Russia] has risen tall and high. Zhirinovsky means war, blood, poverty and final death for Russia. . . . The people have been deceived, deceived by populist slogans, unrealizable promises, and cheap acting." President Yeltsin made similar references to extremism, fascism, and aggressive nationalism in a post–parliamentary elections public appearance on December 22, 1993. See "Yeltsin Vows to Push Ahead with Reforms as he Keeps an Eye on Right-Wing Leader," *Vancouver Sun*, December 23, 1993. Parallels between Yeltsin's and Putin's tactics in instilling fear about what might succeed them are also noted in Payne (2007).

54. See the transcript for the show at http://government.ru/docs/17409/.

55. See Vladimir Putin, "Rossiya: Natsional'nyy vopros" [Russia: the national question], *Nezavisimaya gazeta*, January 23, 2012, at www.ng.ru/politics/2012-01-23/1_ national.html. An English translation is available at http://rt.com/politics/official-word/ migration-national-question-putin-439/.

56. The article also draws heavily from Valery Zorkin. In his own article "Sovremennoye gosudarstvo v epokhu etnosotsial'nogo mnogoobraziya" [The modern state in an era of ethno-social diversity], Zorkin lays out some of the same key ideas, including the failure of multiculturalism and the need to use law to increase people's identification with the government. See *Rossiyskaya gazeta*, September 7, 2011, at www.rg.ru/2011/09/07/ zorkin-site.html.

57. See, for example, Sergei Markov, "The Enlargement of Agencies is Politics: A Fundamental Administrative Reform Will Be Its Logical Continuation," *Strana.ru*, October 17, 2001, translated in *Johnson's Russia List*, October 18, 2001, at www.russialist.org/5496-13.php.

58. See, for example, Valery Tishkov, "Understanding Violence for Post-Conflict Reconstruction in Chechnya," Centre for Applied Studies in International Negotiations (CASIN); Tishkov, "The Rehabilitation of War-Torn Societies Project" (Geneva, January 2001), at www.chechnyaadvocacy.org/conflict/Tishkov.pdf; and Tishkov (2004).

59. This is all very clearly laid out in Tishkov (1997). Several Russian bloggers immediately noticed Putin's reliance on Tishkov's work in this article. They also highlighted some direct appropriations from a 2009 monograph Tishkov wrote with two colleagues on the importance of stressing Russia's multiethnicity in its education system. See, for example, Alexander Morozov's blog at http://amoro1959.livejournal.com/1687369.html.

60. See "Rodina Mat' Zovet!" in White (1988), p. 123, plate 6.7.

61. Zegers and Druick (2011) have several examples of Soviet posters referencing historical figures and their role in saving the Russian state. One poster from July 1942, for example, shows the images of, among others, Alexander Nevsky, Dmitry Donskoi, and Mikhail Kutuzov with the slogan "Let the valiant image of our great ancestors inspire us in this war." Zegers and Druick (2011), p. 84. A similarly themed poster evokes the number of wars fought against the Germanic peoples (Teutonic Knights, Prussians, Germans) across Russian history: "Always, in all times and ages, Russian soldiers have beaten/clobbered the Prussians. At the Neva—defeated. Under Ivan the terrible—defeated. Under Suvorov—defeated. Under Brusilov—defeated. They were defeated in the Ukrainian Civil War. We will finish the German vermin off once and for all." Zegers and Druick (2011), p. 243.

62. For a more detailed discussion, see Gvosdev (2009). Gvosdev looks at Vladislav Surkov's, and thus Putin's, appropriation of the ideas and themes of a range of key Russian thinkers and émigré writers from the early twentieth century. The revival of the works of Ilyin, Trubetskoi, Gumilev, and others in the 1990s is also discussed in Fiona Hill's 1998 Harvard history Ph.D. dissertation.

63. Petro (1995), pp. 93–95.

64. Paul Robinson of the University of Ottawa writes: "Like Stolypin . . . Ilyin believed that the source of Russia's problems was an insufficiently developed 'legal consciousness' (*pravosoznaniye*). Given this, democracy was not a suitable form of government. He wrote that 'at the head of the state there must be a *single will*.' Russia needed a 'united and strong state power, *dictatorial* in the scope of its powers.' At the same time, there must be clear limits to these powers. The ruler must have popular support; organs of the state must be responsible and accountable; the principle of legality must be preserved and all persons must be equal under the law. Freedom of conscience, speech, and assembly must be guaranteed. Private property should be sacrosanct. Ilyin believed that the state should be supreme in those areas in which it had competence, but should stay entirely out of those areas in which it did not, such as private life and religion. Totalitarianism, he said, was 'godless.'" Paul Robinson, "Putin's Philosophy," *The American Conservative*, March 28, 2012, at www.theamericanconservative.com/articles/putins-philosophy/.

65. See, for example, Andrei Soldatov and Irina Borogan, "The Mindset of Russia's Security Services: A Mix of Orthodox Christianity, Trails of Slavic Paganism and a Pride in Being Successors to the Soviet and Byzantine Empires, Both Destroyed by the Western Crusaders," *Agentura.ru*, December 29, 2010, at www.agentura.ru/english/dossier/mindset/. In this article, Soldatov and Borogan discuss Putin's focus on Ilyin, and Ilyin's own writings on how to combine Christian values, Russian patriotism, and the duty of a military officer. The authors also point out the links between Ilyin's ideas and Vladislav Surkov's conception of Sovereign Democracy, as well as discussing how the FSB, the successor to the KGB, strengthened its ties to the Russian Orthodox Church in the 2000s—including restoring the Cathedral of St. Sophia of God's Wisdom next to the FSB headquarters on Moscow's

Lubyanka Square. See also Vladimir Putin, Annual Address to the Federal Assembly of the Russian Federation, April 25, 2005; Vladimir Putin, Annual Address to the Federal Assembly of the Russian Federation, May 10, 2006; and "Stenograficheskii otchet o zasedanii Gosudarstvennogo Soveta. 'O pervoocherednykh merakh po realizatsii gosudarstvennoy sistemy profilaktiki pravonarushenii i obespecheniyu obshchestvennoy bezopasnosti'" [Stenographers report on the session of the State Council. "On priority measures for implementing the state system protecting against violations of the law and ensuring public security], June 29, 2007, at http://archive.kremlin.ru/appears/2007/06/29/1953_type63378_136505.shtml.

66. Steven Lee Myers, "For a New Russia, New Relics," *New York Times*, October 9, 2005. Ilyin, along with Stolypin, Chicherin, and a panoply of Russian reformist tsars and literary figures, features in Mikhalkov's October 2010 manifesto. Mikhalkov, *Pravo i pravda: Manifest prosveshchennogo konservatizma*.

67. See Zakharovich (June 3, 2009).

68. Ivanov, "Russian Social Life and Thought," in Isham (1995), pp. 23–37, specifically pp. 27–28; and Khakimov (1997). More than three-quarters of Russian territory lies in Asia, although most of its population is concentrated in Europe. See also Orlando Figes's reference to the Eurasianist movement in exile and its founding manifesto "Exodus to the East," which was published in 1921. Figes (2002), pp. 423–24. The revival of Eurasianist thought in the 1990s was also discussed in Fiona Hill's 1998 Harvard history Ph.D. dissertation.

69. See, for example, the collection of the essays of some of the Eurasianists and a critique of their philosophy in Novikova and Sizemskaya (1993). See also Laruelle (2008); Torbakov (2003); and Torbakov (2008).

70. See Gleb Bryanski, "Russia's Putin wants to Build 'Eurasian Union,'" Reuters, October 3, 2011. This is also an old idea dating back to the 1990s. In his 1995 memoirs, the KGB's Filipp Bobkov, for example, references the idea of a Eurasian Union, linking it conceptually to the CIS (Bobkov, 1995, p. 379).

71. Keenan, Szporluk, and Rumer (1997).

72. Lev Gumilev's ethnographic works, such as *Etnogenez i biosfera Zemli* [Ethnogenesis and the Earth's biosphere] (1989), were the most popular. Russia's preeminent scholar of ethnicity Valery Tishkov—who Putin drew heavily on in his campaign article on the Russian national question—offers a critique of Gumilev's theories, and an assessment of the impact of his work, in his groundbreaking 1997 book on ethnicity and nationalism in Russia. See Tishkov (1997).

73. For a detailed discussion of the work of Vladimir Nabokov and its resonance in Putin's Russia of the 2000s, see Khrushcheva (2008).

74. Nabokov (2004), p. 51. *Pnin* was first published in the United States by Doubleday in 1957.

75. For participants in the Valdai Discussion Club see http://valdaiclub.com/authors/.

76. See http://archive.premier.gov.ru/eng/events/news/17409/ and www.moskva-putinu.ru/.

77. Authors' personal notes from Valdai Discussion Club meeting with Vladimir Putin in the Rus' Sanatorium in Sochi, September 6, 2010.

78. Putin, address to the State Duma, April 11, 2012.

79. Cited in Waldron (1998), pp. 47–48.

CHAPTER 6

1. Putin, his then wife, Lyudmila, and Putin's secretary at the time, Marina Yental'tseva, relate the story in some detail in Gevorkyan, Timakova, and Kolesnikov (2000), pp. 113–18.

2. A link to a facsimile of the original founding document for the Ozero cooperative listing all of the members is provided on *Antikompromat,* a website maintained by Russian

researcher Vladimir Pribylovsky, in the section detailing elements of Putin's biography at www.anticompromat.org/putin/putinbio.html. The specific link to the document is at www.anticompromat.org/putin/ozero.html. The document lists Vladimir Putin, Vladimir Yakunin, Vladimir Smirnov, Andrei Fursenko, Sergei Fursenko, Yury Kovalchuk, Nikolai Shamalov, and Viktor Myachin as the founding members of the Ozero dacha cooperative. Another article, Viktor Yushkin, "Lyudi kak teni" [People like shadows], *Postimees* (Estonia), September 20, 2007, at http://rus.postimees.ee/200907/glavnaja/mnenie/22618.php, lists the group members and discusses the evolution of their various careers and fortunes since 2006. According to one account, Vladimir Yakunin claims that the idea to found the dacha community was his. It came "after a visit by Yakunin and his business partners to a dacha owned by Putin in the area." Max Delany, "An Inside Track to President Putin's Kremlin," *St. Petersburg Times,* October 2, 2007, at www.sptimes.ru/index.php?action_id=2&story_id=23175. The region where the dacha community was established, the Priozersk district, was also the same area where Putin's close associate Viktor Zubkov spent his career as a farm director and Communist Party official in the Soviet period.

3. Lilia Shevtsova, cited in Martin Sieff, "Scandal Reveals Russia's Power Struggle," United Press International, August 31, 1999 (accessed through Nexis.com). In his book on Stolypin, Peter Waldron argues that Stolypin's outsider status, his comparative lack of bureaucratic experience, and his seeming reluctance to accept his first post in the Russian government in the Ministry of Internal Affairs was likely one of the selling points to those who appointed him. "His ministerial colleagues no doubt felt that Stolypin could be outmaneuvered in the St. Petersburg bureaucratic environment" (Waldron, 1998), p. 48. Similar miscalculations were made repeatedly about Vladimir Putin in the 1990s.

4. For a discussion of the KGB under Yury Andropov see Fedor (2011). Chapter two of Galeotti (1997) offers an analysis of Andropov and his political impact in the USSR. Many of the people who worked for Andropov in the CPSU Secretariat in the 1960s would go on to become prominent colleagues and proponents of Mikhail Gorbachev's reforms in the 1980s.

5. For a thorough discussion of this period and the schism between Honecker's GDR and Gorbachev's USSR see Glaeser (2011); see also Doder and Branson (1990), p. 230.

6. Doder and Branson (1990), pp. 344–45.

7. See, for example, Gessen (2012), pp. 62–64.

8. Reuth and Bönte's 1993 German language book, which discusses Operation Luch, describes how the center of covert opposition to German leader Eric Honecker was in Dresden, and the Dresden Communist Party head, Hans Modrow, was the key figure. According to the authors, Operation Luch lasted from September 1985 to November 1989—almost exactly the time of Putin's posting in Dresden. They relate that Operation Luch was directed from the top of the KGB in Moscow, notably by the then head of the First Directorate, Vladimir Kryuchkov. Kryuchkov later became head of the KGB and was a member of the group that staged the 1991 coup against Gorbachev. In the second half of the 1980s, however, Kryuchkov was a critical ally of Mikhail Gorbachev (although clearly trying to manipulate him). If indeed Operation Luch actually existed and Dresden was the focus, it is hard to imagine that Putin was posted there for five years without taking some part. The KGB group posted in Dresden numbered only a half dozen men. If Putin was part of Operation Luch, that means he would have been involved in recruiting and running East Germans in and outside the government, using the standard methods of blackmail and persuasion. For his part, in *Ot pervogo litsa,* Putin denies being involved in Operation Luch. He does admit its existence in a general sense and says that "it involved working with the political leadership of the GDR." Gevorkyan, Timakova, and Kolesnikov (2000), pp. 65–66.

9. See, for example, Yevgenia Albats, "Who is Vladimir Putin? Why Was He Chosen as Yeltsin's Heir?," in "Who is Putin? Excerpts from *Frontline*'s Interviews," *Frontline:*

Return of the Czar, PBS, at www.pbs.org/wgbh/pages/frontline/shows/yeltsin/putin/putin. html. Albats asserts that "he frequently traveled to West Germany." Putin, however, denies he ever traveled to West Germany during his time in Dresden, in Gevorkyan, Timakova, and Kolesnikov (2000), p. 62.

10. In *Ot pervogo litsa*, Putin states that his work in Dresden "was political intelligence—obtaining information about political figures and the plans of the potential opponent . . . we considered the main opponent to be NATO." Gevorkyan, Timakova, and Kolesnikov (2000), p. 62. He also says that he did look "for information about political parties, the tendencies inside these parties, their leaders. . . . So work went on in parallel on the recruitment of sources and procurement of information, and also on assessing information and analysis. Entirely routine work." Ibid., pp. 62–63. (As we will stress in the Case Officer chapter, chapter 8, in Putin-speak, references to a job being "routine" or "boring" are often a signal that it was in fact extremely important.)

11. Gevorkyan, Timakova, and Kolesnikov (2000), p. 61.

12. Ibid., p. 60.

13. Ibid., p. 70.

14. Ibid., pp. 71–72.

15. Ibid., pp. 72–73. Putin's reference to water barriers or *vodorazdely* is a very specific one. It likely refers to the use of waterways in Berlin, along with the Berlin Wall, as means of dividing the city, and the designation of the river Elbe as part of the border between West and East Germany.

16. Ibid., p. 77.

17. Ibid., p. 77

18. Ibid., p. 80.

19. Ibid., p. 77.

20. See Aron (2012).

21. See also Josephine Woll, "Glasnost: A Cultural Kaleidoscope," in Balzer (1991), pp. 105–17.

22. Aron (2012), pp. 38–39.

23. Ibid., pp. 39–40.

24. Aron (2012) discusses these and other examples in detail in pp. 53–57.

25. See Serge Schmemann, "2 Germanys' Political Divide Is Being Blurred by Glasnost," *New York Times*, December 18, 1988 (accessed through Nexis.com).

26. See Stiehler (2001).

27. Cited in Aron (2012), p. 43.

28. Glasnost essayist Igor Klyamkin, cited in Aron (2012), p. 43.

29. See Aron (2012), pp. 299–302.

30. See Aron's discussion of this in pp. 49–50.

31. Russian music critic Artem Troitsky covers this flourishing of pop culture in his books from the period: *Back in the USSR: The True Story of Rock in Russia* (1988) and *Tusovka: Who's Who in the New Soviet Rock Culture* (1990). Troitsky became an ardent critic of Vladimir Putin in the 2000s and was an active participant in the opposition protests in 2011–12, along with a number of rock stars from the 1980s. See Owen Matthews, "Dumbing Russia Down," *The Daily Beast*, March 22, 2008, at www.thedailybeast.com/newsweek/2008/03/22/dumbing-russia-down.html; and Jeffrey Tayler, "Could This Be the End for Putin's Russia," Bloomberg, December 7, 2011, at www.bloomberg.com/news/2011-12-07/could-this-be-the-end-for-putin-s-russia-jeffrey-tayler.html.

32. Gevorkyan, Timakova, and Kolesnikov (2000), p. 64, "Volodya khorosho rasskazivayet anekdoty" [Volodya tells jokes well].

33. Ibid., p. 85.

34. Russian journalist Oleg Kashin emphasized this point in a presentation at the Brookings Institution on March 29, 2012, as did analyst Maria Lipman of the Carnegie

Endowment for International Peace Moscow Center at a meeting at the Brookings Institution on April 25, 2012.

35. Putin's idea of *dostroika,* finishing up the construction or completion of a specific project that is already under way, contrasts sharply with the Gorbachev era conception of perestroika, or reconstructing and restructuring, with its implications of transformation into something new. Putin's use of *dostroika* at a time of mounting calls for political change in Russia in 2011–12 was clearly intended as a rejection of and an alternative to the ideas of a new perestroika that circulated after 2008 while Dmitry Medvedev was Russian president.

36. See, for example, the German language documentary and portrait of Vladimir Putin, *Ich, Putin* (I, Putin), of February 2012 at www.ardmediathek.de/ard/servlet/content/3517136?documentId=9651826. The authors are grateful to Manfred Huterer for alerting them to this documentary, which was broadcast on German TV. It was also shown on Russia's NTV channel in May 2012.

37. See the earlier reference to this episode, pp. 63–64.

38. Viktor Borisenko quote, as cited in Blotskiy (2002), p. 76.

39. Gevorkyan, Timakova, and Kolesnikov (2000), p. 21. Some of Putin's fellow judo teammates, like Arkady Rotenberg, head of the St. Petersburg–based energy service company Stroygazmontazh, have emerged as among Russia's richest new businessmen in the 2000s. See, for example, Gleb Bryanski, "Putin's Judo Partner Jumps in Russia's Rich List," Reuters, February 13, 2011, at www.reuters.com/article/2011/02/14/russia-rich-idUSLDE71C02X20110214; and Simon Shuster, "Vladimir Putin's Billionaire Boys Judo Club," *Time,* March 1, 2011, at www.time.com/time/world/article/0,8599,2055962,00.html. Like Vladimir Putin, Arkady Rotenberg and his brother, Boris, who is also a successful businessman, credit the discipline and competitive edge their judo training gave them as one of the main drivers of their success in politics and business.

40. See Putin's references to training rather than smoking in *Ot pervogo litsa,* p. 21.

41. Authors' interviews with Vladimir Putin's contemporaries at LGU in the 1970s. Some of these contemporaries noted that the LGU Law Faculty was undergoing a period of dramatic transformation in the 1970s. Prominent professors—mostly liberal Jews—were being pushed out on the direct instructions of the Leningrad Communist Party leadership in favor of more conservative faculty members. As one contemporary emphasized: "To the extent that the tenor of the place was changing, [Putin] was an outsider to the people who dominated in the past and those who were more like him had not come to dominate the place yet." Authors' written exchange with former LGU student, July 3, 2012.

42. Russian analyst Pavel Baev, presentation at the Brookings Institution, February 16, 2010.

43. Gessen (2012), pp. 43–70. Gessen talks about how Putin, in some interviews, deliberately calls himself a "little thug."

44. The full transcript of the call-in show is at http://government.ru/docs/17409/.

45. See Owen Matthew's discussion of Putin's indulgence in "class warfare," in www.thedailybeast.com/newsweek/2012/05/27/meet-igor-the-tank-engineer.html. See also Alexander Bratersky and Natalya Krainova, "Putin Offers Senior Post to Tank Worker Who Scorned Protesters," *Moscow Times,* May 21, 2012, at www.themoscowtimes.com/news/article/putin-offers-senior-post-to-tank-worker-who-scorned-protesters/458826.html#ixzz1yZOgLbi9.

46. Maria Lipman presentation at the Brookings Institution, April 25, 2012. Another observer noted that "the domineering, aggressive, often crude boss is . . . a classic Soviet or Russian type. . . . Many people who I would call 'average Russians' often seemed to admire such assertive types, and approve of behavior that [people] in the West would often consider rude . . . such behavior by Putin is populist in origin, more than anything else." Authors' written exchange with senior U.S. diplomat who served in both the USSR and Russia for extended periods, July 2012.

47. See, for example, Miriam Elder, "Vladimir Putin Takes Oleg Deripaska to Task," *The Telegraph*, June 4, 2009, at www.telegraph.co.uk/news/worldnews/europe/russia/5446293/Vladimir-Putin-takes-Oleg-Deripaska-to-task.html; Zakharovich (June 9, 2009).

48. See, for example, "Putin Plays the Role of the Good Tsar," *Moscow Times*, editorial, April 28, 2004, at www.themoscowtimes.com/opinion/article/putin-plays-the-role-of-good-tsar/231296.html; Miriam Elder, "Putin Relying on Support outside Moscow to Win Back Presidency," *The Guardian*, March 2, 2012, at www.guardian.co.uk/world/2012/mar/02/putin-support-outside-moscow-for-presidency.

49. Dmitry Babich, cited in Anna Arutunyan, "The Romanov Legacy in Russia," in the *Rossiyskaya gazeta* and *Telegraph* online English-language supplement, *Russia Now*, July 6, 2010, at www.telegraph.co.uk/sponsored/russianow/features/7875545/The-Romanovs-and-Russia.html.

50. "Blagotvoritel' Vladimir Putin" [The philanthropist Vladimir Putin], *Vedomosti*, editorial, April 11, 2012, at www.vedomosti.ru/opinion/news/1626178/gerojblagotvoritel.

51. Ibid.

52. This story was related to the authors by a Russian colleague who in turn heard it directly from the politician in question (whom he named to us). We have not attempted to verify this episode independently, but we consider our source trustworthy, and the politician's particular predicament is documented.

53. Authors' interview with Putin LGU contemporary. Related in Washington, D.C., in May 2011.

54. The English-language title of the film is *Kidnapping Caucasian Style*. See a brief description of the film on the IMDb website at www.imdb.com/title/tt0060584/.

55. The Perm group's film disappeared from YouTube, but can be found at http://trinixy.ru/2008/03/03/dmitrijj_medvedev_kak_vse_nachinalos_138_mb.html.

56. See "Vladimir Putin Threatened to Hang Georgia Leader 'by the Balls,'" *The Telegraph*, November 3, 2008, at www.telegraph.co.uk/news/worldnews/europe/russia/3454154/Vladimir-Putin-threatened-to-hang-Georgia-leader-by-the-balls.html.

57. The Petka of the original joke was not from the Caucasus, he was merely uneducated. However, later versions of the joke were usually told about a Georgian. A large part of Chapaev's appeal as a hero figure for the Soviets was his background as an uneducated and illiterate peasant, who was nonetheless a worldly and gifted tactician. Petka, Chapaev's aide-de-camp—also a character from real life—was even simpler. The 1934 film *Chapaev*, which was based on a book of the same name by Dmitry Furmanov, was a Soviet blockbuster. In 1941, Chapaev was resurrected in a short "agitational" (propaganda) film produced and aired within weeks after the Nazi invasion, in which the hero calls on the Soviets to defeat the Germans. "Chapaev is with you always," he reassures the moviegoers. See *Chapayev* and *"Chapayev s nami"* (the agitprop sequel) at www.imdb.com. An illustrative selection of Chapaev jokes in English can be found at www.anecdotoff.com/category/funniest-jokes/funniest-chapayev-jokes and also in a review of the basic genres of Russian jokes at www.lonweb.org/links/russian/lang/036.htm. As Russian colleagues underscore, Chapaev-Petka jokes were "rampant" in the USSR by the early 1980s and people would know "dozens of them."

58. The authors, who were not among those getting the joke, thank Nikolai Zlobin for letting them in on it immediately after the dinner.

59. Putin's political rival Gennady Zyuganov is a renowned aficionado of Soviet-era jokes with several anthologies to his name, including *100 anekdotov ot Zyuganova* [100 anecdotes from Zyuganov] (2007).

60. See Gleb Bryanski, "Putin: on the Pulse or out of Touch with Russia," Reuters, December 15, 2011, at www.reuters.com/article/2011/12/15/us-russia-putin-showman-idUSTRE7BE1PG20111215.

61. Putin, address to the State Duma, April 11, 2012. See "Predsdatel' Pravitel'stva Rossiyskoy Federatsii V.V. vystupil v Gosudarstvennoy Dume s otchyotom o dealte'nosti Pravitel'stva Rossiiskoy Federatsii za 2011 god" [Chairman of the Government of the Russian Federation V.V. Putin appeared before the State Duma with the report on the activity of the Government of the Russian Federation for 2011], April 11, 2012, at http://government. ru/docs/18671/. The English version is at http://government.ru/eng/docs/18671/. It is worth noting that Putin, the Leningrad native, tells this Soviet-era joke that lampoons not only Soviet agriculture but also the privileged status of Moscow. A former senior U.S. diplomat, who served in the USSR during the period this particular joke dates from, notes: "By the early to mid-1980s just about everyone there knew the Soviet system wasn't working. One of my friends from the Russian Ministry of Foreign Affairs told me a popular private toast at the time, even in the Central Committee of the CPSU, was *K uspekhu nashego beznadezhnogo dela!* [To the success of our hopeless endeavor]. These guys weren't all outsiders, but they had become cynics." Authors' written exchange with senior U.S. diplomat, July 30, 2012.

62. Putin, address to the State Duma, April 11, 2012.

63. Ibid.

CHAPTER 7

1. An excellent review and analysis of the specifics of this period in St. Petersburg is Volkov (2002). Economic interactions in the St. Petersburg and Russian systems of the 1990s were marked by a complete absence of trust between and among the respective actors. The official institutions that created trust at an impersonal level were missing with the collapse of the Soviet system. There was no new legislative framework in place, so there was no rule of law, and no code of business ethics. In many respects this is still the situation in Russia today. In this entirely lawless system, where no one could be assumed to be honest, no transactions could be guaranteed to deliver a set of goods or services without some kind of personal connection or means of enforcement to make informal contracts work.

2. Putin address to State Duma, April 11, 2012. See "Predsdatel' Pravitel'stva Rossiyskoy Federatsii V.V. vystupil v Gosudarstvennoy Dume s otchyotom o dealte'nosti Pravitel'stva Rossiiskoy Federatsii za 2011 god" [Chairman of the Government of the Russian Federation V.V. Putin appeared before the State Duma with the report on the activity of the Government of the Russian Federation for 2011], April 11, 2012, at http://government. ru/docs/18671/. The English version is at http://government.ru/eng/docs/18671/.

3. International Monetary Fund, "Russian Federation Completes Early Repayment of Entire Outstanding Obligations to the IMF," Press Release No. 05/19, January 31, 2005, at www.imf.org/external/np/sec/pr/2005/pr0519.htm.

4. Authors' calculations from data from International Monetary Fund, *World Economic Outlook Database*, April 2012.

5. See the discussion in chapter 3, "The Survivalist."

6. For details on the dependence of Russia's economic performance on oil prices, see various articles by Clifford Gaddy and Barry Ickes.

7. Putin, address to the State Duma, April 11, 2012.

8. See Daniel Mitchell, "Russia's Flat Tax Miracle," March 24, 2003, at www.heritage. org/research/commentary/2003/03/russias-flat-tax-miracle; and Daniel Mitchell, "Flat Tax Is the Way of the Future," March 20, 2006, at www.heritage.org/research/commentary/ 2006/03/flat-tax-is-the-way-of-the-future.

9. See Anders Aslund, "The President's Turn Away from the Market," *Moscow Times*, November 8, 2006, at www.iie.com/publications/opeds/oped.cfm?ResearchID=684.

10. David Ignatius, "Humbled Masters at Davos," *Washington Post*, February 1, 2009, at www.washingtonpost.com/wp-dyn/content/article/2009/01/30/AR2009013002726.html.

11. The generally underappreciated fact that Putin chose not to reverse the "loans-for-shares" agreements is central to the arguments by Clifford Gaddy and Barry Ickes in their work on "Putin's Protection Racket."

12. Vladimir Putin, "Predsedatel' Pravitel'stva Rossiyskoy Federatsii V.V. Putin vstretil'sya s chlenami byuro pravleniya Rossiyskogo soyuza promyshlennikov i predprini-mateley" [Chairman of the Government of the Russian Federation V.V. Putin met with members of the executive committee of the Russian Union of Industrialists and Entrepreneurs], April 21, 2011, at http://government.ru/docs/14934/. The English version of the text is at http:// government.ru/eng/docs/14934/.

13. See Josef Stalin, "Political Report of the Central Committee," December 18, 1925. (This document is widely available on the Internet in English.)

14. See Clifford Gaddy and William Gale, "Demythologizing the Russian Flat Tax," *Tax Notes International* 43 (March 2005), pp. 983–88, at www.brookings.edu/~/media/research/files/articles/2005/3/14russia%20gaddy/20050314gaddygale.pdf.

15. One American student who was in Leningrad during the 1970s noted that "the illegal economy was particularly well-developed in Leningrad in the 1970s. Sailors and foreign tourists brought in lots of stuff. The KGB (the *Bol'shoy dom*) was pretty strict, but they could not shut down all of the informal marketplaces that sprang up all over the city. Everybody got what stuff they could, and barter was the primary form of commerce. The KGB watched the university [LGU] particularly closely, although the Africans were more of a target than we westerners, because they engaged in more trading and speculation. We had one Brit in our dorm who was doing a brisk business all year in western records (Beatles, Stones, and so on). The KGB let him get close to the end of his year, and then denounced him in the local press and had him expelled. We theorized they waited so long because they were also benefitting from the flow of western music coming into the city. I have no indication how this all may have affected Putin, but it is an environment which he certainly knew intimately." Authors' written communication with a U.S. 1970s exchange student at LGU, July 30, 2012.

16. Masha Gessen, for example, discusses the fact that in the early 1970s Putin's parents had an exceedingly rare stroke of luck and won a car, which they gave to their son, Vladimir. This was a remarkably lavish gift. As Gessen points out, "the number of cars per thousand people in the USSR barely reached sixty (compared with 781 in the United States). A car cost roughly as much as a dacha." Gessen suggests that this gift fell into a pattern of Putin pursuing "luxury items" in his university student days, often by spending "his summers working on far-slung construction sites, where the pay was very good." She notes that after his first summer at university, for example, the young Vladimir Putin "joined classmates in traveling straight from the Far North to the Soviet south, the town of Gagry [Gagra] on the Black Sea in Georgia, where he managed to spend all his money in a few days. The following year, he returned to Leningrad after working on a construction site, and spent the money he had made on an overcoat for himself—and a frosted cake for his mother." See Gessen (2012), pp. 55–56.

17. See Angus Maddison, "Historical Statistics of the World Economy: 1–2008 AD," at www.ggdc.net/maddison/Historical_Statistics/horizontal-file_02-2010.xls.

18. Angus Maddison, "Statistics on World Population, GDP and Per Capita GDP, 1–2008 AD," available at www.ggdc.net/MADDISON/oriindex.htm.

19. Authors' calculations from data on U.S. oil production from U.S. Energy Information Administration (EIA) and on Soviet oil production from Goskomstat SSSR, *Narodnoye khozaystvo SSSR*, various years.

20. Notwithstanding the macro perspective on the Russian economy, although Leningrad was in a better position than other Soviet cities, at the micro level the situation

was somewhat mixed, as one of Vladimir Putin's fellow students described: "While at LGU in the '70s, Leningrad was generally better supplied than any other city except Moscow. Nonetheless, by mid-April 1972, cabbage and carrots had disappeared from even the peasant markets. We ate sorrel grass for salad, and counted ourselves lucky that potatoes, bread, and groats were in reliable supply. In 1971 the siege was still alive in the popular memory of *Leningradtsi*. People talked freely in private about what their family had done, where they had been, how they had survived, not just in public propaganda events or media. We lived OK in Leningrad in the 70s . . . [but] [e]verybody carried an *ovoska,* the just-in-case bag to tote spur of the moment purchases when you were lucky enough to find something. Leningrad was also better supplied than much of the USSR with some foreign goods, due to the large numbers of Scandinavians that came in on short boat or bus tours to buy cheap booze, and stuff smuggled in by sailors in the merchant fleet. This was Putin's youthful environment: not necessarily one of privation, but also far from secure. One looked for food every day, and one could have really bad days, especially when your [student] stipend was low." Authors' written communication with former 1970s U.S. exchange student at LGU, July 30, 2012.

21. Before beginning a discussion of the role the KGB likely played in shaping Vladimir Putin's understanding of the market economy, it is worth stating that we do not subscribe to one particular version or myth of the KGB and the market. This is the myth that as KGB officers had unique access to classified material, and were in an equally unique position to observe Western societies, they were able to see for themselves the "superiority" of the free market economy. According to this narrative, as a result of their firsthand exposure, many KGB officers became strong adherents of the market long before other Russians. Russian oligarch Alexander Lebedev underscored this myth in a December 2007 interview. Lebedev is a former KGB officer, who was a contemporary of Vladimir Putin in the institution but posted to London in the late 1980s while Putin was in Dresden. In the 1990s and 2000s, Lebedev transformed himself into a banker and businessman with a broad range of investments in Russia and abroad, and a seeming penchant for supporting progressive and charitable causes—including acquiring Russia's *Novaya gazeta* and two ailing British newspapers, London's *Evening Standard* and *The Independent.* In an interview with the *New York Times,* Lebedev asserted that some of "his generation of Soviet spies" had become ardent "free-market enthusiasts" and "reformers" having been able to see firsthand "the great gap in economic development between the West and the Soviet Union in the 1980s." Andrew Kramer, "Former Russian Spies Are Now Prominent in Business," *New York Times,* December 18, 2007, at www.nytimes.com/2007/12/18/business/worldbusiness/18kgb.html?_r=1. If Lebedev's assertion is true, then every KGB agent who was stationed in a Western country would be inclined to be pro-Western, engaged in business, a supporter of liberal economic measures, and potentially also a proponent of political reform. For generations, however, KGB officers observing the West at close quarters showed no great propensity for advocating free market or other reforms. Lebedev's comments were clearly meant to burnish his past as a former KGB agent and to provide a rationale for his new incarnation. We argue in the book that most people like Alexander Lebedev and Vladimir Putin who grew up in the Soviet Union got their understanding of the market economy in a piecemeal fashion. In Putin's case, he did not acquire it wholesale from his training and service in the KGB. Putin himself frequently refers to different experiences that shaped his view, in his early life, in East Germany, in St. Petersburg, and in Moscow in the late 1990s.

22. Donald Rayfield, in *Stalin and His Hangmen,* describes Dzerzhinsky as the "economic overlord." His formal economic position was chairman of the USSR Supreme Economic Council. Dzerzhinsky was simultaneously head of the *Cheka* and then its successor, the OGPU. Rayfield (2004), pp. 97–103.

23. Russian economist Valery Lazarev has described the gulag (*Glavnoye upravleniye ispravitel'no-trudovykh lagerey i koloniy,* or chief administration of corrective labor camps

and colonies) as "a system of coerced labor disguised as a penitentiary institution." It was "a huge 'corporation' with hundreds of establishments" and a "millions-strong labor force." Valery Lazarev, "Conclusions," in Gregory and Lazarev (2003), p. 190.

24. See Hill and Gaddy (2003), p. 86. The original information is from Ivanova (1997), p. 136, cited in Smirnov, Sigachev, and Shkapov (1998), p. 72, note 212.

25. See, for example, discussion of Beria in Rayfield (2004), pp. 455–69.

26. This is the symbol of the KGB, see Rayfield (2004), p. 23—"The KGB also adopted the *Cheka* symbols of the sword and the shield: the shield to defend the revolution, the sword to smite its foes."

27. Note: Soviet oil production *levels* did not decline; the *growth rate* declined. Oil production grew, but more slowly than before.

28. Gustafson (1991).

29. U.S. Energy Information Agency, *Annual Energy Review 2010*, Table 5.1b, "Petroleum Overview, 1949–2010," at www.eia.gov.

30. Leslie H. Gelb, "Who Won the Cold War?," *New York Times*, August 20, 1992, accessed through Nexis.com.

31. One American who first went to Leningrad as a student in the early 1970s and then returned a decade later observed the shift in perceptions over this time period in his personal encounters: "When I was at LGU in the early '70s I could still find Soviets who genuinely believed that the system might work. At that time the experience after World War II had been one of relatively steady, although not always uninterrupted, improvement in social and economic conditions. By the time I returned in the early 1980s, this was clearly no longer the case." Authors' written exchange with former 1970s U.S. exchange student at LGU, July 30, 2012.

32. Putin, speech at the Assembly of the Russian Academy of Sciences, May 18, 2010. See "Predsedatel' Pravitel'stva Rossiyskoy Federatsii V.V. Putin vystupil na Obshchem sobranii Rossiyskoy akademii nauk" [Chairman of the Government of the Russian Federation V.V. Putin gave a speech at the Assembly of the Russian Academy of Sciences], May 18, 2010, at http://government.ru/docs/10609/. The English version is at http://government.ru/eng/docs/10609/. These remarks may have been Putin's first public reference to the fact that he himself may have been one of those stealing technological secrets during his time in Dresden. The closing comments were not included in the English version of the speech on the prime minister's website, which only provides the opening remarks. The full text is available in the Russian version. The authors have noted in the course of their research that it is often the case that when Putin makes a controversial comment or "off-color" remark the English version is "cleaned up," but the Russian version retains the original. The authors are grateful to Richard Burger and Veronika Kupriyanova-Ashina for alerting them to this speech and to the discrepancy between the two versions in this particular case.

33. Putin often talks about seeking to join the KGB from his childhood, and has related a story about going to the KGB headquarters in Leningrad while he was still in high school to ask to sign up. The KGB representative who received him advised him to first go to university and get a law degree. See Gevorkyan, Timakova, and Kolesnikov (2000), p. 25.

34. In April 1985, as the Gorbachev era began, Chebrikov was promoted to full member of the Politburo. (The USSR's Defense Minister Sokolov, by contrast, remained only a candidate member, underscoring the relative greater weight of the KGB at this juncture in the Soviet system.)

35. "Zhivoye tvorchestvo naroda. Doklad M.S. Gorbacheva. Vsesoyuznaya nauchno-prakticheskaya konferentsiya" [The living accomplishment of the people. Report by M.S. Gorbachev. All-Soviet scientific-practical conference], *Izvestiya*, December 11, 1984.

36. The best economic history of the GDR is Steiner (2007).

37. World oil prices peaked in January–February 1981, dropped continuously for over 5 years (well into 1986), stayed low for the next 13 years, and did not start to recover until 1999.

38. Steiner (2007), p. 227.

39. This is all very relevant to the situation Putin witnessed happening in the 1990s under Yeltsin and which he appeared to face himself in 2012, as we will discuss in chapter 10.

40. Rahr (2008), pp. 75–79.

41. Ibid., pp. 73–74.

42. Ibid. Putin's formal position was deputy to the vice rector for international affairs, Yury Molchanov.

43. At some point in this period, Putin is reported to have shifted from being a full-time KGB officer to the institution's "active reserve." He presumably remained in this capacity until he officially resigned from the KGB in August 1991. The sequencing and dates in the various biographical materials are unclear.

44. In early interviews in 2000 with Russian analysts about Mr. Putin's work in St. Petersburg in the 1990s, it was clear that Putin's links to the KGB were common knowledge and also that Sobchak was well aware of Putin's continued connections. Russian journalist Yevgenia Albats, for example, notes that "if you talk to those who worked in the mayor's, Sobchak's, office of the time they will tell you that all of them were perfectly aware that Putin was assigned to this new democratically elected Mayor to watch after him, to advise him. . . ." See Yevgenia Albats, "Who is Vladimir Putin? Why Was He Chosen as Yeltsin's Heir?," in "Who is Putin? Excerpts from *Frontline*'s Interviews," *Frontline*, "Return of the Czar," PBS, at www.pbs.org/wgbh/pages/frontline/shows/yeltsin/putin/putin.html.

45. Gaddy (1996), pp. 27 and 155.

46. See Charap (2004); and Sakwa (2009), p. 140. Samuel Charap writes that "Putin's daily work as chair of the Petersburg Committee on Foreign Relations [Committee for External Relations] and vice-mayor encompassed a wide array of responsibilities, including attracting foreign investment, fostering economic development, arranging visits by foreign dignitaries, and coordinating with the federal bureaucracies in St. Petersburg." Charap also relates an interview with one of Putin's associates in this period who asserted that "St. Petersburg is practically a mini-model of Russia. . . . [Putin's] work here was a good school of management. Here, the quantity and variety of contacts, the need to take different kinds of decisions, and take them fast, are extreme." Richard Sakwa notes that companies operating in St. Petersburg in this period had to establish "close links with the St. Petersburg mayor's office, and in particular with Putin (at the head of the foreign economic relations office in the city from June 1991) and [Igor] Sechin."

47. Putin cited in Blotskiy (2002), p. 327.

48. Khodorkovskiy and Nevzlin (1992). The authors thank Thane Gustafson for this reference.

49. Gleb Pavlovsky interview with *The Guardian*, January 24, 2012.

50. Authors' computations from data from the Russian State Statistics Service.

51. Ibid.

CHAPTER 8

1. Gessen (2012), p. 140.

2. *Banditskiy Piterburg* (Bandit St. Petersburg) is an iconic and extremely popular Russian TV series that premiered on NTV in May 2000 and was considered to sum up the entire decade of the 1990s. Basic information about the series is available on www.imdb.com. The information for the first episode, "Baron," including a series of informal reviews, is at www.imdb.com/title/tt0245602/.

3. Gessen (2012), pp. 122–25. In 2000, when Vladimir Putin was elected president for the first time, Marina Salye publicly released her report and supporting documentation

from her investigation, before retreating from public life to live in a remote village in Russia's Pskov region. (Gessen references both the original 1992 report and Salye's 2000 facsimile documentation in the notes for p. 122 of her book, which are on p. 298 of *The Man without a Face*.) Salye emerged again as a vocal member of the St. Petersburg opposition during the 2011–12 parliamentary and presidential election protests, but died suddenly of a heart attack at age 77 in March 2012. See "Prominent Putin Critic Dies at 77," RFE/RL Russian Service, March 21, 2012, at www.rferl.org/content/salye_putin_critic_dies/24523142.html.

4. An unsubstantiated 2010 report claims the original documents "disappeared" in the period between 1997 and 1999. This was when Putin held the post of head of the Main Control Directorate (GKU) of the Russian presidential administration and then became director of the FSB. It was also when the St. Petersburg legislature (to which the archives of the St. Petersburg City Council had been transferred in 1994) was headed by people close to Putin. See Kravtsov, Novoselov, and Mironov (2010).

5. Salye as cited in Gessen (2012), p. 121.

6. Clifford Gaddy and Barry Ickes describe the barter phenomenon and its motivations in the 1990s in *Russia's Virtual Economy* (2002).

7. Putin's letter is appendix 3 in the Salye report. Aven replied to Putin on February 1, 1992, and the Russian ministry of economics authorized Putin's committee to issue licenses on March 25, 1992. By this time Putin and his associates had already issued a number of licenses. Sal'ye (2000).

8. Gevorkyan, Timakova, and Kolesnikov (2000), pp. 90–91. Also Gessen (2012), p. 122.

9. See Rahr (2008), pp. 88–89.

10. See Matt Bivens, "Waiting for Vladimir Putin," *Moscow Times*, March 4, 2000, accessed through Nexis.com. Bivens offers a detailed discussion of the St. Petersburg food scandal and of other events involving Putin in the city in the 1990s in his lengthy article. See also Oleg Lurie, "Food for St. Petersburg," *Novaya gazeta*, No. 10, March 2000, p. 5, accessed through Nexis.com in English; and David Filipov, "Putin's Record Suggests Alliance with Insiders Deals as City Officials Raise Reformer Doubts," *Boston Globe,* March 24, 2000, accessed through Nexis.com.

11. In November 2014, Aven ranked number 264 on the *Forbes* magazine's world's leading businessmen and billionaires list. He ranked number 22 among Russia's billionaire oligarchs. See www.forbes.com/profile/pyotr-aven/.

12. See Viktor Yushkin, *Lyudi kak teni* [People like shadows], *Postimees* (Estonia), September 20, 2007, at http://rus.postimees.ee/200907/glavnaja/mnenie/22618.php.

13. Rahr (2000), pp. 94–95.

14. In the interview transcript published on the Russian prime minister's website, this is translated into English as "credulity." See http://government.ru/eng/docs/3192/. The Russian version is at http://government.ru/docs/3192/. *Doverchivost'* shares the same root as the word *doveryay,* in the famous Russian phrase *Doveryay, no proveryay!*—"Trust, but verify!"—which U.S. president Ronald Reagan was fond of quoting in his meetings with Soviet leaders and which he had been told was a well-known Russian proverb. Newspaper and other accounts that refer to the phrase almost invariably claim that it was one of Lenin's favorite sayings. This seems to be a myth, since the phrase never occurs in any of Lenin's published speeches or writings.

15. Rahr (2000), p. 99.

16. Ibid., p. 102. See earlier discussion of the 1995–96 Russian Duma and presidential election campaigns, pp. 21–24.

17. See Sobchak (1999).

18. Rahr (2000), p. 104.

19. Ibid., pp. 105–06. Yakovlev was reelected as mayor in 2000 and was then replaced by Valentina Matvienko before being briefly dispatched as the presidential envoy to the Southern Federal District from 2003 until the terrorist attack on Beslan. Yakovlev was then shifted to the position of deputy prime minister and Russian minister for regional development from 2004 to 2007. The various online biographical sketches of Yakovlev report that he retired from his official positions in 2007.

20. Rahr (2000), p. 106.

21. Ibid., pp. 106–07.

22. Rahr (2008), p. 89.

23. Rahr (2000), p. 95.

24. See "Meeting with Members of the Valdai International Discussion Club," Sochi, Russia, September 14, 2007, at http://archive.kremlin.ru/eng/speeches/2007/09/14/1801_type82917type84779_144106.shtml. The Russian version is at http://archive.kremlin.ru/appears/2007/09/14/2105_type63376type63381type82634_144011.shtml.

25. See Viktoriya Voloshina, "Piterskaya shkola razvedki" [The St. Petersburg school of intelligence], *Izvestiya*, November 2, 2001, at http://izvestia.ru/news/254165. One of Zubkov's most important protégés was his son-in-law, Anatoly Serdyukov, who served as Russian defense minister from 2007 to 2012. Serdyukov had no security or military background when he was appointed to this position in 2007. He was the director of a large furniture company, who then went on to succeed his father-in-law at the St. Petersburg tax directorate, before coming to Moscow in his own turn to head the Russian Federal Tax Service. Given his financial and management skills, Serdyukov was assigned the primary task of curbing graft. He was to get the military budget in order, as well as bypass recalcitrant generals in pushing forward with military reform. See Mark Galeotti, "Reform of the Russian Military and Security Apparatus: An Investigator's Perspective," in Blank (2012).

26. In his response to the Valdai Discussion Club session in Sochi on September 14, 2007, Putin was quite explicit about the work of *Rosfinmonitoring:* "This is, after all, an analytical service that collects information about financial institutions and government organizations, a massive amount of information. . . . Business circles in Russia repeatedly talked about the risks when we decided to create this organization. People were afraid that, in contemporary Russia, the concentration of confidential information in one agency would adversely affect business. This did not happen. . . . At the same time, the service has worked effectively. The information it has collected has led to criminal proceedings against thousands of people, 521 of whom have been found guilty by the courts. That number over that period of time is comparable to the number of persons involved with the justice system and convicted by courts in the major European countries. In the United States during the same time period twice as many people were convicted, in European countries, an average of 500-plus people." See http://archive.kremlin.ru/eng/speeches/2007/09/14/1801_type82917type84779_144106.shtml.

27. Putin, "Conversation with Heads of Local Bureaus of Leading U.S. Media Outlets," June 18, 2001, in English at http://archive.kremlin.ru/eng/speeches/2001/06/18/0000_type82915type84779_143577.shtml and in Russian at http://archive.kremlin.ru/appears/2001/06/18/0002_type63376type63380_28569.shtml.

28. Gevorkyan, Timakova, and Kolesnikov (2000), pp. 40–41. "Vovka" and "Volodya" are both diminutives of Vladimir, along with "Vova."

29. Murawiec and Gaddy (2002)

30. Putin, meeting with young officials from the law enforcement organs, November 10, 2003. See "Stenograficheskiy otchet o vstreche s molodymi sotrudnikami pravookhranitel'nykh organov" [Stenographers report on meeting with young officials from the law enforcement organs], November 10, 2003, at http://archive.kremlin.ru/text/appears/2003/11/55331.shtml. It is interesting to note that this idea has also been

expressed by Putin's aide, Vladislav Surkov. As so often is the case, Surkov echoes a "Putinesque" idea in much more flowery language than his boss. In a conversation with Russian investigative journalist Yelena Tregubova, Surkov boasted that he "categorically rejected all forms of tyranny and violence—from the esthetic point of view, of course." So you do not advocate repressive measures? Tregubova asked. Of course not, replied Surkov: "That's so primitive! That's for the dull and lazy. Just arrest someone and force them to do something? Any qualitative process by definition has to be complicated. A process of long and agonizing agreement is much more complicated than a dictatorship, but it is also much more beautiful!" See Tregubova (2003), p. 342.

31. See earlier discussion of the "Andropov levy" in the text, pp. 109–10.

32. Bobkov (1995)

33. Ibid., pp. 204–07.

34. Ibid., p. 257.

35. Ibid., pp. 259–60.

36. Ibid., pp. 267–68. Medvedev corroborates this story in one of his own books; see Medvedev (2006), pp. 221–22.

37. Bobkov (1995), p. 268.

38. See earlier references to Operation Luch, including note 8 on p. 438.

39. The best source for understanding the specific skills and methods of the case officer working with double agents is the book by British World War II era spy John Masterman, *The Double Cross System*. Masterman ran the system of double agents for Britain's MI5 during the war to deceive German intelligence and the high command about Allied war plans. Masterman's basic concept was: How can you control and manipulate people who are your enemies? Your choice is to destroy them or to use them, and in wartime the latter proved particularly effective. Masterman's book was first written as a private record and report on how the system worked in 1945. It was then published by Yale University Press in 1972 as *The Double Cross System in the War of 1939 to 1945*.

40. Grigoriy Volchek, "Sluzhba v KGB – plyus dlya politika" [KGB Service—A plus for a politician], *Zvezda* (Perm'), June 15, 2000, www.nevod.ru/local/zvezda/archive.html.

41. Ibid.

42. Ibid.

43. As we have noted elsewhere, there is some uncertainty in the various sources, and in Mr. Putin's official biographies, about when exactly he shifted from being a "regular" KGB agent to the institution's "active reserve," and what his exact status was within the KGB (and for how long) after he joined the Sobchak administration and became deputy mayor.

44. Vladimir Putin, "From an Interview with the Canadian CBC and CTV Channels, the Globe and Mail Newspaper and the Russian RTR Television," December 14, 2000, at http://archive.kremlin.ru/eng/speeches/2000/12/14/0001_type82916_135565.shtml. Putin has frequently sought out former U.S. Secretary of State Henry Kissinger as an interlocutor during his tenure at the top of the Russian state and just as frequently has repeated this specific quote about all decent people starting their careers in intelligence. It also features as an anecdote in *Ot pervogo litsa*, pp. 80–81. Henry Kissinger's career in intelligence was, however, very different from Putin's. Kissinger was a private in U.S. Army Intelligence in World War II and was assigned there as a native German speaker. As is the case with Putin's personalized references to Russian historical figures and other world leaders, the comparison is made to bolster and legitimize his own biography, career, and position. During Kissinger's visit to Russia in June 2012 to participate in the St. Petersburg Economic Forum, he had another separate meeting with President Putin, who made a point, again, of stressing how long their acquaintance extended. In an excerpt of their discussion, available on the president's website, Putin reminded Kissinger that "our personal relations, they began while I was working as deputy mayor of St Petersburg, back in the mid-1990s. You came here as the head of the Russian-American commission." Putin told Kissinger: "I am very glad that we have maintained these

relations to this day." See "Vladimir Putin met with former US Secretary of State Henry Kissinger," June 21, 2012, at http://eng.special.kremlin.ru/news/4060. Mr. Putin is referring in this interview to a commission set up in 1992–93 under the auspices of the Center for Strategic and International Studies in Washington, D.C., and co-chaired by Anatoly Sobchak and Henry Kissinger. The goal of the commission was to assist the city of St. Petersburg in identifying foreign investors to help convert its defunct defense plants into commercial factories and turn around other manufacturing operations. See Scott Shane, "Cold Warrior Kissinger Sells Old Nemesis Russia," *Baltimore Sun*, June 24, 1993, at http://articles.baltimoresun.com/1993-06-24/news/1993175015_1_petersburg-cold-warrior-russian. It is not clear, however, how much actual direct contact Putin and Kissinger had in the context of this commission, as we will discuss in chapter 12.

45. Strictly speaking, the Russian term for the call-in show is *pryamaya liniya* or direct line, but it is referred to by Putin's PR team in English as the *Hot Line*.

46. RIA Novosti staff would explicitly reinforce this point to participants before the Valdai Discussion Club meetings with Mr. Putin—noting that the meetings were "all about the questions" and challenging Putin. Angus Roxburgh makes the same point about Putin relishing the questions in his description of the Valdai Club in Roxburgh (2012), p. 195.

47. Vladimir Putin, *Hot Line,* December 24, 2001. "Stenogramma 'Pryamoy linii' Prezidenta Rossiyskoy Federatsii V.V. Putina" [Transcript from "Direct line" with the President of the Russian Federation V.V. Putin], December 24, 2001, at http://archive.kremlin.ru/appears/2001/12/24/0001_type82634type146434_28759.shtml.

48. See Medvedev (2006), p. 135.

49. Authors' interviews with Russian press and PR representatives at the November 7–11, 2011, Valdai Discussion Club meetings in Moscow.

50. A series of articles and video clips depicting Mr. Putin's arrival in Pikalyovo and his meeting with Deripaska are at www.cbsnews.com/8301-503543_162-5071988-503543.html; www.reuters.com/article/2009/06/04/russia-putin-idUSL445098320090604; and www.youtube.com/watch?v=0MntxIPL8xo&feature=related.

51. The meeting at the Alfa Bank branch with Alfa president Pyotr Aven in Novosibirsk was on October 22, 2008, and is available on the Russian prime minister's website at www.government.ru/docs/2210/. The United Russia activists meeting was on October 23, 2008; see www.government.ru/docs/2211/.

52. The clip was uploaded on July 30, 2010, and is available at www.youtube.com/watch?v=8f5wXsB-Yp8 under the title of "Kak narod poslal Putin na ****" [How the people told Putin to go to ****].

53. Ibid.

54. Gessen (2012), pp. 164–75.

55. Kolesnikov (2005).

56. Kolesnikov's story as related in Gessen (2012), p. 170.

57. Kolesnikov (2005), pp. 38–39; also cited in Gessen (2012), p. 170.

58. Gessen (2012), p. 171.

59. Gevorkyan, Timakova, and Kolesnikov (2000), pp. 69–72. Also see Blotskiy (2002), pp. 259–66.

60. Gevorkyan, Timakova, and Kolesnikov (2000), p. 69.

61. Ibid., p. 71.

62. Ibid.

63. Blotskiy (2002), p. 263.

64. Ibid., p. 264. This seems to have been intended by Putin as a self-serving element in the narrative to underscore his superior German language skills. The Russian-language exchange in Blotsky (2002) is as follows: [someone from the crowd] "And who are you?" [Mr. Putin] "A translator"; [someone from the crowd] "Translators don't speak German that well." Putin told his interlocutors that the building they had massed before was an

extra-territorial Soviet military building covered by an inter-state agreement with the GDR (which was why all the cars outside had East German registration plates) and it had nothing to do either with the *Stasi* or the East German armed forces.

65. See Gaddy and Ickes (2009).

66. See Gaddy and Ickes (2011a).

67. The particular reason why Putin ended up in the property management department is one of the many murky aspects of Putin's initial move to Moscow. There is evidence that Putin already had a relationship with that Kremlin agency while he was in St. Petersburg. John Evans, the U.S. consul general in St. Petersburg in 1994–97, relates that the Kremlin property agency had at one point called on Putin to help with a particularly sensitive issue on its behalf. The Kremlin wanted the city of St. Petersburg to reassign, for Russian presidential use, a residential property designated for Americans and other foreigners. President Yeltsin's daughter needed a "dacha" when she visited St. Petersburg. This piece of property seemed ideal, even though it was already occupied. Putin stepped in to resolve this potentially embarrassing dispute, and thereby bolstered his reputation with the office that turned out to be his future employer. Author interview with John Evans, Washington, D.C., June 26, 2014.

68. Ibid.

69. Andrey Kolesnikov, "Aleksey Kudrin zaveshchal svoye kreslo Vladimiru Putinu" [Alexei Kudrin bequeaths his chair to Vladimir Putin], *Segodnya*, March 28, 1997, accessed through Eastview. The Russian word translated here as "menacing" is *groznaya*, which is often rendered in English as "fear" or "awe-inspiring," "threatening," or "terrible" (as in Ivan Grozny, the infamous Russian Tsar, "Ivan the Terrible").

70. "Soveshchaniya: Za poryadok vzyalis' vseryez" [Meetings: taking order seriously], *Rossiyskiye vesti*, May 21, 1997 (accessed through Eastview).

71. Gaddy and Ickes (2011a).

72. See Michael Gordon, "Russia's Former Head of Privatization Faces Bribery Charge," *New York Times*, October 2, 1997, accessed on ProQuest. Uneximbank was headed by Vladimir Potanin, the oligarch who had served in the Yeltsin government as first deputy prime minister from August 1996 until March 1997 and was known to be close to Chubais.

73. After being ousted from the government, Anatoly Chubais was assigned to head RAO UES, Russia's massive power utility, and maintained his close ties to President Yeltsin and the Kremlin. In this capacity, he is on record as having no principled objection to Putin being made Yeltsin's successor-designate in 1999, although he was skeptical about whether the choice would work. He expressed reservations that there was insufficient time in 1999–2000 to transform a publicly unknown, behind-the-scenes figure like Putin into a national politician. He clearly also had some unease with the prospect of Vladimir Putin becoming president. See, for example, the extracts from Boris Yeltsin's memoirs: "*Prezidentskiy marafon*" [The presidential marathon], *Ogonyok*, September 29, 2000; and "Chubays Denies Intrigue, Expresses Support for the President," *Komsomolskaya pravda*, October 20, 2000 (Internet versions from FBIS, the Foreign Broadcast Information Service, in English). Nonetheless, Chubais continued to play key roles in critical state-led entities throughout Putin's presidency and premiership. In 2012, Anatoly Chubais was the head of the Russian Nanotechnology Corporation, having served for a decade at RAO UES.

74. The oligarchs were in a vulnerable situation because of the questionable legality of their wealth before the 1996 "loans-for-shares" deal with the Yeltsin government as well as during that contentious process (they often used particularly nasty means to force "insiders" to sell their shares). Putting this issue aside, even the disclosure of legal financial information can be fatally dangerous to a corporation. See Gaddy and Ickes (2011a).

75. Ibid.

76. Vladimir Putin, "Vstupitel'noye slovo na vstreche s doverennymi litsamy" [Opening remarks at a meeting of high-level campaign workers], February 28, 2000, at http://archive.kremlin.ru/appears/2000/02/28/0000_type63374type63376_122120.shtml. The English version is at http://archive.kremlin.ru/eng/text/speeches/2000/02/28/0000_type82912type84779_123954.shtml. The actual quote in Russian is "the equidistant position of all subjects of the market from power" (*ravnoudalennoye polozheniye vsekh sub'yektov rynka ot vlasti*). One of the implications was that business people, oligarchs, would not be given formal government positions in the future, as Vladimir Potanin and Boris Berezovsky had been after 1996. This did not necessarily mean, however, that government officials would be precluded from positions on the boards of companies where the state had a significant interest, which was a notable factor in Russia in the 2000s.

77. The use of disappropriation is very specific here—it means to remove something that has been allocated to someone, often to reassign it to someone else. What has been given can also be taken away. The idea of disappropriation underscores a core concept within the Putin system that the assets the oligarchs own are not exactly their private property. They acquired the assets in deals with the Kremlin and thus became the stewards of this property on behalf of the Kremlin (or the state). This was also the essence of the arrangement between the tsar and the aristocrats in imperial Russia, who received large grants of land and also bonded serfs in return for service and loyalty to the autocrat. This arrangement retarded the development of private property rights in Russia even before the 1917 Revolution and the imposition of the communist system with its emphasis on communal property. For a detailed discussion see Pipes (1999).

78. The meeting is covered in detail in a four-part BBC documentary charting the rise of Putin to the Russian presidency and his time in office. See *Putin, Russia and the West* (Norma Percy, director), first aired on BBC2 in January 2012. In the documentary, there is a scene immediately after the meeting where oligarch Mikhail Khodorkovsky notes that "now we know what *vlast'* wants from us." The Khodorkovsky quote comes in Part 1, Minute 12:20.

79. Gaddy and Ickes (2009). The Surkov quotes come from Tregubova (2003), pp. 349–50.

CHAPTER 9

1. Gleb Pavlovsky interview with *The Guardian*, January 24, 2012. Although Pavlovsky does not make this reference in the interview, it is worth noting that the term "prohibitory system" comes from English political, legal, and moral philosopher Jeremy Bentham (1748–1832), who outlined a set of principles for states to adopt in creating penal, commercial, and other legal codes. In 1814–15, Bentham offered his assistance to Tsar Alexander I of Russia in reforming and codifying the complete laws of the Russian Empire. The tsar did not accept his offer. For a good general reference, see Rosen (2004).

2. Gleb Pavlovsky in *The Guardian* interview, for example, underscores the arbitrary nature of this decision, refuting Putin's own claim in September 2011 that he and Dmitry Medvedev had firmly decided from the outset that they would switch positions in 2012: "It's a complete myth that Putin and Medvedev agreed years ago that Putin would return. They may have talked about that 100 times. This is politics. It remained an open question. . . . of course they probably had a discussion about what would happen [if something didn't go right] . . . there could not have been a formal agreement." Pavlovsky notes that he thought the so-called *rokirovka,* the Medvedev-Putin swap, was a mistake and had spoken out against even the possibility of it in April 2011—which was when he was sacked as an adviser to the Kremlin, "on the direct order of the White House, i.e. on the personal order of Putin."

3. This was the view of senior European and U.S. officials the authors privately interviewed for this book.

4. Gleb Pavlovsky addresses this speculation directly in his interview with *The Guardian:* "There was a great deal of tension in the tandem. . . . In the White House [prime minister's office], there was a constant fear that Medvedev would sack the government suddenly. And that would create a completely different situation. And this fear reached its maximum in spring 2011." See also Ellen Barry, "Key Question Is Left Open as Medvedev Faces Media," *New York Times,* May 18, 2011, at www.nytimes.com/2011/05/19/world/europe/19russia.html?partner=rss&emc=rss; and Nikolai Zlobin, "Russia's leaders Dmitry Medvedev and Vladimir Putin should back each other," originally published in *Vedomosti,* reproduced and translated in *The Telegraph,* November 2, 2010, at www.telegraph.co.uk/sponsored/russianow/opinion/8105352/Russias-leaders-Dmitry-Medvedev-and-Vladimir-Putin-should-back-each-other.html.

5. The *Institut sovremennogo razvitiya* (INSOR) (Institute for Contemporary Development) and other similar think tanks were established in Russia under the tutelage of President Medvedev and the Kremlin to generate new ideas about reforming the state and its institutions and how to tackle the economic crisis and other critical political issues. The head of INSOR, Igor Yurgens, was a well-respected Russian businessman with extensive international contacts and considerable experience of establishing analytical centers. Deputies at the institute also included individuals who had served directly on the staff of the presidential administration. INSOR's official website is at www.insor-russia.ru/en. Igor Yurgens was routinely outspoken on the need for political change in Russia. See, for example, Igor Yurgens online interview on September 21, 2011, with the newspaper *Kommersant,* at www.kommersant.ru/doc/1778346; and Sergei Loiko, "In Russia, Medvedev's Key Advisor to Leave Post: Russian Activist Igor Yurgens Talks about the Future of the Council on Human Rights and the Return to Office of President Vladimir Putin," *Los Angeles Times,* June 28, 2012, at www.latimes.com/news/nationworld/world/la-fg-russia-qa-20120629,0,3197541.story.

6. See Luke Harding, "Russian President Sacks Moscow Mayor: Dmitry Medvedev Orders Out Veteran Yuri Luzhkov Citing 'Loss of Confidence,' Bringing 18-Year Domination to an End," *The Guardian,* September 28, 2010, at www.guardian.co.uk/world/2010/sep/28/russian-president-sacks-moscow-mayor. Gleb Pavlovsky comments on this episode in the following way: "Medvedev insisted that Luzhkov must go, and achieved that—Putin didn't like that because it was a very powerful gesture." Gleb Pavlovsky interview with *The Guardian,* January 24, 2012.

7. Gleb Pavlovsky interview with *The Guardian,* January 24, 2012. Putin also made the same comments in his presentations at the Valdai Discussion Club meeting on September 14, 2007, at the presidential dacha in Sochi, as well as in other interviews and exchanges in the period from 2007 to 2008. He stressed that it was important to ensure that everything was not "always in the hands of one man" given all the issues on the national agenda that needed to be addressed. He was, again, quite transparent in setting out his goals for the tandem.

8. Gleb Pavlovsky interview with *The Guardian,* January 24, 2012.

9. Authors' private meetings with former presidential aides in preparation for this book.

10. Putin used the metaphor of the Russian system operating like a "Swiss watch" (which could also be a Swiss clock, as the Russian word *chasy* is used for both watch and clock) at the Valdai Discussion Club dinner meeting in Sochi on September 14, 2007. He then used it repeatedly in subsequent sessions in the same context. Authors' personal notes from 2007–11 Valdai Discussion Club meetings. See also, for example, "Personifitsirovat' 'Plan Putin' nepravil'no, no pri vykhode iz krizisa mnogoye delayetsya v ruchnom upravleniy—Putin" [Personifying "Putin's Plan" is not correct, but before exiting from the crisis

much will have to be done in manual control—Putin], ITAR-TASS, October 18, 2007; and "We have taken positive steps in construction over the past few years. For example, housing construction has reached 60 million square meters per year. This is a good figure. However, it is mainly the effect of day-to-day 'manual control.' Unfortunately, no effective model has been created yet to regulate the construction industry automatically." Vladimir Putin, at a meeting on improving oversight, regulatory, and licensing policies and government services in construction, March 15, 2010, at www.government.ru/eng/docs/9744/.

11. This concept was also outlined in the 1997 *poslaniye*, which focused on coordinating legislation and reducing contradictions and redundancies in legislative acts at all levels across the Russian Federation. The 1993 Russian constitution is at the center of Putin's vision for the *pravovoye gosudarstvo*, or law-governed state, as we have already discussed.

12. See Burnham and Trochev (Summer 2007).

13. In June 2012, as we discuss later in the chapter, Putin appointed a Russian official specifically to help guide businesses through court cases. Alexander Bratersky, "Newsmaker: Small Business Lobbyist Titov Named Business Ombudsman," *Moscow Times*, June 21, 2012, at www.themoscowtimes.com/mobile/article/460818.html. The Russian government has also allowed its citizens to take political abuse cases to the European Court of Human Rights, with mixed results. See William Pomeranz, "Russia and the European Court of Human Rights: Implications for U.S. Policy," Kennan Institute seminar summary, May 3, 2011, at www.wilsoncenter.org/publication/russia-and-the-european-court-human-rights-implications-for-us-policy.

14. See the conference proceedings from "The Russian Constitution at Fifteen: Assessments and Current Challenges to Russia's Legal Development," Kennan Institute, March 19, 2009, at www.wilsoncenter.org/sites/default/files/KI_090623_Occ%20Paper%20304. pdf.

15. See, for example, Dmitri Trenin, "Putin's Russia Is Embracing Czarism: Trud Interviews Dmitri Trenin," *Trud*, November 14, 2006, at www.carnegieendowment. org/2006/11/16/putin-s-russia-is-embracing-czarism-trud-interviews-dmitri-trenin/9pg.

16. A good example is the article by Yevgeniya Albats and Anatoliy Yermolin, "Korporatsiya 'Rossiya': Putin s druz'yami podelili stranu" ["Russia," Inc.: Putin and his friends have divided up the country], *Novoe Vremya/The New Times*, No. 36, October 31, 2011. The centerpiece of the article was a large fold-out display of a tower of corporate interests linked to Putin, all color-coded by their backgrounds as *siloviki*, non-*silovik* St. Petersburgers, members of the Ozero dacha collective, and "children, relatives, friends and close associates." In their article, Albats and Yermolin erroneously attribute the origin of the term, Russia, Inc., to one of us. In fact, the term itself is an old and common one. What is important is to distinguish the actual meaning of the Russia, Inc. concept.

17. Private author interviews with GE executives in the United States in 2010–12.

18. See "Strategic Planning: Building up Reserves," pp. 81–85.

19. See "From Dresden to Business Developer in St. Petersburg," pp. 147–49.

20. See "Strategic Planning: Building up Reserves," pp. 81–85.

21. King and Cleland (1978), p. 11.

22. In private conversation with the authors, a pair of Russian oligarchs described their role in similar terms: "Our job is to stick to and optimize our business and not dabble in politics [the strategic agenda]." Washington, D.C., spring 2008.

23. King and Cleland (1978), p. 11.

24. At the November 2011 Valdai Discussion Club meeting, Putin continuously pointed out in response to questions that most, if not all, of Dmitry Medvedev's policies were his, Vladimir Putin's, or set in close consultation with him. From authors' personal notes.

25. Gaddy and Ickes describe Russia as an "inverted funnel" economy: Value is created in the narrow neck of the oil and gas sector and then flows to a broad base of the rest of industry. See Gaddy and Ickes (2011b).

26. The Russian leadership has shown little inclination to encourage entry into this sector by smaller firms. The number of companies operating in Russia's oil and gas sectors is around 160, for example, while the United States has over 22,000.

27. See "The Oligarchs' Dilemma: Mr. Putin's Solution," pp. 186–89.

28. See "The Food Scandal Revisited," pp. 154–60.

29. See p. 160.

30. The title of chapter 3 of Putin's dissertation is "A concept for formation of trans-portation-technological port complexes in the northwest Russian Federation." Finnish economist Pekka Sutela describes this issue as Putin's concern with "logistics sovereignty." See Sutela (2012), p. 35.

31. A decree issued by President Boris Yeltsin, "O merakh po vozrozhedeniyu torgogo flota Rossii" [On measures to resurrect Russia's commercial fleet], Decree No. 1513, December 3, 1992, called on the government to adopt a program to restore the physical and institutional infrastructure of Russian commercial shipping, including seaports and rail access to them. In the follow-up to Yeltsin's decree, a number of committees were established that included members from the St. Petersburg mayor's office. Vladimir Putin, the deputy mayor in charge of international business development, was likely one of those taking part.

32. The two most prominent pipeline projects of Putin's tenure have been Nord Stream, which transports natural gas from Russia's Baltic coast to Germany and came into opera-tion in 2011–12; and South Stream, a similar pipeline project to transport natural gas from Russia's Black Sea coast to southeastern Europe, which has yet to reach the construction phase. See the Nord Stream pipeline consortium official website for detailed information at www.nord-stream.com/press-info/library/. South Stream's official website is at http://south-stream.info/index.php?id=2&L=1. Further details and analysis of Putin's pipeline and other energy sector priorities are available on journalist Steve LeVine's online blog at www.stevelevine.info.

33. A detailed account of how Putin established control over the strategic companies that make up Russia, Inc. is beyond the scope of this book. The account on the following pages and in the accompanying notes only scratches the surface. Suffice it to say that in many cases it took a great deal of effort and time on Mr. Putin's part to acquire real con-trol. Each of the target companies had its own peculiarities and required a special opera-tion. Of all the takeover operations, the one aimed at Gazprom was the most important but also the most difficult and delicate. Gazprom's role in Putin's system is unique owing to its dual status as both the single largest rent producer and the most important rent distributor in the country. It, of course, had to be brought under Putin's personal control. At the same time, a simple frontal assault to seize control and install reliable subordinates inside Gazprom was unthinkable because of the risk that a power struggle might disrupt its vital role in distributing resource rent and supporting huge sections of the population and industry. It took Putin over two years after he became president to orchestrate the complete ousting of Gazprom's incumbent director, Rem Vyakhirev, and install his own man, Alexei Miller. Some particularly enlightening episodes of that takeover operation may be found in Panyushkin, Zygar, and Reznik (2008).

34. This does not imply, however, that there are not other trusted lieutenants who play critical roles in other state sectors for CEO/President Putin. These two stand out in terms of the length of time they have spent working close to Vladimir Putin throughout his career and in the specific roles they have played at important junctures.

35. See the detailed profile of Igor Sechin by Irina Reznik and Irina Mokrousova, "Igor' Sechin, pervyy vozle Vladimira Putina" [Igor Sechin, first alongside Vladimir Putin], *Vedomosti,* March 19, 2012, at www.vedomosti.ru/library/news/1541119/pervyj_vozle_putina. The introduction to the profile asserts that "acquaintances of Sechin give him a variety of titles: Putin's secretary, aide, adjutant, soldier, sometimes more insulting ones,

but all of them agree that the main concept of his function is not self-enrichment and not even the creation of a regime of personal power in and of itself, but implementing the will and desires of his patron, which for him coincide with societal welfare." In another article in *Vedomosti*, by Oksana Gavshina, Maksim Tovkaylo, and Yekaterina Derbilova, "Chto ozhidayet 'Rosneft' pod rukovodstvom Sechina?" [What awaits "Rosneft" under Sechin's leadership?], *Vedomosti*, May 23, 2012, at www.vedomosti.ru/companies/news/1774296/ sechin_soberet_neft, one source for the article notes that even as CEO of Rosneft, Sechin "will go to Putin directly. Sechin isn't a person but a function: When he's told to do something, he does it." Like many other figures in Putin's inner circle, Igor Sechin has close links to a number of key figures. Sechin's daughter is married to the son of Vladimir Ustinov. The elder Ustinov, who has served as both Russian justice minister and Russia's prosecutor general, led the first legal cases against Mikhail Khodorkovsky and the YUKOS energy company in the 2000s. YUKOS assets acquired by Rosneft after the company's dissolution now form a substantial part of Rosneft's core operating units. See *Moscow Times* profile of Igor Sechin at www.themoscowtimes.com/mt_profile/igor_sechin/433774.html. See also Coll (2012).

36. *Vedomosti* claimed that this particular project was drawn up by the export arm of the Kirishi oil refinery—the company Kirishineftekhimeksport, or Kineks. See Reznik and Mokrousova, March 19, 2012. It should also be noted here that the Kirishi oil refinery was the source of the oil that Putin licensed to be exported in the 1991–92 oil-for-food deal. Presumably its export division, Kineks, played a role in the transactions. One of the early executives of Kineks in the 1990s was Gennady Timchenko, who was, until March 2014, also the co-owner of Gunvor, one of the largest global oil trading companies. Although Gunvor is primarily based in Switzerland it has substantial Russian interests, including in selling and exporting a portion of Rosneft's oil production. See Timchenko's profile in *Forbes*'s Billionaires List at www.forbes.com/profile/gennady-timchenko/. Timchenko, a dual Finnish and Russian citizen, is purportedly connected to Putin from the time they overlapped in St. Petersburg in the early 1990s. Timchenko has other business interests in Russia, including in Novatek, one of Russia's largest independent gas producers. He is also a sponsor of the contemporary St. Petersburg judo club where Putin trained as a young man. See Andrew Kramer and David Herszenhorn, "Midas Touch in St. Petersburg: Friends of Putin Glow Brightly," *New York Times*, March 1, 2012, at www.nytimes.com/2012/03/02/world/ europe/ties-to-vladimir-putin-generate-fabulous-wealth-for-a-select-few-in-russia.html. In 2008–09, Timchenko sued *The Economist* for suggesting even closer links between himself, Gunvor, and Putin. See "Grease My Palm," *The Economist*, November 29, 2008, and the publication's subsequent clarification of the relationship between Timchenko, Gunvor, and Putin, "Gennady Timchenko and Gunvor International BV," *The Economist*, July 30, 2009, at www.economist.com/node/14140737. In May 2012, coinciding with Putin's inauguration as president for the third time, *The Economist* produced another lengthy article on Gunvor and its oil trading practices: "Gunvor: Riddles, Mysteries and Enigmas," *The Economist*, May 5, 2012, at www.economist.com/node/21554185. In July 2012, Timchenko reportedly decided to move the headquarters of his Volga Resources investment company, which holds and manages his various assets, to Moscow from Switzerland. See "Timchenko Moves Headquarters to Moscow," *Moscow Times*, July 20, 2012, at www.themoscowtimes.com/ business/article/timchenko-moves-headquarters-to-moscow/462357.html.

37. Zubkov (2000).

38. Nikolai Tokarev was educated and worked in mining and geology. Many sources claim that he was in the KGB and that he served with Putin in the GDR in the 1980s. Tokarev's current official biography (from the Transneft website) makes no reference to a career in the KGB. It states that he worked in the presidential property office 1996–99, which is where Vladimir Putin served when he first came to Moscow in 1996–97. In

August 1999, Tokarev was appointed vice president for international affairs and projects of Transneft. In September 2000, he left Transneft to head the Russian oil company Zarubezhneft, and on September 11, 2007, he was named president of Transneft. Given that his first position at Transneft in 1999 was as head of security, one can assume that he does have a background in the KGB.

39. Some 70 percent of all Russian refined oil products (domestic and exported) are transported by rail. Troika, *Russia Oil and Gas Atlas,* January 2012, p. 39.

40. See previous references to Yakunin on pp. 67–68 and p. 186. See also Douglas Busvine and Stephen Grey, "Special Report: Russian Railways' family connections," *Reuters,* July 25, 2012, at www.reuters.com/article/2012/07/25/us-russia-railways-idUSBRE86O06U20120725.

41. Yakunin is another Putin associate who is thought to have a KGB background, a supposition based on strong circumstantial evidence about his background (including education as an expert on ballistic missiles, two years' service as head of the international department of the Yoffe Institute of Physics in Leningrad, and a five-year posting with the Soviet delegation to the United Nations in the 1980s). Like many other individuals around Putin, he does not appear ever to have publicly confirmed or denied his alleged ties to the KGB. See Max Delany, "An Inside Track to President Putin's Kremlin," *St. Petersburg Times,* October 2, 2007, at www.sptimes.ru/index.php?action_id=2&story_id=23175.

42. It is interesting to note the similarity between Yakunin's path to the head of Russian Railways and that of Tokarev in Transneft. Both were initially appointed to be deputies under an older head and served in that position for a while. Such a procedure makes sense. The position as deputy gave them time to learn the ropes, since neither had any previous expertise in the industries they were later to command. However, in view of the previous expertise each is said to have—as KGB specialists in "working with people"—the position as deputy also provided the classic opportunity to observe, monitor, and gather information about *people* in the organization.

43. Vladimir Yakunin, like others in Putin's circle, also has a connection to the shipping business in St. Petersburg. His first position in Moscow was in 2000 as deputy minister for transportation in charge of seaports. See Delany, "An Inside Track to President Putin's Kremlin," *St. Petersburg Times,* October 2, 2007.

44. The company's website is at www.oaoosk.ru/.

45. For details on the methods of rent sharing, see Gaddy and Ickes (2011). It is worth noting that Russian oligarchs have also been encouraged by the Kremlin to branch out from the commodities and manufacturing sectors into hi-tech and emerging retail sectors, including the new media, resulting in the emergence of a whole new group of Russian billionaires (or even richer billionaires) in the last decade. See the *Forbes* Billionaires List at www.forbes.com/billionaires/list/. For example, Alisher Usmanov, who manages the investment arm of Gazprom, has also owned stakes in Facebook as well as the online retailers Groupon and Zynga, in addition to the Russian newspaper *Kommersant* and massive holdings in steel and telecommunications. He comes in on the *Forbes* list at number 40 with $18 billion (in November 2014). Vladimir Potanin, who first built up huge holdings in Russian metallurgy through the "loans-for-shares" deal in the 1990s, is also the owner of one of Russia's largest media groups, ProfMedia. He comes in at number 86 with $13.7 billion. Yury Milner, Alisher Usmanov's business partner, now specializes primarily in social networking and tech investments that have included Facebook, Groupon, Zynga, and Russia's Mail.ru, among many others (including Chinese online retailers). He comes in on the November 2014 *Forbes* list at number 1,010 with $1.8 billion.

46. Vladimir Putin: "I've been a military functionary [*chinovnik*], a civilian functionary, all my life. . . . Do I feel like I am a functionary? Of course, I do. Because even if it's on a high level, it is still in the service of the state, and service presupposes certain obligations,

and they have to be met. . . . In that sense, we're all functionaries." Vladimir Putin, television interview on the program "Geroy dnya so Svetlanoy Sorokinoy na NTV" [Hero of the day with Svetlana Sorokina on NTV], November 24, 1999, at http://tvoygolos.narod. ru/elita/elitatext/1999.11.24.htm.

47. Putin put explicit emphasis on his decision to bolster the importance of the position of prime minister, both in the September 14, 2007, Valdai Discussion Club meeting in Sochi—when he first signaled that he intended to step into the position—and again in statements in 2008–09 when he became prime minister. Authors' personal notes from Valdai Discussion Club sessions.

48. In this interview, Putin was frank about bringing people into the Kremlin primarily on the basis of their personal connections to him—including some who had previously worked with him in the KGB. "I have brought some of them to the Kremlin. These people work on my staff. I have known them for many years and I trust them. This is the main reason why I have brought them along. . . . It has nothing to do with ideology. It's only a matter of their professional qualities and personal relationships." See "Vladimir Putin Arises from Murky Background of KGB to Become Acting President of Russia," *Nightline* (Friday Night Special), ABC News, March 24, 2000 (transcript, with Mr. Putin speaking through a translator), accessed through Nexis.com.

49. Igor Sechin did two stints as a military interpreter with Soviet forces in Africa, which presumably put him under the supervision of the GRU, military intelligence. He was called out of his undergraduate studies in romance languages in 1982 to work in Mozambique for two years. After graduating with degrees in teaching French and Portuguese from Leningrad State University in 1985, he served two years in the Red Army, again as an interpreter, including service in Angola. Sechin was never in the KGB, but he is said to nurture fantasies of being a spy—which may explain why he seems to have allowed, and even encouraged, the mythmaking about his being a *silovik*, which seems to be used as a synonym for the KGB in some commentaries. See Reznik and Mokrousova, March 19, 2012. Private conversations with former Russian presidential administration aides tend to confirm this version of Sechin's background. The former aides asserted that Sechin had been made an "honorary colonel" by Putin at some point during his Kremlin service and mostly as an "inside joke." The GRU connection and the related idea of Sechin as a spy feature prominently in press articles on Sechin. See, for example, Andrew Kramer, "In Bid for BP's Stake of Venture, a Former Spy Becomes the Focus," *New York Times*, July 25, 2012, at www.nytimes.com/2012/07/25/business/global/rosneft-opens-talks-on-buying-bps-stake-in-oil-joint-venture.html.

50. Putin has been quoted as saying of Sechin: "I value him for his professionalism, his grasp. He is able to see something through to the end. If he takes on a job, you can be sure that it will be done." See Gavshina, Tovkaylo, and Derbilova, May 23, 2012.

51. We use the term ombudsman here in its original Scandinavian sense of a "representative" or trusted intermediary between the state and other external groups and interests, not in the more modern form of an independent arbiter or watchdog who acts in the public interest on a particular issue.

52. Igor Shuvalov was also the point person for Russia's World Trade Organization bid and membership, which was eventually pushed through in 2012.

53. In a private conversation with the authors, one former presidential administration aide observed of Dmitry Medvedev's role as president that "someone has to have tea with dignitaries." In private meetings in Berlin in May 2012, a number of senior political advisers to European leaders noted that as prime minister, Vladimir Putin had, in their view, deliberately avoided anticipated meetings with their heads of state in the period from 2008 to 2012. Dmitry Medvedev had invariably been substituted or the meeting had sometimes not taken place at all.

54. This issue was a common theme in author interviews with Russian analysts and officials in preparation for this book. Gleb Pavlovsky also makes this point in his extensive interview with *The Guardian*, including in reference to his own role as a Kremlin adviser.

55. See, for example, the discussion in Brian Whitmore, "The Unraveling: The Tandem's Slow Death," *The Power Vertical* (blog), RFE/RL, April 2, 2012, at www.rferl.org/content/how_the_tandem_disintegrated/24535389.html; and Charles Clover and Catherine Belton, "Inside the Kremlin," *Financial Times Weekend Magazine*, May 5/6, 2012, pp. 26–31.

56. In the Soviet period, the Communist Party at various times actively encouraged debate on some policy issues among party members at all levels of the hierarchy, but expected full compliance with decisions once they were made by the top leadership.

57. Former *Washington Post* Moscow bureau chiefs Peter Baker and Susan Glasser discuss this directly in "After Beslan," the epilogue to their 2005 book, *Kremlin Rising*, on pp. 371–82.

58. PBS's *Wide Angle* produced an excellent documentary with a range of supporting analytical material on the September 2004 school siege in 2005. This is available at www.pbs.org/wnet/wideangle/episodes/beslan-seige-of-school-1/introduction/246/. The siege occurred simultaneously with the first Valdai Discussion Club meeting, which resulted in a back and forth between Putin and the invited guests on the crisis and its aftermath in the presidential dacha on the outskirts of Moscow for more than four hours. There were also real-time meetings with other Russian government officials who were trying to contend with the flow of events.

59. Sergei Shoigu, another of Mr. Putin's key operational managers, was moved from the position of emergencies minister to governor of the critical Moscow region in May 2012. As we will discuss later, Putin appointed Shoigu as defense minister in late 2012.

60. Ironically, Putin rolled out this stock anecdote in late 2011 and 2012 to justify the very opposite policy response to 2004—adjusting the vertical of power through the return to elected regional officials to inculcate a renewed sense of responsibility. Seemingly forgetting that he had used the tale of the irresponsible official before in an earlier meeting with the Valdai Discussion Club group, he returned to it at the November 11, 2011, meeting in reference to a question about his plans to restore direct elections at the regional level. Authors' personal notes.

61. The main theme of Putin's speech at the June 2012 St. Petersburg Economic Forum was the importance of government effectiveness. The full speech is available in English at http://eng.kremlin.ru/news/4056 and in Russian at http://kremlin.ru/transcripts/15709. Video footage is at http://2012.forumspb.com/#.

62. Alexei Kudrin's sustained and highly praised performance as finance minister is perhaps the clearest example of the confluence of personal relationships *and* professional qualifications at the very top of Mr. Putin's Russian system. Elsewhere in the government, and also in the presidential administration, there has been some effort to bring in young reform-minded technocrats and appoint them to key operational (but not decisionmaking) positions across the apparatus. In February 2009, President Medvedev initiated the government's technocratic drive, when the Kremlin announced that it had drawn up a list of 100 members of a "high-potential" managerial pool, the so-called *zolotaya sotnya* (golden hundred). This list included 36 people from federal agencies, 23 from regional administrations, 31 from business, and 10 from science, education, and nonprofit organizations. The Kremlin declared that it would draw on the list in making future government appointments. Examples of technocratic appointments and the *zolotaya sotnya* include the central bank head, Elvira Nabiullina, who has an economics degree from Moscow State University and also served as Russian minister of economic development and trade; Deputy Prime Minister Arkady Dvorkovich, who did part of his economics training at Duke University in the United States, in addition to Moscow State University and Moscow's New Economic School; and the Central Bank of Russia's first deputy governor, Ksenia Yudaeva, the former chief economist at Russia's Sberbank, who became head of a major government economics task force and was then appointed director of the presidential administration's "expert department," as well as "sherpa" to the G-20. Yudaeva earned a Ph.D. in

economics from the Massachusetts Institute of Technology and worked for a period as a senior analyst for the Carnegie Institute for International Peace's Moscow Center. See the official link to the Kremlin announcement of this list at "Kadrovy rezerv" (Cadres reserve) at http://archive.kremlin.ru/articles/kadry.shtml. The contrast between the accomplished technocrats who have been brought into the government in the 2000s and those in the inner circle, whose positions derive primarily from their proximity to Putin, is an issue that crops up repeatedly in discussions of Russian governance and economic development as, for example, in author interviews with senior international financial institution officials in Washington, D.C., in July 2012.

63. In a May 2012 editorial, the Russian newspaper *Vedomosti* discusses the complexities of operating in these parallel worlds and talks about the phantom-people (*lyudi-prizraki*) in the Russian apparatus—the people who are not household names, who work hard and work honestly in the ordinary world, putting forward ideas and writing reports, but who know all the time that someone else makes the real decisions. See "Tsar'-klyuch-nik" [Tsar-steward], *Vedomosti,* May 21, 2012.

64. For examples of the many recent journalistic accounts of Putin's new crony oligarchs, see Andrew E. Kramer and David M. Herszenhorn, "Midas Touch in St. Petersburg: Friends of Putin Glow Brightly," *New York Times,* March 1, 2012, at www.nytimes.com/2012/03/02/world/europe/ties-to-vladimir-putin-generate-fabulous-wealthfor-a-select-few-in-russia.html; and Catherine Belton and Charles Clover, "Putin's People," *Financial Times,* May 30, 2012, at www.ft.com/cms/s/0/8d0ed5ce-aa64-11e1-899d-00144feabdc0.html#axzz26w16zruc.

65. Arkady Rotenberg, who was part of Putin's Leningrad judo team in his youth, underscored this in an extremely frank interview with the Russian edition of *Forbes* magazine in July 2012. Since the 1990s, Rotenberg has transformed himself into a billionaire businessman specializing in banking and construction, as well as in Putin's priority energy pipeline and transportation sectors. In the interview, Rotenberg refuted the *Forbes* journalist's accusations that he enjoys a privileged position and secures lucrative projects and contracts only because of his relationship with Putin. Rotenberg pointed out that he has to perform and perform well in these sectors: "These were big, difficult, and responsible projects that had to be completed within tight deadlines. There are few people in our country who can do that kind of thing. . . . Unlike my friends, I am not entitled to make a mistake, because it is not only a question of my reputation. . . . Vladimir Vladimirovich does not protect me. If I was to involve myself not in business but in some other practices, he would not say: 'He must not be touched; he is a good guy!' If some people can make a living out of doing bad things, that is unacceptable to me." In other words, in Rotenberg's and Putin's views of how the crony oligarch system works, it is not "corruption" when your friends get lucrative contacts *if* they get the job done. Corruption is when people abuse their position, privilege, or connections for personal gain at the expense of getting the job done (the specific job that Putin wants done). From Vladimir Putin's perspective, the reason you give the contacts to your friends, the crony oligarchs, is because you can make them understand that very crucial point. Rotenberg states explicitly that Putin would not protect him if he were to abuse the responsibility he has been given. See Aleksandr Levinskiy, "Yesli by menya ne piarili kak druga Putina, tak i biznes byl by pokhuzhe" [If I had not been hyped as a friend of Putin's, my business would have fared a bit worse], *Forbes Russia,* July 23, 2012, at www.forbes.ru/sobytiya/lyudi/84415-esli-menya-ne-piarili-kak-druga-putina-tak-i-biznes-byl-po-huzhe. The article's subtitle is, in English, "How Arkadiy Rotenberg changed from being a sportsman and cooperative member into the biggest contractor for the state and state monopolies."

66. In *Ot pervogo litsa,* pp. 181–83, in addition to mentioning Dmitry Medvedev, Alexei Kudrin, and Igor Sechin as close and trusted associates at the outset of his presidency, Putin singles out two others. They are Sergei Ivanov, then secretary of the Russian

Security Council, who served in the Leningrad branch of the KGB, and Nikolai Patrushev, who replaced Putin as the head of the KGB/FSB in 1999. Every single one is connected to Leningrad/St. Petersburg. See Gevorkyan, Timakova, and Kolesnikov (2000).

67. Cited in Simon Shuster, "Vladimir Putin's Billionaire Boys Judo Club," *Time*, March 1, 2011.

68. Putin frequently refers to Mikhail Khodorkovsky breaking the terms of the original deal he made with the oligarchs in 2000 to stay out of politics. This was seen by some in Khodorkovsky's own inner circle as one of the factors in his arrest on charges of tax evasion in 2003. See Gessen (2012), pp. 242–43; and Coll (2012), pp. 264–66, p. 271, and p. 275. In June 2012 (as we will discuss in chapter 10), Anatoly Sobchak's daughter, Ksenia Sobchak, a prominent Russian media figure and supporter of the Russian opposition movement, was the target of a raid by the Russian interior ministry police, who seized an estimated €1 million and $500,000 in cash from her home safe and threatened her with prosecution for tax evasion. Most commentators assumed that she was being punished for having "betrayed" Vladimir Putin. See, for example, Brian Whitmore, "Ksenia and Vladimir," *The Power Vertical* (blog), RFE/RL, June 18, 2012, at www.rferl.org/content/ksenia-anatolevna-and-vladimir-vladimirovich/24618330.html.

69. See, for example, Catherine Belton, "Analysis: A Realm Fit for a Tsar," *Financial Times*, November 30, 2011, at www.ft.com/intl/cms/s/0/69d1db86-1aa6-11e1-ae14-00144feabdc0.html#axzz26w16zruc; and "Putin's Watch Collection Dwarfs His Declared Income," *Moscow Times*, June 8, 2012. The article and a related video are at www.themoscowtimes.com/news/article/putins-watch-collection-dwarfs-his-declared-income/460061.html. This is also a major point of discussion in Masha Gessen's chapter "Insatiable Greed," pp. 227–60, and has been the subject of reports by members of the Russian opposition. See, for example, Boris Nemtsov and Leonid Martiniuk, "Zhizn' raba na galerakh: dvortsy, yakhty, avtomobili, samolyoti and drugiye aksessuary" [Life of a galley slave: palaces, yachts, automobiles, airplanes and other accessories], August 2012, on Boris Nemtsov's website at www.nemtsov.ru/?id=718577.

70. When Putin first came to Moscow in 1996, he began work in the Kremlin presidential property agency, which is the central repository of privileges and perks for those inside the government system. The Kremlin agency oversees the allocation of dachas and official cars to government officials, airplane leases for private and government jets, and preferential access to presidential medical facilities among many other things. This initial Kremlin position would have given Putin a firsthand view of who exactly had access to what.

71. Viktor Zubkov as cited in Yelena Vladimirova, "Gryaznyye den'gi" [Dirty money], *Trud*, September 14, 2002, at www.trud.ru/issue/article.php?id=200209141640203.

72. In their 2008 book about Gazprom, Valeriy Panyushkin, Mikhail Zygar', and Irina Reznik relate the case of Yakub Goldovsky, one of the original owners of the energy company SIBUR, in which Goldovsky first acquired a stake during the "loans-for-shares" period of the 1990s. In 2001, Gazprom acquired SIBUR. Golodovsky was arrested. According to the book's authors, he had been offered a deal to cash out, but he refused. Golodovsky was later asked why he did not leave on good terms (*uyti po-khoroshemu*), and he replied that he was an independent businessman, had created the company for himself and his children, and did not want to leave it nor sell it to Gazprom. In December 2011, Goldovsky had reemerged—presumably rehabilitated on the basis of a new deal—as one of the key players in a new entity, the United Petrochemical Company, owned by the massive Moscow-based conglomerate AFK Sistema. The head of Sistema, Yevgeny Yevtushenkov, another of Russia's top oligarchs and billionaires, was one of the closest associates of Yury Luzhkov and his businesswoman wife, Yelena Baturina, during Luzhkov's long tenure as Moscow's mayor. In April 2012, Yevtushenkov offered the former mayor a seat on the board of United Petrochemical Company, apparently stressing to Luzhkov that "the leadership [of Russia] did not object."

All of these complexities are related in "Luzhkov voshel v sovet direktorov Obedinennoy neftekhimicheskoy kompanii" [Luzhkov enters the board of directors of the United petrochemical company], *Vedomosti,* June 26, 2012, at www.vedomosti.ru/companies/news/2179270/luzhkov_vojdet_v_sovet_direktorov_obedinennoj. Linking back to others in the circles around Putin, the SIBUR company's website now indicates that it is partially owned by Gennady Timchenko and his business partner Leonid Mikhelson (who also co-owns Novatek with Mr. Timchenko). See http://sibur.com/about/controls/directors/. Sistema's Yevtushenkov fell into his own trouble in 2014, ostensibly as a result of an ownership dispute over the energy company Bashneft. See, for instance, Courtney Weaver, "Russian Oligarch Yevtushenkov Placed under House Arrest," *Financial Times,* September 17, 2014, and much subsequent media coverage.

73. The contours and mechanics of this system are also discussed in Ledeneva (2006); Lucas (2008); and Monaghan (2012), pp. 1–16. Mark Galeotti provides an analysis of the enduring tradition of corruption as a tool of statecraft in Russia in "Who's the Boss: Us or the Law? The Corrupt Art of Governing Russia," in Lovell, Ledeneva, and Rogatchev (2000).

74. "Castling" is the only move in chess that allows two pieces to be moved at the same time. It involves switching positions between the king and a rook.

75. This story was related to the authors in private discussions with former presidential administration aides who were present for some of these announcements. Putin made similar references at the Valdai Discussion Club meetings in 2007 and 2008.

76. The full transcript of the call-in show is at http://government.ru/docs/17409/.

77. This point was made by Vladislav Surkov in his 2000 interview with journalist Yelena Tregubova (see p. 189).

78. Tregubova (2003), p. 147. This analysis of Putin's treatment of Nazdratenko is from Gaddy and Ickes (2011a).

79. See Albats and Yermolin (2011). Albats and Yermolin note that many of the new faces in Russian political and business circles are in fact the children or in-laws of those already well ensconced in the inner circle and thus already known or connected to Putin.

80. In May 2012, Putin purportedly cancelled a planned visit to the United States for the G-8 meeting because he had to attend to all the decisions related to the selection of a new Russian cabinet personally. See Josh Rogin, "Putin Not Coming to the U.S. for G-8," *Foreign Policy,* May 9, 2012, at http://thecable.foreignpolicy.com/posts/2012/05/09/putin_not_coming_to_us_for_g_8.

81. See Fiona Hill, "Dinner with Putin: Musings on the Politics of Modernization in Russia," Brookings Foreign Policy Trip Reports, No. 18, October 2010, at www.brookings.edu/research/2010/10_russia-putin-hill.aspx.

82. In 2009, Ramzan Kadyrov reportedly told a Russian newspaper: "I am wholly Vladimir Putin's man. I shall never betray Putin; I shall never let him down. I swear by the Almighty: I would rather die 20 times." Cited in Yaffa (2012).

83. Gleb Pavlovsky interview with *The Guardian,* January 24, 2012.

84. Roxburgh (2012). The description of Roxburgh's role in Moscow is at pp. xi–xiii. Also, author interviews with Roxburgh and other Ketchum colleagues working with the Peskov team during the research for this book.

85. Roxburgh (2012), pp. 183–91. Roxburgh also describes, on pp. 193–95, how the Valdai Discussion Club, which fell under the oversight of Dmitry Peskov, was first conceived and launched in 2004. The intent was to provide a group opportunity for some foreign journalists and experts to have much-coveted access to Putin himself and other top officials. The Kremlin would give individuals in the group the chance to ask a question directly and receive a transmission, an answer, back from Vladimir Putin. Peskov's team then intended that the foreign journalists and experts would "transmit" this response, as well as a favorable impression from the overall experience, to a larger audience in their

subsequent articles and presentations. Putin himself stated this openly in 2007: "We'd be glad if you would transmit something of what you learn to your readers and viewers, to combat the strong stereotypes that exist in the West." The Putin citation is on p. 195 of Roxburgh's book.

86. See "Obama Tells Russia's Medvedev More Flexibility after Election," Reuters, March 26, 2012, at www.reuters.com/article/2012/03/26/us-nuclear-summit-obama-medvedev-idUSBRE82P0JI20120326.

87. The ironic and humorous aspects of this incident, with much emphasis on the "transmission" of information "to Vladimir," were heavily featured in the Western media. See, for example, Jon Stewart, "The Borscht Whisperer" episode on *The Daily Show* on Comedy Central, March 28, 2012, at www.thedailyshow.com/watch/wed-march-28-2012/march-28--2012---pt--3.

88. Josh Gerstein, "Barack Obama meets with Vladimir Putin," *Politico,* July 7, 2009, at www.politico.com/news/stories/0709/24621.html. Putin and Obama only met for a second time in June 2012 during the G-20 meeting in Los Cabos, Mexico, after Putin had pulled out of an earlier planned meeting in the United States in May for the G-8 summit.

89. Author interviews with senior advisers to top European leaders in Berlin in May 2012 and other similar discussions with European and U.S. officials in 2009–12. World leaders felt they had to start again in building relations with Putin when he moved back into the presidency in May 2012. Many considered they had less insight into and less feel for the man than they did in 2000. Joshua Yaffa, in a *Foreign Affairs* review of Masha Gessen's and Angus Roxburgh's 2012 books on Putin, noted that he remained "a mysterious figure" and "ultimately, an unknowable subject." See Yaffa (2012).

90. See note 42, p. 440, for previous citation.

91. Author interviews in 2012 with U.S. and European officials, who variously identified Russian Security Council secretary Nikolai Patrushev, presidential foreign policy adviser Sergei Prikhodko, Deputy Prime Minister and now presidential Chief of Staff Sergei Ivanov, and presidential adviser Vladislav Surkov as their "transmitters."

92. At the June 2012 St. Petersburg Economic Forum, for example, Putin held a well-publicized private meeting with Russian and international oil company executives. See the account of this meeting on the Russian presidential website at http://news.kremlin.ru/news/15716. Christopher Helman in *Forbes* magazine notes that "when sorting through the rankings of the world's 25 biggest oil companies and looking at who controls and influences the biggest of big oil, one thing becomes clear: no industry leader has more sway, has twisted more arms or made more deals than Russian President Vladimir Putin." See "The World's 25 Biggest Oil Companies," *Forbes* [online], July 16, 2012, at www.forbes.com/sites/christopherhelman/2012/07/16/the-worlds-25-biggest-oil-companies/.

93. See "Alcoa Inc: obrashcheniya k investitsionnomu ombudsmenu Shuvalovu pomogli reshit' problemy kompanii" [Alcoa Inc: turning to the investment ombudsman Shuvalov helped to resolve problems for the company], *Vedomosti,* June 23, 2012, at www.vedomosti.ru/politics/news/2091862/alcoa_inc_obraschalsya_s_prosbami_k_investicionnomu#ixzz1yzw5GMM8.

94. Ibid. In the same timeframe, also at the St. Petersburg Economic Forum in June 2012, President Putin officially created another business ombudsman, naming Boris Titov, the former head of a Russian business group *Delovaya Rossiya,* to the position. Titov's role was to assist company and business owners in navigating court battles during legal disputes, which Putin acknowledged were a growing problem in Russia at this juncture. Putin's announcement of this appointment is available on the Kremlin website at http://news.kremlin.ru/news/15709.

95. Some sources claim that Matthias Warnig is a former East German secret police agent whom Putin first got to know during his posting to Dresden in the 1980s. Warnig personally denies this but does not deny the close and very friendly ties he forged with

Putin in St. Petersburg in the 1990s when he was working at Dresdner Bank and Putin was head of the Committee for External Relations. Author interviews with Matthias Warnig in Washington, D.C., in June 2009. See also Dirk Banse and others, "Circles of Power: Putin's Secret Friendship with Ex-Stasi Officer," *The Guardian,* August 13, 2014, at www.theguardian.com/world/2014/aug/13/russia-putin-german-right-hand-man-matthias-warnig.

96. Author interviews with energy executives from several U.S. and European companies in 2012. In August 2012, the Russian version of *Forbes* magazine published a lengthy analysis of Warnig's relationship with Putin and role in the Russian energy sector: Aleksandr Levinskiy, Irina Malkova, and Valeriy Igumenov, "Kak Mattias Warnig stal samym nadezhnym 'ekonomistom' Putina" [How Matthias Warnig became the most reliable 'economist' for Putin], *Forbes.ru,* August 28, 2012, at www.forbes.ru/sobytiya/vlast/103069-kak-chekist-iz-gdr-stal-samym-nadezhnym-ekonomistom-putina-rassledovanie-forbe.

97. Igor Sechin's status in the transmission system far surpasses that of Igor Shuvalov, as an often repeated, possibly apocryphal, anecdote from inside the Kremlin corridors underscores. Sechin and Shuvalov share a first name and patronymic—Igor Ivanovich—which would be used both to address and refer to them in a work setting. The anecdote, which has been told to us by a variety of interlocutors, is as follows: Putin tells one of his aides to summon Igor Ivanovich for a meeting. The aide asks, *"Kakoy Igor' Ivanovich?"* [Which Igor Ivanovich?], to which Putin replies, *"Nastoyashchiy!"* [The real one]. The aide and everyone else immediately knows this is Igor Ivanovich Sechin, not Shuvalov.

98. Kirill Mel'nikov, "Igor' Sechin nashel al'ternativu pravitel'stvu. On sozdayet sobstvennyy Neftyanoy klub" [Igor Sechin has found an alternative to the government. He's creating his own "oil club"], *Vedomosti,* June 8, 2012, at www.vedomosti.ru/companies/news/1833019/sechin_na_prieme and www.vedomosti.ru/newspaper/article/282241/sechin_na_prieme.

99. See Clifford Gaddy, "Pudrin Lives," Brookings Institution, September 11, 2011, at www.brookings.edu/research/opinions/2011/09/30-russia-gaddy.

100. Kudrin made allusions to this possibility in a series of interviews and more private discussions in the period between December 2011 and April 2012. See interview with Alexei Kudrin, *Ekho Moskvy,* December 13, 2011, at www.echo.msk.ru/programs/dozor/838597-echo/; also authors' notes from Alexei Kudrin presentation in Washington, D.C., April 19, 2012.

101. Douglas Busvine, "Russia's Kudrin Stays in Mix with New Task Force," Reuters, April 5, 2012, at www.reuters.com/article/2012/04/05/russia-kudrin-idUSL6E8F515C20120405. Masha Gessen, Maria Lipman, and Oleg Kashin all noted Alexei Kudrin's active outreach to the Russian protest and opposition movements during presentations at the Brookings Institution in March–April 2012.

CHAPTER 10

1. See also the lead article, "Putin's Russia. Call Back Yesterday," *The Economist,* March 3–9, 2012, at www.economist.com/node/21548949.

2. The announcement was made by Dmitry Medvedev at the United Russia party convention, where it was greeted with enthusiastic applause. Ellen Barry, "Putin Once More Moves to Assume Top Job in Russia," *New York Times,* September 24, 2011, at www.nytimes.com/2011/09/25/world/europe/medvedev-says-putin-will-seek-russian-presidency-in-2012.html?pagewanted=all. Although Russian public opinion surveys in September–October 2011 showed what appeared at first to be an indifferent response among the population to the announcement, Putin's poll ratings slipped relative to the past. See the opinion poll by Russia's leading polling agency Levada taken just after Putin's September 2011 announcement: "Vladimir Putin i ego tretiy srok" [Vladimir Putin and

his third term], October 7, 2011, Levada Center, at www.levada.ru/07-10-2011/vladimir-putin-i-ego-tretii-srok. The Levada agency also maintains an approval index for Vladimir Putin and Dmitry Medvedev at www.levada.ru/indeksy. The index shows a dip in their approval after the announcement.

3. Michael Idov, "The New Decembrists," *The New Yorker*, January 22, 2012. The title refers to the Russian Decembrist Revolt of 1825.

4. Russian journalist Oleg Kashin made similar comments in a meeting at the Brookings Institution on March 29, 2012. He noted that, as president, Dmitry Medvedev had sent out signals that there would be change, and a lot of people believed in this. Even though they were well aware that Medvedev was a close associate and personal friend of Vladimir Putin, Medvedev was still seen as the representative of a new generation of Russian politicians—especially as he had no affiliation with the KGB or other security services. Kashin observed ruefully that when Putin announced in September 2011 that he would return, "it was clear that we were now stuck with Putin. There would be no change. . . . I will have spent my whole adult life with Putin in power. I was 19 when he came in. I am 32 now. I could be 44 when he leaves" (from authors' personal notes). Political analyst Mikhail Dmitriyev made a similar comment with regard to the older generation. These people, "45 years and older," he wrote, were calculating how they would now be fated to conclude their entire working lives under the same man. Mikhail Dmitriyev, "Voshli v stadiyu samorazrusheniya [We have entered a stage of self-destruction], *Vedomosti*, October 20, 2011, at www.vedomosti.ru/opinion/news/1397603/kradenoe_solnce#ixzz1bInfOSEM.

5. The Levada Center polling results cited here and in the following text may be found at www.levada.ru/.

6. See chapter 4 for an earlier discussion of the establishment of this entity in May 2011.

7. Will Englund, "Putin Booed by Russian Fight Fans, in Rare Public Show of Disapproval," *Washington Post*, November 21, 2011, at www.washingtonpost.com/world/putin-booed-by-russian-fight-fans-in-rare-public-show-of-disapproval/2011/11/21/gIQAxUOrhN_story.html; Ellen Barry, "In Russia, Evidence of Misstep by Putin," *New York Times*, November 27, 2011, at www.nytimes.com/2011/11/28/world/europe/vladimir-putin-of-russia-begins-presidential-bid.html. In author personal interviews with representatives of the Ketchum public relations agency who were working with the Kremlin in this period, they noted the overall difficulties of the presidential election campaign, commenting in general terms that it was always difficult, in any political context, to get a candidate reelected for a third term.

8. One newspaper article claimed that in the 2012 presidential election, Putin's campaign had to spend approximately ten times the amount per vote that Dmitry Medvedev's campaign had spent in 2008, with most of the expenditures going to ensuring media coverage, campaign posters, and other promotional materials. See Yevgeniya Korytina and Tatyana Kosobokova, "Putinu golosa rossiyan oboshlis' v 10 raz dorozhe, chem Medvedevu" [Russians' votes cost Putin ten times more than Medvedev], *RBK Daily*, No. 43, March 12, 2012, at www.rbcdaily.ru/2012/03/12/focus/562949983220042.

9. Three of the four candidates opposing Putin—Communist Party leader Gennady Zyuganov, Liberal Democratic Party of Russia head Vladimir Zhirinovsky, and the Just Russia Party's Sergei Mironov—were all well-trod fixtures of the Russian political scene with long-established records of losing presidential elections. The newcomer was oligarch Mikhail Prokhorov. The official results in descending order were Putin 63.60 percent; Zyuganov 17.18 percent; Prokhorov 7.98 percent; Zhirinovsky 6.22 percent; and Mironov 3.85 percent. Tsentral'naya izbiratel'naya komissiya Rossiyskoy Federatsii [Central Election Commission of the Russian Federation], "Dannye o predvaritel'nikh itogakh golosovaniya vybory Prezidenta Rossiyskoy Federatsii" [Information on the preliminary voting results from the election for president of the Russian Federation], at www.vybory.izbirkom.ru.

10. Vote results by city calculated by the authors from district-level results reported by the Central Election Commission at www.vybory.izbirkom.ru. Nine of Russia's 25 largest

cities gave Putin less than 53 percent of the vote: Moscow, Vladimir, Omsk, Irkutsk, Voronezh, Novosibirsk, Yaroslavl, Ulyanovsk, and Barnaul.

11. Medvedev seemed to express some sympathy with the protesters in what was essentially his farewell address as president on April 26, 2012, when he remarked that "it's good when the destiny of the country and its political processes depend on more than the will of one person, who does whatever pops into his head." See Marc Bennetts, "One Man Rule Bad for Russia—Medvedev (Wrap)," RIA Novosti, April 26, 2012, at http://en.rian.ru/russia/20120426/173070543.html.

12. Alexei Kudrin presentation in Washington, D.C., April 2012. Authors' discussions with members of Kremlin economic task force and leading Kremlin-associated think tank director in London, May 2012.

13. See Natalya Galimova, "Vladimir Ryzhkov: 'Posle vyborov budet massovoye begstvo lyudey. Sakharova i Bolotnaya uyedt'" [Vladimir Ryzhkov: 'People will flee en masse after the elections. Those from Sakharov and Bolotnaya will leave'], *Moskovskiy komsomolets,* February 29, 2012, at www.mk.ru/politics/interview/2012/02/29/676987-vladimir-ryizhkov-posle-vyiborov-budet-massovoe-begstvo-lyudey-saharova-i-bolotnaya-uedut.html. Sakharov and Bolotnaya refer to Moscow locations where street protests took place.

14. Ibid.

15. Russia's Levada polling agency provides an overview analysis of the age, educational and professional backgrounds, and political views of the protesters at www.levada.ru/13-02-2012/opros-na-mitinge-4-fevralya. A further analysis of the composition of people participating in protests in both December 2011 and February 2012 is at Boris Dubin, "Yakimanka i Bolotnaya 2.0: Teper' my znayem kto vse eti lyudi!" [Yakimanka and Bolotnaya 2.0: Now we know who all these people are!], *Novaya gazeta,* February 10, 2012, at www.novayagazeta.ru/society/50949.html. Yakimanka and Bolotnaya refer to the locations of two of the biggest street protests in Moscow.

16. See "Putin Warns 'Mistakes' Could Bring Back '90s Woes," RFE/RL, October 17, 2011, at www.rferl.org/content/putin_mistakes_could_bring_back_1990s_woes/24362626.html. There are 52 separate references to the 1990s, the beginning of the 2000s, the fall of USSR, or the late Soviet period, in Vladimir Putin's seven 2012 presidential campaign articles. Only Putin's final article on foreign policy has no reference at all, while his first introductory article hammers home the point 14 times.

17. See Guy Faulconbridge and Gleb Bryanski, "Putin Invokes History's Lions for Return to the Kremlin," Reuters, November 1, 2011, at www.reuters.com/article/2011/11/01/us-russia-putin-heroes-idUSTRE7A024W20111101.

18. See, for example, Russian journalist Mikhail Fishman's article, "Prokisshaya" [Turning sour], *Vedomosti,* June 29, 2012, accessed through Eastview. Fishman rebuffed Putin's constant references to Stolypin by retorting: "Stolypin is not a hero-reformer, he is simply a familiar name, a mustached man from the schoolbook of history." He also noted that "traditions . . . are good for advertising beer, but they don't convert into political capital. The best Russian monarchist is still Nikita Mikhalkov . . . because everyone understands that this is the movies, it's not a political program . . . The Russian tsars . . . have a rich past but have nothing for the future."

19. See earlier discussion of Putin and *dostroika* in chapters 4 and 6. It is worth noting that Putin never actually uses this term in any of his campaign articles in 2012.

20. Andrew Osborne, "Vladimir Putin Accuses Hillary Clinton of Inciting Protests," *Daily Telegraph,* December 8, 2011. A selection of photographs from the protests is available on the Russian blogging site livejournal.ru at http://toma-gramma.livejournal.com/783603.html.

21. "Frankly speaking, when I saw on TV what some of them were wearing on their chests, I'll tell you, though it might be somewhat inappropriate, I thought they were some weird symbols for the fight against AIDS–condoms, if you'll excuse me. It struck me as odd

that they would unpack them first, but upon a closer look, I saw that they weren't condoms after all." See "A Conversation with Vladimir Putin: Continuation," December 15, 2011, at http://archive.premier.gov.ru/eng/events/news/17409/. The Russian version is at http://archive.premier.gov.ru/events/news/17409/.

22. See "Predsedatel' Pravitel'stva Rossiyskoy Federatsii V.V. Putin vystupil v Gosudarstvennoy Dume s otchyotem o deyatel'nosti Pravitel'stva Rossiyskoy Federatsii za 2011 god" [Chairman of the Government of the Russian Federation V.V. Putin presented a report to the State Duma on the activity of the Government of the Russian Federation for the year 2011], April 11, 2012, at http://archive.premier.gov.ru/events/news/18671/.

23. Kremlin adviser Vladislav Surkov was much more circumspect about this designation of the protesters as a minority and spoke out about it publicly in an interview with the Russian newspaper *Izvestiya* in December 2011. In the interview, Surkov, who was then first deputy head of the Russian presidential administration, underscored that Russia had changed and the way of doing politics had changed. "We are already in the future," he asserted, "and the future is not peaceful." He identified the protesters as "the best part of our society, or, more correctly, the most productive part, which is demanding respect." Of course, Surkov argued, "you can underscore that those who have taken to the streets are a minority. This is the case, but, on the other hand, what a minority!" He noted that "tomorrow's leaders" would emerge from out of this minority. See Elena Shishkunova, "Vladislav Surkov: Sistema uzhe izmenilas'" [Vladislav Surkov: The system has already changed], *Izvestiya*, December 22, 2011, at http://izvestia.ru/news/510564. According to Gleb Pavlovsky in his various interviews, it was for expressing sentiments like this that Vladislav Surkov was removed from his position in the presidential administration before Putin returned to the Kremlin in 2012. Surkov was not gone for long. From December 2011 to May 2013, he served as a deputy prime minister in the Russian government; but in September 2013 he moved back to the Kremlin to pick up an assignment as an adviser to the president on Abkhazia, South Ossetia, and relations with Ukraine.

24. See Vladimir Putin, "Stroitel'stvo spravedlivosti. Sotsial'naya politika dlya Rossii" [The construction of justice. Social policy for Russia], *Komsomolskaya pravda*, February 13, 2012, at http://kp.ru/daily/3759/2807793/.

25. Florida (2002), p. 249.

26. In July 2012, a disastrous flood in Russia's Black Sea region again brought anger to the fore with the failure of local authorities either to provide adequate warning of the impending catastrophe or to deal with the ensuing relief effort. Putin flew quickly to Krymsk, the most severely affected of the local towns, and several local officials were sacked. His team's PR efforts were as poorly received as his earlier interventions during the raging summer fires of 2010. Repeated natural disasters and crises, since the sinking of the *Kursk* and the terrorist siege of the school in Beslan, underscored the weak capacity of the Russian state to provide services for the population. They highlighted the inability of Putin's vertical of power to respond at anything other than the highest level in a timely and decisive fashion. If something needed to be done, then it would only be done if Putin went there to do it. See Ellen Barry, "After Russian Floods, Grief, Rage and Deep Mistrust," *New York Times*, July 10, 2012, at www.nytimes.com/2012/07/11/world/europe/after-russian-floods-grief-rage-and-deep-mistrust.html.

27. At one point toward the end of his January 2012 interview with David Hearst and Tom Parfitt, Pavlovsky returned to the events of 1993 and the "shooting of the [Russian] White House." Pavlovsky underscored that "in the Kremlin establishment . . . there has been an absolute conviction that as soon as the Kremlin is shifted, or if there is some mass popular pressure, the appearance of a popular leader, then everybody will be annihilated. . . . A feeling of vulnerability. As soon as someone is given the chance—not necessarily the people, maybe the governors, maybe some other faction—they will physically destroy the establishment, or we'll have to fight and destroy them instead."

28. Gleb Pavlovsky interview with *The Guardian*, January 24, 2012.

29. Pavlovsky makes this point in his interview. "Bol'she net cheloveka, kotoryy ska-zal by emu: 'Ne nado, Vladimir Vladimirovich'" [There's no one left who could tell him: "Vladimir Vladimirovich, don't!"], *Novoye Vremya/The New Times*, September 10, 2012, at http://newtimes.ru/articles/print/56884/.

30. Yegor Gaidar told this story many times in private and public. One version is related by Valeriy Zavarotnyy in "Kamikadze," *Ezhednevnyy zhurnal*, June 12, 2012, at www.ej.ru/?a=note&id=11847.

31. Fiona Hill and Clifford G. Gaddy, "Putin's Next Move in Russia: Observations from the 8th Annual Valdai International Discussion Club," Brookings Institution, December 12, 2011, at www.brookings.edu/research/interviews/2011/12/12-putin-gaddy-hill.

32. Ellen Barry, "Resolute Putin Faces a Russia That's Changed," *New York Times*, February 23, 2012, at www.nytimes.com/2012/02/24/world/europe/a-resolute-putin-faces-a-changing-russia.html. In another element worthy of a tsar, on this same occasion (as he had on many others) Putin kept the Valdai Discussion Club participants waiting for several hours before arriving for the dinner. In author interviews with journalists, oil company executives, senior European and U.S. officials, and others between 2010 and 2012, waiting for an audience with Putin was a common theme. In July 2012, after President Putin kept his Ukrainian counterpart Viktor Yanukovych waiting for a scheduled meeting in the Crimean city of Yalta, the issue became the subject of press scrutiny. Russian journalist Andrei Kolesnikov noted: "This habitual lateness of Putin's can be read in different ways, as a character trait or his way of demonstrating his attitude toward others. . . . But only God is above him now. He's person No. 1, and he can afford to be late whenever he wants." See Fred Weir, "Got an Appointment with Vladimir Putin? Better Bring a Book," *Global News* (blog), *Christian Science Monitor*, July 18, 2012, at www.csmonitor.com/World/Global-News/2012/0718/Got-an-appointment-with-Vladimir-Putin-Better-bring-a-book.

33. Bobkov (1995), p. 40.

34. Ibid., p. 284.

35. Bobkov notes that it was evident that "the more bans you set up, the sharper would be the reaction of the intelligentsia. And in the end, there was no doubt that there would be some who would be prepared to break the law." Ibid., pp. 259–60.

36. Ibid., pp. 355–61.

37. Ibid., p. 213 and p. 257.

38. "Putin welcomes the young to speak out their position," ITAR-TASS, December 15, 2011, at http://en.itar-tass.com/archive/666509 (accessed through Nexis.com in English); "Spokesman says Putin is true liberal, welcomes "healthy" opposition pressure," BBC Monitoring Former Soviet Union—Political, March 26, 2012 (accessed through Nexis.com in English); and "Putin's chief of staff denies that new law on demos restrictive," Russia and CIS General Newswire, June 22, 2012 (accessed through Nexis.com in English).

39. See chapter 8 for previous references to von Benckendorff.

40. See Douglas Busvine, "Russia's Kudrin Stays in the Mix with New Task Force," Reuters, April 5, 2012, at www.reuters.com/article/2012/04/05/russia-kudrin-idUSL6E8F515C20120405. See also Alexei Kudrin's official website: http://akudrin.ru/news/.

41. See, for example, the May 5, 2012, open letter signed by Kudrin and others associated with the Committee for Citizens' Initiatives, "Shansy na dialog mezhdu obshchestvom i vlast'yu snizilis'" [The chances of dialogue between society and the authorities have been reduced], at http://akudrin.ru/news/shansy-na-dialog-mezhdu-obshchestvom-i-vlastyu-snizilis.html.

42. In private interviews with the authors in June and July 2012, members of the U.S. administration and European officials also noted that Alexei Kudrin had presented himself and the Committee of Citizens' Initiatives to them in this fashion.

43. In a presentation at the Brookings Institution on March 5, 2012, journalist and author Masha Gessen, who had become a leading member of the Russian opposition protests, noted of Alexei Kudrin's new role that the former finance minister had "a stellar reputation on all fronts. I have no idea how someone can have that reputation after staying with Vladimir Putin for 20 years and even as the extent of corruption in his patron's government has become clear to everyone. He still needs to prove that he can be an effective communicator and negotiator . . . but the reputation of Kudrin is important, especially his international reputation. Russians like this." Oleg Kashin—who was also playing a role in the protests at this juncture—remarked in his presentation at the Brookings Institution on March 29, 2012, that Kudrin seemed ill-prepared for such a public political role after his years in "dark rooms, counting money for the Kremlin."

44. This was the view, for instance, of Russian analyst Maria Lipman in her presentation at the Brookings Institution on April 25, 2012, based on meetings with Russian officials.

45. See, for example, John Lloyd, "Master of Nostalgia: Vladimir Putin Has Played Expertly to Russia's Emotions during His Years at the Centre of Power—but at What Cost?," *Financial Times*, January 28/29, 2012, at www.ft.com/intl/cms/s/2/7f623772-467d-11e1-85e2-00144feabdc0.html#axzz26w16zruc; "Russia's 'Revolutionary' Situation," RFE/RL, June 12, 2012, at www.rferl.org/articleprintview/24612283.html; and David Hearst, "Will Putinism See the End of Putin," *The Guardian*, February 27, 2012, at www.guardian.co.uk/world/2012/feb/27/vladimir-putin-profile-putinism/print. Dmitriyev noted in his interview for *The Guardian*'s profile of Putin that he had detected a steady deterioration of Putin's political brand since 2006 in the focus groups he conducted. In another interview with David Hearst, Russian investigative journalist Andrei Soldatov recounted his own meetings within the ranks of the younger generation of security service colonels, who also felt cut off from advancement and thus resentful of the older cohort FSB generals who were "all men Putin personally knew and appointed." This resentment left the younger colonels unwilling to share information on the critical shifts in Russian public opinion with their older superiors.

46. Lloyd, "Master of Nostalgia," *Financial Times*, January 28/29, 2012.

47. Kirill's remarks are available in Russian on the patriarch's website, at www.patriarchia.ru/db/text/1932241.html.

48. For more elaboration of this idea, see Keenan (1986).

49. See "Vozmozhnyye rezul'taty prezidentskikh i parlamentskikh vyborov" [Possible results of presidential and parliamentary elections], Levada Center, September 5, 2013, at www.levada.ru/05-09-2013/vozmozhnye-rezultaty-prezidentskikh-i-parlamentskikh-vyborov.

50. These polls are reviewed in Sberbank Investment Research, "Russia Economic Monthly. February 2014—Creative Chaos," at www.sberbank-cib.ru/eng/research/research.wbp.

51. The others were the Rose Revolution in Georgia in 2003 and the Tulip Revolution in the Central Asian country of Kyrgyzstan in 2005.

52. See Steven Lee Myers, "Putin Reforms Greeted by Street Protests," *New York Times*, January 16, 2005, at www.nytimes.com/2005/01/16/international/europe/16moscow.html?_r=0. In part, these so-called anti-monetization protests reflected Russian citizens' deep-seated lack of faith in the government. The government was taking tangible benefits away from pensioners and, in return, promising compensation in monetary form. Based on their experience in the 1990s, when their pensions were not paid for prolonged periods and they were never compensated for the arrears, Russian pensioners did not believe they would ever see the money. Another reason for the strong negative reaction was that pensioners, including war veterans for instance, would be denied long-standing special

privileges such as free ridership on public transportation and entry to museums and theaters. They would have to stand in line and pay in cash like everyone else. It was an affront to the minimal dignity they felt they deserved.

53. "Russia Says 'Hooligans' Attacked Tajik Train," RFE/RL's Tajik Service, October 30, 2013, at www.rferl.org/content/tajik-train-attack-/25153112.html.

54. See "Rossiyane o migratsii i mezhnatsional'noy napryazhennosti" [Russians on migration and intra-ethnic tensions], Levada Center, November 5, 2013, at www.levada. ru/05-11-2013/rossiyane-o-migratsii-i-mezhnatsionalnoi-napryazhennosti.

55. Alexei Navalny's blog can be found at http://navalny.livejournal.com/.

56. See the discussion of this in Fiona Hill and Hannah Thoburn, "The Populist Threat to Putin's Power," Brookings Institution's Up Front Blog, November 15, 2013, at www. brookings.edu/research/opinions/2013/11/15-populist-threat-putin-power-hill-thoburn.

57. Zachary A. Goldfarb, "S&P downgrades U.S. credit rating for first time," *Washington Post,* August 6, 2011, at www.washingtonpost.com/business/economy/sandp-considering-first-downgrade-of-us-credit-rating/2011/08/05/gIQAqKeIxI_story.html. The article begins: "Standard & Poor's announced Friday night that it has downgraded the U.S. credit rating for the first time, dealing a symbolic blow to the world's economic superpower in what was a sharply worded critique of the American political system."

58. "IMF Survey: Global Financial System Risks Escalate," September 21, 2011, at www.imf.org/external/pubs/ft/survey/so/2011/new092111a.htm.

59. Stock market data available at Yahoo Finance, at http://finance.yahoo.com/stock-center/.

60. See "Rossiyane o svoyey zhiznennoy situatsii" [Russians on their living situation], Levada Center, October 14, 2013, at www.levada.ru/14-10-2013/rossiyane-o-svoei-zhiznennoi-situatsii; and Ellen Barry, "The Russia Left Behind," *New York Times,* October 13, 2013, at www.nytimes.com/newsgraphics/2013/10/13/russia/.

61. See chapter 5.

62. In his cornerstone economic policy document during the 2012 presidential campaign, Putin never mentioned targets for GDP growth—something he had typically done in earlier years. Rather, he stressed that the global economy today was fraught with "risks" and "threats." "In these circumstances," he wrote, "we must ensure sustainable progressive development of our economy and try to shield our citizens from the hardships of crises as much as possible." Vladimir Putin, "O nashikh ekonomicheskikh zadachakh" [On our economic tasks], January 30, 2012, at http://archive.premier.gov.ru/events/news/17888/0. In English at http://archive.premier.gov.ru/eng/events/news/17888/.

63. See "Sovmestnaya press-konferentsiya s Prezidentom Kazakhstana Nursultanom Nazarbayevym po itogam rossiysko-kazakhstanskikh peregovorov" [Joint press conference with President of Kazakhstan Nursultan Nazarbaev on the results of Russian-Kazakh talks], May 22, 2008, at http://kremlin.ru/transcripts/183.

64. Authors' personal notes from Valdai Discussion Club dinner meeting Q&A with President Putin, Moscow, November 11, 2011.

65. For more detailed discussions of the case of Alexei Navalny, see, for example, Peter Beaumont, "Alexei Navalny: Firebrand Bidding for Russia's Soul," *The Guardian,* August 10, 2013, at www.theguardian.com/theobserver/2013/aug/11/sergei-navalny-liberal-hero-bidding-for-russia-soul; and Andrew Roth, "Court Orders House Arrest, and No Internet, for Fierce Critic of Putin," *New York Times,* March 1, 2014, at www.nytimes.com/2014/03/01/world/europe/aleksei-navalny.html.

66. For a full discussion of Putin's treatment of Pussy Riot, see Gessen (2014).

67. "Russian Opposition Figures Udaltsov, Razvozzhaev Sentenced to Prison," RFE/RL, July 24, 2014, at www.rferl.org/content/udalstov-razvozzhayev-trial-verdict-guilty-bolotnaya/25468624.html.

68. See, for example, Brian Whitmore, "Ksenia and Vladimir," *The Power Vertical* (blog), RFE/RL, June 18, 2012, at www.rferl.org/content/ksenia-anatolevna-and-vladimir vladimirovich/24618330.html.

69. See Leonid Bershidsky, "Parsing the Marriage of Russia's Paris Hilton," *Bloomberg View*, February 2, 2013, at www.bloombergview.com/articles/2013-02-05/ parsing-the-marriage-of-russia-s-paris-hilton.

70. See Julia Ioffe, "A Week before the Olympics, the Kremlin Is Attacking Russia's Last Independent TV Channel," *The New Republic*, January 31, 2014, at www.newrepublic. com/article/116434/putin-attacks-dozhdtv-russias-last-independent-tv-channel.

71. See Putin's comments about Alexei Navalny being accused of corruption in a press conference and interview with AP on September 3, 2013. In the interview, Putin never referred to Navalny by name. He only mentioned "this gentleman" [*etot gospodin*]—a conscious denial of respect and a distancing tactic. After much public criticism of Putin's refusal to say Navalny's name, the Russian president did so in a conversation with journalist Alec Luhn. See "Putin Finally Says Navalny's Name, Journalist Tweets," *Moscow Times*, September 20, 2013, at www.themoscowtimes.com/news/article/putin-finally-says-navalnys-name-journalist-tweets/486380.html.

72. In an October 2013 poll by Russia's Levada Center, for example, 55 percent of respondents indicated that they saw the prosecution of 28 protesters arrested in May 2012 as aimed at "frightening the public's pro-opposition spirit." See "Bolotnoye delo" [The Bolotnaya Square affair], Levada Center, October 4, 2013, at www.levada.ru/04-10-2013/ bolotnoe-delo.

73. See Hill and Thoburn, "The Populist Threat to Putin's Power," Broookings Up Front Blog.

74. "Russia's NATO envoy appointed deputy PM for defense industry," RIA Novosti, December 23, 2011, at http://en.ria.ru/russia/20111223/170446490.html.

75. See "Putin Tells Zhirinovsky to 'Tone it Down,'" *Moscow Times*, November 8, 2013, at www.themoscowtimes.com/news/article/putin-tells-zhirinovsky-to-tone-it-down/489148.html?id=489148.

76. During the authors' exchanges with Russian participants at the Valdai Discussion Club meeting in Moscow in November 2011, including a session with Zhirinovsky himself, Russian political technologist Andranik Migranyan openly spoke of Zhirinovsky's links with the Russian intelligence services and of the role he had been assigned to play in the 1990s in channeling Russian nationalist sentiment. In a comment to the authors Migranyan quipped: "The difference between our fanatics and your fanatics [in the U.S.], is that yours believe what they're saying. Ours are only pretending" (from authors' notes).

77. Rogozin was also, however, kept under the close watch of the Kremlin during his time with Rodina, a fact that was underscored directly to the authors by one of his minders, Vladimir Frolov, during meetings in Moscow on the fringes of the Valdai Discussion Club meeting in September 2005.

78. See Bullough (2013).

79. See "Rossiyane o dele pussy riot" [Russians on the Pussy Riot case], Levada Center, July 31, 2012, at www.levada.ru/31-07-2012/rossiyane-o-dele-pussy-riot.

80. Putin said this during an interview with the Associated Press and Russia's First Channel. See "Interv'yu Pervomu kanalu i agentstvu Assoshieyted Press" [Interview with First Channel and the Associated Press], September 4, 2013, at http://kremlin.ru/ transcripts/19143.

81. See Vladimir Putin, "Poslaniye Prezidenta Federal'nomu Sobraniyu" [Message of the President to the Federal Assembly], December 12, 2012, at http://kremlin.ru/news/17118.

82. Vladimir Putin, "Poslaniye Prezidenta Federal'nomu Sobraniyu" [Message of the President to the Federal Assembly], December 12, 2013, at http://kremlin.ru/transcripts/ 19825. When talking about the "chaotic darkness," Putin used the Old Church Slavonic

word *t'ma* rather than the modern Russian word for darkness, *temnota*. In premodern Russia, the word *t'ma* referred not just to darkness but also to something "uncountable"—a host, a multitude, thousands. The Mongol hordes that swept into the old Russian principalities from Siberia were a *t'ma*. Their multitudes brought a period of darkness to Russian lands. The word *t'ma* itself is, in fact, Mongolian. It is the plural form of the word *tumen*, which was a unit of 10,000 men at arms. Putin did not use this term casually.

83. Brett Forrest, "Putin's Party," *National Geographic*, January 2014, at http://ngm.nationalgeographic.com/2014/01/sochi-russia/forrest-text).

84. See Peter Finn, Carol D. Leonnig, and Will Englund, "Tamerlan Tsarnaev and Dzhokhar Tsarnaev Were Refugees from Brutal Chechen Conflict," *Washington Post*, April 19, 2013, at www.washingtonpost.com/politics/details-emerge-on-suspected-boston-bombers/2013/04/19/ef2c2566-a8e4-11e2-a8e2-5b98cb59187f_story.html.

85. See Owen Matthews, "Russia Tests 'Total Surveillance' at the Sochi Olympics," *Newsweek*, February 12, 2014, at www.newsweek.com/2014/02/14/russia-tests-total-surveillance-sochi-olympics-245494.html.

86. In the case of Khodorkovsky, Putin did not absolve the oligarch of any misdeeds. In commenting on his release, Putin made sure to put his emphasis on the punishment that the Russian system had meted out: "Very recently he . . . appealed to me with a request for a pardon. He has already spent over ten years in prison; this is a serious punishment. He refers to circumstances of a humanitarian nature: his mother is ill. I believe that, in view of all these circumstances, the appropriate decision can be made, and in the near future a decree on his pardoning will be signed." "Press–konferentsiya Vladimira Putina" [Press conference by Vladimir Putin], December 19, 2013, at http://kremlin.ru/transcripts/19859. Khodorkovsky's mother was indeed gravely ill and died in August 2014.

87. In a profile of Ernst, Joshua Yaffa wrote for *The New Yorker* that "Ernst is an unmatched figure in Russia's official culture, where statist boosterism combines with high production values to create the image of a vital nation under one leader—Putin—to whom there is no alternative. Ernst's aesthetic sensibility defines the annual Victory Day parade, on May 9, as well as Putin's yearly call-in shows, televised marathons that can run for more than four hours, in which he fields questions from factory workers in the Urals and concerned mothers in the Far East." See Joshua Yaffa, "Putin's Master of Ceremonies," *The New Yorker*, February 5, 2014, at www.newyorker.com/news/news-desk/putins-master-of-ceremonies.

88. See James Poniewozik, "Russian through History: The Sochi Olympics Opening Ceremonies," *Time*, February 8, 2014, at http://time.com/6025/russian-through-history-the-sochi-olympics-opening-ceremonies/#6025/russian-through-history-the-sochi-olympics-opening-ceremonies/.

89. See Vladimir Putin, "Interv'yu predstavitelyam telekanalov 'Pervyy,' VGTRK, NTV, RBK" [Interview with representatives from television channels, Channel One, VGTRK, NTV, and RBK], February 25, 2014, at http://kremlin.ru/transcripts/20336.

CHAPTER 11

1. On Putin's accusations against Hillary Clinton, see chapter 10.

2. See "Russia's Putin Signs NGO 'Foreign Agents' Law," Reuters, July 21, 2012, at www.reuters.com/article/2012/07/21/us-russia-putin-ngos-idUSBRE86K05M20120721.

3. See chapter 10.

4. In his March 18, 2014, speech in the Kremlin, marking the annexation of Crimea, Putin asserted: "We understand what is going on, we understand that all of these actions [by the West in Ukraine since the color revolutions] were directed against Ukraine, and against Russia, and against integration in the Eurasian space." See Vladimir Putin,

"Obrashcheniye Prezidenta Rossiyskoy Federatsii" [Address by the President of the Russian Federation], March 18, 2014, available on the Kremlin's website archive (in Russian) at news.kremlin.ru/news/20603/print. An English translation is available at eng.news.kremlin.ru/news/6889/print.

5. In his March 18, 2014, speech, Putin claimed: "Some Western politicians are already frightening us not just with sanctions [in response to Crimea], but also with the potential intensification of [our] internal problems. I would like to know what they have in mind: the actions of some kind of fifth columns—all kinds of "national-traitors"—or do they consider that they can worsen the socio-economic situation of Russia and by this they can provoke people's discontent? We look upon any statements like these as irresponsible and obviously aggressive and we will respond to this accordingly." See Putin, "Obrashcheniye Prezidenta Rossiyskoy Federatsii" [Address by the President of the Russian Federation], March 18, 2014, Moscow.

6. General Makhmud Gareyev is a distinguished military historian and decorated World War II veteran. He is a former deputy chief of the General Staff of the Armed Forces of the USSR and the president of Russia's Academy of Military Sciences. Gareyev was also the chief military adviser to President Najibullah of Afghanistan from 1989 to 1991.

7. General Gareyev's speech on "Threat Perceptions: The View from Moscow" was given at a conference on "Forecasting Russian Military Reform and Modernization to 2020," co-organized by a number of U.S. think tanks on July 28, 2010. Gareyev was initially recommended as a participant by Yegor Gaidar during a November 2009 visit to the United States. The citations are taken from the text of General Gareyev's speech (in Russian), which was circulated at the event, and author notes from the Q&A and discussion with General Gareyev.

8. This is a line from Putin's address to the Russian people after the 2004 terrorist attack on the school in Beslan. Putin went on to say that those who were trying to tear Russian territory away were always helped by others who "help, I suppose, because Russia—as one of the strongest nuclear powers in the world—still represents a threat for some parties. Therefore, this threat has to be eliminated. And terrorism—this is, of course, only an instrument for the achievement of these goals." See Vladimir Putin, "Obrashcheniye Prezidenta Rossii Vladimira Putina" [Address by the President of Russia Vladimir Putin], September 4, 2004, at http://archive.kremlin.ru/text/appears/2004/09/76320.shtml.

9. Thomas Wright, director of the Brookings Project on International Order and Strategy, presentation on "The Return of Revisionist States," at the Brookings Institution, Washington D.C., June 5, 2014. For a longer discussion on why other powers have largely not feared American aggression and "generally accepted American power," see Kagan (2012).

10. In his March 18, 2014, Kremlin speech Putin noted that "there was already an announcement made in Kyiv about Ukraine joining NATO as soon as possible. What would that prospect have meant for Crimea and Sevastopol [the home port of the Russian Black Sea Fleet]? It would have meant that in the city of Russian military glory a NATO fleet could have appeared, [and] that a threat would have sprung up for the whole of southern Russia—not some sort of ephemeral threat, something entirely concrete." See Putin, "Obrashcheniye Prezidenta Rossiyskoy Federatsii" [Address by the President of the Russian Federation], March 18, 2014.

11. In Russian, Putin said, directly: "Nu chto Rossiya? Opustila golovu i smirilas', proglotila etu obidu. Nasha strana nakhodilas' togda v takom tyazhyolom sostoyanii, chto prosto ne mogla real'no zashchitit' svoi interesy." See Putin, "Obrashcheniye Prezidenta Rossiyskoy Federatsii" [Address by the President of the Russian Federation], March 18, 2014.

12. See Vladimir Putin, "Soveshchaniye poslov i postoyannykh predstaviteley Rossii" [Meeting of ambassadors and permanent representatives of Russia], July 1, 2014, at http://kremlin.ru/transcripts/46131.

13. See, for example, Krastev (2014) and Mead (2014).

14. Sergei Glazyev, as an economic adviser to Putin and one of the leading Russian commentators on Ukraine, was included on the United States sanctions list of individuals targeted for their activities during the crisis; see, for example, Henry Meyer and Stephen Bierman, "Putin Allies Targeted by U.S., EU Sanctions over Ukraine Crisis," Bloomberg, March 17, 2014, at www.bloomberg.com/news/2014-03-17/putin-allies-targeted-by-u-s-sanctions-over-ukrainian-standoff.html. In July 2014, the Ukrainian government launched an official probe into the activities of Gennady Zyuganov and other Russian nationalist politicians in the Ukraine crisis, accusing them of potentially funding separatist forces in the Donetsk region; see "Ukraine Launches Probes of Zyuganov, Zhirinovsky," RFE/RL, August 1, 2014, at www.rferl.org/content/zyuganov-zhirinovsky-avakov-kolomoyskiy-probe/25469971.html.

15. In June 2013, when he announced the official separation and divorce from his wife, Lyudmila Putina, Putin even intimated that this unfortunate episode was the result of his service to the Russian state. His complete devotion to Russia had left no time for personal relationships. Vladimir Putin, the president, the man, was essentially married to the state. See Ol'ga Marandi, "Vladimir i Lyudmila Putiny ob"yavili o razvode" [Vladimir and Lyudmila Putin announce divorce], *Moskovskiy komsomolets,* June 6, 2013, available (in Russian) at mk.ru/politics/russia/article/2013/06/06/865914-vladimir-i-lyudmila-putinyi-obyavili-o-razvode.html.

16. In his address, Putin declared that "Russia should not only preserve its geopolitical demand—it should increase the demand, [Russia] should be demanded [or needed] by our neighbors and partners. . . . This concerns our economy, culture, science, education and diplomacy. . . . And, last, but not least, this concerns our military might, which guarantees Russia's security and independence." See Vladimir Putin, "Poslaniye Prezidenta Federal'nomu Sobraniyu" [Message of the President to the Federal Assembly], December 12, 2012, (in Russian) at kremlin.ru/news/17118.

17. See Peter Baker, "Pressure Rising as Obama Works to Rein in Russia," *New York Times,* March 2, 2014, at www.nytimes.com/2014/03/03/world/europe/pressure-rising-as-obama-works-to-rein-in-russia.html?_r=0. Baker, the *New York Times* White House correspondent, sourced Merkel's comment from unnamed U.S. officials briefed on a telephone conversation between Merkel and Obama. Baker's story was also picked up in the German press ("Merkel schimpft: Putin lebt in einer anderen Welt" [Merkel complains: Putin is living in another world], *Bild,* March 3, 2014, at bild.de/politik/ausland/krim/merkel-schimpft-im-obama-telefonat-ueber-putin-34911584.bild.html) and elaborated on by the *New York Times* Berlin correspondent (Alison Smale, "Ukraine Crisis Limits Merkel's Rapport With Putin," *New York Times,* March 12, 2014, at www.nytimes.com/2014/03/13/world/europe/on-ukraine-merkel-finds-limits-of-her-rapport-with-putin.html?_r=0). Although no official transcript for the chancellor's remark exists, in German press circles the prevailing view was that Merkel *had* made this comment. It was consistent with other remarks she had made about the Russian president and his views in off-the-record meetings and interviews (author discussion with Martin Klingst, Washington bureau chief of *Die Zeit,* March 31, 2013).

18. Vladimir Putin, "Obrashcheniye Prezidenta Rossiyskoy Federatsii" [Address by the President of the Russian Federation], March 18, 2014.

19. In a private discussion with the authors in Washington, D.C., on March 31, 2014, the CEO of a leading European company with regular access to Kremlin inner circles told the authors that he had just met with a top Russian oligarch, who made the same point. The oligarch had flown to their meeting directly from a ceremony with President Putin to celebrate the successful completion of the 2014 Sochi Winter Olympics. Putin told the oligarch that he had been "forced" to annex Crimea. There was no alternative. The threat from the West in Ukraine was too strong.

20. See "V Kremle vrucheny premii deyatelyam kul'tury i premii za proizvedeniye dlya detey" [In the Kremlin, awards were given to cultural figures and awards for works for children], March 25, 2014, available (in Russian) at kremlin.ru/transcripts/20638.

21. See "Minkul't: "Rossiya ne Evropa"" [Ministry of culture: "Russia is not Europe"], *Colta*, April 4, 2014, at www.colta.ru/news/2779, and Garrison Golubock, "Culture Ministry Affirms 'Russia is not Europe,'" *Moscow Times*, April 7, 2014, at www.themoscowtimes. com/arts_n_ideas/article/culture-ministry-affirms-russia-is-not-europe/497658.html. This citation comes from a draft of the report that had not been formally approved. *Kommersant* subsequently reported on May 17, 2014, that the document was to be toned down and that the Tolstoy quote, to the effect that "Russia is not Europe," would not be in the final version; see www.kommersant.ru/doc/2473782. The report itself, "Osnovy gosudarstvennoy kul'turnoy politiki," was published on May 15, 2014, in the Russian government's official newspaper, *Rossiyskaya gazeta*, at www.rg.ru/2014/05/15/osnovi-dok.html. See also note 2 to chapter 4 on Vladimir Medinsky's May 2012 appointment to the Culture Ministry.

22. Poe (2003), p. 66.

23. Ibid., preface, p. xii.

24. Ibid., pp. 17–18.

25. Ibid., p. 23.

26. Keenan (1986), p. 139.

27. Poe (2003), pp. 30–32.

28. Ibid., p. 32.

29. Ibid., pp. 38–45.

30. Ibid., p. 45.

31. See also the discussion in Hill and Gaddy (2003), pp. 7–10 and pp. 26–28.

32. See, for example, the collection of articles in Eklof, Bushnell, and Zakharova (1994).

33. Poe points out that Muscovite Russia was the only continental state to control and close its borders to foreigners (Poe, 2003, p. 57).

34. Ibid., pp. 50–51.

35. Pipes (1974).

36. Pipes (1999).

37. Poe (2003), p. 51.

38. Ibid., p. 52.

39. Keenan (1986), p. 164.

40. Poe (2003), p. 51.

41. Ibid., p. 62,

42. Ibid., p. 52.

43. Ibid., p. 53.

44. Neil MacFarquhar, "Putin Strives to Harness Energy of Russian Pilgrims for Political Profit," *New York Times*, August 2, 2014, at www.nytimes.com/2014/08/03/world/europe/from-pilgrims-putin-seeks-political-profit.html?_r=0.

45. See Andrey Illarionov's blog post: "The Rape of Chersonesus Vladimirom Tavricheskim," March 27, 2014, *Ekho Moskvy*, at echo.msk.ru/blog/aillar/1287568-echo/. For the Russian Orthodox Church's presentation of Saint Vladimir, see the entry "Svyatoy ravnoapostol'nyy velikiy knyaz' Vladimir" [The Holy, Apostolic Great Prince Vladimir], on the official website of the Moscow Patriarchate at www.patriarchia.ru/db/text/910305.html.

46. Poe (2003), p. 66.

47. Ibid., p. 58.

48. See Putin, "Obrashcheniye Prezidenta Rossii Vladimira Putina" [Address by the President of Russia Vladimir Putin], September 4, 2004, available in Russian at http://archive.kremlin.ru/text/appears/2004/09/76320.shtml.

49. Lenin's foreign experience was far greater than Putin's. He and some of his close associates spent nearly two decades living in various major European cities, including London and Paris, before returning to Russia to take advantage of the 1917 Revolution. Josef Stalin was an exception. He remained in his native region in the Caucasus, except for repeated, and generally very brief (because he usually escaped), periods of exile in Siberia. Stalin's longest stay abroad was one month in Vienna in 1912, when he was doing research and writing for his study of the Russian Empire's nationalities question.

50. For further background on the Russia-Germany relationship, see Laqueur (1990) and chapter 1, "Comrades in Misfortune: The USSR and Germany," in Stent (1999).

51. Images of some of the graffiti can be seen at www.rarehistoricalphotos.com/reich-stag-covered-graffiti-seized-nazis-red-army-1945/. See also Baker (2002).

52. Detailed information on the book, the film, and the author of *Seventeen Moments of Spring,* with further links to sources, may be found on the Wikipedia pages for each. The best Russian-language site for information on all aspects of the book and film (including a section on some choice Stirlitz jokes) is mgnoveniya.ru/kniga/. It is generally assumed that the KGB commissioned Semyonov to write the Stirlitz book series (he wrote 12 in all, over a span of 25 years) as part of the campaign to glorify the Soviet secret service and help recruit young cadres to the organization in the so-called Andropov levy (see chapter 6). It was published in English in 1978 as *The Himmler Ploy.* See Semenov (1978).

53. See Simis (1982), pp. 195–96. Simis is the father of leading U.S. analyst Dimitri Simes, president of the Washington, D.C.–based Center for the National Interest. For more information on Simis and his work, see Patricia Sullivan, "Konstantin Simis; Critic of Soviet Corruption," *Washington Post* (obituary), December 17, 2006, at www.washingtonpost.com/wp-dyn/content/article/2006/12/16/AR2006121600909.html.

54. Gevorkyan, Timakova, and Kolesnikov (2000), p.70 (see chapter 4 for a full formulation of this idea).

55. See LeVine (2008).

56. See, for example, Julia Ioffe, "Putin's Press Conference Proved Merkel Right: He's Lost His Mind," *New Republic,* March 4, 2014, at www.newrepublic.com/article/116852/merkel-was-right-putins-lost-his-mind-press-conference; and Evan McMurry, "Here Are All The People Who Think Putin Has Straight Up Lost His Mind," *Mediaite,* March 4, 2014, at www.mediaite.com/tv/here-are-all-the-people-who-think-putin-has-straight-up-lost-his-mind.

57. In an off-the-record private meeting in 2008, to discuss Russia's statements and Moscow's interpretation of the circumstances surrounding the outbreak of the war with Georgia, one extremely high-ranking U.S. official slapped his forehead and exclaimed: "Why don't these people think like us?" Other U.S. officials asserted that the Russians' and Putin's perspectives on the conflict were simply not valid. They did not conform to U.S. views, and there was no point in analyzing and trying to understand them (author personal notes from the meeting). The contentious and opposing nature of the U.S. and Russian rhetoric around the war with Georgia, and each side's failure to recognize the position of the other, is captured by Angela Stent in her book *The Limits of Partnership: U.S.-Russian Relations in the Twenty-First Century,* in chapter 7, "From Kosovo to Georgia: Things Fall Apart," pp. 159–76.

58. Multiple author interviews with members of the chancellor's staff and cabinet in Berlin and in Washington, D.C., between 2011 and 2014.

59. Kornelius (2013), p. 182.

60. Ibid., pp. 181–82.

61. This incident was referred to frequently in author interviews with members of the chancellor's staff and cabinet in Berlin and in Washington, D.C., between 2011 and 2014.

62. Shore (2014), p. 81.

63. Author interview with the head of the Dresden office of the German newspaper *Die Zeit* in Dresden, Germany, on February 6, 2014.

64. See Thumann (2005). A senior foreign policy correspondent for *Die Zeit*, Thumann undertook an extensive research project on the relationship between Chancellor Schroeder and President Putin. He presented a summary of his conclusions at a conference of the Transatlantic Academy of the German Marshall Fund in Washington, D.C., on June 30, 2005, at www.gmfus.org/archives/2005/06/.

65. See Tony Patterson, "Gerhard Schroeder's Birthday Party with Vladimir Putin Angers Germany," *The Telegraph*, April 29, 2014, at www.telegraph.co.uk/news/world news/europe/ukraine/10795042/Gerhard-Schroeders-birthday-party-with-Vladimir-Putin. html.

66. See "Meeting with Helmut Schmidt," December 22, 2013, at eng.kremlin.ru/ news/6398.

67. Sophie Friederike Auguste of Anhalt-Zerbst was born in Stettin, Pomerania, in the Kingdom of East Prussia in 1729—now the city of Szczecin in the province of West Pomerania in Poland. As Catherine the Great (1762–96), Princess Sophie became the quintessential Russian ruler, immersing herself in Russian culture. Over time, her European roots and her "Germanness" were lost and almost forgotten.

68. The transcript report of the Körber Stiftung roundtable is available in German at www.koerber-stiftung.de/internationale-politik/bergedorfer-gespraechskreis/protokolle/ protokoll-detail/BG/russland-und-der-westenbrinternationale-sicherheit-und-reformpoli-tik.html. Putin's intervention at the roundtable was also related by British academic Timothy Garton Ash in a July 20, 2014, article in the *New York Times*, at www.nytimes. com/2014/07/20/opinion/sunday/protecting-russians-in-ukraine-has-deadly-consequences. html?ref=opinion&_r=1. Garton Ash used Putin's intervention to make the point that Putin had expressed nationalist views long before Russia's intervention in Crimea. In fact, Putin's comments at the roundtable were entirely in keeping with the tone and substance of other Russian participants, including then First Deputy Defense Minister Andrey Kokoshin, who conveyed strong warnings about the risk that Russians and other former Soviet peoples would want to change the existing facts on the ground for themselves at some point in the future. In an exchange with then German defense minister Volker Rühe, Kokoshin said: "It is possible that a people in some part of the collapsed Soviet Union will come to a different decision than we expect. Because now they themselves are determining political action. We should not close our eyes to such possibilities. We absolutely cannot rule out surprises in this respect" (*Möglicherweise kommt ein Volk in irgendeinem Teil der zerfallenen Sowjetunion zu einem anderen Entschluß, als wir dies vorhersehen; denn jetzt bestimmt es selbst das politische Handeln. Vor solchen Möglichkeiten darf man die Augen nicht verschließen. Hier sind durchaus Überraschungen nicht auszuschließen*). These 1994 exchanges in St. Petersburg took place against the backdrop of the final withdrawal of the last Soviet soldiers from Germany. Defense Minister Volker Rühe and the German government were heavily involved in helping to provide housing back in Russia for the returning servicemen and their families. The withdrawal from Germany was seen by the Russian leadership as far more orderly and cordial than across the border in the Baltic states in the same timeframe, where Russian forces felt they were being unceremoniously kicked out under Western pressure.

69. Vladimir Putin, "Obrashcheniye Prezidenta Rossiyskoy Federatsii" [Address by the President of the Russian Federation], March 18, 2014, available on the Kremlin's website archive (in Russian) at http://news.kremlin.ru/news/20603. An English translation is available at http://eng.news.kremlin.ru/news/6889.

CHAPTER 12

1. A detailed analysis of the course of the U.S.-Russian relationship over this period can be found in Stent (2014).

2. Author private interview in March 2010.

3. In a private meeting with the authors in April 2013, a very senior U.S. official also confirmed that Putin showed no curiosity whatsoever in the United States, unlike the Chinese and other world leaders with whom he had met.

4. When Medvedev visited the United States in 2010, he made an effort to learn as much as he could about aspects of the United States that interested him, particularly technology. He spent significant time in Silicon Valley, visiting Apple headquarters and the offices of Russian company Yandex.ru and opening a Twitter account at Twitter headquarters. Medvedev also met with the CEOs of Cisco and Google, chatted with California governor and movie star Arnold Schwarzenegger, had hamburgers with President Obama at Ray's Hell Burger in Washington, D.C., and spoke to an open audience at the Brookings Institution. For more, see Andrew Clark, "Dmitry Medvedev Picks Silicon Valley's Brains," *The Guardian*, June 23, 2010, at www.theguardian.com/business/2010/jun/23/dmitry-medvedev-silicon-valley-visit.

5. Stanley Meisler, "Circus of '59: Khrushchev's U.S. Tour Recalled," *Los Angeles Times*, May 30, 1990, at articles.latimes.com/1990-05-30/news/vw-234_1_nikita-khrushchev.

6. See Fischer (1997). This review contains excerpts from KGB files, translated by KGB defector Oleg Gordievsky, as well as translated materials from the East German intelligence files, obtained from the GDR government archives after the reunification of Germany. Fischer discusses here how the CIA also stepped up its psychological warfare operations, or PSYOP Program, beginning in 1981 to encourage the idea that the United States might indeed attack the USSR and keep the Soviets on edge and guessing about U.S. intent: "The purpose of this program was not so much to signal U.S. intentions to the Soviets as to keep them guessing what might come next. The program also probed for gaps and vulnerabilities in the USSR's early warning intelligence system." The Soviets set up their own strategic warning program in response to keep tabs on the Americans, Operation RYAN.

7. Fischer (1997). See, in particular, the section on "The Soviet Intelligence Alert and Operation RYAN."

8. Ibid. See the section on "RYAN: Retaliatory or Preemptive Strike? February 1983 (excerpt from KGB cable translated by Oleg Gordievsky)." The cable went on: "For instance, noting the launching of strategic missiles from the continental part of the USA and taking into account the time required for determining the direction of their flight in fact leaves roughly 20 minutes' reaction time. This period will be considerably curtailed after deployment of the 'Pershing-2' missile in the FRG, for which the flying time to reach long-range targets in the Soviet Union is calculated at 4-6 minutes."

9. See Claire Duffin, "Civil Servants Prepared 'Queen's Speech' for Outbreak of World War III," *The Telegraph*, August 1, 2013, at www.telegraph.co.uk/news/uknews/queen-elizabeth-II/10212063/Civil-servants-prepared-Queens-speech-for-outbreak-of-World-War-Three.html.

10. The speech is available in video and written form in the Ronald Reagan presidential archives. The transcript is at www.reaganfoundation.org/pdf/Remarks_Annual_Convention_National_Association_Evangelicals_030883.pdf.

11. See "The Day After" (1983) and "Threads" (1984) in the Internet Movie Database, at www.imdb.com/title/tt0085404/ and www.imdb.com/title/tt0090163/.

12. See the poster details in the collections of the Victoria and Albert Museum in London, at http://collections.vam.ac.uk/item/O76710/gone-with-the-wind-poster-houston-john/. The poster was initially designed by artists Bob Light and John Houston for the

British left-wing newspaper *The Socialist Worker* in 1981. In the early to mid-1980s it became widely available through British retail outlets and was especially popular on college campuses. It was also reprinted and sold in the United States. An image of the poster is available at http://www.politicalgraphics.org/cgi-bin/album.pl?photo=30presidential_rogues_02%2F065_PG_06468.jpg.

13. A full archive and history of the Greenham Common camp can be found in the UK National Archives, and online at http://apps.nationalarchives.gov.uk/a2a/records.aspx?cat=106-5gcw&cid=-1#-1.

14. Fischer (1997). This period in 1983 was the backdrop to U.S. journalist Leslie Gelb's discussion with the chief of the Soviet General Staff, Marshal Nikolai Ogarkov, about the USSR's growing concern about not being able to keep up with the military in the United States. It also framed the KGB's instructions to all of its personnel and allies to steal Western technological secrets, which is something that Vladimir Putin and his colleagues set about doing in Leningrad and then Dresden (see chapter 7).

15. In various interviews, Markus Wolf commented on the instructions from the KGB to set up the task forces that "our Soviet partners had become obsessed with the danger of a nuclear missile attack . . . [but] [l]ike most intelligent people, I found these war games a burdensome waste of time, but these orders were no more open to discussion than other orders from above." See Wolf with McElvoy (1997), p. 222.

16. Fischer (1997). See the sections on "The Enduring Trauma of BARBAROSSA" and "Conclusion: The War Scare Was for Real."

17. The Reagan audio recording can be found at www.youtube.com/watch?v=wgSSRE27GQ0.

18. See Jason Saltoun-Ebin and Andrea Chiampan, "The Reagan Files: From the Euro-Missiles Crisis to the Intermediate Range Nuclear Forces Treaty, 1979–1987," October 17, 2011, at www.thereaganfiles.com/inf-treaty.html.

19. Pepper (2012).

20. Ibid., p. 23.

21. Author interview with John Evans, Washington, D.C., June 26, 2014.

22. See Pepper (2012), p. 44. P&G CEO John Pepper's son, David, became an assistant to the program, which set out to promote the development of the St. Petersburg region. In his book, John Pepper writes: "My son David recalled Putin in those days as 'rough, quiet, direct,' a powerful complement to Sobchak's charismatic, inspirational leadership." As noted in note 44, pp. 449–50, the goal of the commission was to assist the city of St. Petersburg in identifying foreign investors to help convert its defunct defense plants into commercial factories and turn around other manufacturing operations.

23. See Scott Shane, "Cold Warrior Kissinger Sells Old Nemesis Russia," *Baltimore Sun*, June 24, 1993, at articles.baltimoresun.com/1993-06-24/news/1993175015_1_petersburg-cold-warrior-russian.

24. Putin likes to suggest that his acquaintance with Kissinger has extended in an uninterrupted temporal line since the 1990s. For more on Putin's relationship with Kissinger, see note 44, p. 449.

25. See the section "The Oligarchs' Dilemma: Mr. Putin's Solution," in chapter 8 for Putin's offer of protection to the oligarchs. In the wake of Russia's 1998 financial crisis, a vicious anti-Semitic campaign blamed the Jewish oligarchs, and specifically Boris Berezovsky, for the collapse and the suffering of Russians. The most vocal extremist was a member of parliament from the Communist Party, General Albert Makashov. When other Duma members demanded that the communists censure or even expel Makashov from the party, party leader Gennady Zyuganov refused. Zyuganov's own anti-Semitic rhetoric included such statements as: "Our people . . . cannot turn a blind eye to the aggressive, destructive role of Zionist capital in ruining Russia's economy and plundering her property owned by all." Hoffman (2003), p. 445. As head of the Federal Security Service (FSB) since

July 1998, Putin was a central figure in the Makashov affair. Following a direct threat made by Makashov to Berezovsky on November 11, 1998, the latter wrote to Putin and begged Putin personally to protect him, not only from Makashov but also from a unit inside the FSB that Berezovsky claimed had threatened him already in 1997. Putin's FSB was the agency that had to decide whether Makashov's anti-Semitic statements qualified as a crime. The FSB ruled in February 1999 that they did not. This is recounted in "The Reemergence of Political Anti-Semitism in Russia," Anti-Defamation League, 2001, at archive.adl.org/russia/russian_political_antisemitism_1.html.

26. See *Ot pervogo litsa,* pp. 14–15. Putin talks about how the elderly couple "loved" him and how he would often spend half the day playing in their section of the apartment. He also talks of an early visit he made to Israel in 1993 as part of an official delegation from the St. Petersburg council.

27. In private author interviews with senior Israeli officials in July and October 2013 at the Brookings Institution in Washington, D.C., the officials confirmed Putin's personal connections with individual Soviet Jewish émigrés to Israel, and his efforts to meet with them during official visits. One former Israeli ambassador to Moscow stressed how Putin would extol the virtues of Israel and express his admiration for Israel's economic and military success in high-level meetings with his counterparts. He would also get somewhat carried away in the process: "He thinks he knows our interests and what's best for our security better than we do," the diplomat observed.

28. Michal Margalit, Polina Garaev, "I Was Vladimir Putin's Teacher," *Ynetnews.com,* March 29, 2014, at www.ynetnews.com/articles/0,7340,L-4504539,00.html.

29. See Ellen Barry, "In Big New Museum, Russia Has a Message for Jews: We Like You," *New York Times,* November 9, 2012, at www.nytimes.com/2012/11/09/world/europe/russias-new-museum-offers-friendly-message-to-jews.html?_r=0. The official website for the Jewish Museum and Tolerance Center in Moscow is at www.jewish-museum.ru/en.

30. Russian, like some other languages, has the same word, *zhertvy,* for "sacrifices" and "victims."

31. See "Vstrecha s Prezidentom Izrailya Shimonom Peresom" [Meeting with President of Israel Shimon Peres], November 8, 2012, at www.kremlin.ru/news/16772.

32. Peres continued: "Thirty million Soviet citizens died in that war. They saved the world from disaster. I want to pay tribute to their memory and to the Soviet and Russian peoples for their heroism. The Russian people fought against the Nazis' massive war machine, not retreating until they had reached the gates of Berlin and liberated the whole world from this most terrible danger that threatened all of humanity. This was liberation for the world, for humanity, and for my people. The Nazis tried to wipe out my people. They killed 6 million Jews, including 1.5 million children. I thank you as a citizen of the world, and I thank you as a Jew. This victory enabled us to live again and become an independent people once more. . . ." See "Statements for the Press Following Russian-Israeli Talks," November 8, 2012, in English at eng.news.kremlin.ru/transcripts/4601/.

33. In the Soviet period, anti-Semitism was formally rejected and outlawed by the state, but the USSR embraced an official anti-Zionist policy as part of its struggle against the cosmopolitan, capitalist West. See, for example, the extensive discussion in Antonella Salomoni, "State Sponsored Anti-Semitism in Postwar USSR: Studies and Research Perspectives," *Quest. Studies in Contemporary Jewish History,* April 1, 2010, at www.questcdecjournal.it/focus.php?id=212. See also the discussion of the *Protocols of the Elders of Zion* in the final chapter of this book.

34. In 2004, Manzhosin was promoted to replace Prikhodko as head of the presidential administration's foreign affairs department. Prikhodko was elevated to a higher rank in the presidential administration, and then in 2012 moved from the Kremlin to the Russian government, becoming deputy prime minister in 2013.

35. In February 2003, the authors and a group of other scholars from the Brookings Institution were given an audience with Alexander Manzhosin in the Kremlin as part of a study trip to Moscow to discuss U.S.-Russian relations. The meeting with Manzhosin was arranged through a personal contact in the presidential administration, not through the Russian Embassy in Washington, D.C., and the North America desk in the Russian Ministry of Foreign Affairs, which had otherwise helped to organize the trip. The representative of the ministry's North America desk confessed that he was unable to set up the meeting in the Kremlin as they had no regular contact with Prikhodko and had never even met Manzhosin (no one at the U.S. Embassy in Moscow at the time had either!). The foreign ministry official asked to accompany the Brookings team to the meeting so he could "see Manzhosin for himself." The official was initially denied entry by the Kremlin guards because he was "not one of ours" (*ne nash*), that is, not from the presidential administration. It took a series of appeals to the guards' supervisors to get him into Manzhosin's office with the rest of the group.

36. Goldgeier and McFaul (2003). See the section on "NATO is a Four-Letter Word," pp. 183–210.

37. Ibid., p. 188.

38. Ibid., p. 184.

39. Ibid., p. 191. On the debate about what had been promised to Russia in the early 1990s regarding NATO's future expansion, see Sarotte (2014)

40. See Körber Stiftung, "Europa—aber wo liegen seine Grenzen?" [Europe—but where do its frontiers lie?], 104th Bergedorfer Gesprächskreis [104th Bergedorf Roundtable], Warsaw, Königsschloss, 1995, at www.koerber-stiftung.de/fileadmin/bg/PDFs/bnd_104_de.pdf.

41. Goldgeier and McFaul (2003), p. 201.

42. "Dr. Michael Haltzel Shares Insights on the Balkan Wars and NATO Enlargement . . . ," American Hungarian Federation, August 26, 2011, at www.americanhungarianfederation.org/news_CEEC_USEngagement_2011_Haltzel.html.

43. Goldgeier and McFaul (2003), pp. 208–10.

44. Ibid., p. 247.

45. NATO's intervention also shook the Russian public. Polls conducted by VTsIOM, the predecessor polling agency to the Levada Center, showed that the share of Russians polled who had a negative view of the United States rose from barely 20 percent to well over 50 percent in the first half of 1999. Levada Center data as reported in Sberbank Investment Research, "Russia Economic Monthly," July 2014.

46. See Vladimir Putin, "Obrashcheniye Prezidenta Rossiyskoy Federatsii" [Address by the President of the Russian Federation], March 18, 2014, available on the Kremlin's website archive (in Russian) at news.kremlin.ru/news/20603. An English translation is available at eng.news.kremlin.ru/news/6889.

47. Goldgeier and McFaul (2003), p. 249. For an American diplomat's side of the story, see Talbott (2002), chapter 12, "Hammer and Anvil."

48. Ibid.

49. See Putin, "Obrashcheniye Prezidenta Rossiyskoy Federatsii" [Address by the President of the Russian Federation], March 18, 2014.

50. See Goldgeier and McFaul (2003), pp. 261–62.

51. Ibid., p. 263.

52. Ibid., p. 264.

53. For a personal account by someone who interacted with Putin during the Kosovo events, see Strobe Talbott, "Vladimir Putin's Role, Yesterday and Today," *Washington Post*, March 21, 2014. Talbott, former deputy secretary of state in the Clinton administration, described his meeting with Putin in the latter's capacity as head of the Russian Security Council. Putin's role in Russia's intervention in Kosovo, notes Talbott, "remains a mystery."

54. Ibid.

55. See Goldgeier and McFaul (2003), pp. 282–83.

56. See Akhmadov and Daniloff (2013).

57. Vladimir Putin, "Why We Must Act," *New York Times*, November 14, 1999, at www.nytimes.com/1999/11/14/opinion/why-we-must-act.html.

58. See "Terror Strikes—and Putin Proposes an Antiterrorist Alliance," in Stent (2014), pp. 62–66. Russian military commanders also tried to draw direct comparisons between Chechnya and the NATO bombing campaign in Yugoslavia in a different way, explaining that they were simply emulating NATO's strategy in trying to deal with the terrorist operations in Chechnya; see Michael Gordon, "Imitating NATO: A Script Is Adapted for Chechnya," *New York Times*, November 28, 1999, at www.nytimes.com/1999/09/28/world/imitating-nato-a-script-is-adapted-for-chechnya.html.

59. Stent (2014), pp. 62–63.

60. "Vneshnepoliticheskiye kontakty—zayavleniye dlya pressy i otvety na voprosy po okonchanii rossiysko-bel'giyskikh peregovorov" [Foreign political contacts—statements for the press and answers to questions at the conclusion of Russian-Belgian negotiations], Kremlin Archive website, October 2, 2001, at http://archive.kremlin.ru/appears/2001/10/02/0002_type63377type63380_28650.shtml.

61. Stent (2014), p. 67.

62. Ibid., p. 69. See also Hill (2002)

63. Stent (2014), p. 69. This is a quote from an interview that Stent conducted with former Russian Foreign Minister Igor Ivanov.

64. Ibid.

65. See the section "Chechnya, Again" in Goldgeier and McFaul (2003), pp. 267–86.

66. See Stent (2014), pp. 69–72.

67. See Vladimir Putin, "Vstrechi s predstavitelyami razlichnikh soobshchestv" [Meetings with representatives of different communities], September 15, 2001, at http://archive.kremlin.ru/appears/2001/09/15/0003_type63376type63377_28632.shtml.

68. Authors' notes from Gareyev presentation in Washington, D.C., in 2010.

69. For a detailed discussion of Russian attitudes toward U.S. ballistic missile defense, including extensive interviews with Russian officials, see Lilly (2014).

70. Manzhosin's statements to the Brookings group were consistent with those made by Kremlin officials in the same timeframe to representatives in the U.S. Embassy in Moscow. Manzhosin's overall point was that Hussein had got himself caught in an elaborate bluff to convince his domestic opponents, Iran and other hostile regional states, and Washington that he had a WMD arsenal. His goal was to bolster his internal authority and deter any would-be attackers. Instead, by resisting international weapons inspections, Hussein ended up with the very outcome he feared. Manzhosin claimed, at the time, that the real threat of WMD proliferation was from Pakistan—an allusion to the network of top Pakistani nuclear scientist Abdul Qadeer (A.Q.) Khan, which was providing nuclear technology to North Korea, Libya, and Iran (although Manzhosin did not elaborate on this point). Authors' notes from meeting with the deputy head of the presidential Foreign Affairs Department, Alexander Manzhosin, February 6, 2002, Kremlin, Moscow.

71. This was repeated to the authors on numerous occasions by Polish foreign minister Radosław Sikorski, who is fond of a good international affairs joke. Whether Putin actually uttered this remark—and if he did, whether he meant it as a joke—is unclear.

72. Authors' notes from meeting with Sergei Ivanov, September 7, 2004, Ministry of Defense, Moscow.

73. Goldgeier and McFaul (2003), p. 365. The idea that Russia had disappeared as a threat to the United States by the end of the 1990s is the theme and conclusion of the last chapter of Goldgeier and McFaul's book, "Lessons," pp. 330–65.

74. Putin's time in power has thus far encompassed three American presidents: Bill Clinton, George W. Bush, and Barack Obama. James Goldgeier, Michael McFaul, and

Angela Stent meticulously chart out the evolution of U.S.-Russian relations under these three presidents in their books. They take the narrative from the 1990s to 2002 (in the case of Goldgeier and McFaul) and from the 2000s to 2013 (in the case of Stent). These and other accounts provide a wealth of firsthand, real-time reporting, which captures the atmosphere of each period. All three authors were, at various junctures, part of the action, not just analysts and observers. Goldgeier worked at the U.S. State Department and the National Security Council in 1995–96 during the Clinton administration. Michael McFaul was heavily involved in U.S. technical assistance projects on the ground in Russia in this period, and one of the most prominent American commentators on Russian affairs. In 2009, he became one of the architects of Russia policy in the Obama administration, serving in the White House and then as ambassador to Moscow from 2012 to 2014. Angela Stent was on the Policy Planning Staff in the State Department from 1999 to 2001 and then served on the National Intelligence Council as the top analyst on Russia from 2004 to 2006. Their analyses and insights show that the U.S. and Russian presidents all inhabited different worlds physically and mentally. The leaders consistently found it difficult to see things from the other's perspectives and to acknowledge each other's threat perceptions.

75. The Baltic states secured independence from Russia after World War I. The United States and other countries did not recognize the Soviet Union's reincorporation of the states after World War II.

76. See Stent (2014), pp. 97–123, for a detailed discussion of Russian responses to the color revolutions and Russian government interpretations of events.

77. For more information on the policies related to the Bush administration's "Freedom Agenda," see the George W. Bush archives at www.georgewbush-whitehouse.archives.gov/infocus/freedomagenda/; Yerkes and Wittes (2006); and Paulette Chu Miniter, "Why George Bush's Freedom Agenda Is Here to Stay," *Foreign Policy*, August 21, 2007, at www.foreignpolicy.com/articles/2007/08/20/why_george_bushs_ldquofreedom_agendardquo_is_here_to_stay_.

78. See Vladimir Putin, "Obrashcheniye Prezidenta Rossiyskoy Federatsii" [Address by the President of the Russian Federation], March 18, 2014, available on the Kremlin's website archive (in Russian) at http://news.kremlin.ru/news/20603. An English translation is available at http://eng.news.kremlin.ru/news/6889.

79. Stent (2014), p. 10.

80. See, for example, the text of "Cheney's Speech in Lithuania," *New York Times*, May 4, 2006, at www.nytimes.com/2006/05/04/world/europe/04cnd-cheney-text.html?pagewanted=all&_r=0.

81. See Anne Kornblut, "Cheney Shoots Fellow Hunter in Mishap on a Texas Ranch," *New York Times*, February 13, 2006, at www.nytimes.com/2006/02/13/politics/13cheney.html. The *Today* show video and an analysis of the interview are available at www.nbcnews.com/id/12355000/ns/world_news-europe/t/putin-takes-swipe-cheney-over-criticisms/. The Kremlin's official transcript of the interview is at http://archive.kremlin.ru/appears/2006/07/12/1130_type63379_108507.shtml. In the interview, Putin made a series of his own strong public statements, calling for a global system of security to replace the U.S.-dominated unipolar system, and criticizing the United States very sharply over Iraq.

82. Vladimir Putin, "Speech and the Following Discussion at the Munich Security Conference on Security Policy," February 10, 2007, at http://archive.kremlin.ru/eng/speeches/2007/02/10/0138_type82912type82914type82917type84779_118123.shtml.

83. Stent (2014), pp. 147, 149.

84. Vladimir Putin, "Press Statement and Answers to Journalists' Questions Following a Meeting of the Russia-NATO Council," April 4, 2008, at http://archive.kremlin.ru/eng/text/speeches/2008/04/04/1949_type82915_163150.shtml.

85. Cited in Stent (2014), p. 161.

86. Ibid., pp. 238–39. The authors, who were in Berlin for an international conference hosted by the German Council on Foreign Relations that coincided with Medvedev's visit,

had several meetings with Russian and German officials, who stressed that Medvedev's speech had been coordinated with his German hosts in advance. The Russians had presented it as a "last ditch attempt" to find a new form of co-existence between Moscow and the Euro-Atlantic security institutions. The hope was that a "fresh face" in the Kremlin and a constructive approach might make some progress where Putin's assertive stance in Munich and Bucharest had failed.

87. Stent (2014), pp. 168–76.

88. Ibid., pp. 211–34.

89. Putin declared Qaddafi's death an "outrage" (bezobraziye) in his November 11, 2011, meeting with the Valdai Discussion Club, which also covered many of these same issues (authors' notes).

90. Vladimir Putin, "A Plea for Caution from Russia: What Vladimir Putin Has to Say to Americans about Syria," New York Times, September, 11, 2013, at www.nytimes.com/2013/09/12/opinion/putin-plea-for-caution-from-russia-on-syria.html?_r=0. The op-ed was published on September 11 but is listed on the website as published on September 12.

91. Stent (2014), p. 274.

CHAPTER 13

1. See Gaddy and Hill (2002).

2. Cited in Figes (2003). The quote is from a famous interview Stolypin gave in October 1909 explaining his reform agenda.

3. Putin forged a personal connection with Bush during their first meeting in Slovenia in July 2001—an encounter marked by President Bush's much-cited comment in their joint press conference that he had looked Putin in the eye and got "a sense of his soul" (see "Press Conference by President Bush and Russian Federation President Putin," Brdo Castle, Brdo Pri Kranju, Slovenia, July 16, 2001, available in full at www.georgewbush-whitehouse.archives.gov/news/releases/2001/06/20010618.html). See also Stent (2014), pp. 60–66, for an overview of the Slovenia meeting and the interactions between Putin and Bush. On numerous occasions during Bush's two terms in office, including during sessions with the participants of the Valdai Discussion Club, Putin would make a point of stressing his personal regard for George W. Bush irrespective of any tensions in the bilateral political relationship.

4. This assessment was hammered home to the authors in every meeting with top Russian officials in preparation for the book, including in comments made by President Putin in the Valdai Discussion Club sessions.

5. A picaresque novel is a type of fiction where the central character progresses through a series of episodic adventures. Cervantes's Don Quixote, Mark Twain's Adventures of Huckleberry Finn and The Adventures of Tom Sawyer, and Nikolai Gogol's Dead Souls are examples of this genre.

6. See Akiner and Barnes (2001).

7. See, for example, Meier (2004), p. 118.

8. See Gall and de Waal (1998), pp. 56–75. For a detailed discussion of the World War II deportations to both Central Asia and Siberia, see Nekrich (1981).

9. As an example, see Putin's televised speech to the Russian people after the tragedy at Beslan. Vladimir Putin, "Obrashcheniye Prezidenta Rossii Vladimira Putina" [Address by the President of Russia Vladimir Putin], September 4, 2004, at http://archive.kremlin.ru/text/appears/2004/09/6320.shtml.

10. Vladimir Putin, "Vystupleniye na parade, posvyashchennom 56-y godovshchine Pobedy v Velikoy Otechestvennoy voyne" [Speech at the parade commemorating the 56th anniversary of victory in the Great Patriotic War], May 9, 2001, at http://archive.kremlin.ru/appears/2001/05/09/0001_type63374type82634type122346_28544.shtml.

11. See discussion in chapter 12 about the February 2003 meeting between the Brookings delegation and Alexander Manzhosin in the Kremlin.

12. Herspring and Kipp (2001). The citation is on p. 14.

13. Ibid., p. 15.

14. Ibid., p. 16.

15. Vladimir Putin, "Speech and the Following Discussion at the Munich Security Conference on Security Policy," February 10, 2007, at http://archive.kremlin.ru/eng/speeches/2007/02/10/0138_type82912type82914type82917type84779_118123.shtml.

16. In their early analysis of Putin, Herspring and Kipp noted: "Watching Putin deal with Moscow's foreign debt is especially interesting. He wants nothing more than to pay it." Herspring and Kipp (2001), p. 15.

17. On the importance of financial sovereignty for Putin, see the section "Deploying Russia's Financial Reserves" in chapter 5 of this book.

18. Private author interviews with German officials in meetings in Washington, D.C., and Berlin between 2009 and 2013. This story was repeated to the authors on multiple occasions with several small variants in the phrasing.

19. Vladimir Putin, "Zasedaniye Soveta Bezopasnosti" [Meeting of the Security Council], July 22, 2014, at http://kremlin.ru/transcripts/46305.

20. After Chavez's death, Putin expressed some dissatisfaction with how Chavez had run Venezuela's economy. See "Vladimir Putin Answered Journalists' Questions at the End of his Trip to Vologda," March 7, 2013, at http://eng.kremlin.ru/news/5095.

21. Michael Birnbaum, "Ukraine Factories Equip Russian Military Despite Support for Rebels," *Washington Post,* September 15, 2014, at www.washingtonpost.com/world/europe/ukraine-factories-equip-russian-military-despite-support-for-rebels/2014/08/15/9c32cde7-a57c-4d7b-856a-e74b8307ef9d_story.html.

22. See, for example, Vladimir Putin, "Meeting with Russian Ambassadors and Permanent Representatives in International Organizations," July 9, 2012, at http://eng.kremlin.ru/news/4145. In this meeting, for example, Putin stated: "Let me stress again that deepening the integration process in the CIS [Commonwealth of Independent States] is the core of our foreign policy and is our strategic objective. It is Russia, Kazakhstan, and Belarus, of course, who together form the driving force of this integration, having already formed the Customs Union and now starting to work together within the common economic space." See also Vladimir Putin, "Annual Address to the Federal Assembly," April 26, 2007, at http://archive.kremlin.ru/eng/speeches/2007/04/26/1209_type70029type82912_125670.shtml.

23. See Hill and Gaddy (2003) for a further discussion of this issue; also see Lo (2008).

24. China's new president, Xi Jinping, made things a little easier for Putin in 2013 by selecting Russia for his first foreign visit as Chinese leader and by then proceeding to embrace his own more personalized leadership style. See David Herszenhorn and Chris Buckley, "China's New Leader, Visiting Russia, Promotes Nations' Economic and Military Ties," *New York Times,* March 22, 2013, at www.nytimes.com/2013/03/23/world/asia/xi-jinping-visits-russia-on-first-trip-abroad.html?pagewanted=all&_r=0; and Cheng Li, "Xi Jingping's Inner Circle" (two-part series), *China Leadership Monitor,* January/July 2014, available at www.brookings.edu/research/papers/2014/01/30-xi-jinping-inner-circle-li, and www.brookings.edu/research/articles/2014/07/18-xi-jinping-inner-circle-friends-li.

25. See also Sergei Karaganov's article "Vpered k Velikomu okeanu" [Toward the Great Ocean], *Rossiiskaya gazeta* (Federal issue), No. 6464, August 26, 2014, at www.rg.ru/2014/08/26/usilenie.html.

26. Fiona Hill and Bobo Lo, "Putin's Pivot: Why Russia Is Looking East," *Foreign Affairs,* July 31, 2013, at www.foreignaffairs.com/articles/139617/fiona-hill-and-bobo-lo/putins-pivot.

27. Hours after the Chinese ships had moved into the Sea of Okhotsk, the Russian Ministry of Defense mobilized (what was to that date) the largest land and sea military exercise in its Eastern Military District since the end of the Cold War. Putin flew out east

to Chita, close to Russia's land border with China, and then to Sakhalin to review the ad hoc maneuvers personally. In author interviews on Russian-Japanese-Chinese relations in Tokyo in October 2013, Japanese military analysts reported that their Russian interlocutors told them directly (albeit privately) that Moscow had launched the military exercise to signal its displeasure to Beijing. China had taken Russia by surprise by sending its ships on the "scenic route" home. After cruising past Sakhalin and other islands, the Chinese vessels also sailed around Japan before heading to Chinese waters. For more on this delicate relationship, see Fiona Hill, "Gang of Two: Russia and Japan Make a Play for the Pacific," *Foreign Affairs,* at www.foreignaffairs.com/articles/140288/fiona-hill/gang-of-two.

28. These are three islands—Etorofu (Iturup in Russian), Kunashiri (Kunashir in Russian), and Shikotan—and a group of islets, the Habomais, which the Soviet Union took from Japan in 1945. The disputed islands lie at the southern tip of the Kuril Islands chain that extends from Japan's northernmost territory of Hokkaido to Russia's Kamchatka Peninsula.

29. See Hill (2013).

30. Author interviews with Japanese officials in Tokyo on Japan's relations with Russia, October 2013.

31. As American scholar Bruce Jones pointed out in a 2014 analysis of the BRICS countries and their efforts to set up a "BRICS bank" as a source of international lending for development projects: "All of the BRICS but Brazil have suffered under Western sanctions at one time or another, and they tend to reject as a matter of principle the application of sanctions as a tool of international relations." In setting up a bank and consolidating their relations, the countries "were seeking to limit their own exposure to American financial muscle-flexing. They want to diversify their relationships beyond the West." The BRICS were not a new alliance. They were a group of countries brought together by "a shared desire to increase their freedom of action in the international system . . . [and] . . . an interest in curtailing Western dominance." See Jones (2014).

32. See Stent (2014), pp. 215–22.

33. Putin and Medvedev both, at different junctures in September and October 2011, indicated that they had discussed this possibility in 2007, in advance of the creation of the tandem power arrangement. See, for example, "Interv'yu s predsedatelem pravitel'stva RF Vladimirom Putinom" [Interview with the Prime Minister of the Russian Federation, Vladimir Putin], *Perviy Kanal,* October 17, 2011, www.1tv.ru/news/polit/188478.

34. Author interviews with senior German officials in 2011–12.

35. Author interviews with representatives of the Ost-Ausschuss der Deutschen Wirtshaft (Committee on Eastern European Economic Relations, which is the organization of German industry investing in Russia and Eastern Europe) in Washington, D.C., and Berlin in 2012–13. On the specific situation of the auto-manufacturing industry, see Fiona Hill and Clifford Gaddy, "Putin's Next Move in Russia: Observations from the 8th Annual Valdai International Discussion Club," Brookings Institution, December 12, 2011, which offers observations from the authors' visit to Russia's Kaluga region, at www.brookings.edu/research/interviews/2011/12/12-putin-gaddy-hill.

36. For a full discussion, see Fidelius Schmid and Holger Stark, "In the 'Land of the Enemy': Spies Strain German-Russian Ties," *Spiegel Online,* July 2, 2013, at www.spiegel.de/international/world/trial-of-russian-spies-in-germany-strains-diplomatic-relations-a-908975.html.

37. See Markus Dettmer and Christian Reiermann, "Bailing out Oligarchs: EU Aid for Cyprus a Political Minefield for Merkel," *Spiegel Online,* November 5, 2012, at www.spiegel.de/international/europe/german-intelligence-report-warns-cyprus-not-combating-money-laundering-a-865451.html. In author interviews with German officials,

frequent reference was made to the general conclusions of the BND report, which had been presented to the German government and members of parliament.

38. See, for example, Section 18, "Relations with Russia on Protracted Conflicts" in Vaisse and Dennison (2013), and Philip Remler, "Negotiation Gone Bad: Russia, Germany, and Crossed Communications," Carnegie Europe, August 21, 2013, at http://carnegie europe.eu/publications/?fa=52712&reloadFlag=1.

39. In author interviews in Berlin in May 2013 and February 2014, and also at an international conference in Paris in May 2014, German Foreign Ministry officials noted somewhat ruefully that they had finally concluded Moscow had no desire to resolve the Transnistria conflict. Russia was more interested in the process of engaging bilaterally with Germany on a high-profile European foreign policy issue than in reaching the endgame. Dealing directly with Germany kept the EU and the United States out of the issue for the duration of the negotiations. It gave Moscow more control and the ideal small number of players to deal with. And Transnistria, the Germans realized, was ultimately too important a lever in Moscow's foreign policy in its neighborhood to relinquish. The desire to reunify its territory and the denial of reunification kept Moldova on Moscow's leash. It also kept Moldova away from NATO—especially after 2008 when Russia's war with Georgia signaled what could happen to countries with secessionist republics if they ignored Moscow's warnings. Moscow had made it very clear to Tbilisi and to European interlocutors that it had recognized Abkhazia and South Ossetia to punish Georgia for its NATO bid.

40. For analysis of the data until February 2014, see Hannes Adomeit, "Collapse of Russia's Image in Germany: Who Is to Blame?," *Eurasia Outlook*, Carnegie Moscow Center, February 18, 2014, at http://carnegie.ru/eurasiaoutlook/?fa=54540. For the period until May 2014, see ARD-Deutschlandtrend, "Vertrauenswürdige Partner Deutschlands," at www.tagesschau.de/inland/deutschlandtrend2238.pdf.

41. See Robert Coalson, "As Merkel Heads for Russia, Moscow Is in for a Schockenhoff," RFL/RL, November 16, 2012, at www.rferl.org/content/news-analysis-merkel-putin-schockenhoff/24768692.html. Schockenhoff produced a second version of his report in July 2014 in response to the crisis in Ukraine, available in English at http://schockenhoff.de/download/140701_Russia_Paper_EN.pdf.

42. Multiple author interviews in Washington, D.C., and Germany with Andreas Schockenhoff and other CDU representatives and German journalists in 2013–14. See also Alison Smale, "Germany Puts Curbing Russia Ahead of Commerce," *New York Times*, August 13, 2014, at www.nytimes.com/2014/08/14/world/europe/ukraine-crisis-hardens-germany-against-russia-an-old-partner.html?_r=0.

43. It should be noted that Putin did not abandon his appeals to Germany even after the Ukraine crisis had unfolded. In his March 18, 2014, speech on the annexation of Crimea, he reminded Germans of Russia's support for its reunification at the end of the Cold War.

44. This remark was made by Konstantin Simonov on the radio program *Polnyy Albats*. See Yevgenia Albats, *Polnyy Albats*, Ekho Moskviy, April 24, 2014, at http://echo.msk.ru/programs/albac/1304074-echo/.

45. Gevorkyan, Timakova, and Kolesnikov (2000), pp. 155–56.

46. Ibid., p. 156.

47. See Fiona Hill, "Dinner with Putin: Musings on the Politics of Modernization in Russia," October 2010, Brookings Foreign Policy Trip Reports, No. 18, at www.brookings.edu/research/reports/2010/10/russia-putin-hill.

48. In all the versions, God sends a message to the world's religious leaders that he will send another flood to punish mankind, but this time there will be no dry land. The world will stay underwater. Everyone will drown. Most of the religious leaders implore their followers to be pious, repent, and come to terms with their fate in the time left. But

the rabbi goes to his people and says: "My people (or my fellow Jews), we have to learn to live under water."

49. See Guy Rolnik, "Taking Stock/Learn to Breathe Under Water," *Haaretz,* February 9, 2009, at www.haaretz.com/print-edition/business/taking-stock-learn-to-breathe-under-water-1.269722.

50. Putin's telling of the joke in February 2012 was related to us by Nikolai Zlobin, who was present in the closed meeting with Putin's "authorized campaign representatives" (*doverennyye litsa*) on February 29, 2012.

51. Authors' notes from November 1, 2013, meeting at the Brookings Institution in Washington, D.C. As this was a private meeting and he had not written about these discussions with Putin or spoken about them publicly, the journalist requested that his comments be used without attribution.

52. King and Cleland (1978), pp. 55–56.

53. As American political commentator Charles Cooke relates in a *National Review* piece in July 2011: "In the late 1950s, a journalist asked incumbent British prime minister Harold Macmillan what he considered was most likely to blow his government off course. In an answer that has gone down in history—perhaps as much for its Edwardian construction as its content—Macmillan replied, 'Events, dear boy, events.'" This response hits at a fundamental truth, and one that can be combined with Harold Wilson's most famous aphorism: "A week is a long time in politics." See Charles Cooke, "Events, Dear Boy, Events," *National Review,* July 18, 2011, at www.nationalreview.com/corner/272089/events-dear-boy-events-charlie-cooke.

54. These comments were relayed to the authors in private meetings with senior Georgian officials in 2009 and 2010.

55. Dmitry Medvedev, "Poslaniye Federal'nomu Sobraniyu Rossiiskoi Federatsii" [Message to the Federal Assembly of the Russian Federation], November 5, 2008, at http://archive.kremlin.ru/appears/2008/11/05/1349_type63372type63374type63381type82634_208749.shtml.

56. See Stent (2014) and Asmus (2010).

57. See discussion in chapter 12.

58. Helene Cooper and Thom Shanker, "After Mixed U.S. Messages, a War Erupted in Georgia," *New York Times,* August 12, 2008, at www.nytimes.com/2008/08/13/washington/13diplo.html?pagewanted=all&_r=0.

59. This point is well made in the final report of the Independent International Fact-Finding Mission on the Conflict in Georgia. The mission was set up in December 2008 by the Council of the European Union, with Swiss diplomat Heidi Tagliavini appointed as its head, to investigate the origins and causes of the August war. The final report was formally presented to the Council of the EU, the Organization for Security and Cooperation in Europe, the UN, and the governments of Russia and Georgia on September 30, 2009, and can be accessed at www.ceiig.ch/Report.html.

60. Thom Shanker, "Russians Melded Old-School Blitz with Modern Military Tactics," *New York Times,* August 17, 2008, at www.nytimes.com/2008/08/17/world/europe/17military.html?pagewanted=all&_r=0.

61. Medvedev, "Poslaniye Federal'nomu Sobraniyu Rossiiskoi Federatsii" [Message to the Federal Assembly of the Russian Federation], November 5, 2008.

62. Ibid.

63. The immediate response by some military experts after the 2008 Georgia war was remarkably similar to the response after the 2014 Crimea operation. A comparison of two articles in the *New York Times* shortly after each conflict is instructive. See Shanker, "Russians Melded Old-School Blitz with Modern Military Tactics," *New York Times,* August 17, 2008, and C. J. Chivers and David Herszenhorn, "In Crimea, Russia Showcases

a Rebooted Army," *New York Times*, April 2, 2014, at www.nytimes.com/2014/04/03/world/europe/crimea-offers-showcase-for-russias-rebooted-military.html.

64. Fred Weir, "In Georgia, Russia Saw Its Army's shortcomings," *Christian Science Monitor*, October 10, 2008, at www.csmonitor.com/World/Europe/2008/1010/p01s01-woeu.html. For a Russian expert assessment of the performance of the Russian military as well as an analysis of the war and the actions of the Georgian forces, see Pukhov (2010).

65. It is worth noting here again that Chechnya was seen as the nadir, the tombstone, of the Russian military. The two wars in Chechnya confirmed for military professionals and analysts at home and abroad that the Russian military was no longer an effective fighting force. It could not even accomplish an operation on its own territory let alone project itself abroad. For more, see Lieven (1998).

66. On Serdyukov's background, see note 25, p. 448.

67. Nikolai Makarov, "Vremya razgil'dyaystva, populizma i demagogii zakonchilos'" [The time of slipshod efforts, populism, and demagogy is over], *Voyenno-promyshlennyy kur'yer*, February 8, 2012, at http://vpk-news.ru/articles/8597.

68. See Putin's 2012 election campaign article on the military and the importance of military innovation: "Vladimir Putin: Byt' sil'nymi: garantii natsional'noy bezopasnosti dlya Rossii" [Vladimir Putin: To be strong is the guarantee of Russia's national security], *Rossiyskaya gazeta*, February 20, 2012, at www.rg.ru/2012/02/20/putin-armiya.html.

69. Executive order 603, May 7, 2012, "O realizatsii planov (programm) stroitel'stva i razvitiya Vooruzhennykh Sil Rossiyskoy Federatsii, drugikh voysk, voinskikh formirovaniy i organov i modernizatsii oboronno-promyshlennogo kompleksa" [On implementing plans (programs) for building and developing the Armed Forces of the Russian Federation, other troops, military units and agencies, and modernizing the military-industrial complex], at http://kremlin.ru/acts/15242. Also see Executive order 604, May 7, 2012, "O dal'neyshem sovershenstvovanii voyennoy sluzhby v Rossiyskoy Federatsii" [On further improvements to military service in the Russian Federation], at http://kremlin.ru/acts/15253.

70. The assessment by Congressional Research Service analyst Jim Nichol is an example: "Compared to Russia's previous attempts to revamp its armed forces, the current reform effort has gone further in altering the force structure and operations of the armed forces, according to most observers. However, the reforms face daunting delays, modifications, and setbacks. It remains highly uncertain whether Russia will be able to marshal the budgetary and demographic resources to field a substantially professional military with high readiness, as planned, or to modernize its ailing defense industries to obtain a new array of weaponry over the next 10 years." Nichol (2011).

71. In a speech given at NATO's Parliamentary Assembly Committee meeting in Vilnius, Lithuania, and republished on his blog at Ekho Moskviy, Illarionov writes that "this war was carefully planned and prepared over the period of several years." See Andrei Illarionov, "Chetvertaya mirovaya voina," [The fourth world war], *Ekho Moskvy*, June 12, 2014, at www.echo.msk.ru/blog/aillar/1338912-echo/.

72. See note 68, above, for Putin's article. See note 69, above, for his decrees.

73. Putin's proposed amendments to the defense law were not enacted by the Duma until April 5, 2013. The text of the changes is at www.consultant.ru/document/cons_doc_LAW_144635/#p21. The list of new defense planning documents is in "Ukaz Prezidenta Rossiyskoy Federatsii ot 23 iyulya 2013 g. No. 631, 'Voprosy General'nogo shtaba Vooruzhennykh Sil Rossiyskoy Federatsii'" [Decree of the President of the Russian Federation of July 23, 2013, No. 631 on "Questions of the General Staff of the Armed Forces of the Russian Federation"], available at http://stat.doc.mil.ru/documents/quick_search/more.htm?id=11807834@egNPA.

74. An English-language translation of Gerasimov's January 2013 speech with comments can be found at Mark Galeotti's blog, "The 'Gerasimov Doctrine' and Russian Non-Linear War," *In Moscow's Shadows*, July 6, 2014, at http://inmoscowsshadows.

wordpress.com/2014/07/06/the-gerasimov-doctrine-and-russian-non-linear-war/. Galeotti is a British professor at New York University who specializes in research on the Russian security and intelligence services, as well as organized crime.

75. General Gareyev's 2010 speech in Washington, D.C., went through the same points as Gerasimov. See note 7, p. 473.

76. See Mark Galeotti's blog, "The 'Gerasimov Doctrine' and Russian Non-Linear War," *In Moscow's Shadows*.

77. Ibid.

78. Valeriy Gerasimov, "General'nyy shtab i oborona strany" [The general staff and the defense of the country], *Voyenno-promyshlennyy kur'yer*, February 5, 2014, at http://vpk-news.ru/articles/18998.

79. Vladimir Putin, "Soveshchaniye o vypolnenii gosoboronzakaza" [Meeting on implementation of the defense order], May 14, 2014, at http://kremlin.ru/transcripts/21021.

80. "Peskov: Kreml' proanaliziruyet resheniye vostoka Ukrainy po referendumu" [Peskov: The Kremlin is analyzing the decision of eastern Ukraine on a referendum], RIA Novosti, May 8, 2014, at http://ria.ru/politics/20140508/1007012830.html.

81. For instance, the Kremlin website announced on May 2, 2014, that Putin was receiving "all information" on the military situation in southeast Ukraine "in operational mode" (*v operativnom rezhime*). See http://kremlin.ru/news?since=02.05.2014&till=02.05.2014. The Russian Ministry of Defense defines *operativnyy rezhim* as "a set of operational rules, measures, and norms aimed at stabilizing the military-political and military-strategic situation, maintaining high combat readiness of troops (forces), deterring (containing) the escalation of an armed conflict, preventing possible aggression by the enemy, and, if necessary, organizing entry into war and successfully conducting initial operations. The operational mode may be introduced in peacetime or a period of threat." See http://encyclopedia.mil.ru/encyclopedia/dictionary/details_rvsn.htm?id=7660@morfDictionary.

82. Gerasimov, "General'nyy shtab i oborona strany" [The general staff and the defense of the country], *Voyenno-promyshlennyy kur'yer*, February 5, 2014.

CHAPTER 14

1. On this point, see Sergey Brezkun, "Ne radi podgotovki k novym voynam, a dlya isklyucheniya ugrozy voyny. U Rossii yest' lish' odin nadezhnyy soyuznik—yeyo yadernoye oruzhiye" [Not for the sake of preparing for new wars but for ruling out the threat of war. Russia has but one reliable ally—its nuclear arsenal], *Voyenno-promyshlennyy kur'yer*, February 8, 2012. Brezkun, a professor at the Academy of Military Sciences and a protégé of Army General Makhmud Gareyev, argues that if Russia has a nuclear force properly configured for massive retaliation and if it makes clear that it is prepared to use it in response to any attack, nuclear or non-nuclear, it frees Russia's hands. "Russia can permit itself any actions aimed at guaranteeing its security and historical future—up to and including, for example, support of those forces in the post-Soviet space that want their country to become part of the Russian Federation or the Union State."

2. See Stent (2014), pp. 241–42.

3. Tom Parfitt, "Vladimir Putin Consoles Exposed Russian Spies with 'Singalong,'" *The Guardian*, July 25, 2010, at www.theguardian.com/world/2010/jul/25/vladimir-putin-russian-spy-ring. The song "From What the Motherland Begins" can be heard at www.youtube.com/watch?v=9mhXpu9Eoj8.

4. Ibid.

5. Putin made the allegation that Chubais was "surrounded" by CIA operatives in his nationally broadcast *Hot Line* program in April 2013, "Pryamaya liniya s Vladimirom Putinym" [*Hot Line* with Vladimir Putin], April 25, 2013, at http://kremlin.ru/transcripts/17976. Chubais's response came the next day. See "Chubais schital slukhami dannyye o rabote v TsRU dvukh sovetnikov" [Chubais dismisses reports that two advisers worked for CIA as rumors], RIA Novosti, April 26, 2013, at http://ria.ru/politics/20130426/934784673.html.

6. Human rights activist Lyudmila Alexeyeva, for instance, was quoted by the Russian newspaper *Nezavisimaya gazeta* as saying: "I am happy . . . that Snowden has been granted asylum in our country." See "Russian Press Hail Snowden Asylum Move," *BBC News*, August 2, 2013, at www.bbc.com/news/world-europe-23548785.

7. See Steven Pifer, "Edward Snowden in Moscow: A Case Study in Diplomatic Mismanagement," Brookings Institution's Up Front Blog, August 9, 2013, at www.brookings.edu/blogs/up-front/posts/2013/08/09-snowden-moscow-diplomatic-mismanagement-pifer. See also Stent (2014), pp. 269–71.

8. See, for example, Cornelius Rahn and Leon Mangasarian, "Germans Hail Snowden as NSA Evokes Stasi Seizing Lives of Others," Bloomberg, July 10, 2013, at www.bloomberg.com/news/2013-07-10/germans-hail-snowden-as-nsa-evokes-stasi-seizing-lives-of-others.html; and "Stateless in Moscow: Germany Rejects Asylum for Snowden," *Spiegel Online*, July 3, 2013, at www.spiegel.de/international/germany/germany-has-rejected-edward-snowden-asylum-application-a-909128.html.

9. An audio recording of the phone call can be found online at www.youtube.com/watch?v=KIvRljAaNgg.

10. This section and these comments are based on extensive author interviews in 2014 with German officials, business representatives, and journalists in Washington D.C., Munich, and Berlin.

11. The Russian organization GOLOS, which means both "vote" and "voice" in Russian, is active in exposing election corruption and violations and in training election monitors around Russia. Its online interactive "Map of Violations" chronicled the many problems with the December 2011 parliamentary elections and helped spark the protest movement. Consequently, it was one of the first groups targeted by the Kremlin crackdown. For more, see "Golos Election Monitoring NGO Fined under New Law," RFE/RL, April 25, 2013, at www.rferl.org/content/russian-election-monitoring-golos-trial/24968090.html.

12. David M. Herszenhorn, "New Russian Law Assesses Heavy Fines on Protesters," *New York Times*, June 8, 2012, at www.nytimes.com/2012/06/09/world/europe/putin-signs-law-with-harsh-fines-for-protesters-in-russia.html?_r=0.

13. Alexander Grigor'yev, "Vladimir Markin: 'Navalnyy smozhet borot'sya s korruptsiyey i iz tyur'my'" [Vladimir Markin: 'Navalny can fight against corruption from prison'], *Izvestiya*, April 12, 2013, at http://izvestia.ru/news/548376.

14. "Putin Ally Lambasts Western Values Embodied by Conchita Wurst," Reuters, May 15, 2014, at www.reuters.com/article/2014/05/15/us-germany-russia-idUSKBN0DV0YB20140515.

15. See Miriam Elder and Chris McGreal, "USAid Ordered out of Moscow as Putin's Protest Crackdown Continues," *The Guardian*, September 18, 2012, at www.theguardian.com/world/2012/sep/18/usaid-moscow-putin-protest.

16. Early in his presidency, Putin sent similar signals with a series of arrests and trials of Russian analysts and former U.S. intelligence officers who had entered the Russian private sector. They were singled out for actions and contacts that would never have raised any flags in the West. See Herspring and Kipp (2001), p. 11, and Scott Peterson and Fred Weir, "Pope Case a Resurgence for Russian Spy Agency," *Christian Science Monitor*, December 6, 2000, at www.csmonitor.com/2000/1206/p1s3.html.

17. For example, Alisher Usmanov, who made his fortune in metals and then branched out into telecommunications and media holdings, for a time owned 10 percent of Facebook and was heavily invested in Apple. See Ilya Khrennikov and Yuliya Fedorinova, "Billionaire Usmanov Aims at China after Apple, Facebook Sale," Bloomberg, March 18, 2014, at www.bloomberg.com/news/2014-03-17/billionaire-usmanov-turns-to-china-after-selling-apple-facebook.html. A former business associate of Usmanov's, Yury Milner, also successfully invested in Western social media companies. On top of owning Mail.ru, which in turn owns VK.com, Russia's largest social network, *Forbes* reports that "Milner was one of the first major backers of Facebook in 2009 and has since steered investments in a handful of late-stage Internet giants like Groupon (IPO 2011), Zynga (IPO 2011), Spotify, and Airbnb through DST Global, the investment fund he manages. Having led a reported $400 million funding round in Twitter in 2011, DST's stake was worth $1.2 billion at the time of the company's IPO in November. Milner himself has also piled money into a string of earlier-stage companies, including 23andMe, Genapsys, and Coursera." See "#35: Yuri Milner," *Forbes*, at www.forbes.com/profile/yuri-milner/.

18. See the discussion in Herspring and Kipp (2001), p. 10.

19. Ewan MacAskill, "Putin Calls Internet a 'CIA Project' Renewing Fears of Web Breakup," *The Guardian*, April 24, 2014, at www.theguardian.com/world/2014/apr/24/vladimir-putin-web-breakup-internet-cia.

20. See Rebecca DiLeonardo, "Russia President Signs Law Re-Criminalizing Libel and Slander," July 30, 2012, at http://jurist.org/paperchase/2012/07/russia-president-signs-law-re-criminalizing-libel-and-slander.php.

21. Blogs that received over 3,000 daily hits were required to register as official media outlets. Users of open Wi-Fi networks had to show their identification before use. For more on these laws, see "Russia Internet Blacklist Law Takes Effect," *BBC News*, October 31, 2013, at www.bbc.com/news/technology-20096274; Michael Birnbaum, "Russian Blogger Law Puts New Restrictions on Internet Freedoms," *Washington Post*, July 31, 2014, at www.washingtonpost.com/world/russian-blogger-law-puts-new-restrictions-on-internet-freedoms/2014/07/31/42a05924-a931-459f-acd2-6d08598c375b_story.html; "Russia Demands Internet Users Show ID to Access Public Wifi," Reuters, August 8, 2014, at www.reuters.com/article/2014/08/08/us-russia-internet-idUSKBN0G81RV20140808. Cable carriers and print publications that formerly had enjoyed a degree of freedom were also brought under new leadership. And Pavel Durov, the owner and founder of Russia's most popular social media site, VKontake, was compelled to leave his position as general director and sell his shares in the company after refusing to share user data with the government. Durov left Russia. See Miriam Elder, "CEO of 'Russian Facebook' Says He Was Fired and That the Social Network Is Now in the Hands of Putin Allies," *BuzzFeed*, April 21, 2014, at www.buzzfeed.com/miriamelder/ceo-of-russian-facebook-says-he-was-fired-and-that-the-socia#2frolnd. The attack on independent TV station Dozhd' is addressed in chapter 10.

22. See, for example, Jill Dougherty, "Everybody Lies: The Ukraine Conflict and Russia's Media Transformation," Shorenstein Center on Media Politics and Public Policy, Discussion Paper Series D-88, July 2014, at http://shorensteincenter.org/everyone-lies-ukraine-conflict-russias-media-transformation/.

23. "Ukaz Prezidenta Rossii RF ot 20.10.2012 N 1416 'O sovershenstvovanii gosudarstvennoy politiki v oblasti patrioticheskogo vospitaniya'" [Presidential Decree of October 20, 2012, No. 1416, 'On improving state policy on patriotic education'], October 20, 2012, at http://graph.document.kremlin.ru/page.aspx?1;1630683.

24. Anna Pushkarskaya and Taisiya Bekbulatova, "Kreml' prodolzhit obucheniye za rubezhom" [The Kremlin continues its education abroad], *Kommersant*, October 2, 2013, at www.kommersant.ru/doc/2309989.

25. Underscoring this point, in May 2014 Putin signed a law making it illegal to question or deny either Nazi crimes or the Soviet role in World War II. The message

was that once an official version of history was established, it became an immutable fact. It was not open to reinterpretation. See Alexei Anishchuk, "Russia's Putin Outlaws Denial of Nazi Crimes," Reuters, May 5, 2014, at www.reuters.com/article/2014/05/05/us-russia-putin-nazi-law-idUSBREA440IV20140505.

26. See Gabrielle Tétrault-Farber, "RIA Novosti Staff to Remain 'In Demand' at New Agency," *Moscow Times,* December 11, 2013, at www.themoscowtimes.com/news/article/ria-novosti-staff-to-remain-in-demand-at-new-agency/491236.html.

27. See also "Revamp Underway at State News Agency RIA Novosti," RIA Novosti, March 11, 2014, at www.themoscowtimes.com/news/article/revamp-underway-at-state-news-agency-ria-novosti/495869.html.

28. See "Russian News Agency RIA Novosti Closed Down," *BBC News,* December 9, 2013, at www.bbc.com/news/world-europe-25299116.

29. During his August 2014 trip to Latin America to attend the BRICS summit, Putin secured Argentina's agreement to broadcast Russia's RT over its airwaves round-the-clock. Argentina became the first South American country to broadcast RT Spanish, a major success for the Kremlin media team. See "The Opinion-Makers: How Russia Is Winning the Propaganda War," *Spiegel Online,* May 30, 2014, at www.spiegel.de/international/world/russia-uses-state-television-to-sway-opinion-at-home-and-abroad-a-971971.html.

30. This claim was bolstered by RT signing on former CNN host Larry King for a regular show in 2013. See Lloyd Grove, "Larry King's Russian TV Dilemma: 'It Would Be Bad If They Tried to Edit Out Things. I Wouldn't Put Up With It,'" *Daily Beast,* March 6, 2014, at www.thedailybeast.com/articles/2014/03/06/larry-king-s-russian-tv-dilemma-it-would-be-bad-if-they-tried-to-edit-out-things-i-wouldn-t-put-up-with-it.html#.

31. For a full rundown of Kiselyov's statements, see Stephen Ennis, "Dmitry Kiselev: Russia's Chief Spin Doctor," *BBC News,* April 1, 2014, at www.bbc.com/news/world-europe-26839216.

32. See Peter Pomerantsev, "Russia and the Menace of Unreality," *The Atlantic,* September 9, 2014, at www.theatlantic.com/international/archive/2014/09/russia-putin-revolutionizing-information-warfare/379880/.

33. See Oliver Bullough, "Inside Russia Today: Counterweight to the Mainstream Media, or Putin's Mouthpiece?," *New Statesman,* May 10, 2013, at www.newstatesman.com/world-affairs/world-affairs/2013/05/inside-russia-today-counterweight-mainstream-media-or-putins-mou; and the website for Julian Assange's show on RT: http://rt.com/tags/the-julian-assange-show/.

34. See Andrew Higgins, "Populists' Rise in Europe Vote Shakes Leaders," *New York Times,* May 26, 2014, at www.nytimes.com/2014/05/27/world/europe/established-parties-rocked-by-anti-europe-vote.html?_r=0. See also Charles Grant, "Marine Le Pen and the Rise of Populism," Center for European Reform, July 20, 2011, at www.cer.org.uk/insights/marine-le-pen-and-rise-populism, and Torreblanca and Leonard (2013).

35. See Stephen Fidler, "Putin Depicts Russia as a Bulwark Against European Decadence," *Wall Street Journal*'s Real Time Brussels blog, September 20, 2013, at http://blogs.wsj.com/brussels/2013/09/20/putin-depicts-russia-as-a-bulwark-against-european-decadence/, and Nina Khrushcheva, "Putin's New 'Values Pact,'" Reuters, March 26, 2014, at http://blogs.reuters.com/great-debate/2014/03/26/putins-new-values-pact/.

36. See "'France Is Plagued by Bankruptcy and Mass Immigration'—Marine Le Pen," RT, July 1, 2013, at http://rt.com/news/marine-le-pen-interview-448/, and Patrick Wintour and Rowena Mason, "Nigel Farage's relationship with Russian media comes under scrutiny," *The Guardian,* March 31, 2014, at www.theguardian.com/politics/2014/mar/31/nigel-farage-relationship-russian-media-scrutiny.

37. As we have already discussed in chapters 3 and 4, in addition to his official position as head of the strategically important Russian railroads, Vladimir Yakunin sponsors and heads a number of Russian patriotic and religious organizations. See Max Delany, "An

Inside Track to Putin's Kremlin," *Moscow Times,* September 28, 2007, at www.themoscow times.com/news/article/an-inside-track-to-putins-kremlin/194008.html. Yakunin has, in essence, served as the Kremlin's "Lord of the Rails," taking charge of and overseeing the physical and metaphysical infrastructure binding Russia together. In the tsarist era, the railroads and the church were similarly fused together. The church blessed the inauguration of the new Russian railway network and used it to expand its reach across Russia's vast territory. Famous icons traveled around the country by rail to be viewed by the faithful—a practice that Yakunin has continued. See Sophia Kishkovskiy, "In Russian Chill, Waiting Hours for Touch of the Holy," *New York Times,* November 23, 2014, at www.nytimes.com/2011/11/24/world/europe/virgin-mary-belt-relic-draws-crowds-in-moscow.html?_r=0. For a sample of Yakunin's conservative views, see "Vladimir Yakunin: Homosexuality Is the Same Threat as Environmental Pollution," Moscow, May 25, 2011, available at www.pravoslavie.ru/english/46736.htm and www.interfax-religion.com/?act=news&div=8484. In March 2014, shortly before the annexation of Crimea, Yakunin accused the United States and a "global financial oligarchy" of trying to destroy Russia. He asserted that the separation of Ukraine from Russia was the revival of a long-established CIA plot. See Catherine Belton, "US Accused of 'Trying to Destroy Russia,'" *Financial Times,* March 6, 2014.

38. This approach was picked up on and flagged by a number of external conservative commentators. See, for example, Kaylan (2014).

39. Private author interview in Washington, D.C., September 2014. The August 2014 conference "Russia, Ukraine, Novorossia: Global Problems and Challenges" was held in Yalta, Crimea, and brought together nationalist figures from around Europe and Russia. Significantly, Putin adviser Sergei Glazyev was one of the keynote speakers. See Catherine Fitzpatrick, "Kremlin Advisor Glazyev Speaks in Yalta, Surrounded by Separatists and European Far Right," *The Interpreter,* August 30, 2014, at www.interpretermag.com/russia-this-week/#4057. See also Polyakova (2014).

40. Putin first spoke of this is his 2012 address to the Federal Assembly. See Vladimir Putin, "Address to the Federal Assembly," December 12, 2012, at http://eng.kremlin.ru/transcripts/4739.

41. "Timchenko Moves Headquarters to Moscow," *Moscow Times,* July 20, 2012, at www.themoscowtimes.com/business/article/timchenko-moves-headquarters-to-moscow/462357.html.

42. See, for example, "South America Cashes in on Russian Food Ban," Deutsche Welle, August 8, 2014, at www.dw.de/south-america-cashes-in-on-russian-food-ban/a-17842215.

43. Vladimir Putin, remarks in a video linkup with the West Alpha drilling rig in the Kara Sea, August 9, 2014, in Russian at http://kremlin.ru/transcripts/46421.

44. See Högselius (2013). The approach worked. In the wake of the Soviets' 1968 invasion of Czechoslovakia, the demands to sanction the USSR foundered when individual countries broke ranks and scrambled to conclude deals with the Soviet Union at the expense of other Western countries.

45. See, for instance, Anatoly Chubais's article on the topic from October 2003, "Missiya Rossii v XXI veke" [Russia's mission in the twenty-first century], *Nezavisimaya gazeta,* October 1, 2003, at www.ng.ru/ideas/2003-10-01/1_mission.html. Russian American scholar Nina Khrushcheva has noted on this point that as "Putin put it himself, 'natural resources offered the key to Russia 'regaining its former might.' Indeed, 'Russia's natural resource potential defines its special place among industrialized countries.' So mankind would once again tremble with respect and fear, this time not of the prospect of a Red Army invasion, but of a Gazprom cutoff of gas." Khrushcheva (2008), pp. 27–29.

46. Author interview with leading U.S. distressed asset manager who represented Russian corporations in many of these deals, Washington D.C., August 2014.

47. The fact that BP's own investment options were more limited and that it had taken a financial drubbing after the Gulf spill meant that it would have less room for maneuver in its new relationship with Rosneft. Putin sent a clear signal that BP's vulnerability was

a source of leverage for Russia when he met with BP chief executive Robert Dudley in January 2011. Putin said: "We're also aware of the problems that BP has encountered very recently in the Gulf of Mexico. But you know, we Russians have a proverb: 'One beaten man is worth two unbeaten ones.'" BP, in other words, was like the serf who is worth more once he's been whipped and learned his place. "Predsedatel' Pravitel'stva Rossii V. V. Putin provyol rabochuyu vstrechu s rukovodstvom kompanii 'British Petroleum'" [Prime minister V. V. Putin conducted a working meeting with the management of the company, British Petroleum], January 14, 2011, at http://archive.premier.gov.ru/events/news/13857/. On Russia's Mistral purchase, see the detailed *Defense Industry Daily* report at www.defensein-dustrydaily.com/russia-to-order-french-mistral-lhds-05749/. The Mistral purchase became a major headache for the French government in 2014 after the imposition of EU sanctions. Whether or not to deliver the completed ships to Russia became a point of domestic and international contention. For more, see Sharon Muthoni and Ryan Faith, "The Russia-France Warship Deal Is Turning into a Total Mess," *Vice News,* November 22, 2014 (https://news.vice.com/article/the-russia-france-warship-deal-is-turning-into-a-total-mess).

48. Guy Adams, "Revealed: The Knights, Peers and Even Members of the Royal Family Who Are Now on the Payroll of Russian Oligarchs," *Mail Online,* July 23, 2014, at www.dailymail.co.uk/news/article-2703574/Revealed-The-knights-peers-members-Royal-Family-payroll-Russian-oligarchs.html.

49. See Česlovas Iškauskas, "Third Energy Package: Dispute between Russia and the EU," *Geopolitka,* March 23, 2001, at www.geopolitika.lt/?artc=4561.

50. James Kanter and Andrew E. Kramer, "Europe Threatens Gazprom with Antitrust Action," *New York Times,* October 3, 2013, at www.nytimes.com/2013/10/04/business/international/europe-threatens-gazprom-with-antitrust-action.html?_r=0. See also Tim Boersma, "Europe's Energy Dilemma," Brookings Institution, June 18, 2014, at www.brookings.edu/research/articles/2014/06/18-europes-energy-dilemma-boersma.

51. For one of many examples of Putin's personal engagement on the issue of the Third Energy Package, see the public discussion between Putin and EU Commission president José Manuel Barroso in February 2011. Putin stated, among other things, that "this 'third energy package' is obviously detrimental to our energy companies. [It amounts to] de facto confiscation of property." See "Prime Minister Vladimir Putin and President of the European Commission José Manuel Barroso give a news conference following the meeting of the Russian government and the EU Commission," February 24, 2011, at http://archive.premier.gov.ru/eng/events/news/14257/. Putin also emphasized this point at the November 2011 Valdai Discussion Club meeting.

52. See Emily Young, "Russian Money in Cyprus: Why Is There So Much?," *BBC News,* March 18, 2013, at www.bbc.com/news/business-21831943.

53. Shaun Walker, "Cyprus Bailout—The Russian Angle: Vladimir Putin Hits out at 'Unjust and Dangerous' Bank Levy," *The Independent,* March 18, 2013, at www.independent.co.uk/news/world/europe/cyprus-bailout--the-russian-angle-vladimir-putin-hits-out-at-unjust-and-dangerous-bank-levy-8539502.html.

54. Authors' discussions with German, UK, and EU officials in May 2014.

55. In theory two other entities, the Commonwealth of Independent States and the Eurasian Economic Community (EvrazEC), were already in place to do just this, but they had essentially been abandoned by the other members. Putin bemoaned the failure of these entities in his March 18, 2014, speech, hinting that it might not have been necessary even to promote the Eurasian Union, or even end up annexing Crimea, had Ukraine and the other former Soviet states not kept leaving Russia's economic and political institutions. A senior Russian business executive made this exact same point in a private interview with the authors in early 2013—another example of key Russian figures echoing Putin's comments.

56. "Russia Pushing for EU Visa-Free Travel Deal in January," RIA Novosti, December 6, 2013, at en.ria.ru/russia/20131207/185311112/Russia-Pushing-for-EU-Visa-Free-Travel-Deal-in-January.html.

57. Author private interviews with senior EU officials in multiple meetings from November 2013 to September 2014.

58. See Stent (2014), p. 168.

59. See, for example, Andrey Kurkov, "Is Ukraine Next?," *New Statesman,* September 4, 2008, at www.newstatesman.com/europe/2008/09/russia-ukraine-georgia.

60. See Clifford Levy, "Ukraine Woos Russia with Lease Deal," *New York Times,* April 21, 2010, at www.nytimes.com/2010/04/22/world/europe/22ukraine.html.

61. When he fled the country in February 2014, Yanukovych left behind a rather surprising paper trail of how much money he had siphoned from the state coffers. A group of Ukrainian journalists has since posted many of the documents online at www.yanukovychlinks.org. For more, see Mikhail Bushuev, "'Yanukovych Leaks' Documents Abuse of Office," Deutsche Welle, March 16, 2014, at www.dw.de/yanukovych-leaks-documents-abuse-of-office/a-17499525.

62. The links between Yanukovych's corruption and Putin's Russia are well chronicled in a 2014 report by the Legatum Institute, Bullough (2014), and in Anders Aslund, "Payback Time for the 'Yanukovych Family,'" Peterson Institute for International Economics, December 11, 2013, at http://blogs.piie.com/realtime/?p=4162.

63. After the February 2014 events, the authors were told by several senior European officials that Putin had personally intervened by phone with Yanukovych during the negotiations apparently to get him to sign the agreement. In their view, Putin was as shocked as everyone else when Yanukovych took off. He felt completely betrayed by the whole process and suspected that the Europeans had somehow orchestrated this. Other European officials had their own suspicions that it was Putin who had pulled the plug on Yanukovych and had instructed him to leave Ukraine during the phone call. They pointed to the fact that the Russian envoy to the talks, Ombudsman for Human Rights Vladimir Lukin, did not actually sign the final version of the agreement. See "Russia's Ombudsman Explains Why He Didn't Sign Agreement in Kiev," TASS, February 22, 2014, at http://en.itar-tass.com/russia/720391. Whatever the case may be, Yanukovych's flight was a moment of high drama and a major turning point in the crisis.

64. "Extracts from Putin News Conference on Ukraine," Reuters, March 4, 2014, at reuters.com/article/2014/03/04/ukraine-crisis-putin-extracts-idUSL6N0M13BN20140304.

65. Putin spoke of the Eurasian Union as "a project to preserve the identity of the people who inhabit the historic Eurasian space." See Leon Neyfakh, "Putin's Long Game? Meet the Eurasian Union," *Boston Globe,* March 9, 2014, at www.bostonglobe.com/ideas/2014/03/09/putin-long-game-meet-eurasian-union/1eKLXEC3TJfzqK54elX5fL/story.html.

66. Putin referred to the customary story that his namesake, Grand Prince Vladimir of Kyiv, had assumed Christianity on behalf of Russia through his baptism in Khersones in Crimea—to become the holy Prince Vladimir of Putin's March 18, 2014, speech.

67. See Vladimir Putin, "Konferentsiya Pravoslavno-slavyanskiye tsennosti—osnova tsivilizatsionnogo vybora Ukrainy" [Conference on Orthodox and Slavic values—The basis of Ukraine's civilizational choice], July 27, 2013, at http://kremlin.ru/transcripts/18961.

68. See Katarzyna Jarzynska, "Patriarch Kirill's Game over Ukraine," Center for Eastern Studies, August 14, 2014, at www.osw.waw.pl/en/publikacje/osw-commentary/2014-08-14/patriarch-kirills-game-over-ukraine.

69. Kyiv's interim government signed the political provisions of the association agreement on March 24, 2014, after Moscow's annexation of Crimea.

70. See "Ukraine Crisis: Transcript of Leaked Nuland-Pyatt Call," *BBC News,* February 7, 2014, at www.bbc.com/news/world-europe-26079957.

71. Several senior European officials told the authors in interviews that Putin had complained vehemently to them about these appearances in Kyiv and had accused both the United States and the EU of funding the protests.

72. At a Russia-EU summit in January 2014, Putin said: "Second, as for advice to Ukraine on what to do and how to do it, I think the Ukrainian people are quite capable of deciding this for themselves. In any case, Russia has no intention of ever intervening. I can imagine how our European partners would react if at the height of the crisis in Greece or Cyprus, say, our foreign minister turned up at one of the anti–European Union meetings there and began making appeals to the crowd." See "Russia-EU summit," January 28, 2014, at http://eng.kremlin.ru/transcripts/6575. At the Seliger youth camp in August 2014, Putin said: "Our Western partners, with the support of fairly radically inclined and nationalist-leaning groups, carried out a coup d'état there. No matter what anyone says, we all understand what happened. There are no fools among us. We all saw the symbolic pies handed out on the Maidan. This information and political support, what does it mean? This was a case of the United States and European countries getting fully involved in a change of power, an anti-constitutional change of power carried out by force." "Vladimir Putin at the Seliger 2014 National Youth Forum," August 29, 2014, at http://eng.kremlin.ru/transcripts/22864.

73. See Vanessa Mock, "Russia, Ukraine Deadlocked in Gas Talks," *Wall Street Journal*, June 11, 2014, at http://online.wsj.com/articles/russia-extends-ukraine-gas-talks-deadline-1402475375.

74. See Clifford G. Gaddy and Barry W. Ickes, "Ukraine: A Prize Neither Russia nor the West Can Afford to Win," Brookings Institution, May 22, 2014, at www.brookings.edu/research/articles/2014/05/21-ukraine-prize-russia-west-ukraine-gaddy-ickes.

75. See, for example, Simon Shuster, "Putin Says Ukraine's Revolutionaries Are Anti-Semites. Is He Right?," *Time*, March 6, 2014, at http://time.com/14289/ukraine-putin-anti-semites/#14289/ukraine-putin-anti-semites/.

76. Putin used this term on a few occasions, including during his annual televised call-in session with the Russian population on April 17, 2014. The transcript for the sessions is at http://kremlin.ru/news/20796. The term "Novorossiya" was applied to lands around the Black Sea conquered from the Ottoman Empire during the reign of Catherine the Great in the eighteenth century, and included the city of Odesa, which became the region's administrative center in the nineteenth century. Large parts of Ukrainian territory with its Orthodox population were also referred to as Little (or Lesser) Russia (*Malaya Rossiya*), first in ecclesiastical and later in political documents from the late fourteenth century until the Russian Revolution.

77. The Kremlin solemnly noted that the Russian president's brother was interred in a mass grave at the St. Petersburg cemetery. See "70-letiye snyatiya blokadiy Leningrad" [The 70th anniversary of the lifting of the siege of Leningrad], January 27, 2014, at http://kremlin.ru/news/20110.

78. This is based on author personal interview with Lynn Berry, the Moscow bureau chief for the Associated Press, in Washington, D.C., April 3, 2014. Berry, one of the longest-serving foreign correspondents in Moscow, closely monitored the content of the Russian media in this period and the timing of specific broadcasts. Note that at this juncture of World War II, the territory of Ukraine was under German occupation and the Crimean city of Sevastopol—which was then part of the Russian republic and not Ukraine—was also under siege.

79. See Vladimir Putin, "Obrashcheniye Prezidenta Rossiyskoy Federatsii" [Address by the President of the Russian Federation], March 18, 2014, available on the Kremlin's website archive (in Russian) at http://news.kremlin.ru/news/20603/print. An English translation is available at http://eng.news.kremlin.ru/news/6889/print.

80. Both during and after World War II, Soviet leader Josef Stalin ordered many of those who had found themselves under occupation by the Germans to be deported en masse, imprisoned in the gulag, or simply shot. In some cases there was no evidence of mass collaboration beyond the efforts of the invading German forces to exploit minority grievances against the Soviets as they moved deeper into the USSR. Ukrainian nationalist

partisans were among these alleged fifth columns, along with Estonians, Latvians, Georgians, and entire ethnic groups such as the Crimean Tatars and the Chechens, whose settlement on the fringes of the state had exposed them to the earliest phases of the invasion. See Nekrich (1981) and previous note on the Chechen deportations. See chapter 10, note 84, on p. 472.

81. During the Russian Revolution, Vladimir Lenin and the Bolsheviks tried to harness Ukrainian nationalist thinkers to their political struggle. Lenin also attempted to use Ukrainian nationalism as a counterweight to Russian nationalism, which he feared would undermine his centralized Communist Party and new supranational socialist state. It was Lenin who pushed for the territories of "New Russia" to be incorporated into the Ukrainian Socialist Republic—specifically to reduce the size of the Russian Republic and dilute the appeal of Russian nationalism. After Lenin's death, Ukrainian Communist Party leaders demanded more autonomy from Moscow, and, in response, Soviet leader Josef Stalin purged the Ukrainian political leadership. By the late 1930s, Ukraine had been brutalized by Stalin's rural collectivization and urbanization policies, which resulted in a devastating famine. See also Pipes (1997).

82. See Anderson (2000), pp. 325–51. Anderson recounts how, in the very early stages of the war, Germans singled out Ukrainians for preferential treatment. Nazi political ideologue Alfred Rosenberg had conceived of a hierarchy of peoples in Eastern Europe: "a sort of racial ladder, where Ukrainians occupied the highest position, with Poles, Russians and sundry 'Asiatics' scattered below them. Jews . . . belonged at the very bottom. . . . As the German offensive carried . . . into the Caucasus . . . Caucasians (Georgians, for example) [were afforded] status similar to that of Ukrainians." Ukraine's sizable Jewish population bore the brunt of Nazi brutality, and many were also killed by nationalist partisans. The occupying force's favorable treatment of Ukrainians and others was, however, short-lived.

83. See Matt Ford, "Good News from Ukraine: Everyone Still Hates Hitler," *The Atlantic*, March 20, 2014, at www.theatlantic.com/international/archive/2014/03/good-news-from-ukraine-everyone-still-hates-hitler/284489/. For a synopsis of the history of Ukraine's relations with Russia and the impact of World War II as it specifically relates to the events of 2014, see Timothy Snyder, "Ukrainian Extremists Will Only Triumph if Russia Invades," *New Republic*, April 17, 2014, at www.newrepublic.com/article/117395/historic-ukrainian-russian-relations-impact-maidan-revolution. A revised version of this article, "The Battle in Ukraine Means Everything: Fascism Returns to the Continent It Destroyed," was published in the *New Republic* on May 11, 2014, at www.newrepublic.com/article/117692/fascism-returns-ukraine.

84. See, for instance, Putin's November 5, 2014, meeting with young academics and history teachers at http://kremlin.ru/news/46951, where he argued that the Molotov-Ribbentrop Pact gave the Soviet Union time to modernize its army for an "inevitable" war with Nazi Germany. See also Anthony Faiola, "A Ghost of World War II History Haunts Ukraine's Standoff with Russia," *Washington Post*, March 25, 2014, at www.washington post.com/world/a-ghost-of-world-war-ii-history-haunts-ukraines-standoff-with-russia/2014/03/25/18d4b1e0-a503-4f73-aaa7-5dd5d6a1c665_story.html.

85. During Putin's meeting at the Russian youth camp in Seliger in August 2014, he essentially defined four categories of Russians: 1) [implicit] loyalists; 2) "official" oppositionists—parliamentary parties—who differ with the Kremlin on a number of issues but demonstrated their patriotism by backing the annexation of Crimea; 3) the "patriotic" part of the "non-systemic opposition"; and, finally, 4) those in the non-systemic opposition "who feel differently." Putin made it clear that he considered the first three categories to be *nash* [ours]; the last category was clearly not. Those in that category were traitors for all intents and purposes, and *chuzhoy* [alien]. Putin also went on to remind Russian politicians on the Left (the communists) of *their* own "dirty secret": the Bolsheviks were also traitors to Russia. They undermined the state during World War I (as we will note later). So no

matter what good the communists might have done subsequently, including in World War II, they were also not free of sin. See "Vladimir Putin at the Seliger 2014 National Youth Forum," August 29, 2014, at http://eng.kremlin.ru/transcripts/22864.

86. See the section "A System Based on Distrust" in chapter 9.

87. See, for example, Alexandra Odynova, "WikiLeaks: Putin's 'Personal Gripe' with Estonia Result of WWII Betrayal," *Moscow Times,* September 6, 2011, at www.the moscowtimes.com/news/article/wikileaks-putins-personal-gripe-with-estonia-result-of-wwii-betrayal/443254.html.

88. "Russian Parliament Passes Bill on Using Troops Abroad," RIA Novosti, October 23, 2009, at http://en.ria.ru/military_news/20091023/156570108.html.

89. A hasty Russian parliamentary resolution gave Putin the right to take action in defense of Russians and Russian interests in Crimea and elsewhere on the territory of Ukraine. See Shaun Walker and Harriet Salem, "Russian Parliament Approves Troop Deployment in Ukraine," *The Guardian,* March 1, 2014, at www.theguardian.com/world/2014/mar/02/russia-parliament-approves-military-ukraine-vladimir-putin.

90. In private discussions at the Brookings Institution, one Russian analyst and scholar from Moscow observed that around the crisis in Ukraine and the annexation in Crimea, Putin's references to the Russian Federation were couched in the idea that Russia/*Rossiya* was much bigger, far more, than the contemporary official federalized state. For Putin, the scholar asserted, "the Russian Federation is [was] only an 'ugly stop' on the way back to the revival of Great Russia."

91. See "More Russians Support Annexation of Crimea, Poll Shows," *Moscow Times,* September 2, 2014, at www.themoscowtimes.com/news/article/more-russians-support-annexation-of-crimea-poll-shows/506247.html. At the Seliger Youth Forum in August 2014, Putin noted how widespread domestic support for the annexation of Crimea was in Russia. He said: "Now with regard to the nationally oriented opposition, whether there is one. Yes, of course there is. I spoke about the parliamentary parties. Remember the fierce competition during the 2012 presidential campaign? I already spoke about it. It was tough and absolutely uncompromising, and sometimes even somewhat indecent, I think, but nevertheless. And the way people united around the events in Crimea, when everyone felt and understood that we are right." See "Vladimir Putin at the Seliger 2014 National Youth Forum," August 29, 2014, at http://eng.kremlin.ru/transcripts/22864.

92. Author discussion in July 2014 with World Bank representative and Central Asia expert.

93. See, for example, "Orban Renews Autonomy Call for Hungarians in Ukraine," Reuters, May 17, 20914, at www.reuters.com/article/2014/05/17/us-ukraine-crisis-hungary-autonomy-idUSBREA4G04520140517. Putin and Russia also received words of support for the annexation of Crimea from some of the European Right, including France's Marine Le Pen. See "Crimea Is Historically Part of Russia, Referendum Was Legitimate—Marine Le Pen's Spokesman," *Voice of Russia,* March 20, 2014, at http://voiceofrussia.com/2014_03_20/Crimea-is-historically-part-of-Russia-referendum-was-legitimate-Marine-Le-Pens-spokesman-4640/.

94. At a reception for veterans of World War II/Great Patriotic War, Putin explained: "The unity of our multinational, multiconfessional nation is the greatest legacy of our victory [over Germany in World War II]." See "Torzhestvennyy priyom po sluchayu Dnya Pobediy" [Reception in honor of Victory Day], May 8, 2014, at http://kremlin.ru/news/20988.

95. See Courtney Weaver, "Chechens Join Pro-Russians in Battle for East Ukraine," *Financial Times,* May 27, 2014, at www.ft.com/intl/cms/s/0/dcf5e16e-e5bc-11e3-aeef-00144feabdc0.html#axzz33EOnse4i.

96. Alexei Makarkin, deputy director of the Moscow-based think tank Center for Political Technologies, cited in Gabrielle Tétrault-Farber, "Chechens in Ukraine Capture

Public Interest," *Moscow Times,* May 28, 2014, at www.themoscowtimes.com/news/article/chechens-in-ukraine-capture-public-interest/501105.html.

97. This was consistent with Putin's commentary in the March 18, 2014, speech when he criticized the Bolsheviks for giving away historic Russian territory to their new Soviet republic of Ukraine; or when he chastised the Bolsheviks (see chapter 3) for effectively destroying the Russian Orthodox Church and other indigenous religions in the 1920s and 1930s and thus depriving the state of useful tools for mobilizing the support of the population.

98. Vladimir Putin, "Vserossiyskiy molodyezhniy forum 'Seliger-2014'" [All-Russian Youth Forum 'Seliger 2014'] August 24, 2014, http://news.kremlin.ru/transcripts/46507.

99. See, for example, Ellen Barry, "Foes of America in Russia Crave Rupture in Ties," *New York Times,* March 15, 2014, at www.nytimes.com/2014/03/16/world/europe/foes-of-america-in-russia-crave-rupture-in-ties.html, and Paul Ames, "Europe's Far Right Is Rootin' for Putin," *Global Post,* April 10, 2014, at www.globalpost.com/dispatch/news/regions/europe/140409/europe-far-right-rootin-for-putin.

100. See Mackinder (1904) and Dugin (1997).

101. Simon Shuster, "Russia Embraces Europe's Far Right Even As It Fears 'Contagion,'" *Time,* May 27, 2014, at http://time.com/#120650/russia-europe-far-right/. Also see an appearance by Prokhanov on the television channel Russia24, at www.vesti.ru/videos/show/vid/581823/cid/7/.

102. The citation is from Shuster in *Time.*

103. See, for example, Oleg Shynarenko, "Alexander Dugin: The Crazy Ideologue of the New Russian Empire," *Daily Beast,* April 2, 2014, at www.thedailybeast.com/articles/2014/04/02/alexander-dugin-the-crazy-ideologue-of-the-new-russian-empire.html#.

104. Ellen Barry of the *New York Times* told the authors in March 2014 that Prokhanov himself had told her this in interviews. He had expressed surprise, as well as appreciation, that he was called into action by the Kremlin, after years of generally sitting on the sidelines.

105. See Paul Sonne, "Russian Nationalists Feel Let Down by Kremlin, Again," *Wall Street Journal,* July 4, 2014, http://online.wsj.com/articles/russian-nationalists-feel-let-down-by-kremlin-again-1404510139

106. See chapter 12.

107. See, for instance, the books by Tat'yana Gracheva, *Nevidimaya Khazariya* [Hidden Khazariya] and *Svyataya Rus protiv Khazarii* [Holy Rus' against Khazariya], which offer a purportedly nonfictional account of a set of international plots, dating far back into history, where Jewish interests, now led by the United States and U.S.-dominated international institutions, seek to compromise and constrain Russia and the Russian Orthodox Church. Gracheva is a colonel in the Red Army and head of the foreign languages and literature department of the General Staff Academy. Her books may not have been widely read in Russia (they are available on Amazon UK's website), but they were published by Putin's close associate, Vladimir Yakunin, through one of his subsidiary companies. The authors were presented with a copy of the first book by Yakunin personally. When the authors asked him about the book, Yakunin stressed that it was important to give everyone's point of view a voice and that there was an audience for this kind of book. Yakunin has made similar inferences to Gracheva's stories about Jewish American plots in his own publications and public appearances. Yakunin's book *New Technologies of Struggle against Russian Statehood* (Yakunin 2013) is available in Russian at http://rusrand.ru/dev/novye-tehnologii-borby-s-rossijskoj-gosudarstvennostju. An example of Gracheva's ideas may be seen in her nearly two-hour-long video lecture on YouTube at www.youtube.com/watch?v=8E18AZbjyvk. The film was produced in 2009 at the studios of the Holy Trinity Monastery in Sergeyev Posad. Gracheva is presented as a "political scientist and department head at the Military Academy of the General Staff of the Armed Forces of the Russian Federation." The film's credits state that it was produced with financial support from a

presidential grant. On Gracheva's anti-Semitism, see also Shimon Briman, "Antisemits-kaya bomba v Genshtabe rossiyskoy armii" [Anti-Semitic bomb in the general staff of the Russian army], August 4, 2009, at http://izrus.co.il/diasporaIL/article/2009-08-04/5727.html#ixzz38zF4pK1K.

108. Vladimir Putin, "Vstrecha s predstavitelyami mezhdunarodnykh obshchestvennykh i religioznykh organizatsiy" [Meeting with representatives of international public and religious organizations], July 9, 2014, at http://kremlin.ru/transcripts/46180, in Russian. In English at http://eng.kremlin.ru/transcripts/22635. In July 2014, Putin met with Jewish representatives in Sevastopol in Crimea to commemorate the Holocaust. See "At Crimean Holocaust Event, Putin Burnishes His Image as Defender of Minorities," *Haaretz,* at www.haaretz.com/jewish-world/jewish-world-features/.premium-1.605696. For additional background, see Anshel Pfeffer, "The New Dilemma for Jews in Ukraine," *Haaretz,* February 25, 2014, at www.haaretz.com/jewish-world/jewish-world-news/.premium-1.576372#!.

109. The cartoon is at http://kprf.ru/party-live/cknews/127574.html. For the persistence and prevalence of such cartoons, see Kotek (2009).

110. The authors personally spotted a copy of the *Protocols* on sale in a Russian Orthodox bookstore in Tver in 2004.

111. See Vladislav Goncharov's foreword to the 2005 fantasy *The Moscow Labyrinth,* by Oleg Kulagin. See also Peter Pomerantsev, "How Putin Is Reinventing Warfare," *Foreign Policy,* May 5, 2014, at www.foreignpolicy.com/articles/2014/05/05/how_putin_is_reinventing_warfare.

112. Blurbs about the seven novels in the series "Battlefield Ukraine," published by Eksmo, are available at http://fiction.eksmo.ru/filter/serie/ukraina-pole-boya-fantastiches-kiy-boevik_ID344973/. On Eksmo's status as Russia's largest publishing house, see Eugene Gerden, "Eksmo and AST: Russia's Two Publishing Giants Merge," at http://publishingperspectives.com/2014/01/eksmo-and-ast-russias-two-publishing-giants-merge/.

113. The long-established role of novels and literature in framing and reframing Russian politics is laid out in Khrushcheva (2008).

114. The entire program, lasting over an hour, was broadcast on a major Russian television station, Rossiya 2. The full video can be watched at www.vesti.ru/broadcasts/show/id/35731/. Among its many dimensions, the extravaganza was a deliberate perversion of Western popular culture, ranging from rip-offs of shows such as the Blue Man Group and *Stomp,* with masked, painted men drumming, the film *Clockwork Orange,* and The Who's "Tommy," to Pink Floyd's "The Wall," and a host of other U.S. and British shows. Giant hands reached down from the skies (U.S. hands wearing an American eagle insignia ring) toward the participants in the staged protests, accompanied by the menacing sounds of the alien invaders from the film version of *The War of the Worlds.*

115. Indeed, Putin even commissioned a commemorative coin to mark the occasion, and a commemorative medal for the Russian armed forces, which noted the "Return of Crimea" and the dates of February 20, 2013, to March 18, 2014, for the duration of the campaign.

116. As Russian American scholar and Nabokov expert Nina Khrushcheva has put it, this was the epitome of "'Putinism' (an all-inclusive hybrid Brezhnevism, communism, KGB-ism, market-ism with some remaining freedoms) as a comforting 'golden mean' between radical reforms and strong-arm rule." Khrushcheva (2008), p. 29.

117. Vladimir Putin, "Meeting with Representatives of State Duma Political Party Groups," Yalta, Crimea Republic, August 14, 2014, at http://eng.kremlin.ru/news/22820.

118. In an August 2014 Levada Center poll, when asked to select the answer that best explained the Ukrainian leadership's desire to move toward Europe and away from Russia, 52 percent of respondents said that they agreed with the statement that "Ukraine has become a marionette in the hands of the West and the United States, who are pursuing an anti-Russian policy." See "Ukrainskiy krizis: deystviya rukovodstva Ukrainy i Rossii" [The crisis in Ukraine: the actions of Ukraine and Russia], Levada Center, August 12, 2014, at www.levada.ru/12-08-2014/ukrainskii-krizis-deistviya-rukovodstva-ukrainy-i-rossii.

119. This is the only instance in the book where Putin uses the term "mission." Gevorkyan, Timakova, and Kolesnikov (2000), p. 133.

120. For example, in a poll conducted in September 2014 by GfK Ukraine, the polling agency found a marked increase in the numbers of Ukrainians who would support Ukraine's entry into NATO. See, "Bil'she polovini ymovirhikh viybortsiv za vstup Ukraini do NATO ta proti miru na umovakh peredachi teritoriy pid kontrol' Rosiyi," [More than half of likely voters are for the entry of Ukraine into NATO and against a peace [settlement] under terms transferring territory to Russian control], GfK Ukraine, September 29, 2014, at www.gfk.ua/ua/news-and-events/press-room/press-releases/pages/politics-290914.aspx.

121. Gevorkyan, Timakova, and Kolesnikov (2000), p. 160.

BIBLIOGRAPHY

Abdulatipov, Ramazan "O federativnoy i natsional'noy politike Rossiyskogo gosudarstva" [On the federal and national policies of the Russian state], *CMG Bulletin,* June 1995.

Akhmadov, Ilyas, and Nicholas Daniloff, *Chechnya's Secret Wartime Diplomacy: Aslan Maskhadov and the Quest for a Peaceful Resolution* (New York: Palgrave McMillan, 2013).

Akiner, Shirin, and Catherine Barnes, *Politics of Compromise: The Tajikistan Peace Process* (London: Conciliation Resources, Accord Series, 2001). Online at www.c-r.org/accord-article/tajik-civil-war-causes-and-dynamics.

Albats, Yevgeniya, and Yermolin, Anatoliy, "Korporatsiya 'Rossiya': Putin s druz'yami podelili stranu" ["Russia" Inc.: Putin and his friends have divided up the country], *Novoe Vremya/The New Times,* No. 36, October 31, 2011.

Alexseev, Mikhail, "Overcounting Russia's Muslims: Implications for Security and Society," PONARS Eurasia Policy Memo No. 27, August 2008 (www.gwu.edu/~ieresgwu/assets/docs/pepm_027.pdf).

Anderson, Truman O., "Germans, Ukrainians and Jews: Ethnic Politics in Heeresgebiet Süd, June–December 1941," *War in History,* Vol. 7, No. 3 (2000).

Andrew, Christopher, and Vasili Mitrokhin, *The Sword and Shield* (New York: Basic Books, 1999).

Antonenko, Oksana, *New Russian Analytical Centers and Their Role in Political Decisionmaking* (Harvard University, John F. Kennedy School of Government: Strengthening Democratic Institutions Project, February 1996).

Aron, Leon, *Yeltsin: A Revolutionary Life* (New York: St. Martin's Press, 2000).

———, *Roads to the Temple: Truth, Memory, Ideas, and Ideals in the Making of the Russian Revolution, 1987–1991* (Yale University Press, 2012).

Ascher, Abraham, *P. A. Stolypin: The Search for Stability in Late Imperial Russia* (Stanford University Press, 2002).

Asmus, Ronald, *A Little War That Shook the World: Georgia, Russia, and the Future of the West* (New York: Palgrave Macmillan, 2010).

Azadovskii, Konstantin, "Russia's Silver Age," in Heyward Isham (ed.), *Remaking Russia: Voices from Within* (Armonk, N.Y.: M. E. Sharpe, 1995).

Baker, Frederick, "The Red Army Graffiti in the Reichstag, Berlin," in Christopher Chippindale and George Nash (eds.), *European Landscapes of Rock-Art* (London: Routledge, 2002).

Baker, Peter, and Susan Glasser, *Kremlin Rising* (New York: Scribner, 2005).

Batuman, Elif, "The Bells: How Harvard Helped Preserve a Russian Legacy," *The New Yorker*, April 27, 2009.

Berlin, Isaiah, *Russian Thinkers* (Harmondsworth, Middlesex: Penguin Books, 1978).

Bestuzhev, I. B., *Bor'ba v Rossii po voprosam vneshney politiki, 1906–1910* [The struggle in Russia over questions of foreign policy, 1906–1910] (Moscow: Akademiya nauk SSSR, 1961).

Billington, James H. *The Icon and the Axe: An Interpretive History of Russian Culture* (New York: Knopf, 1966).

Blotskiy, Oleg, *Vladimir Putin: doroga k vlasti* [Vladimir Putin: the road to power] (Moscow: OSMOS-PRESS, 2002).

———, *Vladimir Putin: istoriya zhizni* [Vladimir Putin: history of a life] (Moscow: Mezhdunarodnye otnosheniya, 2002).

Bobkov, Filipp Denisovich, *KGB i vlast'. 45 let v organakh gosudarstvennoy bezopasnosti* [The KGB and the regime. 45 years in the institutions of state security] (Moscow: Izd. "Veteran MP," 1995).

Brown, Archie, *The Gorbachev Factor* (Oxford University Press, 1996).

Burnham, William, and Alexei Trochev, "Russia's War between the Courts: The Struggle over the Jurisdictional Boundary between the Constitutional Court and the Regular Courts," *American Journal of Comparative Law*, Vol. 55, No.3 (Summer 2007).

Bullough, Oliver, *The Last Man in Russia: The Struggle to Save a Dying Nation* (New York: Basic Books, 2013).

———, "Looting Ukraine: How East and West Teamed Up to Steal a Country," Legatum Institute's Transitions Forum, July 2014 (www.li.com/activities/publications/looting-ukraine-how-east-and-west-teamed-up-to-steal-a-country).

Bush, George W., *Decision Points* (New York: Crown, 2010).

Chaadayev, Pyotr, *Philosophical Letters* (1826–31), first published in journal *Teleskope* (1836).

Charap, Samuel, "The Petersburg Experience: Putin's Political Career and Russian Foreign Policy," *Problems of Post-Communism*, Vol. 51, No. 1 (January–February 2004).

Chinyaeva, Elena, "The Search for the 'Russian Idea,'" *Transition*, June 1997.

Chubays, Igor, *Ot russkoy idei k ideye novoy Rossii* [From the Russian idea to the idea of a new Russia] (Moscow: Izd. "GITIS," 1996)

Chubays, Igor, and Vladimir Vedrashko (eds.), *Novyye vekhi: Obshchestvennyy al'manakh demokraticheskoy nauchno-publitsistechskoy mysly o rossiyskoy probleme* [New signposts: A societal almanac of democratic scholarly commentary and political thought on the Russian problem] (Moscow: Izd. Prava cheloveka, 1996).

Clover, Charles, and Catherine Belton, "Inside the Kremlin," *Financial Times Weekend Magazine*, May 5/6, 2012, pp. 26–31

Coleman, Fred, *The Decline and Fall of the Soviet Empire* (New York: St. Martin's Press, 1996).

Coll, Steve, *Private Empire: ExxonMobil and American Power* (New York: Penguin Press, 2012).

Colton, Timothy J., *Yeltsin: A Life* (New York: Basic Books, 2008).

Dawisha, Karen, *Putin's Kleptocracy: Who Owns Russia?* (New York: Simon and Schuster, 2014).

Doder, Dusko, and Louise Branson, *Gorbachev: Heretic in the Kremlin* (New York: Penguin, 1990).

Dukes, Paul (ed.), *Russia and Europe* (London: Collins & Brown, 1991).

Dugin, Alexander, *Osnoviy geopolitiki: geopoliticheskoye budushche Rossii* [The foundations of geopolitics: the geopolitical future of Russia] (Moscow: Arktogeya, 1997).

Dunlop, John, *The Rise of Russia and the Fall of the Soviet Empire* (Princeton University Press, 1993).

The Economist, "Russia's Regions: Fiefs and Chiefs," January 25, 1997

———, "Anatoly Sobchak, a Flawed Reformer, Died on February 20th, Aged 62," February 24, 2000.

———, "Chechnya and the North Caucasus. And They Call It Peace: Vladimir Putin's Presidency began in Chechnya; the Region Is Restive as It Ends," February 28, 2008

———, "Grease My Palm," November 29, 2008.

———, "Gennady Timchenko and Gunvor International BV," July 30, 2009 (www.economist.com/node/14140737).

———, "Briefing: Putin's Russia. Call Back Yesterday," March 3–9, 2012 (www.economist.com/node/21548949).

———, "Gunvor: Riddles, Mysteries and Enigmas," May 5, 2012 (www.economist.com/node/21554185).

Eklof, Ben, John Bushnell, and Larissa Zakharova (eds.), *Russia's Great Reforms, 1855–1881* (University of Indiana Press, 1994).

EPI Center, *Social Policies in Russia*, No.2 (26).

Evangelista, Matthew, *The Chechen Wars: Will Russia Go the Way of the Soviet Union?* (Brookings, 2002).

Falkus, M. E., *The Industrialization of Russia, 1700–1914* (London: Macmillan, Studies in Economic and Social History, 1972)

Fedor, Julie, *Russia and the Cult of State Security* (New York: Routledge, 2011).

Fiefer, Gregory, "The Price of Progress—Life in Kadyrov's Grozny Permeated by Fear," RFE/RL, August 11, 2009 (www.rferl.org/content/The_Price_Of_Progress_Life_In_Kadyrovs_Grozny_Permeated_By_Fear/1797452.html).

Fieldhouse, D. K., *Economics and Empire 1830–1914* (Cornell University Press, 1973).

Figes, Orlando, *A People's Tragedy: A History of the Russian Revolution* (New York: Viking, 1996)

———, *Natasha's Dance* (New York: Picador, 2002).

———, "In Search of Russia," *New York Review of Books*, October 23, 2003.

Fischer, Benjamin B., *A Cold War Conundrum: The 1983 Soviet War Scare* (CIA: Center for the Study of Intelligence Publications, 1997) (www.cia.gov/library/center-for-the-study-of-intelligence/csi-publications/books-and-monographs/a-cold-war-conundrum/source.htm).

Florida, Richard, *The Rise of the Creative Class* (New York: Basic Books, 2002).

Forbes Billionaires List, March 2012 (www.forbes.com/billionaires/list/).

Forrest, Brett, "Putin's Party," *National Geographic*, January 2014 (http://ngm.nationalgeographic.com/2014/01/sochi-russia/forrest-text).

Freeland, Chrystia, *Sale of the Century: Russia's Wild Ride from Communism to Capitalism* (New York: Crown Books, 2000).

Fuller, William, *Strategy and Power in Russia, 1600–1914* (New York: Free Press, 1992).

Gaddy, Clifford G., *The Price of the Past: Russia's Struggle with the Legacy of a Militarized Economy* (Brookings, 1996).

———, "Pudrin Lives!" *Brookings Institution Opinion*, September 30, 2011 (www.brookings.edu/opinions/2011/0930_russia_gaddy.aspx).

Gaddy, Clifford, and William G. Gale, "Demythologizing the Russian Flat Tax," *Tax Notes International*, no. 43, March 2005 (www.brookings.edu/~/media/research/files/articles/2005/3/14russia%20gaddy/20050314gaddygale.pdf).

Gaddy, Clifford, and Fiona Hill, "Putin's Agenda, America's Choice: Russia's Search for Strategic Stability," Brookings Policy Brief Series No. 99, Brookings Institution, April 2002 (www.brookings.edu/research/papers/2002/05/russia-gaddy).

Gaddy, Clifford G., and Barry Ickes, *Russia's Virtual Economy* (Brookings, 2002).

———, "Putin's Third Way," *The National Interest* (January/February 2009).

———, "Russia after the Global Financial Crisis," *Eurasian Geography and Economics*, Vol. 51, No. 3 (2010) (www.brookings.edu/~/media/research/files/articles/2010/5/russia%20financial%20crisis%20gaddy/05_russia_financial_crisis_gaddy.pdf).

———, "Putin's Protection Racket," in Likka Korhonen and Laura Solanko (eds.), *From Soviet Plans to Russian Reality* (Helsinki: WSOYpro Oy, 2011a).

———, "The Russian Economy to 2020: The Challenge of Managing Rent Addiction," in Maria Lipman and Nikolay Petrov (eds.), *Russia in 2020: Scenarios for the Future* (Washington, D.C.: Carnegie Endowment for International Peace, November 2011b).

Gaddy, Clifford C., and Andrew Kuchins, "Putin's Plan: The Future of 'Russia Inc.,'" *Washington Quarterly* (Spring 2008).

Gaidar, Yegor, translated by Antonina W. Bouis, *Collapse of an Empire: Lessons for Modern Russia* (Brookings, 2007).

Galeotti, Mark, *Gorbachev and His Revolution* (London: Palgrave Macmillan, 1997).

———, "Who's the Boss: Us or the Law? The Corrupt Art of Governing Russia," in S. Lovell, A. Ledeneva, and A. Rogatchev (eds.), *Bribery and Blat in Russia* (London: Macmillan, 2000).

———, "Reform of the Russian Military and Security Apparatus: An Investigator's Perspective," in Stephen Blank (ed.), *Can Russia Reform? Economic, Political, and Military Perspectives* (U.S. Army War College Strategic Studies Institute, 2012).

———, "Putin, Kudrin and the Real Stolypin," *In Moscow's Shadows* (blog), January 6, 2012 (http://inmoscowsshadows.wordpress.com/2012/01/06/putin-kudrin-and-the-real-stolypin/).

Gall, Carlotta, and Thomas de Waal, *Chechnya: Calamity in the Caucasus* (New York University Press, 1998).

Gellner, Ernest, *Nations and Nationalism* (Cornell University Press, 1983).

Gerschaft, Mikhail, "The Economic Grounds for Russian Nationalism," *PRISM*, Vol. I, No. 22, Part 4 (October 20, 1995).

Gessen, Masha, with Stephane Lavoue, "Dead Soul," *Vanity Fair* (October 2008).

Gessen, Masha, *The Man without a Face: The Unlikely Rise of Vladimir Putin* (New York: Riverhead Books, 2012).

———, *Words Will Break Cement: The Passion of Pussy Riot* (New York: Riverhead, 2014).

Gevorkyan, Nataliya, Natali'a Timakova, and Andrey Kolesnikov, *Ot pervogo litsa: razgovory s Vladimirom Putinom* [From the first person: conversations with Vladimir Putin] (Moscow: Vagrius, 2000).

Geyer, Dietrich, *Russian Imperialism: The Interaction of Domestic and Foreign Policy 1860–1914* (Yale University Press, 1987).

Glaeser, Andreas, *Political Epistemics: The Secret Police, the Opposition, and the End of East German Socialism*, Chicago Studies in Practices of Meaning (University of Chicago Press, 2011).

Goble, Paul, "Orthodoxies Old and New," *RFE/RL Analysis from Washington*, January 23, 1997.

Goldgeier, James M., and Michael McFaul, *Power and Purpose: U.S. Policy toward Russia after the Cold War* (Brookings, 2003).

Goldstein, Judith, and Robert Keohane (eds.), *Ideas and Foreign Policy: Beliefs, Institutions and Political Change* (Cornell University Press, 1993).

Goskomstat SSSR, *Narodnoye khozaystvo SSSR* (multiple years).

Gracheva, Tat'yana, *Nevidimaya Khazariya* [Hidden Khazaria] (Ryazan': Zerna, 2009).

Gracheva, Tat'yana, *Svyataya Rus' protiv Khazarii* [Holy Rus' against Khazaria] (Ryazan': Zerna, 2009).

BIBLIOGRAPHY

Gumilev [Gumilyov], Lev, *Etnogenez i biosfera Zemli* [Ethnogenesis and the biosphere of the Earth] (Leningrad: Izd. Leningradskogo gosudarstvenogo universiteta, 1989).

———, *Geografiya etnosa v istoricheskiy period* [The geography of ethnoses in the historical period] (Leningrad: Nauka, 1990).

Gustafson, Thane, *Crisis amid Plenty: The Politics of Soviet Energy under Brezhnev and Gorbachev*, RAND Corporation Research Study (Princeton University Press, 1991).

Gvosdev, Nikolas, "Review Essays: Russia's Future," *Orbis*, Spring 2009.

Hajda, Lubomyr, and Mark Beissinger (eds.), *The Nationalities Factor in Soviet Politics and Society* (Boulder, Colo.: Westview Press, 1990).

Haldeman, H. R. *The Ends of Power* (New York: Times Books, 1977).

Harding, Luke, *Expelled: A Journalist's Descent into the Russian Mafia State* (New York: Palgrave MacMillan, 2012).

Henderson, James, and Simon Pirani (eds.), *The Russian Gas Matrix: How Markets Are Driving Change* (Oxford University Press, 2014).

Herspring, Dale R., and Jacob Kipp, "Understanding the Elusive Mr. Putin," *Problems of Post-Communism*, Vol. 48, No. 5 (September/October 2001), pp. 3–17.

Helman, Christopher, "The World's 25 Biggest Oil Companies," *Forbes* [online], July 16, 2012 (www.forbes.com/sites/christopherhelman/2012/07/16/the-worlds-25-biggest-oil-companies/).

Henze, Paul, "Circassian Resistance to Russia," in Marie Bennigsen Broxup (ed.), *The North Caucasus Barrier: The Russian Advance towards the Muslim World* (New York: Palgrave Macmillan, 1992).

Hill, Fiona, "In Search of Great Russia: Elites, Ideas, Power and the State, and the Pre-Revolutionary Past in the New Russia, 1991–1996," unpublished Ph.D. dissertation in history, Harvard University, 1998.

———, "Putin and Bush in Common Cause? Russia's View of the Terrorist Threat after September 11," *The Brookings Review*, Summer 2002 (www.brookings.edu/research/articles/2002/06/summer-pakistan-hill).

———, "Governing Russia: Putin's Federal Dilemmas," *New Europe Review*, January 2005.

———, "Gang of Two: Russia and Japan Make a Play for the Pacific," *Foreign Affairs*, November 27, 2013 (www.foreignaffairs.com/articles/140288/fiona-hill/gang-of-two).

Hill, Fiona, and Clifford Gaddy, *The Siberian Curse: How Communist Planners Left Russia Out in the Cold* (Brookings, 2003).

———, "Vladimir Putin and the Uses of History in Russia," *The National Interest* (January-February 2012).

Hill, Fiona, and Pamela Jewett, *Back in the USSR: Russia's Intervention in the Internal Affairs of the Former Soviet Republics and the Implications for United States Policy toward Russia*, Strengthening Democratic Institutions Project, John F. Kennedy School of Government, Harvard University, January 1994.

Hoffman, David, *The Oligarchs: Wealth and Power in the New Russia* (New York: Public Affairs, 2003).

Högselius, Per, *Red Gas: Russia and the Origins of European Energy Dependence* (New York: Palgrave, 2013).

Hughes, James, "Moscow's Bilateral Treaties Add to Confusion," *Transition*, September 20, 1996.

Hutchins, Chris, with Alexander Korobko, *Putin* (Leicester, UK: Matador, 2012).

Idov, Michael, "The New Decembrists," *The New Yorker* (January 22, 2012).

International Monetary Fund, "Russian Federation Completes Early Repayment of Entire Outstanding Obligations to the IMF," Press Release No. 05/19, February 2, 2005 (www.imf.org/external/np/sec/pr/2005/pr0519.htm).

————, "IMF Survey: Global Financial System Risks Escalate," September 21, 2011 (www.imf.org/external/pubs/ft/survey/so/2011/new092111a.htm).

————, *World Economic Outlook Database*, April 2012.

Ivanov, Vyacheslav, "Russian Social Life and Thought," in Heyward Isham (ed.), *Remaking Russia: Voices from Within* (Armonk, N.Y.: M. E. Sharpe, 1995).

Ivanova, G. M., *GULAG v sisteme totalitarnogo gosudarstva* [The GULAG in the system of a totalitarian state] (Moscow, 1997).

Jack, Andrew, *Inside Putin's Russia* (Oxford University Press, 2004).

Jelavich, Barbara, *St. Petersburg and Moscow: Tsarist and Soviet Foreign Policy 1814–1974* (Indiana University Press, 1974).

Jones, Bruce D., "The BRICS and Their Bank," *The American Interest*, July 26, 2014 (www.the-american-interest.com/articles/2014/07/26/the-brics-and-their-bank/).

Judah, Ben, *Fragile Empire: How Russia Fell In and Out of Love with Vladimir Putin* (Yale University Press, 2013).

Kagan, Robert, *The World America Made* (New York: Knopf, 2012).

Kaylan, Melik, "Kremlin Values: Putin's Strategic Conservatism," *World Affairs Journal*, May/June 2014. (www.worldaffairsjournal.org/article/kremlin-values-putin%E2%80%99s-strategic-conservatism).

Keenan, Edward L., "Muscovite Political Folkways," *Russian Review*, Vol. 45, No. 2 (April 1986).

Keenan, Edward, Roman Szporluk, and Boris Rumer, Presentation: *The Many Faces of Eurasianism*, Davis Center for Russian Studies, Harvard University, Occasional Seminar, January 28, 1997.

Kennan Institute, "The Russian Constitution at Fifteen: Assessments and Current Challenges to Russia's Legal Development," March 19, 2009 (www.wilsoncenter.org/sites/default/files/KI_090623_Occ%20Paper%20304.pdf).

Khakimov, Rafael (ed.), *Evraziystvo: za i protiv* [Eurasianism: for and against], Panorama-Forum (Kazan), Vol. 8, No.1 (1997).

Khodorkovskiy, Mikhail, and Leonid Nevzlin, *Chelovek s rublyom* [Man with a ruble] (Moscow: Menatep-Inform, 1992).

Khrushcheva, Nina, *Imagining Nabokov: Russia between Art and Politics* (Yale University Press, 2008).

————, *The Lost Khrushchev: A Journey into the Gulag of the Russian Mind* (Mustang, Okla.: Tate Publishing, 2014).

King, William R., and David I. Cleland, *Strategic Planning and Policy* (New York: Van Nostrand Reinhold, 1978).

Kirkpatrick, Jeane, *The Withering Away of the Totalitarian State* (Washington, D.C.: AEI Press, 1990).

Kissinger, Henry, *Diplomacy* (New York: Touchstone, 1994).

Klebnikov, Paul, *Godfather of the Kremlin* (New York: Harcourt, 2000).

Kochan, Lionel, and Richard Abraham, *The Making of Modern Russia*, 2nd ed. (Harmondsworth, Middlesex, UK: Penguin Books, 1983)

Kokoshin, Andrey, "Natsional'naya bezopasnost' i voyennaya moshch' Rossii" [National security and military might of Russia], final chapter of draft book, Moscow, 1995.

————, *Reflections on Russia's Past, Present and Future*, Strengthening Democratic Institutions Project, John F. Kennedy School of Government, Harvard University, June 1997.

————, *Soviet Strategic Thought, 1917–91* (MIT Press, 1998).

Kolesnikov, Andrey, *Ya Putina videl!* [I saw Putin!] (Moscow: Eksmo, 2005).

Körber Stiftung, "Europa—aber wo liegen seine Grenzen?" [Europe—but where do its frontiers lie?], 104th Bergedorfer Gesprächskreis [104th Bergedorf Roundtable], Warsaw, Königsschloss, 1995 (www.koerber-stiftung.de/fileadmin/bg/PDFs/bnd_104_de.pdf).

Kornelius, Stefan, *Angela Merkel: The Chancellor and Her World* (London: Alma Books, 2013).

Kotek, Joel, *Cartoons and Extremism: Israel and the Jews in Arab and Western Media* (Portland, Ore.: Vallentine Mitchell, 2009)

Korytina, Yevgeniya, and Tat'yana Kosobokova, "Putinu golosa rossiyan oboshlis' v 10 raz dorozhe, chem Medvedevu" [Russians' votes cost Vladimir Putin ten times more than Medvedev], *RBC Daily*, No. 43, March 12, 2012 (www.rbcdaily.ru/2012/03/12/focus/562949983220042).

Kramer, Mark, "The Myth of a No-NATO-Enlargement Pledge to Russia," *Washington Quarterly* (April 2009).

Krastev, Ivan, "Russian Revisionism: Putin's Plan for Overturning the European Order," *Foreign Affairs*, March 3, 2014 (www.foreignaffairs.com/articles/140990/ivan-krastev/russian-revisionism).

Kravtsov, Yuriy, Viktor Novoselov, and Sergey Mironov, "Dos'ye na Putina v Sankt-Peterburge. Narkotiki, bandity, vorovstvo i KGB" [Dossier on Putin in St. Petersburg. Narcotics, bandits, theft, and the KGB], January 15, 2010 (http://rospres.com/hearsay/5833/).

Kudrin, Aleksey, and others, "Shansy na dialog mezhdu obshchestvom i vlast'yu snizilis'" [The chances of dialogue between society and the authorities have been reduced], Committee for Citizens' Initiatives, May 5, 2012 (akudrin.ru/news/shansy-na-dialog-mezhdu-obshchestvom-i-vlastyu-snizilis.html).

Laqueur, Walter, *Russia and Germany* (New Brunswick: Transaction Publishers, 1990).

Lacquer, Walter, *Black Hundred: The Rise of the Extreme Right in Russia* (New York: HarperCollins, 1993).

Laruelle, Marlene, *Russian Eurasianism: An Ideology of Empire* (Woodrow Wilson Press/Johns Hopkins University Press, 2008).

Lazarev, Valery, "Conclusions," in Paul R. Gregory and Valery Lazarev (eds.), *The Economics of Forced Labor: The Soviet Gulag* (Hoover Institution Press, 2003).

Lebed', Aleksandr, *Za derzhavu obidno* [It makes you ashamed of your homeland] (Moscow: Moskovskaya pravda, 1995).

———, "International Aspects of Russia's Development," presentation at the German Society of Foreign Policy, Bonn, January 1997 (transcript obtained from the German Society of Foreign Policy).

Ledeneva, Alena, *How Russia Really Works* (Cornell University Press, 2006).

Leonova, Kseniya, "Slovesnyi zanos: Avtory rossiiskoi konstitutsii vspominayut, kak v dokument zaneslo slovo, blagodarya kotoromu Vladimir Putin smog poiti na tretii prezidentskii srok" [The authors of the Russian constitution reflect on how the document formulated the words that enabled Vladimir Putin to go for a third presidential term], *Esquire*, March 2, 2012 (http://esquire.ru/constitution-75).

LeVine, Steve, *Putin's Labyrinth: Spies, Murder and the Dark Heart of the New Russia* (New York: Random House, 2008).

Levinskiy, Aleksandr, Irina Malkova, and Valeriy Igumenov, "Kak Mattias Warnig stal samym nadezhnym 'ekonomistom' Putina," [How Matthias Warnig became the most reliable "economist" for Putin] *Forbes.ru*, August 28, 2012 (www.forbes.ru/sobytiya/vlast/103069-kak-chekist-iz-gdr-stal-samym-nadezhnym-ekonomistom-putina-rassledovanie-forbe).

Li, Cheng, "Xi Jinping's Inner Circle" (two-part series), China Leadership Monitor, January/July 2014 (www.brookings.edu/research/papers/2014/01/30-xi-jinping-inner-circle-li and www.brookings.edu/research/articles/2014/07/18-xi-jinping-inner-circle-friends-li).

Lieven, Anatol, *Chechnya: Tombstone of Russian Power* (Yale University Press, 1998).

Lieven, Dominic, *The Aristocracy in Europe, 1815–1914* (Columbia University Press, 1992).

———, *Nicholas II: Twilight of the Empire* (New York: St. Martin's Press, 1993).

Lilly, Bilyana, *Russian Foreign Policy toward Missile Defense: Actors, Motivations and Influence* (New York: Lexington Books, 2014).

Lo, Bobo, *Axis of Convenience: Moscow, Beijing, and the New Geopolitics* (Brookings, 2008).

Lough, John, "The Place of the 'Near Abroad' in Russian Foreign Policy," *RFE/RL Research Report*, Vol. 2, No. 11, March 12, 1993.

———, "Defining Russia's Relations with Neighboring States," *RFE/RL Research Report*, Vol. 2, No. 20, May 14, 1993.

Lucas, Edward, *The New Cold War* (New York: Palgrave MacMillan, 2008).

Mackinder, H. J., "The Geographical Pivot of History," *Geographical Journal*, London, Vol. 23, No. 4 (April 1904), pp. 421–44 (accessed on JSTOR).

Malinova, Ol'ga, "Tema proshlogo v ritorika prezidentov Rossii" [The theme of the past in the rhetoric of Russia's presidents"], *Pro et Contra* (May–August 2011).

Markov, Sergei, "The Enlargement of Agencies Is Politics. A Fundamental Administrative Reform Will Be Its Logical Continuation," *Strana.ru*, October 17, 2001, translated in *Johnson's Russia List*, October 18, 2001 (www.cdi.org/russia/johnson/5496-13.cfm).

Masterman, Sir John C., *The Double Cross System in the War of 1939 to 1945* (Yale University Press, 1972).

Matthews, Owen, "Dumbing Russia Down," *Newsweek/Daily Beast*, March 22, 2008 (www.thedailybeast.com/newsweek/2008/03/22/dumbing-russia-down.html).

———, "Meet Igor the Tank Engineer," *Newsweek/Daily Beast*, May 28, 2012 (www.thedailybeast.com/newsweek/2012/05/27/meet-igor-the-tank-engineer.html).

McDaniel, Tim, *The Agony of the Russian Idea* (Princeton University Press, 1996).

McDonald, David, *United Government and Foreign Policy in Russia: 1900–1914* (Harvard University Press, 1992).

McFaul, Michael, *Russia's Unfinished Revolution: Political Change from Gorbachev to Putin* (Cornell University Press, 2001).

McNeil, Robert (ed.), *Russia in Transition 1905–1914: Evolution or Revolution?* (Huntington, N.Y.: Robert E. Krieger Publishing Company, 1976).

Mead, Walter Russell, "The Return of Geopolitics: The Revenge of the Revisionist Powers," *Foreign Affairs*, May/June 2014 (www.foreignaffairs.com/articles/141211/walter-russell-mead/the-return-of-geopolitics).

Medvedev, Roy, *Neizvestnyy Andropov* [The unknown Andropov] (Rostov-na-Donu: Feniks, 1999).

———, *Andropov* (Moscow: Molodaya gvardiya, 2006).

Meier, Andrew, *Chechnya: To the Heart of a Conflict* (New York: W. W. Norton, 2004).

Merridale, Catherine, *Red Fortress: History and Illusion in the Kremlin* (New York: Metropolitan Books, 2013).

Mikhalkov, Nikita, *Pravo i pravda: Manifest prosveshchennogo konservatizma* [Law and truth: a manifesto of enlightened conservatism] (Moscow: Rossiyskiy fond kul'tury, "Sibirskiy tsiryul'nik," 2010) (http://polit.ru/kino/2010/10/26/manifest.html).

Milyukov, Pavel, *Russia and its Crisis* (University of Chicago Press, 1906).

———, "The Representative System in Russia," in J. D. Duff (ed.), *Russian Realities and Problems* (Cambridge University Press, 1917).

Mitchell, Daniel, "Russia's Flat Tax Miracle," Heritage Foundation, March 24, 2003 (www.heritage.org/research/commentary/2003/03/russias-flat-tax-miracle).

———, "Flat Tax Is the Way of the Future," Heritage Foundation, March 20, 2006 (www.heritage.org/research/commentary/2006/03/flat-tax-is-the-way-of-the-future).

Monaghan, Andrew, "The Vertikal: Power and Authority in Russia," *International Affairs*, Vol. 88, No. 1 (2012).

Moskoff, William, *The Bread of Affliction: The Food Supply in the USSR During World War II*, Soviet and East European Studies, No. 76 (Cambridge University Press, August 8, 2002).

Murawiec, Laurent, and Clifford Gaddy, "The Higher Police: Vladimir Putin and his Predecessors," *The National Interest* (Spring 2002).

Nabokov, Vladimir, *Pnin: A Novel* (New York: Knopf, 2004).

Nemtsov, Boris, and Leonid Martinyuk, "Zhizn' raba na galerakh: dvortsy, yakhty, avtomobili, samolyoti and drugiye aksessuary" [The life of a galley slave: palaces, yachts, automobiles, airplanes and other accessories], August 2012 (www.nemtsov.ru/?id=718577).

Nekrich, Aleksandr M., *The Punished Peoples: The Deportation and Fate of Soviet Minorities at the End of the Second World War* (New York: W.W. Norton, 1981).

Nichol, Jim, "Russian Military Reform and Defense Policy," Congressional Research Service, August 24, 2011 (http://fas.org/sgp/crs/row/R42006.pdf)

Novikova, L. I., and I. N. Sizemskaya (eds.), *Rossiya mezhdu Evropy i Azii: evraziyskiy soblazn* [Russia between Europe and Asia: the Eurasian temptation] (Moscow: Nauka, 1993).

Official Kremlin International News Broadcasts, "Press Conference by Russia's Choice Leaders Yegor Gaidar and Sergei Kovalev," December 13, 1993.

Orwell, George, *1984* (London: Secker and Warburg, 1949).

Panyushkin, Valeriy, and Mikhail Zygar', with Irina Reznik, *Gazprom: Novoye russkoye oruzhiye* [Gazprom: the new Russian weapon] (Moscow: Zakharov, 2008).

Partlett, William, "Separation of Powers without Checks and Balances: The Failure of Semi-Presidentialism and the Making of the Russian Constitutional System, 1991–1993," in William Simons and Tatiana Borisova (eds.), *The Legal Dimension in Cold War Interactions: Some Notes from the Field*. Law in Eastern Europe Series (Leiden: Brill, 2012).

———, "Vladimir Putin and the Law," *Brookings Institution Commentary*, February 28, 2012 (www.brookings.edu/opinions/2012/0228_putin_law_partlett.aspx).

———, "Liberal Revolution, Legality, and the Russian Founding Period," *Review of Central and East European Law*, No. 1 (2013).

Payne, Marissa, "Putin's Criticisms of Extreme Russian Nationalism Are Politically Motivated," *World Politics Review* (February 19, 2007).

Pepper, John, *Russian Tide: Proctor and Gamble Enters Russia. Building a Leadership Position in the Midst of Unprecedented Change* (Cincinnati, Ohio: John Pepper, 2012).

Petro, Nikolai N., *The Rebirth of Russian Democracy: An Interpretation of Political Culture* (Harvard University Press, 1995).

Pipes, Richard, *The Formation of the Soviet Union: Communism and Nationalism 1917–1923* (Harvard University Press, 1964).

———, *Russia under the Old Regime* (New York: Charles Scribner's Sons, 1974).

———, *The Russian Revolution* (New York: Alfred A. Knopf, 1990).

———, *The Formation of the Soviet Union: Communism and Nationalism 1917–1923*, rev. ed. (Harvard University Press, 1997).

———, *Property and Freedom* (New York: Alfred A. Knopf, 1999).

———, *Russian Conservatism and Its Critics: A Study in Political Culture* (Yale University Press, 2005).

Plokhy, Serhii, *The Last Empire: The Final Days of the Soviet Union* (New York: Basic Books, 2014).

Podberezkin, Aleksey, "Russkiy put'"[The Russian path], *Avtograf* (May 22–June 6, 1997).

Poe, Marshall, *The Russian Moment in World History* (Princeton University Press, 2003).

Polyakova, Alina, "Strange Bedfellows: Putin and Europe's Far Right," *World Affairs Journal*, September/October 2014 (www.worldaffairsjournal.org/article/strange-bedfellows-putin-and-europe%E2%80%99s-far-right).

Pomerantsev, Peter, "Putin's Rasputin," *London Review of Books*, Vol. 33, No. 20 (October 20, 2011).

Pomeranz, William, "Russia and the European Court of Human Rights: Implications for U.S. Policy," Kennan Institute seminar summary, May 3, 2011 (www.wilsoncenter.org/publication/russia-and-the-european-court-human-rights-implications-for-us-policy).

Prevost-Logan, Nicole," Moscow Reclaims Its Past," *Archaeology* (July/August 1997).

Prozorov, Sergei, "Russian Conservatism in the Putin Presidency: The Dispersion of a Hegemonic Discourse," Danish Institute for International Studies Working Paper, 2004 (www.diis.dk/graphics/publications/wp2004/spz_russian_conservatism.pdf).

Pukhov, Ruslan (ed.), *The Tanks of August* (Moscow: Centre for Analysis of Strategies and Technology, 2010) (www.cast.ru/files/The_Tanks_of_August_sm_eng.pdf).

Putin, Vladimir Vladimirovich, "Strategicheskoye planirovaniye vosproizvodstva mineral'no-syr'yevoy bazy regiona v usloviyakh formirovaniya rynochnykh otnosheniy (Sankt-Peterburg i Leningr. obl.) [Strategic planning of the reproduction of the mineral resource base of a region under conditions of formation of market relations (St. Petersburg and Leningrad oblast)]." A dissertation submitted in pursuit of the degree of candidate of economic sciences, St. Petersburg State Mining Institute named for G. V. Plekahnov, St. Petersburg, 1997.

Putin, Vladimir, with Nataliya Gevorkyan, Natalya Timakova, and Andrei Kolesni-kov, *First Person: An Astonishingly Frank Self-Portrait by Russia's President Vladimir Putin* (New York: Public Affairs, 2000).

Ra'anan, Uri, Maria Mesner, Keith Armes, and Kate Martin (eds.), *State and Nation in Multi-Ethnic Societies: The Breakup of Multinational States* (Manchester University Press, 1991).

Radio Free Europe/Radio Liberty (RFE/RL), "Putin Warns 'Mistakes' Could Bring Back '90s Woes," October 17, 2011 (www.rferl.org/content/putin_mistakes_could_bring_back_1990s_woes/24362626.html).

———, "Prominent Putin Critic Dies at 77," Russian Service, March 21, 2012 (www.rferl.org/content/salye_putin_critic_dies/24523142.html).

———, "Russia's 'Revolutionary' Situation," June 12, 2012 (www.rferl.org/article printview/24612283.html).

Raeff, Marc, *The Decembrist Movement* (Englewood Cliffs, N.J.: Prentice-Hall, 1966).

Rahr, Alexander, *Wladimir Putin: Der "Deutsche" im Kreml* [Vladimir Putin: the "German" in the Kremlin] (Munich: Universitas, 2000).

———, *Putin Nach Putin*: *Das Kapitalistische Russland am Beginn einer neuen Weltordnung* [Putin after Putin: a capitalist Russia at the beginning of a new world order] (Berlin: Universitas Verlag, 2008).

RAU Corporation, *Kontseptsiya natsional'noy bezopasnosti Rossiyskoy Federatsii v 1996–2000 godakh* [National security concept for the Russian Federation from 1996–2000] (Moskva: Obozrevatel', 1995).

Raviot, Jean-Robert, "Fédéralisme et Gouvernement Régional en Russie" [Federalism and regional governance in Russia], *Politique Étrangère*, Paris, December 1996.

Rayfield, Donald, *Stalin and His Hangmen: The Tyrant and Those Who Killed for Him* (New York: Random House, 2004).

Reddaway, Peter, and Dmitri Glinski, *The Tragedy of Russia's Reforms: Market Bolshevism against Democracy* (Washington, D.C.: United States Institute of Peace, 2001).

Reuth, Ralf Georg, and Andreas Bönte, *Das Komplott: Wie es wirklich zur deutschen Einheit kam* [The conspiracy: the real story of German unification] (Munich: Piper, 1993).

"RF-SNG: Strategicheskiy kurs. Ukaz Prezidenta Rossiyskoy Federatsii ob utverzhdenii strategicheskogo kursa Rossiyskoy Federatsii s gosudarstvami--uchastnikami Sodruzhestva nezavisimykh gosudarstv" [RF-CIS: Strategic course. Decree of the President of the Russian Federation on establishing the strategic course of the Russian Federation with the state-participants in the commonwealth of independent states], Decree no. 940, September 14, 1995, in *Dipkur'er*, No. 16/18, 1995.

Riasanovsky, Nicholas, *Nicholas I and Official Nationality* (University of California Press, 1959).

Rice, Condoleezza, *No Higher Honor* (New York: Crown, 2011).

Ries, Nancy, "Potato Ontology: Surviving Postsocialism in Russia," *Cultural Anthropology*, Vol. 24, No. 2 (May 2009).

Robinson, Paul, "Putin's Philosophy," *The American Conservative*, March 28, 2012 (www.theamericanconservative.com/articles/putins-philosophy).

Rosen, F., "Bentham, Jeremy," *Oxford Dictionary of National Biography* (Oxford University Press, 2004) (www.oxforddnb.com/view/printable/2153).

Rothgeb, John M., Jr., *Defining Power: Influence and Force in the Contemporary International System* (New York: St. Martin's Press, 1993).

Roxburgh, Angus, *The Strongman* (New York: I. B. Tauris, 2012).

Ruspres, "Vitse-mayor Putin za bor'bu s monstrom KGB. Zapis' 1996 goda," [Vice-Mayor Putin in favor of struggling with the KGB monster. Recording from 1996] (www.rospres.com/government/2766/ [Russian-language website]).

Russian Federal State Statistics Service, *Statistical Yearbook for 2011*.

Russian Ministry of Economic Development [Minekonomrazvitiya Rossii], "Innovatsionnaya Rossiya–2020 (Strategiya innovatsiyonnogo razvitiya Rossiyskoy Federatsii na period do 2020 goda)" [Innovative Russia–2020 (Strategy for the innovative development of the Russian Federation for the period until 2020)], 2010 (www.economy.gov.ru/minec/activity/sections/innovations/doc20101231_016?presentationtemplate=docHTMLTemplate1&presentationtemplateid=2dd7bc8044687de796f0f7af753c8a7e).

Sachs, Jeffrey, Testimony before the United States Senate Committee on Banking, Housing and Urban Affairs, February 5, 1994.

———, "Toward *Glasnost* in the IMF: Russia's Democratization Policy and the International Monetary Fund," *Challenge*, Vol. 37, No. 3 (May–June 1994).

Safire, William, "On Language: The Near Abroad," *New York Times Magazine*, May 22, 1994.

Sakwa, Richard, *Putin: Russia's Choice* (London and New York: Routledge, 2007).

———, *The Quality of Freedom: Khodorkovsky, Putin and the Yukos Affair* (Oxford University Press, 2009).

Salomoni, Antonella, "State Sponsored Anti-Semitism in Postwar USSR: Studies and Research Perspectives," *Quest: Studies in Contemporary Jewish History*, April 1, 2010 (www.quest-cdecjournal.it/focus.php?id=212).

Sal'ye, Marina, "V. Putin–'prezident' korrumpirovanoy oligarkhii!" [V. Putin–'president' of a corrupt oligarchy!], Glasnost' Foundation, March 18, 2000 (www.anticompromat.org/putin/salie.html).

Sarotte, Mary Elise, "A Broken Promise?: What the West Really Told Moscow about NATO Expansion," *Foreign Affairs*, September-October 2014, pp. 90–97 (www.foreignaffairs.com/articles/141845/mary-elise-sarotte/a-broken-promise).

Schäffer, Sebastian, "Still All Quiet on the Eastern Front? The European Union's Eastern Partnership One Year after the Prague Summit," *CAP Perspectives*, No. 2, Center for Applied Policy Research, June 2010.

Sechin, Igor' Ivanovich, "Ekonomicheskaya otsenka investitsionnykh proyektov transita nefti i nefteproduktov (na primere nefteproduktoprovoda Kirishi--Batareynaya)"

[Economic evaluation of investment projects for transit of petroleum and petroleum products (the example of the Kirishi-Batareynaya petroleum product pipeline)]. A dissertation submitted in pursuit of the degree of candidate of economic sciences, St. Petersburg State Mining Institute named for G. V. Plekhanov, St. Petersburg, 1998.

Semenov, Julian, *The Himmler Ploy* (Terra Haute, Ind.: Popular Library, 1978).

Shakhrai, Sergei, "Official Memorandum to President Boris N. Yeltsin," No. 1576, March 1995, reproduced in Rafael Khakimov "Federalization and Stability: A Path Forward for the Russian Federation," *CMG Bulletin*, June 1995.

Shevtsova, Lilia, *Putin's Russia* (Washington D.C.: Carnegie Endowment for International Peace, 2005).

Shore, Zachary, *A Sense of the Enemy: The High-Stakes History of Reading Your Rival's Mind* (Oxford University Press, 2014).

Shuster, Simon, "Vladimir Putin's Billionaire Boys Judo Club," *Time*, March 1, 2011 (www.time.com/time/world/article/0,8599,2055962,00.html).

———, "The Empire Strikes Back: Putin Sends in the Storm Troopers," *Time*, December 7, 2011.

Simis, Konstantin, *USSR: The Corrupt Society. The Secret World of Soviet Capitalism* (New York: Simon and Schuster, 1982).

Simmons, Ernest J. (ed.), *Continuity and Change in Russian and Soviet Thought* (Harvard University Press, 1955).

Smirnov, M. B., S. P. Sigachev, and D. V. Shkapov, "Sistema mest zaklyucheniya v SSSR. 1929–1960" [The prison system in the USSR, 1929–1960], in M. B. Smirnov (ed.), *Sistema ispravitel'no-trudovykh lagerey v SSSR, 1923–1960: Spravochnik* [The system of correctional work camps in the USSR, 1923–1960: a reference] (Moscow: Zven'ya, 1998).

Snyder, Jack, *Myths of Empire: Domestic Politics and International Ambition* (Cornell University Press, 1991).

Snyder, Timothy, *Bloodlands: Europe between Hitler and Stalin* (New York: Basic Books, 2010).

Sobchak, Anatoliy, "The New Soviet Union—Challenges in the Development of a Law-Abiding State," *Stetson Law Review*, Vol. XX (1990).

———, *Dyuzhina nozhey v spinu: Pouchitel'naya istoriya o rossiyskikh politicheskikh nravakh* [A dozen knives in the back: an instructive tale of Russian political norms] (Moscow: Vagrius-Petro-News, 1999).

Soldatov, Andrei, and Irina Borogan, "The Mindset of Russia's Security Services: A Mix of Orthodox Christianity, Trails of Slavic Paganism and a Pride in Being Successors to the Soviet and Byzantine Empires, Both Destroyed by the Western Crusaders," *Agentura. ru*, December 29, 2010 (www.agentura.ru/english/dossier/mindset/).

———, *The New Nobility* (New York: Public Affairs, 2010).

Solnick, Stephen L., *Stealing the State: Control and Collapse in Soviet Institutions* (Harvard University Press, 1998).

Stalin, Josef [Iosif], "Political Report of the Central Committee," December 18, 1925.

Steiner, Andre, *Von Plan zu Plan: Eine Wirtschaftsgeschichte der DDR* [From plan to plan: an economic history of the GDR] (Berlin: Aufbau, 2007).

Stent, Angela, *Russia and Germany Reborn: Unification, the Soviet Collapse, and the New Europe* (Princeton University Press, 1999).

———, *The Limits of Partnership: U.S.-Russian Relations in the Twenty-First Century* (Princeton University Press, 2014).

Stepanov, Vladimir, "The Gray Cardinal Leaves the Kremlin," *Russia Beyond the Headlines*, December 28, 2011.

Stiehler, Hans-Jörg, *Leben ohne Westfernsehen. Studien zur Mediennutzung und Medienwirkung in der Region Dresden in den 80er Jahren* [Life without western television. Studies on media use and media impact in the Dresden region in the 1980s] (Leipzig: Universitätsverlag, 2001).

Sumner, B. H., *Peter the Great and the Emergence of Russia* (New York: Collier Books, 1962).

Sutela, Pekka, *The Political Economy of Putin's Russia* (London and New York: Routledge, 2012).

Szporluk, Roman, *Communism and Nationalism: Karl Marx versus Friedrich List* (Oxford University Press, 1988).

Talbott, Strobe, *The Russia Hand* (New York: Random House, 2002).

Taylor, Brian D., *State Building in Putin's Russia: Policing and Coercion after Communism* (Cambridge University Press, 2011).

Thumann, Michael, "Russia and Germany, Schroeder and Putin: Cabinet Diplomacy 21st Century Style," GMF Conference paper, June 2005 (www.gmfus.org/doc/Thumann %20paper%20Schroeder%20Putin.pdf).

Tishkov, Valery, *Ethnicity, Nationalism and Conflict In and After the Soviet Union: The Mind Aflame* (London, Thousand Oaks, and New Delhi: International Peace Research Institute Oslo and United Nations Research Institute for Social Development, 1997).

———, "The Rehabilitation of War-Torn Societies Project," Geneva, January 2001 (www. chechnyaadvocacy.org/conflict/Tishkov.pdf).

———, "Understanding Violence for Post-Conflict Reconstruction in Chechnya," Centre for Applied Studies in International Negotiations (CASIN), Geneva, January 2001.

———, *Chechnya: Life in a War-Torn Society* (University of California Press, 2004).

Torbakov, Igor, "From the Other Shore: Reflections of Russian Émigré Thinkers on Soviet Nationality Policies, 1920s–1930s," *Slavic and East European Information Resources*, Vol. 4, No. 4 (2003).

———, "Understanding Classical Eurasianism," in Ingmar Oldberg (ed.), *Sven Hedin and Eurasia: Knowledge, Adventure, and Geopolitics* (Stockholm, 2008).

Torreblanca, Jose Ignacio, and Mark Leonard, "The Continent-Wide Rise of Euroscepticism," Policy Memo, European Council on Foreign Relations, May 2013 (www.ecfr.eu/ page/-/ECFR79_EUROSCEPTICISM_BRIEF_AW.pdf).

Tregubova, Yelena, *Bayki kremlyovskogo digger* [Tales of a Kremlin digger] (Moscow: Ad Marginem, 2003).

Treisman, Daniel, "Loans for Shares Revisited," Working Paper 15819 (Cambridge, Mass.: National Bureau of Economic Research, March 2010) (www.nber.org/papers/w15819).

Trochev, Alexei, *Judging Russia: Constitutional Court in Russian Politics: 1990–2006* (Cambridge University Press, 2008).

Troika, *Russia Oil and Gas Atlas*, January 2012.

Troitsky, Artem, *Back in the USSR: The True Story of Rock in Russia* (London and Boston: Faber & Faber, 1988).

———, *Tusovka: Who's Who in the New Soviet Rock Culture* (London: Omnibus, 1990).

U.S. Energy Information Agency, "Petroleum Overview, 1949–2010," *Annual Energy Review 2010* (www.eia.gov).

Vaïsse, Justin, and Susi Dennison (eds.), "European Foreign Policy Scorecard," European Council on Foreign Relations, 2013, available www.ecfr.eu/scorecard/2013.

van der Does de Willebois, Emile, Emily M. Halter, Robert A. Harrison, Ji Won Park, and J. C. Sharman. *The Puppet Masters: How the Corrupt Use Legal Structures to Hide Stolen Assets and What to Do about It* (Washington, D.C.: IBRD/World Bank, 2011).

Venturi, Franco, *Roots of Revolution: A History of the Populist and Socialist Movements in Nineteenth Century Russia* (New York: Grosset & Dunlap, The Universal Library, 1966).

Vile, M. J. C., *Constitutionalism and the Separation of Powers*, 2nd ed. (Indianapolis: Liberty Fund, 1998).

Vishnevskiy, Boris, "Zhestkim kursom Chubaysa [Chubais's hard line] 1990–1999," "Analiticheskaya zapiska po kontseptsii perekhoda k rynochnoy ekonomike v SSSR (fragment)" [Analytical notes for the conception for the transition to a market economy in the USSR], "Apple Orchard," Internet forum (www.yabloko.ru/Forums/Main/index. html).

Volkov, Vadim, "Anatoly Sobchak (1937–2000): Leading Representative of Capitalist 'Reform' in Russia," World Socialist Website, March 10, 2000 (www.wsws.org/articles/ 2000/mar2000/sobc-m10.shtml).

———, Violent Entrepreneurs: The Use of Force in the Making of Russian Capitalism (Cornell University Press, 2002).

Waldron, Peter, Between Two Revolutions: Stolypin and the Politics of Renewal in Russia (Northern Illinois University Press, 1998).

Walicki, Andrzej, The Slavophile Controversy: History of a Conservative Utopia in Nineteenth Century Russian Thought (Clarendon Press and Oxford University Press, 1975).

———, A History of Russian Thought from the Enlightenment to Marxism (Stanford University Press, 1979).

White, Stephen, The Bolshevik Poster (Yale University Press, 1988).

White, Stephen, Richard Rose, and Ian McAllister, How Russia Votes (Chatham, N.J.: Chatham House Publishers, 1997).

Whitmore, Brian, "Andropov's Ghost," The Power Vertical (blog), RFE/RL, February 9, 2009 (www.rferl.org/content/Andropovs_Ghost/1467159.html).

———, "The Unraveling: The Tandem's Slow Death," The Power Vertical (blog), RFE/RL, April 2, 2012 (www.rferl.org/content/how_the_tandem_disintegrated/24535389.html).

———, "Ksenia and Vladimir," The Power Vertical (blog), RFE/RL, June 18, 2012 (www. rferl.org/content/ksenia-anatolevna-and-vladimir-vladimirovich/24618330.html).

Wilson, Andrew, Virtual Politics: Faking Democracy in the Post-Soviet World (Yale University Press, 2005)

Wolf, Markus, with Anne McElvoy, Man without a Face: The Autobiography of Communism's Greatest Spymaster (New York: Times Books/Random House, 1997).

Woll, Josephine, "Glasnost: A Cultural Kaleidoscope," in Harley Balzer (ed.), Five Years That Shook the World: Gorbachev's Unfinished Revolution (Boulder, Colo.: Westview Press, 1991).

Wortman, Richard S., Scenarios of Power Myth and Ceremony in Russian Monarchy from Peter the Great to the Abdication of Nicholas II (Princeton University Press, 2006).

Yaffa, Joshua, "Reading Putin: The Mind and the State of Russia's President," Foreign Affairs, July/August 2012.

Yakunin, V. I., and others, Novyye tekhnologii bor'by s rossiyskoy gosudarstvennost'yu [New technologies of struggle against Russian statehood], (Moscow: Nauchnyy ekspert, 2013).

Yavlinsky, Grigory, Reforms from Below: Russia's Future (Moscow: EPIcenter, Nika Print, 1994).

Yeltsin, Boris, translated by Catherine Fitzpatrick, The Struggle for Russia (New York: Times Books, 1994).

———, Midnight Diaries (New York: Public Affairs, 2000).

Yerkes, Sarah, and Tamara Wittes, "What Price Freedom? Assessing the Bush Administration's Freedom Agenda," Brookings Institution Center for Middle East Policy Analysis Paper Series, September 2006 (www.brookings.edu/research/papers/2006/09/ middleeast-wittes).

Zakharovich, Yuri, "Putin Pays Homage to Ilyin," Eurasia Daily Monitor (Jamestown Foundation), Vol. 6, No. 106 (June 3, 2009).

————, "Putin Resolves Protest in Pikalevo," *Eurasia Daily Monitor* (Jamestown Foundation), Vol. 6, No. 110 (June 9, 2009).

Zegers, Peter Kort, and Douglas Druick (eds.), *Windows on the War: Soviet TASS Posters at Home and Abroad, 1941–1945* (Yale University Press, 2011).

Zen'kovich, Nikolay, *Putinskaya Entsiklopediya: Sem'ya. Komanda. Opponenty. Preyemniki* [The Putin encyclopedia: Family. Colleagues. Opponents. Followers] (Moscow: Olma Press, 2006).

Zor'kin, Valeriy, *Muromtsev* (Moscow: Yuridicheskaya literatura, 1979).

————, *Chicherin* (Moscow: Yuridicheskaya literatura, 1984).

Zubkov, Viktor Alekseyevich, "Sovershenstvovaniye nalogovogo mekhanizma mineral'no-syr'yevogo kompleksa (na primere Leningradskoy oblasti)" [Improvement of the tax mechanism of the mineral resource complex (the example of Leningrad oblast)]. A dissertation submitted in pursuit of the degree of candidate of economic sciences, St. Petersburg State Mining Institute named for G. V. Plekhanov, St. Petersburg, 2000.

Zyuganov, Gennadiy, *Derzhava* [Great power] (Moscow: Informpechat, 1994).

————, Report to Congress of the Communist Party of the Russian Federation (CPRF), April 22, 1997 (official transcript in English obtained from the CPRF).

————, *100 Anekdotov ot Zyuganova* [100 anecdotes from Zyuganov] (Moscow: ITRK, 2007).

WEBSITES FOR PUTIN MATERIAL

Some of the older material for Putin's 2000–08 presidencies, as well as for the 2008–12 presidency of Dmitry Medvedev: www.archive.kremlin.ru/

Material for Putin's time as prime minister 2008–12: www.government.ru/

Portal for Putin's post–May 2012 presidency: www.kremlin.ru/

Antikompromat, a website maintained by Russian researcher Vladimir Pribylovskiy, has many reports relating to Vladimir Putin: www.anticompromat.org/putin/

"Conversation with Vladimir Putin. A Continuation," website promoting Putin's annual *Hot Line* television call-in shows: www.moskva-putinu.ru/

Federal State Statistics Service (*Rosstat*, called *Goskomstat* in the Soviet period): www.gks.ru/wps/wcm/connect/rosstat/rosstatsite/main/

Levada Center: www.levada.ru/

Tsentral'naya izbiratel'naya komissiya Rossiiskoi Federatsii [Central election commission of the Russian Federation], "Dannye o predvaritel'nykh itogakh golosovaniya vybory Prezidenta Rossiiskoi Federatsii" ["Information on the reported voting results from the election for the President of the Russian Federation"]: www.vybory.izbirkom.ru

Valdai Discussion Club: valdaiclub.com.

INDEX